Femini
and
Catholic Moral Tradition

Readings in Moral Theology No. 9

Edited by
Charles E. Curran
Margaret A. Farley
and
Richard A. McCormick, S.J.

PAULIST PRESS
New York/Mahwah, N.J.

Cover design by Tim McKeen.

Library of Congress Cataloging-in-Publication Data

Feminist ethics and the Catholic moral tradition / edited by Charles
E. Curran, Margaret A. Farley, and Richard A. McCormick.
p. cm.—(Readings in moral theology ; no. 9)
Includes bibliographical references.
ISBN 0-8091-3669-4 (alk. paper)
1. Feminist ethics. 2. Feminist theology. 3. Sexual ethics.
4. Social ethics. 5. Catholic Church—Doctrines. I. Curran,
Charles E. II. Farley, Margaret A. III. McCormick, Richard A.,
1922– . IV. Series.
BJ1395.F448 1996
241'.042'082—dc20 96-24598
CIP

Published by Paulist Press
997 Macarthur Boulevard
Mahwah, New Jersey 07430

Printed and bound in the
United States of America

Contents

PART FOUR: BIOETHICS

PART FIVE: SOCIAL ETHICS

Acknowledgments

The articles reprinted in *Feminist Ethics and the Catholic Moral Tradition: Readings in Moral Theology No. 9* appeared in the following publications and are reprinted here with permission:

Margaret A. Farley, "Feminist Ethics," in James F. Childress & John Macquarrie, eds., *The Westminster Dictionary of Christian Ethics* (Louisville: Westminster John Knox Press, 1986), pp. 229–231, revised; Susan A. Ross, "Feminist Theology: A Review of Literature: The Context," *Theological Studies* 56 (1995), 327–41; Elisabeth Schüssler Fiorenza, "Discipleship and Patriarchy: Early Christian Ethos and Christian Ethics in a Feminist Theological Perspective," in *The Annual: Society of Christian Ethics* (Scholars Press, 1982), pp. 131–72—originally appeared in *Bread Not Stone* (Boston: Beacon Press, 1984, 1995); Christine E. Gudorf, "Encountering the Other: The Modern Papacy on Women," *Social Compass* 36 (1989), 295–310; Maria Pilar Aquino, "Women's Contribution to Theology in Latin America: The Theological Method," in *Our Cry for Life: Feminist Theology from Latin America* (Maryknoll, N.Y.: Orbis, 1993), pp. 109–130; Ada Maria Isasi-Diaz, "Defining Our *Proyecto Historico: Mujerista* Strategies for Liberation," *Journal of Feminist Studies in Religion* 9 (Spring/Fall, 1993), 17–28; M. Shawn Copeland, "Wading Through Many Sorrows: Toward a Theology of Suffering in Womanist Perspective," in Emilie M. Townes, ed., *A Troubling in My Soul: Womanist Perspectives on Evil and Suffering* (Maryknoll, N.Y.: Orbis, 1993), pp. 109–29; Margaret A. Farley, "A Feminist Version of Respect for Persons," *Journal of Feminist Studies in Religion* 9 (Spring/Fall, 1993), 182–98; Lisa Sowle Cahill, "Feminist Ethics, Differences, and Common Ground," revised, *Catholic Theological Society of America Proceedings* 48 (1993), 65–83; Barbara H. Andolsen, "Whose Sexuality? Whose Tradition? Women, Experience, and Roman Catholic Sexual Ethics," in Ronald M. Green, ed., *Religion and Sexual Health: Ethical, Theological, and Clinical Perspectives* (Dordrecht: Kluwer, 1992), pp. 55–77; Marie Augusta Neal, "Sociology and Sexuality: A Feminist Perspective," *Christianity and Crisis* 39 (May, 1979), 118–22—originally appeared in Franz Bockle and Jacques-Marie Pohler, *Concilium* 100 (Nijmegen: Strichting Concilium); Christine E. Gudorf, "Western Religion and the Patriarchal Family," in Ronald M. Green, ed., *Religion and Sexual Health: Ethical, Theological, and Clinical Perspectives* (Dordrecht: Kluwer,

1992), 99–117; Mary E. Hunt, “Friendship as Inspiration: A Study in Theo-Politics,” in *Fierce Tenderness: A Feminist Theology of Friendship* (New York: The Crossroad Publishing Company, 1991), 57–85; Toinette Eugene, “While Love Is Unfashionable: Ethical Implications of Black Spirituality and Sexuality,” in Barbara Andolsen, Christine E. Gudorf, Mary Pellauer, eds., *Women's Consciousness/Women's Conscience* (Minneapolis: Winston Press, 1985), 121–41—reprinted by permission of HarperCollins Publishers, Inc.; Barbara Hilkert Andolsen, “Elements of a Feminist Approach to Bioethics,” in Paul F. Camenisch, ed., *Religious Methods and Resources in Bioethics* (Dordrecht: Kluwer, 1994), pp. 227–57; Maura A. Ryan, “The Argument for Unlimited Procreative Liberty: A Feminist Critique,” *Hastings Center Report* 20 (July/August, 1990), 6–12; Paul Lauritzen, “Whose Bodies? Which Selves? Appeals to Embodiment in Assessments of Reproductive Technology,” in Lisa Sowle Cahill & Margaret A. Farley, eds., *Embodiment, Morality, and Medicine* (Dordrecht: Kluwer, 1995), pp. 113–26; Sidney Callahan, “Abortion and the Sexual Agenda: A Case for Pro-Life Feminism,” *Commonweal* 123 (April 25, 1986), 232–38; Patricia Beattie Jung, “Abortion and Organ Donation: Christian Reflections on Bodily Life Support,” in Patricia Beattie Jung & Thomas A. Shannon, eds., *Abortion and Catholicism: The American Debate* (New York: Crossroad, 1988), 141–71; Anne E. Patrick, “Toward Renewing ‘The Life and Culture of Fallen Man’: *Gaudium et Spes* as Catalyst for Catholic Feminist Theology,” in Judith A. Dwyer, ed., *Questions of Special Urgency: The Church in the Modern World Two Decades After Vatican II* (Washington, D.C.: Georgetown University Press, 1986), pp. 55–78; Christine Firer Hinze, “Bridge Discourse on Wage Justice: Roman Catholic and Feminist Perspectives on the Family Wage,” in *The Annual: Society of Christian Ethics* (Georgetown University Press, 1991), pp. 109–132; Carol Coston, “Women's Ways of Working,” in John A. Coleman, ed., *One Hundred Years of Catholic Social Thought: Celebration and Challenge* (Maryknoll, N.Y.: Orbis, 1991), pp. 256–69; Rosemary Radford Ruether, “Healing the World: The Sacramental Tradition,” in *Gaia and God: An Ecofeminist Theology of Earth Healing* (San Francisco: HarperCollins, 1992), pp. 229–53; Mary C. Segers, “Feminism, Liberalism, and Catholicism,” in R. Bruce Douglass & David Hollenbach, eds., *Catholicism and Liberalism: Contributions to American Public Philosophy* (Cambridge: University Press, 1994), pp. 242–68; Francine Cardman, “Liberating Compassion: Spirituality for a New Millenium,” *The Way* 32 (January, 1992), 5–12

Foreword

This ninth volume in our *Readings in Moral Theology* proved especially challenging. Once feminist ethics was chosen as the organizing theme, we had to narrow the focus, so huge and varied is the literature. In accord with the purpose of our series we focus on feminist ethics insofar as it interacts with the Catholic moral tradition, and we try to show the diversity within feminist ethics. We also determined, with few exceptions, to select more recent writings. We realize that such a narrowing leads to the omission of some other highly desirable material: for example, a more historical approach would emphasize the original contributions of scholars such as Rosemary Radford Ruether and Elisabeth Schüssler Fiorenza. All we could do was try to assemble a representative sample of this abundant literature. It is our hope that textual and footnote references will provide further invitations to explore beyond our offerings.

Next we had to develop organizing topics under which we would group the essays. We decided on: Overview, General Theory, Interpersonal and Familial Relations, Bioethics, and Social Ethics. Clearly other categories could have been chosen. Moreover, these are not mutually exclusive categories, especially in light of the feminist insistence that the personal is political.

The editors of the first eight volumes were males. To continue that policy would be clearly inappropriate given our organizing theme in this volume. For this reason a third editor has been added for this volume. Not only that, however. We consulted broadly on both the desirability and possible contents of our volume. Without exception we received very insightful and helpful responses. Obviously, none of our consultants is responsible for any defects in our selection. But all contributed to the overall value of the book. We wish to thank, in alphabetical order, the following: Barbara Hilkert Andolsen, Lisa Sowle Cahill, Sidney Callahan, Francine Cardman, Dolores L. Christie, M. Shawn Copeland, Cynthia S.W. Crysdale, Mary A. Elsbernd, Rosemarie E. Gorman, Christine E. Gudorf, Mary E. Hunt, Ada María Isasi-Díaz, Elizabeth A. Johnson, Patricia Beattie Jung, Cathleen Kaveny, Sally A. McReynolds, June O'Connor, Anne E. Patrick, Jean Porter, Rosemary Radford Ruether, Susan A. Ross, Maura A. Ryan, Patricia A. Schoelles, Susan L. Secker, Joan H. Timmerman, and Diane Yeager.

It is our conviction that the Catholic tradition will only be enriched if it takes seriously the voices of women like those mentioned above. This *Readings in Moral Theology No. 9* hopes to contribute to that purpose.

Charles E. Curran
Margaret A. Farley
Richard A. McCormick, S.J.

Part One

OVERVIEW

1. Feminist Ethics

Margaret A. Farley

This chapter first appeared in *The Westminster Dictionary of Christian Ethics* in 1986.

In its most general sense "feminist ethics" refers to any ethical theory that locates its roots in feminism, especially in the contemporary feminist movement. "Feminism" is itself a much contested term, but in its most fundamental meaning it represents a position, a belief, a perspective, a movement, that is opposed to discrimination on the basis of gender. It is, therefore, opposed to sexism in all of its forms, whether within institutional structures and practices, attitudes and behaviors, or ideologies, beliefs, and theories that establish and reinforce gender discrimination. In terms of social structure, feminism is opposed to gendered patterns of domination and subordination, gendered role differentiation, gender-biased unequal access to goods and services. In addition, feminism is opposed to other forms of unjust discrimination and patterns of domination; it includes in its analysis the socially constructed connections among gender, race, class, age, sexual orientation, and other particular characterizations that can be the basis of discrimination and oppression.

Positively, feminism aims ultimately at equality of respect and the concrete well-being of all persons regardless of gender. To move toward this aim, however, feminism is necessarily pro-women (but *not* thereby anti-men). Since sexism has been and remains pervasively discrimination against women, feminism aims to correct this bias by a bias for women. This includes a focal concern for the well-being of women and a taking account of women's experience in coming to understand what well-being means for both women and men.

Feminist theory appears in a variety of disciplines, including philosophy, the social and behavioral sciences, and theology. It is also expressed in principles of interpretation for literary and historical texts and for religious scriptures. All feminist theory incorporates a firm methodological commitment to maintaining a focus on the experience of women as a primary source. Like feminism in general, feminist theory traces its origins to women's growing awareness of the disparity between received traditional interpretations of their identity and function and their own experience of themselves and their lives. Hence, major tasks undertaken by feminist scholars include the critique of sources of sexism (religious, social, political, economic); retrieval of women's history and pro-women myths; reconstruction of theories of the human persona and the human community. As feminist theories developed, the commitment to the well-being of women required a widening attention to the experience of all women and therefore a serious consideration of the diversity of women's historical and cultural contexts and experiences.

There is pluralism and controversy within feminism, and hence within feminist ethics. Differences are sometimes identified according to analyses of the causes of sexism and strategies to correct it. Thus, for example, a liberal feminist ethic advocates the extension of the liberal tradition of political rights to women and a corresponding reform of policies of gender discrimination. It challenges liberalism to consistency and to true impartiality in its recognition of and respect for every human person. A socialist feminist ethic, however, notes the ongoing failure of liberal theory and policies to emancipate women. This ethic, therefore, critiques the "additive" approach of liberalism and focuses on changing the structures related to production in society in order to secure economic parity and autonomy for women. Radical feminist ethics appears in several strands, but gender analysis is central to its many approaches. From its perspective, patriarchy is neither a mere anomaly in an otherwise liberal system nor a form of domination solely derivative from economic systems. It is less concerned with issues of individual autonomy than with issues of community in which gendered power relations are exposed and transformed.

Beyond the frequently blurred categories of liberal, socialist, and radical feminism, disagreements in feminist ethics occur over recognizable fault lines such as particularity versus universality, context versus principles, and justice versus care as approaches to ethical problems or the highest expression of moral character. There is also disagreement when feminists address more specific ethical issues such as reproductive technologies, pornography, protective labor laws, population crises, and ecological dangers.

Despite the pluralism in feminist ethics, there are generally shared issues and basic values. Major questions that have produced common ethical concerns include: human agency, embodiment (especially in terms of sexuality), the nature of the human self, moral development, patterns of human relationships (both personal and political), the value of the world of nature. Revisionist interpretations of these questions have yielded strong theories of the relation between reason and emotion, the positive possibilities of desire, love, anger, the place of the individual within community, the structure of human and religious virtue, the importance of dispositions for caring as well as dispositions for justice.

Methodologically, feminist ethics has been open to both deontological and consequentialist patterns of reasoning. On the one hand, it has taken seriously the possibility that human actions can be judged unethical insofar as they contradict values intrinsic to the concrete reality of persons. On the other hand, feminist ethics sustains a concern for consequences, for an ethical evaluation of means in relation to ends and of parts in relation to the whole; overall it is favorable to an ecological view of reality, and it allows the relativization of values in situations of conflict.

Feminist ethics as a systematic discipline is new enough and sufficiently diverse that it is difficult to generalize its substantive principles. One way of identifying them could go something like this. The most fundamental substantive principle is the principle that women are fully human and are to be valued as such. The content of this principle differs significantly from similar but nonfeminist affirmations. It is not, for example, to be mistaken for the view that women are human, though derivatively and partially so. Rather, feminist belief about the humanness of women is specified by the inclusion of further principles of equality and autonomy, and it is qualified by a principle of mutuality.

The insistence on the combination of principles of autonomy, equality, and mutuality differentiates feminist ethics from some other ethical approaches. Feminist ethics wants to specify the formal principle of "equal treatment for equals," noting the necessity of discerning who are equals in terms of basic humanity. Moreover, feminist ethics rejects strong theories of gender complementarity that, in the name of "different but equal" identifications, disguise patterns of inequality. Many feminist ethicists insist, therefore, that the essential feature of personhood, which modern philosophy identified as a capacity for free self-determination (autonomy), be appropriated for women as well as for men. On this basis, the feminist principle of equality, of the equal right of all persons to respect as persons, is maintained.

Feminist ethics, however, extends the principle of equality to some version of a principle of equitable sharing. That is, out of women's experience of disadvantage and their perception of the disadvantaged histories of other groups, feminists argue for a universalized right of all to an equitable share in the goods and services necessary to human life and basic happiness. Feminist ethics generally includes, therefore, a positive form of the principle of equality, one based not only on the self-protective right of each to freedom, but on the participation of all in human solidarity.

Closely aligned with this, feminist ethics could be described as rejecting a view of human persons that is self-isolating. Hence, it tends to combine some form of the principle of mutuality with the principle of equality. Its basis for doing this is a view of human persons that identifies relationality along with autonomy as an essential need and possibility. Feminist ethicists insist, then, on a corrective to liberal philosophy insofar as it fails to understand persons as embodied subjects, with a capacity and a need for union with other persons. But feminist ethics generally also sees itself as a corrective to romantic theories of sociality, organic models of society, or theories of complementarity in which relation is all, without regard for free agency or for personal identity, power, and worth, which transcend roles.

An effort to identify methodological and substantive principles for feminist ethics must be qualified by acknowledging that some feminist ethicists prefer to avoid the language of "principles" altogether. This follows recognition of past abuses where principles were used to oppose, rather than serve, the well-being of persons and relations, and where principles were maintained without any acknowledgment of the historical and social nature of human knowledge. It also takes account of postmodern critiques of essentialism, giving serious attention to the social construction of human self-understandings. The diversity in women's own experience argues against too much reliance on abstract principles and too easy universalization of meanings. Yet feminism's commitments to gender (and racial, religious, etc.) equality make it wary of unmitigated relativism as well. Hence within feminist ethics there is an effort to work out a theory that will take account of particularity but not altogether rule out universal norms. In this effort, feminist ethics is both challenged and enriched by the work of womanist and *mujerista* ethicists, as well as the ethical analyses provided by many other women whose particular experience is essential to the overall ethical task.

Some feminist ethical reflection can be more specifically described as Christian feminist ethics. This includes much of what has already been noted, but also a more direct concern with issues shaped by Christian belief and theology. Thus, for example, Christian feminist ethics takes a critical stance in relation to past theological justification of the inferiority of women to men. It challenges the distinction of male and female as polar opposites (representing mind/body, reason/emotion, activity/passivity, autonomy/dependency). It opposes the association of women with religious symbols of evil, but it is also opposed to religious "pedestalism," or the expectation that women will be more virtuous than men. A Christian feminist ethics takes seriously the feminist critique of Christianity as a religion that can lead to the exaltation of dependence and suffering. It shares the critique made of Christianity and other religions insofar as they present gendered expectations that women should exist more for the service of others (indeed, the whole species) than should men. As Christian and feminist, then, it takes as one of its tasks the development of a theory of moral and religious development and a feminist theory of virtue. Christian feminists have also identified problems with traditional concepts of *agape,* and they seek to balance principles of equality and mutuality with the concept of self-sacrifice. Christian feminists are, moreover, concerned with the formulation of theories of justice that will illuminate more adequately every form of human and Christian relationship (and that will thereby address more adequately issues of power, violence, responsibility, and social cooperation).

2. Feminist Theology: A Review of Literature

Susan A. Ross

This chapter first appeared in *Theological Studies* in 1995.*

According to Sandra Schneiders's useful definition, feminism is a comprehensive ideology, rooted in women's experience of sexual oppression, which engages in a critique of patriarchy, embraces an alternative vision for humanity and the earth, and actively seeks to bring this vision to realization.[1] Feminist theology may be considered that part of this quest for justice which is concerned with critical analysis and liberating retrieval of the meaning of religious traditions. In the roughly 35 years of its existence, contemporary feminist theology has produced a vast, international body of literature that ranges across all of the theological specialties and beyond. The notes that follow revisit several salient themes and debates in the area of systematic theology, although no hard and fast division obtains between this discipline and feminist ethics and biblical hermeneutics.[2]

The current intellectual ferment first came to expression in Valerie Saiving (Goldstein)'s now-classic 1960 article, "The Human Situation: A Feminine View," in which she raised the question of the applicability of prevailing theological statements to all human beings. Her own suggestion, that teachings about sin as pride or will-to-power and about redemption as negation of self or self-giving love might look very different from the perspective of women's experience, struck a deep chord.[3] Since then, virtually every aspect of inherited theology has been scrutinized for the ways in which its context has shaped its content, the two being inextricably linked.

In 1985 Mary Jo Weaver identified six tasks for feminist academicians.[4] The first three involve pointing out the absence of women in a field, recognizing that whatever knowledge about women in fact exists has been trivialized, and searching out the lost traditions of women. Much work on these initial tasks was undertaken during the 1970s and early 1980s. The other three tasks entail reading old texts in a revisionary way, challenging the discipline methodologically, and working toward a truly integrated field. In the last ten years these latter tasks have been taken up with enthusiasm and rigor by feminist theologians, resulting in works that not only fall under the general rubric of systematic theology but also stretch the boundaries of what has been understood to be systematic theological discourse.

While earlier (i.e., pre-1980) feminist theologians could be characterized as either "radical" or "reformist" in view of their relation to patriarchal traditions,[5] no such classification can be made now. This is due to the diversity that prevails in approaches to the constructive tasks of theology, to the point where feminist theolo*gies* would be more accurate nomenclature. Even the term "feminist" is problematic, given its association with largely white, middle-class, well-educated women. In the U.S., the "womanist" theology of African-American women and the *mujerista* theology of Hispanic women now take their place at the table, along with the insights of Asian-American women. Indeed, attention to diversity, otherness, and difference has emerged as an essential methodological concern of feminist theologies.[6] This shows itself in several ways.

First, the recourse to experience is a major though controverted move in all women's theologies. As in Saiving's essay, "women's experience" in distinction to the claim of "common human experience" functions as a theological resource and criterion.[7] Yet it became increasingly evident in the 1980s that the nature of that experience needed more careful scrutiny. Does the appeal to experience refer to bodily, socialized, psychological, historical, religious, political, cultural, racial, class, or economic experience?[8] Is it an appeal to their own experience by white women who fail to consider the difference that race makes, thereby effectively erasing women of color the way traditional male theology overlooked all women?[9] Ann O'Hara Graff has pointed out that "there is no unified body of women's experience, but rather there are multiple forms and multiple dimensions of women's experience,"[10] proposing that this multiplicity can be located in three "key complexes": social location, language, and the quest for human wholeness. "*Whose* experience?" has become a key question, and the answer is not easily arrived at. Yet there can be no doubt that experience continues to be central and that the particularity of that experience is increasingly critical for feminist theologies.

Second, attention to difference is also to the fore in analyses of subjectivity and language. While theologies influenced by postmodernism declare the death of the subject, feminist theologies question its demise just as women have begun to name themselves as acting subjects of their own history.[11] Concern for community as intrinsic to the self is likewise central to feminist theologies which question Western individualism and its concomitant idea of the isolated self apart from relationships and social location.[12] The role of language and reason in relation to the role of emotion in human life is a related question, as is the power of voice for defining subjectivity.[13] Indeed, "hearing one another into speech" has been one of the defining metaphors of feminist theologies.[14] In short, concerns for the nature of the self, the self's embeddedness in communities, and the power of language to constitute the self are central to feminist reflection and another entry point for the emergence of difference.

Third, diversity emerges as feminist theologians continue to grapple with the patriarchal nature of traditional religions, resulting in the boundaries being pushed among denominational divides and between these and postpatriarchal religions. Since a concern for justice is at the root of all feminist theologies, creative fidelity to tradition requires hermeneutics of both suspicion and retrieval in order to wrest resources that support the full humanity of women. The extent to which inherited theological traditions provide resources for feminist theologies is a much-debated question. Answers range from Elizabeth Johnson's rich retrieval of Sophia for language about God,[15] to Kwok Pui-lan's affirmation of her Asian pagan/Christian identity,[16] to Emily Culpepper's use of Christianity as compost for the growth of new religious traditions.[17]

As the following notes make clear, feminist theologies may be pluralist in nature but they are united by a shared passion for justice for women. Visions of right relations and well-being in ecclesial and societal human communities as well as between human beings and the earth continue to inspire the work, while the lives and struggles of actual women around the world provide the resources and the ultimate test of the adequacy of all feminist theologies.

The Physical and Social Context for Feminist Theology and Spirituality

This section will review recent literature in feminist theology that provides foundational categories drawn from the contextual linkage of theology and location, both physical and social. Beginning with embodiment, the ever-widening and intersecting relationships with self, other, community, and cosmos serve to ground feminist theologies and provide bases from which to reconceive new models of self and God, as well as the inherited theological tradition.

Embodiment

Feminists and traditionalists alike argue that embodiment is central to the Christian tradition.[18] But given the wide range of meanings which embodiment can assume, there is no one definitive feminist perspective on embodiment. What distinguishes feminist theological treatments of embodiment are these related features: (1) a suspicion of views that see women as being more "naturally" embodied than are men;[19] (2) a rejection of a dualist framework (e.g., body–soul) for conceptualizing embodiment;[20] (3) a concern to place embodiment in a historical and social context;[21] (4) an extension of embodiment as a value to wider issues, such as the nature of the person, norms for moral action, and the human relationship to the earth;[22] (5) a celebration of embodiment in new forms of ritual and liturgy.[23]

The "suspicion" with which feminist theology holds theories which link women to body and nature is a basic issue for feminist theologians. This linkage has often been the grounds for establishing a dualistic hierarchy of mind and soul over body, in which men are identified with mind/soul and women with body. Yet there is also a feminist concern to value the "distinctiveness" of women's embodied experience.[24] While recognizing that menstruation, pregnancy, and childbirth are distinctively female experiences, feminists note that their meaning across cultures may vary widely.[25] There is no "purely natural" experience that is not at the same time mediated by culture.[26] Thus feminists reject views that assign an essential "femininity" to women without a critical examination of what such a term implies.[27] Likewise, feminists see the "complementarity" of masculine and feminine, especially as it is used in magisterial documents, as a new form of dualism.[28]

Christine E. Gudorf's critical approach to embodiment stresses the importance of "bodyright" as the right to control one's own body. She observes that the absence of bodyright is a heritage of Western patriarchal mind/body dualism. The failure to value bodyright results in such serious personal and social ills as violence against women and children and compulsory military service, especially for minority groups.[29] Similarly, Delores Williams and Cheryl Townsend Gilkes argue that the embodied experiences of African-American women have been particularly vulnerable to control and exploitation by others.[30] Bodily integrity—freedom from violence, harassment, surrogacy, and freedom to choose or refrain from sexual intimacy—is essential for full personhood for women.

Constructively, feminist theologians (as well as feminists in other disciplines) argue that a greater appreciation for the embodied character of human existence has the potential to transform our understanding of what it means to be human, challenging prevailing notions of rationality and autonomy as superior to affectivity and interdependence. Beverly Wildung Harrison has sounded this theme, which has been echoed, in various ways by Paula Cooey, Mary Ellen Ross, and Linell Cady, to mention only a few.[31] An "embodied morality" is one in which one's rationality and emotions are integrated, and one which considers the concrete, as well as the theoretical, consequences of one's actions, and which celebrates the joys and the delights of women's sexuality.[32]

Ecofeminist concerns will receive more detailed attention below, but it is worth pointing out here the connection between hierarchical and dualist conceptions of the relation between soul and body with those of the human to the natural world. This connection was recognized 20 years ago in Rosemary Ruether's *New Woman, New Earth,*[33] and it has been developed at length in her *Gaia and God: An Ecofeminist Theology of Earth Healing.*[34]

Finally, the focus on embodiment in feminist sacramental and liturgical theologies is important to note. In a 1987 essay, Christine Gudorf observed that male control of the sacraments represents a ritualization of what is ordinarily women's realm (feeding, caring for the sick, etc.). The solution, she argued, lies in men's greater participation in daily life and women's greater involvement in sacramental administration.[35] In discussing the role of "emancipatory language" in liturgy, Marjorie Procter-Smith writes: "Language that makes women's experience visible must therefore recognize the physical realities of women's lives," and she goes on to emphasize negative as well as positive dimensions of women's embodiment.[36] Ann Patrick Ware, in a critique of the Easter Vigil, notes the persistence of dualistic metaphors (which have historically served women badly), the use of overwhelmingly male language, and the frequent reference to the sacrificial death of Christ.[37] In the same volume, Sheila Redmond discusses how family violence is all too often ignored in liturgy. This denial perpetuates a division between the private, domestic sphere of the body and the public sphere, suggesting that the bodily and psychic pain experienced by many needs no public or ritual acknowledgement.[38] In "God's Embodiment and Women: Sacraments," I emphasize the bodily tie which connects the sacraments and human life, and argue for a serious consideration of women's ambiguous experience of sacraments.[39]

The emphasis on embodiment and the role of mothering has also been an important theme.[40] Most of the essays in the anthology *The Will to Arise: Women, Tradition and the Church in Africa* concern the role of sexuality and marriage in women's lives.[41] The authors of these essays argue, in differing ways, for an integration of women's embodied experience in marriage and motherhood into ritual and symbol. The importance of incorporating one's own cultural experience into ritual is also crucial. Hispanic women theologians, both *mujerista* and Latin-American, emphasize the importance of the family and are critical of feminist views which argue for women's equality in an individualist sense that ignores the ties of women to families and children.[42] They share a concern for integrating popular culture into religious praxis and reflection. Similarly, Korean theologian Chung Hyun Kyung as well as Chinese theologian Kwok Pui-Lan argue for incorporation of women's religiosity, within its cultural context, into Christian ritual.[43]

While embodiment remains a crucial and essential element of feminist theology, it is also an ambiguous element. While any "special" or "distinctive" knowledge of women through the body is always mediated through social structures, it is also impossible to escape biological reality.[44]

Mutuality and Friendship

The embodied self lives in a context of relationships. As with the category of embodiment, feminist theologians are critical of conceptions of the self which abstract from physical and social context. The work of Mary E. Hunt, as well as that of Janice Raymond and Carter Heyward, has stressed friendship as a foundational relationship for women, more important affectively (and, they argue, also morally) than the traditional association of women with marital or parental relationships.[45] As a model for "right relation," Hunt's conception of friendship challenges classic models, such as Aristotle's or Augustine's, for their inherent inequality. Insights from women's friendships include their potential availability to everyone, their ambiguous and fluid nature, and their qualitative, rather than quantitative, dimension.[46]

For most feminist theologians, mutuality as a normative principle counters hierarchical structures of relationship, which are, at best, viewed by feminists with suspicion. This concern carries over into almost every dimension of feminist theology, encompassing relationships with God, other human beings, and the nonhuman world.[47] Carter Heyward argues that homosexual friendship provides a better model for real mutuality in relationship than do heterosexual relationships: ". . . in our present social order, mutual sexual relationships are available largely in same-sex relationships. I have come to believe that it is unwise to expect true personal equality—mutuality of common benefit—between women and men in a sexist society."[48] Jacqueline Grant, however, argues that "discipleship" provides a more "empowering" model for equality in relationship and explicitly rejects models of "service" and "servanthood," especially for African-American women, given their imposed servanthood in slavery and beyond.[49]

Although too complex an issue to treat in detail here, the influence of object-relations theory and other psychoanalytic theories warrants mention.[50] Object-relations theory focuses on the relationship between mother and child and on the "pre-Oedipal" period in childhood development.[51] In brief, feminists who use object-relations theory argue that because women remain overwhelmingly the primary parent for young children (at least in industrialized Western society), boys must learn to separate from their mothers to become individual persons, while girls (who are potential mothers) see their selfhood in relationship.[52] These developmental issues have serious repercussions for theology, especially in relation to conceptions of God and God's relation to humanity, as well as for ethics.

Mutuality thus takes on a normative quality in feminist theology, serving to criticize oppressive and hierarchical relationships and to model new possibilities.

Social Location

The embodied, related self also comes from a distinct social and cultural environment. While earlier (white) feminist theology tended to generalize about "women's experience," assuming commonalities across cultures, more recent theology has emphasized the distinct issues that concern women of diverse backgrounds.

Most prominent in the American scene are the voices of African-American and U.S. Hispanic women.

In a 1990 roundtable discussion,[53] six African-American woman scholars debated the usefulness of the term "womanist" as an appropriate nomenclature for African-American women scholars in ethics and theology. Cheryl Sanders argued that "womanist" is problematic, rooted in secular culture, and of questionable value to Christians. The five respondents to Sanders (Katie G. Cannon, Emilie M. Townes, M. Shawn Copeland, bell hooks, and Cheryl Townsend Gilkes) all defended the term, with Copeland arguing that it "makes visible and gives voice to African-American women scholars in religion who are in the process of crafting a distinct perspective that takes the experiences and traditions of black women as a source for theologizing on the black experience."[54] In a 1992 article, Diana L. Hayes writes of becoming aware of her own voice and the need to work for liberation "not just of self but for others."[55] The work of Cannon,[56] Townes,[57] Delores S. Williams,[58] and Renita Weems[59] draws on the long-neglected history of African-American women as well as the Bible in giving birth to a theology which is rooted in the survival through centuries of oppression of strong women and men.

In many cases, womanist theology has taken (white) feminist theology, as well as traditional (male) theology, to task for its use of certain metaphors and values. Katie Cannon suggests that "truth-telling" may not always be of primary importance in ethics for the oppressed;[60] Jacqueline Grant has argued strongly against the model of Jesus as "servant," given the long history of African-American servitude.[61] Nearly all womanist theologians draw heavily on the fiction of African-American women writers, as well as on the long-neglected history of African-American women.[62]

The term *mujerista* as an analogous term for Hispanic feminists was also discussed in a subsequent roundtable discussion.[63] Ada María Isasi-Díaz defines *mujerista* theology: "As a liberative praxis, *mujerista* theology is a process of enablement for Hispanic women insisting on the development of a strong sense of moral agency, and clarifying the importance and value of who we are, what we think, and what we do."[64] In her own work, Isasi-Díaz emphasizes the importance of her method, "ethnomethodology," based in a critical approach to social sciences and the life stories of Hispanic women.[65] This method seeks to make explicit the connections between the community and theology by drawing on the life experiences of Hispanic women.

María Pilar Aquino, a Mexican educated in Spain and now teaching in the U.S., develops a systematic perspective on Hispanic women's experience that is based in Latin America in her book *Our Cry for Life.*[66] Rooted in the liberation theology of Latin America, as well as the work of Elisabeth Schüssler Fiorenza and Karl Rahner, Aquino's theology emphasizes its collective nature, which is enriched by the originality, resistance, creativity, solidarity, hope, and freedom of the experiences of women in Latin America.[67]

The social reality of injustice and struggle defines the work of women theologians, but in a particularly important way for non-Western and poor women. Thus, questions that may be of more import in the North American scene (like the issue of women's ordination) are less significant than concerns for equality within marriage,[68] for freedom from sexual exploitation and domestic violence,[69] and for sheer economic survival.

Social location also serves to challenge received theological definitions and categories. The concept of sin, for example, has a highly developed social character in womanist and *mujerista* theology and "engages both a hermeneutic of suspicion and a hermeneutic of resistance," especially in relation to theologies that promote such virtues as patience and forebearance.[70] "Sin is not a matter of disobedience but of not being for others," says one of the women interviewed in *Hispanic Women.*[71] Similarly, virtues are related to social context and cannot be assumed to have the same significance for all women, much less all human beings.[72]

As "difference" has emerged as a critical issue for women-centered theological efforts, painful questions have arisen concerning ways in which women from different social locations can share concerns and sources. How is "difference" acknowledged without reduction to a mere acknowledgment of one's own social location? Toinette Eugene laments what typically occurs in writings by white women: "After the disclaimer [of one's social location], nothing again indicates that difference is recognized."[73] Another problem arises from the "appropriation" of material by those who do not share the same social location.[74] That difference must *make* a difference remains more an ideal than a reality.

Ecofeminism

The physical context which makes all of earthly life possible is the ecosystem. As feminist, womanist, and *mujerista* theologians have developed "new patterns of relationship,"[75] the relationship of human beings to the nonhuman world has been one of special concern. Hierarchical relations of domination/submission have had devastating consequences for women and for the earth, especially when the creation narratives seem to support such relations.[76]

As Rosemary Ruether and Sallie McFague have suggested, new understandings of the doctrine of creation are needed. Indeed, Ruether begins *Gaia and God* with a chapter on three creation stories (the *Enuma Elish, Genesis,* and the *Timaeus*) and argues that contemporary science suggests a new creation story, one that portrays the origin of life as fundamentally interrelational.[77] Similarly, Sallie McFague argues for an "organic" model for creation which "supports both radical individuality and difference while at the same time insisting on radical interdependence of all the parts."[78] Elizabeth Johnson suggests that a consideration of "Creator Spirit" as Wisdom can better support a theology of interrelation.[79]

Ruether, McFague, and Johnson see the potential within the Christian tradition to reformulate and reenvision the relationship between God and humanity, and between human beings and the nonhuman world. But other feminists find this retrieval of Christian tradition unsuccessful. Emily Culpepper suggests that Christianity might serve as "compost," helping to fertilize new forms of relating to the sacred.[80] Thealogian Carol Christ questions the value placed by patriarchal religions on human self-consciousness, since it elevates some species over others;[81] she suggests that humanity "consider whether there is any reality 'higher' than the finite, the earth, that which changes."[82] Ruether shares this suspicion of the fear of finitude, and asks whether Christian eschatology has refused to accept the inevitable limitations of earthly existence.[83]

The consequences of a distorted relationship to the earth have had a disproportionate effect on poor women, men, and children.[84] Indeed, a critique of the devastating repercussions of unequal power relations is at the core of feminist theology and spirituality, as women envision and live into new forms of relationship. Here, the boundaries between systematic theology and ethics begin to dissolve, as the concern for justice and right relation extends into every dimension of life.

Notes

*The overall planning for this survey was done by Elizabeth A. Johnson, C.S.J., who also wrote the Introduction with Susan A. Ross. The section on "The Physical and Social Context for Feminist Theology and Spirituality" was written by Susan A. Ross; that on "Key Religious Symbols: Christ and God" was written by Mary Catherine Hilkert, O.P.

1. Sandra Schneiders, *Beyond Patching: Faith and Feminism in the Catholic Church* (New York: Paulist, 1991) 15.

2. For recent treatments in *TS* of feminist biblical scholarship and ethics, see Phyllis Trible, "Five Loaves and Two Fishes: Feminist Hermeneutics and Biblical Theology," *TS* 50 (1989) 279–95; Lisa Sowle Cahill, "Notes on Moral Theology: Feminist Ethics," *TS* 51 (1990) 49–64. Cahill writes, "Virtually by definition, feminist theology is 'moral' theology or ethics" (50).

3. *Journal of Religion* 40 (1960) 100–12; reprinted in Carol Christ and Judith Plaskow, eds., *Womanspirit Rising: A Feminist Reader in Religion* (San Francisco: Harper & Row, 1979) 25–42. See also Judith Plaskow, *Sex, Sin and Grace: Women's Experience and the Theologies of Reinhold Niebuhr and Paul Tillich* (Washington: University Press of America, 1980).

4. *New Catholic Women: A Contemporary Challenge to Traditional Religious Authority* (San Francisco: Harper & Row, 1985) 154–55.

5. See *Womanspirit Rising* 1–17.

6. The struggle is reflected in a dialogue between two colleagues: Susan Secker, "Women's Experience in Feminist Theology: The 'Problem'

or the 'Truth' of Difference," *Journal of Hispanic/Latino Theology* 1 (1993) 56–67; and Jeanette Rodriguez, "Experience as a Resource for Feminist Thought," ibid. 68–76. For a helpful theological perspective on the category of "difference" using the thought of Bernard Lonergan, see Cynthia Crysdale, "Horizons That Differ: Women and Men and the Flight from Understanding," *Cross Currents* 44 (1994) 345–61.

7. Consult Rosemary Radford Ruether, *Sexism and God Talk: Toward a Feminist Theology* (Boston: Beacon 1983), or Anne Carr, *Transforming Grace: Christian Tradition and Women's Experience* (San Francisco: Harper and Row, 1988), in contrast with David Tracy, *Blessed Rage for Order: The New Pluralism in Theology* (New York: Crossroad, 1975).

8. See Anne Carr, "The New Vision of Feminist Theology," in *Freeing Theology: The Essentials of Theology in Feminist Perspective,* ed. Catherine LaCugna (San Francisco: Harper Collins, 1993) 5–29, at 22–23.

9. Susan Brooks Thistlethwaite, *Sex, Race, and God: Christian Feminism in Black and White* (New York: Crossroad, 1989), esp. 11–26.

10. "The Struggle to Name Women's Experience: Assessment and Implications for Theological Construction," *Horizons: Journal of the College Theology Society* 20 (1993) 230.

11. See Barbara Christian, "The Race for Theory," *Feminist Studies* 14 (1988) 67–79; Jane Flax, *Thinking Fragments: Psychoanalysis, Feminism and Postmodernism in the Contemporary West* (Berkeley: University of California, 1990).

12. Catherine Keller, *From a Broken Web: Separation, Sexism and Self* (Boston: Beacon, 1986) is one such analysis from a white Western woman, while Ada María Isasi-Díaz, *En la Lucha (In the Struggle): A Hispanic Woman's Liberation Theology* (Minneapolis: Fortress, 1993) underscores that self-in-community is more representative of women in nondominant cultures.

13. See Rebecca Chopp, *The Power to Speak: Feminism, Language, God* (New York: Crossroad, 1989); and Mary McClintock Fulkerson, *Changing the Subject: Women's Discourses and Feminist Theology* (Minneapolis: Fortress, 1994).

14. The phrase is from Nelle Morton, *The Journey Is Home* (Boston: Beacon, 1985).

15. *SHE WHO IS: The Mystery of God in Feminist Theological Discourse* (New York: Crossroad, 1992).

16. "Claiming a Boundary Existence: A Parable from Hong Kong," *Journal of Feminist Studies in Religion* 3 (1987) 121–24.

17. "The Spiritual, Political Journey of a Feminist Freethinker," in *After Patriarchy: Feminist Transformations of the World Religions,* ed.

Paula Cooey, William Eakin, and Jay McDaniel (Maryknoll, N.Y.: Orbis, 1991) 146–65.

18. See, e.g., Pope John Paul II, *Love and Responsibility,* trans. H. T. Willetts (New York: Farrar, Straus, and Giroux, 1981); Susan A. Ross, " 'Then Honor God in Your Body' (1 Cor. 6:20): Feminist and Sacramental Theology on the Body," *Horizons* 16 (1989) 7–27; Maria Theresa Porcile-Santiso, "Roman Catholic Teaching on Female Sexuality," in Jeanne Becker, ed., *Women, Religion and Sexuality: Studies on the Impact of Religious Teachings on Women* (Philadelphia: Trinity, 1990) 192–220; Lisa Sowle Cahill, *Women and Sexuality,* 1992 Madaleva Lecture in Spirituality (New York: Paulist, 1992).

19. See Sherry B. Ortner's classic article "Is Female to Male as Nature is to Culture?" in Michelle Zimbalist Rosaldo and Louise Lamphere, eds., *Woman, Culture and Society* (Stanford: Stanford University, 1974) 67–87, and further discussion in Carol MacCormack and Marilyn Strathern, eds., *Nature, Culture and Gender* (Cambridge: Cambridge University, 1980).

20. This is a theme repeatedly emphasized by Rosemary Radford Ruether; see *New Woman, New Earth: Sexist Ideologies and Human Liberation* (New York: Seabury, 1975) and *Sexism and God-Talk: Toward a Feminist Theology* (Boston: Beacon, 1983).

21. Carolyn Walker Bynum, *Holy Feast and Holy Fast: The Religious Significance of Food for Medieval Women* (Berkeley: University of California, 1987); idem., *Fragmentation and Redemption* (New York: Zone, 1991); Martha Reinecke, " 'This is My Body': Reflections on Abjection, Anorexia, and Medieval Women Mystics," *Journal of the American Academy of Religion* 58 (1990) 245–65; Giles Milhaven, "A Medieval Lesson on Bodily Knowing: Women's Experience and Men's Thought," *Journal of the American Academy of Religion* 57 (1989) 341–72; Margaret Miles, *Carnal Knowing: Female Nakedness and Religious Meaning in the Christian West* (Boston: Beacon, 1989).

22. Paula M. Cooey, Sharon A. Farmer, and Mary Ellen Ross, eds., *Embodied Love: Sensuality and Relationship as Feminist Values* (San Francisco: Harper and Row, 1987); see Christine E. Gudorf, *Body, Sex, and Pleasure: Reconstructing Christian Sexual Ethics* (Cleveland: Pilgrim, 1994). Feminist ethics warrants, and has received, separate surveys of its own; see, e.g., Lisa Sowle Cahill, "Notes on Moral Theology: Feminist Ethics," *TS* 51 (1990) 49–64; "Professional Resources," *Annual of the Society of Christian Ethics* (1994) 257–305, with special focus on method, ecofeminism, and womanist ethics; and Lois K. Daly, ed., *Feminist Theological Ethics: A Reader* (Louisville: Westminster/John Knox, 1994). I will

focus my attention on the broader foundational issues underlying feminist theology, which by definition includes ethics (see Cahill, "Notes").

23. Barbara Walker, *Women's Rituals: A Sourcebook* (San Francisco: Harper and Row, 1990); Marjorie Procter-Smith, *In Her Own Rite: Constructing Feminist Liturgical Tradition* (Nashville: Abingdon, 1990); Marjorie Procter-Smith and Janet R. Walton, eds., *Women at Worship: Interpretations of North American Diversity* (Louisville: Westminister/John Knox, 1993). For a thorough and elegant consideration of theoretical issues in ritual, see Catherine Bell, *Ritual Theory, Ritual Practice* (Oxford: Oxford University, 1992). Mary Collins provides a helpful overview in her "Principles of Feminist Liturgy," in *Women at Worship* 9–26; See also Rosemary Radford Ruether, *Women-Church: Theology and Practice of Feminist Liturgical Communities* (San Francisco: Harper and Row, 1985).

24. The "distinctiveness" of women's experience, especially embodied experience, is debated among feminists. French feminists, notably Helene Cixous, Luce Irigaray, and Julia Kristeva, interpret this as "essential" to women. See Toril Moi, ed., *French Feminist Thought: A Reader* (Oxford: Blackwell, 1987); also C. W. Maggie Kim, Susan St. Ville, Susan Simonaitis, eds., *Transfigurations: Theology and the French Feminists* (Minneapolis: Fortress, 1993). American feminists tend to look toward social and historical forces, rather than biological or "natural" ones, to explain "difference"; for a helpful discussion, see Anne E. Carr, *Transforming Grace: Christian Tradition and Women's Experience* (San Francisco: Harper and Row, 1988).

25. Anne E. Carr and Elisabeth Schüssler Fiorenza, eds., *Motherhood: Experience, Institution, Theology* (Edinburgh: Clark, 1989); also Carr and Schüssler Fiorenza, eds., *The Special Nature of Women?* (London: SCM, 1991); Mercy Amba Oduyoye and Musimbi R. A. Kanyoro, eds., *The Will to Arise* (Maryknoll, N.Y.: Orbis, 1992); and, for a contemporary Western perspective, Susan Bordo, *Unbearable Weight: Feminism, Western Culture and the Body* (Berkeley: University of California, 1993). See also Clarissa W. Atkinson, *The Oldest Vocation: Christian Motherhood in the Middle Ages* (Ithaca: Cornell, 1991); Phyllis H. Kaminski, " 'Reproducing the World': Mary O'Brien's Theory of Reproductive Consciousness and Implications for Feminist Incarnational Theology," *Horizons* 19 (1992) 240–62.

26. See Gudorf, *Body, Sex;* Mary Douglas, *Purity and Danger: An Analysis of the Concepts of Pollution and Taboo* (London: Ark, 1984); idem., *Natural Symbols: Explorations in Cosmology* (New York: Pantheon, 1970).

27. See, e.g., John Paul II, *Mulieris dignitatem* no. 10, in *Origins* 18 (October 6, 1988) 261, 263–83, at 269.

28. Rosemary Radford Ruether, "Catholicism, Women, Body and Sexuality: A Response," in *Women, Religion and Sexuality* 221–32; see also Mary Aquin O'Neill, "The Mystery of Being Human Together," in Catherine M. LaCugna, ed., *Freeing Theology: The Essentials of Theology in Feminist Perspective* (San Francisco: Harper, 1993) 139–60.

29. Gudorf, *Body, Sex,* esp. chap. 6.

30. Delores Williams, "A Womanist Perspective on Sin," in Emilie M. Townes, ed., *A Troubling in My Soul: Womanist Perspectives on Evil and Suffering* (Maryknoll, N.Y.: Orbis, 1993) 139–49; Cheryl Townsend Gilkes, "The 'Loves' and 'Troubles' of African-American Women's Bodies: The Womanist Challenge to Cultural Humiliation and Community Ambivalence," in Townes, *Troubling* 232–49. See also Williams, *Sisters in the Wilderness: The Challenge of Womanist God-Talk* (Maryknoll, N.Y.: Orbis, 1993).

31. Beverly Wildung Harrison, "The Power of Anger in the Work of Love," in Carol S. Robb, ed., *Making the Connections: Essays in Feminist Social Ethics* (Boston: Beacon, 1985) 3–21; see Cooey, Farmer, and Ross, *Embodied Love,* and Paula Cooey, "The Redemption of the Body: Post-Patriarchal Reconstruction of Inherited Christian Doctrine," in *After Patriarchy: Feminist Transformations of the World Religions* (Maryknoll, N.Y.: Orbis, 1991) 106–30.

32. See Joan M. Tronto, *Moral Boundaries: A Political Argument for an Ethics of Care* (London: Routledge, 1993). The literature on "care" ethics is extensive; for a helpful survey, see Cynthia Crysdale, "Gilligan and the Ethics of Care: an Update," *Religious Studies Review* 20 (1994) 21–28; Mary D. Pellauer, "The Moral Significance of Female Orgasm: Toward Sexual Ethics That Celebrates Women's Sexuality," *Journal of Feminist Studies in Religion* 9 (Spring and Fall 1993) 161–82.

33. See n. 3 above.

34. Ruether, *Gaia and God: An Ecofeminist Theology of Earth Healing* (San Francisco: HarperSan Francisco, 1992).

35. "The Power to Create: Sacraments and Men's Need to Birth," *Horizons* 14 (1987) 296–309.

36. Procter-Smith, *In Her Own Rite* 68.

37. *Women at Worship* 83–106. See Hilkert, below, for more discussion of sacrifice in relation to Christology.

38. Sheila Redmond, " 'Remember the Good, Forget the Bad': Denial and Family Violence in a Christian Worship Service," *Women at Worship* 71–82.

39. Susan A. Ross, "God's Embodiment and Women: Sacraments," in *Freeing Theology,* 185–209; see also idem., "The Bride of Christ and the Body Politic: Body and Gender in Pre-Vatican II Marriage Theology," *Journal of Religion* 71 (1991) 345–61.

40. Carr and Schüssler Fiorenza, *Motherhood;* Bonnie Miller-McLemore, *Also a Mother: Work and Family as Theological Dilemma* (Louisville: Westminster/John Knox, 1994); also Virginia Held, *Feminist Morality: Transforming Culture, Science and Politics* (Chicago: University of Chicago, 1993).

41. *The Will to Arise* (above n. 25); see also Ursula King, ed., *Feminist Theology from the Third World,* (Maryknoll, N.Y.: Orbis, 1994) for an extensive and very helpful compilation of essays.

42. See Ada María Isasi-Díaz and Yolanda Tarango, *Hispanic Women: Prophetic Voice in the Church* (Maryknoll, N.Y.: Orbis, 1988, 1992); Isasi-Díaz, *En la Lucha (In the Struggle): A Hispanic Women's Liberation Theology* (Minneapolis: Fortress, 1993); see also her earlier articles, "*Mujerista* Theology's Method: A Liberative Praxis, A Way of Life," *Listening* 27 (Winter 1992) 41–54; "Silent Women Will Never Be Heard," *Missiology* 7 (1979) 295–301.

43. *Struggle to Be the Sun Again: Introducing Asian Women's Theology* (Maryknoll, N.Y.: Orbis, 1990); Kwok Pui-Lan, *Chinese Women and Christianity: 1860–1927* (Atlanta: Scholars, 1992); idem, "Claiming a Boundary Existence: A Parable from Hong Kong," *Journal of Feminist Studies in Religion* 3/2 (Fall 1987) 121–24.

44. For a perspective which recognizes both the biological and the social, see Paula M. Cooey, *Religious Imagination and the Body: A Feminist Analysis* (New York: Oxford University, 1994).

45. Mary E. Hunt, *Fierce Tenderness: A Feminist Theology of Friendship* (New York: Crossroad, 1991); idem., "Lovingly Lesbian: Toward a Feminist Theology of Friendship," in Robert Nugent, ed., *A Challenge to Love: Gay and Lesbian Catholics in the Church* (New York: Crossroad, 1983) 135–55; Janice Raymond, *A Passion for Friends: Toward a Philosophy of Female Affection* (Boston: Beacon, 1986); Carter Heyward, *Our Passion for Justice* (Cleveland: Pilgrim, 1984); idem., *Touching Our Strength: The Erotic as Power and the Love of God* (San Francisco: Harper, 1989).

46. Hunt, *Fierce Tenderness* 110.

47. See, e.g., Sallie McFague's delineation of the message of Jesus as inclusive and nonhierarchical, in *Models of God: Theology for an Ecological, Nuclear Age* (Philadelphia: Fortress, 1987) 45–57.

48. Carter Heyward, "Sexuality, Love and Justice," in Judith Plas-

kow and Carol P. Christ, eds., *Weaving the Visions: New Patterns in Feminist Spirituality* (San Francisco: Harper and Row, 1989) 293–301; see also Susan Nelson Dunfee, *Beyond Servanthood: Christianity and the Liberation of Women* (Washington: University Press of America, 1989).

49. Jacqueline Grant, "The Sin of Servanthood and the Deliverance of Discipleship," in Townes, *Troubling* 199–218; see also her *White Women's Christ and Black Women's Jesus* (Atlanta: Scholars, 1989).

50. Probably the most influential work has been Nancy Chodorow, *The Reproduction of Mothering* (Berkeley: University of California, 1978).

51. Diane Jonte-Pace, "Object Relations Theory, Mothering, and Religion: Toward a Feminist Psychology of Religion," *Horizons* 14 (1987) 310–27; idem., "Situating Kristeva Differently: Psychoanalytic Readings of Woman and Religion," in David Crownfield, ed., *Body/Text in Julia Kristeva: Religion, Women, and Psychoanalysis* (Albany: State University of New York, 1992). For two related studies using psychoanalytic categories to interpret ritual, see Nancy Jay, *Throughout Your Generations Forever: Sacrifice, Religion and Paternity* (Chicago: University of Chicago, 1992), and William Beers, *Women and Sacrifice: Male Narcissism and the Psychology of Religion* (Detroit: Wayne State, 1992).

52. The most complete treatment of object-relations theory for feminist theory remains Catherine Keller, *From a Broken Web: Separation, Sexism, and Self* (Boston: Beacon, 1986).

53. "Roundtable Discussion: Christian Ethics and Theology in Womanist Perspective," *Journal of Feminist Studies in Religion* 5/2 (Summer 1990) 83–112.

54. M. Shawn Copeland, "Roundtable" 101.

55. "Church and Culture: A Black Catholic Womanist Perspective," in William O'Brien, ed., *The Labor of God: An Ignation View of Church and Culture* (Washington: Georgetown University, 1991), 73; see also Jamie Phelps, O.P., "Choose Life: Reflections of a Black African-American Roman Catholic Woman Religious Theologian," in Melanie H. May, ed., *Women and Church: The Challenge of Ecumenical Solidarity in an Age of Alienation* (Grand Rapids: Eerdmans, 1991).

56. Katie G. Cannon, *Black Womanist Ethics* (Atlanta: Scholars, 1988).

57. Emilie M. Townes, *Womanist Justice, Womanist Hope* (Atlanta: Scholars, 1993); idem., *Troubling*.

58. Delores S. Williams, *Sisters in the Wilderness: The Challenge of Womanist God-Talk* (Maryknoll, N.Y.: Orbis, 1993).

59. Renita Weems, *Just a Sister Away* (San Diego: LuraMedia, 1988).

60. Katie G. Cannon, *Black Womanist Ethics;* idem., "Moral Wisdom in the Black Women's Literary Tradition," in Plaskow and Christ, *Weaving the Visions* 281–92.

61. Grant, *White Woman's Christ and Black Woman's Jesus.*

62. This is true of (white) feminist theologians who have also used African-American women's fiction as a resource for theology; see Sharon D. Welch, *A Feminist Ethic of Risk* (Minneapolis: Fortress, 1990).

63. Ada María Isasi-Díaz et. al., "Roundtable Discussion: *Mujeristas:* Who We Are and What We Are About," *Journal of Feminist Studies in Religion* 8 (Spring 1992) 105–25. See also Isasi-Díaz's earlier essay, "Toward an Understanding of Feminismo Hispano in the U.S.," in Barbara Hilkert Andolsen, Christine E. Gudorf, and Mary D. Pellauer, eds., *Women's Consciousness, Women's Conscience: A Reader in Feminist Ethics* (Minneapolis: Winston, 1985) 51–61.

64. Isasi-Díaz, "*Mujeristas*" 108.

65. Ada María Isasi-Díaz, *En la Lucha* 62–79; see also *Hispanic Women.*

66. María Pilar Aquino, *Our Cry for Life: Feminist Theology from Latin America,* trans. Dinah Livingstone (Maryknoll, N.Y.: Orbis, 1993); note that Aquino does not use the term "mujerista," preferring "feminist" as qualified by social location.

67. See chap. 5, "Methodological Premises for Theology from the Perspective of Women," *Our Cry for Life* 81–108.

68. Aruna Gnanadason, "Towards an Indian Feminist Theology," in Virginia Fabella and Sun Ai Lee Park, eds., *We Dare to Dream: Doing Theology as Asian Women* (Maryknoll, N.Y.: Orbis, 1989) 117–26; Judith Mbula Behemuka, "Social Changes and Women's Attitudes toward Marriage in East Africa," in Oduyoge and Kanyoro, *The Will to Arise* 119–34.

69. Marianne Katoppo, "The Church and Prostitution in Asia," in King, *Feminist Theology from the Third World* 114–22; Yayori Matsui, "Violence Against Women in Development, Militarism, and Culture," ibid. 124–33; but see also Joanne Carlson Brown and Carole R. Bohn, eds., *Christianity, Patriarchy, and Abuse: A Feminist Critique* (Cleveland: Pilgrim, 1989) for a North American perspective.

70. M. Shawn Copeland, " 'Wading Through Many Sorrows': Toward a Theology of Suffering in Womanist Perspective," in Townes, *Troubling* 109–29.

71. Isasi-Díaz and Tarango, *Hispanic Women* 90.

72. Katie G. Cannon, "Moral Wisdom in the Black Women's Literary Tradition," on truth-telling, in Plaskow and Christ, *Weaving* 281–92; Jacqueline Grant, "The Sin of Servanthood," on service, in Townes, *Trou-*

bling 199–218; Emilie M. Townes, “Living in the New Jerusalem: The Rhetoric and Movement of Liberation in the House of Evil,” on obedience, in Townes, *Troubling* 78–91.

73. “Special Section on Appropriation and Reciprocity in Womanist/ Mujerista/Feminist Work,” *Journal of Feminist Studies in Religion* 8 (Fall 1992) 91–123.

74. For a revealing account of this situation in women’s literature, see Katherine J. Mayberry, “White Feminists Who Study Black Writers,” *Chronicle of Higher Education,* 12 October 1994, A48. For a Native American woman’s view, see Andy Smith, “For Those Who Were Indian in a Former Life,” in Carol J. Adams, ed., *Ecofeminism and the Sacred* (New York: Continuum, 1993) 168–71.

75. See Margaret Farley, “New Patterns of Relationship: Beginnings of a Moral Revolution,” *TS* 36 (1975) 627–46.

76. See the very helpful survey by Mary Ann Hinsdale, “Ecology, Feminism and Theology,” *Word & World* 11 (1991) 156–64; Rosemary Ruether, *New Woman, New Earth; Gaia and God.* See also Elizabeth A. Johnson, *Woman, Earth and Creator Spirit* (New York: Paulist, 1993); Elizabeth Dodson Gray, *Green Paradise Lost* (Boston: Roundtable, 1979).

77. Ruether, *Gaia and God* 15–58.

78. Sallie McFague, *The Body of God: An Ecological Theology* (Minneapolis: Fortress, 1993) 28.

79. Johnson, *Woman, Earth and Creator Spirit.*

80. “The Spiritual, Political Journey of a Feminist Freethinker,” in Cooey, Eakin and McDaniel, *After Patriarchy* 146–65.

81. “Rethinking Theology and Nature,” in *Weaving the Visions* 314–25.

82. “Reverence for Life: The Need for a Sense of Finitude,” in *Embodied Love* 51–64.

83. *Sexism and God-Talk* 257.

84. See Shamara Shantu Riley, “Ecology Is a Sistah’s Issue Too: The Politics of Emergent Afrocentric Ecowomanism,” in *Ecofeminism and the Sacred* 191–204.

Part Two

GENERAL THEORY

3. Discipleship and Patriarchy: Early Christian Ethos and Christian Ethics in a Feminist Theological Perspective

Elisabeth Schüssler Fiorenza

This chapter first appeared in *The Annual: Society of Christian Ethics* in 1982.

INTRODUCTION

The studies of ethics in the New Testament and its various themes and problems are vast, and the discussions on the use of the Bible in Christian moral theology are numerous.[1] To summarize the contents of the literature on Biblical ethics and to discuss its theoretical-theological aspects adequately in a short paper would be presumptuous. To assume a relationship and interaction between Christian ethics and early Christian ethos, between contemporary moral theological reflection and first century ethical instruction, is conventional but nevertheless difficult to assess. The hermeneutic-methodological problems raised by the actual encounter of a predominantly philosophical-systematic mode of inquiry with a historical-critical mode of analysis are complex and far from being resolved. Nevertheless a scholarly consensus seems to have emerged that the common ground for the two disciplines is given in the church since the "community of Christian Scriptures" is also the "community of moral discourse." Not only do the Scriptures provide resources for the church's moral discourse and its systematic reflection in Christian ethics, but they also form and guide the Christian community as a people "who derive their identity from a book."[2] The moral authority of the Bible is grounded in a community that is capable of sustaining Scriptural authority in faithful remembrance, liturgical celebration, ecclesial governance and continual reinterpretation of its own Biblical roots and traditions.

Situating the authority and significance of Scripture for Christian ethics in the community of faith[3] positively assimilates the results of Biblical scholarship which has for a long time stressed that the community of Israel and of early Christianity is the *Sitz im Leben* of Biblical writings. Biblical texts have to be read in their communal social, religious contexts and to be understood as faith-responses to particular historical situations.[4] No systematization of Biblical moral injunctions, therefore, seems possible. It is misleading to speak about a uniform Biblical or New Testament ethics since the Bible is not a book but a "bookshelf," a collection of various literary texts that span almost a millennium of ancient history and culture. True, some similarities in themes or affinities in religious perspectives can be established. But such a systematization of themes and such a unification of perspectives depends on the selective activity of the Biblical interpreter, the systematic construction of the ethicist, or the one-sided selection of the church rather than on the unilateral and clear-cut authority of Scripture itself. Therefore neither the Biblical nor the moral theologian can eschew hermeneutical reflection and critical evaluation of Biblical traditions.

While the pluriformity of Biblical ethos and ethics is long recognized and the concomitant quest for the "canon within the canon" is much debated in Biblical scholarship,[5] the discussions among ethicists on the authority of the Bible and its use in moral discourse seem not to center on the need for a critical *evaluative* hermeneutics[6] of the Bible and Christian tradition. Remembrance can be nostalgic, and reinterpretation of oppressive traditions can serve to maintain the *status quo*. The history of the church and its appeal to the authority of Scripture shows that Biblical traditions are not only life-giving but also death-dealing. The appeal to Scripture has authorized, for example, persecution of Jews, burning of witches, torture of heretics, national wars of Europe, the subhuman conditions of American slavery, and the anti-social politics of the Moral Majority.

The political appeal to the moral authority of the Bible can be dangerous if it is sustained by the "community of the forgiven" but not by the *ecclesia semper reformanda.* It can be dangerous, especially if the Christian community is shaped by the remembrance of "the historical winners" while abandoning the subversive memory of innocent suffering and of solidarity with the victims of history.[7] In short, the Bible and its subsequent interpretations are not only sources for liberation but also resources for oppression. It can be a resource not only for solving moral problems and generating moral challenges, but also for legitimizing dehumanization and violence. The moral character of its theological vision and the moral injunctions of its traditions must be assessed and adjudicated in critical theological discourse if Scripture is to function as revelation "given for the sake of our salvation."[8]

It is obvious by now that this caveat shares in the moral impetus and theoretical insights of political and liberation theologies which do not seek to use Scripture "as an ideology for justifying the demands of the oppressed"[9] but rather strive to rescue the Biblical vision of liberation from the ideological distortions of those who have formulated, interpreted, and used the Bible against the cultural and ecclesial victims of the past and the present.

From its inception feminist interpretation and concern with Scripture has been generated by the fact that throughout Christian history the Bible has been used to halt the emancipation of slaves and of women, on the one hand, and to justify such emancipation, on the other hand. Elizabeth Cady Stanton has eloquently summed up the negative use of the Bible as a weapon against women's demand for political and ecclesial equality:

> From the inauguration of the movement for woman's emancipation the Bible has been used to hold her in the "divinely ordained sphere" prescribed in the Old Testament and New Testament. The canon and civil law, church and state, priests and legislators, all political parties and religious denominations have alike taught that woman was made after man, of man, an inferior being, subject to man. Creeds, codes, Scriptures and statues are all based on this idea.[10]

As in the last century so also today the Bible is used against the women's liberation movement in society and church. Whenever women protest against political discrimination, economic exploitation, social inequality, and secondary status in the churches, the Bible is invoked because it teaches the divinely ordained subordination of women and the creational differences between the sexes. Anti-ERA groups, the cultural Total Woman Movement, and the Moral Majority appeal to the teachings of the Bible on the family and Christian womanhood. These right-wing political movements, which defend the American Family in the name of Biblical Christianity,[11] do not hesitate to quote the Bible against shelters for battered women, for physical punishment of children, and against abortion, even in case of rape or child-pregnancy.

Yet throughout the centuries the Bible has not only served to justify theologically the oppression of slaves and women. It has also provided authorization for Christian women and men who rejected slavery and patriarchal subjection as unchristian. This dialectical use of the Bible in the moral-theological discourse of the church could be amply documented. A careful survey of the history of Biblical interpretation would show that in the church's moral discourse on women's role and dignity, certain key-passages have emerged and had *formative* historical impact.[12] Such key passages are, e.g., Gal 3:28, the appeal to the women prophets of the Old and New Testaments and the gospel stories of Mary and Martha or of the Woman at the Well.

Key texts for the moral-theological justification of the patriarchal limitation and repression of women's leadership and roles include, e.g., Gn 2–3 and especially the prescriptive New Testament trajectory of texts demanding the submission and silence of women in patriarchal marriage and church. No doubt, the church as the community of moral discourse is shaped by this Scriptural trajectory of *Haustafeln* (household codes) and their faithful remembrance and reinterpretation. The church's dominant structures and articulations are patriarchal and until very recently its moral and theological leadership has been exclusively male. The ongoing formative power of these Biblical texts has led to the silencing and marginalization of women in the church and legitimized our societal and ecclesial exploitation by patriarchal family and church structures. In contemporary democratic society the Bible and Biblical religion serve often to strengthen politically anti-democratic elements and trends by reproducing ancient patriarchal structures of inequality and slave-like conditions in the family and the economy. The political alliance of anti-ERA and anti-abortion forces with conservative Biblical religion becomes understandable in light of these Scriptural texts.

At this point the objection could be raised that such an assessment of the "politics and ethics of Biblical remembrance" not only seriously misconstrues the church's moral discourse on Scripture but also overestimates the political function of the Bible as historical-cultural formation. However the political strength of such right-wing movements as the Moral Majority documents how certain Biblical remembrances can be employed successfully in the contemporary political struggle. This continuing cultural-political influence of the Bible has been, in my opinion, largely overlooked by many in the contemporary feminist movement, who have written off both organized religion and traditional "family" rather than branding the patriarchal structures and elements within Biblical religion and family. Such a feminist wholesale rejection of religion has played into the hands of the present conservative political backlash.

Finally, the contention that the political right and Christian feminists equally misuse the Bible for their own purposes by resorting to proof-texting requires a scholarly historical and theological assessment of such proof-texts cited in the contemporary political struggle. In other words, public discussion needs to move from more generalized moral political discourse in church and society to disciplined theological scholarship if we are to assess the *political* function of Biblical remembrance, i.e., if we are to judge the impact of Biblical traditions and texts on the contemporary Christian community and on American culture that is still largely, if superficially, shaped by Biblical religion. What I propose here is a development of Biblical ethics that does not presuppose the apolitical character of Scripture and assume that *all* Biblical tradition and texts have the authority of Scripture and promote the "common good" merely be reason of their inclusion in the canon.

I do not assume in such a disciplined discourse that the Biblical exegete will provide only the historical cultural "data" for systematic reflection and moral theological evaluation, since such a division of labor would neglect the insights of the hermeneutical discussion itself. Instead I envision a disciplined dialogue between Biblical scholars and moral theologians that enhances the critical-reflective competence of the whole Christian community. In what follows I will attempt such a discourse. I will first sketch the historical critical assessment of one New Testament ethical tradition and its theological significance and meaning for today as asserted by Biblical scholars. Then I will seek to *evaluate* such Biblical theological interpretations from a feminist perspective and discuss the elements of a feminist critical *evaluative* hermeneutics.

Because of the contemporary political discussion the so-called New Testament *Haustafeln* and their scholarly interpretation suggest themselves as a test-case of my proposal for the collaboration of Biblical scholars and Christian ethicists in the service of the Christian community as a community of moral discourse. My critical exploration of the *Haustafel* trajectory and its discussion in contemporary exegetical scholarship is meant, therefore, as an invitation to investigate methodologically the same Biblical tradition from the scholarly perspective and with the theoretical tools of Christian ethics. The purpose is to develop Biblical ethics as an "evaluative hermeneutics" of Biblical traditions and of the Christian communities they have shaped and are still shaping.

I. Historical Critical Analyses of the *Haustafel* Trajectory

Scholars of early Christianity have already opened up such a critical historical discussion and theological evaluation of the household code trajectory although they have not explicitly acknowledged its political dimensions. It is significant that in the past ten years or so scholarly interest and investigation of these texts has increased precisely at the time when the women's movement in the churches has developed momentum and urgency. The most recent works of Balch,[13] Clark,[14] and Elliott[15] testify to this growing scholarly interest, whereas those of Niederwimmer,[16] Crouch,[17] and Thraede[18] mark the entrance into this period.

During the same time works on women in the Bible also have proliferated. However, whereas these works usually concede or make explicit their inspiration by the women's movement, academic studies generally profess their allegiance to the so-called, disinterested, value-neutral paradigm of historical critical scholarship. They therefore reject as unscientific any suggestion that they also might be determined by questions of contemporary relevance and political commitments. Yet a critical review of historical interpretations and theological-hermeneutic justifications of the *Haustafel* ethic can illustrate the hermeneutical dependence of scholarly interests and historical evaluations on their contemporary societal situations.

The texts which are classified as *Haustafel*—a label derived from Lutheran *Ständelehre*—consist of three pairs of relationships: wife-husband, slave-master, and father-children. Each pair receives reciprocal admonitions. The central interest of these injunctions lies in the enforcement of the submission and obedience of the socially weaker group—wives, slaves, and children—on the one hand, and in the authority of the head of the household, the *paterfamilias,* on the other hand.

The complete form of the *Haustafel* is only found in Col 3:18—4:1 and Eph 5:22—6:9. It is not found in the rest of the trajectory (1Petr 2:18—3:7; 1Tim 2:11–15; 5:3–8; 6:1–2; Tit 2:2–10; 3:1–2; 1Clem 21:6–8; Ign Pol 4:1—6:2; Pol 4:2—6:1; Did 4:9–11; Barn 19:5–7). One must therefore ask whether the three pairs of reciprocal relationships found only in Colossians and Ephesians are characteristic for the form as such or whether the pattern of submissiveness[19] must be seen as the most significant element of the trajectory. This pattern of subjection does not always need to include all six social status groups addressed in Collossians and Ephesians. It sometimes mentions only some of the subordinate groups. It also can include obedience to the political powers of the state or address the governance of the Christian community. The injunction to submissiveness is already found in the authentic Pauline letters, e.g., in Rm 13 and 1 Cor 14. It therefore cannot be attributed solely to what exegetes call Early Catholicism.[20] While this pattern of submissiveness functions differently in different early Christian documents and their social-ecclesial historical contexts, the "household dimension"[21] does seem nevertheless characteristic for this trajectory. It conceives not only of family but also of church and state in terms of the patriarchal household. The Christian community soon comes to be called "the household of God" and from the time of Augustus the Roman emperor is himself understood as the *pater patriae*.[22]

Much of the discussion of the household codes has focused on their historical-religious background, as well as on their theological meaning and authority or their "Christian" character. Most recent research, however, has raised significant questions as to their philosophical provenance and their social function especially in view of emancipatory tendencies in the first century.

Philosophical Provenance. Recent discussions seem to have accomplished a significant breakthrough with respect to the philosophical provenance of the code. Although some exegetes maintained that the *Haustafel* was uniquely Christian[23] because it addressed the subordinate group as moral agents, for some time the majority of scholars believed that the *Haustafel* was patterned after the Stoic code of duty[24] and was probably mediated by Hellenistic Jewish propaganda. Now this scholarly consensus seems to give way to another interpretation. It does not exclude the parallel of the Stoics and it has the added virtue of accounting for the three pairs of subordinate relationships and reciprocal admonitions.

Independently from each other the classicist Thraede and the New Testament scholars Lührmann, Balch, and Elliott have contended that the *Haustafel* texts share in the Aristotelian philosophical trajectory concerning household management (*oikonomia*) and political ethics (*politeia*). If this is the case a quite different political philosophical tradition than the Stoic code of duties is present, one concerned with the relationships between rulers and ruled in household and state. Here the patriarchal household is the point of reference and the *Haustafeln* would better be named in my opinion, as "patterns of patriarchal submission."

Exegetes have long recognized that the *Haustafel* trajectory christianizes patriarchal social and ecclesial structures. What the recent research has done is clarify the philosophical-political underpinnings of this pattern. Aristotle, in contrast to the Sophists, stressed that the patriarchal relationships in the household and the city, as well as their concomitant social differences, are based not on social convention but on "nature." He therefore insisted that the discussion of political ethics and household management begin with marriage, defined as the union of natural ruler and natural subject (Pol. I 1252a 24–28). Balch's research documents a growing interest among diverse philosophical directions and schools in the first century to reassert this Aristotelian political ethos, albeit often in a modified, milder form.[25]

The *Haustafel* ethic of the New Testament shares in this stabilizing reception of Aristotelian ethics and politics. The studies of the social world of early Christianity, recognizing the significant role of the house-church for the early Christian mission suggested that the patriarchal ethics of the household expresses the ethos of the early Christian mission. G. Theissen, for example, suggests that the radical ethos of the Jesus movement was a-familial and ascetic, whereas the communities of the Christian missionary movement in the upcoming Greco-Roman urban centers were characterized by a softened form of patriarchalism, which with Troeltsch he terms *Liebespatriarchalismus*.[26]

J.H. Elliott follows this line of argument and seeks to show that the ethical instructions for the household in 1 Peter derive their significance from their rootedness in the early Christian missionary community as the "household of God." He elaborates the function and significance of the household for Greco-Roman politics and in the traditions of the Old and New Testaments. He concludes his survey with the observation:

> Historically the *oikos* was the fundamental social locus and focus of the Christian movement. . . . It was not merely individuals but entire households who were converted and transformed by the good news of human reconciliations and of the new possibilities of life in the community. . . . As a socially revered institution with honorable goals and values, this extended Christian family posed no necessary threat to existing political institutions. To the contrary, focus on the familial nature and character of the Christian community enabled the movement to accentuate precisely those virtues of social life which were held in respect by society as a whole.[27]

This line of argument, however, is based on the unproven assumption that the *house-church* was structured in keeping with the ethics of the household code and represented a Christian form of the patriarchal household. This assumption overlooks the fact that the house-church was not congruent with the existing household, since the conversion of whole households was not the norm in early Christianity. Indeed, the Christian missionary movement conflicted with the existing order of the patriarchal household because it converted *individuals* independently of their social status and function in the patriarchal household. Christian mission caused social unrest because it admitted wives and slaves as well as daughters and sons into the house-church, even when the *paterfamilias* was still pagan and had not converted to Christianity. The pagan accusation that Christian mission was subversive and destroyed patriarchal household structures was still made in the second century. It is not a misunderstanding or slander but an accurate perception of the social implications of conversion to Christianity. The *Haustafel* ethics is an attempt to mitigate the subversive impact of religious conversion on the patriarchal order of the house and of society.

Social Function. The social implications of religious conversion were realized in the house-church as the discipleship community of equals. Independently of their fathers and husbands women had membership and leadership in the Christian missionary movement.[28] Even in the beginning of the second century female and male salves still expected their freedom to be purchased by the Christian community, as the letters of Ignatius and the *Shepherd of Hermas* document. Paul's letter to Philemon, the only New Testament writing addressed to a house-church, mentions a woman among the leadership of the church in Philemon's house. (Later exegetes understand her to be Philemon's wife though she is not so designated by Paul.) In this letter Paul insists with all the means of ancient rhetoric that Onesimus must be accepted into the house-church as a "beloved sibling," both as a Christian and as a human being.[29]

According to Mark's gospel the discipleship of equals is the community of brothers and sisters who do not have a "father." It is the "new family" which has replaced all the natural-social kinship ties of the patriarchal family. It does not consist of rulers and subjects, of relationships of superordination and subordination. According to Paul it is the *ekklesia*—the "assembly of the saints"—who have equal access to God in the Spirit and are therefore coequal members in the body of Christ. Social roles in this *ekklesia* are not based on natural-social difference but on charismatic giftedness.

Sociologist R. Nisbet seems to have captured this ethos of the house-church better than some exegetes and theologians. He stresses the profoundly communal character of early Christianity and maintains that conflict was "the very essence of Christianity's relation to its age." This conflict was a conflict of values and allegiances between the Christian community and the Roman patriarchal family:

> Christianity like all evangelizing religions addressed its message to individuals—men, women, and children. And so long as the family remained an intact structure, just so long did its very structure act to mediate, even to interfere with the proselytizing efforts of the missionaries of Christ. The strategy from the Christian point of view was thus a vital and almost obvious one: to denigrate so far as possible the historic and still deeply rooted kinship tie and offer the community of Christians itself as the only real and true form of kinship.[30]

Nisbet points to the emancipatory implications of such an ecclesial self-understanding for women. By offering the community as the new familial kinship structure the Christian movement disengaged women from their traditional patriarchal family roles and limitations.

The following statement of the classicist E. A. Judge seems to contradict this observation. However, when it is more precisely understood as referring to the *Haustafel* ethics rather than to all New Testament writings, it makes the same point:

> With regard to the household obligation, the NT writers are unanimous; its bonds and conventions must at all costs be maintained. . . . There is of course . . . the interest of

> the patronal class . . . but the primary reason no doubt is that the entrenched rights of the household as a religious and social unit offered the Christians the best possible security for their existence as a group. Any weakening here would thus be a potentially devastating blow to their own cohesion, as well as having revolutionary implications from the point of view of the public authorities.[31]

Nevertheless Judge seems to think that the house-church was governed by the "principles of fraternity" and that it presented a threat only "if enthusiastic members failed to contain their principles within the privacy of the association and thus were led into political indiscretions or offenses against the hierarchy of the household."[32] Such an argument overlooks, however, that the conversion of women, slaves, and young people who belonged to the household of an unconverted *paterfamilias* already constituted such a potential political offense against the patriarchal order. It could not but be considered an infringement of the political order as well, insofar as the patriarchal order of the house was considered the paradigm for that of the state. Since the patriarchal *familia* was the nucleus of the state, conversion of the subordinated members of the house who were supposed to share in the religion of the *paterfamilias* constituted a subversive threat.

The prescriptive *Haustafel* trajectory attempted to soften this threat by asserting the congruence of the Christian ethics with that of patriarchal house and state. It did not continue the ethos[33] of the house-church, with its voluntary and collegial structures, but sought to modify it and bring it into line with the structures of patriarchal family and society. In doing so it patriarchalized not only the early Christian ethos of "fraternity" or better said, of the discipleship of equals, but also the structures of the Christian community. However, its paraenetic and prescriptive character indicates that such a patriarchalization was not yet accomplished even in the beginning of the second century.

Emancipatory Societal Tendencies in the First Century. While the *Haustafel* trajectory participated in the dominant patriarchal ethos of Greco-Roman society, that of co-equal discipleship shared in the more egalitarian aspirations of Roman society.[34] It was so threatening precisely because it participated in a general economic development and cultural mood that allowed for the greater freedom and independence of women from patriarchal control. K. Thraede has chided New Testament scholars for theological misconstrual of the meaning inherent in the *Haustafel* trajectory because they do not take into account the lively public discussion which had ensued on the "nature" and role behavior of women in the first century.[35] Since the economic independence and the civil emancipation of women, especially wealthy women, had increased, the *patria potestas* often amounted to little more than legal fiction. Moreover, Augustean legislation, while professing to strengthen the traditional patriarchal family, actually undermined it, insofar as the emperor increasingly coopted the powers of the *paterfamilias*.

Most of the literary statements and philosophical reflections on the nature and role of women are ruminations and prescriptions of educated men. They must be understood as arguments seeking to deal with a more emancipative social situation. On the one hand there are those who nostalgically conjure up the patriarchal beginnings of Rome and the impeccable behavior of Roman ancestral matrons, in order to demand the strict exercise of the *patria potestas*. On the other hand are those who stress the equality of women with men in nature, education, and social standing although they usually do not go so far as to advocate complete equality of social role.

Thus the reactivation of the Aristotelian ethos that maintains the social differences as *natural* differences between women and men, as well as between slaves and freeborn, has to be seen within the context of this cultural-political debate. When seen within this context, the *Haustafel* trajectory not only christianizes this patriarchal Aristotelian ethics of inequality but also humanizes and modifies it, insofar as it obliges the *paterfamilias* to love, consideration, and responsibility. Seen from the perspective of women and slaves, however, it is a serious setback since it does not strengthen Roman cultural tendencies to equality and mutuality between women and men.

By reenforcing the patriarchal submission of those who according to Aristotle, must be ruled, the early Christian ethos of coequal discipleship loses its capacity to structurally transform the patriarchal order of family and state. And adapting the Christian community to its patriarchal society, the *Haustafel* ethos opens up the community to political cooptation by the Roman empire. That such a cooptation process required centuries to complete speaks for the vitality of the early Christian ethos of co-equal discipleship. In the process, however, the vision of *agape* and service, mutuality and solidarity among Christians no longer connotes a "new reality" but is reduced to mere moral appeal. Submission and obedience, but not equality and justice, became institutionalized by the patriarchal ethos. Insofar as this ethos was not restricted to the household but also adopted by the house-church, Christian faith and praxis no longer provided a structural-political alternative to the dominant patriarchal culture. The church's preaching of the gospel and its hierarchical-patriarchal structures became a contradiction that robbed the gospel of its historically transformative power. However, such a historical-theological interpretation of early Christian development stands in tension with the prevailing scholarly interpretations of the *Haustafel* trajectory.

II. Biblical Theological Evaluation of the *Haustafel* Ethics

Biblical interpretation always entails theological assessment and justification. So it remains for us from a feminist perspective to discuss the types of contemporary theological evaluations that are proposed as justification for the Christian character of this early Christian pattern of patriarchal submission. It appears that the following three distinct types of argument have emerged: necessary adaptation, goodness of creation, and subversive subordination.

Necessary Adaptation. The survival of the church in a patriarchal culture required an adaptation of its ethos and structures to the patriarchy of Greco-Roman society. Whenever such an adaptation is viewed negatively, it is pointed out that the *Haustafeln* belong only to the later New Testament and apostolic writings but are not found in genuine Pauline letters. Therefore they are a deformation of the early Christian ethos and of the Pauline gospel and have to be understood as the outcome of early Catholicism. Such an adaptation of the gospel to its bourgeois society is usually ascribed to the disappearance of imminent eschatologial expectations.[36]

Another version of this theological justification argues that the household codes strengthened the "cohesiveness" of the Christian group and provided institutional patterns which enabled the church to survive.[37] Whereas the Jesus movement was a conflict movement, the early Christian missionary movement was integrative because of its ethos of love-patriarchalism. The process of ecclesial patriarchalization was, in this view, the historically necessary development from charism to office, from Paulinism to early Catholicism, from a millenarian radical ethos to a privileged Christian establisment, from the egalitarian structures of the beginnings to the hierarchical order of the Constantinian church.

This sociological-historical justification maintains that the patriarchalization of the early Christian movement was necessary if Christian communities were to grow, develop, and become historically viable. The institutionalization of the egalitarian Christian movement could not but adopt patriarchal institutional structures. This theological justification, however, overlooks the fact that the house-church already presents an *institutional* structure which was patterned after that of *collegia* and not after the patriarchal household. The *Haustafel* trajectory would not have been formulated if other Christian institutional options had not already existed. By arguing for the necessity of the patriarchal character of the church as an *institution,* this sociological-historical justification *implicitly* maintains that the *institutional* church is inherently patriarchal and therefore has to be exclusive of the institutionalized leadership of women.

Goodness of Creation. Some, especially German Lutheran, interpreters argue that the household code trajectory had a positive theological function insofar as it prevented the emigration of early Christians from "the world." The injunctions of the New Testament *Haustafeln* affirm the goodness of creation, even though the later texts of the trajectory do exhibit the inherent oppressive tendencies of the patriarchal pattern of submission. This second type of justification understands the *Haustafel* trajectory as a social alternative to an unworldly, ascetic ethos that engendered flight from the world and withdrawal from society and cultured life. The ethics of the household code in turn sustains the "worldliness of the New Testament," it says an energetic "yes" to the goodness of creation, and affirms marriage and family. In the *Haustafel* ethics the order of creation, of marriage, family, and work, is accepted but not cosmologically justified and idealized. Instead this Christian ethics "is subordinated to the command of the Lord and especially oriented toward the well being of the other."[38] The linking of the household code ethics to the command of the *Kyrios* enables Christians to live critically in the preordained structures of society.[39] In a similar fashion W. Schrage asserts:

> Diesem Herrn aber, so betonen die Haustafeln, gehört der Gehorsam nicht in einer gettohaft von der Welt abgegrenzten Sphäre, in die man sich weltflüchtig asketisch zurückzieht, nicht in reiner Innerlichkeit oder allein in einem kirchlichen Binnenbereich, sondern auch in den gesellschaftlichen sozialen Bereichen . . . Christen sollen auch als Ehemänner und Frauen, als Vater und Kinder, als Herren und Sklaven ihre *nova obedientia* bewähren, auch wenn die Sozialstrukturen dadurch weder christlich gemacht noch gar durch sie das Heil erwartet wird . . . Gewiss die Sozialgebilde werden nicht destruiert aber sie werden auch nicht als starre Institutionen sanktioniert.[40]

Thraede has aptly characterized such a panegyric of the *Haustafel* ethos as so much theological "*eisegesis.*" And in spite of his own theological justification, E. Schweizer has conceded that the dynamics of the *Haustafel* trajectory tends to preserve the freedom and social privilege of the *adult, free, male* Christian and to ensure the subjection of the socially weaker partner on Christian terms. In later texts the care for the partner, especially the socially weaker partner, recedes more and more into the background, even when love of neighbor is never completely forgotten. This theological evaluation of the *Haustafel* texts therefore not only asserts the androcentric character of Christian ethics but overlooks the fact that in speaking about the goodness of the world, marriage and creation, it ascribes such goodness to oppressive patriarchal societal and ecclesial structures.

Subversive Subordination. The last type of apologetic argument also seeks to justify the *Haustafel's* patriarchal ethics on theological grounds. This justification claims that the ethos of Jesus is expressed in the household codes because they reinforce Jesus' call to service. The codes therefore advocate an ethics of "revolutionary subordination." Such "subordination means the acceptance of an *order* as it exists, but with the new meaning given to it by the fact that one's acceptance of it is willing and meaningfully motivated."[41] Such a theological assertion mistakenly presupposes that Greco-Roman ethics did not address the role of subordinate persons in the social and moral order. It also overlooks the fact that Jesus' call to service in the gospels is addressed to those in power, to those who are first in the community but *not* to those who are least. It is addressed to "friends" and not to subordinates. This call, therefore, functions not as religious motivation for maintaining the existing patriarchal *Herrschaftsverhältnisse* in society and church but has as its goal the praxis of the early Christian ethos of co-equality in discipleship. Such equality is conceded by this third theological evaluation, but only in the *religious,* personal, individual sphere:

> But if we are to understand the point of this passage we must assume that the women *had* heard that message. Otherwise they would not be taking off their veils, especially not during the worship service. Thus the retention of the veil when a woman would rise to speak in the congregation. . . . also became a symbol of that double movement: first of the enfranchizing impact of the gospel upon woman in that she may rise to speak and can function *religiously* (emphasis added) as far more than simply a member of the household of her father or husband, and secondly of her acceptance of the order of society within which her role is to be lived out. Here again as in the *Haustafeln* there is a clear reminder that this relationship of subordination and superordination is not a difference in worth. . . . To accept subordination within the frame-

> work of things *as they are* (emphasis added) is not to grant the inferiority in moral or personal value of the subordinate party.[42]

One is surprised to find such an advocacy of "things as they are" formulated in a work which seeks to recapture those social dimensions of the Biblical vision of reality "which stand in creative tension with the cultural functions of our age and perhaps any age." However this insistence on subordination becomes understandable when one observes that the dominant structures of our culture and society are understood as being determined by "sweeping egalitarianism." In his critique of K. Stendahl, J.H. Yoder asks: "What if, for instance, the sweeping, doctrinaire egalitarianism of our culture, which makes the concept of the 'place of women' seem either laughable or boorish, and makes that of 'subordination' seem insulting should turn out really (in the 'intent of God', or in long run social experience) to be demonic, uncharitable, destructive of personality, disrespectful of creation, and unworkable?"[43] Thus Yoder defends the New Testament pattern of patriarchal submission because it motivates Christian slaves and women to accept "things as they are." He maintains that we today must advocate it because its injunctions are out of step with contemporary convictions "present ever since the age of Lincoln but propagated still more sweepingly with the currency of civil rights and women's liberation rhetoric." Yet a careful analysis of American economic-political realities could have documented that in contemporary society "egalitarianism" does not determine social-political institutions and economic policies. Reaganite-type politics testify every day to this.

In sum: All three attempts to explicate the ethics and ethos expressed in the *Haustafel* trajectory are prepared to justify on theological grounds the historical and contemporary discrimination and oppression of those whose "nature" predisposes them to be "ruled" in patriarchal structures. The sociological-theological justification argues that the continuing existence and historical power of the institutional church legitimizes such patriarchal structures; the predominantly Lutheran justification maintains the goodness of the "world" and creation as concomitant with patriarchal structures, and the social-ethical approach of Barthian theology legitimizes the pattern of patriarchal submission as religious motivation for accepting the *status quo* of patriarachal social structures. All three proposals affirm the patriarchal character of Biblical revelation and of the Christian church as well as document the ideological function of Biblical theology and ethics. They support the post-Biblical feminist claim that Christian theology and church are inherently sexist.

III. A Feminist Evaluative Hermeneutics of the Bible

Recognizing that androcentric language and patriarchal traditions have erased women from history and made them "non-beings," post-Biblical feminists argue that Biblical religion is not retrievable for feminists who are committed to the liberation of women. Biblical religion ignores women's experience, speaks of God in male language, and sustains women's positions of powerlessness by legitimizing women's societal and ecclesial subordination as well as male dominance and violence against women, especially against those caught in patriarchal marriage relationships. Therefore it is argued that feminists must leave behind Biblical religion and reject the authority of the Bible because of its androcentric patriarchal character. Revisionist interpretations are at best a waste of time and at worst a further legitimization of the prevailing sexism of Biblical religion. They are, therefore, a co-optation of women's energy and of the feminist movement. Feminist vision and praxis is rooted in the contemporary experience of women and does not derive its legitimacy from the Christian past and the Bible.

Although this post-Biblical feminist critique of Biblical religion must be taken seriously, it must also be pointed out that such a feminist strategy is in danger of too quickly conceding that women have no authentic history within Biblical religion. It therefore too easily relinquishes women's feminist Biblical heritage. Yet Western feminists cannot afford to deny our Biblical heritage if we do not want to strengthen the powers of oppression that deprive people of their own history and engender the reality constructions of androcentric texts and patriarchal scholarship. Moreover such a feminist strategy cannot sustain solidarity and commitment to *all* women whether they are "liberated" or not.[44] It cannot respect the positive self-identity and vision that women still derive from Biblical religion. Post-Biblical feminism must either neglect the positive Biblical influences on contemporary women or declare women's involvement with Biblical religion as "false consciousness." However any social and cultural feminist transformation in Western society must deal constructively with Biblical religion and its continuing impact on American culture. American women are not able to completely discard and forget our personal, cultural, and religious history. We will either transform Biblical history and religion into a new liberating future or continue to be subject to its patriarchal tyranny.

Feminist Christian theologians have responded in different ways to the challenge of post-Christian feminism and have sought to develop different hermenutical frameworks for spelling out theologically what it means to be a self-identified woman and a Christian. We have, therefore, developed different analyses and approaches to the interpretation and evaluation of Biblical religion in general, and Biblical texts in particular. In my own work I have attempted to formulate a feminist Christian theology as a "critical theology of liberation."[45] I have done so with reference to contemporary oppression of women in society and church, especially my own church, as well as with respect to the Bible and early Christian history.

In the context of such a feminist theology I have sought to develop a feminist Biblical hermeneutics as a critical evaluative hermeneutics.[46] Such a hermeneutics not only challenges androcentric constructions of Biblical history in language but also critically analyzes androcentric texts in order: *first* to arrive at the lived ethos of early Christians that developed in interaction with its patriarchal cultural contexts; and *second* to critically determine and evaluate its continuing structures of alienation and liberation. Such an evaluative feminist hermeneutics uses the critical analytical methods of historical Biblical scholarship on the one hand and the theological goals of liberation theologies on the other hand, but focuses on the historical struggles of women in patriarchal culture and religion.

First: Historical-critical scholarship has worked out the pluralism of Biblical faith experience, ethos, and community. It has shown that Biblical texts are embedded in the historical experiences of Biblical people and that the Bible must be understood in the context of believing communities. It is therefore necessary to reconstruct as carefully as possible not only the structure of Biblical texts but also the paradigms of Biblical faith and Biblical communities shaped by these faith-experiences. However, this interpretative paradigm of historical-critical scholarship often understands the Bible theologically as the prime model of Christian faith and community that defines and controls the contemporary community of faith.

A feminist critical hermeneutics of liberation seeks to read the Bible in the context of believing communities of women, of the "church of women." It realizes that a feminist re-vision and transformation of Biblical history and community can only be achieved in and through a critical evaluation of patriarchal Biblical history and androcentric texts. It recognizes, as a hermeneutic feminist principle, that being woman and being Christian is a social, historical, and cultural ecclesial process. What it means to be a Christian woman is not defined by essential female nature or timeless Biblical revelation but grows out of the concrete social structures and cultural-religious mechanisms of women's oppression as well as our struggles for liberation, selfhood, and transcendence. Feminist identity is not based on the understanding of women as defined by female biology or feminine gender differences and societal-ecclesial roles but on the common historical experience of women as an oppressed people,[47] collaborating with our oppression and at the same time struggling for our liberation in patriarchal Biblical history and community. A feminist critical hermeneutics of the *Haustafel* texts has the aim, therefore, to become a "dangerous memory" that reclaims our foremothers' and foresisters' sufferings and struggles in and through the subversive power of the critically remembered past.

Such a critical feminist hermeneutics is distinct from a neo-orthodox feminist hermeneutics that derives the "canon" of feminist Christian faith and ethos from the Bible and therefore isolates the "liberating" impulses of Biblical vision from its oppressive aspects. Such a hermeneutics therefore seeks to distinguish between historically limited patriarchal traditions and the liberating Biblical tradition,[48] between the liberative essence of the revealed text[49] and its historical patriarchal-cultural expression, between the liberating prophetic critique[50] and the Bible's historical-cultural deformations. Such a neo-orthodox feminist hermeneutics seems sometimes more concerned with establishing the revelatory authority of certain Biblical texts or traditions than with carefully analyzing the particular roots and historical structures of women's oppression and struggles for liberation in patriarchal Biblical history and religion. Such a hermeneutics is, as a result, in danger of formulating a feminist Biblical apologetics instead of sufficiently acknowledging and exploring the oppressive function of patriarchal Biblical texts in the past and in the present. It would be a serious and fatal mistake to relegate the *Haustafel* trajectory, for example, to culturally conditioned Biblical traditions no longer valid today and thereby overlook the authoritative-oppressive impact these texts still have in the lives of Christian women.

A *feminist* "politics and ethics of Scriptural remembrance" that shapes the Christian community as a community of moral discourse must keep alive the sufferings and hopes of Biblical women and other "subordinate" peoples[51] in order to change and transform the patriarchal structures and ideologies of the Christian churches shaped by the New Testament pattern of patriarchal submission and silence. In the final analysis a critical feminist hermeneutics of the Bible has to call patriarchal Biblical religion to personal and structural *metanoia* of feminist praxis before it can proclaim that the communities shaped by the Scriptures are "the community of the forgiven." In the last analysis such an evaluative hermeneutics of liberation is not just geared to the liberation of women but also toward the emancipation of Biblical religion from patriarchal structures and ideologies so that the "gospel" can again be recognized as "the power of God for salvation" (Rm 1:16).

Second: The critical evaluation of the *Haustafel* trajectory and its scholarly interpretations has highlighted that its patriarchal ethics was asserted over and against an "egalitarian" Christian ethos. Biblical and moral theologians have labeled this ethos as unrealistic enthusiasm, gnostic spiritualism, ascetic emigration, or antinomian behavior that did not take seriously the given patriarchal structures of its everyday life and world. Early Christian women and slaves who took the gospel of freedom seriously are thereby disqualified and their faith experience and praxis is rendered rationally or theologically suspect. Yet such a decision for the historical feasibility and theological orthodoxy of the Biblical pattern of patriarchal submission over and against the "unworldliness" or "heresy" of the egalitarian ethos implies a historical-theological evaluation that is not derived from the New Testament itself. Such an evaluative interpretation acknowledges, however, that the New Testament testifies to such an early Christian ethos of coequal discipleship. Otherwise scholars could not disparage it.

A feminist critical hermeneutics that derives its canon from the struggle of women and other oppressed peoples for liberation from patriarchal structures must, therefore, call such scholarly interpretations and evaluations to accountability, and must carefully analyze their theological-political presuppositions and social-ecclesial interests. By making explicit its own evaluative feminist canons of liberation it can reclaim the early Christian ethos of the discipleship of equals as its own Biblical roots and heritage. In doing so it engenders a paradigm shift in Biblical ethics insofar as it does not appeal to the Bible as its primary source but begins with women's own experience and vision of liberation.

In such a feminist evaluative paradigm the Bible and Biblical revelation no longer function as a timeless archetype but as a historical prototype open to feminist theological transformation.[52] The Bible is not the controlling and defining "court of appeals" for contemporary Biblical feminist theology and community but its *formative* root-model. Only in such a way can Biblical revelation become liberated from its imprisonment in androcentric language and cultural-historical patriarchy. Only in and through a critical evaluative process of feminist hermeneutics can Scripture be used as resource in the liberation struggle of women and other "subordinated" people. The vision and praxis of our foresisters who heard the call to co-equal discipleship and acted in the power of the Spirit must be allowed to become a transformative power that can open up a feminist future for Biblical religion.

Third: Such a feminist Biblical future depends not only on the faithful remembrance of the oppression and liberation of women in Biblical history but also on the critical exploration of the continuing effects of the *Haustafel* trajectory in our own time and democratic society. Such a feminist evaluative exploration is not only rooted in the personal experience of women but also utilizes feminist scholarship and scientific theoretical discussion. While feminist theology has severely criticized and challenged present-day patriarchal church structures, it has not sufficiently utilized the theoretical feminist critique of marriage and family as the place of women's patriarchal oppression. It has concentrated on the analysis of cultural dualisms, but not sufficiently explored their ideological roots in patriarchal societal structures.

Susan Moller Okin, a political philosopher, has shown that the Aristotelian political ethics of the *Haustafel* is still operative in contemporary American democratic society. Although the patriarchal family has been modified in the course of history, nevertheless political philosophy still works with the Aristotelian premise that the free propertied man is the full citizen, whereas

> all the other members of the population—slaves and artisans as well as women—exist in order to perform their respective function for the few free males who participate fully in citizenship. The "nature" of all these groups of people are defined in terms of their satisfactory performance of their conventional functions.[53]

However, whereas for the Greeks the private, secluded sphere of the household was important primarily as an economic base, in modern times it is also crucial as a highly important aspect of affective life. Since the wife is responsible for the private sphere of the household, even a liberal philosopher such as John Stuart Mill asserts that she can only take on outside responsibilities after she has successfully taken care of *her* domestic responsibilities.

Even though liberalism is supposed to be based on individualism and to understand society as constituted of "independent, autonomous, units" it is clear, according to Moller Okin, that in spite of this individualistic rhetoric, the "family" and not the adult human individual is the basic political unit of liberal as of non-liberal philosophers. The adult members of a family are assumed to share all the same interests. Yet, whenever a conflict of interest occurs between husband and wife, the presumption in political and legal philosophy has been that such a conflict of interest must be decided by the male head of the household. Moreover, the public political sphere of "man's world' is defined by competition and self-interest but not by values of compassion, love and altruism, since such values are relegated to the private sphere of the home as women's domain. To legally and politically recognize women as individual citizens in their own right would, therefore, entail a change of the family structure and of political philosophy. Moller Okin concludes:

> If our aim is a truly democratic society, or a thoroughly democratic theory, we must acknowledge that anything but a democratic family with complete equality and mutual interdependence between the sexes will be a severe impediment to this aim.[54]

She also points out that the radical feminist critique of marriage and family has to be specified both as a critique of *patriarchal* household and societal relationships and an affirmation of interpersonal relationships of adult members who live in a "familial" community. Moreover, feminists have to recognize that woman's oppression is not constituted by her biological endowments but by her function in the patriarchal family as a cultural-political creation.

> It is not the fact that women are the primary reproductive agents of society, in itself, that has led to their oppression, but rather that reproduction has taken place within a patriarchal power structure, has been considered a private rather than a social concern, and has been perceived as dictating women's entire lives, and as defining their very nature.[55]

Although Moller Okin did not analyze the political implications of the New Testament *Haustafel* trajectory, she has documented that the Aristotelian political ethics of natural inequality has shaped Western political philosophy and society. A truly democratic society therefore would necessarily presuppose not only a radical change of the patriarchal family but also a radical transformation of the patriarchal churches into communities of equality and mutual interdependence, since not only the family but also the Christian churches have an important socializing function in American society.

The early Christian ethos of co-equal discipleship in community could provide a model for the "new family" as adult community of equality, mutuality and responsibility for the home *and* for the "world." It could provide a model for the restructuring of the "patriarchal household of God" into a kinship community without clerical fathers and spiritual masters not patterned after the biological patriarchal family. A feminist critical hermeneutics of liberation seeks to reactivate this early Christian ethos for today so that it can become a transformative historical model for the ordering of interpersonal communities, society, and the churches.

Because early Christian writers introduced the prescriptive Aristotelian ethics of patriarchal submission and patristic writers advocated an ascetic rejection of marriage and women, they together prevented a Christian understanding of marriage and family committed to the radical discipleship of co-equals.[56] Insofar as the patriarchal household and misogynist asceticism, but not the radical discipleship of women and men and as equals, have become the structural models for the dominant institutional churches, Christian theology and communal praxis have not developed ecclesial structures capable of challenging the societal separation of the private sphere as the sphere of interpersonal love sustained by the self-sacrifice of women and the public sphere as a sphere of brutal self-interest and competition. It has, therefore, failed to develop communal structures capable of socializing children into the Christian values of co-equality in community, *diakonia,* and discipleship, rather than into the cultural values and patriarchal roles of superordination and subordination, of masculinity and femininity.

Now that historical critical scholarship has proven the New

Testament *Haustafel* to be a christianized form of Aristotelian ethics, and feminist critical analyses have shown its destructive impact on women and the community of co-equal discipleship, the church as the community of moral discourse is clearly challenged anew to incarnate the early Christian vision and praxis of co-equality in community. True, both the ethos of co-equal discipleship and of the patriarchal pattern of submission can claim Scriptural authority and canonicity. Both are expression of believing communities in the first century and today. Insofar as the patriarchal pattern of submission has decisively formed Christian tradition and communal structures it can claim even greater historical influence and institutional powers for its own vision of how to live as a Christian community.

Nevertheless feminist theology, as a critical theology of liberation, must reject the theological Scriptural claims of this patriarchal pattern because of its oppressive effects on the life of women and other subordinated peoples. A feminist critical hermeneutics has as its canon the liberation of *all* women from oppressive structures, patriarchal institutions, and internalized values. It therefore interprets, retrieves and evaluates Biblical texts and communal structures. It accepts or rejects them as well as their political-social functions in terms of its own canon of liberation. A feminist critical ethics that is committed to the liberation struggle of women and the whole church, therefore, insists that the ethos and praxis of co-equal discipleship must transform the patriarchal *Haustafel* ethics and its institutional structures, if women and the Christian church are to have a feminist Christian future.

Notes

1. For a review and discussion of the hermeneutical and methodological issues involved see among others: E. LeRoy Long, Jr., "The Use of the Bible in Christian Ethics. A Look at Basic Options," *Interpretation* 9 (1965), 149–162; Charles Curran, "Dialogue with the Scriptures: The Role and Function of the Scriptures in Moral Deliberation and Justifica-

tion," in *Catholic Moral Theology in Dialogue* (Notre Dame: Fides Publishers, 1972), 24–64; James M. Gustafson, "The Place of Scripture in Christian Ethics: A Methodological Study," *Interpretation* 24 (1970), 430–455; Allen Verhey, "The Use of Scripture in Ethics," *Religious Studies Review* 4 (1978), 28–39; James Childress, "Scripture and Christian Ethics. Some Reflections on the Role of Scripture in Moral Deliberation and Justification," *Interpretation* 34 (1980), 371–380; and the very useful book of Bruce C. Birch and Larry L. Rasmussen, *Bible and Ethics in the Christian Life* (Minneapolis: Augsburg Publishing House, 1976).

2. Stanley Hauerwas, "The Moral Authority of Scripture. The Politics and Ethics of Remembering," *Interpretation* 34 (1980), 356–370, 367.

3. See e.g. Bernhard Fraling, "Glaube und Ethos: Normfindung in der Gemeinschaft der Gläubigen," *Theologie un Glaube* 63 (1973), 81–105 and the diverse writings of James Barr, especially his contribution "The Bible as Document of Believing Communities," in Hans Dieter Betz (ed.), *The Bible as a Document of the University* (Chico: Scholars Press, 1981), 24–47.

4. For a discussion of different paradigms and heuristic models in Biblical interpretation see my article "For the Sake of Our Salvation. Biblical Interpretation as Theological Task," in Daniel Durken (ed.), *Sin, Salvation, and the Spirit* (Collegeville: Liturgical Press, 1979), 21–39.

5. For a helpful review of the problem see Jean Charlot, *New Testament Disunity: Its Significance for Christianity Today* (New York: E. P. Dutton, 1970).

6. For the definition of ethics as "an evaluative hermeneutics of history" see Gibson Winter, *Elements for a Social Ethics. Scientific and Ethical Perspectives on Social Process* (New York: Macmillan, 1966) and Thomas W. Ogletree, "The Activity of Interpreting in Moral Judgment," *The Journal of Religious Ethics* 8 (1980), 1–25. Ogletree proposes an "historical style" in ethics as an "explication of meanings forming the life worlds of representative actors in concrete situations."

7. See Johann Baptist Metz, *Faith in History and Society. Toward a Pratical Fundamental Theology,* trans. By David Smith (New York: Crossroad Books, 1980), 88–118, 185–199.

8. For this expression see "The Constitution on Divine Revelation of Vatican II." Cf. Walter Abbott and Joseph Gallagher (eds.), *The Document of Vatican II* (New York: American Press, 1966), 119. Salvation must not be restricted to the salvation of the soul from sin, but must be understood as total human wholeness and liberation.

9. Stanley Hauerwas, *ibid.*, 356. Like Metz, Hauerwas uses as key

interpretive categories memory and narrative/story, but neglects how Metz spells out their critical implications. Insofar as Hauerwas asserts that the church is the "community of the forgiven" without asking it to repent and to reject its oppressive traditions, he does not do justice to the memory of the innocent victims in history. Thus his theology has no room for a critical hermeneutics of liberation.

10. Elizabeth Cady Stanton, *The Original Feminist Attack on the Bible. The Woman's Bible,* intro. By Barbara Welter, repr. of 1895 ed. (New York: Arno Press, 1974), 7.

11. See Linda Gordon and Allen Hunter, "Sex, Family, and the New Right. Antifeminism as a Political Force," *Radical America* 11 (1978), 9–25; Charlene Spretnak, "The Christian Right's 'Holy War' Against Feminism," in *The Politics of Women's Spirituality* (New York: Anchor Books, 1982), 470–496.

12. See my article " 'You are not to be called Father': Early Christian History in a Feminist Perspective," *Cross Currents* 39 (1979). 301–323 for a methodological discussion of these dynamics.

13. David L. Balch, *Let Wives be Submissive: The Domestic Code in 1 Peter,* SBL Monograph Series 26 (Chico: Scholars Press, 1981).

14. Stephen B. Clark, *Man and Woman in Christ. An Examination of the Roles of Men and Women in Light of Scripture and the Social Sciences* (Ann Arbor: Servant Books, 1980).

15. John H. Elliott, *A Home for the Homeless. A Sociological Exegesis of I Peter. Its Situation and Strategy* (Philadelphia: Fortress Press, 1981).

16. Karl Niederwimmer, *Askees und Mysterium,* FRLANT 113 (Gottingen: Vandenhoeck & Ruprecht, 1975).

17. James E. Crouch, *The Origins and Intention of the Colossian Haustafel,* FRLANT 109 (Göttingen: Vandenhoeck & Ruprecht, 1972).

18. Klaus Thraede, "Frau," in *Antike und Christentum* 6 (1970), 197–267.

19. William Lillie, "The Pauline House-Tables," *The Expository Times* 86 (1975), 179–183 acknowledges the "pattern of submission" as characteristic for the household code texts. For a christological justification of this pattern of subordination see Else Kähler, *Die Frau in den Paulinischen Briefen* (Zürich: Gotthelf Verlag, 1960). For a Feminist Evangelical interpretation of the pattern as a pattern of "mutual submission" see Virginia Ramey Mollenkott, *Women, Men & the Bible* (Nashville: Abingdon, 1977) and Letha Scanzoni and Nancy Hardesty, *All We're Meant to Be. A Biblical Approach to Women's Liberation* (Waco: Word Books, 1975).

20. For a review of the discussion see Ulrich Luz, "Erwägungen zur Entstehung des 'Frühkatholizismus'," *Zeitschrift für die Neutestamentliche Wissenschaft* 65 (1974), 88–111.

21. Dieter Lührmann, "Wo man nicht mehr Sklave und Freier ist. Ueberlegungen zur Struktur frühchristlicher Gemeinden," *Wort und Dienst* 13 (1975), 53–83.

22. Ronald Syme, *The Roman Revolution* (Oxford: University Press, 1939), 509–24.

23. Among others see David Schroeder, *Die Haustafeln des Neuen Testaments* (unpublished dissertation Hamburg, 1959) whose thesis was taken over and popularized in English by John H. Yoder.

24. For a review of this position and its main representatives see the works of Crouch, Balch, and Elliott.

25. See Klaus Thraede, "Zum historischen Hintergrund der 'Haustafeln' des NT," *Jahrbuch für Antike und Christentum. Ergänzungsband* 8 (1981), 359–368; Kathleen O'Brien Wicker, "First Century Marriage Ethics: A Comparative Study of the Household Codes and Plutarch's Conjugal Precepts," in James Flanagan and Anita W. Robinson (eds.), *No Famine in the Land* (Missoula: Scholars Press, 1975), 141–153; David Balch, "Household Ethical Codes in Peripatetic, Neopythagorean, and Early Christian Moralists," in Paul J. Achtemeier (ed.), *Society of Biblical Literature Seminar Papers II* (Missoula: Scholars Press, 1977), 397–404.

26. Gerd Theissen, "Itinerant Radicalism: The Tradition of Jesus' Sayings from the Perspective of the Sociology of Literature," in *The Bible and Liberation. Political and Social Hermeneutics* (Berkeley: Radical Religion, 1976), 84–93. Id., *Sociology of Early Palestinian Christianity* (Philadelphia: Fortress Press, 1978) and his forthcoming essays *The Social Setting of Pauline Christianity. Essays on Corinth* (Philadelphia: Fortress Press, 1982).

27. John H. Elliot, ibid., 198.

28. See my article "Word, Spirit, and Power. Women in Early Christian Communities," in Rosemary R. Ruether and Eleanor McLaughlin (eds.), *Women of Spirit* (New York: Simon and Schuster, 1979), 29–70 and "Women in the Pre-Pauline and Pauline Churches," *Union Seminary Quarterly Review* 33 (1978), 153–166.

29. For an excellent discussion of the "slavery passages" see Peter Trummer, "Die Chance der Freiheit," *Biblica* 56 (1975), 344–368 and the commentaries to Philemon.

30. Robert A. Nisbet, *The Social Philosophers: Community and Conflict in Western Thought* (New York: Thomas Y. Cromwell, 1973), 178.

31. Edwin A. Judge, *The Social Patterns of Christian Groups in the*

First Century: Some Prolegomena to the Study of New Testament Ideas of Social Organization (London: Tyndale, 1960), 75f.

32. Ibid., 76.

33. For the distinction between *ethos* and *ethics* see Leander E. Keck, "Ethos and Ethics in the New Testament," in James Gaffney (ed.), *Essays in Morality and Ethics* (New York: Paulist Press, 1980), 29–49. For the interrelation between house-church and collegia see Abraham Malherbe, *Social Aspects of Early Christianity* (Baton Rouge: Louisiana State University, 1977).

34. See Susan Treggiari, "Roman Social History: Recent Interpretations," *Histoire Social. Social History* 8 (1975), 149–164 and Wayne A. Meeks, "The Image of the Androgyne," *History of Religion* 13 (1974), 167–180, for a review of the literature.

35. Klaus Thraede, "Aerger mit der Freiheit. Die Bedeutung von Frauen in Theorie und Praxis der alten Kirche," in Gerda Scharffenroth (ed.), *Freunde in Christus werden . . .* (Gelnhausen/Berlin: Burckhardthaus, 1977), 35–182.

36. See the discussion of the literature by Georg Strecker, "Strukturen einer neutestamentlichen Ethik," *Zeitschrift für Theologie und Kirche* 75 (1978), 117–146; Siegfried Schulz, "Evangelium und Welt. Hauptprobleme einer Ethik des Neuen Testaments," in Hans Dieter Betz and Luise Schottroff (eds.), *Neues Testament und christliche Existenz,* Festschrift H. Braun (Tübingen: JCB Mohr, 1973), 483–501.

37. See John G. Gager, *Kingdom and Community. The Social World of Early Christianity* (Englewood Cliffs: Prentice Hall, 1975) and Gerd Theissen, "Itinerant Radicalism," ibid., 91f.

38. Eduard Schweizer, "Ethischer Pluralismus im Neuen Testament: die Haustafeln," in *Beiträge zur alttestamentlichen Theologie,* Festschrift W. Zimmerli (Göttingen: Vandenhoeck & Ruprecht, 1979), 397–413.412.

39. Leonhard Goppelt, *Der erste Petrusbrief,* ed. by Ferdinand Hahn, MeyerK (Göttingen: Vandenhoeck & Ruprecht, 1978), 163–177.

40. Wolfgang Schrage, "Zur Ethik der neutestamentlichen Haustafeln," *New Testament Studies* 21 (1974/75), 1–22.22.

41. John Howard Yoder, *The Politics of Jesus. Vicit Agnus Noster* (Grand Rapids: W. B. Eerdmans, 1972), 175.

42. Ibid., 185.

43. Ibid., 176 n. 22. See also Stanley Hauerwas, ibid., 370.

44. See for example Mary Daly's feminist stance in *Beyond God the Father* (Boston: Beacon Press, 1973) which conceives of "sisterhood as anti-church" and in *Gyn/Ecology. The Metaethics of Radical Feminism* (Boston: Beacon Press, 1978) which redefines sisterhood in terms of "the

bonding of the Selfs" who have "escaped" from patriarchal space as "the territory of non-being." This understanding of "sisterhood" no longer can sustain feminist solidarity with all women because it does not understand the feminist movement as the "bonding of the oppressed" but as the gathering of the ideologically "pure," as "the network of Spinsters and Amazons."

45. Elisabeth Schüssler Fiorenza, "Feminist Theology as a Critical Theology of Liberation," *Theological Studies* 36 (1975), 605–626. Carol S. Robb, "A Framework for Feminist Ethics," *The Journal of Religious Ethics* 9 (1981), 48–68, and especially the very helpful introductions by Carol Christ and Judith Plaskow (eds.), *Womanspirit Rising. A Feminist Reader in Religion* (New York: Harper & Row, 1979).

46. See my articles, "Interpreting Patriarchal Traditions," in Letty Russell (ed.), *The Liberating Word. A Guide to Nonsexist Interpretation of the Bible* (Philadelphia: Westminister Press, 1976), 39–61 and "Toward a Feminist Biblical Hermeneutics: Biblical Interpretation and Liberation Theology," in Brian Mahan and L. Dale Richesin (eds.), *The Challenge of Liberation Theology. A First World Response* (New York: Orbis Press, 1981), 91–112. See also Elizabeth Fox-Genovese, "For Feminist Interpretation," *Union Seminary Quarterly Review* 35 (1979/80), 5–14; Ernst Feil, " 'Konfessorische' Implikationen der Wissenschaft. Folgerungen für die theologische Ethik," *Herder Korrespondenz* 34 (1980), 28–37.

47. For a similar but distinct approach see Beverly Wildung Harrison, "The Power of Anger in the Work of Love. Christian Ethics for Women and Other Strangers," *Union Seminary Quarterly Review* 36 (1981), 41–57; Eleanor Humes Haney, "What is Feminist Ethics? A Proposal for Continuing Discussion," *The Journal of Religious Ethics* 8 (1980).

48. For this distinction cf. Letty Russell, *Human Liberation in a Feminist Perspective—A Theology* (Philadelphia: Westminister Press, 1974).

49. Phyllis Trible, *God and the Rhetoric of Sexuality* (Philadelphia: Fortress Press, 1978) uses the metaphor of the Biblical Text "wandering through history to merge past and present."

50. This position is succinctly stated by Rosemary Radford Ruether, "The Feminist Critique in Religious Studies," *Soundings* 64 (1981), 388–402.400: "Liberationists would use the prophetic tradition as the norm to critique the sexism of the religious tradition. Biblical sexism is not denied, but it loses its authority. It must be denounced as a failure to measure up to the full vision of human liberation of the prophetic and gospel messages."

51. See Elisabeth Schüssler Fiorenza, "Sexism and Conversion," *Network* 9 (1981), 12–22.

52. For this distinction between archetype and prototype see Rachel Blau DuPlessis, "The Critique of Consciousness and Myth in Levertov, Rich, and Rukeyser," *Feminist Studies* 3 (1975), 199–221.

53. Susan Moller Okin, *Women in Western Political Thought* (Princeton: University Press, 1979), 276.

54. Ibid., 289. See also Nannerl O. Koehane, "Speaking from Silence. Women and the Science of Politics," *Soundings* 64 (1981), 422–436.

55. Susan Moller Okin, ibid., 296.

56. See also Beverly Wildung Harrison, "Some Problems for Normative Christian Family Ethics," *Selected Papers, 1977. The American Society of Christian Ethics* (Waterloo: The Council on the Study of Religion, 1977), 72–85; Barbara Hilkert Andolson, "Agape in Feminist Ethics," *The Journal of Religious Ethics,* 9 (1981), 69–81.

4. Encountering the Other: The Modern Papacy on Women

Christine E. Gudorf

This chapter first appeared in *Social Compass* in 1989.

1. Women in Public and Private Realms

Papal teaching on women illustrates the clash that exists between papal social teaching on the one hand and papal teaching on the private realm of Church and family on the other.[1] Since women belong to and are treated by the popes as being part of both realms, papal teaching on women has a schizophrenic quality. Papal social teaching on politics, economics and social policy in the public realm is characterized by a social-welfare liberalism assuming equality, pluralism, democracy, social dynamism and optimism about creating a just egalitarian order through gradual altruistic efforts within existing social structures.

Papal teaching on the private realm, on the other hand, continues to be characterized by assumptions of static institutions rooted in divine and natural law, hierarchy and paternalism. Both private-realm institutions of Church and family interact with the public realm. But in the papal perspective, the Church's interaction with the world is largely limited to the gift of its teachings; the world offers little to the Church other than a field for evangelization. Pope John Paul II agrees with Pope John XXIII that (social scientific) study of the world only shows the Church how to present its eternal truths more effectively.[2] The family is similarly understood as "the church of the home" whose chief role is as refuge from an inhumane world.[3] The world's influence on the family is usually portrayed as detrimental and to be resisted. In short, the social relations the Church teaches as appropriate for the world are not appropriate for Church or family.

1.1. Social Teaching on Women

The public-realm teaching on women since the early 1960s has focused on the equality of women, their right to be accorded equal education, work, pay and political rights, and to be protected from discrimination against their gender.[4] Before Vatican II, popes assumed and explicitly taught women's inequality and subordination to men, as well as condemned advocates of both women's equality and public roles for women.[5] The Second World War seems to have been the transition point; the fact that women both held jobs while men fought and, especially in Europe, worked after the war due to the death of husbands, fathers and potential spouses, led to an acceptance of women's need to enter the public realm through employment. Pius XII recognized both this fact and the fact that women's entry into the public realm made it necessary for them to acquire rights there. But he hoped that, for the good of the family, women would not exercise all their new-found rights.[6]

Since the time of John XXIII the popes have repeated the message that women are equal and should be granted equal rights. Whereas earlier teaching had defined the paternal role as governing, protective and supportive (in a material sense), and the maternal role in terms of indiscriminate love, personal service, and religious and moral instruction,[7] the Council and succeeding popes make fewer gender distinctions between the educative role of parents.[8]

Most contemporary commentary, secular as well as ecclesiastical, on papal teaching on women concentrates on the recent social teaching on women's equality and the need to end discrimination against women. One reason for this is that the language of liberal rights is found in the more authoritative, and more accessible, papal documents, such as social teaching encyclicals. This liberal message is also more familiar and understandable to secular writers. Nevertheless, the great bulk of papal treatment of women contains a very different message and is found in less well-known sermons and addresses, especially in more devotional speeches on Mary and the saints, and in addresses to local groups.

Another interesting note is that the theme of women's equality is not elaborated to the same extent as are the devotional private-realm messages. The popes do not describe or condemn specific discriminative practices against women. Over half of all US women workers have quit their job or been fired because of sexual harassment,[9] which is certainly not an exclusively US phenomenon; but on this issue the popes are silent. Violence against women, whether by rape or battery, is similarly a massive problem all over the world, affecting up to one out of every four families in the USA;[10] and yet the popes are silent. Unlike many other areas of papal teaching, there are no personal stories or remarks from the popes about public roles for women, no models advocated for emulation. When examples of Mary and the saints are presented as models, the aspects of their lives which are highlighted are never responsible leadership or public careers, but rather their role as background supporters who help share the world through prayer and child-rearing. For example, John Paul II wrote of Mary as "the woman who is honoured as Queen of Apostles without herself being inserted into the hierarchical constitution of the Church. Yet this woman made all hierarchy possible because she gave to the world the Shepherd and Bishop of our souls."[11] The teaching on traditional roles for women seems much more deeply rooted in the personal life and spirituality of John Paul II (and that of his predecessors) than is the egalitarian message, however strongly he intellectually supports equality of the sexes.

1.2. Private-realm Teaching on Women

Because of the shift to affirming the equality of women, papal teaching on the private realm required changes not always gracefully achieved. John XXIII insisted on both the equality of women and the authority of husbands in the family: "Within the family, the father stands in God's place. He must lead and guide the rest by his authority and the example of his good life."[12] He later explained:

> It is true that living conditions tend to bring about almost complete equality of the sexes. Nevertheless, while their justly proclaimed equality of rights must extend to all the claims of personal and human dignity, it does not in any way imply equality of functions.
>
> The Creator endowed woman with natural attributes, tendencies and instincts, which are strictly hers, or which she possesses to a different degree from man; this means woman was also assigned certain tasks.
>
> To overlook this difference in the respective functions of men and women or the fact that they necessarily complement one another, would be tantamount to opposing nature: the result would be to debase woman and to remove the true foundation of her dignity.[13]

John never fully describes how the different and complementary functions of men and women are unequal, but he does go on to refer to an argument often made by his predecessors: to claim full equality for women would be to jeopardize all rights for women. His predecessors claimed for the Church the achievement of having elevated the dignity and status of women chiefly through elevating marriage—the intimate but hierarchically ordered link between men and women.[14] The implication is that women accept unequal status in marriage in return for some benefits and protection, or that women can press for equality which so offends men that men will deny any status and protection to women. The nature of men will not allow women full equality. John's assumption that hierarchy is natural, that all social units require a head because authority cannot be shared but only wielded by some over others,[15] is undoubtedly linked to this pessimistic view of men's nature.

Since the time of John XXIII we rarely find women urged to submit to the headship of their husbands, although this was common before the Second World War.[16] Nor is women's nature described in the same traditional terms. Pope Benedict XV bewailed that one of the worst effects of the First World War was the removal of fathers and husbands from the home, which allowed immorality to flourish there.[17] Pius XI condemned Communism for advocating the removal of women from the "tutorship of man," and female athletics for threatening women's virtue.[18] Post-Vatican II popes have not elaborated this female need for moral control and protection. Even more striking is that since formal acceptance of women's equality was given there have been no papal descriptions of women's nature as making them less capable of reason. The claim of women's irrationality and consequent inability to discriminate was the source of the central inconsistency in pre-Vatican II papal teaching on women. For the early twentieth-century popes had adopted pedestalized understandings of woman as the superior religious and moral force *at the same time* as they insisted that woman's nature made her incapable of competent choice. Papal acceptance of women as innately religious and moral was clearly determined more by women's greater acquiesence to Church authority in an age when the Church as an institution was under siege, than by Church teaching on male and female nature.

1.3. Equality and Pedestalization

Despite the shift toward equality for women in Church social teaching, papal teaching on the nature and role of women still demonstrates a romantic pedestalization of women. The predominant theme is motherhood. This is as true of John Paul II today as it was of Pius XII in the 1940s and 1950s. Women are understood to have been created to be mothers,[19] either physically, as wives, or spiritually as with women religious. One arresting aspect of John Paul's thought is that motherhood is not an element of what it is to be a woman, but rather that motherhood defines womanhood.[20] Like his predecessors, John Paul prefers the teaching of 1 Tim. 2:15, that women are saved through motherhood, to Jesus' teaching that women will be saved and venerated not for their maternity but for their participation in the larger project of the Kingdom of God (Lk. 11:27–28, Mk. 3:31–35).

John Paul II represents the "biology is destiny" school of thought with regard to women and shares with others in that school the failure to understand the male sex in similar biological terms. In fact, despite the inadequacy of John Paul's teaching on women (and that of his predecessors) the greater problem is its treatment of men. In an attempt to persuade women to acquiesce to traditional divisions of power which favor men, the popes have lifted women's pedestal so high as to deny in many ways the basic humanity and Christian potential of men.

Like his predecessors, John Paul often speaks of a mother's role in the family as "irreplaceable,"[21] and deals with motherhood by referring to the example of Mary, "who conceived spiritually before she conceived physically."[22] Conception and birth are miraculous moments for John Paul II. He sees them as central to the feminine mystique:

> What is happening in the stable, in the cave hewn from rock, is something very intimate, something that goes on "between" mother and child. No one from outside has access to it. Even Joseph, the carpenter from Nazareth, is but a silent witness.[23]

> . . . we should stand by the expectant mother; [that] we should devote special care to mothers and to the great event that is peculiarly theirs: the conception and birth of a human being. This event is the foundation on which the education of a human being builds. Education depends upon trust in her who has given life.
>
> Motherhood is a woman's vocation. It is a vocation for all times; it is a vocation today. The words of a song popular among young people in Poland comes to my mind at this moment: "The mother who understands everything and in her heart embraces each of us." The song goes on to say that the world has a special "hunger and thirst" for this motherhood which is woman's "physical" and "spiritual" vocation, as it is Mary's.[24]

While childbirth can perhaps be described as an experience touching woman alone, John Paul's placing of conception in the same category raises serious questions about his understanding of sexual intercourse. Furthermore, his description of mothers alone as "detecting the cry of the infant" or understanding children and loving each of them, excludes men from relational intimacy in the family. John Paul II's understanding of the role of men in families often seems to revolve around material support. Men's role is, like Joseph's, to remain loyal to one's wife and to the children to whom she is linked by a mysterious love, even though men are excluded from that mysterious love. "Do not abandon her!" he writes to husbands about their wives.[25] After all, "such was the mystery in which Mary was included, but Joseph was unaware of this mystery."[26]

No wonder that men abandon women and children in large numbers if they share John Paul's understanding of men as being excluded from the central relationship in families. In an age when economic necessity and less economic discrimination against women combine to pressure many women to take on part of men's traditional role as breadwinner, what is left for men to value in their familial role?

Two decades ago John XXIII addressed the issue of working wives and mothers. In an address to working women, he said:

> Everyone knows that outside work, as you might naturally expect, makes a person tired and may even dull the personality; sometimes it is humiliating and mortifying besides. When a man comes back to his home after being away for long hours and sometimes after having completely spent his energies, is he going to find in it a refuge and a source for restoring his energies and the reward that will make up for the dry, mechanical nature of the things that have surrounded him?
>
> Here again there is a great task waiting for women; let them promise themselves that they will not let their contacts with the harsh realities of outside work dry up the richness of their inner life, the resources of their sensitivity, of their open and delicate spirit; that they will not forget those spiritual values that are the only defense of their nobility; last of all, that they will not fail to go to the fonts of prayer and sacramental life for the strength to maintain themselves on a level with their matchless mission.

> They are called to an effort perhaps greater than that of men; if you take into consideration women's natural frailty in some respects and the fact that more is being asked of them. At all times and in all circumstances they are the ones who have to be wise enough to find the resources to face their duties as wives and mothers calmly and with their eyes wide open; to make their homes warm and peaceful after the tiring labours of daily work, and not to shrink from the responsibility of raising children.[27]

Evidently John believed that jobs do not damage and deplete women to the same extent that they do men. Most of the world agrees; government studies in the USA show that married working women put in working weeks averaging 72 to 76 hours, compared with their husbands' average working week of 42 hours.[28] When women return from work, they begin their second job at home, with an average of less than two hours a week of assistance from their husbands. How can this be reconciled with the papal proclamations of women's equality?

Recent popes, including John Paul II in particular, insist that in seeking to free women from discrimination societies must prevent employment from detracting from women's irreplaceable role in the family.[29] Although the policies to achieve this end are yet unclear, John Paul's suggestions seem to revolve around pressure to keep married women from jobs by providing economic incentives for them to stay home.[30] There is no attempt to redistribute the work of the home between the spouses, even in the present before such schemes could be implemented. Furthermore, the implementation of such schemes is far beyond the capability of most nations of the world. In the Third World it is not uncommon for half the men to lack stable employment. Many scrape by in the informal sector with help from wives who work as ambulatory vendors or servants and then return home to take up their second job. In such nations, incomes for housewives are utopian dreams.

Women have often been described by sociologists as carrying the double burden of paid employment and housework/childcare. In the passage quoted earlier John adds another burden for women: that of responsibility for the emotional and spiritual well-being of the family, for making the home into an intimate refuge. Both Paul VI and John Paul II seem to assume that this psychological burden is naturally and exclusively women's.[31] This burden is perhaps more debilitating for women than extra hours of work.

It is inescapable that papal assertions of sexual equality are best understood to refer to equal dignity in the eyes of God. But equal dignity should connote some equality in vocation. If men's only responsibility is to support the family materially, how is his vocation the equal of the wife's, much less the working wife's? Can men be regarded as other than deficient humans when they seem to carry few relational responsibilities? How can they be Christians? Where are men's opportunities for personal service, for sensitivity, for love in any intimate sense? If men's roles in the family do not teach them to be sensitive to the needs of others, to the demands of justice within the home, how can they possibly love well? How will their sons have models for learning to love well as men?

Furthermore, if men lack the compassion and nurturance of women and if these gifts of women are required to keep the home as a refuge for men and children to counteract the harshness of the public sphere, then there can be no conversion of the public sphere. The call to evangelize the world becomes impossible when the only people considered capable of creating true human community are restricted to domestic refuges.

1.4 Gender Complementarity

Papal assumptions of gender complementarity[32] are problematic in themselves, even without the added complexity of historical shifts in gender roles. The problem is that traditional assertions of gender complementarity have the effect of positing both men and women as being incomplete outside marriage. More recent treatment of complementarity tends to explain gender complementarity in terms of human sociality.[33]

It is necessary to affirm that we are inherently social, that we become human through social relations, and grow through exposure to different kinds of people. It is also necessary to oppose the typically modern assumption of autonomous selves for whom social relations are voluntary and not intrinsic. We do need to relate to both men and women in order to develop our own gender identity successfully and to enrich our ability to relate to different people. But gender complementarity in papal teaching reaches much further than this; it assumes that traits and roles are essentially sex-based, so that a man will be more different from all women than from any man. Because of this, our most intimate human relationship, the marital relationship, is assumed to be the place where we come face to face with our complement and thus are made whole through the challenge to communicate with and bond to this opposite.

But the popes seem to forget their teaching on complementarity of the sexes when they discuss celibacy. Not only are celibates who lack the intimate marital bond with an opposite not characterized in terms of a lack of wholeness and completeness, but they are not encouraged to develop close non-sexual relationships with their sexual opposites in order to compensate for the lack of sexual intimacy which more normally forces growth in wholeness.[34] In fact, the segregation of seminarians from women continues to be a major concern of the popes, in opposition to recent trends in the USA and other countries.[35] Despite data circulating among bishops regarding low levels of emotional development and interpersonal relationships, and high levels of alcoholism, depression and sexual activity among Catholic priests,[36] we do not find John Paul II supporting relationships with women as being valuable in the priestly formation process. It has become clear that in a society where intimacy is more or less restricted by convention to sexual, especially marital, relationships, those forbidden marriage will be relationally deprived. Such analysis usually leads to the conclusion that celibates and all of us would benefit from sanctioning greater emotional intimacy in non-sexual relationships such as friendships with both sexes, rather than limiting necessary intimacy to relationships not accessible to all.

But papal thought is not open to this direction for two reasons: fear of sexuality, especially of women, and fear for the stability of marriage. Friendships between the sexes are regarded as dangerous threats to celibacy both for priests and single laity because of the presumed power of the sex drive. Given the patriarchal structure of the Church and the training of the clergy, the threat to celibacy represented by the sex drive is interpreted as a threat from women, and becomes intertwined with historic conceptions of women as polluting. Even within marriage intimacy is understood to be easily corrupted by sexual desire, which John Paul II cannot distinguish from lust. He is thoroughly classical in this regard. Both Augustine and Thomas Aquinas agreed that sexual desire is both sinful and difficult to avoid within marriage; only the great good of procreation made this constant temptation to sin tolerable within marriage.[37]

The second reason for resisting a call for a diffusion of intimate non-sexual relationships within society is rooted in papal fear for the stability of marriage. As we have seen, recent popes present women as being natural nurturers and intimates, compassionate sharers who create webs of relationships around them. The popes, especially John Paul II, see women as domesticating men by offering them the intimacy only available within the refuges created by women. Men are not viewed as naturally bound to family as women are. Instead, women bind men to family through men's need for intimacy—for unconditional acceptance, for sexual gratification, for nurture—which traps him into the role of husband and father, tames his natural drive toward unrooted competition and achievement, and binds him to the home. His tie is to woman, and only through her to children. His role within this family, which both gratifies him and traps him, is material support, a role in which he must be able to take pride if his benefits from the arrangement are to outweigh his sacrifice. Even if the popes believed that intimacy were possible outside the family, they might well suppress it in order to protect the family institution.

Such an understanding of gender roles agrees with much of the data of contemporary sociologists. Women's dependence on men through marriage is largely material; the primary result of divorce for women in the USA is poverty for themselves and their children.[38] Children are regarded as being much more closely bound to mothers than to fathers; the vast majority of children are awarded by mutual agreement to the mother in cases of divorce although this is slightly less common than in the recent past.[39]

Men's psychological need for women seems to be much greater than women's need for men. In the USA married men suffer less anxiety, depression and emotionally related health problems than single or divorced men; divorced and widowed men remarry more often and much sooner than divorced or widowed women.[40] Married women, on the other hand, tend to higher degrees of depression, anxiety and mental illness than both husbands and single women. Men have greater problems adjusting to divorce and death of a spouse than do women.[41]

Papal concern for the stability of family, and reluctance to support any equality which might free women of double workloads and men for growth in relationality, is undoubtedly influenced by traditional theology of marriage.

Saint Augustine, for example, proposed the primary purposes of marriage to be first, producing offspring, and second, a cure for lust and formation of a marital bond (ordered to partnership in the rearing of children).[42] The papal view is distinctly clerical—that is, it is based on children's experience of marriage as revolving around them and their needs, rather than on spouse's experience of marriage. Since the 1960s' debate on contraception there have been vocal assertions by laity of an understanding of marriage contrary to that of St. Augustine and the clergy. Key to these lay perceptions is an understanding of intimacy neither as a by-product of procreation nor as a commodity offered by wives to trap husbands into material support, but a mutual creation which exists for its own sake. An important aspect of this marital intimacy is sexual intercourse, central neither for the sake of procreation nor as an outlet for human lust. Collette Potvin, the wife in one of the three couples appointed to the Pontifical Commission on Population, the Family and Birth during Vatican II represented many of the laity when she responded to a cleric on the Commission who had just asked whether the sex act was necessary for married couples. As reported by Robert Kaiser:

> She described herself as "simply a wife, married 17 years, with five children." She had had three miscarriages and a hysterectomy; perhaps from that point of view she had a clearer point of view than the scientists and the theolo-

> gians. She looked up at the group, hesitated a moment, then dared a needed preamble: "To understand woman, you need to stop looking at her as a deficient male, an occasion of sin, or an incarnation of the demon of sex, but rather as Genesis presents her: a companion to man. Where I come from, we marry primarily to live with a man of our choice. Children are a normal consequence of our love and not the goal. The physiological integrity of the conjugal act is less important than the repercussions of that love on the couple and on their family. And that conjugal act is the principal way we have of showing our love for each other."
>
> . . . Because no one had dared speak so plainly, she would. Directly and with no false modesty, she explained what lovemaking meant to her and Laurent (her husband) "Marvellous moments," she said, "when each of us accepts the other, forgives the other, and can give the best of ourselves to the other." The morning after such a communion, she said, she felt more serene, more patient with her children more loving to everyone. Nothing contributed more to her family equilibrium. She described the spiritual sense of well being that accompanied what she called "the conjugal orgasm": "a sense of joy, a feeling of accord on every level"—and all of it accompanied by "a rainbow of wonderful tingling sensations."[43]

For many laypeople, the papal teaching on marriage fails to understand the great power and gift that resides in marriage as a sacrament. It trivializes marriage by assigning to it a physical goal beyond the relationship itself. Papal teaching on marital sex can be compared with teaching Christians to have faith in order to be saved from hellfire, rather than because faith is a fulfilling way of life, a joyous communion with God and neighbor. The sacramental sign in marriage is sexual orgasm, and the nature of sacramental signs is that they create what they celebrate: in marriage, mutual love.[44] Intercourse is more than an expression of love, certainly more than an outlet for lust or a reward offered men for their fidelity to family. And like the eucharist, another sacramental sign, it should be encouraged as a part of the life of faith.

If the popes could understand that this intimate relationship between equals is central, and the birth of children only an expression, although an important one, of marital love, then perhaps John Paul might not see fathers as so peripheral to family. His fixation on the biological link between mother and child is not necessary when the experience of the couple themselves is that this child is a mutual creation of their love and a challenge to that love to grow and expand to include this child. If John Paul could recognize the existence of strong mutual sexual love between men and women, then perhaps he would realize that men are capable of intimacy and nurture, and that women need not carry the burden of providing intimate, nurturing refuges for society, but can share the task of humanizing the world with men.

2. Women in the Church

Between the beginning of the pontificate of Paul VI and today the question of women's roles in the Church has become a major one. Paul VI was not especially sensitive to this issue. In 1964 he addressed a group of women religious:

> We will let you in on a little secret in this regard: We have given orders that some devout ladies are to attend as auditors several of the solemn ceremonies and several of the General Congregations of the coming Third Session of the Second Vatican Council; what we have in mind are those congregations that will discuss matters of particular concern to the lives of women. Hence we will have present at an ecumenical council, perhaps for the first time, a representation, of women—only a small one, obviously, but still significant, and you might say, symbolic—from you sisters first of all, and then from the great Catholic Women's organizations.
>
> Women will thus know just how much honor the

> Church pays to them in the dignity of their being and of their mission on the human and the Christian levels.[45]

Women today are more likely to read this gesture as an important symbol of how *little* the Church regards them and their role. Paul was similarly dense when he made statements about "the right and duty of all the baptized—men and women alike—to share as responsible members of God's people in the mission of the church."[46] For he connected such statements with seemingly contradictory decisions, as in his *motu proprio. Ministeria quaedam,* of 15 August 1972, which revised the norms concerning the ministries of lector and acolyte:

> Mother Church earnestly desires that all the faithful should be led to that full, conscious and active participation in liturgical celebrations which is demanded by the very nature of the liturgy. Such participation by the Christian people as a "chosen race, a royal priesthood, a holy nation, a purchased people" is their right and their duty by reason of their baptism. In the restoration and promotion of the sacred liturgy, this full and active participation by all the people is the aim to be considered before all else, for it is the primary and indispensable source from which the faithful are to derive the true Christian spirit; and therefore the pastors of souls must zealously strive to achieve it by means of the necessary instruction, in all their pastoral work.[47]

Since women normally consider themselves among "the faithful," "the Christian people," and the baptized, it is difficult to understand number VII of Paul's new norms: "In accordance with the venerable tradition of the church, installation in the ministries of lector and acolyte is reserved to men."

With the publication of the *Declaration on the Question of the Admission of Women to the Ministerial Priesthood,* approved by Paul VI on 15 October 1976,[48] the place of tradition in making decisions about the role of women in the Church became acute. The declaration contained a total of five arguments against the ordination of women, three of which are clearly arguments based on tradition: that Jesus was a male, that the apostles were all male, and that in 2000 years the Church has only ordained males to the priesthood. Scripture scholars and historians have raised numerous objections to these characterizations.[49] A fourth argument is from the nature of signs: a sign must resemble that which it signifies, and since women cannot resemble the maleness of Jesus, they are excluded from priesthood. In reflecting on this argument it is interesting to note that women, like men, are held to be made in the image and likeness of God, but not, evidently, in the image and likeness of Jesus, our fellow human.

The last reason given by the declaration for not ordaining women is an argument from sexual symbolism: the Church is feminine, the bride of a male Christ; it would therefore be inappropriate (symbolic homosexuality) to have a female Christ-figure ministering to the bride, the Church.[50] That such an argument ever saw the light of day says a great deal about the level of theology in the Church today.

Since John Paul II became pontiff he has continued to reiterate Paul VI's message that both men and women are called to participate within the roles appropriate to them.[51] He has permitted some easing of restrictions on women in the roles of lector and eucharistic minister largely through the action of national bishops' conferences, especially in situations of need, but has generally insisted on the authority of the norms.

One of the most interesting notes in John Paul's speeches is the similarity, probably unintended, between his understandings of the material and the priestly role and character. Essential to both is that they be other-directed, that they live lives of self-sacrifice that the love of God may bear fruit in those for whom they sacrifice. John Paul says that the priest renounces human fatherhood to "seek another kind of fatherhood and even another kind of motherhood, for he is mindful of the Apostle's words about the children whom he begot and brought to birth."[52]

While John Paul does not call mothers, like priests, to renounce conjugal love and material possessions, the mother as well as the priest is called to sacrifice self and personal freedom in order to love and nurture others. He describes priesthood, like motherhood, as a special talent, a vocation, which calls for serious preparation and self-discipline,[53] although the capacity for motherhood is held to be inherent in all women, unlike priesthood, which is a call for the few. Both priests and the married are called to purity and chastity. "Purity consists in the first place in containing the impulse to sexual desire," John Paul said in a 1981 address to families,[54] and went on to present two aspects of conjugal chastity: "abstention and control," which have obvious affinities with priestly celibacy. Both vocations, to motherhood and priesthood, are understood by John Paul to be full time, in that women with minor children should be in the home and not forced to other labor, just as priests are not to hold other jobs outside their priestly role.

2.1 Integrating Women: Not Possible

How should this papal tradition on women be interpreted? I would suggest that the first step is to assert that the popes, following Christian theological tradition, having understood woman as "The Other." Simone de Beauvoir explained that woman has been defined by men who understand themselves as the subject, the Absolute, and woman as The Other.[55] Woman is therefore defined in terms not of her similarities to man but of her differences. Historically the chief difference noted has been her reproductive capacity. Besides defining woman in terms of motherhood, this reproductive difference has been the source for menstrual taboos which attempt to restrict the power that women share with nature. Defining woman in terms of her reproductive differences has also created the image of woman as cause of male sexual desire, which is responsible for notions of feminine evil in many different guises.[56] Papal understandings of woman as essentially Other and Dangerous come into conflict not only with the modern demand for equal justice for men and women. Understandings of woman as Dangerous and Other conflict even more directly with idealized, romantic papal understandings of woman and the feminine. These have been created in the Church as substitutes for the participation of real flesh-and-blood women who define themselves and have refused to accept the pedestal offered by the Church in return for their conformity to patriarchal notions of femininity.

Anthropologist Sherry Ortner's analysis of gender in terms of nature and culture is very relevant to the papal understanding of women. Ortner argues that men are socially understood to be creators of culture because they transform raw nature, while women are understood to be closer to nature, placed midway between nature and culture.[57] Women are related to culture, but their chief task is reproduction, which is a part of nature, and socialization of the young, which entails struggling with raw nature (represented by children) in an attempt to pass on culture.

Religion is a cultural enterprise. It represents an attempt to control nature through the use of ritual, to create meaning and structure for the natural world, to create human community as distinct from the realm of nature. If women are understood to be more distanced from culture, of which religion is a part, and more closely tied to nature, which religion struggles to transform, it is no wonder that there is resistance to women as primary agents of religion.

One of the ways in which religion attempts to transform nature is by co-opting and transforming its activities and powers. This is the role of ritual. It is no secret that the signs in the central rituals of Roman Catholicism, the sacraments, are modeled on activities from the realm of nature. But I would suggest that beyond this the signs of the sacraments represent a religious attempt to replicate functions which, in the historic division of labor, are predominantly feminine.[58] Baptism replicates birth, eucharist replicates women's preparation and serving of meals, anointing of the sick represents women's role in caring for the sick and dying, and marriage attempts to regulate the procreative function of women in patriarchal forms.

Confirmation functions today as a puberty ritual. Such rituals are, however, not usually exclusively male, since they are social attempts to signify the coming of adulthood for boys who lack the sudden, public, physical sign of maturity that menarche provides girls.[59] And reconciliation is feminine, although perhaps less so than the other sacraments, in that it lifts the role of the mother as peacemaker and judge of children's behavior and character formation to adult levels, presided over by priest as mother.

In these replications of feminine activities, priestly functions are predominantly feminine. It is not surprising that John Paul II describes motherhood and priesthood similarly. Nor is it surprising that Christian denominations most resistant to women as priests/ministers are those with strong sacramental traditions. The sacraments replicate the natural activities of women while claiming that the replications are more real, more effective, more powerful than the originals, because they are spiritual as opposed to natural. So John Paul II wrote: "He [the priest] is the witness and dispenser of a life other than earthly life."[60]

Soul-body dualism is central to present interpretations of sacraments, for the sacraments claim superiority over the natural acts of birthing, feeding, reconciling, mating, nursing and rites of passage precisely because they are spiritual, while these acts are "merely" natural. This is why we so often hear in homilies that baptism is the real birth of a child, its birthday as a child of God, or that eucharist is real food for "man does not live by bread alone." Real birth is presided over by men; real food is administered by men; real contrition is witnessed by men. It was evidently not enough to claim that in sacraments men also create and nurture life; the claim is that through male priests men—and only men—create and nurture *real* life. John Paul II quotes St. Augustine to this effect: "Two parents have given us the birth that leads to death; two parents have given us the birth that leads to life. The parents that have given us birth for death were Adam and Eve; the parents who give us birth for life are Christ and the Church."[61] By implication, the mother who gave birth to us gave us only birth for death, while the priest who baptized us gave us birth for life.

There is no space here to give examples of other religions and cultures which replicate women's natural roles in sacred ceremonies from whose power women are excluded.[62] It is clear that in such ceremonies where the powerful action is created by all the participants, women are totally excluded; where the powerful action is attributed to one person (the priest/shaman) women are allowed among the recipients, but are barred from the administrator role. Such patterns exist as one of many different ways that males express feelings of fear of and exclusion from the central life-giving functions of human community. The priest becomes a representative of all men, a symbol of all men's ability to give and nurture human life like, and even more powerfully than, women.

But the true value of sacraments should lie not in their ability to displace the natural roles which provide their sacramental signs but in their ability to integrate the natural with the spiritual. Sacraments should direct us back to our natural activities, convinced of their spiritual power for good and open to the grace those activities can impart.

If it is true that the popes understand women in terms of their differences from men, especially in terms of motherhood, and if they see priestly life as motherhood raised to a higher spiritual level, then women cannot ever expect to be integrated into the Church. The inequality of women, and men's fear of women, has been an important formative influence on the self-understanding of the Church as well as on human history in general. We must dismantle and reconstruct the original division of labor which assigned women primary responsibility for reproducing and nurturing human life. Until men are more than peripheral bread-winners in the family, until men are equal partners in the natural world of reproducing and nurturing human life, men are liable to rebel against the power women exercise in this domain and seek compensation in cultural—religious, political and social—activities which assure them of their power and importance over women.

Notes

1. See Christine E. Gudorf, "Renewal or Repatriarchialization? Responses of the Roman Catholic Church to the Feminization of Religion," *Horizons,* Fall 1983.

2. John XXIII, *Mater et Magistra, Acta Apostolicae Sedis* (*AAS*) 53 (1961) pp. 456–7, 236–9; *Pacem in Terris, AAS* 55 (1963), pp. 301, 160.

John Paul II took this position in "Liberatatis Nuntius," 6 August 1984. He told the Peruvian bishops that he not only approved this document written by Ratzinger but wrote opening sections of it. *The Pope Speaks* (*TPS*) 29, pp. 289–310.

3. "Este hora," address in Mexico, 28 January 1979, in *TPS* 24, p. 66; *Familiaris Consortio,* No. 51, *TPS* 27, pp. 3, 214.

4. *Gaudium et Spes,* Nos 52, 60, *AAS* 58 (1966), pp. 1073–4, 1080–1; *Pacem in Terris,* No. 15, *AAS* 55 (1963), p. 261; *Octogesima Adveniens,* No. 16, *AAS* 63 (1971), p. 413; *Justitia in Mundo,* Pt III, *AAS* 63 (1971), pp. 933–41; *Familiaris Consortio,* Nos 22, 23, *AAS* 74 (1982), pp. 106–9.

5. Pius XI, "Lux veritatis," 25 December 1931, *AAS* 23 (1931), p. 516; *Divini Redemptoris, AAS* 29 (1937), p. 71; *Casti Connubii, AAS* 22 (1930), pp. 549–50 Pius XII, address to Catholic Action, 24 April 1943, *AAS* 35 (1943), p. 34; also see Chapter 5 in Christine E. Gudorf, *Catholic Social Teaching on Liberation Themes* (Lanham, MD: University Press of America, 1980).

6. Address to Italian women, *AAS* 37 (1945), pp. 291–2.

7. *Gaudium et Spes,* Nos 50, 52, 103, *AAS* 58 (1966), pp. 1070–2, 1073–4, 24 September address to US bishops, "It is a Real Joy," *TPS* 28, pp. 360–5; "Sono lieto," 9 March 1985, *TPS* 30, p. 358; "Considerando che," 22 October 1983, *TPS* 29, pp. 78–85.

8. An excellent example is Pius XII's treatment of women in "Le vingt cinquiéme," 28 July 1955, *Osservatore Romano,* 28 July 1955, or his 21 October 1945 address, *AAS* 37 (1945), p. 292.

9. The documentary "The Workplace Hustle" describes two studies conducted during the 1980s, one by the US Department of Labor, the other by the US Department of Health and Human Services.

10. Between 25 per cent and 50 per cent of women in the USA have experienced at least one attempted or completed rape; between 15 and 21 per cent of women who have been married in the USA have been battered. See Diana Russell, *Rape in Marriage* (New York: Macmillan, 1983), pp. 64, 57, 89.

11. "Mary, Sign of Hope for All Generations," 7 October 1979, *TPS* 24, pp. 366–70.

12. *Ad Petri Cathedram, AAS* 51, (1959), pp. 509–10.

13. "Convenuti a Roma," *AAS* 53, (1961), p. 611; translation, *TPS* 7, p. 345.

14. Leo XIII, *Arcanum, Acta Sanctae Sedis* 12, p 390; Pius XI, *Casti Connubii, AAS* 22 (1930), pp. 567–8, Pius XII, "Dilette figlie," *TPS* 3, p. 367; 10 September 1941 address *Atti e discorsi* 4, pp. 111–12.

15. *Pacem in Terris, AAS* 55 (1963), p. 270.

16. Leo XIII, *Quod Apostolici Muneris,* 28 December 1878, *AAS* 11, pp. 373–4; Pius XII, *Casti Connubii, AAS* 22 (1930), pp. 549–50; Pius XII, 10 September 1941 to newly-weds, *Atti e discorsi* 3, pp. 224–5; "Der Katolische Deutsche," 17 July 1952, *AAS* 44 (1952), pp. 718–19.

17. *Divini Redemptoris, AAS* 29 (1937), p. 71.

18. "A Lei, Vicario Nostro," *AAS* 20 (1928), pp. 136–7.

19. "E'giunto al termine," 10 January 1979, *TPS* 24, p. 82; *Laborem exercens,* No. 19, *AAS* 73 (1981), pp. 626–9; *Familiaris Consortio,* No. 25, *AAS* 74 (1982), pp. 107–9; "I am Pleased," 7 June 1984, *TPS* 29, p. 250.

20. John Paul II, "Motherhood, which is women's 'physical' and 'spiritual' vocation, as it is Mary's," in "E'giunto al termine," *TPS* 24, p. 182.

21. "Laborem exercens," No. 19, *AAS* 73 (1982), pp. 107–9.

22. "Mary, Hope of All Generations," 7 October 1979, *TPS,* 24, pp. 366–70.

23. "Chi troviamo," 25 December 1978, *TPS* 24, p. 166.

24. "All'indirizzo," 22 December 1979, *TPS* 24, pp. 181–2.

25. "Family Stability and Respect for Life," 19 March 1981, *TPS* 26, pp. 174–9.

26. Ibid.

27. "Ci e gradito," *Osservatore Romano,* 8 December 1960, *TPS* 7, pp. 172–3.

28. Heidi I. Hartman, "The Family as the Locus of Gender, Class and Political Study: The Example of Housework," *SGINS* 6 (Spring 1981), pp. 379–80; Wanda Minge Klevana, "Does Labor Time Decrease with Industrialization? A Survey of Time Allocation Studies," *Current Anthropology* 21 (June 1980), pp. 283–5.

29. "E'giunto al termine," *TPS* 24, p. 182; *Laborem exercens,* No. 19, *AAS* 73 (1981), pp. 625–9; *Familiaris consortio, AAS* 74 (1982), pp. 107–9.

30. "Considerando che," (Charter of Rights of the Family), 22 October 1983, article 10, *TPS* 29, pp. 78–85; "I am Pleased," 7 June 1984, *TPS* 29, p. 250.

31. "A tutti," 8 December 1974, *Osservatore Romano,* 10 December 1974; "Soyez les bienvenues," 18 April 1975, *Osservatore Romano,* 19 April 1975.

32. Pius XII, address to Italian women, 21 October 1945, *AAS* 37 (1945), pp. 291–2; "Convenuti a Roma," *AAS* 53 (1961), p. 611; *Gaudium et Spes, AAS* 58 (1966), p. 1074; "Apres plus," *TPS* 21, p. 165; "Soyex les bienvenues," 18 April 1975, *TPS* 20, p. 37; "Parati semper," 31 March 1985, *TPS* 30, p. 210.

33. Vincent Genovesi, SJ's *In Pursuit of Love: Catholic Morality*

and Human Sexuality (Wilmington, DE: Michael Glazier, 1987), for his description and discussion of Ruth T. Barnhouse, "Homosexuality," *Anglican Theological Review* 58 (1976), pp. 107–24, 129–30, and her *Homosexuality: A Symbolic Confusion* (New York: Seabury, 1977), pp. 172–4. See also Edward A. Malloy, *Homosexuality and the Christian Way of Life* (Lanham, MD: University Press of America, 1981), p. 88.

34. John Paul II does not address the need for any personal relationships in priestly training other than priest-priest, except with prayer relationships, where relationship with Mary is advocated strongly. Traditionally, the feminine symbols of Mary and the "Mother" Church replace all real-live women. See John Paul II, "Augustinem Hipponensem," 28 August 1986, *TPS* 31, p. 363, and also "Este hora," 28 January 1979, *TPS* 24, pp. 49–67.

35. For example, John Paul argues against making the priest more like the laity in "Ecce nunc," 16 March 1986, *TPS* 31, p. 163.

36. See *The National Catholic Reporter* coverage of clerical AIDS, homosexuality, pedophilia and active heterosexuality over the past two years, especially Bill Kenkelen, "Priests" AIDS Deaths," 12 December 1986; Jason Berry, "Homosexuality, Pedophilia: 'no direct linkage'," 6 March 1987, and the extensive two-part study of priestly sexuality/lifestyle by Jason Berry in the 27 February and 6 March 1987 issues.

37. Augustine, *On Marriage and Concupiscence,* Book 1, Chapter 17, No. 15; St. Thomas Aquinas, *Summa theologiae* 1, pp. 98, 2.

38. "Twenty Facts on Women Workers," US Department of Labor, Office of the Secretary, Women's Bureau, 1982.

39. Gwendolyn L. Lewis, "Changes in Women's Role Participation," Irene Frieze (ed.), *Women and Sex Roles* (New York: Norton, 1978).

40. Jessie Bernard, *The Future of Marriage* (New York: World, 1972).

41. Ibid.

42. Augustine, *On Marriage and Concupiscence,* Book 1, Chapter 19, No. 7.

43. Robert Blair Kaiser, *The Politics of Sex and Religion: A Case History in the Development of Doctrine* (Kansas City: Leaven, 1985), pp. 141–2.

44. Charles A Gallagher et al., *Embodied in Love: Sacramental Spirituality and Sexual Intimacy* (New York: Crossroad, 1986).

45. "E motivo," 8 September 1964, *TPS* 10, p. 17.

46. "Soyex les bienvenues," 19 April 1975, *TPS* 20, p. 38.

47. "Ministeria quaedam," 15 August 1972, *AAS* 64 (1972), p. 530.

48. 15 October 1976, *AAS* 69 (1977), p. 98.

49. Leonard and Arlene Swidler (eds), *Women Priests: A Catholic Commentary on the Vatican Declaration* (New York: Paulist, 1977).

50. *AAS* 69 (1977), p. 98.

51. "Inaestimabile donum," 3 April 1980, *TPS* 25, p. 103, approved by John Paul II, written by James R. Knox, Prefect for the Congregation of Sacraments and Divine Worhsip; "Unity in the Love for which Christ Prayed," 4 October 1979, *TPS* 24, pp. 328–34; "Catechesi Tradendae," 16 October 1979, *TPS* 25, pp. 44–45.

52. "Novo incipiente," 8 April 1979, *TPS* 24, p. 245.

53. "Il nostro," 20 December 1978, *Osservatore Romano,* 21 December 1978; also "Ecce nunc," 16 March 1986, *TPS* 21, p. 164.

54. "Scrive San," 28 January 1971, *TPS* 26, p. 278.

55. Simone de Beauvoir, *The Second Sex,* trans H. M. Parshley (New York: Knopf, 1964; orig. pub. Paris: Librairie Gallimard, 1949), Introduction.

56. Rosemary R. Ruethner, *Sexism and God-Talk* (Boston: Beacon, 1983), Chapter 7.

57. Sherry B. Ortner, "Is Female to Male as Nature is to Culture?" in M. Z. Rosaldo and L. Lamphere (eds.), *Women, Culture and Society* (Stanford, CA: Stanford University Press, 1975), pp. 67–87.

58. See Christine E. Gudorf, "The Power to Create: Sacraments and Men's Need to Birth," *Horizons,* Fall 1987.

59. Evelyn S. Kessler, *Woman, An Anthropological View* (New York: Holt, Rinehart and Winston, 1976), p. 24.

60. John Paul II, "Ecce nunc," 16 March 1986, *TPS* 31, p. 163.

61. John Paul II, "Augustinem Hipponensem," 28 August 1986, *TPS* 31, p. 376 quoting Augustine, *Serm* 22, 10.

62. Some examples can be found in Gudorf, op. cit. note 58.

5. Women's Contribution to Theology in Latin America

Maria Pilar Aquino

This chapter first appeared in *Our Cry for Life: Feminist Theology from Latin America* in 1993.

The Theological Method

It is clear that liberation theology from the perspective of women in Latin America must be set in the broad context of Latin American liberation theology, although feminist theology has particular features because of the social and epistemological locations from which it is articulated.[1] Theology done by women shares in the liberation process of the poor, but pays special attention to the liberation of women who are triply oppressed.

Broadening the field to include women's vision and speech is a way of criticizing and correcting the androcentric position of liberation theology, which would be hard to perceive without this contribution from women. Their contribution profoundly modifies the expression and content of liberation theology to date, including even the very concept of *liberation*. In principle, this term bore the meaning of *liberation of the whole of man and all men . . . without excluding any man*. The perspective of women reviews the total meaning of liberation, with two results. On the one hand, it criticizes patriarchal structures, androcentric vision, and *machista* attitudes in the whole social context of oppression. On the other hand, it includes women in the production of knowledge, the making of theology, and the creation of a new liberating reality. This is not just a change of language, but also a change in liberation theology's *epistemological horizon*.

As María Clara Bingemer points out, today it is recognized that women's entry into the field of theological reflection "brings with it a new way, a new method of thinking and expressing theology."[2] What does this new way, this new method consist of? What are its characteristics? As a first response I note a few observations made by Elsa Tamez, who begins by explaining this theology's methodological links with liberation theology and then goes on to point out the advance it represents with respect to theology in general: "Liberation theology," says Tamez,

> does not remove the experience of oppression from the experience of God, or the life of faith; it has demonstrated another methodology in making its point of departure the practice of liberation within this context. Women involved in the theological arena welcome this way of doing theology; dealing with concrete experience means dealing with things of daily significance, and that means also dealing with relationships between men and women.[3]

Indeed, daily life becomes its *point of departure,* whereas in a large part of traditional theology there is a tendency to avoid or spiritualize Christians' daily lives. The perspective of women emphasizes a change of attitude toward daily life without neglecting the transformation of power structures.

The Primacy of Desire

In the past, theology has generally given primacy to rationality. Theology done by women starts from actual experience and therefore, as María Clara Bingemer stresses, "is closely and indissolubly linked to desire."[4] This is trying to give back to theology its full power to express life, which is also made up of sensitivity, generosity, affection, and silence.[5] It must recognize women and men's spiritual experiences, as they try to love and seek justice in their daily lives. Hence women doing theology feel that the primacy of rationality must be replaced by the primacy of desire. The cold and cerebral character of the purely scientific

> must give way to a new system which springs from the desire that lies deep within human beings and which includes and mixes sensitivity and rationality, generosity and efficiency, experience and reflection, desire and rigor. *God is love,* says scripture (1 Jn 4:8). If this is so, God must be first and foremost an object of desire—not of necessity, not of rationality. Theology—which is reflection and discourse about God and God's Word—must therefore be driven and warmed by the flame of desire.[6]

This means that reason, science, and systematic rigor must not suffocate the Greater Desire, or domesticate the divine *Pathos,* or extinguish the flame of the Spirit.[7]

In doing theology women incorporate the primacy of desire, because purely rational concepts do not take sufficient account of experience. This methodology is inherent in the way women work and think. María Clara Bingemer points out that,

> it is unthinkable for women to divide themselves into compartments and consider their theological work as a purely rational activity. Impelled by desire, a totalizing force that penetrates their whole being, women's theological work is done with the body, heart, and hands, as well as with the head. The mature fruit that is beginning to emerge from their fertile wombs is a result of slow and patient meditation on deep and intense experiences of life, confronted with the traditions of the past, the pilgrimage of the people of Israel and of the church. Here the Spirit, who is the divine desire poured out upon history and humanity, finds fertile soil. As well as constantly and faithfully referring to Jesus of Nazareth as the ultimate and definitive norm, it opens the future with infinite possibilities for invention and new ways of expressing the Christian mystery.[8]

Therefore the language of poetry, play, and symbol becomes an appropriate way of expressing the understanding and wisdom of the faith, because it is the means of expressing the human person's deepest and most genuine aspirations and desires.[9]

If we think of desire as fundamental to life or as the primary vital impulse, then clearly Latin America is a continent where desire is systematically threatened and denied fulfillment. Hence, Bingemer observes,

> the liberation process begins to occur when the poor become aware of the desires repressed inside them and allow them to emerge. They are let out like a cry and felt as a motive force impelling them to struggle. It is in this liberation of desire that theology is called upon to speak and in our particular case, theology done by women.[10]

In a context where life itself is threatened, attacked, and violated, where the masses are struggling to assert their right to act, liberation theology from the perspective of women is called upon to take up women's words and deepest desire, for life and hope in the midst of pain and struggle. For Bingemer,

> being a woman means knowing how to combine experience and practice, how to fight oppression, how to glimpse amid many misfortunes the superabundance of grace. In the midst of great contradictions women have the power to integrate and perceive contrasts and differences in a unifying and enriching way. They can contemplate and discern in the pain of the cross the breath of hope and the weight of glory that is now beginning to shine. They do not lose the thread of desire, which from the depths of disfigured reality groans with unutterable groans announcing the delivery of a New Creation that is now appearing.[11]

Desire activates women's capacity to be integrated, integrating, and full of hope. It gives them immeasurable strength, perceived as a gift to be shared generously for the benefit of the oppressed, theology, and the church, for the sake of their common liberation. Thus Latin American women understand that theology is merely a response of faith to God's merciful manifestation in the present-day reality of the immense suffering masses of humanity. Driven by desire, it is an attempt to eradicate their own suffering and that of others, and to restore the deepest desire of the poor and oppressed. By stressing the primacy of desire, this theological viewpoint

> inaugurates new ways of listening to Revelation, of speaking about the experience of faith, of reading and interpreting God's word, thinking and working on the great themes of theology. All this is done through being possessed by desire that inflames and summons, that keeps the flame of love burning without being consumed, against everything that threatens to extinguish it. It leads all creation, wounded by sin back to the Great Desire from which it came.[12]

The Option for Women in the Option for the Poor

Liberation theology from women's perspective is indissolubly linked to the option for the poor. Its origin and basis is the Latin American reality, the urgent reality of the martyrdom, and the hope of the poor. It is directed toward promoting life and overcoming oppression. Nevertheless, the women's perspective gives a special place to one aspect of the option for the poor: it wants to reach the questions, historical and spiritual experiences, knowledge, memory, desires, and expectations of women, not only as part of this suffering world, but primarily *as women.* It is important to stress this aspect because on occasion, even when the option for the poor is recognized as fundamental to liberation theology, women are often neglected. Liberation theology fails to see them as a collective group that experiences in multiple forms the profound inequalities in society and theology.[13] So, for a theology that makes women's vision and interests explicit, the option for the poor becomes in particular an option for poor women.[14]

This option also becomes its principal hermeneutic perspective. Thus this theology is enabled to develop a fruitful dialectic—between the social location from which we learn about the problem to be examined and the epistemological location from which we put this knowledge to use—in order to deal adequately with our problems in a way that furthers the process of women's liberation.[15] In Latin America, says Ivone Gebara,

> the poor have many faces: workers, peasants, beggars, abandoned children, lost young people and others. They are men and women, but now we need to single out the women. The poor woman today is poorest of the poor. She is the other: bleeding and burdened, housewife, mother, daughter, wife. She is both subject and object of our option for the poor.[16]

The option for poor women must obviously look inward. We must look into ourselves. We must also look outward: to commitment, social struggle, militant action. Both these aspects are very necessary because the risk of lacking inner unity becomes ever greater as historical urgency increases. So the option for poor women assumes a *woman's option for herself.*[17] The option for the poor and for herself is not something outside a woman's self and work. Gebara notes that women's participation in popular social movements is often described without touching upon the nucleus of this commitment: the necessary fist step toward themselves, the call to accept themselves and welcome themselves as women first and foremost.[18] This is a journey into self that restores a woman's inner unity. She is reborn as a woman, discovers the creative source of her being, and comes back into contact with her own roots. This inner journey is necessary in order to open herself to others:

> "To love others like oneself" is a key phrase for Christians and also for others. It tries to show how love of others is not distinct from love of self or love of self from love of others. They are two poles of the same loving movement and one cannot develop fully without the other. . . . The option for ourself is a personal act but not a solitary one. It also means being open and welcoming to others.[19]

Hence the option for the other springs from the same source. Both flow into a conscious option for a new future of justice and love.[20]

The Practice of Tenderness

As I have emphasized, the starting point for this theology is daily life. It makes a clear option for poor and oppressed women and stresses the primacy of desire over rationality in order to take account of experience. But there are other crucial elements. Ana María Tepedino adds that this theology "also starts from our experiences of faith, lived from the underside of power and authority. From these two starting points we reread revelation and reality with a view not only to individual liberation, but to liberation of an entire people."[21] This theology understands that it must contribute to the transformation of situations and structures that cause misery and dehumanization. Therefore it cannot ignore the culture of patriarchal and *machista* systems, which worsen women's economic and social oppression. As this theology is concerned with daily life it must necessarily incorporate the relations between men and women. "Consequently," Tepedino continues,

> the starting point for feminist theology goes beyond the experience of oppression, the experience of God, and the struggle for justice; it must also be the "practice of tenderness," that is, seeking to create brotherly and sisterly relationships, which should not exist simply between men and women, but also among the elderly, adolescent, and children—and indeed among all people.[22]

This aspect is incorporated into theology because it is part of real life. It is not something outside human experience and reflection on the faith. Warmth and desire lose their fragmentary character as they become integrated as part of the cognitive process. This warmth is the opposite of the historical coldness of a purely conceptual approach. In fact, women's warmth and commitment have not been seen in the language of faith as a deep spiritual experience giving light and content to formal theological discourse. In this respect Ivone Gebara observes that:

> The persistence of women in the struggle for life and the restoration of justice have been linked together and lived out as expressions of faith, as the presence of God in the struggles of history. Many women see in these developments the expression of their desire to struggle for a more human world, in which certain values presently dormant may be aroused, where people can accept affection, where life may triumph over the powers of death.[23]

The practice of tenderness humanizes theological discourse and restores its meaning for the daily life of the oppressed, and it also integrates women's experience into theology.

Feminist Analytical Tools

In this theology—as in all liberation theology—the social sciences become vitally important for knowing and transforming the situation, especially that of poor and oppressed women.[24] I have already indicated some fundamental elements in the use of socio-analytic methods from the perspective of women [Chapter 1].* It should also be noted that theology from the perspective of women critically adopts the scientific method used by liberation theology. However, inasmuch as certain disciplines do not help it analyze and change the real situation of Latin American women, this theology finds it necessary to resort to others that do move toward women's liberation. Some of the analysis done by Latin American theologians has not contributed to the understanding of women's oppression and has even clearly shown an androcentric point of view. Hence the importance of interdisciplinary feminist investigation stressed by women in their theology. Ivone Gebara notes:

*In *Our Cry for Life.*

> We cannot fail to recall the inestimable contribution of the social sciences—anthropology, psychology, and different theories about language—as elements that have been changing, directly or indirectly, women's understanding of themselves. These same elements have contributed to the emancipation of women's power in the social dimension of human relations and in the way these relations are organized.[25]

Nevertheless, we cannot say that to date liberation theology from the perspective of Latin American women has developed an analytic method capable of encompassing women's problems. This points to an inner methodological weakness and is also a big challenge for feminist theology in our context.

María José Rosado Nuñez's remarks are important here: "In Latin America, when we tried to understand our societies and the way they function to produce a situation of structural injustice that is unacceptable from the Christian point of view, we turned to the social sciences. We looked to European writers, including non-religious ones, for the explanation we lacked to support our theological thinking."[26] If we want to understand and transform oppressive situations unacceptable to women as part of humanity and the church, we must resort to the sciences that help us understand women's particular situation, that is to say, *feminist theory,*[27] and not just that relating to theology but also to other areas, including anthropology and philosophy, from the Latin American viewpoint. The important task is to understand "fully what happens in the unequal and unjust relationships existing between women and men in society and the church."[28] Feminist work is trying to find new answers, new ideas, new paradigms, new ways of understanding that are more whole and that do not exclude people. Whereas men's analyses tend to conceal women's real oppression, feminist analysis makes explicit the oppressive structures working against women, men, and those depending on them. Hence Rosado Nuñez suggests that:

> We must overcome certain prejudices in relation to first-world feminist theory, seek from it what can help us under-

> stand things that are happening in our own countries. . . . We should approach these theories critically, making use of what is helpful, and adding what is peculiar to us in Latin America. We can correct these theories when what they say does not seem valid from our perspective of commitment to the cause of liberation for the poor and the transformation of society.[29]

On the other hand, Latin American feminist theory is already quite well developed—as I have shown [in this book]—and it can act as our reference point. Although this field is of particular interest to women, it should also interest male theologians, because, as I have repeatedly said, women's liberation is not just a matter for women. In liberation theology it is a matter of equal liberation for all.

Tasks and Methods of Feminist Theology

This theological work by women is interested in gathering the historical and spiritual experiences of oppressed women, looking at them, and interpreting them in the light of faith in order to contribute to their own liberation and the liberation of all humanity. Therefore everything that has to do with the creation, re-creation, and defense of life for the poor and for women's work of solidarity has theological significance for their particular way of understanding the faith. Women's activities to secure their own survival and that of those who depend on them intrinsically bear the seal of compassion, solidarity, justice, love, freedom, and passion for God's cause in the cause of the poor, together with large doses of strength, daring, and courage. In these personal and collective activities women discover the signs of God's presence.[30] They are therefore related to the contents of the faith and are where, above all, scripture is read and critically interpreted, along with the church's living tradition, the systematic formulations of theology, and the teachings of the church. For women the key to this reading is *life*,[31] and their hermeneutic starting point is the option for poor and oppressed women along with the option for the poor. Hence we arrive at theology's second stage. For this, a contextual and particularized method is proposed, which Ana María Tepedino summarizes as follows:

> Feminist theology in the Latin American context arises out of the realities of daily life. This theology (a) seeks to know life through personal experience as well as through human and social science; (b) seeks to interpret in the light of the Bible (with the understanding that God's revelation was given to human beings and articulated in human language, thus depending on a culture in time and in space—and accordingly, it can both oppress and liberate); we have to discover the sense that the Spirit reveals to us today through the ancient text of the Bible, and (c) tries to retrieve and give name to the experience of women in a patriarchal society in order to redeem the past, transform the present, and prepare for tomorrow.[32]

This summary gives a general idea of the process followed by liberation theology from the perspective of women. However, before describing some characteristics of its method I want to list the tasks it faces. This is a provisional list:

1. To discover and interpret the saving historical value of reality in the light of new theological criteria, such as the New Creation, full humanity, God's *basileia,* God's reign, the new earth, equal discipleship, salvation, grace, sin, compassion, justice, power of the Spirit in the whole community, and others. It is a matter of giving positive value to projects and tendencies that give salvation a historical setting and anticipate God's liberation plan. Likewise, this theology denounces and rejects situations generating inequality, injustice, and exclusion of some people. It condemns the androcentric and *machista,* because they are at odds with the Christian vision. This criticism is not only of the reality today but also of the androcentric dynamics of scripture, tradition, Christian theology, and social and ecclesial structures promoting sexism, racism, and classism, and ecclesial and social colonialism.[33]

2. To unmask and dismantle theological formulations that support and perpetuate the interpretation of humanity and its

history in terms of the androcentric patriarchal vision, which marginalizes the experience, knowledge, and contributions of women. On the one hand, such a theology consciously seeks to bring women's contributions to light, and on the other, to restore to theological language the power to touch the vital heart of human life.[34]

3. To recognize and describe women's history, showing their presence when many would like them to be invisible. If revelation and divinity are presented with a male character and serve to legitimate women's powerlessness and subordination, feminist theology must denounce these tendencies and show forth God's presence and revelation in women, who are also mediators of grace and God's presence in mind and body. In their bodies they prove the mystery of real life and therefore experience God in a special way.[35]

4. To show up the rigid positions, supported by androcentric and patriarchal dogma, which not only imprison the *real truth* of human life with its hopes and miseries and conceal the sin committed against the poor and oppressed, but also block the life-giving power of the Spirit. As well as systematically opposing divine grace, these rigid positions show their ignorance of the hermeneutic structure of all knowledge, which is not pure, sterilized, totally objective, and disinterested. Thus Christian theologies, primitive writings, and doctrine are not definitive and do not wholly explain the meaning of human life inasmuch as they set aside and conceal women. Those who stubbornly exclude women are opposing divine revelation itself. On the other hand, women's perspective proposes a point of view able

> to view life as the locus of the simultaneous experience of oppression and liberation, of grace and lack of grace. Such perception encompasses what is plural, what is different, what is other . . . to grasp in a more unified way the oppositions and contradictions, the contrasts and differences as inherent to human life. . . . Such behavior enables them [the women] to avoid taking dogmatic and exclusive stances, and to perceive or intuit the real complexity of what is human.[36]

5. To recover and reconstruct the words, gestures, memory, symbols, experiences, desires, and struggles of the women who preceded us and who have left us a legacy of resistance, leadership, and commitment to the defense of life. This task is particularly urgent in our case, given the aggressive nature of the conservative neo-colonialist projects intent on reconquering Latin America for their own interests. These interests are obviously not those of Latin American women and the impoverished masses. In this task women have a fundamental role.[37] This work of reconstruction has three complementary strands. We must reconstruct: (a) our own history of Latin America; (b) biblical, theological, and ecclesial history in solidarity with women in other contexts; and (c) humanity's harmony with the earth, stressing women's ancestral closeness to it.[38]

6. To affirm and rescue what is theological in every authentically liberating process, regardless of its theological definition. The theological criterion of authenticity does not lie in words, but in the work of real liberation. Liberation theology done by women affirms the presence or absence of God according to whether or not both women and men are incorporated as actors with full rights in historical situations.[39]

Liberation theology done by women stresses certain key qualities. These qualities help to distinguish this theology from liberation theology in general. We remember that from its beginning this theology has been a specific form of women's struggle for their right to life.[40] The Final Statement of the Latin American Conference entitled "Theology from the Perspective of Women," identifies the key characteristics of its methodology. This theology sees itself as:

> —Unifying, bringing together different human dimensions: strength and tenderness, happiness and tears, intuition and reason.
>
> —Communitarian and relational, bringing together a vast number of experiences that express something lived and felt, in such a way that people recognize themselves in this reflection and feel challenged by it.
>
> —Contextual and concrete, with its starting point being

> the geographical, social, cultural, and ecclesial reality of Latin America, which detects the community's vital issue. This theological activity bears the mark of the everydayness of life as a site where God is made manifest.
>
> —Militant, in the sense of taking part in the totality of our peoples' struggles for liberation at local and global levels.
>
> —Marked by a sense of humor, joy, and celebration, virtues that safeguard the certainty of faith in the God who is with us.
>
> —Filled with a spirituality of hope whose starting point is our situation as women, and which expresses strength, suffering, and thanksgiving.
>
> —Free, with the freedom of those who have nothing to lose; and open, capable of accepting different challenges and contributions.
>
> —Oriented toward refashioning women's history, both in the biblical texts and in those figures of women, who, acting out of their own situation, are symbols of struggle and resistance, wisdom and leadership, solidarity and fidelity, justice and peace.[41]

These features, together with those I have noted [in previous chapters], give feminist theology a special character with respect to liberation theology in general. Feminist theology stresses the wholeness of human experience and attempts to reconstruct women's history. It stresses that its exercise of theological understanding is animated by the Spirit and aims to build something new:

> We have discovered these characteristics, fully aware that it is the Holy Spirit who arouses us and moves us. The same Spirit draws us women out of our own lack of self-esteem and out of the oppression we experience because of our gender, toward an effort to break out of old frameworks, and to build a new person (woman/man) and a new society.[42]

Finally, we should emphasize the inclusive nature of this theology done by women. Women are not trying to replace men with women but are working to overcome the evils that cause death and inhumanity for women and men. Through their theology women want to contribute to a change that will cease to make the difference between men and women the cause of their inequality.[43]

The Hermeneutics of Suspicion and Daring

Investigations into the field of biblical hermeneutics from the perspective of Latin American women are beginning to look promising. There is great interest in studying the Bible because of the importance it has in women's lives, especially in the base communities. As in other areas, the rereading of the Bible in a way that supports women's human integrity and their liberation struggle is more likely to happen in the daily life of the Christian communities than at the level of systematic study. All over Latin America and the Caribbean there is a growing desire to *name* a new vital force that has entered women's lives: a reencounter between liberative biblical revelation and women's liberation process. In various countries meetings, workshops, seminars, and study days are being devoted to rereading the Bible from the perspective of women; a few works also have been published.[44] These concerns center around three key areas. First, there is the certainty that, although the Bible was long withheld from the people by the clergy, it belongs to the people of God, the poor and oppressed, and therefore also to women. Second, there is a growing awareness that forms of *machismo* are also to be found in the Bible; it contains negative remarks about women and is couched in androcentric language. These texts and traditions cannot be divinely inspired, especially when through Jesus' life and ministry we discover that God does not condone any discrimination against women. Third, stress is laid on the importance of reading the biblical texts in the context in which they were written and also in terms of the everyday experiences of the reader,[45] with readers being aware of their own situation.

Two important points are made about interpreting the Bible. The first is that God's saving will—carried out fully in Jesus Christ and accepted by the men and women who were with him—is not just localized in the biblical text. This is not simply a factual account of historical events that occurred, but includes interpretations assigning theological value to these events. Therefore the biblical text is conditioned by its socio-historical context and is the product of an androcentric and patriarchal socio-religious order. Often the text is patriarchal, and the writer has a patriarchal point of view. Therefore it contains values and traditions, some oppressive and others liberating. So it is necessary to adopt a critical position that notes the texts, traditions, and values—with their subsequent interpretations—that support the subordination of women, and also those that strengthen women's position as persons with full rights. As Gebara and Bingemer note:

> The written text should always generate within us the suspicion, or better, questions about what has not been written, what has been lost, or what has been omitted by choice. A written text is always selective. The author or authors choose some events they believe important, and they interpret them, while leaving aside others which from another perspective might be regarded as the most important.[46]

We must, they continue, bear in mind that if the good news of the reign of God is for humanity as a whole,

> this must of necessity involve the participation of men and women, even if the texts written by men and from a patriarchal viewpoint leave out the active participation of women. . . . That is the reason why we must take up a critical stance that can open space for us to reconstruct and recover the history of the past and thereby grasp the revelation of the God of life in the lives of women as well.[47]

The latter point recognizes that divine revelation is not exhausted in the biblical writings. It continues to operate in the historical process of human liberation, in the signs of life present in the people's advance, in personal and collective activities that humanize life and generate relationships of greater solidarity, participation, and justice.[48]

God's revelation is also present in women's liberation struggles, and those of all the oppressed under the auspices of divine grace and the power generated by the constant activity of the Holy Spirit. Women's work in interpreting the Bible takes these aspects into account. This means that present experience of women's oppression and liberation is a criterion for discerning where and how God acts in the Bible and in life.[49] So, as Gebara and Bingemer point out, women interpreting the Bible turn to it not only in order to understand the texts of the past and the stories it tells as illustrations, but primarily to "understand and reactivate the past for the sake of today's liberation struggles."[50]

The Importance of the Bible in Women's Lives

It is striking what an important role the Bible plays in women's lives in Latin America. In the base communities it is called "the light of our lives," "source of energy, spirituality, and commitment," "word of life that strengthens my faith," "liberating word that illuminates the value of the whole human person." For these communities the Bible is the word of God, the power, and good news that nourishes them.[51] Starting from experience, likenesses are sought in the biblical story, which is reread to relate Bible and life in a simple and creative way, giving priority to faithfulness to life rather than abstract reflection.

Everyday experience is understood in the light of liberating biblical events anticipated by the women and men who participated in the decisive events of revelation. Thus biblical study is not done purely for its own sake. As Tereza Cavalcanti notes "In women's hands the Bible is transformed in the base communities into a dynamic force for the transformation of society and the church. Reading and interpreting it give members a new awareness of liberation, which they express with joy and humor."[52] In readings that link Bible and life there is critical stress on what does and does not correspond. Some examples include the certainty that we cannot infer or justify male superiority from the Bible by referring to Genesis; women's struggle for survival and to defend life finds references in Exodus; women's leadership, wisdom, strength, authority and solidarity is encountered in countless women in the Bible; women's new awareness of their value, their full rights to humanity, can be inferred from Jesus' liberating behavior in his relations with women; women's committed, believing, critical, and innovative participation is to be found in Mary, the mother of Jesus; the equality sought in the church relates to the women in the primitive Christian movement; women's suffering can be linked to the experiences of many people in the Bible as well as to their hopes and songs of joy and victory.[53] It is clear that in Latin America the process of women's liberation has gained energy from the Bible and new meanings are found in the Bible arising out of present experience.

We may note the special way in which women in the base communities establish this dialogue between Bible and life. Ivone Gebara notes the fact that many women

> are especially gifted with a deep intuition about human life and able to counsel, to intuit problems, to express them, to give support, to propose solutions, and to confirm the faith of many people. They explain biblical passages on the basis of their experience and respond to doctrinal questions by simplifying them and setting them on the level of existential reality. Some of these women are illiterate.[54]

Indeed they are, but this is not an obstacle. Tereza Cavalcanti observes that many "memorize words and stories from the scriptures, applying them to different circumstances. . . . Adopting the biblical language as their own they read events in the light of faith."[55] This is not a single reading. The dialogue to which I refer takes place in a critical spirit: "the critical consciousness awakened by reading God's word in contact with real life leads them to discover certain forms of *machismo* both in present-day society and in the Bible itself and the church. Then there are denunciations and protests against sexual discrimination, which is not always recognized by society or even by the members of the base communities themselves."[56] In many cases their way of reading the Bible places women in situations of real conflict within their families, in their own communities, or with the religious or civil authorities. Supported by the good news of the gospel and the power of the Spirit, they dare to claim their rights and the rights of their people.[57] Many of these matters arising from the experience of oppression and liberation have deepened research into biblical hermeneutics, as we shall see.

Feminist Suspicion as a Theoretical Category in Biblical Interpretation

One of the primary insights women bring to their study of the Bible is the option for the poor. They point out that "any reading of the word of the Lord must be a reading from the viewpoint of the poor. When Jesus explains the scriptures, he rereads them (Lk 4:16ff) in the light of his own situation as a poor person and in terms of his struggle for justice. Rereading the Bible means trying to understand its central message in order to live by it in the daily struggle."[58]

The perception that Bible reading in Latin America should be done from the viewpoint of the poor is of crucial importance for exegesis and biblical hermeneutics. This change leads to a rediscovery of the Bible. People have begun to see it as subversive, because it supports the struggle of the poor for liberation. Many men and women in various Latin American countries have suffered persecution simply because they had a Bible. As Elsa Tamez says: "This rereading of the Word from the point of view of the poor has been consolidated and has become so evident that Holy Scripture is regarded as a threatening or dangerous book by some sectors of society that do not share a preferential option for the poor. . . . Some religious circles have even decided to avoid biblical discussions. Do they fear the Bible?"[59] This shows the dominant view—that the Bible is neutral—fails to recognize its own underlying position and that underlying the biblical text, thereby depriving it of its spiritual power and also weakening its historical efficacy. In spite of this "the ancient book of Christianity has indeed become new and defiant when it is read from the perspective of the poor."[60]

Nevertheless, gradually the *suspicion* arose that we cannot take for granted that reading the Bible from the viewpoint of the poor and reading it from women's point of view automatically correspond. This means it is necessary to make poor and oppressed women's interests explicit in order to avoid generalizations that overlook them. According to Tamez, the core of the problem appears to be that the poor "find that the Word reaffirms in a clear and direct way that God is with them in their fight for life. Women who live in poverty, however, even when they are aware that the strength of the Holy Spirit is on their side, do not know how to confront the texts that openly segregate them. These texts sound strange and surprising to someone who is not familiar with the culture of the biblical world and believes in a just and liberating God."[61]

Latin American exegesis and hermeneutics have long emphasized the great biblical liberating processes, which are clearly about the liberation of the oppressed—Exodus, the prophets, the gospel. This is a necessary task in our context, but it has failed to consider the biblical texts and traditions referring to women's oppression and liberation. They have been ignored or regarded as secondary "because the main criterion has been to experience God as a God of life who has a preferential option for the oppressed, including women."[62] Thus women's exclusion was regarded as something not fundamental, an afterthought. This attitude in hermeneutics is consistent with the way in which women's problems have been postponed or considered secondary in other fields.

Part of the problem lies in the encounter and mutual reinforcement between two deeply *machista* and patriarchal cultures: our present society and the culture of the biblical world.[63] Attempts to overcome this have not been adequate. The first thing necessary for reaching a nonsexist (and also non-classist and non-racist) understanding of the Bible is *to take the problem seriously.* Reading the Bible solely from the point of view of the poor may overlook the relations between the sexes, as well as concealing the biblical traditions that have contributed to the consolidation of the sex-gender system with men on the top, which was and continues to be the determining factor in the subordination of women today.

In Tamez's opinion it is important to consider three key points. First, it is necessary to be critically aware of the conditioning that goes with every reading of the Bible. Often anti-feminist readings are determined by a long tradition that imposes on the text an ideological slant deriving from a patriarchal and androcentric society. These readings may be even more negative for women than the text itself. One example is the reading of Genesis, chapter 3, which has become the basis for "creating a mythical framework that legitimizes women's inferiority and their submission to men."[64] Such a reading of this text raises the reader's androcentric views of women to the category of a divine ordinance. The same thing happens with other texts, and the result is "a legitimation and legislation, as if it were holy, of an order unfavorable to women. Women are called, therefore, to deny the authority of those readings that harm them."[65]

Second, says Tamez, even when women succeed in rescuing certain texts and reading them in a liberating sense, they cannot always find their meaning *for women* because these texts merely reflect the inferiority accorded to women. In this case "its exegesis will show only the patriarchal ideology of the author, the commentator, the culture, and the historic moment in which the text was elaborated."[66] Women can merely make explicit and denounce these traditions and texts that oppress them. Nevertheless, the existence of texts that are clearly *machista* does not destroy the Bible's central message, which is intrinsically liberating. Therefore, Tamez says:

> From my point of view, it is precisely the Gospel's spirit of justice and freedom that neutralizes antifemale texts. A reading of the Bible that attempts to be faithful to the Word of the Lord will achieve that goal best when it is done in a way that reflects the liberating meaning of the Gospel, even when sometimes fidelity to the Gospel forces the reader to distance herself or himself from the text.[67]

In this case it is important to recognize that texts and traditions promoting women's inferiority and legitimating their subordination "are not normative; neither are those texts that legitimize slavery normative."[68]

Third, she says, it is necessary to reevaluate the principle of biblical authority. There is a contradiction in Latin American women's experience of reading the Bible. They regard it as the word of God, therefore having the authority of revelation, but they do not agree with patriarchal and *machista* texts and do not put them into practice. But those occupying positions of power in the church resort to these same texts to call women to obedience when their activities become a threat. So, can we say that these misogynist texts and patriarchal traditions that oppress women belong to revelation? Should we allow them the theological authority of Christian revelation? Tamez claims that this means we must "reformulate the principle of biblical authority, from the point of departure of our Latin American reality."[69] This must be done not only in order to criticize the patriarchal texts but also to reread the entire Bible from a point of view that does not exclude women.

New Guidelines for Reading the Bible

The formulation of theological criteria for the critical evaluation of biblical texts and traditions has always been recognized as a necessary task by the church. Throughout history various hermeneutic models have been followed. These have been competently analyzed by Elisabeth Schüssler Fiorenza.[70] Despite the variety of models, biblical research from the perspective of women requires its own particular criteria in order to bring out women's experience of struggle against oppression, which is normally overlooked by androcentric hermeneutics. It is becoming ever more necessary to formulate new guidelines with sufficiently inclusive and liberating criteria so that the Bible ceases to be used as an instrument of women's oppression. Women must be enabled to link their struggle for liberation with biblical revelation, which is life, fulfillment, and justice.

Tamez proposes three indispensable guidelines for rereading the Bible in terms of Latin American women. These are an initial approach to the large task that remains to be undertaken in the future. The questions Latin American women are asking about the Bible have given rise to what we call "hermeneutical audacity."[71]

First, Tamez indicates that for a Latin American rereading of the Bible it is necessary to adopt a dialectical process of *distancing and approaching.* We need to distance ourselves from traditional interpretations that we have assimilated over the centuries. We must really challenge the underlying presuppositions, interpretative models, and traditions, which have been consciously or unconsciously internalized over the years in a one-sided reading of the Bible. This means being *suspicious* of our own conditioning and that of the text. If we are not aware of these presuppositions or "prereadings," they will continue to act as keys to interpretation, blocking out other more liberating ones. So this distancing means "take up the Bible as a new book, a book that has never been heard or read before."[72] We also need to approach the text with the questions that arise from our daily lives, questions about our pain, joy, hope, hunger, repression, celebration, and struggle.[73] The dialectical relationship between these two processes will enable us to arrive at the meaning of revelation for women in their struggle today and also to reformulate the principle of biblical authority.[74]

In the second place, although the task of interpreting the Bible from women's point of view emphasizes women's specific interests, it must still keep the hermeneutic perspective of *the poor.* For Latin American women, the Bible must be read from the standpoint of the values, sufferings, and expectations of the Latin American masses, for whom the present system offers nothing but death or an inhuman life.[75] In Latin America any reading claiming to be liberating must start from the poor and oppressed. As Tamez reiterates:

> They are in a privileged place, hermeneutically speaking, because we conceive of the God of life as One who has a preferential option for the poor. Besides, the mystery of God's reign is with them because it has been revealed to them (Mt 11:25). Therefore, a reading from a woman's perspective has to go through this world of the poor. This will be a guarantee that it has a core theme of liberation, and it will shed light on the other faces of the poor, such as blacks and native peoples. This kind of reading will also give us methods to develop specific approaches to salvation in each of their situations.[76]

This key will enable us to abolish the use of texts and traditions and their *machista* interpretations to oppress women.

Third, a reading of the Bible that aims to eliminate women's oppression requires a *clear feminist consciousness.* Without it we may not recognize the oppressive dimensions present in the biblical texts and traditions. This means, Tamez continues, that:

> To read the Bible from a woman's perspective, we must read it with women's eyes, that is to say, conscious of the existence of individuals who are cast aside because of their sex . . . and a conscious effort is needed to discover new women-liberating aspects, or even elements in the text that other perspectives would not bring to light.[77]

It is not only texts referring to women that need to be read critically, but the whole Bible. This new awareness should not be exclusive to women but shared with men, so that they too may be enabled to read the Bible in a nonsexist way. Feminist awareness in biblical interpretation contributes to broadening the field of research, because women bring their own experience of struggle against oppression.

> They can pose new "ideological suspicions" not only to the culture that reads the text but also to the heart of the text itself by reason of being a product of patriarchal culture. Furthermore, their "ideological suspicions" are also applied to biblical tools, such as dictionaries, commentaries, and concordances, tools that are regarded as objective because they are scientific, but that are undoubtedly susceptible to being biased by sexism.[78]

Finally I should point out—with Elsa Tamez—the need to advance the field of Latin American biblical hermeneutics from the perspective of women and starting from our own historical circumstances. We need to take into account the contributions of other biblical scholars, who are developing new criteria and new hermeneutic models consistent with women's liberation and the liberation of the oppressed in general. This is the case with

Elisabeth Schüssler Fiorenza with her major work *In Memory of Her.*[79] The methodology she proposes supports the common feminist task.

Notes

1. We understand that both locations must be articulated and at the same time maintain their relative autonomy. "The unity of these two locations also requires their autonomy, because while the epistemological location guarantees methodological coherence, the social one provides the themes to be analyzed. This is most important, because in the very act of choosing a topic and rejecting others you are saying where this theme comes from. . . . Of course the social location occupied by philosophers [women theologians, in our case] is no guarantee of the internal quality of their discourse. But it does constitute the necessary condition for this same philosophical theory [theological in this case] to choose a particular theoretical object and present a style appropriate for its communication. So both locations need one another and complement each other: one contributes the theme, the other the method" (J. Francisco Gómez Hinojosa, *Intelectuales y pueblo. Un acercamiento a la luz de Antonio Gramsci* [DEI, San José, Costa Rica, 1987], pp. 225–26).

2. María Clara Bingemer, "Chairete: Alegrai-vos a mulher no futuro da teología da liberção," *REB* 48/191 (1988), p. 571.

3. Elsa Tamez, "Introduction: The Power of the Naked," in *Through Her Eyes: Women's Theology from Latin America* (Orbis Books, Maryknoll, N.Y., 1989), p. 4.

4. Bingemer, "Chairete," p. 572.

5. "The time of silence is the time of living encounter with God and of prayer and commitment; it is a time of 'staying with him' (John 1:39). As the experience of human love shows us, in this kind of encounter we enter depths and regions that are ineffable. When words do not suffice, when they are incapable of communicating what is experienced at the affective level, then we are fully engaged in loving. And when words are incapable of showing forth our experience, we fall back on symbols, which are another way of remaining silent. For when we use a symbol, we do not speak; we let an object or gesture speak for us. . . . This is why images of human love are so often used in the Bible in speaking of the relations

between God and the people of God" (Gustavo Gutiérrez, *On Job: God-Talk and the Suffering of the Innocent* [Orbis Books, Maryknoll, N.Y., 1987], p. xiv).

6. Bingemer, "Chairete."

7. Ibid., p. 573.

8. Ibid.

9. Ibid., p. 574. Everyday poetic and playful language is used by the Spanish biblical scholar Dolores Aleixandre in her writing (see Dolores Aleixandre, "María cómplice de nuestra espera, ruega por nosotros," *Sal Terrae* 11 (1984), pp. 785–91; "La arcilla y el tesoro (con minúsculas, por favor . . .)," *Sal Terrae* 10 (1987), pp. 719–30; "La estatua de Nabucodonosor y otros sueños," *Sal Terrae 11 (1988), pp. 785–92; "Profetas alcanzados y alterados por Dios," Sal Terrae* 2 (1990), pp. 93–106.

10. Bingemer, "Chairete."

11. Ibid., p. 575.

12. Bingemer, "Chairete."

13. The oppression suffered by women is a profound oppression, incomparably worse than that suffered by the poor man (Gustavo Gutiérrez in Elsa Tamez, *Against Machismo: Interviews* [Meyer-Stone Books, Oak Park, Illinois, 1987], p. 40).

14. Hence Ivone Gebara's contribution, "Option for the Poor as an Option for the Poor Woman," *Concilium* 194 (1987), p. 113.

15. For the articulation of the locations in the dialectic between theory and practice, see Gómez Hinojosa, note 1 above.

16. Gebara, "Option for the Poor as an Option for the Poor Woman," p. 113.

17. Ibid., pp. 111–12.

18. Ibid.

19. Ibid., pp. 112–13.

20. Ibid., pp. 116–17.

21. Ana María Tepedino, "Feminist Theology as the Fruit of Passion and Compassion," *With Passion and Compassion: Third World Women Doing Theology,* Virginia Fabella and Mercy Oduyoye, eds. (Orbis Books, Maryknoll, N.Y., 1988), p. 165.

22. Ibid., p. 166.

23. Gebara, "Women Doing Theology in Latin America," in *With Passion and Compassion: Third World Women Doing Theology,* p. 133.

24. Ibid., p. 132; Elsa Tamez, "The Power of the Naked" in *Through Her Eyes: Women's Theology from Latin America,* Elsa Tamez, ed. (Orbis Books, Maryknoll, N.Y., 1989), p. 5.

25. Gebara, "Women Doing Theology in Latin America," p. 132.

26. María José Rosado Nuñez, Interview in Elsa Tamez, *Las mujeres toman la palabra* (DEI, San José, 1989), p. 41.

27. Ibid.

28. Ibid.

29. Ibid.

30. As João B. Libanio and María Clara Bingemer write: "The reign of God will not come ostentatiously. You will not be able to say: 'It is here or it is there' (Lk. 17:20–21). So there is no transparency in a liberation movement that enables us to see, so to speak, in its waters the clear and perfect image of God's reign. This would be an audacity and human presumption. But, on the other hand, from the criteria of charity, justice, freedom, love for the poor and others offered us by the gospel we can hope that God is near in these movements. And in that hope and faith we approach them, either to analyze them theoretically or commit ourselves politically with them. And with that hope we trust those who die in them to God" (*Escatología cristiana* [Paulinas, Madrid, 1985], pp. 132–33).

31. Tepedino, "Feminist Theology as the Fruit of Passion and Compassion," p. 166.

32. Ibid.

33. Leonardo Boff, *Faith on the Edge: Religion and Marginalized Existence* (Orbis Books, Maryknoll, N.Y., 1991), p. 63; Juan José Tamayo-Acosta, *La teología de la liberación. Implicaciones sociales y políticas* (Ediciones de Cultura Hispanica, Madrid, 1990); Elisabeth Schüssler Fiorenza, "Editorial," *Concilium* 182 (1985), p. 14.

34. Cf. Gebara, "Women Doing Theology in Latin America," p. 131; Elisabeth Schüssler Fiorenza, *In Memory of Her: A Feminist Theological Reconstruction of Christian Origins* (Crossroad, New York, 1983), pp. xv–xvi.

35. Cf. Tepedino, "Feminist Theology as the Fruit of Passion and Compassion," p. 167; Schüssler Fiorenza, "Breaking the Silence—Becoming Visible," *Concilium* 182 (1985), p. 14.

36. Gebara, "Women Doing Theology in Latin America," p. 132; see also Tamayo-Acosta, *Para comprender la teología de la liberación,* p. 13; Schüssler Fiorenza, *In Memory of Her,* pp. 48–49.

37. Tereza Cavalcanti, "Sobre la participación de las mujeres in el VI Encuentro Intereclesial de las CEB" in María Pilar Aquino (ed.), *Aportes para una teología desde la mujer* (Biblia y Fe, Madrid, 1988), p. 135; Schüssler Fiorenza, *In Memory of Her,* pp. 30–34.

38. On this point see Tereza Cavalcanti, "Produzindo teología no Feminino plural: A propósito do III Encontro Nacional de Teología na perspectiva da mulher," *Perspectiva Teológica* 20 (1988), pp. 362ff.

39. Boff, *Faith on the Edge: Religion and Marginalized Existence,* pp. 62–63; Tamayo-Acosta, *La teología de la liberación. Implicaciones sociales y políticas.*

40. Cf. "Final Document: Intercontinental Women's Conference (Oaxtepec, Mexico, Dec. 1–6, 1986,) in *With Passion and Compassion: Third World Women Doing Theology,* pp. 184–90.

41. In Tamez, *Through Her Eyes: Women's Theology from Latin America,* p. 151.

42. Ibid., pp. 151–52.

43. Rosado Nuñez, in Tamez, *Las mujeres toman la palabra,* p. 46.

44. As often happens in theology and pastoral studies, many of the works are collective. In general, the writings gather the procedure, contents, results, and commitments reached by the communities. See, for example, *Mulher-Comunidade: a nova mulher,* in *Pastoral da Mulher pobre* (Vozes, Petrópolis, 1988), pp. 65–108; L. Ferreira, "La vocación pastoral de la mujer según la biblia," in Jorge Pixley, *La mujer en la construcción de la Iglesia* (DEI, San José, 1986), pp. 55–106; Raquel Rodríguez, "Esperanza contra esperanza: Perspectivas bíblico-teológicas de la pobreza desde la mujer latinoamericana," *Pasos* 20 (1988), pp. 1–9; idem, "La mujer y su autoridad en la Nueva Creación," *Vida y Pensamiento* 6/2 (1986), pp. 33–41; Ana María Tepedino, "Jesús e a recuperação do ser human o mulher," *REB* 48/190 (1988), pp. 273–82; idem, *Mulheres discípulas nos Evangelhos-discipulado de iguais,* master's thesis, Pontifical Catholic University of Rio de Janeiro, April, 1987; M. V. González Apaza, *Leer el evangelio desde la mujer* (Quelco, Oruro, 1988), pp. 103–18; R. M. Figur Messer, *A historia de Tamar com Judá,* photocopied text, 1986; I. Rodríguez Caldeira, *A revelação de um Deus partidario,* photocopied text, 1985; Tereza Cavalcanti, "The Prophetic Ministry of Women in the Hebrew Bible," in Elsa Tamez, *Through Her Eyes,* pp. 118–39; María Teresa Porcile, "El derecho a la belleza en América Latina," in *El rostro femenino de la teología* (DEI, San José, 1986), pp. 85–107; V. Moreira da Silva, "La mujer en la teología: Reflexión bíblico-teológica" in *Mujer latinoamericana, iglesia y teología* (MPD, Mexico, 1981), pp. 140–66; Elsa Tamez, "Meditación bíblica sobre la mujer en Centroamérica," *Vida y Pensamiento* 6/2 (1986), pp. 53–57; idem, "Justicia y justificación en ocasión de la deuda externa en América Latina," *Vida y Pensamiento* 6/2 (1986), pp. 11–13; "The Woman Who Complicated the History of Salvation," *Cross Currents* 20 (1986), pp. 129–39; idem, "Women's Rereading of the Bible," in Virginia Fabella and Mercy Oduyoye, *With Passion and Compassion,* pp. 173–83; María Pilar Aquino, "Praxis ministerial hoy: La respuesta del Tercer Mundo," *Revista de Teología Bíblica* 46 (1990), pp. 116–39; idem, "Beinaventurados los

perseguidos por causa de la justicia y los que buscan la paz," *Sal Terrae* 12 (1989), pp. 895–907.

45. Ivone Gebara and María Clara Bingemer, *Mary, Mother of God, Mother of the Poor* (Orbis Books, Maryknoll, N.Y., 1990), p. 27.

46. Ibid., pp. 28–29.

47. Ibid., p. 29.

48. "Final Document," in *The Challenge of Basic Christian Communites. Papers from the International Ecumenical Congress of Theology, February 20–March 2, São Paulo, Brazil,* Sergio Torres and John Eagleson, eds. (Orbis Books, Maryknoll, N.Y., 1981), p. 235.

49. Cf. Encuentro Latinoamericano sobre la Situación de la mujer en América Latina (DEI, San José, 1989). This criterion must be methodologically incorporated into the task of biblical interpretation. It also serves as a norm for evaluating the traditions, texts, and interpretations of the Bible as well as for reformulating the principle of biblical authority.

50. Gebara and Bingemer, *Mary, Mother of God, Mother of the Poor,* p. 31. Biblical reflection in Latin America "tries to be sensitive to the questions that are welling up in a Church whose place among the poor demands a faithful, and at the same time renewed, rereading of the scriptures," Tereza Cavalcanti, "The Prophetic Ministry of Women in the Hebrew Bible," p. 119.

51. Cavalcanti, "Sobre la participación de las mujeres in el VI Encuentro Intereclesial e las CEB," pp. 131–32.

52. Ibid., p 131.

53. Within the limits of this book it is not possible to describe all the works on rereading the Bible written by women in Latin America. But here I describe the sort of rereading of the Bible that is being done in terms of the daily experience of women in the base communities and the popular social movements. See note 44 above.

54. Gebara, "Women Doing Theology in Latin America," p. 126. Such dialogue is characteristic of women doing theology.

55. Cavalcanti, "Sobre la participación de las mujeres in el VI Encuentro Intereclesial de las CEB," pp. 131–32.

56. Ibid., p. 132.

57. Many women have to face *machismo* from their husbands, who see women's new awareness as incompatible with the "proper" tasks of a wife and mother in the home. On the other hand, when husbands join in the base communities, they gradually acquire an attitude of more solidarity.

58. Final Statement of Women's Theological Congress ("Mujer Latinoamericana: Iglesia y Teología") in Cora Ferro et al., *Mujer latinoamericana: Iglesia y Teología* (MPD, Mexico, 1981), p. 214.

59. Tamez, "Women's Rereading of the Bible," p. 174.

60. Ibid. For a view of the whole of biblical hermeneutics in liberation theology with an extensive bibliography, see Tamayo-Acosta, *Para comprender la teología de la liberación,* pp. 98–114.

61. Tamez, "Women's Rereading of the Bible," p. 174.

62. Ibid.

63. Ibid., p. 175.

64. Ibid., p. 176.

65. Ibid.

66. Ibid.

67. Ibid.

68. Ibid.

69. Ibid., p. 177.

70. For the different hermeneutic models or paradigms used up till now by biblical research, see Elisabeth Schüssler Fiorenza, "Toward a Feminist Biblical Hermeneutics: Biblical Interpretation and Liberation Theology," in *The Challenge of Liberation Theology,* Brian Mahan and L. Dale Richesin (eds.), (Orbis Books, Maryknoll, N.Y., 1984), pp. 91–112.

71. The term was first used by Tamez in *Against Machismo: Interviews,* pp. 143–47.

72. Tamez, "Women's Rereading of the Bible," p. 178.

73. Ibid.

74. Ibid.

75. In the Latin American context we cannot avoid the significance of death and life. It is a key theme to all liberating thought on biblical theology. In fact, there is no Latin American country that is not in turmoil. The long history of crimes in El Salvador against innumerable unknown men and women goes on day after day, although sometimes public opinion is aroused by a particular outrage such as the massacre on November 16, 1989, of two women and six Jesuit priests. Thousands fall defending life against systems of death that oppress, impoverish, and kill. I want to stress this point to serve as a reference for what it means to speak about life and death and Latin America. These facts call for justice and collective solidarity, so that God may be seen *really* to be the God of Life and on the side of the oppressed.

76. Tamez, "Women's Rereading of the Bible," p. 179.

77. Ibid.

78. Ibid., p. 180.

79. Schüssler Fiorenza, *In Memory of Her.* See also her *Bread not Stone: The Challenge of Feminist Biblical Interpretation* (Beacon Press, Boston, 1984); and "Toward a Feminist Biblical Hermeneutics: Biblical Interpretation and Liberation Theology."

6. Defining our *Proyecto Histórico*: *Mujerista* Strategies for Liberation

Ada María Isasi-Díaz

This chapter first appeared in *Journal of Feminist Studies in Religion* in 1993.

When the present is limiting—oppressive—one looks to the future to find a reason for living. Historically, religion has been used to encourage the poor and the oppressed to postpone hopes and expectations to "the next world." But liberation theologies turn the focus of the hopes and expectations of the poor and the oppressed from the next world to this world. It is for this reason that liberation theologies are feared and opposed by those interested in maintaining the status quo.

In this article I will explore the hopes and expectations of Hispanic women as grounded in reality and aimed at historical fruition. It is the contention of *mujerista* theology that the *proyecto histórico* (historical project) of Latinas is one of the key elements in constructing our future reality.[1] We are guided and motivated by our hope for a future in which we can live fully.

Mujerista theology uses the term *proyecto histórico* to refer to the historical specifics needed for our liberation. Though the plan is not a detailed one, a blueprint, it is "a historical project defined enough to force options,"[2] about the actual structure of our churches and of all social, political, and economic institutions of society. Hispanic women's *proyecto histórico* is articulated here in relation to our understanding of liberation. This articulation is not only an explanation but also a strategy: it aims to help shape our understandings and actions in our day-to-day struggle to survive, and to help shape our identity as Latinas.[3] This articulation is a prediction of "our hopes and dreams toward survival,"[4] of our struggle—*la lucha.* It is an articulation springing from our lived experience as Hispanic women.

The first part of this article explains how salvation is intrinsically linked to liberation, the relationship between liberation and our present struggle to survive, and the different aspects of liberation. In the second, third and fourth parts I explore from a *mujerista* perspective each of these aspects of liberation.

Salvation and Liberation: Two Aspects of One Process

Understanding salvation and liberation as two aspects of the same process is grounded in the belief that there is but one human history that has at its very heart the history of salvation. By "history of salvation" I refer to what we believe are divine actions—creation, incarnation, redemption—as well as our human responses to them. For us Latinas, salvation refers to having a relationship with God, a relationship that does not exist if we do not love our neighbor. Our relationship with God affects all aspects of our lives, all human reality. As Latinas become increasingly aware of the injustices we suffer, we reject any concept of salvation that does not affect our present and future reality. For us salvation occurs in history and is intrinsically connected to our liberation.[5]

For Hispanic women, liberation has to do with becoming agents of our own history, with having what one needs to live and to strive toward human fulfillment. Liberation is the realization of our *proyecto histórico,* which we are always seeking to make a reality while accepting that its fullness will never be accomplished in history. Liberation is realized in concrete events which at the same time point to a more comprehensive and concrete realization.[6] For Latinas to talk about salvation, liberation, and the coming of the kin-dom[7] of God are one and the same thing. Historical events are never clearly nor completely the fulfillment of the kin-dom of God but they affect such fulfillment; they are "eschatological glimpses," part of the unfolding of the kin-dom which we do not make happen but for which we have a certain responsibility.

The realization of the kin-dom of God—liberation—is related to our present reality. Our *proyecto histórico* is not divorced from the present but rather is rooted in it, giving meaning and value to our daily struggle for survival. The present reality of Hispanic women makes it clear that in order to attain what we are struggling for we need to understand fully which structures are oppressive, to denounce them, and to announce what it is we are struggling for.[8] Our struggle for liberation has to start with an analysis of the root causes of our oppression. Such an analysis will show our oppression to be multifaceted—an intersection of ethnic prejudice, sexism, and economic oppression, all of which are intrinsic elements of patriarchal and hierarchical structures. Only after a deep analysis of its causes are we able effectively to denounce our oppression.

Denunciation, as part of the process of rooting Latinas' *proyecto histórico,* is a challenge to present reality in the name of the future. Such a challenge consists not only of criticizing, reproaching, and attacking those who maintain the structures that oppress us, but must also include repudiating such structures, not aspiring to participate in them, and refusing to benefit from them.[9] *Mujerista* theology's role in this denunciation is to move from being a resource for social criticism from the perspective of Hispanic women, to being sociocritical from our point of departure,[10] from using what we know to do a social critique of the reality that we live, to analyzing our own reality using a sociocritical perspective. This we do by insisting on our preferred future from the very beginning and by allowing it to ground our theological task, which we understand to be a liberative praxis.

Merely to denounce, without having a sense of what we believe our future should be, is irresponsible. For denunciation of oppression to be effective Hispanic women must also announce—proclaim what we are committed to bringing about. In this context annunciation, like analysis and denunciation, is indeed a liberative praxis, an exercise with tangible results. Analysis of oppression must lead to action. Annunciation is an intrinsic part of our insistence on the fullness of life against all odds and in spite of all obstacles. Such insistence is incarnated in the concrete daily struggle of Hispanic women that makes tomorrow a possibility for ourselves or for our children. Our annunciation becomes reality in our struggle to find and/or create spaces for self-determination, a key factor in the struggle for liberation. The challenge to be agents of our own history is what pushes us to do the analysis, to denounce those who oppress us, and to engage in building a future society with different values, no matter how foolish our efforts appear to those with power.[11]

Liberation is a single process that has three different aspects or levels.[12] These aspects must not be confused or identified in any simplistic way. Each one maintains its specificity; each is distinct but affects the others, one is never present without the others. They are never separate.[13] These three aspects of liberation also serve as points of entry into the struggle for liberation. For Hispanic women these levels of liberation are concrete aspects of our *proyecto histórico.* We refer to these aspects of liberation as *justicia, libertad,* and *comunidad de fe* (justice, freedom, and faith community).

Since these three aspects of liberation are simultaneous and interconnected, it is difficult to speak about them separately. I do so to distinguish each from the others, to explain and understand how they interrelate without confusing them. The specifics discussed as part of each of these three elements are not to be understood as relating only to that element. Each of the specifics has implications for, relates to, all three elements.[14]

Libertad

In Hispanic women's struggle for survival we must take great care not to oppose structural change to personal liberation. What is "personal" for us Latinas is neither individual nor necessarily private. For us the term *individual* carries a pejorative meaning, a sense of egocentrism and selfishness that we believe to be inherently bad since it works against what is of great value to us, our communities. Our sense of community keeps us from arrogating a sense of privacy to all aspects of the personal. Therefore, for us *libertad personal* means being aware of the role we play in our own oppression and in the struggle for liberation; it means being conscious of the role we must play as agents of our own history. *Libertad personal* requires self-determination, refusing to be controlled by outside forces, whether these are materialistic, economic, or psychological.[15] *Libertad personal* means recognizing the interior aspiration for personal freedom as a truly powerful one, as both motive and goal of liberation.[16]

Libertad as an element of liberation for us Hispanic women happens, then, at both the psychological level and the social level. The two main obstacles to *libertad* among Latinas are apathy and fear. As an oppressed group within one of the richest countries in the world, Hispanic women view their liberation as such an immense task that a common response is apathy: we often think our task is beyond accomplishing no matter how hard we try. For example, there are community groups that have been struggling for over twenty years for better housing and they have accomplished little or nothing. For them, for all who struggle for a long time accomplishing little, apathy appears as a protection against frustration. And, for those of us for whom the *proyecto histórico* becomes a motivational factor strong enough to enable us to shake off our apathy, our next struggle is with fear. Our fear is not mainly the fear of failing—fear of trying and not accomplishing what we set out to do—but rather the fear of being coopted by the status quo.[17]

A central and powerful myth of the status quo in the United States tells all those who come here, as well as everyone in the world, that, because this is the best of all societies, whether one accomplishes what one wants depends on the individual. It depends on whether one is ambitious enough, gets a good education (available to everyone as the myth maintains), and is willing to work hard and sacrifice.[18] This myth is constant and pervasive. It contributes significantly to the negative self-image of Hispanic women who cannot get ahead, not because we do not try hard, but because of socioeconomic realities that militate against us in all areas of life. A negative self-image is indeed oppressive but this myth is insidious because it fills us with fear and often robs us of even envisioning our *proyecto histórico*.

In order to counteract apathy and fear, we have to work together, study together, think together, devise strategies together. Second, we must articulate the details of our *proyecto histórico* at the same time that we elaborate its vision. Making our preferred future a reality requires more than vague generalities. Latinas' *proyecto histórico* has to be specific enough for each of us to know how we are to participate in the struggle to make it a reality, and what our task will be when it becomes a reality. We have to develop concrete programs and plans that will help us move forward—no matter how small the step we are able to take—so that we do not lose heart.

Only when we know the concrete details can we be agents of our own history, face our shortcomings and our fears, and the tremendous obstacles that we find along the way. We can mitigate our fear of an unknown future by insisting on particulars, by having a concrete vision of the future. The more tangible our *proyecto histórico* becomes, the more realizable it will be; as it moves from vision to plan we will be able to transfer the skills of everyday survival to the task of building our preferred future.

Comunidad de Fe

Hispanic women's relationship with the divine is a very intimate one. This relationship is not only a matter of believing that God is with us in our daily struggle, but also of relating to God the same way we relate to all our loved ones.[19] We argue with God, barter with God, get upset with God, are grateful and recompense God, use endearing terms for God.[20] This intimate relationship with the divine is at the heart of our *comunidad de fe.* For Latinas it makes no sense to say one believes in God if one does not relate to the divine on a daily basis.

Because Hispanic women relate intimately to the divine, we know that sin hurts such a relationship, for sin, like liberation, is personal, but not private. The reflections of grassroots Latinas about evil give a clear sense of their understanding of sin.

> Sin is not a matter of disobedience but of not being for others. Not going to church is not a sin. But not to care for the children of the community—that is a sin, a crime! And the women take direct responsibility for what they do or do not do. Though they have a certain sense of predestination, they do not blame anyone but themselves

> for what goes wrong. On the other hand, God is given credit for the good that they do, the good that occurs in their lives.[21]

For grassroots Latinas sin is first and foremost whatever negatively affects us as members of a community and the community itself.

The analysis that our *proyecto histórico* demands can help us understand that sin affects not only us and our communities but it is also present in the structures of our churches and society. We need to understand that there are sinful structures that have been set up to maintain the privilege of a few at the expense of the many. Our analysis of oppressive structures will help us understand that sin is "according to the Bible the ultimate cause of poverty, injustice, and the oppression in which [we] . . . live."[22]

To understand the structural implications of sin, Latinas need to actualize our sense of *comunidades de fe* and establish praxis-oriented communities, which bring together personal support and community action, and which include our religious understandings and practices as an organizing principle. Though indeed we have much to learn from the Base Ecclesial Communities that are at the heart of the Latin American liberation struggle, our *comunidades de fe* have to develop their own characteristics based on our lived experiences and our needs.[23]

The first thing we have to accept is that, for the most part, we will not be able to depend on church structures and personnel to help us develop our communities because they are often part of the problem. Although, perhaps, we will find help in the few national Latina organizations that claim to be committed to the struggle for liberation, ultimately we have to depend on ourselves.

Second, our *comunidades de fe* must find ways of relating to community organizations. Where there are no community organizations, the *comunidades de fe* will have to function as such. We must resist the temptation to let our *comunidades de fe* become "support groups" that separate our lives into realms, severing the personal from the communal, the spiritual from the realm of justice.

Third, the *comunidades de fe* must be ecumenical. Our ecumenism must take into consideration *religiosidad popular*—popular religiosity. The common ground of our *comunidades de fe* must be the struggle for liberation and not the fact that we belong to the same church.

Finally, the *comunidades de fe* must develop their own models of leadership. We need communal leadership that recognizes and uses effectively the gifts of Hispanic women; communal leadership that understands that power belongs to the community. Our leaders can exercise power only insofar as the community allows them and they must be held strictly accountable for their use of the power of the community. Because it is the community that has power, there must be a variety of leaders, all of whom use their gifts to build the community. Lastly, the leaders of the community must nurture and promote the qualities listed here so that Latinas' *comunidades de fe* can contribute effectively to the building of our *proyecto histórico*.

Justicia

Justice as a virtue does not refer only or mainly to an attitude but to a tangible way of acting and being; it involves not only personal conduct but also the way social institutions are organized and operate. Justice is not only a matter of taking care of the basic needs of the members of society, nor is it a utilitarianism that insists on the greatest happiness of the majority of people.[24] Justice is more than the Marxist principle "to each according to one's needs."[25] For *mujerista* theologians justice is all of this and much more. Justice is a Christian requirement: one cannot call oneself a Christian if one does not struggle for justice.

Our understanding of justice is based on the lived experience of Hispanic women, an experience that has as its core multifaceted oppression. In *mujerista* theology justice is a matter of permitting and requiring each person to participate in the production of the goods needed to sustain and promote human well-being; it has to do with rights and with the participation of all Latinas in all areas of life. Justice is indeed understood as the "common good." But striving for the common good can never be done at another's expense. The common good is to be judged by the rights and participation of the poorest in society; it cannot be defined as placing the rights of individuals over against the rights and participation in society of others, particularly the poor. The common good has to do with a "holistic welfare" and not just with the barest physical necessities of life. In *mujerista* theology justice is concretely expressed by being in effective solidarity with and having a preferential option for Latinas.[26]

Effective solidarity with Hispanic women is not a matter simply of agreeing with, being supportive of, or being inspired by our cause. Solidarity starts with recognizing the commonality of responsibilities and interests all of us have despite differences of race/ethnicity, class, sex, sexual preference, age. Those who wish to be in solidarity with Hispanic women must affirm and defend the community of interests, feelings, purposes and actions of the poor and the oppressed. The two main, interdependent elements of solidarity are mutuality and praxis. Mutuality keeps solidarity from being a merely altruistic praxis by making clear that while solidarity benefits the poor and the oppressed, the salvation and liberation of the rich and the oppressors depend on it. Solidarity is truly praxis: in order for there to be a genuine community of interests and purposes between the oppressed and the oppressor, there must be radical action that makes oppression impossible. Thus, for solidarity to be a praxis of mutuality it has to struggle to be politically effective; it has to have as its objective radical structural change.[27]

Effective solidarity with Latinas demands a preferential option for the oppressed. This preferential option is not based upon our moral superiority, but on the fact that Hispanic women's point of view, "pierced by suffering and attracted by hope, allows them, in their struggles, to conceive another reality. Because the poor suffer the weight of alienation, they can conceive a different project of hope and provide dynamism to a new way of organizing human life *for all.*"[28] Solidarity with Latinas as oppressed people is a call to a fundamental moral option, an option that makes it possible and requires one to struggle for radical change of oppressive structures even when the specifics of what one is choosing are not known. Indeed, only with a radical change of oppressive structures can the specifics of new societal structures begin to appear.

Conclusion

The ability of Hispanic women to conceive "another reality," a different social, political and economic structure, is greatly hampered, as I have explained, by the powerful myth about the possibility of success for everyone in this country. Poor and oppressed women in the shanty towns that surround Lima, Perú, for example, know very well that they will never be able to live—except as maids—in San Isidro, one of the rich neighborhoods in that city. Knowing that they cannot benefit from the present societal structures helps them to understand the need for and to work toward radical change. But it is not unusual to find Latinas living in the most oppressed conditions in the inner cities of the United States who think that if they work hard and sacrifice themselves, their children will benefit from the present order, that they will eventually have the material goods and privileges this society claims to offer all. I believe that this possibility, which becomes a reality for only the tiniest minority of Hispanic women and/or their children, hinders our ability to understand structural oppression. It keeps us from understanding that if we succeed in the present system it will be because someone else takes our place at the bottom of the socioeconomic-political ladder.

In order to avoid the temptation to overcome oppression individually and at the expense of others, Latinas must continue to set up strong community organizations. Such organizations are a key element in constructing our own identity and strengthening our moral agency; they are fertile settings for our liberative praxis. They provide spaces for us to gather our political will and power.[29] Without strong community organizations we will not be able to make our *proyecto histórico* a reality.

Our community organizing will be helped if those with privileges in this society are willing to stand in solidarity with us and use their privileges to bring about radical change. On our part, Latinas must embrace the mutuality of solidarity. This means that we have to be open to the positive role that those who are not part of our community but who have become our "friends" by being in solidarity with us can play in our struggle for liberation. By culture and socialization Hispanic women are not separatists; we do not exclude others from our lives and from *la lucha,* nor do we struggle exclusively for ourselves. We extend this same sense of community to those who are in solidarity with us. They can enable us in our process of conscientization; they can help us see the deception behind the myth of success. They can assist us in getting rid of the oppressor within who at times makes us seek vengeance and disfigures our *proyecto histórico* when we seek to exchange places with present day oppressors.[30]

At present the unfolding of our *proyecto histórica* requires that Hispanic women organize to bring about in the United States a national commitment to full employment and an adequate minimum wage; redistribution of wealth through redistributive inheritance and wealth taxes; comparable remuneration for comparable work regardless of sex, sexual preference, race/ethnicity, age, and so forth; economic democracy that would transform an economy controlled by a few into the economy of a participatory community; health care—with emphasis on preventive health care—available to all; changes in the economics of the family that will encourage more "symmetrical marriages, allow a better balance between family and work for both men and women, and make parenting a less difficult and impoverishing act for single parents" (the majority of whom are women);[31] access to political office for Hispanic women and men (to insure adequate representation of our community); restructuring of the educational system so that our children and others can study Hispanic culture and Spanish; restructuring the financing of public education so that its quality does not depend on the wealth of the neighborhood served by a given school but is the responsibility of the whole community of that area, region, or state; more diverse images in public communication, including entertainment TV and movies, so that the values of Latinas can begin to influence the culture of the nation at large.

Working for such changes will enhance our ability to build coalitions with other oppressed groups struggling for liberation. It will strengthen our communities of struggle and enable us to survive as we experience ourselves as self-defining moral agents.[32]

Hispanic women's *proyecto histórico* is based on our lived experience and is an intrinsic element of our identity as a community of struggle. Our *proyecto histórico* is not a fully developed historical societal model but we believe it is specific enough to be a moral imperative and an adequate basis for moral norms and values.

It has been argued that the subjectivity of lived experience makes it an inadequate normative base. But the fact is that so-called adequate normative bases, such as various different theories of justice, spring from the understandings of particular groups of men, based on *their* experiences. Thus the liberative praxis of Latinas, having as its source our lived experience, is an adequate base for moral norms and values because it enables moral agency and empowers us to understand and define ourselves—to comprehend what our human existence is all about and what its goal is.[33]

Mujerista theologians refuse to reduce theology to a formal, disciplinary discourse in which adequacy is defined by certain intellectual criteria as they are understood by those who control the cultural and academic apparatus.[34] *Mujerista* theology is indeed an attempt to deconstruct the dominant normative understanding of theology as a disciplinary method, in order to place theology at the heart of Latinas' daily life where the norm is *hacer lo mejor que se puede aunque no sea necesariamente lo más bueno*—to do what one is able to do, though it might not always be the best thing—in order to survive.[35]

Notes

Dedication: To Beverly Harrison, my adviser at Union Theological Seminary for seven years, as an expression of gratitude for her sisterly solidarity and her adamant insistence on the centrality of the socio-economic-political understandings and models in theology and ethics. *Adelante,* Bev.

1. *Mujerista* theology is a liberation theology having as its source the lived experience of Hispanic women. Its articulation is in infancy, but its practice is generations old, for *mujerista* theology is about continuing the tradition of our *abuelitas, madres, tías, y comadres,* who have struggled to survive on a daily basis.

2. José Miguez Bonino, *Doing Theology in a Revolutionary Situa-*

tion (Philadelphia: Fortress Press, 1975), 38–39. Chapter 3 of this book is perhaps the most detailed description of the meaning of *proyecto histórico* by a Latin American liberation theologian. *Mujerista* theology appropriates this term critically according to our lived experience.

3. Since there is no consensus in our communities on whether to use *Hispanic* or *Latina,* I will alternate the two. Among ourselves we hardly ever use either but instead identify ourselves by our country of origin or that of our ancestry; we call ourselves, Cuban, Puerto Rican, Mexican-American, etc.

4. Audre Lorde, "Poetry Is Not a Luxury," in her *Sister Outsider* (Trumansburg, N.Y.: Crossing Press, 1984), 37. See Ada María Isasi-Díaz and Yolanda Tarango, *Hispanic Women: Prophetic Voice in the Church* (1988; reprint Minneapolis: Fortress Press, 1993), chap. 3, where we explain how the struggle for survival is not only a matter of economics but also of cultural survival. In this article Latinas/Hispanic women is intended to summon images of inequality and subordination and to evoke a sense of collective identity, a claim to group self-definition and self-determination, and an insistence on setting our own agenda.

5. See Gustavo Gutiérrez, *A Theology of Liberation* (Maryknoll, N.Y.: Orbis Books, 1988), xxxix, 83–91. Also see Gustavo Gutiérrez, *The Truth Shall Make You Free* (Maryknoll, N.Y.: Orbis Books, 1990), 14–16, 116–21.

6. Gutiérrez, *Theology of Liberation,* 94.

7. I do not use *kingdom* or *reign* because of their sexist and classist connotations. *Kin-dom* is preferred because it also includes a sense of community, of shared responsibility for survival and welfare.

8. Using Paulo Freire, Gutiérrez sees the relationship of what he calls "utopia" to historical reality as appearing under two aspects: denunciation and annunciation. See, Gutiérrez, *Theology of Liberation,* 136–40.

9. This is why we avoid using the terms *minority* or *marginalized.* These labels communicate the way the dominant group sees us and not the way we see ourselves; they imply that what we want is to participate in present structures which are oppressive. We see ourselves as a group that has a significant contribution to make precisely because we demand radical change of oppressive structures.

10. See the comments of Larry Rasmussen, *Christianity and Crisis,* October 22, 1990.

11. For the effectiveness of this understanding of struggling to build a preferred future see Renny Golden, *The Hour of the Poor, The Hour of Women* (New York: Crossroad, 1991).

12. We have appropriated Gutiérrez's understanding of the three levels or aspects of the process of liberation. The specifics of each of these aspects arise from our lived experience as Hispanic women.

13. Gutiérrez refers to the "Chalcedonian Principle" and uses the Chalcedonian language regarding the two natures of the one person Jesus, in order to clarify the distinctiveness and intrinsic unity of the three aspects of liberation. In this, *mujerista* theology follows Gutiérrez quite closely. The distinctiveness of Hispanic women's struggle, however, will come in the "content" of each of the three aspects of the process of liberation. See Gutiérrez, *The Truth,* 120–24.

14. Following the venerable tradition referred to in Acts 1:26, I cast lots to decide the order in which to deal with these three aspects of liberation! I know some will try to see in the order a certain priority of importance or relevance. That is indeed *not* my intention.

15. The only reason a *balsero,* a young man who escaped from Cuba in a makeshift raft, could give me for risking his life was the lack of *libertad* he experienced in Cuba. I assumed that for him, influenced by US propaganda, *libertad* had to do with accessibility to consumer goods, with a better material life. But I was wrong. For him *libertad* had to do with self-determination, with wanting something different and being able to work towards making it a reality. Whether one agrees or disagrees with his assessment of the present Cuban situation, his understanding of *libertad* and his willingness to risk his life for it has helped me to understand what I and other Latinas mean by *libertad.*

16. Compare with Gutiérrez, *The Truth,* 132–34.

17. This fear is compounded by the fact that seeing ourselves as different from the status quo is an intrinsic element of what it means for us to be Latina/Hispanic women. See Ada María Isasi-Díaz, *En La Lucha—In the Struggle: A Hispanic Women's Liberation Theology* (Minneapolis: Fortress Press, 1993), chap. 1.

18. The best proof of this mindset is the name of the US government program for Puerto Rico in the middle decades of this century: "Operation Bootstrap." The Puerto Ricans understood very clearly the American expression that was behind that title and they responded painfully and cleverly, "How do you expect us to lift ourselves by our bootstraps when we do not even have boots?"

19. I use the word *God* here not to refer to one divine being but rather as a collective noun that embraces God, the saints, dead ones whom we love, manifestations of the Virgin (not always the same as manifestations of Mary the mother of Jesus), Jesus (not very similar to the Jesus of the Gospels), Amerindian and African gods, and so forth.

20. To the accusation that this places us in the ranks of the neo-orthodox, the charismatics and/or the fundamentalists, we answer that Latinas have not been part of the "modern experiment"; that the kind of belief in the divine that for the enlightened, scientific mind signifies a lack of autonomous, critical, rational thought, is for us a concrete experience that we use as a key element in the struggle for liberation. See Christine Gudorf, "Liberation Theology's Use of Scripture: A Response to First World Critics," *Interpretation: A Journal of Bible and Theology* (January, 1987): 12–13.

21. Isasi-Díaz and Tarango, *Hispanic Women,* 90.

22. Gutiérrez, Theology of Liberation, 24.

23. For a concise articulation of what Base Ecclesial Communities are and the role they play in Latin America, see Pablo Richard, "The Church of the Poor in the Decade of the 90s," *LADOC* 21 (Nov./Dec., 1990): 11–29.

24. See, John Stuart Mill, *Utilitarianism* (New York: Bobbs-Merrill, 1957).

25. See also Acts 4:35!

26. For an excellent short analysis of six major theories of justice, see Karen Lebacqz, *Six Theories of Justice* (Minneapolis: Augsburg Publishing House, 1986).

27. For a more comprehensive analysis of the meaning of solidarity, see Ada María Isasi-Díaz, "Solidarity: Love of Neighbor in the 1980s," in *Lift Every Voice: Constructing Christian Theologies from the Underside,* ed. Susan Brooks Thistlethwaite and Mary Potter Engels (San Francisco: Harper & Row, 1990).

28. José Miguez Bonino, "Nuevas Tendencias en Teología," *Pasos* (1985): 22.

29. Fernando Romero, "*Sentido práctico y flexibilidad popular,*" *Páginas* 111 (October 1991): 43.

30. For an amplification of this theme, see Isasi-Díaz, "Solidarity," 37.

31. Teresa L. Amott and Julie A. Matthaei, *Race, Gender and Work* (Boston: South End Press, 1991), 346–48.

32. Romero, 45–47.

33. Isasi-Díaz and Tarango, *Hispanic Women,* 77–80, 109–110.

34. We are not denying the need for consistency and coherence as part of needed moral and theological criteria, but we must also take into consideration the practicality and flexibility of Hispanic women's everyday lives, since these qualities are essential for their survival. Mainline

intellectuals often consider practicality and flexibility to be inconsistent, incoherent and contradictory.

35. Pedro A. Sandín-Freimant, "Domesticating the Theology of Liberation: A Deconstructive Reading of Clodovis Boff's *Theology and Praxis*," *Apuntes* 7, no. 2 (Summer 1987): 27–41.

7. "Wading Through Many Sorrows": Toward a Theology of Suffering in Womanist Perspective

M. Shawn Copeland

This chapter first appeared in *A Troubling in My Soul: Womanist Perspectives on Evil and Suffering* in 1993.

Suffering is universal, an inescapable fact of the human condition; it defies immunities of all kinds.[1] Suffering despoils women and men irrespective of race or tongue, wealth or poverty, learning or virtue; disregards merit or demerit, reward or punishment, honor or corruption. Like sun and rain, suffering comes unbidden to the just and the unjust alike.

Suffering always means pain, disruption, separation, and incompleteness. It can render us powerless and mute, push us to the borders of hopelessness and despair. Suffering can maim, wither, and cripple the heart; or, to quote Howard Thurman, it can be a "spear of frustration transformed into a shaft of light."[2] From some women and men, suffering coaxes real freedom and growth, so much so that Thurman insists we literally see the change: "Into their faces come a subtle radiance and a settled serenity; into their relationships a vital generosity that opens the sealed doors of the heart in all who are encountered along the way."[3] From other women and men, suffering extracts a bitter venom. From still others, suffering squeezes a delicious ironic spirit and tough laughter. Consider the Gullah [woman's] proverb: "Ah done been in sorrow's kitchen and ah licked de pots clean."[4]

As a working definition, I understand suffering as the disturbance of our inner tranquility caused by physical, mental, emotional, and spiritual forces that we grasp as jeopardizing our lives, our very existence. Evil is the negation and deprivation of good; suffering, while never identical with evil, is inseparable from it. Thus, and quite paradoxically, the suffering caused by evil can result in interior development and perfection as well as in social and cultural good. African Americans have encountered monstrous evil in chattel slavery and its legacy of virulent institutionalized racism and have been subjected to unspeakable physical, psychological, social, moral, and religious affliction and suffering. Yet, from the anguish of our people rose distinctive religious expression, exquisite music and song, powerful rhetoric and literature, practical invention and creative art. If slavery was the greatest evil, freedom was the greatest good and women and men struggled, suffered, sacrificed, and endured much to attain it.

This essay is a theological meditation on "the maldistribution, negative quality, enormity, and transgenerational character" of the suffering of Black women.[5] Such particularizing of suffering requires neither qualification nor apology. However, there can be no ranking of oppression or suffering; no men or women are excluded from the canon of anguish. Indeed, the historic suffering of the Jewish people and the oppression of the hundreds of thousands of indigenous peoples of the lands of the Americas weigh heavily in any discussion of ethnic suffering.[6] Further, the specificity of this essay neither discounts the humiliating racism Black men suffer, nor does it undermine the grievous sexism women of all races and cultures endure. Rather, I hope that the reader shall situate this particularizing of suffering within the ongoing Christian theological effort to respond to the human condition in new and graced ways.

The focus of this three-part essay is not the formal, self-conscious and bold contemporary articulation of womanist theology for an authentic new world order, but rather its roots in the rich historic soil of Black women's experiences of suffering and affliction during the centuries of chattel slavery. In the first section of the essay, enslaved or fugitive Black women speak for themselves.[7] Scholars estimate that Black women wrote about 12 percent of the total number of extant slave narratives, although none of these is as well known as the narratives by fugitive and emancipated men.[8] Mary Helen Washington observes that male slave narrators often render Black women invisible or relegate them to subordinate roles. When Black women are referenced in men's narratives, they are depicted as "the pitiable subjects of brutal treatment, or benign nurturers who help the fugitive in his quest for freedom, or objects of sentimentality."[9] Black women slave narrators offer a stiff antidote to the (hegemonic) cultural stereotypes that Black men seem to have imbibed. As Hazel Carby points out, when these women relate and interpret their experiences on their own terms, they disclose a very different sense of themselves:

> In the slave narratives written by black women the authors placed in the foreground their active roles as historical agents as opposed to passive subjects; represented as acting their own visions, they are seen to take decisions over their own lives. They document their sufferings and brutal treatment but in a context that is also the story of the resistance of that brutality.[10]

Only by attending to Black women's feelings and experiences, understanding and reflection, judgment and evaluation about their situation, can we adequately challenge the stereotypes about Black women—especially those stereotypes that coalesce around that "most popular social convention of female sexuality, the 'cult of true womanhood.' "[11]

The centerpiece of this first section is the story of emancipated fugitive slave Harriet Jacobs [Linda Brent], *Incidents in the Life of a Slave Girl.*[12] Jacobs' controversial narrative is quite likely, "the only slave narrative that takes as its subject the sexual exploitation of female slaves—thus centering on sexual oppression as well as on oppression of race and condition."[13] Here, we apprehend not only the intersection of gender and race and class, but a most excruciating form of the suffering of enslaved Black women.

Womanist theology claims the experiences of Black women as proper and serious data for theological reflection. Its aim is to elucidate the differentiated range and interconnections of Black women's gender, racial-ethnic, cultural, religious, and social (i.e., political, economic, and technological) oppression.[14] Hence, a womanist theology of suffering is rooted in and draws on Black women's accounts of pain and anguish, of their individual and collective struggle to grasp and manage, rather than be managed by their suffering. Drawing from these narratives, the second section discusses those resources that support Black women's resistance to evil and the third section sketches the basic elements of a theology of suffering from womanist perspective.

Black Women's Experiences of Suffering

Composite narratives and interviews with emancipated men and women, as well as their children and grandchildren, have given us a picture of daily plantation life.[15] These include chronicles of the horrors and anguish they endured under chattel slavery: the auction block with its rupture of familial bonds, the brutalization of human feeling, savage beatings and mutilation, petty cruelty, and chronic deprivation of human physical and psychological needs. But accounts of the rape and sexual abuse of enslaved Black women are told reluctantly, if at all. James Curry, after his escape, recounting some of the "extreme cruel[ties] practised upon [some] plantations" around Person County, North Carolina, asserted "that there is no sin which man [sic] can commit, that those slaveholders are not guilty of." And Curry lamented, "It is not proper to be written; but the treatment of females in slavery is dreadful."[16] Still, some men and women dared to write and speak about that dreadful treatment—the coarse and vulgar seduction, rape, abuse, and concubinage of Black women under chattel slavery.

Lizzie Williams, who had been held on a plantation near Selma, Alabama, relayed the fear and resignation that overtook so many Black women. "Many de poor nigger women have chillen for de massa, dat is if de massa mean man. Dey just tell de niggers what to do and dey know better dan to fuss."[17] The following reports are bitter reinforcements:

One former slave repeated this story:

> Ma mama said that a nigger 'oman couldn't help herself, fo' she had to do what de marster say. Ef he come to de

> field whar de women workin' an tell gal to come on, she had to go. He would take one down in de woods an' use her all de time he wanted to, den send her on back to work.[18]

And another former slave told this plaintive account:

> My sister was given away when she was a girl. She told me and ma that they'd make her go out and lay on a table and two or three white men would have sex with her before they'd let her up. She was just a small girl. She died when she was still in her young days, still a girl.[19]

Fourteen-year-old Louisa Picquet escaped from the sexual advances of one slave owner, only to be sold to another with similar intentions. Years later in an interview, the emancipated Picquet recalled:

> Mr. Williams told me what he bought me for, soon as we started for New Orleans. He said he was getting old, and when he saw me he thought he'd buy me and end his days with me. He said if I behave myself he'd treat me well: but, if not, he'd whip me almost to death.[20]

Compelled to serve as Williams' housekeeper, caretaker for his sons from a former marriage, and his mistress, Picquet also bears four children by Williams. When the interviewer questions her about her life with Williams, Picquet reveals her innermost anguish: "I thought, now I shall be committin' adultery, and there's no chance for me, and I'll have to die and be lost. Then I had this trouble with him and my soul the whole time."[21] Picquet tells her interviewer that she had broached these concerns with Williams often. But his response, she says, was to curse and to argue that her life with him was not an impediment to her religious conversion. Picquet continues:

> But I knew better than that. I thought it was of no use to be prayin', and livin' in sin. . . . I begin then to pray that he might die, so that I might get religion; and then I

> promise the Lord one night, faithful, in prayer, if he would just take him out of the way, I'd get religion and be true to Him as long as I lived.[22]

Sometime later, Williams became ill and died.

In what is most likely the first female slave narrative from the Americas, Mary Prince describes her anger at a slaveholder's lewd intentions and her own efforts at personal modesty:

> [Mr. D—] had an ugly fashion of stripping himself quite naked, and ordering me then to wash him in the tub of water. This was worse to me than all the [beatings]. Sometimes when he called me to wash him I would not come, my eyes were so full of shame. He would then come to beat me. One time I had plates and knives in my hand, and I dropped both plates and knives, and some of the plates broke.[23]

Mr. D— struck her and Mary Prince declares, "at last I defended myself, for I thought it was high time to do so. I then told him I would not live longer with him, for he was a very indecent man—very spiteful, and too indecent; with no shame for his servants, no shame for his own flesh."[24] With that, she walked out and went to a neighboring house. And although Mary Prince is compelled to return the next morning, the slaveholder hires her out to work. Her daring gains her some small measure of relief.

Under the pseudonym Linda Brent, Harriet Jacobs gives us a detailed presentation of the psychological and sexual torment to which she was subjected. Like other fugitive female narrators, Jacobs writes her story neither "to attract attention" to herself, nor "to excite sympathy for [her] own sufferings." Rather, she seeks "to arouse the women of the North to a realizing sense of the condition of millions of women in the South, still in bondage, suffering what I suffered, and most of them far worse."[25]

Born in 1818 to an enslaved mulatto couple, Jacobs describes her childhood in which she and her brother were "fondly shielded" from the harsh reality of their condition. Neither dreamt that they were like "merchandise, [only] trusted to [their parents] for safe keeping, and liable to be demanded of them at any moment."[26] Jacobs' father's reputation and skill as a carpenter earned him unusual privileges and a substantial income, a portion of which he paid annually to the woman who owned him. Allowed to manage his own affairs, her father provided a relatively comfortable home and living for his wife and two children. "His strongest wish," Brent writes "was to purchase his children; but, though he several times offered his hard earnings for that purpose, he never succeeded."[27] The little girl's happiness is marred irrevocably by the death, first of her mother, then that of the female slaveholder, who was also her mother's foster sister. Family and friends had expected the woman to emancipate the children; after all, their mother and grandmother had been trusted family servants and she had promised Jacobs' dying mother that "her children should never suffer for any thing." Yet, the slaveholder's will bequeathed Linda to a five-year-old niece. Looking back more than thirty years, Jacobs wrote mournfully and sagely that "the memory of a faithful slave does not avail much to save her children from the auction block."[28] It is this broken promise that consigns twelve-year-old Linda and her ten-year-old brother William to the household of Dr. and Mrs. Flint.

At fifteen with the onset of her puberty, like Louisa Picquet and Mary Prince, Harriet Jacobs' Linda Brent is confronted by the persistent, unwelcome lewd advances by the male head of the household.

> I now entered my fifteenth year—a sad epoch in the life of a slave girl. [Dr. Flint] began to whisper foul words in my ear. Young as I was, I could not remain ignorant of their import. I tried to treat them with indifference or contempt. . . . He tried his utmost to corrupt the pure principles my grandmother had instilled. He peopled my young mind with unclean images, such as only a vile monster could think of. I turned from him with disgust and hatred. But he was my master. I was compelled to live under the same roof with him—where I saw a man forty years my senior daily violating the most sacred commandments of nature. He told me I was his property; that I

> must be subject to his will in all things. My soul revolted against the mean tyranny. But where could I turn for protection? No matter whether the slave girl be as black as ebony or as fair as her mistress. In either case, there is no shadow of law to protect her from insult, from violence, or even from death; all these are inflicted by fiends who bear the shape of men. The mistress, who ought to protect the helpless victim, has no other feelings toward her but those of jealousy and rage.[29]

Flint sought not only to satiate his lust, but to wreak his twisted will-to-power, to conquer Linda Brent's body and defile her spirit.

> My master met me at every turn, reminding me that I belonged to him, and swearing by heaven and earth that he would compel me to submit to him. If I went out for a breath of fresh air, after a day of unwearied toil, his footsteps dogged me. If I knelt by my mother's grave, his dark shadow fell on me even there.
>
> When I succeeded in avoiding opportunities for him to talk to me at home, I was ordered to come to his office, to do some errand. When there, I was obliged to stand and listen to such language as he saw fit to address me.[30]

Brent's revulsion and repulsion are unshakable, even as the physician is consumed by a life of revenge. Flint refuses to sell Brent to the freeborn colored man who wishes to marry her. Flint's insults, taunting, and physical abuse force Brent to break off her engagement.

> [The doctor] had an iron will and was determined to keep me, and to conquer me. My lover was an intelligent and religious man. Even if he could have obtained permission to marry me while I was a slave, the marriage would give him no power to protect me from my master. It would have made him miserable to witness the insults I should have been subjected to. And then, if we had children, I

> knew they must "follow the condition of the mother." What a terrible blight that would be on the heart of a free, intelligent father! For his sake, I felt that I ought not to link his fate with my own unhappy destiny.[31]

Flint has a small house built in a secluded place, a few miles outside of town—away from his wife and home. He intends to keep Brent as his mistress; but she vows "never [to] enter it." Brent writes, "I had rather toil on the plantation from dawn till dark; I had rather live and die in jail, than drag on, from day to day, through such a living death."[32] Emotionally distraught, feeling "forsaken by God and man [sic]," Brent acquiesces emotionally and sexually to the sympathy, romantic overtures, and eloquence of the white unmarried gentleman, Mr. Sands.[33]

> So much attention from a superior person was, of course, flattering; for human nature is the same in all . . . It seemed to me a great thing to have such a friend. By degrees, a more tender feeling crept into my heart . . . Of course, I saw whither all this was tending. I knew the impassable gulf between us; but to be an object of interest to a man who is not married, and who is not her master, is agreeable to the pride and feelings of a slave, if her miserable situation has left her any pride or sentiment. It seems less degrading to give one's self, than to submit to compulsion.[34]

Brent describes her decision as "a headlong plunge into the abyss," and admits a mixture of motives: "Revenge and calculations of interest were added to flattered vanity and sincere gratitude for kindness. . . . [A]nd it was something to triumph over my tyrant even in that small way."[35] Jacobs' Brent is convinced that the physician will be so outraged at her sexual and emotional choice of Sands that he will sell her. She is just as convinced that Sands will buy her and that she easily can obtain her freedom from him. When Flint orders Brent to move into the completed cottage, she adamantly and triumphantly refuses.

> I told him I would never enter it. He said, "I have heard enough of such talk as that. You shall go, if you are carried by force; and you shall remain there."
>
> I replied, "I will never go there. In a few months I shall be a mother."
>
> He stood and looked at me in dumb amazement, and left the house without a word. I thought I should be happy in my triumph over him. But now that the truth was out, and my relatives would hear of it, I felt wretched. Humble as were their circumstances, they had pride in my good character. Now, how could I look them in the face? My self-respect was gone! I had resolved that I would be virtuous, though I was a slave. I had said, "Let the storm beat! I will brave it till I die." And now how humiliated I felt.[36]

Brent used her body, her sex, to gain some measure of psychological freedom from Flint. Although she wounds her grandmother in the process, she is never completely alienated from this good woman, even when she bears her second child by Sands. When Brent hears that her newborn is a girl, she is pained. "Slavery is terrible for men; but it is far more terrible for women. Superadded to the burden common to all, *they* have wrongs, and sufferings, and mortifications peculiarly their own."[37]

Flint is relentless; Brent takes the only and hazardous course open to her. She runs away, resolving "that come what would, there should be no turning back," staking her future on liberty or death. Concealed, first by a friend, then by the wife of a prominent slaveholder, Brent eludes meticulous search for some weeks. Then, following a carefully devised plan involving Brent disguising herself as a sailor, hiding for a few days in a swamp, and darkening her face with charcoal, friends and relatives hide Brent beneath the sloping crawl space of her grandmother's house. For nearly seven years, Linda Brent lived undetected in this garret—nine feet long, seven feet wide, three feet high, accessible only through a carefully constructed and hidden trapdoor that led to a storeroom. Deprived of light and air, with no space to stand or move about, Brent is assailed by insects and heat in the summer and frostbite in winter. But she insists, she was not without comfort; brief conversations with her relatives, the discovery of a small gimlet that she uses to bore three small holes to increase light and air, and the voices—and most importantly the purchased freedom—of her son and daughter. Only her grandmother, aunt, uncle, brother, and a trusted friend knew her whereabouts. During those nearly seven years, Flint threatened and harassed her family and traveled three times to New York to search for Linda Brent who was "practically in his own back yard."[38]

Huddled in her cramped garret, observing the street through a tiny hole in the boards, Brent is an invisible, yet recording witness to the pathos of the world the slaveholders made. One day she notices an enslaved woman passing her grandmother's gate weeping and muttering to herself. This woman, Brent's goodly grandmother tells her later, had been turned out by the mistress of the house and forbidden to return. The wife of the slaveholder had seen the slave woman's baby for the first time, "and in the lineaments of its fair face she saw a likeness to her husband." The very next day this nineteenth-century Hagar and her child were sold to a Georgia trader. On another occasion, Brent sees another enslaved woman "rush wildly by, pursued by two men" and records her affliction. The "wet nurse of her mistress's children," the woman had committed some offense and subsequently was "ordered to be stripped and whipped. To escape the degradation and the torture, she rushed to the river, jumped in, and ended her wrongs in death."[39] Such treatment is corroborated by both Mary Prince and Mattie Jackson. Prince relays her own experience: "To strip me naked—to hang me up by the wrists and lay my flesh open with the cowskin, was an ordinary punishment for even a slight offence."[40] And Mattie Jackson tells of the similar brutish behavior of slaveholder Benjamin Lewis: "He used to extend his victim, fastened to a beam, with hands and feet tied, and inflict from fifty to three hundred lashes, laying their flesh entirely open, then bathe their quivering wounds in brine."[41]

Mary Prince remembers the brutal death of Hetty, an enslaved woman who was especially kind to her in her youth. She and the other slaves of this plantation believe that Hetty's premature death was caused by a beating she received during her pregnancy.

> One of the cows had dragged the rope away from the stake to which Hetty had fastened it, and got loose. My master flew into a terrible passion, and ordered the poor creature to be stripped quite naked, notwithstanding her pregnancy, and to be tied up to a tree in the yard. He then flogged her as hard as he could lick, both with the whip and the cow-skin, till she was all over streaming with blood. He rested, and then beat her again and again. Her shrieks were terrible. Poor Hetty was brought to bed before her time, and was delivered after severe labour of a dead child. She appeared to recover after her confinement, so far that she was repeatedly flogged by both master and mistress afterward; but her former strength never returned to her. Ere long her body and limbs swelled to a great size; and she lay on a mat in the kitchen, till the water burst out of her body and she died. All the slaves said that death was a good thing for poor Hetty; but I cried very much for her death. The manner of it filled me with horror. I could not bear to think about it; yet it was always present to my mind for many a day.[42]

Prince is forced to take over many of Hetty's duties, including the care of the cows. Once again, a cow slips its tether. The cow wanders into a garden, and eats some sweet-potato slips; Prince is blamed. Capt. I—, the slave master, finds Prince milking a cow. He takes off his boot and strikes her with it in the small of the back. The frightened cow kicks over the pan, spilling the milk. The accident is the slaveholder's fault, but it fuels his rage at Prince and he beats her. "I cannot remember how many licks he gave me then, but he beat me until I was unable to stand, and till he himself was weary." Prince runs away to her mother who is held on a nearby farm. Her mother, Prince tells us, "was both grieved and glad" to see her: "grieved because [Prince] had been so ill used, and glad because she had not seen [her daughter] for a long, long, while." Prince's mother hid her in a hole in nearby rocks and brought her food late each evening. But her father takes her back to the slaveholder. Not surprisingly, Prince is fearful of return.

When they arrive, her father entreats Capt. I— "to be a kind master" to his daughter in the future. But Prince speaks up boldly:

> I then took courage and said that I could stand the floggings no longer; that I was weary of my life, and therefore I had run away to my mother; but mothers could only weep and mourn over their children, they could not save them from cruel masters—from whip, the rope, and the cow-skin. [Capt. I—] told me to hold my tongue and go about my work, or he would find a way to settle me. He did not, however, flog me that day.[43]

For five years Prince remained a slave in this household, flogged and mistreated almost daily, until she was sold and shipped away from her parents and siblings.

Harriet Jacobs, Mary Prince, Louisa Picquet, Mattie Jackson and all the many thousand women gone were caught in the vicious nexus spawned in chattel slavery—full and arrogant self-assertion of white male power and privilege, white female ambivalence and hatred, the subjugation of Black women and men. These and so many other women were caught, but not trapped. To be sure, these are narratives of staggering affliction—human lives are seized, uprooted, and attacked directly and indirectly, in psychological, intellectual, cultural, social, physical dimensions.[44] Clearly these narratives expose maldistributed suffering, for Black women endured torments precisely because they were Black women and all Black women—enslaved or free—were potential victims. Neither is the suffering disclosed here pedagogically motivated, nor is it some form of spiritually beneficial asceticism. And since such suffering was meant to break, not temper, the spirit, it is of negative quality. Not infrequently, the beatings and abuse these women withstood ended in death. And, finally, their suffering extended for more than three hundred years, striking mother, daughter, granddaughter, great-granddaughter, great-great-granddaughter. Again: These are narratives of affliction, but not narratives of despair; the women may be caught, but they are not trapped. These Black women wade through their sorrows, managing their suffering, rather than being managed by it. In the next section, we turn to look at their resistance, a characteristic feature of their suffering and struggle and potent element in a theology of suffering in womanist perspective.

Resources of Womanist Resistance

Almost from its emergence, Christianity has been described as the religion of slaves.[45] Space does not allow me to elaborate here the nature and character of the psychic moments, spiritual experiences, preaching and teaching, rituals of passage and praise, spirituals and shouts and dance, visions and vocations that signify the distinctive Afric appropriation, if not reception, of biblical revelation by the enslaved Africans in the Americas. From their aural appropriation of the Bible and critical reflection on their own condition, these men and women shaped and "fitted" Christian practices, rituals, and values to their own particular experiences, religio-cultural expectations, and personal needs.[46] The slave community formed a distinctive image of itself and fashioned "an inner world, a scale of values and fixed points of vantage from which to judge the world around them and themselves."[47]

Christian religion was a fundamental resource for womanist resistance. Many women drank from its well, yet selectively so. Harriet Jacobs was critical of religious hypocrisy speaking of the "great difference between Christianity and the religion of the south."[48] Slaveholders who beat, tortured, and sexually harassed slaves prided themselves on church membership. The planter class held one set of morals for white women, another for white men, and assumed that enslaved women and men had little, if any, capacity for real moral experience, moral agency, and moral virtue. All too often, Christian preaching, teaching, and practice complied. Black women's narratives counter these assumptions and stereotypes as well as discern and embrace a religious standard that exposes the moral hypocrisy of the planter class. Moreover, these women are living witnesses to the power of divine grace, not merely to sustain men and women through such evil, but to enable them to turn victimization into Christian triumph.[49] Jacobs records the lines of this old slave hymn that sings the distinction between a pure or true Christianity and that poisoned by slavery: "Ole Satan's church is here below/Up to God's free church I hope to go."

The attitude of the master class toward worship by slaves was not uniform. On some plantations slaves held independent, and sometimes, unsupervised services of worship; on other plantations, they attended white churches, sitting or standing in designated areas; on still others, they were forbidden to worship at all and they were punished if found praying and singing. Yet the people persisted. Christian biblical revelation held out formidable power. It offered the slaves the "dangerous" message of freedom, for indeed, Jesus did come to bring "freedom for the captive and release for those held in economic, social, and political bondage."[50] It offered them the great and parallel event of Exodus, for indeed, it was for a people's freedom that the Lord God chose, called, and sent Moses. Christian biblical revelation provided the slaves with material for the singular mediation of their pain. The spirituals, "forged of sorrow in the heat of religious fervor,"[51] were an important resource of resistance. In and through these moaned or sung utterances, one woman's, one man's suffering or shout of jubilation became that of a people. The spirituals reshaped and conflated the characters and stories, parables and pericopes, events and miracles of the Hebrew and Christian scriptures. These songs told the mercy of God anew and testified to the ways in which the enslaved people met God at the whipping post, on the auction block, in the hush arbor, in the midnight flight to freedom. The maker of the spiritual sang: "God dat lived in Moses' time/Is jus' de same today." The spirituals served as coded messages, signaling the arrival of Moses in the person of Harriet Tubman or other ex-slaves who went back into Egypt to "tell ole Pharaoh, Let My People Go." "Steal away," sang the maker of the spiritual, "the chariot is comin'." And, if the makers of the spirituals gloried in singing of the cross of Jesus, it was not because they were masochistic and enjoyed suffering. Rather, the enslaved Africans sang because they saw on the rugged wooden planks One who had endured what was their daily portion. The cross was treasured because it enthroned the One who went all the way with them and for them. The enslaved Africans sang because they saw the result of the cross—triumph over the principalities and powers of death, triumph over evil in this world.

The slaves understood God as the author of freedom, of emancipation, certainly. Harriet Jacobs recalls Aggie, an old slave woman and neighbor to her grandmother. When Aggie hears the other old woman weeping, she hurries to inquire. But, when told that the grandmother is weeping because her grandson has escaped North, Aggie's joy admonishes Jacobs' grandmother.

> Is dat what you's cryin fur? Git down on your knees and bress de Lord! I don't know whar my poor chillern is, and I nebber 'spect to know. You don't know what poor Linda's gone to; but you do know whar her brudder is. He's in free parts; and dat's de right place. Don't murmur at de Lord's doings, but git down on your knees and tank him for his goodness.[52]

For the slaves, "the God of the fugitive is a God who offers immediate freedom and deliverance to his [sic] chosen people," even if this deliverance sometimes entails trial and fear.[53]

Even as Linda Brent joins in thanks for her brother's safety, she does not hesitate to question God. Brent's experience of oppression forced her "to retain the right, as much as possible, to resist those things within the [dominant] culture and the Bible that [she found] obnoxious or antagonistic to [her] innate sense of identity and to [her] basic instincts for survival."[54] In the following passage, Brent speaks for so many who puzzled and would puzzle at the maldistribution, enormity, viciousness, and recrudescence of this peculiar suffering.

> I tried to be thankful for my little cell, dismal as it was, and even to love it as part of the price I had paid for the redemption of my children. Sometimes I thought God was a compassionate Father, who would forgive my sins for the sake of my sufferings. At other times, it seemed to me there was no justice or mercy in the divine government. I asked why the curse of slavery was permitted to exist, and why I had been so persecuted and wronged from youth. These things took the shape of mystery,

> which is to this day not so clear to my soul as I trust it will be hereafter.[55]

Harriet Jacobs' Linda Brent has made a space for Alice Walker's Celie. Tormented in heart and mind and body, Celie declares: God "act just like all the other mens I know. Trifling, forgitful, low-down. . . . If he [sic] ever listened to poor colored women the world would be a different place, I can tell you."[56]

For the enslaved community, memory was a vital and empowering act. Remembering gave the slaves access to "naming, placing, and signifying,"[57] and thus the recovery, the reconstitution of identity, culture, and self. Memory, then, was an essential source of resistance. As a young girl, Lucy Delaney's mother, Polly Berry, was kidnapped from Illinois and sold into slavery. Like Harriet Jacobs, Polly Berry's emancipation is bound up in a slaveholder's will that an executor disregards. Delaney writes: "My mother registered a solemn vow that her children should not continue in slavery all their lives, and she never spared an opportunity to impress it upon us, that we must get our freedom whenever the chance offered."[58] Delaney's mother kept alive for her children the memory, promise, and possibility of freedom. Fugitive and emancipated slave narrators remember and recall for us, not only their own experiences and suffering, but those of other enslaved women and men as well. Mary Prince explained her own commitment to their memory simply and eloquently: "In telling my own sorrows," she declared, "I cannot pass by those of my fellow-slaves—for when I think of my own griefs, I remember theirs."[59]

Linda Brent, her grandmother, Mary Prince, and Polly Berry all use language to defend themselves from sexual and physical assault and to gain psychological space and strength. *Language* was a crucial form of resistance. In these narratives, women model audacious behavior: wit, cunning, verbal warfare, and moral courage. These Black women *sass! The Random House Dictionary of the English Language* defines sass as impudent or disrespectful back talk. Enslaved Black women use sass to guard, regain, and secure self-esteem; to obtain and hold psychological distance; to speak truth; to challenge "the atmosphere of moral ambiguity that surrounds them," and, sometimes, to protect against sexual assault.[60]

Joanne Braxton explores the West African derivation of the word *sass,* noting its association "with the female aspect of the trickster." Sass comes from the bark of the poisonous West African sassy tree. Deconcocted and mixed with certain other barks, sass was used in ritual ordeals to detect witches. If the accused survives the potion, she is absolved; if not, the sass poisons, it kills. For enslaved women, sass is a ready weapon; it allows them to "return a portion of the poison the master has offered."[61] There is strong sass in the lines of a song women cutters sang in the Louisiana cane fields: "Rains come wet me/Sun come dry me/Stay back, boss man/ Don't come nigh me."[62] An emancipated slave recalls Sukie, an enslaved Black woman who used her fists and sass to protect herself from the sexual assault of a Virginia slave master. In revenge, he sells her to traders who, the narrator reports, " 'zamined her an' pinched her an' den dey open her mouf, an stuck dey fingers in to see how her teeth was. Den Sukie got awful mad, and she pult up her dress an' tole old nigger traders to look an' see if dey could fin' any teef down there."[63] Strong sass!

Linda Brent uses sass to ward off Flint's sexual and psychological attacks. When the physician mocks her marriage plans, calling her fiancé a "puppy," Brent sasses: "If he is a puppy, I am a puppy, for we are both of the negro race. . . . The man you call a puppy never insulted me." Infuriated, Flint strikes her. Brent sasses again: "You have struck me for answering you honestly. How I despise you!" "Do you know," Flint demands, "that I have a right to do as I like with you—that I can kill you, if I please?" Unbowed, Brent sasses yet again: "You have tried to kill me, and I wish you had; but you have no right to do as you like with me." At this, Flint is enraged, "By heavens, girl, you forget yourself too far! Are you mad?"[64] Indeed, sass is Linda Brent's means of physical and psychological resistance. Brent is *not* mad. Of course, thinking that Brent may be mad makes it is easier for Flint to dismiss her behavior—and salvage his ego. Rather, Brent and her sassing sisters are naming their own standards, claiming their own bodies, their own selves.

An Outline for a Theology of Suffering in Womanist Perspective

It is ironic, perhaps, that a theology of suffering is formed from resources of resistance. It is not womanist perspective that makes it so, but the Christianity of the plantation. In its teaching, theologizing, preaching, and practice, this Christianity sought to bind the slaves to their condition by inculcating caricatures of the cardinal virtues of patience, long-suffering, forebearance, love, faith, and hope. Thus, to distance itself from any form of masochism, even Christian masochism, a theology of suffering in womanist perspective must reevaluate those virtues in light of Black women's experiences. Such reevaluation engages a hermeneutic of suspicion and a hermeneutic of resistance; but that reevaluation and reinterpretation must be rooted in a critical realism that rejects both naive realism and idealism as adequate foundations for a theology of suffering.

Chattel slavery disclosed the impoverished idealism that vitiated the Gospels, left Christianity a mere shell of principles and ideals, and obviated the moral and ethical implications of slavery—for master and slave alike. Likewise, a naive biblicism is impossible: "the Bible has been the most consistent and effective book that those in power have used to restrict and censure the behavior of African American women."[65] Womanist Christian realism eschews naive biblicism, dogmatic moralism, and idealism distanced from critical knowledge of experience, of human reality—of Black women's reality. Thus, a theology of suffering in womanist perspective begins with the acknowledgment of Black women's critical cognitive practice and develops through their distinctive Christian response to suffering.

Recalling her father's stories of slavery, Ruth Shays reflected: "The mind of the man and the mind of the woman is the same. But this business of living makes women use their minds in ways that men don' even have to think about. . . . it is life that makes all these differences, not nature."[66] As a mode of critical consciousness and emancipatory struggle, Black women's critical cognitive practice is glimpsed in the earliest actuated meanings of resistance by captured and enslaved African women in North America. This practice emerged even more radically in the patterned operations of seeing, hearing, touching, smelling, tasting, inquiring, imagining, understanding, conceiving, formulating, reflecting, marshaling and weighing the evidence, judging, deliberating, evaluating, and deciding, speaking, writing. As a mode of critical self-consciousness, Black women's cognitive practice emphasizes the dialectic between oppression conscious reflection of the experience of that oppression, and activism to resist and change it. The matrix of domination is responsive to human agency: the struggle of Black women suggests that there is choice and power to act—and to do so mindfully, artfully.[67]

A theology of suffering in womanist perspective grows in the dark soil of the African-American religious tradition and is intimate with the root paradigms of African-American culture, in general, and African-American women's culture, in particular. Such a theology of suffering attends critically and carefully to the differentiated range of Black women's experiences. It holds itself accountable to Black women's self-understandings, self-judgment, and self-evaluation.

A theology of suffering in womanist perspective repels every tendency toward any *ersatz* spiritualization of evil and suffering, of pain and oppression. Such a theology of suffering seeks, on behalf of the African-American community whose lives and struggles it honors and serves, to understand and to clarify the meaning of the liberating Word and deed of God in Jesus of Nazareth for all women and men who strive against the principalities and structures, the powers and forces of evil. A theology of suffering in womanist perspective is characterized by remembering and retelling, by resisting, by redeeming.

• A theology of suffering in womanist perspective remembers and retells the lives and sufferings of those who "came through" and those who have "gone on to glory land." This remembering honors the sufferings of the ancestors, known and unknown, victims of chattel slavery and its living legacy. As Karen Holloway indicates, this "telling . . . is testimony that recenters the spirits of women, mythic and ancestral, into places where their passionate articulation assures them that neither geography nor history can separate them from the integrity of the essential Word."[68] And that "recentering" revives the living as well. Black women remember and draw strength in their own anguish from hearing and imitating the strategies adopted by their mothers, grandmothers, great-grandmothers, great-great-grandmothers to handle their suffering. These stories evoke growth and change, proper outrage and dissatisfaction, and enlarge Black women's moral horizon and choices.

- A theology of suffering in womanist perspective is *redemptive.* In their narratives, Black women invite God to partner them in the redemption of Black people. They make meaning of their suffering. Over and over again, Black women under chattel slavery endured pain, privation, and injury; risked their very lives, for the sake of the lives and freedom of their children. Praying in her garret, Linda Brent offers her suffering as part of the price of the emancipation of her children. Mattie Jackson recounts that during their escape, her mother fasted for two days, saving what food she had been able to carry away for Mattie and her sister. And, by their very suffering and privation, Black women under chattel slavery freed the cross of Christ. Their steadfast commitment honored that cross and the One who died for all and redeemed it from Christianity's vulgar misuse.
- A theology of suffering in womanist perspective is *resistant.* With motherwit, courage, sometimes their fists, and most often sass, Black women resisted the degradation of chattel slavery. Sass gave Black women a weapon of self-defense. With sass, Black women defined themselves and dismantled the images that had been used to control and demean them. With sass, Black women turned back the shame that others tried to put on them. With sass, Black women survived, even triumphed over emotional and psychic assault.

Moreover, in their resistance, Black women's suffering redefined caricatured Christian virtues. Because of the lives and suffering of Black women held in chattel slavery—the meanings of forebearance, long-suffering, patience, love, hope, and faith can never again be ideologized. Because of the rape, seduction, and concubinage of Black women under chattel slavery, chastity or virginity begs new meaning.

Harriet Jacobs' sexual liaison with Mr. Sands causes her great remorse and she experiences a loss of self-esteem. Indeed, for

Jacobs, this spiritual and existential agony shadows the remainder of her life. A theology of suffering in womanist perspective ought offer her comfort: Does not the sacrifice of her virgin body shield and preserve the virginity of her spirit and her heart? And, of what importance is a virgin body if the spirit and heart are violated, raped, crushed? And can we not hope that in the life of death, Harriet Jacobs has found "god in [her]self and loves her/loves her fiercely?"[69]

Notes

1. The title of this chapter is taken from "The Memoir of Old Elizabeth, a Coloured Woman" (1863) in *Six Women's Slave Narratives,* The Schomburg Library of Nineteenth-Century Black Women Writers, gen. ed., Henry Louis Gates, Jr. (New York: Oxford Paperbooks/Oxford University Press, 1988), 13. For some Christian theological explorations of suffering, see Ladislaus Boros, *Pain and Providence* (New York: Seabury Crossroad Press, 1966); Rosemary Haughton, *The Passionate God* (Ramsey, NJ: Paulist Press, 1981); Arthur C. McGill, *Suffering: A Test of Theological Method* (Philadelphia: Westminster Press, 1982); Dorothee Sölle, *Suffering,* trans. Everett R. Kalin (Philadelphia: Fortress Press, 1975); Simone Weil, "The Love of God and Affliction," in *Waiting for God,* trans. Emma Craufurd (1951; New York: Harper Colophon Books/Harper & Row Publishers, 1973); *Gravity and Grace,* trans. Arthur Wills (New York: G. P. Putnam's Sons, 1952).

2. Howard Thurman, *Disciplines of the Spirit* (1963; Richmond, IN: Friends United Press, 1977).

3. Ibid., 76.

4. Quoted in Mary Helen Washington, "Zora Neale Hurston: A Woman Half in Shadow," in Zora Neale Hurston, *I Love Myself When I Am Laughing . . . And Then Again When I Am Looking Mean and Impressive: A Zora Neale Hurston Reader,* ed. Alice Walker (New York: Feminist Press, 1979), 19.

5. William R. Jones, *Is God A White Racist: A Preamble to Black Theology* (Garden City, NY: Anchor Press/Doubleday, 1973), 21–22. Twenty years ago, Jones sought to provide the new emerging Black theology with what he considered to be a much needed preamble. Black theol-

ogy, Jones asserted, lacked a viable theodicy. What had Black theology to say about divine justice and vindication after centuries of chattel slavery, murder, lynching, rape, and persistent discrimination? How was Black theology to affirm a God of love, of compassion, of mercy, of care? How could Black theology operate as if the goodness of God toward all humankind were an unimpeachable theological axiom? What had Black theology to say about the maldistribution, negative quality, enormity, and transgenerational character of Black suffering? Provocatively to some and blasphemously to others, Jones asked, "Is God a white racist?" He took his title from a line in a poem written in 1906 by W. E. B. DuBois, "Litany at Atlanta," in *The Seventh Son: The Thought and Writings of W. E. B. DuBois,* vol. I, ed. Julius Lester (New York: Random House, 1971), 422–426. In frustration and anguish, DuBois exclaimed:

> *Keep not Thou Silent, O God!*
> Sit not longer blind, Lord God, deaf to our prayer and dumb
> to our dumb suffering.
> Surely Thou, too, art not white, O Lord, a
> pale bloodless, heartless thing! (425)

DuBois' work is part of an often overlooked strand in the African-American theological and literary tradition that puts God on trial because of the nature and character of Black suffering and that ridicules efforts to legitimate and rationalize that suffering on the grounds of divine intervention—future release and vindication. For some representative religious and theological examples, including those suspect of Christianity's value for the enslaved, see Nathaniel Paul, "An Address Delivered on the Celebration of the Abolition of Slavery in the State of New York, July 5, 1827," in *Negro Orators and Their Orations,* ed. Carter G. Woodson (New York: Russell and Russell, 1969); David Walker, "An Appeal" (1829) in *Walker's Appeal/Garnet's Address* (New York: Arno Press & The New York Times, 1969); Frederick Douglass, "On the Union, Religion, and the Constitution," (1847) in *Frederick Douglass: The Narrative and Selected Writings,* ed. Michael Meyer (New York: Modern Library College Editions/ Random House, 1984); Daniel A. Payne, *A Recollection of Seventy Years* (Nashville: Publishing House of the A. M. E. Sunday School Union, 1988). For some representative literary examples, see Georgia Douglas Johnson, *Bronze* (Boston: B. J. Brimmer Company, 1922), 32; Countee Cullen, *Color* (New York: Harper & Brothers, 1925), 3, 20–21, 36–41; idem., *The Black Christ* (Harper & Brothers, 1929); Nella Larsen, *Quicksand and Passing,* ed. Deborah E. McDowell (1928; New Brunswick, NJ: Rutgers

University Press, 1986), especially 109–130, 133–36; Jessie Redmond Fausett, *Plum Bun* (New York: Frederick A. Stokes Company, 1928), 308, 309; Langston Hughes, "Goodbye Christ," *Negro Worker* (November–December 1932); Benjamin E. Mays, *The Negro's God, As Reflected in His Literature* (1938; New York: Atheneum, 1969), 189–244; Zora Neale Hurston, *Dust Tracks on a Road: An Autobiography,* 2d ed., ed. Robert E. Hemenway (1942; Urbana and Chicago: University of Illinois Press, 1984), 266–279; and Alice Walker, *The Color Purple* (New York: Harcourt Brace Jovanovich, 1982), especially, 164–168.

6. For some discussions of Jewish suffering, especially the Holocaust, see Hannah Arendt, *The Origins of Totalitarianism* (London: Allen & Unwin, 1962) *Eichmann in Jerusalem: A Report on the Banality of Evil* (New York: Viking Press, 1964); George L. Mosse, *Toward the Final Solution: A History of European Racism* (London: J. M. Dent & Son, 1978); Henry Friedlander and Sybil Milton, eds., *The Holocaust: Ideology, Bureaucracy, and Genocide* (Millwood, NY: Kraus International Publications, 1980); Alex Grobman and David Landes, eds., *Genocide: Critical Issues of the Holocaust* (Los Angeles: Simon Wiesenthal Centre, 1983); Zygmunt Bauman, *Modernity and the Holocaust* (Ithaca, NY: Cornell University Press, 1989). For some discussion of the suffering of the indigenous peoples of the Americas, see Lewis Hanke, *The First Social Experiments in America: A Study in the Development of Spanish Indian Policy in the Sixteenth Century* (Cambridge, MA: Harvard University Press, 1935); Roy Harvey Pearce, *Savagism and Civilization: A Study of the Indian and the American Mind* (1953; Berkeley: University of California Press, 1988); Vine Deloria, Jr. *Custer Died for Your Sins: An Indian Manifesto* (London: The Macmillan Company/Collier-Macmillan Limited, 1969), *God is Red* (New York: Grosset & Dunlap, 1975); Francis Jennings, *The Invasion of America: Indians, Colonialism, and the Cant of Conquest* (1975; New York: W. W. Norton & Co., 1976); Octavio Paz, *One Earth, Four or Five Worlds,* trans. Helen R. Lane (1983; New York: Harcourt Brace Jovanovich, 1985).

The oppression and violence endemic to white racist supremacy has been a characteristic feature of Black life since the advent of modernity and shows little abatement in the postmodern age. In the United States, white women and men endure no such protracted, intentional, and institutionally authorized spirit numbing affliction, induced merely by their pigmentation. See David Hume, *Essays and Treatises on Several Subjects,* 2 vols. (Edinburgh, 1825), I, 521–22; Immanuel Kant, *Observations on the Feeling of the Beautiful and Sublime* [1764; ET: *Beobachtungen über das Gefühl des Schönen und Erhabenen*], trans. John T. Goldthwait (Berkeley: University of California Press, 1960), 111, 78–79; David Mermelstein, ed., *The Anti-*

Apartheid Reader: South Africa and the Struggle against White Racist Rule (New York: Grove Press, 1987); David Theo Goldberg, ed., *Anatomy of Racism* (Minneapolis, MN: University of Minnesota, 1990); Dominick Lacapra, ed., *The Bounds of Race: Perspectives on Hegemony and Resistance* (Ithaca, NY: Cornell Paperbacks/Cornell University Press, 1991).

7. "The History of Mary Prince, a West Indian Slave" (1831), and Lucy Delaney, "From the Darkness Cometh the Light or Struggles for Freedom" (ca. 1891) in Gates, ed., *Six Women's Slave Narratives.* Sources regarding autobiographical narrative and literary criticism that I have found useful in preparing this essay include Robert B. Stepto, *From Behind the Veil: A Study of Afro-American Narrative,* 2d ed. (1979; Urbana and Chicago: University of Illinois Press, 1991); Charles T. Davis and Henry Louis Gates, Jr., eds., *The Slave's Narrative* (New York: Oxford University Press, 1984); Hazel Carby, *Reconstructing Womanhood: The Emergence of the Afro-American Women Novelist* (Oxford: Oxford University Press, 1987), Joanne M. Braxton, *Black Women Writing Autobiography: A Tradition Within a Tradition* (Philadelphia: Temple University Press, 1988); and Karla F. C. Holloway, *Moorings and Metaphors: Figures of Culture and Gender in Black Women's Literature* (New Brunswick, NJ: Rutgers University Press, 1992).

8. John Sekora and Darwin T. Turner, eds., *The Art of Slave Narrative: Original Essays in Criticism and Theory* (Macomb, IL: Western Illinois University, 1982).

9. Mary Helen Washington, "Meditations on History: The Slave Woman's Voice," in her edited *Invented Lives: Narratives of Black Women, 1860–1960* (Garden City, NY: Anchor Press/Doubleday & Co., 1987), 8. Washington points up the example of Frederick Douglass—whose narratives omit information about his first wife, Anne Murray Douglass. Washington reports that Douglass' silence is countered by the testimony of his eldest daughter who reveals her mother's hand in his escape.

10. Carby, *Reconstructing Womanhood,* 36.

11. Ibid., 21.

12. Harriet Jacobs [Linda Brent], *Incidents in the Life of a Slave Girl* (1861; New York: Harcourt Brace Jovanovich, 1983).

13. Jean Fagan Yellin, "Texts and Contexts of Harriet Jacobs' *Incidents in the Life of a Slave Girl: Written by Herself,*" in Davis and Gates, eds., *The Slave's Narrative,* 263. Only within the last decade has the slave status and racial heritage of the author of *Incidents in the Life of a Slave Girl* been verified. Many interpreters and historians viewed the story as too horrific to be true. Yellin discovered a cache of letters written by

Harriet Jacobs about matters narrated in her autobiography and has been able to establish the truthfulness and substantive accuracy of her account.

14. For a definition of womanist theology, see Toinette Eugene, "Womanist Theology," in *The New Handbook of Christian Theology,* ed. Donald Musser and Joseph Price (Nashville: Abingdon Press, 1992).

15. The earliest major projects to collect and preserve the eyewitness accounts and experiences of the men and women who had been enslaved were begun in the first quarter of the twentieth century at Hampton Institute in Virginia, Southern University in Louisiana, and Fisk University in Tennessee. The Hampton Project resulted in *The Negro in Virginia,* Virginia Writers' Project (New York: Hastings House, 1940). At Southern, interviews were conducted under the direction of John B. Cade and culminated in his "Out of the Mouths of Ex-Slaves," *Journal of Negro History,* 20 (July 1935): 294–337. The two volumes of the Fisk University study have been included in George P. Rawick, ed., *The American Slave: A Composite Autobiography,* 19 vols. (1941; Westport, CT: Greenwood Publishing Co., 1972). These initial efforts to preserve the life stories of our ancestors were given focus and support with the establishment of a comprehensive program of interviews inaugurated and carried through under the auspices of the Federal Writers' Project of the Works Project Administration (WPA) during the years 1936 to 1938. This project began on the local and regional levels, and under the directorship of John Lomax, evolved into a systematic national endeavor. Approximately 2 percent of the total of emancipated African peoples in the United States in 1937 were interviewed. The Slave Narrative Collection consists of more than 10,000 pages of typescript and contains 2,000 interviews.

16. John W. Blassingame, ed., *Slave Testimony: Two Centuries of Letters, Speeches, Interviews, and Autobiographies* (1977; Baton Rouge: Louisiana State University Press, 1989), 138, 128; also, 157–158.

17. Norman R. Yetman, ed., *Voices from Slavery* (New York: Holt, Rinehart and Winston, 1970), 317.

18. Dorothy Sterling, ed., *We Are Your Sisters: Black Women in the Nineteenth Century* (New York: W. W. Norton, 1984), 25; also see Gerda Lerner, ed., *Black Women in White America: A Documentary History* (New York: Random House/Vintage Books, 1973), 45–51, 149–163; also Rawick, ed., *The American Slave,* 174–175.

19. Sterling, ed., *We Are Your Sisters,* 25, 26–31.

20. Bert James Loewenberg and Ruth Bogin, eds., *Black Women in Nineteenth-Century American Life: Their Words, Their Thoughts, Their Feelings* (University Park and London: Pennsylvania State University Press, 1976), 58.

21. Ibid.
22. Ibid.
23. "The History of Mary Prince," 13.
24. Ibid.
25. Jacobs, *Incidents in the Life of a Slave Girl,* xiii–xiv.
26. Ibid., 3.
27. Ibid.
28. Ibid., 6.
29. Ibid., 26–27.
30. Ibid., 27, 30.
31. Ibid., 41.
32. Ibid., 54–55.
33. Ibid., 55.
34. Ibid.
35. Ibid., 54, 56.
36. Ibid., 57.
37. Ibid., 79.
38. Ibid., 101, 97–151; also, Braxton, *Black Women Writing Autobiography,* 32.
39. Jacobs, *Incidents in the Life of a Slave Girl,* 124.
40. "The History of Mary Prince," 7.
41. "The Story of Mattie J. Jackson," in *Six Women's Slave Narratives,* 37.
42. "The History of Mary Prince," 7.
43. Ibid., 8, 9.
44. Weil, "The Love of God and Affliction," 119.
45. See Sölle, *Suffering,* 151–178; Weil, "The Love of God and Affliction," 117–136; Friedrich Nietzsche, "The Antichrist," in *The Portable Nietzsche,* selected and translated, with an introduction, preface, and notes by Walter Kaufmann (New York: Viking Press, 1954), 565–656.
46. Albert Raboteau, *Slave Religion: The 'Invisible Institution' in the Antebellum South* (New York: Oxford University Press, 1975), 213.
47. C. Johnson and A. P. Watson, eds., *God Struck Me Dead* (Philadelphia and New York: Pilgrim Press, 1969), vii.
48. Jacobs, *Incidents in the Life of a Slave Girl,* 77.
49. On a Roman Catholic systematic theological reading, Katie G. Cannon, in her *Black Womanist Ethics* (Atlanta, GA: Scholars Press, 1988), in fact, presents a prologomenon to a womanist ethics. In her dissertation, Cannon researches historically and concretely the social and cultural contexts in which Black women's moral agency dares emerge—thus, the conditions that provoke womanist ethics. Most importantly, Can-

non's reseach allows her to identify categories for women's expression of that agency: invisible dignity, quiet grace, and unshouted courage. See Washington, "Meditations on History," 8; Deborah Gray White, *Ar'n't I a Woman? Female Slaves in the Plantation South* (New York: W. W. Norton & Co., 1985), 119.

50. Thurman, *Deep River and the Negro Spiritual Speaks of Life and Death* (Indianapolis, IN: Friends United Press, 1975), 16.

51. James Weldon Johnson, ed., *The Book of American Negro Spirituals* (New York: Viking Press, 1925), 20. For a comprehensive discussion of the making and history of the spirituals, see John Lovell, Jr., *Black Song: The Forge and the Flame—The Story of How the Afro-American Spiritual Was Hammered Out* (1972; New York: Paragon, 1986).

52. Jacobs, *Incidents in the Life of a Slave Girl,* 135.

53. Melvin Dixon, "Singing Swords: The Literary Legacy of Slavery," in Davis and Gates, *The Slave's Narrative,* 313.

54. Renita J. Weems, "Reading Her Way through the Struggle: African-American Women and the Bible," in *Stony the Road We Trod: African American Biblical Interpretation,* ed. Cain Hope Felder (Minneapolis, MN: Fortress Press, 1991), 63.

55. Jacobs, *Incidents in the Life of a Slave Girl,* 125–126.

56. Walker, *The Color Purple,* 164.

57. Holloway, *Moorings and Metaphors,* 38.

58. Lucy Delaney, "From the Darkness Cometh the Light or Struggles for Freedom," 15–16.

59. "The History of Mary Prince," 12.

60. Braxton, *Black Women Writing Autobiography,* 30.

61. Ibid., 30, 31; see Amanda Smith, *An Autobiography: The Story of the Lord's Dealings with Mrs. Amanda Smith, the Colored Evangelist* (Chicago: Meyer and Brothers, 1893), 386–89.

62. Sterling, *We Are Your Sisters,* 26.

63. Ibid., 27.

64. Jacobs, *Incidents in the Life of a Slave Girl,* 38–39.

65. Weems, "African American Women and the Bible," 62.

66. John Langston Gwaltney, *Drylongso: A Self-Portrait of Black America* (New York: Vintage Books/Random House, 1980), 33.

67. Patricia Hill Collins, *Black Feminist Thought: Knowledge, Consciousness, and the Politics of Empowerment* (Boston: Unwin Hyman, 1990), 52.

68. Holloway, *Moorings and Metaphors,* 187.

69. Ntozake Shange, *For Colored Girls Who Have Considered Suicide/When the Rainbow Is Enuf* (New York: Macmillan, 1977), 63.

8. A Feminist Version of Respect for Persons

Margaret A. Farley

This chapter first appeared in *Journal of Feminist Studies in Religion* in 1993.

My central concern in this essay is with what I shall call *obligating-features of persons*. What is it about persons that requires respect? Does a requirement of respect for persons include enough content to tell us not only *that* we must respect one another but *what* it means to give this respect? These are questions, I believe, that are crucial for current developments in feminist ethical theory, despite some appearances to the contrary.

Concern for a ground of moral obligation may seem anachronistic and even harmful in a time when much of Western ethical theory has discredited or at least moved beyond so-called foundationalist interests. To try to locate a basis for respect for persons is reminiscent of rationalistic projects that seek to tie every moral obligation to one or two indisputable principles. To look for "features" of human persons that bind us to moral actions and attitudes is to run up against problems of essentialism, anthropocentrism, and an abstract universalism that all too easily ignores the particularity and diversity of persons in concrete contexts. Feminist ethical theorists, precisely on the basis of feminist analysis, are skeptical of sheer universalizability as a ground of moral obligation. The modern notion of what it means to be a person all too often either excludes women or makes them disappear into a "generalized other."[1] The better theoretical way may be the postmodernist rejection of the personal subject and self, a dissolution of "person" into a plurality of differences. We would look, then, not for features of personhood, but for a solidarity among fragmented, partial, separate, even oppositional, socially constructed temporary selves.

To try to identify something that is the same in all persons, male or female, whatever their diversity of history and experience, may be dangerous, but it remains nonetheless important. The risks are that we will once again lose sight of human differences, or once again devalue whatever appears as "other" in relation to our norm. We may even end up with one more theory that justifies self-interest on a grand scale, that isolates individuals in their rights to noninterference and to competition, that allows rejection of the social claims of those identified as other.[2] Or we may repeat the mistake of theorizing about persons in a way that collapses the individual into a "collective singular," an organic ideal in relation to which groups and individuals are subordinated to a developing community without regard for their own needs or demands for respect. Despite these risks, there are strong reasons why feminist ethical theory needs to engage the question of obligating-features of persons.

One such need, it seems to me, is at the heart of recent vigorous developments in feminist ethical theory. Here there has emerged a tension between freedom of choice and social determinism.[3] Contemporary feminism is ambivalent toward freedom in the sense of individual autonomy, especially if it is considered the central feature of the human personality. On the one hand, claims to autonomy have been important bulwarks in women's struggle against exploitation and oppression. Freedom of choice is valued as the capacity to fashion one's own self, and its exercise is claimed as an inalienable right in relation to bodily integrity, equality of opportunity, and so forth. But on the other hand, feminists are generally critical of individualistic notions of autonomy as the power of self-legislation and the possibility of a solely self-generated personal self. Many feminist theorists are sympathetic to social constructionist views of the self, convinced by the diversity of women's experiences to forego generalizations even about the value of self-determination. Feminists know that freedom turns up empty when abstracted from social histories and concrete, specific bonds. The theoretical tension between feminist versions of a self-determining and a socially constructed self can perhaps be resolved simply by a notion of freedom limited within historically given possibilities. Yet it remains unclear in much of current (especially postmodernist) feminist theory whether the personal self fragments into its roles, is diffused within a web of social forces, and disappears in a protean process of changing personae. Thus it is at least still worth asking about the status of autonomy as a feature of persons.

There is a second area of feminist ethical theory that illustrates the need to consider obligating-features of persons. Central to the concerns of many feminists today are questions of moral development and an emphasis on what is called an ethics of "care." The fruitful studies of Carol Gilligan, Nel Noddings, and now many others, have provided rich fare for feminist theory both in method and substance. The descriptive beginnings of these theories, however, as well as the normative debates that have followed, leave largely unexplored the underlying issues of why care should be a moral requirement or a developmental ideal. Often included in an ethics of care is a critique of the grounding of an ethics of justice in principled logic and a preference for the grounding of an ethics of care in the concrete reality of persons and relationships. Yet why persons are valuable, or why caring is a sign of moral maturity, are questions whose answers are more often assumed than examined.[4]

A third reason for feminist theory to explore obligating-features of persons lies in a troubled set of questions about the possibility or impossibility of a common or universal morality. Feminists have identified serious reasons both to reject and to promote belief in a common or universal morality.[5] The social construction of moral norms is evident in the history of women's roles and duties. Identification of inadequacies and errors in views of women's "nature," as well as the growing feminist appreciation of cultural and historical diversity among women, have yielded a deep skepticism among feminists about the universality of any moral claims. Yet the moral commitments and political agendas of many feminists make it unacceptable for them to settle for total relativity of moral norms. Thus the question of a basis for a requirement to respect persons remains an important one—especially insofar as it can help to interpret the meaning of respect across, but without indifference to, boundaries of time and culture.

The larger question of this essay might, then, be formulated in terms like these: Is there anything intrinsic to persons that inspires us to care for them, that claims our respect, that awakens our love? Is there anything inherent in persons that forbids us to reduce them to what they can do for us, that prohibits us from invading their bodies or their lives, that requires us to pay attention to their needs and their beauty? There are, of course, additional questions: Do our ethical obligations to one another rise ineluctably from our own dynamism to self-actualization? Are they lodged only in the concrete special relationships we already have? Are there only extrinsic warrants for our obligations to human persons, warrants like the command of God, or our own decision to obligate ourselves through some form of contract, or our vision of a society we are trying to create?

The larger question of love must wait for another day. So must the alternative questions about the grounds of our obligations. Here I will address only what it is about persons that requires our respect. In pursuing this question, I want to consider two "features" of persons that appear to me to require our respect. The first is autonomy, and the second is relationality.

Obligating-Features of Persons

If persons are worthy of respect, they are so as integral beings. That is, everything about human persons seems to call for our respect. What could it mean to talk of respecting persons if all we intended by that was respect for one or two features of their being? This would be abstraction, ahistorical and acultural in the extreme. Yet surely it is not every characteristic of a person that requires respect. Some aspects of persons may, in fact, call for our disrespect (as, for example, cruelty in a person's character). We may affirm other aspects but not consider ourselves bound to do so (as in the case of some idiosyncratic habit a person may have). Because personal beings are complex, some aspects of a person may conflict with other aspects, so that our very respect requires that we acknowledge a priority of one aspect over another (for example, the priority of an individual person's freedom of choice, as expressed in informed consent in a medical context, over her physical well-being).

It is persons we are obligated to respect, not features. Yet if there are intrinsic grounds for this obligation, there must be something *about* persons that claims our respect and tells us what respect must mean. It is according to features, aspects, of persons that we can both establish a general principle of respect for persons and specify its content. The first candidate for such a feature is the one identified by Kant, namely, autonomy.

Autonomy

However maligned Kant's principle of respect for persons has become, and whatever the shortcomings of his focus on rationality and autonomy, Kant's theory stands as a powerful and in many ways still persuasive effort to identify an obligating-feature of persons. Its continuing importance for feminist theory is, of course, under suspicion, and yet it deserves reconsideration. As we have already noted, an early conviction of contemporary feminism was that at the heart of what is good for women is autonomy, or the freedom of self-determination. Because autonomy belongs to women as personal beings with the capacity to determine the ultimate meaning of their own lives, they make claims for respect as persons, valuable in themselves and not only as instruments in the service of the family or community or the human species or men.

Kant argued that every human being is absolutely valuable as an end in itself.[6] Persons are ends in a radical sense (not simply the last in a series of means) because they are autonomous. They are autonomous because of their rationality—more specifically, because of their capacity to recognize in and by themselves what counts as a moral obligation and to resolve to act in accordance with it or not. Autonomy is, therefore, that feature of persons whereby they are not solely determined in their actions by causes external to their own reason and will, not even by their own desires and inclinations. Negatively free (undetermined, uncoerced) in this sense, persons can recognize their own law (reason "legislates" for itself); they are thereby also positively free (self-governing) to determine the meaning of their own lives in an ultimate (moral) sense. This is the basis of human dignity.[7]

The moral response appropriate to and required by this radical personal dignity or worth, is respect. To respect persons as ends in themselves is to *relate* to them as valuable in themselves, not just valuable for me; to *treat* them as absolutely valuable, not just conditionally and contingently valuable. To be an end in oneself is, as Kant put it, to have no market price—to be "not for sale," because nothing else can be of equivalent value; nothing can substitute for a human person whose dignity is of "unconditioned and incomparable worth," whose value is permanent and nonreplaceable.[8] Hence, Kant's famous formula: "Act in such a way that you always treat humanity, whether in your own person or in the person of any other, never simply as a means, but always at the same time as an end."[9] That is, persons are not ever to be used as mere means to other persons' ends; no one is to be wholly subordinated to another's agenda. Individuals and groups are not to achieve their purposes at the expense of other persons' basic needs and purposes. Each and every person is to be respected, whatever their achievements, roles, moral integrity, or any other aspect of their being.

Feminist dissatisfaction with Kant's grounding of human dignity in rationality and freedom echoes the criticisms made by Hegel and Marx, Nietzsche and Lacan, Habermas and Foucault, MacIntyre and Sandel. The problems of Kantian autonomy begin with the disembodied self that it represents. Here, seemingly, is a freedom that needs no social context, no affective ties, no history of desire. Here is a rational freedom that opposes duty to inclination and remains deaf to claims from anything but its own logic. The charges are formalism, indifference to human vulnerability, the delusion of a self-generating self. Finally, insist some feminist theorists, the Kantian self is a model of domination; its task and its goal are self-repression within and mastery of all that is without.[10]

But it may be possible to retain Kant's intuition regarding a capacity for self-determination and a human claim for respect without at the same time adopting Kant's pessimistic view of affectivity, and without following some Kantians into a morality of principles apart from persons and communities. Like most of Kant's critics, feminists may affirm the significance of individual agency and the dignity of individual persons while insisting on a more integrated and more social view of the human self. The first sign that this is possible lies in a fuller reading of Kant himself. Autonomy need not be completely over against affectivity, given Kant's description of the experience of the law;[11] autonomy is not fulfilled in Hobbesian self-protectiveness, but in a "kingdom of ends";[12] human dignity translates into equality, with respect inclusive of the self as well as others, adversaries as well as friends;[13] there are positive duties to persons as well as negative, duties of caring as well as of noninterference;[14] for all of the abstraction from history and from concrete relations, Kant's turn to the self-effects (or can) at the same time a turn to others, in sameness but also in embodied diversity.[15]

Kant's notion of autonomy may be useful, even necessary, for a feminist principle of respect for persons, but it is nonetheless inadequate. Its problems remain multiple, impossible to address here. We can, however, pursue one line of thought suggested by Kant's critics, a line which will allow us to hold on to freedom while exploring its context and its purpose. To do that, we need to examine a second candidate for an obligating-feature of persons: relationality. For feminist theory, relationality is as primordial as is autonomy, though it may be as problematic as well.

Relationality

The relation of human persons to one another is not a new preoccupation in Western philosophy and theology, nor is it particular to feminist theory. Aristotle argued that the human individual is "by nature a social and political being."[16] For Augustine, "there is nothing so social by nature" as human beings (though they are political only as a remedy for sin).[17] Even Kant thought that the goal of the moral life included community.[18] Hegel, Feuerbach, and Marx attempted to show the dependency of the person on the "other" for her or his own personhood, the capacity (and need) for community as structurally fundamental to the person. In the twentieth century there is a persistent concentration on the person as interpersonal and social. It is generally acknowledged that individuals do not just survive or thrive in relation to others; they cannot exist as human persons without some form of fundamental relatedness to others. George Herbert Mead articulated a theory of the social self which critics describe as submerging the individual so completely in the social that identity is lost. Martin Buber turned dramatic attention to the dialogue at the heart of human reality (and strongly influenced the theologies of, for example, H. Richard Niebuhr and Karl Barth). Contemporary communitarianism (as represented in the work of Alasdair MacIntyre, Michael Sandel, Robert Bellah, Stanley Hauerwas, and others) has different interests than continental social ontology or philosophies of dialogue, but it aims no less to place an otherwise autonomous self in the context of relationships.

Among feminists, relationality and community are central personal and political concerns.[19] But, as Marilyn Friedman warns, "communitarian philosophy as a whole is a perilous ally for feminists."[20] Feminist theorists cite a number of reasons for this caution. First, to give traditional communities and relationships normative weight is to risk perpetuating the tyranny of unchosen roles, patterns of domination and subordination, and overall normative complacency regarding the inhumanity of individuals and groups in relation to one another.[21] Second, communitarian ideals (as they are articulated today) may be essentially exclusionary. As Iris Young argues, in privileging unity over difference, the ideal of community both excludes those who are different and suppresses the differences of those who are considered the same.[22] Third, if an emphasis on autonomy leads to a devaluing of the "other," an uncritical focus on community may do nothing to correct this or redeem it.[23] Everything will depend on the kind of relationships one finds or creates and the way in which one participates in them. Feminist ethics needs an understanding of relationality that will yield a *normative* theory of community.

Once again we have a set of questions too numerous and complex to address here. But our central question remains: What are the obligating-features of persons? And now: How is relationality, along with autonomy, to be understood as an obligating-feature of persons, and can we find in it some clues for an ethic that will guide human relationships?

The philosophy of Jean-Paul Sartre is in many ways a strange place to look for insight into the moral significance of relationality.

Few thinkers have been so negative in interpreting interpersonal relations. Few, however, have taken them more seriously. Building on Hegel and Heidegger, on Husserl and finally on Marx, Sartre offered a systematic and original description and appraisal of being-for-others, of sociality or relationality. What is particularly to the point in our explorations is that Sartre was as concerned about autonomy as he was about relationality. In a way, the line from Kant to Sartre is clear and direct.[24] Despite Sartre's interest in relationality, he probably represents an extreme development of the potential in Kant's theory for an atomistic, isolated, competitive individual freedom. And despite Sartre's commitment to autonomy, he finally shows us how destructive relationships can be if they are completely without ethical anchoring. Sartre's philosophy, then, may serve heuristically to help us sort out the relationship between autonomy and relationality, not because he offers us an adequate view of this relationship but because he shows us unwittingly what is at stake if we cannot find a more integrative way. To examine Sartre's analysis is also to remember the profound influence he had on Simone de Beauvoir, and perhaps to understand why her own theory was both a remarkable contribution to feminism and yet has been criticized and even rejected by so many feminists.[25] The problems it incorporated from Sartre may not yet, however, be fully resolved.

For Jean-Paul Sartre, as for Kant, the autonomy of the individual is of central importance.[26] Consciousness functions in Sartre's theory in many ways like rationality in Kant's. Like rationality, consciousness makes the difference between being a person or a thing. Because of consciousness, a person is negatively undetermined and positively self-determining, radically free. Unlike Kantian reason, however, Sartrian consciousness is not so closed in on itself, generating only its own ideas, recognizing the power only of its own law. Indeed, consciousness is born as freedom only when it encounters another person (another consciousness) in the world. In Sartre's view, things that are not conscious exist in the world as passive objects, to be given meaning, used, transformed, "worked" by the freedom of the person. Conscious beings (other persons) are, however, encountered not as passive objects but as centers of freedom, centers of power. Each person, with her freedom, organizes the world into a system of meaning according to her own chosen ends. The encounter with an other threatens this world; for here is another system of meaning, another set of ends. Two worlds of meaning do not simply exist side by side; they encroach on one another, for it is the very construal of one person's world that can be given a different meaning by another person.

Sartre's telling example is familiar by now even to those who have never read him.[27] Human relations are like this: I am outside a door, listening, perhaps peering through a keyhole. I hear footsteps behind me, and I feel the eyes of another on me. However I have understood my own action (whatever meaning I have given it until now), the other who approaches will give it a different meaning. Even if I am responding to the request of someone on the other side of the door to test what can be heard or seen through the keyhole (in which case I believe it is quite reasonable for me to be peering through it), I feel profoundly threatened, "unjustified," by the suspicious stare of the other who comes upon me from behind and who now interprets my action and passes judgment on me as a keyhole-peeper. No longer can I simply determine my own meaning for my actions; someone else threatens psychologically to imprison me, to take away my freedom by imposing a judgment on me, by locking my action and thereby my self into a meaning that is not mine.

According to Sartre, it is only in and through my encounter with another person that I become reflectively conscious and therefore truly free. In concrete relation, autonomy is born. Only through an other do I become a person. But the person-becoming encounter is of a particular kind: My awareness of my capacity and my need to determine myself (through determining my action and meaning) is awakened when my freedom to do so is threatened. It is in experiencing myself being made into an object that I come to know myself as a subject. The most fundamental of human relations, then, are relations of conflict.

So potentially devastating is the block to my freedom in every suspicious stare from an other that it is necessary for me to respond. The threat of objectification is unbearable. I have two options, says Sartre. I can either overpower the gaze of the other, or I can submit to it so fully, absorb it so completely, that I no longer see it. I do the first by psychologically (or even physically) striking out at the other's eyes, overwhelming the other's judgment, taking away the other's meaning. My freedom prevails. I do the second by choosing to objectify myself in the same way that the other has objectified me. This I can do by, for example, identifying myself with a role, deceiving myself into believing that the whole meaning of my self is exhausted in this part that I play, the part that is expected of me. The power of the other's gaze prevails.

For Sartre, it is of the utmost theoretical importance that persons are encountered as embodied beings; it is as body that the individual receives the other's stare. Hence, the paradigm of human relations is to be found in the sexual sphere.[28] Sexuality represents the most basically structured attempt to overcome the subjectivity and freedom of the other. The two fundamental responses to the suspicious state are sadism or masochism. I can try to manipulate the other's suspicious gaze by seduction (attempting to change it into the appraisal I want); failing this, I can turn upon the gaze, making the other my object, subduing the other even through violence and pain. This is the sadistic response. Alternatively, I can let myself be lost in my desire so fully that I am lost in myself, masochistically absorbed by the other (even though I know that the other does not see me as I am), so completely given over to the other that I no longer have to endure the other's gaze. In a conflict of freedoms, I move to suppress the consciousness of the other or to hide from the consciousness of myself.

We have in Sartre's theory a picture of human absurdity. Autonomy and relationality are both fundamental to persons, yet they finally cancel each other out in a futile effort to achieve personal identity. Autonomy needs relationships in order to be actualized; yet in relationships freedom must either crush the autonomy of the other or surrender the autonomy of the self. In either case the relationship is finally destroyed, and autonomy is compromised or at least remains alone, perpetually yearning for itself in an impossible struggle or dream.

The critical question for feminist theory is not whether Sartre has accurately described a large part of human experience, but whether autonomy is inescapably hostile to any but instrumental relationships. We know Kant's answer to such a question: Autonomy requires respect for persons; it requires and makes possible relationships that are more than instrumental. For Sartre, the other is always only the other for me. Freedom's value is only *my* freedom's value. I am not required to treat anyone else as an end; I am compelled to treat everyone else as a means.[29] How, if Sartre is in any way in the tradition of Kant, can he have retained autonomy but lost respect for the other?

In the view of many feminists, the problem lies not only with Sartre but also with Kant. As Nancy Hartsock has put it (though not speaking specifically of Kant), "the philosophical and historical creation of a devalued 'Other' was the necessary precondition for the creation of the transcendental rational subject outside of time and space."[30] Why? Kant's concern for respect for persons was not sufficient to counter the stronger drift of the whole Enlightenment toward the self-defining agent. Moreover, concrete differences in individuals and groups were always "other" to the agent who controlled not only action but meaning. Rationality was never as pure and impartial as it claimed to be, and the myth of incorporating all moral concerns under one perspective has in fact generated exclusion and conflict as much or more than inclusion and harmony of interests. From Kant to Sartre is not as long a way as it seems nor as circuitous.

But can autonomy still require respect for all persons, and can it be correlated with a notion of relationality that requires respect for differences among persons? Can obligating-features of persons call us to move beyond conflict to care, and within care, to justice that is both personal and political?

Respect Revisited

The Value of Persons

Whatever the variations in feminist theory, feminism as a movement has generally presupposed and even been grounded in the conviction that persons are of unconditional value. Insofar as caring for others has been part of women's lives, it has been perceived by women as a commitment to the incomparable worth of those for whom they care. This commitment is renewed when feminists claim the importance of caring and argue for active participation in it not only by women but by men. Feminist critiques of women's caring call into question not the value of persons or the good of care but the social construction of women as caregivers—their sometime adoption of an identity under the historical pressure of gendered power, expectations, and roles.[31] this critique in turn is part of the central claim of feminists that women themselves are of unconditional value, as persons and as women-persons. The buying and selling of women, by whatever cultural disguise, violates the dignity of women who are all ends in themselves.

It is important, then, to keep trying to articulate the unconditional value of persons. If persons are to be valued as ends in themselves, there must be a way to avoid abstracting from their histories and their present needs. If relationships among persons are to incorporate respect, there must be a way to address otherness without devaluing whoever is the other. We must at least try to correct for the kind of theoretical difficulties we have seen in Sartre and Kant.

Persons are ends in themselves because in some way they both transcend themselves and yet belong to themselves. They transcend themselves because their meaning is inexhaustible; they are more than anyone's judgment of them, more than their past and their present, more than the causes that have shaped them, more than the context that allows them to be what they are. In the midst of all the givens of their lives, persons can introduce something new, whether in meaning or action. They alone can take their stance in relation to what happens to them, what they have done, what they will do or commit themselves to do. They can, in a sense, determine the center of themselves and the direction they will take. Because they are capable of this, persons also belong to themselves; their selves and their actions are in some sense their own.

Yet persons, as we know them, do not exist in the world by themselves. No one today would argue that persons are as autonomous as either Kant or Sartre thought they were. To be self-transcendent and self-possessing is neither to be, nor to be inside, a vacuum. Persons are in the world, and the world is in them. They are in society, and society is in them. They are in biological, psychological, cultural history, and their history is in them like the rings of a tree. We are who we are within social, cultural, linguistic contexts, formed in our understandings and our desires. We do not produce our own meaning out of nothing, nor are our actions wholly our own. We take our stance, but who knows what causal forces, or what moral luck, make any stance possible? Thus, if we are free, if we are autonomous, it is not in spite of our world but because we are capable of interaction with our world. In hearing and receiving, knowing and loving, speaking and doing, surrendering and resisting, we become ourselves—able (always more or less) to understand our desires, express our intentions, organize our plans, and reveal our loves.

By freedom, but not only by freedom, persons are both self-transcendent and self-possessing; they are so also by knowledge and love. These are not separable capacities, but mutually qualifying ways of existing—of being and relating. Persons are ends in themselves not only because they can freely determine themselves but because they can know and be known, love and be loved, as both embodied and free. By knowledge, love, and freedom, persons transcend themselves even as they possess themselves. Paradoxically, persons who are terminal centers of life are capable of being centered beyond themselves, finding their home in what they love. The capacity of persons to love one another and the world, and (as theologians and philosophers of religion must surely add) their capacity to love and to love freely what is sacredly transcendent and immanent, makes them worthy of respect.[32]

How can we know that any of this is true, that is more than rhetorical assertion? And even if it makes sense as a characterization of persons, why should any of it create in us an experience of moral obligation? How can persons, ends in themselves, claim respect? Kant had reasons for insisting on autonomy as a central feature of persons, but he did not think it admitted of a priori demonstration. Relationality may equally defy demonstration as an obligating-feature of persons. Reasons can be given (as I am trying to give), and descriptions can be offered. But the claim itself may have to be experienced. Kant noted that "two things fill the mind with ever new and increasing admiration and awe, the oftener and more steadily we reflect on them: the starry heavens above me and the moral law within me. I do not merely conjecture them and seek them as though obscured in darkness or in the transcendent region beyond my horizon: I see them before me, and I associate them directly with the consciousness of my own existence."[33] If Kant had to contemplate the moral law, feminists may have to do no less; only now it is not only a law but concrete persons that must be seen.

Freedom in Relation

We need a way of interpreting autonomy not as sheer self-dependence but as a response to what we already and to what has become possible for us in terms of where we are.[34] In other words, we need an understanding of autonomy as situated. Here, perhaps, is a way to begin: Freedom is not opposed to desire (as Kant thought it was), but desire is not in the first instance free.[35] Shaped as we are in the fabric of our lives, our desires rise not from our free choice but out of what we already are—including our needs and loves, fears and hopes, deprivations and fulfillments. These desires, rising unbidden, nonetheless present themselves to our freedom. Our desires mediate for us the options of freedom. For whenever we are confronted with alternative possible actions, these actions become viable choices only if we desire them in some way.

But desires have not only a history; they arise not only out of the past that has generated our present selves. Here and now desires rise out of some deeper affective response; they rise out of our loves. Loves, too, have a history, and they rise unbidden by our choice. But, like the desires that express them, loves present themselves to our freedom. Every action that we choose is for the sake of some love, whether for ourselves or for another, whether for persons or for things. When we choose our actions, we ratify, identify with, some of our loves (deferring, or refusing to ratify, other loves that are thereby not expressed in action). And the same is true for the desires that come from our loves; we affirm some and refuse to affirm others, letting the ones we affirm issue in action or commitment to action.

Freedom, then, is possible not in spite of our loves and desires, but because of them—because they express who we are and present what can be chosen, because they do not always compel us to remain as we are. Becoming truly one with our loves, and in that process shaping them—sustaining or changing, strengthening or weakening, integrating or fragmenting—that is the possibility and the task of our freedom. Freedom, then, rises out of relationality and serves it. Freedom is for the sake of relationship—with ourselves and with all that can be known and loved.

But what are the possibilities for our love, the possible forms of our relationships? In particular, what are the possibilities of our relating with other persons? Can freedom find and shape relationships whose core is not conflict, whose pattern is not dominance and subordination, whose goal is not exclusion of some for the sake of being included with others?

It is true, as Sartre suggests, that some of our experiences of others are experiences of being threatened; that we seek self-justification whether by mastery or by submission; that we are likely to project on those who are different from us what we ourselves lack (not-I) or fear (passion) or do not understand (the "mysterious") or need (the complement or the narcissistic mirror).

But these are not the only possibilities for relating to others. However serious is the threat of absurdity and tragedy among us, there are multiple testimonies to the experience of shared struggle and the achievement of mutual understanding; and there are continuing proposals for theories that will sustain liberating praxis.[36] An obligation to respect persons requires that we honor their freedom and respond to their needs, that we value difference as well as sameness, that we attend to the concrete realities of our own and others' lives (reminded, if need be, by the power of the most deeply embedded universal). We *can* risk considering seriously the meaning the other gives to the world; building communities of support that have openness to the other at the center of their strength; surrendering our tendencies to omniscience without surrendering to despair; learning the particular content of just and fitting care. In a feminist ethic, respect for persons is both an obligating and a liberating call.

Notes

1. See the carefully nuanced treatment of this concept provided by Seyla Benhabib, "The Generalized and the Concrete Other," in *Feminism as Critique: On the Politics of Gender,* ed. Seyla Benhabib and Drucilla Cornell (Minneapolis: University of Minnesota Press, 1987), 77–95.

2. A helpful addition to the growing literature on these problems is the collection of essays in George Levine, ed., *Constructions of the Self* (New Brunswick: Rutgers University Press, 1992), esp. Agnes Heller, "Death of the Subject?"

3. For an example of the debate on this issue, see Diana T. Meyers, "Personal Autonomy or the Deconstructed Subject: A Reply to Hekman," *Hypatia* 7 (1992): 124–32.

4. A beginning effort to probe these assumptions can be found in Robin S. Dillon, "Care and Respect," in *Explorations in Feminist Ethics: Theory and Practice,* ed. Eve Browning Cole and Susan Coultrap-McQuin (Bloomington: Indiana University Press, 1992), 69–81.

5. See my discussion of this issue in "Feminism and Universal Morality," in *Prospects for a Common Morality,* ed. Gene Outka and John Reeder (Princeton: Princeton University Press, 1992), 170–90.

6. Immanuel Kant, *Groundwork of the Metaphysic of Morals,* trans. H. J. Paton (New York: Harper & Row, 1964), 95–96, 102–103 [427–29, 434–36]. "Absolute" here means unconditional, nor necessarily "unrelated," for example, to God. For the difficulties in interpreting what Kant is saying in this and similar passages, see George Schrader, "Autonomy, Heteronomy, and Moral Imperatives," *Journal of Philosophy* 60 (1963): 65–77; Thomas E. Hill, Jr., "Humanity as an End in Itself," *Ethics* 91 (1980): 84–99; P. C. Lo, *Treating Persons as Ends* (Lanham, Md.: University Press of America, 1987), chaps. 3–4.

7. Kant, *Groundwork,* 102, 103, 107 [435–6, 440].

8. Kant, *The Doctrine of Virtue,* part 2, *The Metaphysics of Morals,* trans. Mary J. Gregor (New York: Harper & Row, 1964), 101 [436].

9. *Groundwork,* 96 [429].

10. See, e.g., Seyla Benhabib, *Critique, Norm, and Utopia: A Study of the Foundations of Critical Theory* (New York: Columbia University Press, 1986), 187; Luce Irigaray, "Any Theory of the 'Subject' Has Always Been Appropriated by the 'Masculine,' " in *Speculum of the Other Woman,* trans. Gillian C. Gill (Ithaca, N.Y.: Cornell University Press, 1985) 133–46; Judith Butler, "Gender Trouble, Feminist Theory, and Psychoanalytic Discourse," in *Feminism/Postmodernism,* ed. Linda J. Nicholson (New York: Routledge, 1990), 324–40.

11. See, e.g., Kant, *Critique of Practical Reasons,* trans. Lewis White Beck (New York Liberal Arts Press, 1956), 161 [158].

12. *Groundwork,* 101–102 [433–35].

13. See the formulation in *Groundwork,* 96 [429].

14. *Doctrine of Virtue,* 44–47 [385–88]; *Groundwork,* 96–98 [429–30].

15. In the *Doctrine of Virtue* [429] Kant takes up briefly the issue of particularities in individuals (such as age, health, sex, wealth, etc.). While they do not of themselves ground a requirement of respect, there is a need, Kant says, to take them into account in the application of ethical duty. This is hardly sufficient to provide the full ethical approach needed in a feminist ethic, but it may at least not finally oppose it.

16. Aristotle, *Nicomachean Ethics* 1097b10–11. For an interesting perspective on this in the context of contemporary ethical concerns, see Martha Nussbaum, "Aristotelian Social Democracy," in *Liberalism and the Good,* ed. R. Bruce Douglass, et.al. (New York: Routledge, 1990), 203–52.

17. Augustine, *City of God* 12.28.

18. For example, see Kant, *Religion Within the Limits of Reason Alone,* trans. Theodore M. Greene and Hoyt H. Hudson (New York: Harper & Row, 1960), 85, 88.

19. Beverly Wildung Harrison identifies this as one of the methodological "basepoints" for feminist ethics in *Our Right to Choose: Toward a New Ethic of Abortion* (Boston: Beacon Press, 1983), 15ff. Important discussions range across disciplines, as for example, Carol Gilligan, *In a Different Voice* (Cambridge: Harvard University Press, 1982); Nel Noddings, *Caring: A Feminine Approach to Ethics* (Berkeley: University of California Press, 1984); Isabel Carter Heyward, *The Redemption of God: A Theology of Mutual Relation* (Lanham, Md.: University Press of America, 1982); Iris Marion Young, *Justice and the Politics of Difference* (Princeton: Princeton University Press, 1990).

20. Marilyn Friedman, "Feminism and Modern Friendship: Dislocating the Community," in *Explorations in Feminist Ethics,* 89.

21. See Friedman, "Feminism and Modern Friendship," 89. See also Rita Manning, "Just Caring," in *Explorations in Feminist Ethics,* 45–54; Margaret Farley, "Feminism and Universal Morality."

22. Young, *Justice and the Politics of Difference,* 12.

23. Nancy Hartsock, "Foucault on Power: A Theory for Women?" in *Feminism/Postmodernism,* 157–75. Part of Hartsock's point in this essay is that an alternative view of the world is needed.

24. The line is interestingly and persuasively drawn in Frederick A.

Olafson, *Principles and Persons: An Ethical Interpretation of Existentialism* (Baltimore: Johns Hopkins Press, 1967).

25. Simone de Beauvoir insisted throughout most of her professional life that she wore "the mantle of disciple and chief spokesperson for Sartre's philosophy." See Deirdre Bair, *Simone de Beauvoir: A Biography* (New York: Summit Books, 1990), 307; also 269. Most starkly relevant here are de Beauvoir's incorporation of a radical notion of freedom in her overall philosophy and her development of women as "other" in *The Second Sex,* trans. H. M. Parshley (New York: Vintage Books, 1952), esp. chap. 6.

26. Here I will draw almost exclusively on Sartre's early thought as articulated in *Being and Nothingness.* It is debatable whether he ever significantly departed from the particular ideas I am examining. Simone de Beauvoir thought he did, apparently, and she resisted this. See Bair, *Simone de Beauvoir,* 446, 516, 580. Other scholars disagree. Michael Theunissen, for example, argues that "Nothing has been altered in the *Critique* with respect to the leading thesis of *Being and Nothingness,* in accordance with which the interhuman relation is primarily a subject-object relationship. Correspondingly, Sartre further affirms that the original intersubjective situation is 'conflict' which can turn into acute 'warfare.' " See Theunissen, *The Other: Studies in the Social Ontology of Husserl, Heidegger, Sartre, and Buber,* trans. C. Macann (Cambridge: MIT Press, 1984), 246. There is a difference, however, in that interhuman conflict becomes no longer a matter of ontological structures but, rather, historical conditions of scarcity. An inchoate treatment of nonconflictual human relations can be found in Sartre's posthumously published *Notebooks for An Ethics,* trans. David Pellauer (Chicago: University of Chicago Press, 1992), esp. 274–94, 368–76, 496–500.

27. Jean-Paul Sartre, *Being and Nothingness,* trans. Hazel E. Barnes (New York: Washington Square Press, 1966), 348–49.

28. Sartre, *Being and Nothingness,* 471–556.

29. "In so far as my project is a transcendence of the present towards the future, and of myself toward the world, I always treat myself as a means and cannot treat the Other as an end." Sartre, *Critique of Dialectical Reason,* trans. Alan Sheridan-Smith (London: NLB, 1976), 112. Both self and other are Hobbesian, and later, Marxian, means.

30. Hartsock, "Foucault on Power," 160.

31. Catherine MacKinnon offers this caution: "Women are said to value care. Perhaps women value care because men have valued women according to the care they give. Women are said to think in relational terms. Perhaps women think in relational terms because women's social

existence is defined in relation to men." See *Toward A Feminist Theory of the State* (Cambridge: Harvard University Press, 1989), 51. For a similar suggestion regarding women's interpretation of their experience in general, see Joan W. Scott, "The Evidence of Experience," *Critical Inquiry* 17 (1991): 773–97.

32. Basil Mitchell maintains, for example, that it is human persons' "capacity to love one another and to love God, rather than their powers of self-legislation" that makes them "proper objects of respect." See *Morality: Religious and Secular* (Oxford: Clarendon Press, 1980), 134. This may be an important place to add a clarification about the limits of this essay. While my focus is on an ethical obligation to respect persons, I do not thereby in any way want to imply that we have no obligation to love God/dess or that we have no obligation to respect and to love beings that are not perceived as persons. Both of these dimensions of a feminist ethic need to be dealt with, though not here.

33. Kant, *Critique of Practical Reason,* 161–62 [158–59].

34. Charles Taylor concludes his remarkable analysis of the trends in modern philosophy with the observation that Hegel's criticism of the autonomous self was a harbinger of the contemporary attempt "to situate subjectivity, by relating it to our life as embodied and social beings, without reducing it to a function of objectified nature." Hegel did not and cannot do it for us, but the task seems clear. See *Hegel and Modern Society* (Cambridge: Cambridge University Press, 1970), 167–69.

35. For a fuller (though still only in sketch form) description of freedom of this sort, see my *Personal Commitments: Beginning, Keeping, Changing* (San Francisco: Harper & Row, 1986), chap. 3.

36. Examples of such theories from a feminist perspective can be found in the work of bell hooks, Seyla Benhabib, Iris Marion Young, and many others. What is particularly helpful is the effort to find a theory that will address both interpersonal and political relations. The problem of otherness in the area of religious pluralism is creatively treated by David Tracy in *Dialogue With the Other: The Inter-Religious Dialogue* (Grand Rapids, Mich.: William B. Eerdmans Publishing Co., 1990). This work has important implications for a general theory about human differences.

9. Feminist Ethics, Differences, and Common Ground: A Catholic Perspective[1]

Lisa Sowle Cahill

This chapter is a revised version of a Presidential Address, which first appeared in *Catholic Theological Society of America Proceedings* in 1993.

Introduction

Feminist theology is thoroughly particular and historical: its beginning point is the experience of women, and that experience is diverse. The increasing variety of feminist theologies emerging in North America and around the globe displays feminism's multiple practical and political concerns.[2] Many feminists rightly hold us accountable to the *differences* among women's situations worldwide.[3] This is an important task, one indispensable to the creativity of feminism. Despite an initial blind spot in middle-class feminism, and fairly persistent backsliding, most feminists do now recognize that it is important not to assimilate all women too quickly to a paradigm of "woman's experience." The experience of privileged, educated women, those with a voice in politics or the academy, should not merely be projected onto the lives of other women who differ by class, race, ethnicity, or even historical era.

Yet, for all its concreteness and plurality, feminist ethics issues a universal moral imperative: Justice for women! The particularity of feminism is complemented by its global mandate. Feminist theology and ethics are committed to equal personal dignity, equal mutual respect, and equal social power for women and men. This does not mean that men and women are identical; it does assume that biological sex differences between them are compatible with social equality and vocations to similar social roles. Men's and women's roles will not be structured justly if they are premised on hierarchy of the sexes, or on the allocation of public roles to one sex, and domestic roles to the other, with a resulting gender-specific separation of spheres. Women's basic needs are the same as those of men; women's potential contributions to the common good are similar to those of men; therefore women's full social participation is as important as that of men; and women's basic human rights are the same also.

Ethics is not just inclusiveness, open dialogue, understanding, taking on other mindsets as an experimental second language, or even a "fusion of horizons" understood as mutual transformation. Ethics in practice is not afraid to be critical, judgmental, persuasive, interventionist, and even coercive. We do in fact, especially as feminists (or as liberation theologians), suppose that we can judge certain practices, institutions, and acts as wrong—for instance, rape, domestic violence, killing or neglect of female children as female, denial of basic health care or education on the basis of sex. We are confident that we should and can work to improve women's situations across cultures. We presume in this process that talk about basic goods and evils is possible, intelligible, and necessary across cultural boundaries and among moral traditions.[4]

Feminist ethics is inherently particular in its origins; but it is universal in its agenda. Feminist ethics begins with the particular, with practice, with experience, with the situation—but out of the particular (not over against it) feminists recognize what furthers or damages "full humanity" for women and men. I want to affirm the particularity of feminist theologies and accept the postmodern critique of abstract definitions of women's and men's natures, while still establishing some intercultural common ground on which to make moral claims. In this essay, I am particularly concerned with women's well-being, social participation, and contributions to the common good.

I will first take up the "postmodern" interpretation of the challenge of cultures. The postmodern insistence on difference is generally accompanied by social and ethical resistance to "domination." Yet practical resistance is difficult to justify theoretically unless one can identify some criteria of what counts as domination or liberation. Although postmodern philosophy's attack on "modern" models of rationality, knowledge, and moral judgment is cogent, it is neither theoretically necessary nor practically prudent to abandon wholesale objectivity and universality as foundations of ethics.[5] Thus, I will reconsider some Aristotelian-Thomistic approaches to moral thinking, especially in light of their reliance on shared basic dimensions of experience and on practical reason. Finally, I find the work of Martha Nussbaum useful in advancing this project, but I will show ways in which Catholic theological feminism qualifies her insights.

I. The Challenge of Cultures in Postmodern Perspective

The 1991 film *No Longer Silent,*[6] documents the struggles of the women of New Delhi to gain better treatment in a culture which subordinates their interests in virtually every sphere to those of men. Even certain protections guaranteed by the Indian constitution are not respected in fact. The outlawed dowry custom is often used as a means of extorting money from a married woman's kin. One figure the film follows is a mother persistently hammering at a bureacratic and sexist legal system to prosecute a son-in-law who burned her pregnant daughter and left her body in his courtyard—because the mother and her husband could not afford to up the dowry ante with the purchase of a motorscooter.

The narrator of *No Longer Silent* is an Indian feminist and organizer of rural women. She notes that among the poor, women are the most poor; among the exploited, the most exploited. Yet women in the audience of a feminist street play smile or titter cautiously as the male character exhorts women, in the name of tradition and religion, to be faithful to their duties to cook, clean, carry wood, raise children, *always in silence,* always within "the lines men have drawn for women." Comments the narrator, "we can laugh at our pain. We can reflect on our own situation and maybe some women who see it will start to work together to change things." The film is produced by Indian women and portrays Indian women and men, both educated and rural, working together to re-create their own cultural traditions. As a visual and spoken medium, rich with the sensible texture of Indian women's lives, the *No Longer Silent* is effective in moving the Western viewer closer to its subjects' worldview. Finally, however, can we claim or expect to have reached a common moral understanding?

In *Remembering Esperanza,* Mark Kline Taylor eloquently stresses the elusiveness of any "universal" perspective. He lists three postmodern traits of theology whose appeal lies precisely in their ability to shatter the arrogance of false claims about moral sameness. Postmodern theology, according to Kline Taylor, values a sense of tradition, celebrates plurality, and consequently resists domination or oppression as "the systemic exercise of authority and power and in burdensome, cruel, and unjust manner."[7] The acknowledgment of tradition also functions to delegitimize any authority's claim to freedom from location or context. This quality of postmodern theology can sponsor resistance to domination, a task which Kline Taylor finds crucial to biblical Christian identity. Surely Mark Kline Taylor represents many other contemporary theologians when he states that the impact of postmodernism's relativizing and pluralist consciousness (especially obvious he believes in feminist critiques of gender difference) can be summarized by saying that "theologians must now, like their colleagues in other fields, work without foundations, i.e., without a touchstone located outside the play of relativizing forces."[8]

The foundationless mission of theology has been accepted—even embraced—by many feminists.[9] Sheila Greave Devaney notes that movements which take historicity as a central concern reject the very idea of "objective, universally valid experience or knowledge," and urges that feminists confront fully "this progressive loss of norms for evaluating claims to truth that we face in the twentieth century."[10] She takes three Catholic feminists to task—Rosemary Radford Ruether, Elisabeth Schüssler Fiorenza, and even Mary Daly—for not having faced up to this loss. Instead, she accuses, they each propose some kind of feminist vision whose worth is misguidedly premised on a correspondence to "ultimate reality."[11] Greave Devaney counters with her own view that acknowledging "radical historicity" requires us to move away from any "ontological" grounds and to get rid of "referential models of knowledge."[12]

Postmodern feminist theological approaches like these are chartered partly by Nietzsche, but perhaps more explicitly and importantly by Foucault, with his positive ethical agenda of disclosure and resistance. Foucault's philosophy is inspired by the problem of the body as a site of power. No wonder that feminists find his work amenable. According to Foucault the very notion of "sexuality" (as opposed to the body and its pleasures) is a historical construct, deployed in the service of bourgeois power.[13] Foucault takes the "reality" of "sexual" experience apart by a historical study in which he argues, for instance, that the ancient Greeks saw the body and sexual passions much differently.[14] Foucault shows that the "nature" of sexual desire, as well as gender expectations of men and women, are variable with culture, and even suggests in a few more extravagant passages that the human body itself is not a cultural constant. In straightforward, if limited, ways this is certainly true, since the pliability of the human face and form have underlain cultural mediations of them from foot-binding and war paint to cosmetic surgery and anorexia. Jean-Francois Lyotard's words resound with the energetic iconoclasm of Foucault and his followers, when the Lyotard warns, in the final lines of *The Postmodern Condition,* against "the fantasy to seize reality" and charges, "Let us wage a war on totality"![15]

Some feminists carry this trajectory to the utmost and envision commensurate pliability of the reproductive functions. Some claim it may even be possible soon to overcome the prenatal division of labor, by redesigning supposedly natural physical capacities.[16] Socialist feminist Alison Jaggar is unafraid of the anti-metaphysical corrollary and summons women to "reconstruct reality" from their own standpoint.[17] Postmodern ethics is not necessarily nihilistic—it is in its own way positive and constructive, for it identifies and seeks to overturn real injustices in the world as "dominations." But postmodern philosophy models its discourse as "war"—an endless series of usurpations in which winners are established by violence and become losers in their turn. Is this philosophy adequate to its own practical program? Foucault, for one, implies in practice both a categorical imperative (Resist domination!) and a basis for truth claims (You can recognize both domination and resistance when you see them). Yet philosophies of otherness and difference have not stopped with dethroning totalitarian philosophical systems. Especially in the hands of academic theorists, they continue guerilla warfare against the commonality of human moral experience, without which intercultural critique stands to lose its moral authority.

II. Reconstructing Common Ground

There is a danger to the moral power of feminist ethics when the particularity which corrects biased interpretations of "nature" or "divine will" is carried to the point of moral incommensurability. Catholic feminists do not, as a rule, cave in to postmodern proposals which either retreat romantically into the epistemological enclosure of tradition, or revel satisfyingly but short-sightedly in the no-holds-barred deconstruction of all cultural ideals. We are generally resistant to the tendency of many philosophical feminists to discount cynically, even eagerly, the availability of truth in any tradition. A central contribution of the Roman Catholic tradition of ethics, indebted to Aristotle as reinterpreted by Aquinas, is commitment to an objective moral order which is knowable at least in its basic shape by all reasonable moral agents, across moral and political communities. This premise undergirds Catholic social ethics. Feminist ethics retrieves and renews this tradition, not in order to overcome particularity, but as an affirmation of the legitimacy and importance to all of us of the most concrete moral struggles.

But a question no less difficult than persistent is how precisely and persuasively to reconstruct a historically accountable sense of the inclusiveness of moral truth. The Enlightenment ideal of abstract reason and universal, ahistorical knowledge has been irretrievably challenged by recent critiques. But relativistic communitarianism is not the only other alternative. Another possibility is to redefine the meaning of objectivity in ethics by reconceiving moral reason as practical.

The Roman Catholic tradition of ethics, conceived in terms of a "natural law," is based on goods to be sought for all persons. It represents a commitment to an objective moral order, knowable by reasonable reflection on human experience, especially on the goods which constitute human flourishing, and the institutions necessary to secure, protect, and distribute them. Although the specific shape of moral practices and institutions varies culturally, all peoples recognize such goods as life, family, marriage, education, government and religion. Prudence is required to realize these values rightly in the complexity and occasionally conflict of a full human life and in a society of persons. Truth in morality emerges from concrete locations, demanding both the affections and the cognitive powers of discernment to guide us in the achievement of "true good" for ourselves and others.[18] But the fact that both Aristotle and Aquinas assume it possible to speak of moral virtue and of reasonably discerned "practical rectitude" in morality, demonstrates that they applied standards of truth and falsity to practical action despite its inevitable contingency. That they were sometimes wrong in their conclusions, especially about women's natural inferiority, does not disprove their method. Rather, it validates the necessity of a constant reexamination and reformation of particular readings of "human experience," informed by critical interaction with other standpoints, past and present.

This approach is validated by critical theory and liberation theology. From a "Third World" perspective, the Argentinian Jesuit Juan Carlos Scannone writes that rationality has to be given a broader definition, including the sapiential and the symbolic. He worries that exaggerated "ambiguity, plurality, and nihilistic deconstruction threaten capacity for communal initiatives characteristic of the common people," as well as "their capacity for hope and collective action." He proposes that philosophies of "communicative reason" as well as, at the practical level, "base neo-communitarianism," can more successfully combine traditional values such as community, solidarity, and gratuitousness, with modern values, such as historical praxis, political pluralism, rationality, and economic structures which are efficient as well as communitarian.[19] From a North American Hispanic perspective, Roberto Goizueta similarly promotes a neo-Aristotelian understanding of rationality, in which a praxis of solidarity not only inherently liberates, but also objectively names injustice and oppression in the light of a more authentic ideal of community.[20]

Robert Schreiter notes that praxis is today understood as "the ensemble of social relationships that include and determine the structures of social consciousness," including both theory and action as dialectical moments within praxis.[21] Insofar as theory reflects on the precise nature of social relationships, it illumines oppression and is the first step toward transformation. But the theological moment is not subsequent to or detached from the experiential and practical; the authenticity of theological claims not only arises from, but is validated by, the quality of the communal praxis theological "truth" is able to engender.

Among Catholic theologians, especially ethicists, there is a working assumption that any two traditions with the occasion for conversation can have a meaningful exchange. When a matter of justice is at stake, communication should not be limited to free exchange of ideas or mutual permeation of horizons; criticism, argument, judgment, and action are required to transform specific situations toward objectively greater human well-being. As we have seen, this is precisely the way feminists and other liberation theologians approach "foreign" traditions and engage them in moral exchange with political results. Serendipitous, if honest, "conversation" is not enough from the Catholic feminist point of view.

The work of the Catholic fundamental theologian, David Tracy, is helpful in establishing a model of intercultural ethics which assumes the possibility of communication without concealing its historical nature. Especially relevant are his notion of "the classic," of "relative adequacy" as a standard of truth, and of "analogy" as a model of knowledge. Any text (or myth, event, work of art, or ritual) comes out of a particular tradition; but a classic text is one which has disclosive power beyond that tradition, an "excess of meaning" able permanently to address the great human questions in an indefinite succession of historical situations.[22] The theory of the classic presupposes the general *reliability* of communication among traditions, by means of their classics.

Further, Tracy suggests a replacement for terms such as objectivity and universality. He expresses the reliability and generalizability of truth judgments in ethics in terms of "analogy." Analogical models of knowledge have a prominent history in the Catholic tradition. What analogy may accomplish for us in intercultural feminist ethics is an ability to affirm similarity in difference, and true knowing without reduction.[23] As Tracy cautions in *Dialogue with the Other,* we should be "suspicious of how easily claims to 'analogy' or 'similarity' can become subtle evasions of the other and the different."[24] Yet, though dignity in the family, adequate health care, a decent education, and fair gender roles in the public realm may not all amount to exactly the same thing in every culture, we *can* understand and evaluate justice and injustice in different cultures by virtue of their resemblance-in-difference to our own experience. Arriving at understanding and truth is a practical rather than a purely speculative process. Tracy proposes a standard of "relative adequacy" for formulations of theological and moral truth: "relative to the power of disclosure and concealment of the text, relative to the skills and attentiveness of the interpreter, relative to the kind of conversation possible for the interpreter in a particular culture at a particular time. Somehow conversation and relatively adequate interpretations suffice."[25] The reason that they suffice for feminist ethics is that they are appropriate to its origin and outcome as practical and historical at both ends—though not "relative" in the strong, deconstructionist sense.

To carry the best of our tradition forward, we require a new, postmodern, account of *rationality*—not a marginalization of rationality as ultimately unnecessary to the assertion of truth claims. We must find a responsible way back to rationality through pluralism. By combining the historical consciousness of postmodern thinkers and the inductive ethical approach of Aristotelian-Thomistic ones, perhaps we can ground truth claims in a culturally mediated but reliable stratum of common human experience. This experience is reflectively understood and shared within a practical process of prudently choosing and acting in ways that further human flourishing. Such a model assumes, beyond merely hoping for, meaningful and productive intercultural ethical exchanges which secure real results for human well-being. Given the crying injustices worldwide of poverty, war, hunger, and oppression of whole peoples, and of women among all peoples, we cannot afford to let our intercultural conversations be merely accidental or serendipitous, nor our agreements merely a matter of luck.

An example of authentic Christian praxis which is already and instrinsically liberating, and engenders feminist theology and action, is given in Maria Pilar Aquino's *Our Cry for Life!*. Aquino is a Mexican feminist working in the U.S. and is a past president of ACHTUS (Academy of Catholic Hispanic Theologians in the U.S.). Of Latin American base communities she writes:

> A genuine perspective of solidarity and equal participation gives rise in the church base communities to an awareness of the grave problems suffered by women and encourages them to take the necessary action to uproot "machismo." In the church base communities women denounce the many injustices that have been committed against them for centuries and summon women and men to struggle collectively to eradicate the ancient evil.[26]

Toward the end of *No Longer Silent,* the narrator gives us a practical manifesto of solidarity and hope which is especially pertinent to cultural variation in the virtually universal suffering of women:[27] "We see ourselves linked to women in other parts of the world in our struggle to go forward." This vision of unity does not wait for a "foundationalist" philosophical rationale, but comes straight out of a practical agenda to address basic human needs. And yet it affirms that women in many different situations worldwide are linked in their moral struggle, are even agreed in fundamental ways on the direction in which "forward" lies.

In an obvious way, cultural variety challenges us to respect cultural differences. But imperialisms of class, race, or continent are not the only dead-end for feminist ethics. Another is the self-silencing of social protest by announcement of plurality as ultimate. Only if a revolutionary critique can be validated as something more than a power shift, can it fend off cynicism and inspire practical work toward a new social consensus.

This project is already being carried forward. Rosemary Radford Ruether's manifesto has become the motto of many Roman Catholic feminists: "The critical principle of feminist theology is the promotion of the full humanity of women." Whatever denies full humanity to women "must be presumed not to reflect . . . the authentic nature of things."[28] Feminist theology begins from the standpoint of women's subordination, and promotes a pro-woman liberating agenda. Catholic feminist theology furthers this agenda in relation to an ideal of full human moral agency and well-being which not only includes men, but measures the goal by a presumably common standard. As Margaret Farley puts it, feminism makes a case for a "common morality" which goes beyond the feminist political agenda as such. Whatever the differences of culture and history, the experience of what it means to be "a human person" makes it possible, even "across time and place," "to condemn commonly recognized injustices and act for commonly desired goals." In her own experience of listening to women from parts of Asia and Africa, and from Central and Latin America, Farley writes, she has encountered feminist theologians who "are as opposed to unmitigated moral relativism as to false and inadequate universalisms."[29]

I submit that women who are practically involved in the most desperate sorts of struggles for women's very lives do not resort to any rhetoric of the incommensurability of worldviews, but appeal straight to the heart of our common humanity. One example: an intercontinental conference of Third World women theologians which met in Mexico in 1986 issued a final document which noted women's different situations, and the centrality of Third World women's faith perspective; but it still concluded with the aim to "deepen our commitment and solidarity work toward *full humanity for all.*"[30] Maria Pilar Aquino also insists that the poverty and dehumanization which result from "patriarchal, imperialistic capitalism" can only be resisted successfully if the "perspective of women accords priority to the achievement of women's human integrity and emphasizes the right of humanity for all women and men."[31]

Many authors placing ethics in an intercultural context have fruitfully highlighted praxis, practical reason, and prudence, in order to renew the foundations of ethics after the postmodern critique. These categories can promote a phenomenological, inductive, and historical epistemology, while preserving a commitment to truth in moral knowledge.

III. Conversation with a Feminist Philosopher

The work of the philosopher Martha Nussbaum provides another model of Aristotelian practical rationality. She asserts truth claims from within an inductive, historical approach, and develops specific applications for women.[32] Cross-cultural debate about justice will certainly proceed, as communication increases among societies.[33] She gives an example of development from a village in Bangladesh which demonstrates that change requires some conception of the good which can be grounded in the experience of culturally different working partners.

An international development agency tried to provide the women from this village with literacy materials to improve their uniformly low status. Like the women in *No Longer Silent,* they worked harder, ate less, got sicker, died earlier, and were less respected than men. However, these women also had no interest in education, since their imaginations were unable to encompass what an educated female life would be like, or what advantages it would bring. They had no role models. The situation called for some standard of change external to the community itself; but it also called for concrete engagement with the community women's experience. Change did not begin until the researchers began to look at women's actual functions and opportunities in more depth, asking what might be important to them over a complete life. At last, the women themselves became involved, in women's cooperatives in the village, which led to transformations on a number of levels, including gender relations and production, as well as education. The Western women and the rural women in Bangladesh were finally able to achieve results, because, despite vast differences in culture, they "recognized one another as fellow human beings, sharing certain problems and certain resources, certain needs for fuller capability and certain possibilities for movement toward capability," as well as with the imagination and humor to identify with one another and envision mutual change.[34]

It is evident to Nussbaum, as an Aristotelian, that the liberal aims of access and liberty are inadequate foundations of real structural change. The Bangladeshi women failed to take advantage of access to education because they could not see why it would matter.

The Western women had to learn that education might not matter much unless other factors changed too. Change required from both "an inquiry into the goodness and full humanness of various functionings, and into the special obstacles faced by deprived groups."[35] They were able to undertake this inquiry together once they engaged at the practical level. Although contentious relativists like to overestimate disagreement, we can and do sit down to discuss hunger or justice or the quality of women's lives with people from other parts of the world and still find it "possible to proceed as if we are all talking about the same human problem."[36]

Nussbaum's constructive account of moral judgment and truth centers both on practical reason and on the reliability of certain aspects of human experience in disclosing the goods which constitute a full human life. (Moral obligation consists in ensuring that all persons enjoy the capability to exercise those functions which lead to the goods constitutive of human flourishing.) She offers a revisable list of these convergent experiences: mortality, the human body (hunger and thirst, need for shelter, sexual desire, mobility), capacity for pleasure and pain, cognitive capability (perception, imagination, thought), early infant development, practical reason, affiliation with other human beings, relatedness to other species and to nature, humor and play, separateness, and strong separateness (the peculiarity of one's whole life, not just spatial and temporal separateness).[37] Of these, she believes, the most distinctively human are practical reason and affiliation (corresponding to Aristotle's definition of "man" as a rational and social animal), and they give a shape to the whole.

Two further basic human experiences might supplement Nussbaum's rendering of human experience: religion[38] and kinship. At least in the sense that all human beings wonder about the origin of the world and an intelligent purpose behind its fortunes, about the human fate after death, about a larger order of reward and retribution for good and evil, about salvation from their own wrongdoing and suffering, and about a unity of all persons and of the natural world in a dimension transcending history, they are open to an experience that could in a broad sense be called "religious."

I also find it odd that Nussbaum does not include kinship as a basic experience, one whose moral interpretation is certainly at the root of many feminist concerns. Nussbaum puts human relationships in the category of "affiliation," which might include kinship, but tends to connote freely chosen relationships (a "liberal" model). She does mention infant development as a special category, though I would tend to see it as a subcategory of embodiment. Perhaps the inclusion of infancy is a way of getting at the parent-child relation without elevating parenthood to the status of an indispensable experience, or involving the issue of whether men and women are related to infants in the same way. Nonetheless I find it obvious that, cross-culturally, all human beings come in some way or other from the bodies of other human beings. This is a fact of the human condition, basic to our experience, and goes beyond free choice. Moreover, at least for the foreseeable future, the combination of one female and one male parent will be indispensable. Because patriarchy survives in and through the social mediation of biological reproduction, especially by enlarging reproduction and attendant duties into women's virtually exclusive function, feminist social concerns are not well served by neglect of this dimension of experience.

An inductive approach to basic human values with universal status is a model which is not only amenable to, but already functional within, feminist theological ethics. Among those constitutive aspects of human being named by Nussbaum, feminists frequently give heightened practical importance to affiliation and to the body, as having special impact on women's experience as moral agents. Others note separateness and strong separateness as lacking in women's experience and as necessary to women's as well as men's well-being.

The concern with affiliation is often expressed in terms of relationality and sociality, as well as the inclusion within justice as fairness of a standard of "care." In *Hispanic Women: Prophetic Voice in the Church,* Ada María Isasi-Díaz and Yolanda Tarango name six presuppositions of their approach, four of which explicitly mention community.[39] Margaret Farley corrects an imbalance between autonomy and relationality, and develops correlative moral norms, justice and care. Feminism can appreciate that, against modern rationalism, "autonomy is ultimately for the sake of relationship," while, against postmodern diffusion of the self into language and social systems, relationship without autonomy is destructive, and, historically, especially so of women.[40]

Pilar Aquino's *Our Cry for Life!* affirms a theology which comes out of a context (praxis), and is therefore specific to the experiences, needs, and insights of women who are not only poor, but also suffer as women because they are women, and, in addition, belong to ethnic or racial groups which are marginalized. The themes of community, solidarity, and embodiment prevail in this book, especially its location of feminist theology within the reality and the interpretation of women's daily lives.

Aquino takes women's reproductive power as a "biological fact," regards maternity as an appropriate and important female role, but refuses to let motherhood override women's other roles. She insists that the social and political interpretation of women's reproduction is the source of their historical and universal domination, even when, as in Western Catholic tradition, that role is idealized. "The problem lies in the politico-ideological treatment of women's power to bear children, not in the power itself."[41]

In summary, Catholic feminists writing today arrange their agenda around those distorted interpretations of the basic human experiences which deprive women of a full human life. Special interests are women's religious experience, embodiment, kinship, affiliation and separateness. Feminists also seek to renew practical reason as accounting for both the particularity of and the common ground in moral experience. They urge recognition of the nonnegotiable and universal imperative of feminist ethics: respect for social equality as part of women's well-being, and for women's social vocations as essential to the flourishing of every human community.

Conclusion

Postmodern critical philosophy, and feminist and other liberation theologies which stress the irreducibility of the particular, rightly repudiate all abstract, patriarchal and oppressive ethics of sex and gender. Yet "difference" does not wipe out what we as human, and more precisely as women, have in common. Commonality exists in and through the different personal and social embodiments of what is still fundamentally *human* experience. For feminist ethics shared meaning and judgment are both necessary in principle and visible in fact. The Catholic moral tradition on sex and gender has evidenced undeniable limits and distortions in many of its actual expressions. But, positively, it upholds the ideal of *reasonableness* in moral discourse about the *basic human goods* of family, parenthood, and cooperation between the sexes (which should not be structured strictly or only by reproductive roles, however). Catholic feminism casts moral understanding in practical, inferential, and revisable forms, but does not see morality as completely relative to social traditions or ideologies. Hence it can give a theoretical justification of women's equality as a cross-cultural human responsibility. A feminist theology which makes moral claims on the basis of common humanity can strengthen support for women worldwide, as they struggle to live, for themselves and others, with human dignity.

Notes

1. This is a revised version of my 1993 Catholic Theological Society of America Presidential Address, "Feminist Ethics and the Challenge of Cultures," (CTSA *Proceedings* 48[1993] 65–83). The address is also incorporated into chapters 1, 2, and 3 of *Sex, Gender, and Christian Ethics* (Cambridge University Press, 1996/forthcoming).

2. Indeed, even the term "feminist" has its own particular point of origin in the concerns of white, educated, middle class, North American women. Women's theology actually takes shape in multiple varieties—including *mujerista,* Latina, womanist, Asian and African. In the present essay, sources from Latin America will be most visible, because the address was delivered in San Antonio, to a professional society in which the work of Latino and Hispanic theologians has been very important. See the works cited in n. 3 below for discussion of differences and commonality among feminists.

3. In 1991, a session of the Women and Religion Section of the American Academy of Religion annual convention brought together Toinette M. Eugene, Ada María Isasi-Díaz, Kwok Pui-lan, Judith Plaskow,

Mary E. Hunt, Emilie M. Townes, and Ellen M. Umansky to discuss the importance of difference and the possibility of moral agreement in women's theology. Their papers were published as "Appropriation and Reciprocity in Womanist/Mujerista/Feminist Work," *Journal of Feminist Studies in Religion* 8 (Fall, 1992) 91–122. These papers are now available in Lois K. Daly, ed., *Feminist Theological Ethics: A Reader* (Louisville, KY: Westminster John Knox Press, 1994), along with many other essays which touch on the same issue. For an influential philosophical statement of the irreducible nature of difference, see Iris Marion Young, "The Ideal of Community and the Politics of Difference," *Social Theory and Practice,* 12/1 (Spring, 1986).

4. It should, but unfortunately does not, go without saying that such dialogue properly includes receptivity to criticism by the dominant culture within a society, or by more powerful nations, as they become aware of their own moral limits in interaction with other traditions. Intercultural critique is not just a matter of "modern" cultures insisting that other traditions grant equality and rights to women. It also requires that North Atlantic industrialized societies recognize such failings as individualism, capitalism, and colonialism.

5. Seyla Benhabib, in *Situating the Self: Gender, Community and Postmodernism in Contemporary Ethics* (New York: Routledge, 1992), confirms this point, but is skeptical of the possibility of agreement on substantive theories of goods. Criticizing and developing the thought of Jurgen Habermas, she offers a neo-Kantian feminist version of "discourse ethics" as an alternative model of moral knowledge. For a more thorough assessment of Benhabib's commitments and contributions, see my *Sex, Gender and Christian Ethics,* chapter 2.

6. International Film Bureau, Inc., 1991. This film came to my attention in the writings of Martha Nussbaum.

7. Mark Kline Taylor, *Remembering Esperanza: A Cultural-Political Theology for North American Praxis* (Maryknoll, NY: Orbis Books, 1990) 37.

8. Ibid., 37.

9. Jane Flax proclaims the death of Man, the death of History, and the death of Metaphysics (*Thinking Fragments: Psychoanalysis, Feminism and Postmodernism in the Contemporary West* [Berkeley: University of California Press, 1990] 32 ff.).

10. Sheila Greave Devaney, "Problems with Feminist Theory: Historicity and the Search for Sure Foundations," in Paula M. Cooey, Sharon A. Farmer and Mary Ellen Ross, eds., *Embodied Love: Sensuality and Relationship as Feminist Values* (San Francisco: Harper and Row, 1987) 92.

11. Ibid., 90. Rebecca Chopp has similarly faulted Rosemary

Ruether for her "abstract" notion of "full humanity," because it seems to postulate "a metahistorical structure" which is "merely realized in historical experience," and to suppose that "we can grasp something independent of our concrete situation" ("Seeing and Naming the World Anew: The Works of Rosemary Radford Ruether," *Religious Studies Review* 15 [1989] 10).

12. "Problems," 93.

13. Michel Foucault, *The History of Sexuality: An Introduction,* trans. Robert Hurley (New York: Random House, 1978). The discourse of sexuality focuses the self-affirmation of the bourgeoisie on the body, via a "technology of sex," and an ever heightening process of medical and psychoanalytic inspection, introspection, and ultimately control. "We are often reminded of the countless procedures which Christianity once employed to make us detest the body, but let us ponder all the ruses that were employed for centuries to make us love sex, to make the knowledge of it desirable and everything said about it precious. . . . The irony of this deployment is in having us believe that our 'liberation' is in the balance" (ibid., 159).

14. Sexual desire was a drive requiring integration into a full life, just as the appetite to eat and drink. The fulfillment of sexual desire was not evaluated so much by the sex of the partners, as by the activity or passivity of their roles. For a free, adult male, master of his own life, only the active role was honorable.

15. *The Postmodern Condition: A Report on Knowledge,* trans. Geoff Bennington and Brian Massumi (Manchester, England: Manchester University Press, 1984) 82.

16. "This transformation might even include the capacities for insemination, for lactation and for gestation so that, for instance, one woman could inseminate another, so that men and nonparturitive women could lactate and so that fertilized ova could be transplanted into women's or even into men's bodies. These developments may seem farfetched, but in fact they are already on the technological horizon" (Alison M. Jaggar, *Feminist Politics and Human Nature* [The Harvester Press: Brighton, Sussex, 1983] 132; see also 76).

17. Ibid., 389. Along the same lines, "socialist feminists view knowledge as a social and practical construct and they believe that conceptual frameworks are shaped and limited by their social origins" (369–70). See also, Sarah Franklin, "Deconstructing 'Desperateness': The Social Construction of Infertility in Popular Representations of New Reproductive Technologies," in Maureen McNeill, Ian Varcoe and Steven Yearley, *The New Reproductive Technologies* (London: The Macmillan Press, 1990) 200–229.

18. As Catholic feminists such as Pilar Aquino, Elsa Tamez, Sidney

Callahan, and Margaret Farley have noted, reason should not be separated in any dichotomous way from the emotions and affections. In a textual analysis of Thomas, Brian Johnstone rejects both a dichotomy between the practical and the speculative reason, and a dichotomy between reason and will, insofar as we seek in action that which attracts us as good (Brian V. Johnstone, C.SS.R., "The Structures of Practical Reason: Traditional Theories and Contemporary Questions," *The Thomist* 50 ([986] 425). See also, Jean Porter, *The Recovery of Virtue: The Relevance of Aquinas for Christian Ethics* (Louisville: Westminster/John Knox Press, 1990), Chapter 4., "The Affective Virtues."

19. Juan Carlos Scannone, "The Debate About Modernity in North Atlantic and Third Worlds," in Claude Geffré and Jean-Pierre Jossua, *The Debate on Modernity* (*Concilium* 1992/6) 84–85.

20. Roberto Goizueta, "Rediscovering Praxis: The Significance of U.S. Hispanic Experience for Theological Method," in Roberto S. Goizueta, ed., *We Are a People!: Initiatives in Hispanic American Theology* (Minneapolis: Fortress, 1993) 67.

21. Robert J. Schreiter, C.PP.S., *Constructing Local Theologies* (Maryknoll, NY: Orbis, 1985)91. Aristotle distinguished *praxis* from both *theoria* and *poiesis,* however.

22. David Tracy, *The Analogical Imagination: Christian Theology and the Culture of Pluralism* (New York: Crossroad, 1981) 14, 102.

23. Ibid., 408.

24. David Tracy, *Dialogue with the Other: The Interreligious Dialogue* (Grand Rapids: Eerdmans, 1990) 42.

25. David Tracy, *Pluralism and Ambiguity* (New York: Harper and Row, 1987) 22–23.

26. *Our Cry for Life! Feminist Theology from Latin America* (Maryknoll, NY: Orbis, 1993) 56. Gustavo Gutiérrez has given this dynamic a classic expression for theology: "Theologians will be personally and vitally engaged in historical realities with specific times and places. They will be engaged where nations, social classes, and peoples struggle to free themselves from domination and oppression by other nations, classes, and peoples. In the last analysis, the true interpretation of the meaning revealed by theology is achieved only in historical praxis," *A Theology of Liberation,* rev. ed. (Maryknoll, NY: Orbis, 1988) 10. See also 12: "The theology of liberation is a *new way* to do theology. Theology as critical reflection on historical praxis is a liberating theology, a theology of the liberating transformation of the history of humankind. . . . This is a theology which does not stop with reflecting on the world, but rather tries to be part of the process through which the world is transformed."

27. See Christine Gudorf, "Women's Choice for Motherhood: Beginning a Cross-Cultural Approach," in Anne Carr and Elisabeth Schüssler Fiorenza, eds., *Motherhood* (*Concilium* 1989/6).

28. *Sexism and God-Talk: Toward a Feminist Theology* (Boston: Beacon Press, 1983) 18, 19. Ruether adds:

> This principle is hardly new. In fact, the correlation of original, authentic human nature (*imago dei*/Christ) and diminished, fallen humanity provided the basic structure of classical Christian theology. The uniqueness of feminist theology is not the critical principle, full humanity, but the fact that women claim this principle for themselves. Women name themselves as subjects of authentic and full humanity (19).

See also, Ruether, "The Development of My Theology," *Religious Studies Review* 15 (1989) 1–4, where she reiterates this principle and affirms the goal of "a redemptive community that encompasses all people."

29. Margaret A. Farley, "Feminism and Universal Morality," in Gene Outka and John P. Reeder, Jr., eds., *Prospects for a Common Morality* (Princeton: Princeton University Press, 1993) 178–79.

30. "Final Document: Intercontinental Women's Conference," in Virginia Fabella, M.M. and Mercy Amba Oduyoye, *With Passion and Compassion: Third World Women Doing Theology* (Maryknoll, NY: Orbis Books, 1989) 184; my italics. On June 16, 1992, *The New York Times* reported that the Global Campaign for Women's Human Rights, backed by 950 women's organizations worldwide, seized the center of attention at a United Nations World Conference in Human Rights, held in Vienna, by showcasing the personal testimony of women about WWII sexual slavery in Japan, the terrorism of the Shining Path in Peru, and the violence against Palestinians under Israeli occupation. Women told of particular experiences of suffering, and joined together in their demand for international recognition of women's human rights.

31. Maria Pilar Aquino, "Doing Theology from the Perspective of Latin American Women," in Goizueta, ed., *We Are a People!,* 91.

32. "Introduction," in Martha Nussbaum and Amartya Sen, eds., *The Quality of Life* (Oxford: Clarendon Press, 1993) 4.

33. "Aristotelian Social Democracy," in R. Bruce Douglass, Gerald R. Mara, and Henry S. Richardson, eds., *Liberalism and the Good* (NY: Routledge, 1990).

34. Ibid., 236–37.

35. Nussbaum, "Aristotelian Social Democracy," 214–15. She takes

the example from Marty Chen, *A Quiet Revolution: Women in Transition in Rural Bangladesh* (Dhaka: BRAC, 1986).

36. Martha Nussbaum, "Non-Relative Virtues: An Aristotelian Approach," *Midwest Studies in Philosophy* 13 (1988) 46–47. This essay is included in *Quality of Life*.

37. Nussbaum, "Aristotelian Social Democracy," 219–224. Certain positive human functionings in these areas are also valued cross-culturally, and it is the capability to so function that morality and policy ought to seek for each human being. The "basic human functional capabilities" are being able to live to the end of a complete human life; to have good health, to avoid nonuseful pain and enjoy pleasurable experiences; to use one's five senses and to imagine, think, and reason; to have attachments to others, to love, to grieve, and to feel gratitude; to form a conception of the good, and to plan one's life around it; to be concerned for animals and nature; to laugh and play, to live one's own life, and to do so in one's own surroundings and context (225). The task of politics is accordingly to structure social life around labor, property, political participation, education, and some pluralism and choice in individual's specific approaches to the good life.

38. Nussbaum explicitly excludes religion, though she allows for religious freedom.

39. *Hispanic Women: Prophetic Voice in the Church* (Minneapolis: Fortress Press, 1992) xvii.

40. Farley, "Feminism and Universal Morality," 181–85.

41. *Our Cry for Life!*, 32.

Part Three

INTERPERSONAL AND FAMILIAL RELATIONS

10. Whose Sexuality? Whose Tradition? Women, Experience, and Roman Catholic Sexual Ethics

Barbara Hilkert Andolsen

This chapter first appeared in *Religion and Sexual Health: Ethical, Theological, and Clinical Perspectives* in 1992.

This essay focuses on the position of women vis-à-vis "tradition"—the process by which a religious community hands on, from generation to generation, the wisdom of the past, in this case, wisdom concerning human sexuality. From my perspective as a woman, the materials concerning sexuality usually encompassed by the phrase "the Roman Catholic tradition" are a painful and sometimes repulsive collection. Misogyny, distrust of the body, and antipathy toward sexuality are found in too many classic Catholic theological sources. Reexamining the tradition from a perspective that affirms women's struggles for sexual wholeness, I have gained a heightened sense of the scope, complexity, and ambiguity of my church's moral memories.

Throughout this essay, I will draw upon examples from the tradition of my religious community, Roman Catholicism. However, questions about tradition raise critical issues for other religious groups, too. Tradition is particularly important as a basis for ethical reflection about sexuality in Judaism, the Eastern Orthodox churches, and Roman Catholicism. It also exerts a more subtle influence on Protestant ethics, despite the propensity of some Protestant ethicists to appeal primarily to a narrow range of historical strata among their traditions, i.e., the Biblical traditions. In all these religious groups, women have rarely possessed the social and religious power necessary to be effective participants in the shaping of corporate religious memories. What Judith Plaskow says of her religious tradition is true, in a somewhat different fashion, for Christianity, too.

> The need for a feminist Judaism begins with hearing silence. It begins with noting the absence of women's history and experiences as shaping forces in the Jewish tradition. . . . Women have lived Jewish history and carried its burdens, but women's perceptions and questions have not given form to scripture, shaped the direction of Jewish law, or found expression in liturgy ([38], p. 1).

Women's perspectives and questions have not contributed in a substantial way to the formation of Christian tradition, either.

In this essay, I approach the examination of Catholic tradition as a feminist. I insist that women must become active participants in the formation of the tradition for their own sake as members of the religious community and for the good of the community as a whole. An adequate assessment of Roman Catholic sexual ethics must include explicit attention to the sexual well-being of women. A renewed sexual ethic must speak meaningfully to Catholic women in very diverse circumstances. Among (but not exhaustive of) the differences which must be taken into account are marital status, fertility or infertility, sexual preference, race, national origin, and economic class. I have tried to remain aware of these variations in writing this essay, but ultimately defining a new Catholic ethic will require a dialogue among many different women.

One feminist criterion for evaluating the church's sexual ethic is a requirement that the church's teachings must acknowledge and enhance the moral agency of women. Basic to all moral agency is what Carol Robb has termed "the capacity for responsible self-direction" ([23], p. xvi). Women and men need an ethic that calls them equally to responsible self-direction in sexual matters. In this essay I propose a substantially revised Roman Catholic sexual ethic that places responsibility for morally appropriate sexual restraint on each individual as a moral agent responsible for his or her sexual behavior and accountable to others for the consequences of his or her sexual choices.

By contrast, throughout most of Catholic history, the official teachers of the church have perpetuated an ethic of male control over female sexuality. The "fathers of the church" have sought to constrain women's sexuality for the sake of men's spiritual well-being. The aid of Catholic women was enlisted in protecting men from their own sexual urges. Female purity and chastity safeguarded men's virtue as well as women's own. The final vestiges of such control of female sexuality are found in the fading, but still perceptible, traces of the "double standard"—male sexual lapses are an understandable result of men's inability to control their raging sexual urges, while women's falls from purity represent grave female failures to contain not only their own sexual passions, but those of their male partners as well.[1]

In addition to proposing an ethic of responsible self-direction for women and men, I stress a code of sexual ethics consistent with a recognition of the equal moral worth of women and men. Exponents of the church's official sexual ethic would insist that their sexual norms are uniquely consistent with the human dignity of man and woman properly understood. Proponents of the hierarchy's teachings contend that they offer a reliable code of sexual morality rooted in the objective natural law. They claim that their moral teachings are congruent with the basic, unchanging structures of human sexuality.[2]

The natural law tradition in the Roman Catholic church has been articulated largely from the vantage point of a clerical caste in the church, because, at least until recently, access to theological education has been closely linked to the clerical state of life. Thus, most of the persons who possessed the formal credentials necessary to contribute to expositions of sexual ethics were celibate men who viewed sexual issues from a limited range of male perspectives. What those in sympathy with the official teachings of the church regard as an objective, rational analysis of the trans-historical, natural (moral) law concerning human sexuality is, in reality, a series of culture-bound explications of those sexual norms which seemed compelling to certain members of the celibate clergy.

The reorientation of tradition that I call for here requires increased attention to the experience of *ordinary folk, especially women*. Contemporary Roman Catholic theology emphasizes that all believers, with their multifaceted experiences of human sexuality, *are the church*. Therefore, the entire community of believers should be at the center of the Roman Catholic tradition. There are differing responsibilities within the church for public articulation of tradition. Nevertheless, it is the witness of Catholic peoples—women and men, gay and straight, sexually active and celibate—to the human wholeness which God holds out to them that provides the central threads in Catholic tradition.

At present, we are far from having adequate interpretations of the living tradition of the entire church. It is very difficult, given presently available historical resources, to recover and reinterpret the faith experiences of those generations of women and men who have been the ordinary members of the church throughout the centuries. So, far too often, Catholic ethicists reduce tradition to a litany of carefully selected excerpts from the writings of prominent theologians and from the statements of popes and church councils. Ethicists who make the standard appeals to tradition become entrapped in a male-defined, elitist intellectual heritage. There is a profound irony in this intellectual captivity. For there is significant hermeneutical evidence that the Jesus community, which was the genesis of the entire Christian faith, was not elitist, at least arguably not patriarchal, and not preoccupied with control of sexual behavior [16], [10].

My review of the "official" tradition of the Roman Catholic church on sexuality in preparation for this essay was profoundly alienating. It often meant seeing human sexual behavior through the eyes of men who are distrustful of women. It frequently involved the disorienting experience of viewing persons like me—others with female bodies—as *the Other*. The images of women offered by the "fathers of the church" seemed as distorted as the reflections in a fun house mirror.

Tertullian's Misogyny Reexamined

Christian men, especially celibate men, have frequently dealt with ambivalence about their own erotic feelings by projecting sexual passion onto women whom they stereotyped as wanton and seductive. There is little that could contribute to female wholeness in those powerful streams of religious tradition in which men view women as seductive bodies that represent serious obstacles in the male path to salvation. Yet, even the most misogynist theological statements may be more complex than they first appear. Paradigmatic for me of the woman-as-evil-temptress view are statements from Tertullian's essay concerning women's appearance—their cosmetics and dress—*De Cultu Feminarum.*

Tertullian was a second century (married) theologian who stressed modesty and chastity as crucial virtues necessary for both men and women to preserve holiness in the interval between baptism and death in the grace of God. Since Tertullian viewed rigorous sexual self-restraint as essential to the Christian life, he strongly discouraged Christian women from engaging in practices that heightened sexual attractiveness. He decried women's use of cosmetics and alluring clothes. In one of his more temperate passages, he advised that a Christian woman should achieve a balance in her appearance—that she should strive for "natural and demure neatness" (II, v, i).

However, in this essay he went beyond a denunciation of fashions that exaggerated a woman's sexual appeal; he recommended that Christian women disguise even *naturally attractive* bodily features. Love of the male neighbor entailed for Tertullian that a woman disguise her physical beauty, so as not to arouse his lust. Tertullian advised: "you must not only shun the display of false and studied beauty, but also remove all traces of natural grace by concealment and negligence, as equally dangerous to the glances of another's eyes." It is not altogether clear what Tertullian would have a naturally beautiful Christian woman do, because he added that he saw no virtue in bodily filth and he was not advocating "an utterly uncultivated and unkempt appearance" (II, ii, v).

In yet another section of this same essay—a section characterized by particularly strong rhetoric—Tertullian descended to misogynist excess. He suggested that new female converts, rather than continuing to practice customs of fashion that accentuated their physical attractions, should have adopted the austere garb of one in mourning—mourning for her sins. Converts might have been expected, he claims, to neglect their appearance, "acting the part of mourning and repentant Eve in order to expiate more fully by all sorts of penitential garb that which woman derives from Eve—the ignominy, I mean, of original sin and the odium of being the cause of the fall of the human race" (I, i, i). Women's natural allures are connected with the sexual appeal of the first woman, Eve, who, in Tertullian's mind, caused the downfall of the human race.

Determining the import of these passages from the tradition for contemporary women in a fair way is a complex challenge. This document is addressed to upper-class, second-century, Christian women, especially to female converts who must learn wholly to reorient their lives in a manner consistent with their new religious commitment. Therefore, *De Cultu* emphasizes issues of women's appearance and virtue. Throughout his writings, Tertullian advocates a high standard of sexual self-restraint for men as well as women. In other works, Tertullian discusses Adam's pivotal role in original sin or describes how humanity—male and female—are heirs to the fall [8]. Moreover, his views on sexual activity reflect a particular ancient Christian mentality concerning sexual indulgence and sexual restraint. This ancient Christian view is in some ways intractably foreign to modern experience ([4], p. xv). In addition, Tertullian's penchant for excessive rigorism ultimately led him to a group called the Montanists who were rejected as heretics by the main body of Christians.

Still, Tertullian is representative of a major strand in Catholic tradition insofar as he places a special burden on women to take responsibility for male sexual behavior without any reciprocal demand addressed to men. He does ask men to curb their sexual passion, even during intercourse with their wives, and to consider a higher life of sexual continence. He also admonishes men to be less vain about their appearance. Although Tertullian describes male vanity more briefly as antithetical to the sober virtue that should characterize the lives of Christian men (*De cultu feminarum,* II, viii), he does not dwell on male sexual allure as a danger to *women's* souls. Here, Tertullian stands near the source of one unfortunate stream in Catholic sexual tradition. This is the stream of tradition in which women are viewed as seductive sexual objects whose sexuality must be constrained for the sake of men's spiritual well-being.

What Judith Plaskow has said of Judaism is true of Roman Catholicism as well, albeit in a somewhat different fashion: "Men define their own sexuality ambivalently—but they define it. And men also define the sexuality of women which they would circumscribe to fit the shape of their own fears, and desire for possession. Women must carve out a sense of sexual self in the context of a system that—here [on issues of sexuality] most centrally—projects them as Other, denying their right to autonomous self-understanding or action" ([38], pp. 91–92).

Broadening the Tradition

The tradition, as it has usually been framed by Catholic ethicists, almost never includes the self-understanding and practices of autonomous women. Instead, as I have indicated, the history of Roman Catholic ethics, including the history of teachings on sexuality, remains largely a chronological account of the ideas of prominent theologians. Throughout much of the church's history very few women have been allowed access to those forms of education that were a prerequisite to making one's view of sexuality intelligible in theological language. The insights of women have rarely found a place among those documentary memories which have been preserved for future generations.

The history of Roman Catholic ethics, in particular, and Christian ethics, in general, is in much the same state as the larger academic discipline of history was several decades ago. Then, secular history was dominated by the study of the activities of diplomats, military leaders, and leaders of state who were overwhelmingly men. The history of Christian ethics *remains* primarily the history of (male) theologians. In Roman Catholic ethics, the statements of ecumenical councils and popes receive heavy emphasis. Secular history as a discipline has been challenged and transformed by new work which deals with social and family history. Many secular historians now give careful attention to the experiences of women and less powerful men. Still, few ethicists interested in the history of Christian ethics have adopted approaches similar to those developed by these historians.

Catholic ethicists should become involved in collaborative scholarship that integrates the experiences of women and less powerful men throughout the history of ethics. In preparation for such a long-term, cooperative scholarly enterprise, I would like to pursue briefly two examples of how our understanding of the Roman Catholic ethical tradition might be broadened by attention to the experiences of these other members of the church. I will explore, first, the bodily piety of certain late medieval women and, second, the protests about the imposition of clerical celibacy from the fourth through the twelfth centuries.

The Body and Medieval Women's Piety

During the later middle ages, women were drawn to the Eucharist as an element in a spirituality that paid special attention to and valued physicality. As with other sacraments of the Roman Catholic church, the Eucharist is rooted in sensual, bodily experience. The doctrine of transubstantiation affirms that Jesus Christ is truly present body and blood in the bread and wine of the Eucharist. This doctrine establishes "an intimate interconnectedness of the physical and spiritual by which physical food can nourish spiritual life . . . the boundaries of body and soul are not absolute, but permeable" ([31], p. 107). Ethicist Giles Milhaven notes: "Unprecedented in Europe was the eagerness of the [medieval] faithful, especially women, to receive the Eucharist, to eat of the bread, drink of the wine, and thus receive Christ within them" ([32], p. 346). Women pressed for more opportunities to be united with the body of Christ through more frequent reception of the Eucharist. Some women even rushed from church to church while Masses were being said in order to receive Communion as often as possible within the same day.

An intense desire to be united with Christ through receiving and becoming one with his body in the Eucharist was consonant with a powerful erotic spirituality in which Christ was received as a lover.[3] The medieval mystic Hadewijch gave particularly eloquent expression to this spirituality when she described one unusually memorable experience of her union with Christ through reception of the Eucharist. Present at morning service on Pentecost, Hadewijch was in a state of keen anticipation of union with Christ. "My heart and my veins and all my limbs trembled and quivered with eager desire. . . ." She longed "to have full fruition of my Beloved, and to understand and taste him to the full." After she had received Communion, Christ, "came himself to me, took me entirely in his arms, and pressed me to him, and all my members felt his [body] in full felicity, in accordance with the desire of my heart and my humanity. So I was outwardly satisfied and fully transported." Then it seemed to her that she and Christ melted into one. "After that I remained in a passing away in my Beloved, so that I wholly melted away in him. . . ." ([24], pp. 280–82). Certain medieval women unabashedly connected physicality and eroticism with the knowledge of God. Milhaven suggests that this bodily piety of medieval women was not incorporated into the high theological tradition of their time or of later ages. "Thomas and other theologians ignored the wisdom growing from sexual love and pleasure" ([32], p. 362).

Yet, to correct the exclusion of medieval women's perspectives from the tradition is again to uncover a complex history. The late medieval female spirituality did include a special attention to physicality—both women's experiences as bodily selves and Christ's bodily experiences. Particularly through reception of the Eucharist, medieval women mystics identified themselves with a Christ who fed the whole community, especially the poor and suffering, with his body. However, that same spiritual tradition was also marked by a propensity to extreme bodily asceticism. As historian Caroline Bynum states, "women's devotion was more characterized by penitential asceticism, particularly self-inflicted suffering" ([5], p. 26). Some of these women deprived themselves of sleep, starved themselves, flogged themselves, and deliberately consumed lice and pus from the wounds of seriously ill patients for whom they cared. Indeed, women were disproportionately represented among those saints who died as a result of severe ascetic practices ([5], p. 76). Bynum emphasizes that such practices can only be understood properly within their historical and cultural context: ". . . what modern eyes see as self-punishment . . . [was to medieval people] imitatio Christi—a fusion with Christ's agony on the cross" ([5], pp. 211–12). She also reminds the reader that medieval people could frequently do little to ameliorate human suffering ([5], p. 245). Therefore, the ability to give suffering spiritual meaning was a precious capacity. The complex interrelationship of physicality, sensuality, concern for the poor and self-inflicted suffering in the religiosity of certain medieval women poses a challenge to me as a twentieth-century ethicist who wants to affirm the moral worth of bodily well-being and pleasure.

Priestly Celibacy and the Purposes of Marriage

The prolonged protest against the imposition of mandatory celibacy for the clergy is another interesting strand in the history of Catholic sexual ethics. Ethicists can enrich their understanding of tradition by using a technique of feminist historiography, i.e., by viewing history from the underside—from the perspective of the devalued members of the community. Ethicists should search for moral wisdom known to historical "losers."[4] In this case, I have in mind the wisdom of those who, in the Roman Catholic tradition at least, struggled unsuccessfully to preserve a married clergy.

The imposition of celibacy involved a protracted struggle, which culminated in the eleventh and twelfth centuries. There were many episodes of resistance. In the fifth century, for example, Synesius of Cyrene agreed to become a bishop only on the condition that it be clearly understood that he would continue to have an active sexual relationship with his wife. He refused to continue their relationship "surreptitiously like an adulterer." He expressed the hope that he would father "many virtuous children" ([17], p. 199). Thus, this upper-class church leader placed a high value on marriage and procreation.

Even a bit earlier, by the fourth century, there was a fierce intellectual controversy over the relative merits of virginity and marriage. Unfortunately the defense of marital sexuality offered by Helvidius, Vigilantius and Jovinian are known to us only second hand through the vituperative rejoinders of Jerome. This well-known case of a loss of primary historical source materials highlights the difficulty of reconstructing the full tradition of the Catholic church. We are far from having sound documentary records from all the persons and about all topics of interest to modern scholars.

After studying eleventh and twelfth century materials from the continuing debate concerning celibacy, historian Anne Barstow indicates that "married clergy and their supporters left a valuable legacy of arguments affirming the goodness of . . . human sexuality, affirmations seldom enough found in medieval theological writings" ([2], p. 155). For a twentieth-century ethicist like me to consider the protestors as a positive part of the tradition, involves immersing myself in the ambiguities of history. Those who opposed mandatory clerical celibacy affirmed positive aspects to sexual activity within marriage and insisted that sexual intimacy with a woman did not prevent a man from functioning effectively as a religious leader.

Yet, medieval arguments against imposition of celibacy present strange and unappealing elements to a modern interpreter as well. A defense of marriage was not necessarily an affirmation of the inherent goodness of sexual pleasure. Reviewing notions of (marital) sexual relationships in Christianity, historian Margaret Miles notes: "A dichotomy between marriage and pleasure was assumed in many writings—marriage being good and pleasure bad. In marriage, sex was tolerated largely for purposes of the continuity of the human race, although some authors can imagine a companionship between husband and wife that is a good in itself." She continues: "Clearly, it was never sexual intimacy or activity itself that Christian authors valued and were grateful for" ([31], p. 155).

In the middle ages, married clergy and their supporters did not appeal to an ideal of marriage as a realm of specially valuable interpersonal emotional and sexual intimacy. Instead, they defended marriage as an institution that let people direct their fierce sexual urges into a socially acceptable channel, thus avoiding sexual sins. The protestors against celibacy frankly acknowledged that marriage was good as a socially necessary relationship that enabled persons to reproduce their kind in a responsible way. They pointed out that for the (nonmonastic) lower clergy, marriage could be an essential economic arrangement in which a man and a woman pooled gender-specific productive skills that were crucial for the day-to-day survival of a household.

The pragmatic concerns of the protestors point toward another area of family and sexual history which ethicists need to reexamine. Even "love" is not a timeless norm in Christian sexual ethics; it has specific meanings in particular historical contexts. A widespread cultural view that loving affection and interpersonal intimacy are primary aims of marriage represents a specific development in modern European and American history.[5] The social ideal of marriage as a loving partnership with sexual intercourse serving an emotionally and spiritually unitive function arose under particular historical circumstances. It was rooted in two historical developments, among others. First was the Reformation and later Protestant emphasis on marriage as a vocation for almost all adults with an increasing emphasis on the "spiritual intimacy" between husband and wife ([42], p. 101). Second was the privatization and sentimentalization of the home that occurred as many types of economic production were removed from the household through industrialization. In the newly privatized home of the middle class, the emotional bonds between family members took on novel importance and intensity. As ethicist James Nelson has recognized:

> The notion of romantic marriage is part of a larger social revolution in the West which, beginning in the seventeenth century, also led to the development of the capitalistic economy and the democratic state. It was a basic reordering of the traditional ways in which persons were understood to relate to each other. Before that time, the more usual assumption had been that people must adapt to society. With that revolution, however, it became commonly believed that social institutions could and should be changed to meet [individual] human needs. That applied to marriage and the sexual relationship ([35], p. 108).

Christian ethicists need to probe the implications of this social revolution in marriage and the family far more carefully than we have yet done. I cannot provide an exhaustive treatment of that subject here, but I would like to call attention to several implications.

It appears that this change in the understanding of spousal relationships began as a modern middle-class experience, articulated in the sermons and writings of Protestant ministers, among other sources. In the later stages of this social transformation of the purposes of marriage, medical experts and a newly emerging class of psychological experts played an increasingly authoritative role. By the late nineteenth and early twentieth century in the United States, the social influence which religious authorities exerted over generally accepted societal norms for sexual behavior had diminished. Medical experts took on a correspondingly greater degree of social power to shape cultural notions of acceptable sexual behavior.[6] The message that married couples received from certain medical authorities was an uplifting one. "By the late Victorian period, medical writers increasingly spoke of sexuality as an important means for enhancing the spiritual unity of husband and wife" ([12], p. 69). The medical advice literature "called attention to the importance of sexuality in personal life, often elevating it as a powerful force imbued with possibilities for heightened marital intimacy and even spiritual transcendence" ([12], p. 67).

It is this modern, romantic ideal of sexual intercourse as an expression of total interpersonal unity that was belatedly adopted in twentieth-century, magisterial Roman Catholic ethics.[7] An indication of the incipient impact of modern views of marriage and sexuality on the teachings of the magisterium is found in the 1930 encyclical, *Casti Connubii.* Having already reiterated the long-standing view that the procreation and education of children was the primary end of marriage, Pius XI went on to praise "the love of husband and wife which pervades all of the duties of married life and holds pride of place in Christian marriage" (Paragraph 23; see also Paragraphs 12–17). Such Christian love between spouses is not based on "the passing lust of the moment." Rather such love represents "a spiritual unity—aimed at the perfection of the character of spouses" (Paragraph 23). Pius even asserted that a marital love that uplifts the moral and spiritual character of the spouses "can in a very real sense . . . be said to be the chief reason and purpose of matrimony" (Paragraph 24). Yet, there remains a serious tension between an incipient acceptance of this modern view of spousal love and an older Catholic view that procreation is the primary end of marital intercourse. The view that emphasizes procreation determined the major thrust of Pius XI's teaching concerning sexual activity within marriage. Pius described the act of sexual intercourse itself as primarily destined for the begetting of children and only secondarily aimed to provide "mutual aid, the cultivation of mutual love, and the quieting of concupiscence" (Paragraph 60). Nevertheless, the express toleration of a couple's decision to engage in sexual intercourse even when conception cannot be expected—read by some commentators at the time as tacit approval of the rhythm method—represented an implicit admission of the value of sexual intercourse sought for the sake of expressing love apart from an intention to beget children (Paragraph 60).[8]

A stronger commitment to marital sexuality as an expression of loving, interpersonal unity was manifest in the section of the Vatican II document, *The Church in the Modern World,* which deals with marriage and the family. The assembled bishops declared that marital love is "uniquely expressed and perfected through the marital act." Sexual intercourse of husband and wife "signify and promote that mutual self-giving by which spouses enrich each other" (Paragraph 49). The language of primary and secondary ends of marriage was abandoned in this document. Instead, the document presented a clear portrait of marriage as an institution in which begetting children and promoting interpersonal intimacy between spouses are coequal aims. Church leaders did acknowledge that, in some circumstances, responsible couples might decide to limit the birth of more children. Yet, if abstinence from sexual intercourse is demanded of the married couple, sexual fidelity and the loving nurture of children already born may be imperiled (Paragraph 51). Still, in one of the contradictory impulses in the Council's documents, the bishops also insisted that there can be no fundamental conflict between the desire for genital contact as an expression of love and the ability to conceive children responsibly. Relying on natural law language, the bishops boldly asserted that there can be no fundamental contradiction between the divine laws pertaining to procreation and those pertaining to authentic conjugal love (Paragraph 51).

A continued emphasis on loving unity and procreation as the (inseparable) fundamental aims of marital intercourse is found in *Humanae Vitae,* the papal encyclical that reaffirmed the condemnation of the use of artificial means of birth control. The irony is that substantial *historical change* in the understanding of marital sexuality is the backdrop against which the encyclical lays claim to be in continuity with prior church teaching. Paul VI presents his letter as based squarely upon consistent ecclesiastical analysis of human sexuality understood as "natural" and, hence, unchanging. He asserts: "That teaching [about contraception], *often set forward by the magisterium,* is founded upon the inseparable connection willed by God and unable to be broken by man on his own initiative, between the two meanings of the conjugal act: *the unitive meaning* and the procreative meaning" (Paragraph 12, emphasis added). The value assigned to "the unitive meaning" of marital intercourse constitutes an important new emphasis influenced by historical developments in the modern period.

Currently, the magisterium of the Roman Catholic church seeks to maintain a combination of procreation and interpersonal unity as the two coequal principal aims of marriage. Liberal Catholic theologians, meanwhile, have come to place their primary emphasis on the capacity of sexual intercourse to serve as an expression of profound interpersonal intimacy between partners. The quality of the love expressed in intercourse becomes a crucial element in evaluating the moral legitimacy of sexual activity, at least between marital partners. Lisa Sowle Cahill provides a good summary of this position when she characterizes contemporary Christian sexual ethics as having "permitted procreation gradually to cede primacy of place to the interpersonal aspects of sexuality. . . . A sexual act may or may not be procreative, but it is always an avenue of personal communication, and a constituent of the most intense and intimate human relationships possible" ([7], p. 141).

This latter normative statement—sexual activity is morally legitimate only when it is an expression of intense interpersonal intimacy—is a culturally based ideal. I suggest that an ideal of intense interpersonal intimacy between heterosexual partners is foreign to the experience of many Christians who have lived in other historical periods. (It may be class bound as well.) I question whether Christians who were socialized in groups in which there were rigid, highly polarized sex roles expected marriage to provide opportunities for profound emotional intimacy. In certain historical and cultural settings, *same-sex* kinship or friendship relationships were an important source of emotional (and, perhaps, sexual) intimacy, particularly for women ([9], pp. 160–96; [41]). To the extent that we recognize explicitly the culture bound nature of the ideal of genital sexual activity as expressive of intensive interpersonal communication, we are free to critique the limitations as well as the benefits of this norm.

The modern recognition of the human person as a being entitled to direct his or her own sexual relationships as well as other social relationships is a genuine moral advance in European and American culture. This personal freedom represents a precious resource for the establishment of sexual relationships characterized by mutual respect and reciprocal self-giving and fulfillment. As a twentieth-century, Euro-American ethicist, I find the belief that sexual intercourse ought to be an expression of reciprocal openness and mutual self-giving very appealing. Still, the cultural vision of a sexual relationship as one of the most powerful expressions of interpersonal love and intimacy is subject to distortion. For example, a facile concept of romantic love can be mistaken for the difficult and fragile process of mutual personal revelation that characterizes genuine interpersonal intimacy. A shallow notion of romantic love lends itself too readily to interpersonal exploitation and irresponsibility. There is a real danger that almost any sexual behavior, no matter how personally or socially destructive, may be condoned because "we really love each other."

In addition, "loving" sexual relationships are not necessarily egalitarian. For example, during the first half of the seventeenth century in England, while Protestant preachers were stressing the importance of love in a Christian marriage, the patriarchal power of husbands and fathers was increasing and the subordination of women was deepening. Historian Lawrence Stone suggests that these two trends may have been interrelated. "Women were now expected to love and cherish their husbands after marriage and were taught that it was their sacred duty to do so. This love, in those cases where it in fact became internalized and real, made it easier for wives to accept that position of submission to the will of their husbands upon which the preachers were also insisting" ([42], pp. 141–42). Romantic love and patriarchal domination can coexist and can even be mutually reinforcing.

The Search for a Usable Tradition

Implicit in my call for collaborative scholarship that would permit us to integrate the historical experiences of women and less ecclesiastically powerful men into the tradition is the hope that such an enriched version of tradition would provide greater resources for a contemporary ethic supportive of sexual wholeness for diverse women. There is enormous work to be done by historians and ethicists before we will know whether that hope can be fulfilled. The search for a "usable history"[9] requires unusual scholarly creativity because the traces of women's historical experiences are often so scanty. Also, it is only certain women—often economically privileged women and, in the Catholic religious tradition, often celibate women—who have had the opportunity to create records reflecting their self-understanding.

Moreover, within recorded historical memory, women have lacked experiences free of influence from their *patriarchal* cultural and social context. For example, although Caroline Bynum wants to emphasize the personal and social meanings that saintly women attached to the practice of rigorous fasting, she also acknowledges that at least some of these women could not transcend entirely the hatred of the female body prevalent in certain aspects of their culture ([5], pp. 216–18). For some of these women, fasting was also a way to chastise their dangerously carnal, female bodies. Thus, I must ask if I can select certain elements of medieval women's piety—those that are consistent with my intuitions about sexual and personal wholeness—and ignore the other parts that seem to threaten an ethic that cherishes the body?

Examining the bodily piety of late medieval women and the resistance against mandatory celibacy has shown me the difficulties of a search for a usable past. Can I be confident that further collaborative scholarship will discover a genuinely "usable" history? Will we find remnants of our foremothers' resistance to male dominance and of women's efforts at self-direction of their lives, particularly their sexual choices? Are there traces of the experiences of female ancestors who valued equality in their sexual relationships? If such memories are uncovered, how do I make ethically useful connections with those memories given the distinctiveness of the experience of women who lived centuries ago in very different social and cultural circumstances?

As human beings, we always carry the past with us in the present. In ethical reflection, as in the rest of life, human beings, individually and corporately, are always reinterpreting and reappropriating elements from the past to move forward in the present. We cannot avoid being selective, for we can never recreate the entire social matrix of some revered period in the past. It seems to me that there is no better alternative than to be honest and self-critical about our reappropriation of various traditions and to be morally accountable to others for the consequences of our use of selected segments of the tradition.

Toward a New Ethic of Erotic Equality

At the beginning of this essay, I spoke about the silence of women throughout the Catholic tradition. Roman Catholic women today must demand an active role in shaping and sustaining Catholic moral traditions. I suggest that an active and influential role for diverse Catholic women would lead to a radical reorientation of Roman Catholicism's sexual ethics. The task confronting contemporary Catholics is to create a sexual ethic consistent with a deep and abiding regard for the worth and dignity of every human person. The Catholic tradition needs to be reshaped, so that it can contribute to the creation of social and cultural conditions that minimize sexual brokenness and support sexual wholeness in our times. We must formulate a sexual ethic that will be consistent with a major, morally positive cultural change now taking place—consistent with the recognition, at last, that women share fully in human dignity. We need to begin to develop a sexual ethic for a culture, which, in the tantalizing words of philosopher Mariana Valverde, "eroticizes equality" ([44], p. 43).

In this final section I will discuss three major concerns which need to be addressed in a renewed Roman Catholic sexual ethic. First, Catholic ethicists must work out the implications of a shift away from an emphasis on procreation as the *telos* which justifies sexual activity to an understanding of procreation as one possible good among others which may be realized through (some) sexual relationships. Second, Catholic ethicists need to name violent or coercive sexual activity, not nonprocreative sexual activity, as the fundamental sexual evil. They should examine the implications of unequal distributions of social power for a sexual ethic rooted in respect for the equal dignity of sexual partners. Third, a renewed sexual ethic should consider not just the restraint of sexual evil, but also the enhancement of sexual satisfaction and sexual intimacy as important components of human fulfillment for many persons.

Reassessing the Human Meaning of Procreation

Roman Catholic ethics must finally come to grips with a profound and deep-seated historical change in the human meaning of procreation. Despite a vigorous rear guard action by the Vatican and certain conservative theologians, many Catholic ethicists and most sexually active Catholics have moved procreation away from the center of sexual morality. Procreation is no longer an unambiguous good, if it ever was. I question whether women who could imagine themselves becoming pregnant would *ever* have developed a sexual ethic that centered on procreation as the primary (unambiguously positive) end of marital intercourse. For women, especially in earlier centuries, multiple pregnancies and births too often represented a serious threat to their survival and that of children whom they had already borne. Many women understand that some pregnancies are extraordinarily burdensome and dangerous and that some infants cannot be offered even the bare minimum conditions for dignified human life.

I suggest that—for a longer historical time than is often recognized—many of the Catholic faithful have realized that they have a moral responsibility to employ effective means to limit births for the good of their family relationships. Catholic couples have been making successful attempts to limit fertility for over two hundred years. By the second half of the eighteenth century in France, for example, the ordinary faithful in large numbers were limiting births and the birth rate declined steeply. Within a century the same trend could be observed in other Catholic nations of Europe ([36], pp. 461–70). Urbanization, advanced industrial economic arrangements, and ecological strains have so transformed social relationships that, barring a sudden, catastrophic depopulation of the globe, responsible and effective control of births is a major moral obligation for heterosexually active, fertile persons.

Women, in particular, are redefining the place of procreation as a moral value in their lives. Women are asserting that an ability to control their own fertility is essential to women's equal participation in other aspects of communal life. This struggle to redefine the meaning of procreation as a good for women may not be a recent historical phenomenon either. Women may have been struggling to come to a new understanding of their procreative responsibilities at prior moments in history in ways ethicists do not yet fully appreciate. For example, John Noonan discusses a Catholic moral treatise addressed to the literate laity of Renaissance Italy. Its author, Cherubino of Siena, castigates women who engage in contraceptive practices to avoid the burdens of pregnancy and motherhood. Noonan comments: "That this motive strikes him as a probable one suggests that already in the late fifteenth century the women of the Italian bourgeoisie were restive in being given only a maternal role" ([36], p. 412). Further scholarly work might reveal to ethicists that "ordinary" Catholic women have long been struggling to assume greater autonomous control over their fertility, precisely in order to act as responsible moral agents. Most women today continue to bear children and many women would describe their maternal relationships as among the most central ones in their lives. Nonetheless, women are asserting ever more strongly that an ability to direct their own reproductive power is essential for their well-being and that of their families.

If the Catholic Church finally put procreation in perspective as an important aspect of human sexuality, but no longer a feature determinative of the moral legitimacy of every act of intercourse, then the church might be able to offer a needed counter cultural witness demanding *social accountability* for the use of procreative power. Fertile, sexually active, heterosexuals do have a serious moral responsibility for new lives which result from their sexual actions. A renewed Catholic sexual ethic would hold such persons accountable to the community for responsible use of procreative power. Such people should be challenged to consider whether they (and their communities) would be able to provide adequate care for a child who might be conceived as a result of their sexual union. If not, they should not have intercourse without employing a reliable means of birth control.

The present Catholic teaching exaggerates the moral significance of procreation for a fertile, married couple; and, perhaps, it underestimates the importance of procreation for those who cannot achieve it through a nuptial embrace. The normative view of sexuality promulgated by the magisterium of the Catholic church extols the interrelated values of love and procreation said to be present in the marital act. Among the problems with that paradigm—as an exclusive ethical reference point—is that it does not provide a helpful basis upon which to develop ethical guidance for infertile heterosexual couples or homosexual persons who wish to become parents. We need to make a fresh examination of ways in which such persons can responsibly be connected to procreation and/or to the nurture of children.

A displacement of procreation from a central position in Catholic ethics will require a reevaluation of the moral weight that we attach to loving companionship and to bodily pleasure in the moral evaluation of sexual behavior. A crucial asset here would be a serious dialogue with gay Catholics, especially lesbian women, whose sexual experiences have been so severely silenced. Some lesbian Catholics have challenging questions to ask about the moral assessment of women's sexuality when it is not defined by men in the service of men and about genuine acceptance of *women's* erotic fulfillment. These are questions for all women, not just those who have genital relations with other women.

Noncoercion, Justice, and Sexual Ethics

The fundamental evil in a revised code of Roman Catholic sexual ethics should not be nonprocreative sexual activity; rather it should be coercive sexual activity. Attention to the harsh reality of sexual violence puts the attractive ideal of the unitive meaning of human sexuality into a larger perspective. Sexual intercourse can be used as an expression of anger or dominance that destroys any possibility of establishing real interpersonal intimacy. Ethicists need to consider the implications for sexual morality of the social science findings that "sexual assaults by *intimates,* including husbands, are by far the most common type of rape" ([15], p. 7, emphasis added).

Several times in this essay, I have used the metaphor of "sexual wholeness." Our lived experience, as women and men, is an experience of sexual brokenness and betrayal as well as sexual healing or wholeness. A revised Catholic sexual ethic would seek to restrain the evil of coercive or violent sexual activity. This may seem a banal normative statement. Of course, coercive sexual activity is morally wrong. But a firm ethic of noncoercive sexual activity is essential, because, in the United States, all women, all children, and an unknown number of men are at risk of sexual exploitation and sexual violence.[10] Sexual coercion—rape (including marital rape), child sexual abuse, or sexual harassment—represents a morally reprehensible expression of hatred or dominance. It is true that "sexual abuse is only peripherally about sex. More often it [is] . . . about humiliation, degradation, anger, and resentment" ([15], p. 18). Still, sexual abuse reveals starkly the broken and evil aspects of our sexuality.

One especially powerful reminder of sexuality deformed by human brokenness is marital rape. By marital rape, I mean the use of violence or the threat of violence by a husband (or ex-husband) to compel his wife to engage in sexual activity against her will. Social science studies show that 10 to 14 percent of married or previously married women report that their husbands used force or threat of force to try to make them submit to sexual activity ([15], pp 6–7; [39], p. 57; [18], pp. 542–43).

The Catholic tradition has even contributed to social blindness toward the reality of marital rape. It did so by defining marriage as a religious contract that created a special conjugal right (*jus ad corpus*), i.e., an exclusive, perdurable right to the sexual use of the partner's body. Each spouse was obligated to render "the marital debt," i.e., have sexual intercourse at the partner's request. In fairness, it should be noted that the wife was excused from her marital duty if intercourse posed a serious threat to her well-being or that of the children or if her husband had become an unfit partner. Classic examples of conditions that nullify a husband's right to sexual intercourse with his wife are insanity or drunkenness. Besides, terms such as "the marital debt" have rarely been used by Catholic ethicists since Vatican II.

Still, the Vatican II ideal of sexual intercourse as an expression of loving intimacy is a hollow mockery without explicit insistence on a prior principle of noncoercive sexual activity. A renewed Catholic sexual ethic must speak clearly and frequently against coercive or violent sexual behavior. Sexual behavior which expresses dominance or hatred must be condemned as a violation of sexual equality.

An adequate sexual ethic—one consistent with a principle of equality between the sexes—must include wide-ranging social analysis. In particular, it would explore the extent to which a lack of gender justice in the economic and social realms is a threat to sexual morality. A complex interrelated system of social structures still supports male privilege and deprives women of equal social power, particularly equal economic power. Because of the unequal social, economic, and cultural power held by women and men *as members of their respective gender groups,* it is very difficult for individual heterosexual partners to achieve genuine equality in any aspect of their lives, including the erotic dimension.

Social injustice undermines an ethic rooted in regard for the equal human dignity of all persons in other ways that are seldom explored in discussions of Catholic sexual ethics. For example, sociological patterns and cultural images exert significant influence over our opportunities to form and sustain positive sexual relationships. We do not all have equal opportunities to form personally fulfilling and interpersonally enriching sexual relationships. Homophobic prejudice and institutional heterosexism reverberate in damaging ways in both heterosexual and homosexual relationships. As Mariana Valverde perceptively notes, so-called sexual liberation is a possibility primarily for "people . . . who are young, economically secure, and without major responsibilities to children or to anyone else" ([44], p. 188). Opportunities for life-enhancing sexual relationships are too often denied persons who fail to conform to societal norms for physical attractiveness or who have noticeable physical or mental impairments. Racial oppression and ethnic prejudice create conditions that introduce special strains into the relationships between some sexual partners. Unjust patterns for allocating social power distort the distribution of opportunities for personally fulfilling and interpersonally enriching sexual relationships.

An Ethic which Enhances the Good of Sexual Fulfillment

A renewed Catholic ethic should define coercive sexual activity as the fundamental evil and analyze social patterns that undermine the equal dignity of sexual partners. Yet, a renewed sexual ethics should not overemphasize the restraint of sexual evil. Rather it should see an important role for ethical guidance which enhances prospects that human beings will experience the goods of sexual satisfaction and sexual intimacy.

Throughout the "official" Roman Catholic tradition, there is a tendency to view sexual desire as a ferocious form of energy that perpetually threatens to surge out of control with profoundly damaging consequences personally, socially and spiritually. This is too simplistic. Sexual feelings and sexual touch are sometimes more tentative and fragile stirrings of a longing for personal affirmation, solace, intimacy or bodily enjoyment. Sexual desire can be severely and lamentably dampened by low self-esteem, interpersonal rejection, despair created by various forms of social oppression, or even mere physical exhaustion. Ethicist Margaret Farley offers wise advice when she reminds us that moral norms for sexual behavior should not focus exclusively on controlling sexual feelings and activities. "Sexuality is of such importance in human life, and in interpersonal relationships, that it needs to be freed, nurtured, and sustained, as well as disciplined, channeled and controlled"

([14], p. 1587). Other Catholic ethicists need to begin to imagine what it would mean to articulate an ethic that frees, nurtures and sustains sexual energy for the sake of personal wholeness and for the sake of the enrichment of our communal lives.

One part of a sexual ethic that nurtures and sustains sexual wholeness would be an enriched notion of the virtue of [sexual] fidelity. The types of commitment between sexual partners that make for human wholeness would need to be reconsidered. The image of faithfulness as a life-long pledge of physical exclusivity in sexual relations is not enough. Faithfulness is a promise to sustain and deepen a relationship in which one is known and valued and knows and values the other. In western culture, women, both gay and straight, have been socialized to integrate our physical desires with our emotional attachments. The yearning to integrate sexual release with loving tenderness is a woman's truth that is worth preserving. (Although women need to be more honest with themselves about whether they sometimes feel sexual desire that is not connected to love.)

Sexual fidelity is a matter of making a promise to oneself and to the other that binds us to the on-going work of loving, rather than simply being carried away by "love." Sometimes the exciting, deeply satisfying quality of sexual joining and the fierceness of erotic passion make it possible for partners to maintain a sound relationship despite hard times. The fidelity that has moral significance is an on-going commitment to be present to one another in all our brokenness and our power. Such commitment is manifest in a steadfast concern for the beloved and for the relationship that allows us to "hold fast when love is not always returned as we had hoped, or when we would have wished," when it "engulfs us far more radically than we had envisaged and stretches us beyond what we had understood as our limits" ([20], p. 189).

If we viewed our sexual energies as a resource to be cherished, we might more easily recognize positive connections between our sexuality and our spirituality. Certain feminists are carefully examining the connection between sexual energy and an even more inclusive "spiritual" force in human experience. (For example: [26]; [34], pp. 180–195; [38], pp. 197–210.) Audre Lorde's essay, "Uses of the Erotic: The Erotic as Power," is an eloquent exposition of these insights. By the erotic, Lorde means a type of energy that fuels genuine sexual passion but also underlies other passionate human feelings and commitments as well. The erotic, according to Lorde, is a sense of internal satisfaction that, once known, challenges us to strive continually to meet our full potential in our personal and corporate lives. The power of the erotic also creates the ability to feel acutely and deeply in the midst of our daily activities. In particular, it unleashes our capacity for joy. Being in touch with the erotic allows us to come together in mutually respectful ways "to share our joy in the satisfying . . . [to] make connection with our similarities and our differences" ([30], p. 59). Optimally, the erotic is thread through our work lives, our political action, and our spiritual experiences as well as our sexual couplings.

Lorde does not deny that the power of the erotic can be misused, but she claims that repression of the erotic is not an effective way to prevent possible abuses.

> We have been raised to fear the yes within ourselves, our deepest cravings. But, once recognized, those which do not enhance our future lose their power and can be altered. The fear of our desires keeps them suspect and indiscriminately powerful. . . . The fear that we cannot grow beyond whatever distortions we may find within ourselves keeps us docile and loyal and obedient, externally defined, and leads us to accept many facets of our oppression as women ([30], pp. 57–58).

When we begin to shape our lives in terms of the erotic, i.e., our own inner knowledge of what gives us joy, we become unwilling to endure powerlessness and oppression passively. As Lorde says: "Recognizing the power of the erotic in our lives can give us the energy to pursue genuine change within our world, rather than merely settling for a shift of characters in the same weary drama" ([30], p. 59). Lorde connects our sexual longings to a deeper, more inclusive yearning for all that is good in human life. As a religious ethicist, I would suggest that this hunger is finally a hunger for contact with divine power.

This way of connecting the sexual in all its bodily intensity with the spiritual has enormous appeal for me. There is a truth here—a truth, I sometimes, but only sometimes, know through my experience of erotic desire. Still, the theme of the positive power of the erotic is recurring often enough in religious feminist discourse that it is time to begin to explore its possible negative facets as well as its obviously attractive aspects. Let me illustrate a few of the questions feminists might begin to explore. Are there nonfeminist cultural sources for this view of the erotic, as well as wellsprings in our own most satisfying personal experiences? Is this celebration of the erotic a feminist rendering—perhaps an unwitting one— of a pervasive, "popular culture" version of Freudian theory? Is it a new way of saying that the sex drive is one of the strongest and most fundamental human urges—one that permeates life, particularly all attempts at cultural creativity? If so, does this idea carry with it any implicit Freudian "baggage" that we would do well to examine and possibly discard? Does the feminist celebration of the erotic have any important similarities to nineteenth-century Romanticism? If so, is it vulnerable to some of the corruptions that plagued the Romantic movement? In suggesting such questions, for which I have no ready answers, I am also suggesting that a feminist ethic of the erotic needs to include an ongoing process of self-criticism.

Such self-criticism is also an important aspect of Catholic women's responsible participation in the process of shaping tradition as members of their church. This struggle of women to become active shapers of sexual morality is a crucial struggle, not just for women's growth in sexual wholeness, *but also for the welfare of the Catholic community.* The entire church—male and female, gay and straight, sexually active and celibate—must engage in a candid reappraisal of the church's teachings about women and human sexuality. If such an honest, far reaching dialogue among a wide range of participants whose insights are truly respected is not given priority soon, the vitality of the church itself will be jeopardized.

Symbolic of the urgency of this task is one recent result of a continuing requirement that ordained ministers be celibate, coupled with an inveterate insistence on an all-male priesthood. There is a serious and rapidly worsening shortage of Roman Catholic priests throughout the world. The shortage of clergy has become so severe, that, in the United States, Catholic bishops are beginning to plan carefully for a time in the not-distant future when many Catholic congregations have no priests available to preside at the Eucharist weekly.

The Sunday Eucharistic liturgy is a central activity of the Roman Catholic community. It is a powerful sign of the unity of believers in the one body of Christ. As a sacrament, it is a sign which effects what it signifies. It creates the bonds of community that it so eloquently symbolizes. Yet, a fear of women and a distrust of sexuality are so deeply ingrained in the personalities of some church leaders, and in certain of the traditions that the bishops are pledged to uphold, that they are willing to jeopardize the celebration of the Eucharist, rather than to allow the body and blood of Christ to be consecrated by any woman or by a man who publicly acknowledges an active sexual life.

If we accept the model of Catholic tradition as a compendium of the sayings of celibate, male theologians, then "the tradition" offers limited resources with which morally serious contemporary women can help men to define an ethic that promotes both sexual wholeness for believers and vitality for the religious community. Now is the time to begin a long-range, collaborative, scholarly project that may allow Catholics to discover a more usable history. Then tradition would include the stories of believing women struggling to deal responsibly with their sexuality.

Catholic women need to contribute to a new sexual ethic, one that is consistent with recognition of the equal worth and dignity of men and women. Such an ethic would recognize that coercive sexual activity, not nonprocreative sexual activity, is the fundamental evil. Ethicists influenced by feminist thought should reexamine the connections between the erotic and a "spiritual" awareness of a divine power that intends wholeness in human lives.

Women need to become full partners in a fundamental reassessment of Roman Catholic sexual ethics. For, unless contemporary Catholicism can come to a better understanding of human sexuality, even its Eucharistic unity may jeopardized. If Catholics—sexually active and celibate, gay and straight, women and men—do not find a way to reorient the tradition where sexuality is concerned, Roman Catholicism's viability as a sensual, sacramental church is threatened.

Notes

1. This particular version of the double standard in which women, who are seen as purer and less passionate beings, are held to a higher standard of behavior is a relatively recent cultural image. At other periods in Western history, women were kept under strict control (at least in the upper classes), not only to protect men from lust, but also to provide external control over women who were viewed as more carnal, less rational, and more prone to sexual promiscuity.

2. There is a vigorous debate underway in contemporary Roman Catholic ethics about the proper understanding of natural law as an ethical concept. In this paragraph and the next one, I refer to a classicist conception of the natural law. A classicist view purports to offer access to moral norms which are certain and unchanging. In the area of human sexuality, norms are frequently apprehended by reflecting on the physical structures of the reproductive organs and by contemplating intercourse as a biological activity. Careful consideration is given to the generative faculties that human beings share with other animals. This view of the natural law continues to be influential, particularly in documents concerning human sexuality issued by the Vatican. For more information about differing conceptions of natural law, see ([21], chapters 15 and 16), [11], and ([37], chapters 13 and 14).

3. Certain male mystics have also used erotic imagery to describe their experiences as persons beloved by Christ.

4. Those who opposed mandatory clerical celibacy are "losers" from the point of view of the official Roman Catholic magisterium which still requires celibacy of its ordained ministers. Protestant church historians who come from Christian traditions that have rejected clerical celibacy have a different perspective on this history. See, for example, [1].

5. This is not to say that loving affection between husband and wife, especially as it might develop during the course of the marriage, was not recognized as a human good. Some writers both ancient and medieval praised such marital affection. For example, Thomas Aquinas spoke of the great friendship between husband and wife. Such sweet bonds develop among human beings, in part, because of the pleasurable unity of copulation (*Summa Contra Gentiles,* III, 123). Yet, this is the same theologian who also said that woman was created to be man's partner in procreation, since in any other human endeavor a man will find another man to be a superior companion (*Summa Theologiae,* I, 98). Loving friendship between husband and wife was recognized by some premodern writers as a wonderful side benefit of matrimony, but

the theologies of the church did not recognize it as a central purpose of either marriage or marital intercourse.

6. If this historical analysis of the growth of medical and psychological professionals' power to influence sexual norms is correct, it raises ethical questions for such professionals. How can this cultural power be used in a socially responsible way?

7. Throughout this essay I will use the term magisterium to refer to the teaching authority of the popes and bishops who, by virtue of their episcopal office, have a special charge to preserve the integrity of the Roman Catholic church's beliefs concerning faith and morals. Some Catholic theologians have also used the term magisterium to speak of a different type of teaching authority in the church exercised by theologians by virtue of their scholarly competence. In this essay magisterium is not used to speak of the contribution of theologians. For further discussions of the two "magisteria," see [13]. For a general treatment of the magisterium, see [43].

8. A similarly complex understanding of nonprocreative, marital sexual activity is reflected in the church's practice of permitting marriage (or continuing sexual activity) when one or both spouses are infertile.

9. Letty Russell used this term, "usable history," in a pioneering work of feminist theology [40].

10. There is a high incidence of rape. Given the prevalence of rape, all women can be described as at risk of being raped. There is a high incidence of child sexual abuse, with some indications that male children are victimized more often than had originally been understood. Therefore, all children can be described as being at risk of sexual abuse. Sexual abuse of adult males does occur. However, it has not often been investigated. It is hard to estimate the risk of sexual abuse faced by nonincarcerated adult men.

Bibliography

1. Bailey, D. S.: 1959, *Sexual Relation in Christian Thought,* Harper and Brothers, New York.

2. Barstow, A.: 1982, *Married Priests and the Reforming Papacy: The Eleventh-Century Debates,* Edwin Mellen Press, New York.

3. Bayer, E.: 1985, *Rape Within Marriage: A Moral Analysis Delayed,* University Press of America, Lanham, Maryland.

4. Brown, P.: 1988, *The Body and Society: Men, Women, and Sexual Renunciation in Early Christianity,* Columbia University Press, New York.

5. Bynum, C.: 1987, *Holy Feast and Holy Fast: The Religious Significance of Food to Medieval Women,* University of California Press, Berkeley.

6. Cahill, L.: 1986, "Sexual Ethics," in J. Childress and J. Macquarrie (eds.), *The Westminster Dictionary of Christian Ethics,* Westminster Press, Philadelphia, pp. 579–583.

7. Cahill, L.: 1985, *Between the Sexes: Foundations for a Christian Ethics of Sexuality,* Fortress Press, Philadelphia.

8. Church, F.: 1975, "Sex and Salvation in Tertullian," *Harvard Theological Review* 68, 83–101.

9. Cott, N.: 1977, *The Bonds of Womanhood: Woman's Sphere in New England, 1780–1835,* Yale University Press, New Haven.

10. Countryman, L. W.: 1988, *Dirt, Greed, and Sex: Sexual Ethics in the New Testament and Their Implications for Today,* Fortress Press, Philadelphia.

11. Curran, C.: 1970, "Natural Law and Contemporary Moral Theology," in *Contemporary Problems in Moral Theology,* Fides Publishers, Notre Dame, IN, pp. 97–158.

12. D'Emilio, J. and Freeman, E.: 1988, *Intimate Matters: A History of Sexuality in America,* Harper and Row, Philadelphia.

13. Dulles, A.: 1980, "The Two Magisteria: An Interim Reflection," *Catholic Theological Society of America, Proceedings* 35, 155–69.

14. Farley, M.: 1978, "Sexual Ethics," in W. Reich (ed.), *Encyclopedia of Bioethics,* Free Press, New York, 4, pp. 1575–1589.

15. Finkelhor, D. and Yllo, K.: 1985, *License to Rape: Sexual Abuse of Wives,* Holt, Rinehart, and Winston, New York.

16. Fiorenza, E.: 1984, *In Memory of Her: A Feminist Theological Reconstruction of Christian Origins,* Crossroad, New York.

17. Fitzgerald, A. (trans.): 1926, *The Letters of Synesius of Cyrene,* Oxford University Press, London.

18. Frieze, I.: 1983, "Investigating the Causes and Consequences of Marital Rape," *Signs: A Journal of Women in Culture and Society* 8, 532–53.

19. Furstenberg, F. et al.: 1987, "Parental Participation and Children's Well-Being after Marital Dissolution," *American Sociological Review* 52, 695–701.

20. Gudorf, C.: 1985, "Parenting, Mutual Love, and Sacrifice," in B. Andolsen, C. Gudorf, and M. Pellauer (eds.), *Women's Consciousness,*

Women's Conscience: A Reader in Feminist Ethics, Winston Press, Minneapolis, pp. 175–91.

21. Gula, R.: 1989, *Reason Informed by Faith: Foundations of Catholic Morality,* Paulist Press, Mahwah, NJ.

22. Harrison, B.: 1983, *Our Right to Choose: Toward a New Ethic of Abortion,* Beacon Press, Boston.

23. Harrison, B.: 1985, *Making the Connections: Essays in Feminist Social Ethics,* ed. C. Robb, Beacon Press, Boston.

24. Hart, C. (trans.): 1980, *Hadewijch: The Complete Works,* Paulist Press, New York.

25. Herman, D.: 1989, "The Rape Culture," in J. Freeman (ed.), *Women: A Feminist Perspective,* Mayfield Publishing Company, Mountain View, CA, pp. 20–44.

26. Heyward, C.: 1984, *Our Passion for Justice: Images of Power, Sexuality, and Liberation,* Pilgrim Press, New York.

27. Heyward, C. et al.: 1986, "Lesbianism and Feminist Theology," *Journal of Feminist Studies in Religion* 2, 95–106.

28. Lebacqz, K.: 1990, "Love Your Enemy: Sex, Power, and Christian Ethics," in D. M. Yeager (ed.), *Annual of the Society of Christian Ethics,* Georgetown University Press, Washington, DC, pp. 3–24.

29. Lewin, T.: 1990, "Father's Vanishing Act Called Common Drama," *New York Times,* 4 June, A18.

30. Lorde, A.: 1984, "Uses of the Erotic: The Erotic as Power," in *Sister Outsider,* Crossing Press, Trumansburg, New York, pp. 53–59.

31. Miles, M.: 1988, *Practicing Christianity: Critical Perspectives for an Embodied Spirituality,* Crossroad, New York.

32. Milhaven, J. G.: 1989: "A Medieval Lesson in Bodily Knowing: Women's Experience and Men's Thought," *Journal of the American Academy of Religion* 57, 341–72.

33. Mitterauer, M. and Sieder, R.: 1982, *The European Family: Patriarchy to Partnership from the Middle Ages to the Present,* University of Chicago Press, Chicago.

34. Mud Flower Collective: 1985, *God's Fierce Whimsy: Christian Feminism and Theological Education,* Pilgrim Press, New York.

35. Nelson, J.: 1978, *Embodiment: An Approach to Sexuality and Christian Theology,* Augsburg Publishing House, Minneapolis.

36. Noonan, J.: 1965, *Contraception: A History of Its Treatment by the Catholic Theologians and Canonists,* New American Library, New York.

37. O'Connell, T.: 1978, *Principles for a Catholic Morality,* Seabury Press, New York.

38. Plaskow, J.: 1990, *Standing Again at Sinai: Judaism from a Feminist Perspective,* Harper and Row, San Francisco.

39. Russell, D.: 1982, *Rape in Marriage,* Macmillan Publishing Company, New York.

40. Russell, L.: 1974, *Human Liberation in a Feminist Perspective—a Theology,* Westminster Press, Philadelphia.

41. Smith-Rosenberg, C.: 1975, "The Female World of Love and Ritual: Relations between Women in Nineteenth-Century America," *Signs: A Journal of Women in Culture and Society* 1, 1–29.

42. Stone, L.: 1977, *The Family, Sex, and Marriage in England 1500–1800,* abridged ed., Harper Colophon Books, New York.

43. Sullivan, F.: 1983, *Magisterium: Teaching Authority in the Church,* Paulist Press, New York.

44. Valverde, M.: 1985, *Sex, Power and Pleasure,* The Women's Press, Toronto.

11. Sociology and Sexuality: A Feminist Perspective

Marie Augusta Neal

This chapter first appeared in *Christianity and Crisis* in 1979.

The relation of sexuality to religious belief can be discussed meaningfully, it seems to me, only within the context of a religious commitment rooted in the gospel injunction to share God's creation with all the people. That context at the present time is the church's commitment to the poor of the world.

As long as the central human need called for was continued motivation to propagate the race, it was essential that religious symbols idealize that process above all others. Given the vicissitudes of life in a hostile environment, women had to be encouraged to bear children and men to support them; child-bearing was central to the struggle for existence. Today, however, the size of the base population, together with knowledge already accumulated about artificial insemination, sperm banking, cloning, make more certain a peopled world.

The more serious human problems now are who will live, who will die and who will decide. The central fear and dread of our times is no longer that the human race might die out but that some people might face extermination for the sake of the others, and these people are the poor of the world.

In such a context the pyramidal structure of decision-making systems, so long modeled on the patriarchal family with its tradition of father-right, is a source of grave anxiety to those with little or no power. At the same time, the fear of being overthrown by the organized masses stimulates those who have power to affirm whatever in the old tradition stands to legitimate their continued right to rule. Christianity, with its gospel message to serve the Lord by serving the oppressed, is caught within these forces. There is the double dread of an elite being served by the masses and of the total extinction that would result if the "enemy" were to get control of the system.

Religious sacralization has always developed around what is feared and dreaded. We are witnessing today the desacralization of the patriarchal family as the model for business firms, industry, government, educational systems and other organizations. Desacralization occurs whenever the unrepresented have learned that people who make decisions for others, who are not members of their interest groups, make these decisions against the outsiders. Self-representation is part of the process of the development of peoples.

Although in the past religion and science affirmed the sacredness and the naturalness of hierarchy and bureaucracy, today these things are called into question because of the exploitative uses to which they have been pressed by the elite in government and industry. Today father-right has been replaced by human rights as the ethical norm for international relations as well as for communal relations under the law. Even though the Roman Catholic Church and the World Council of Churches have affirmed the declaration of these human rights in the United Nations Charter, only now are the fuller implications of their affirmation becoming manifest, as the poor rise up to claim what is rightfully theirs.

The affirmation of human rights makes of equal importance the availability of opportunities for men and women, whites and nonwhites. It provides a new ethic and brings into question long-established white male ascendancy. It affects sexual relations as well as racial relations. In various parts of the world, non-white people and women of all colors are becoming conscious of the assumptions of their inferiority, assumptions systematically enforced through social conditioning in order to provide a legitimization for their relegation to servile tasks in the interest of the dominant males.

Women are searching for ways in which to correct inhuman presuppositions about inferiority and superiority. History is correcting such errors, as people raise to consciousness the tacit assumptions embedded in centuries-old educative materials and other forms of indoctrination. Oppressed peoples demand civil rights and respect; and now women are demanding, beyond these, further knowledge of and control over their own bodies. The way these various factors relate to one another is still obscure to those immersed in a long tradition of the exploitation of persons. Moreover, art and religion frequently compound this obscurity, functioning to refine ambiguities and render them respectable.

A New Awareness

The new concern for human rights arises out of the experience and knowledge of the two-thirds of the world that lives below the level of subsistence, despite the fact that we have the technological potential to provide the health, education and welfare services to remedy that problem. What we lack are the social relations needed to produce and distribute durable goods effectively for human use and to reallocate resources on the basis of human need. The growing consciousness among the poor peoples of the world of their right to participate in the decisions that affect their lives, and to develop the resources of the places where they live rather than to have those resources used in the interest of multinational corporations and the powerful nations of the world, has stimulated the Catholic Church and the World Council of Churches to affirm those rights and to support in the context of the Gospel this movement toward a more human world (Pope John XXIII, 1963; the Second Vatican Council's Pastoral Constitution on the Church; Pope Paul VI, 1967).

It is also this movement that stimulated the re-ordering of priorities for the structure of the church that was evident in the Second Vatican Council's Dogmatic Constitution on the Church, in which the community of the people of God is accorded a priority over the juridical, hierarchical structure designed to minister to its needs. We have only begun to realize the implications of the changing structure of our church. Founded to be a community of peers, all sons and daughters of the same Father, we are beginning to feel the demand for a new symbol of unity; a symbol that is circular and not pyramidal; a symbol that does not associate expressive and instrumental skills but combines them in single units.

In the church today human community needs to be celebrated with all the pomp and ceremony with which father-right has been celebrated in the past. Even to return to the Scripture to find its meaning for our times, new symbols and a new language need to be developed. Theologies are needed that can articulate this new life that is struggling to be recognized as the church. It is a life predicated not on the rule of elites over masses in the image of fathers over children, but on the development of human beings.

The theologies of liberation developing around the issues of oppression in Latin America provide the context for the emergence of new gender-relations between men and women, relations that do not rest primarily on biological differences associated with the bearing of children. Even those theologies, sensitive as they are to the oppression of poor peoples, are not yet couched in language sensitive to the oppression of women.

Juan Luis Segundo's theological method—based on what he calls a hermeneutical circle—provides a way of approaching the problem of sexism. The circle begins with our way of experiencing reality, an experience which gives rise to ideological suspicion. This suspicion, of ideological superstructures in general and of theology in particular, is followed by a new way of experiencing theological reality, an experience that in turn gives rise to a theological suspicion about our customary hermeneutics. This leads to a new way of doing hermeneutics that appeals for a new human reality, thus beginning the whole process anew. Applied to the experience of women's status since the Council, this sequence puts the examinations of the issue of sexuality into an entirely new context. John L. McKenzie describing the Roman Catholic Church in 1969 and Martin Marty, Protestantism in 1974, sense this new context.

The end of the era is forewarned and directed by Pope Paul when, in *The Development of Peoples* and again in *The Eightieth Year Letter* on the anniversary of *Rerum Novarum,* he called Christians to action and urged the laity to transform structures "without waiting passively for orders and directives, to take the initiative freely and to infuse a Christian spirit into the mentality, customs, laws and structures of the community in which they live." All this was said in the context of action for the elimination of injustices. The injustices specifically referred to were the usurpation of the world's resources by one-third of the world, to the exploitation of the other two-thirds.

The right to life of living peoples is systematically denied to two-thirds of the people in social systems in which crumbs from the master's table are awarded in paternalistic fashion to the desperately poor, while the industrial producers and their benefactors deliberate on how they will accord assistance to the poor in future disasters. That part of the church which is caught up in such a system is currently being addressed by another part, a part that has been freed from this structure by meditating on the Gospel in company with the poor, and by the mandate of the Pastoral Constitution on the Church in the Modern World to work with the poor for their own liberation. The dynamic of this confrontation provides the context for addressing issues of sexuality.

Interface of Biology and Culture

What sociology teaches about sexuality is that the ethic the church has continued to reinforce was the common ethic of Western society prior to the development of an enormous population base. Even in 1969 Clifford Allen wrote in his *Textbook of Psychosexual Disorders:* "It seems to me that the essential criterion for normal intercourse is that it is one that tends to fertilize the woman. Intercourse is biologically for this one purpose and any pleasure, excitement, sense of well-being and so on which it produces is merely coincidental and an incitement to do what nature needs to be done." Allen was only saying what needed to be said when what he wrote was still true—that is, when fertilization was "what nature needs to get done." The fact is that nature no longer needs either as much fertilization or even the same mode of fertilization. We can deny it for a while, but the youth of the world will discover the potential for planned population through the education that we have given them.

Once women are recognized as persons fully capable of sexual feeling and not as property, they can no longer be used to satisfy urges as prostitutes, dolls, or wives in bondage. Once women's human right to professional training is provided for in our own schools, as it is now for a few, we can no longer claim that her place alone is in the home. Once the homemaking tasks are shared by men and women, then interpersonal skills will no longer be functionally divided into headwork for men and handwork for women, nor as instrumental activism for men and expressive maintenance for women. Children still need to be socialized, but the task becomes a common one for people sharing a common life-style.

My discipline of sociology teaches me that Catholic doctrine on birth control, abortion and divorce lags behind, even though it follows in the same direction as that of other church groups with less structure and looser decision-making systems—and that all of them are responding slowly to the pressure of population size. The structure of the Catholic Church provides better for the perception of new problems arising from life conditions—such as the conditions of the poor of the world—and accordingly, for directives to respond. It does not provide effectively, however, for the elimination of obsolete forms.

Another thing the theory and practice of sociology reveal is in the area of conditioning. So much that we accept as natural is in fact cultural in origin, and as such may be functionally necessary at one time and functionally autonomous at another. No longer necessary for survival, the conditioning usually serves the interest of some group with power to preserve what is to its advantage to retain. This process has been sustained in the past by the timidity with which members call for administrative accountability. Studies indicate that males are more susceptible than females to cultural conditioning, particularly in the area of sexuality. John Petras in an important essay puts it this way:

> It is the rare study in the field of human sexuality that does not report as a fact the greater potential for the sexual conditioning of males as compared with females. Males have been defined as behaving in an environment that has more to offer, symbolically, in the form of erotic

> stimuli. More recently, we are becoming aware that the prevailing image was due in large part to the assumption that females in Western society lacked a potential for sexual conditioning. It cannot be overemphasized, however, that apart from materials that have emerged from women's liberation, very few individuals have noted this fact. Nearly all the literature has been written by males, and, subtly or otherwise, a definite masculine bias is often reflected (*Sexuality in Society,* Boston, 1973).

Petras predicts for women a potential for greater sexual expressiveness, once they are no longer inhibited by the traditional definition of their passive role in sexual relations, a role reinforced by erotic literature frequently written by men. Knowledge of the more diffuse experience of delight that women experience in their bodies with greater or less intensity has a further implication. It could very well be that the exquisite delight associated with sexual intercourse is a behavior modification systematically reinforced by taboo and ritual to concentrate human desire on the task of propagating the race as long as that task was functionally necessary for its survival, and that the present de-tabooing and experimentation in the area of sexual behavior is a preparation for the newer tasks necessary for the preservation of the race. Thus, the universal ideal would no longer be only to live but to develop humanly and to provide that option for all those who choose life. This of course would include the still voiceless poor of the world.

Reality as Social Construct

Once a discipline like sociology or anthropology begins to reveal comparatively the changing focus of the sacred, the question arises: What determines the concentration of taboo and ritual in one area as compared with another? In the broadest context, language has much to do with this concentration. Recent research in the area of symbolic interaction teaches us how children are socialized to accept as natural what their parents insist is normal, expected and right. Language with special words for status groups teach as normal what is societally structured; in fact, a deference system that is exploitative is preserved by cherished norms.

Sociology can demonstrate that "reality is socially constructed," that "the processes of social interaction constrict the typifications and recipes which make up social reality," that even the dimensions of time and space are socially constructed, and finally "that human thought serves human interest." "The social configuration of the times are in the thought system" (cf. *Rules and Meanings: The Anthropology of Everyday Knowledge,* Mary Douglas, ed.; Maryland, 1973).

These observations have enormous implications for the new interest of the church in the development of community, in contrast with the old sacralization of the family. Our theological language is rooted in patriarchal family terms because of the generic masculine. Despite the fact that Scripture admonishes us to call no one father but "your Father who is in heaven," we have used the word quite freely for heads of families, local churches and countries, and have even permitted business magnates to take a paternal interest in their workers, psychiatrists in their patients, etc. In every case exploitation has followed.

So far has this use of "father" extended that in some cultures a woman is subject first to her father, then to her husband, and in old age to her son. This male dominance prevails with no disturbance to the mindset of the male who allocates the roles. A woman's coming to consciousness of herself as a human being, of the prerogatives that men arrogate to themselves and of their assumptions about women—these processes represent a conscientization that cannot be retracted.

Art, literature, professional writings, and religious practice communicate to the public a whole range of rationalizations embodied in cultural materials—including a church liturgy geared to preserve an ascendancy that the church has now disavowed in theory but not in practice. For women who have chosen ministry as their life's vocation, the situation presents an enormous task. These women ask: How can a Eucharist which calls forth a transformed community be celebrated when the image in which it is cast is not community but patriarchal family? They ask further how we can preserve an ecclesiastical structure which is so male-dominated that the thousands of books and reports written by women to show the anomaly of this situation never come under the purview of men.

Men still write about and research the priesthood without considering the issue of the ordination of women. So concentrated is the question of sexuality on the issues of birth control, abortion and divorce, as well as on the issues of premarital sex and the possibility of a married clergy, that men are not yet aware of the general problem of a male-dominated theological language, liturgy, and the religious education that is denying to women a place to celebrate life in the church.

This problem, already an anguish for a comparatively small number of women, will burst upon our consciousness with a suddenness we will be unable to cope with unless those who dominate the discipline of theology become aware that women are searching the Scriptures in a hermeneutic circle that goes far beyond the issue of unborn life to the issue of human development. Moreover, these women are doing this research with a mandate received directly from their church (through the Pastoral Constitution, for example, and in Pope Paul's encyclical on development). Soon they will discover their common oppression with the poor of the world.

Evidence is accumulating that gives the lie to the division of labor into instrumental activism for men and expressive maintenance functions for women. Human personalities are at once both instrumental and expressive, and call for communal structures which provide for development along both dimensions, not as couples, forming a unity when matched together, but as persons, whole in themselves. Aiming for wholeness men and women can do something effective about the contradictions that are present in the proposals that the church still offers for ethical solutions to problems about life and marriage.

THE LOGIC OF PATRIARCHS

When the right of a fetus to live is affirmed by a body of bishops in clear and unambiguous terms, though the same body could not condemn an unjust war using the same argument, women who bear these fetuses in their bodies and know the history of how they came to be wonder at the arrogant certainty of those who affirm the one while they are too uncertain to condemn the other.

In another contradictory position, a method of birth control by rhythm has been affirmed from 1936 onward, although even now medical research cannot predict the time of ovulation in the menstrual cycle. Nor do the bishops make research funds available for the continuation of this much-needed research. The 70 percent of women whose menstrual cycles do not match the bishops' model can only wonder at the intentions of those who propound such "certainties."

Furthermore, as long as dubious measures are being affirmed, available research on population control is not supported. And finally, the conflict generated between people trained to accept patriarchal dominance will find no adequate resolution in marriage counseling unless the patriarchal model is replaced by an experience of communal participation.

My discipline of sociology in theory and research, and especially my research on the changing structures of religious orders of women, confirms that the major sexual problem for consideration by the church is the human rights of women in the consciousness of men, men who manage the affairs of the church without recognition of their sisters whom they need if ministry, theology and clerical research are to be done adequately. Willingness of women to live in a male-dominated society will decrease rapidly as the rights of *paterfamilias* decline and the implications of full human rights develop. Population size makes it no longer functional to continue subconsciously the social conditioning—operative in art, education and the mass media—which perpetuates father-rights long after we have rejected them intellectually as inhuman and replaced them at the value level with human rights.

When liturgy, church law and theology celebrate in language and intent this human development affirmed by council and decree, then men and women can work out together an ethic for control of life. Until then, what theologians do in this area is painful rationalization, reflecting an experience too narrow to have meaning for those not included in the deliberation about the life they bear or intend to bear. Women are demanding control over their own bodies, over their minds and over their hearts. Men have thought that they themselves had this kind of control but, because of their overrationalized education, what they have falls far short of what is humanly acceptable now that human development, which includes the poor of the world, has become the intended goal of church action and reflection.

A Christian perspective on sexuality will be worked out when men and women set their fantasies aside and in communal encounter face the serious questions of life, love and sacrament. The rules and regulations that will emerge will not resemble the obsolete regulations presently prescribed for men and women with regard to birth control, abortion, divorce and sexual relations outside a context of love.

The current system is no longer credible; the time for the creation of the new community is now. The future of the church rests with those making current decisions in response to the Spirit which is moving all over the land. The problem is rooted in the reality that we are, in gospel terms—a church of the poor—but in historical reality a church that periodically gets captured by those who rule, because they are still the fathers speaking for the children, relatively untouched by the people whose life condition is not yet categorized in sacred language.

12. Western Religion and the Patriarchal Family

Christine E. Gudorf

This chapter first appeared in *Religion and Sexual Health: Ethical, Theological, and Clinical Perspectives* in 1992.

The Judeo-Christian tradition has helped to shape, legitimate, and even sacralize the model of family characteristic of the western world: the patriarchal family. Though the Judeo-Christian tradition neither created nor exclusively controlled the patriarchal family—which both predated it and was manifested in areas outside the influence of both Judaism and Christianity—neither did the Judeo-Christian tradition merely passively accept the patriarchal family, but instead made it central to the religious tradition itself, and even based religious structures on patriarchal assumptions.

Within Christianity in particular, it is necessary to distinguish between the influence of the overall Christian tradition on the family, and the existence within the Christian gospel of a teaching on family contrary to the dominant patriarchal thrust, a teaching which seems to be rooted in the teachings of Jesus himself and to have exercised a great deal of influence in the first century or two of Christianity. In the New Testament, for example, in addition to the patriarchal household codes found in a number of epistles (especially Eph. 5:22–6:9 and Col. 3:18–4:1) which recapitulated prevailing family structure in the Roman empire and accorded with the patriarchal Jewish norms, there are also a number of countervailing passages. In the Gospels, Jesus opposed the generally accepted primacy of familial duty, especially filial duty, in his refusal to interrupt his teaching to see his mother and brothers (Mk 3:31–35), in his refusal to sanction burying one's father before taking up the duties of discipleship (Lk 9:59–62), and in rebutting the woman who blessed his mother for having birthed him ("Blessed rather are those who hear the word of God and keep it!" Lk 11:27–28). While Jesus never directly contravened the dominant/subordinate relationship prescribed for husbands and wives in patriarchy, he did give many examples extraordinary in his time of respect for women, and he demonstrated support for breaking the stereotypically servant role of women in the home (Mary and Martha, Lk 10:38–42). Perhaps the strongest evidence for a New Testament tendency to contravene patriarchy comes from Gal. 3:28 and the examples in Paul's epistles of the leadership roles given to women in the early church, some of whom, like Prisca, shared authority in the church with their husbands ([12], Ch. 5). Yet regardless of the existence of this potential for opposing the patriarchal family within the Christian tradition, from the second century onward such New Testament passages were overshadowed by the development of a patriarchal church that stressed those sections of the New Testament supporting patriarchal relations in the family, such as the household codes.

Today, the passages from the Gospels and the epistles which undermine the legitimacy of the patriarchal model are being lifted up in some quarters of Christianity as the basis for constructing alternative models of Christian family and community [12], [13], [5]. A similar movement is taking place within Judaism, though the primary texts of Judaism are somewhat less explicitly supportive of alternatives to patriarchy, due largely to their greater antiquity and their original social location [7], [38].

In this discussion I will restrict myself to suggesting some of the effects of three specific aspects of the traditional Judeo-Christian model of family: the headship/breadwinner role of husbands/fathers, wives' subordination to husbands and restriction to motherhood and the domestic hearth, and the imperative that children obey parents. These have been standard aspects in Judeo-Christian tradition, culled from the Genesis story of creation (men as breadwinners, women as childbearers subject to men) and from the commandments (children's obedience to parents), and embodied and elaborated in countless stories in both Hebrew and Christian scriptures. Both Jewish and Christian scripture scholars and religious writers have further discussed, elaborated, and confirmed these three aspects of religious teaching on family throughout history up to and including our century [9]. The effects of these three aspects of the traditional family on both contemporary individuals in the family and on society itself are enormous, and frequently destructive. I will examine the effects of these three aspects on the three groups of participants in the modern family: men, women and children.

Effects on Men

The division of roles and power in the traditional family has both privileged and disadvantaged men in varying ways. Since the family has been understood as the primary and basic social unit, the power of men over women and children in the family also served to give men a power, a freedom, in wider society that women, and certainly children, did not have. For example, the chief reason that Thomas Aquinas gives for the impossibility of women becoming priests is that women were created subject to men in families, and for a much narrower purpose (reproduction), so that ordination could not be effective for women (*Summa Theologiae,* III Suppl. Q 39). Similarly Jewish women were not obligated by any of the time bound positive laws—such as on prayer and study of the law—since these would interfere with women's obligations in the home. Because women were ignorant of the law, they were excluded not only as judges, but as witnesses ([19], p. 191). Thus the power of men over women, and their comparative lack of restriction to assigned roles in the family, also conferred on men power outside the family itself. One result of this greater social power and freedom of men has been greater opportunity for personal development and for the formation of identity. Psychologists still find today that men of college age have usually reached a stage in identity formation that most women do not reach before middle age ([45], p. 175).

With social power for men came the power to name and define the world; the material world, the nature of men, women and children, as well as ultimacy itself came to be male-defined. One must be careful not to exaggerate this matter, since rigid hierarchies among men have, throughout history, severely restricted the number of men who exercised social power; for most men, rule over one's own home ("a man's home is his castle") was minimal compensation for exclusion from the male elites who ruled the wider society.

Within the family men's power over women and children tended at many periods in history to be absolute: he determined the place of residence, controlled all family resources regardless of their source, and had the right to use physical force—even to the point of death—to punish women or children or to compel obedience. In some periods and places he could sell them as property, whether in slavery, apprenticeship, or indenture. Within the marital relationship, the greater power of men allowed the sexual double standard, under which women, but not men, were held to celibacy before marriage and fidelity within marriage. Though both later Jewish and all Christian teaching included insistence on chastity, neither tradition rigorously or consistently attacked the double standard, often treating chastity as an impossible ideal for men due to their sexual nature and their social freedom ([33], pp. 227–228; [19], p. 198; [4], pp. 50–52).

To balance this great power of men, the traditional family imposed on men the responsibility of providing material support for the family. Until the modern era most people subsisted from agriculture, in which women and children participated as well. But the responsibility for family support was the husband's. This responsibility was usually onerous, and was made periodically impossible by droughts and floods, wars, epidemics or other social dislocations.

Besides the burden of responsibility for material support, the assignment of work to men, as means of providing family support, has resulted in some serious distortions in men's lives, especially in the contemporary era. Work ideally serves two other purposes in addition to material support. It is human beings' chief method for participating in and contributing to the larger human community. Work also serves as the major activity through which human persons create themselves by learning and developing their talents, encountering and overcoming challenges, and interacting co-operatively with others. In the modern world work is not only very specialized and therefore varied, but chosen by individuals rather than assigned by class or heredity. The emphasis on work as the means to support a man's family, as that which legitimates his participation and role in the family, has overshadowed for many men these other purposes of human work. Many men today do not feel free to choose work through which they can satisfy personal needs or contribute to their societies in ways meaningful to them. Many are trapped in jobs they actively dislike, some in jobs they feel detract from the broader social welfare; they feel obliged to choose work which provides as much material support as possible. Many workers dislike their work so intensely that they understand it as a sacrifice for their families, who in turn owe them respect and obedience—and greater success than the worker himself achieved ([46], Ch. 2; [40], Ch 7). This is a problem not only among the working class, where basic levels of support are often difficult to achieve, but is also true for many middle class men. Many middle class college men feel pressured to prepare for careers in accounting, law, medicine, finance and engineering, and to squelch any satisfaction they might feel in courses which might otherwise lead them to careers as poets, nurses, forest rangers, social workers or teachers. This is a common source of depression among college and university students. It is, of course, closely intertwined with more general social pressure to measure one's worth by the size of one's paycheck. Working women, socialized to think of their salaries as secondary to their spouse's (pin money), and who normally take their social status (and economic class) from their husband's job rather than their own, have not felt nearly the degree of pressure to choose work for its remuneration alone.

Today the breadwinner role of man in the west faces an additional pressure from the increased numbers of working women. In many countries the majority of women—even the majority of married women with children—now work. The reasons vary, and include career ambitions among more educated women, larger numbers of female headed households and ideological pressure in communist states, but the overwhelming majority of women work due to the inability of a single wage to support a family in adequate comfort.

The phenomenon of women working in large numbers causes anxiety in men at three levels: 1) it undermines the historic economic dependency of women and children on men on which men's authority in the family was based, 2) it forces men to work with women as co-workers, and sometimes with women as bosses, though they have been socialized to view women as subordinates, and 3) it calls into question the value of men's contribution to the family. This last is important, and often overlooked. Women's role in the family is much more secure than men's. Subordination to men and restriction to domestic work has often been difficult, and has sometimes resulted in abuse of women, but the role of mother and homemaintainer is comparatively impervious to becoming anachronistic. The tasks involved in women's role change, but they have never, despite some ideologically motivated attempts at collectivization, either been eliminated or successfully reassigned away from women. Thus economic depression and other social dislocations, for all their disastrous consequences on general family welfare, are much more devastating for men than for women, in that they steal from men the activity on which their identity, their place and authority in the family, as well as their livelihood, are based.

The greater security of women's role in the family has been augmented by the romanticization of the family in the last few centuries, which was aimed at camouflaging the power inequities in the family from a culture increasingly critical of power inequities. This romanticization described women's role in the family as being the heart of the family, as the center of warmth and as mediator of love and communication, as the primary source of nurture. The child was represented as innocent and carefree, protected and cherished. Men's role, however, did not require any romanticization, as men did not require convincing as to the benefits of the patriarchal family; their role was still presented in terms of headship and breadwinner. At times religious treatment of the burden of breadwinning suggested that this onerous burden was men's admission price to the warm refuge of the family hearth—a warmth generated by women and children.[1]

In the present when many women and children no longer are dependent upon men's breadwinning, what do men have to offer as the admission price of membership in the family? The relation between men and the rest of the family in the traditional model was based on economic need, not emotional ties, though emotional ties often developed. Mutual love as constitutive of relationships, though advocated for the Christian community as a whole, was not described as central to the family, but was assumed to be naturally present in the relation between mother and children. In the household codes, for example, the husband was to love, the wife to obey; the father was to refrain from provoking children, the children to obey; the injunctions are complementary, but not mutual.

A major effect of the traditional family on men, then, which is only highlighted by the loss of economic dependency of families on men, is the depiction, and consequent socialization of men as emotionally isolated persons who relate to others primarily through power and provision.[2] Men's historic roles of ruler and breadwinner in the family have never demanded interpersonal nurturance skills, though many men have developed these independently. In dominant/subordinate relations, it is always the subordinates who need to develop sensitivity, tact, communication and solidarity skills, which, under greatly unequal divisions of power, are actually survival skills.

Another explanation often given for the lesser relationality of men is the different conditions under which male children deal with the task of gender identity, which children face in their first and second years ([39], pp. 20–25; [8], pp. 50, 274). Since virtually all child care during these early years is provided by women, boys cannot use the modelling technique which girls use for achieving gender identity. The absence of fathers or other males, and the fact that the young boy's closest attachment is to a female, makes his task of gender identity much more anxiety-ridden. Boys' technique for reaching gender identity is a combination of separation from the mother or mother-substitute, and reliance on reinforcement and cognitive learning. In this explanation, the restriction of child care to women (and the resulting absence of men in child care) is an important factor forcing boys to renounce their earliest intimate relation (with a women) in favor of more impersonal cognitive learning if they are to feel themselves men. The implications for men's later capacity for intimacy and for later attitudes toward women are potentially serious.

Today we face massive evidence that at social-psychological levels men are increasingly isolated, anxious, and emotionally repressed, and that these conditions are potentially lethal. Their socialization in and for the traditional family has not equipped them in great numbers for child nurturance or for the emotional self-disclosure necessary for the close friendships and mutual, intimate marriages which become more necessary in modern society as more traditional forms of community and intimacy disintegrate under the influence of mobility and urban anonymity. There is a shift in the masculine paradigm now occurring in the West, largely under socio-economic pressure, which emphasizes the co-operative teamwork required of labor in a mechanized age rather than the stoic physical strength and endurance of traditional masculinity ([39], Ch. 10). This shift, toward masculine interpersonal skills and more mutual forms of relationship, which is now in its early stages and is largely limited to middle class workers, is greeted warmly by many women desirous of more mutuality and intimacy in relationships with men. There is no better way to sell women's magazines then headlines promising: "How to Get Your Man to Know and Share His Feelings"; "How Men Can Learn to Parent Well"; "How Spouses Can Be Partners." Yet men's socialization in and for the traditional family is a primary obstacle to this paradigm shift. The situation of many western men today bears eloquent witness to the cliche that it is lonely at the top. Headship and responsibility for breadwinning have deprived many men of some important human experiences, pressuring them to find identity in power and responsibility.

At a social level, the headship of men in the family has been so accepted that there have been few checks on the illegitimate use of men's power in the family. Today we face horrendous statistics regarding men's abuse of women and children, both inside and outside the family. In the U.S. domestic violence occurs in 10–21 percent of all families, with men as the almost exclusive perpetrators of this violence ([32], p. 11; [42], pp. 21–22). Studies show that between 20–48 percent of women are victims of serious sexual assault by males,[3] with a marital rape rate of 14 percent ([42], pp. 57, 64). Over 30 percent of girls and 10 percent of boys are sexually molested [43]–and the overwhelming majority of the offenders are men. 4.5 percent of all girls in this society are sexually abused by their fathers ([44], p. 10). While there are traditional Jewish and Christian teachings on family which condemn such practices, the religious legitimation of the power of men in families conditions some men to understand wives and children as possessions they may use as they wish, thus undermining the bans. Religious traditions have exhibited peculiar blind spots which also promoted abuse. Christianity long understood marriage as entailing the gift of one's body to the spouse in perpetuity,[4] so that the churches, and the Christian states, until very recently failed to recognize the possibility of rape in marriage. Still today not all the United States recognize marital rape, the largest single type of violent rape, and until 15 years ago no state recognized it. In Judaism also there has been some blindness to illegitimate exercise of men's power in families. The Mosaic law's list of relationships covered by the incest ban includes bans on a man uncovering the nakedness of his mother, his sisters, his granddaughters, his father's wives, his daughters-in-law, his aunts by blood and marriage, his sisters-in-law, but not his own daughters (Lev. 18:7–16), though father-daughter incest is one of the most prevalent, most violent, and most damaging type of adult-child incest ([44], pp. 231–232). The women covered by the ban were understood as the property of another man, while his daughters were his. In the Decalogue, men are forbidden to covet not only their neighbor's house, ox, ass, manservant or maidservant, but also his wife—another piece of his property (Ex. 20:17). In the Mosaic law, if a man rapes a betrothed virgin, he is sentenced to death; if he rapes an unbetrothed virgin, he must pay her father the bride price and marry her (Deut. 22:25–29). The injury done is understood to be to the victim's father or betrothed, not to her; she can be married off to her rapist.

Effects on Women

Just as there are some disadvantages to men in the power given to men in the patriarchal family, there are some limited benefits which accrue to women despite their subordination and restriction to home and motherhood. Chief among the positive benefits are a capacity for and interest in relationship with others which frequently produces among women intimate friendship, varying degrees of solidarity, and nurturing bonds to children. One must be careful not to understand these as inherent in women; just as some men resist male socialization to develop these qualities, so some women do not develop these qualities. But by comparison to men as a group, women are inclined to be much more relational and to develop skills for nurturing intimacy. For example, studies of conversation among male groups and female groups demonstrate that men are more likely to interrupt one another, discuss impersonal subjects and events rather than feelings or relationships, and to compete with one another for the speaker role. In contrast, women's groups demonstrate attempts to include women who have been silent, to share feelings and discuss relationships, and seem to lack the dominance hierarchy so central to men's groups ([2], pp. 292–299).

Yet for all the importance of these relational skills, the overall effects of women's role in the family have been negative. The understanding that women were created to be full time mothers and domestic workers has resulted in economic discrimination against women for millennia. Even today in the US the average female wage for full time workers is less than 2/3 that of men, though women as a group are better educated than men. The channeling of the majority of women into "women's work," sometimes called pink collar work, makes "comparable worth" campaigns difficult to implement, and so women's work continues to be underpaid. Furthermore, the majority of married women who do work today find that they, compared to their husbands, carry a "double burden" [1]. They share the burden of supporting the family, in addition to virtually the entire burden of child care and domestic work. Working wives have a workday of ten to twelve hours; they average workweeks of 76 hours ([18], p. 379 in [1]). Studies of men's labor in the home report that husbands spend from .3 to 1.3 hours per day in child care or domestic labor ([37], p. 285 in [1]). Thus in the contemporary world what might once have been an equitable division of labor—though not of power—between men and women in the patriarchal family has become blatantly inequitable as women share the burden of men's traditional role, while men fail to share the burden of women's traditional role.

The definition of women as made to be mothers within the patriarchal family contributed to an understanding of women as body, as inherently carnal, during centuries when all things material, and especially the body, were understood as morally dangerous and inferior to the spiritual soul, which characterized men. It was the possession of the soul that was understood to make humans reflect the image and likeness of God; yet Christianity tended to follow Augustine's dictum that men possessed the image and likeness of God in themselves, women only when joined to a man (De Trinitate, IV, 6). The carnality which characterized women for most of Christian history was understood to justify men's control of female bodies. This not only allowed the sexual abuse of women described above, but produced many other variations of female loss of control of their bodies. It was decided that the evil seductiveness of female flesh (to men!) should be covered and kept out of sight; women who failed to heed this decision were considered to have invited random abuse. Women's carnality was considered to be redeemed only through childbirth (1 Tim. "Yet woman will be saved through childbearing, if she continues in faith and love and holiness, with modesty"). Because childbearing was women's function, until recently Christianity has forbidden women any reproductive control over their bodies: no contraception, no abortion, and no right to refuse intercourse in marriage, even though frequent childbearing endangered women's lives, and millions of women died in childbirth. Women still struggle for control over their bodies with a largely male medical establishment,[5] which, it is charged, has developed medical procedures contrary to women's interests, such as widespread caesarean sections, induced births, unnecessarily radical hysterectomies and mastectomies, not to mention the development of the horizontal birthing position which extends labor time [48], [16].

But perhaps the most negative effects of women's role in the family have been on women's personalities and identities. Many women in the West feel a lack of individual identity. Longer lives and shorter periods of child bearing and rearing have left many women feeling as if they have drifted through their lives fulfilling assigned roles without any sense of themselves as individuals. Universities, churches, and volunteer organizations benefit from attempts of middle class women to fill this void; marriages are strained as women seek to expand their interests and test their capacities in new ways. There is frequent feminist discussion of women as spiders sitting on a web and unable to distinguish themselves from their webs: they are daughters, sisters, wives and mothers, but they fear that apart from these relations they do not exist, and are therefore dependent [27]. The contemporary understanding of the human person as autonomous contributes to their dissatisfaction [27], [47]. This is the reverse of the situation of many men, who have constructed the identity which women feel the lack but are constrained from the relationality which women feel defines them.

Passivity is often described as characteristic of women. One element of passivity under increasing attention is fear. There is little doubt that most women live in fear, to greater or lesser degrees, of male anger and aggression. A cursory review of the statistics on domestic battering and sexual abuse makes this understandable. But we are coming to understand that the 20, or 30 or 40 percent of women who personally suffer the various types of male abuse are not the only women who live in fear. The knowledge that one's mother, sister, friend or neighbor (not to mention many anonymous women in the daily news) has been beaten, raped, or molested is sufficient to provoke fear of men's anger and aggression. Even fathers teach girls to fear violence, or at least coercion, from males; many end their warnings with "I know; I was once a young man." In fact, parents of both sexes teach women from the time that they are little girls that men are to be feared at some level. "Don't talk to strange men, don't accept rides, be careful to travel in groups, always carry money for a cab or phone." The very measures we teach our girl children to make them safe, alert young women that there is danger out there, and it is male. Mothers often counsel children to avoid or to appease Daddy when he is angry (whether the anger is appropriate or not), thus teaching children that Daddy's anger is potentially dangerous. Fear has a debilitating effect on persons; the greater the level of fear, the more energy must go to coping with the fear, and less is left for other activities. A great deal of many women's energy gets used coping with fear and attempting to avoid, deflect, or distract men from men's anger and violence, not to mention coping with the familial after-effects of anger and violence.

Is it any wonder that religious women are increasingly admitting to problems with relating to a male God we call Father? It seems clear that the Judeo-Christian tradition, so long as it continues to identify God as male and father, and so long as women's experience of males is tinged with fear of anger and violence, will have great difficulty in overcoming traditional understandings of God as strict judge, swift to anger and terrible in his wrath.

But explorations of anger have expanded from considerations of the effects of men's anger and violence to deal with the phenomenon of anger in women. Many writers increasingly point to anger as both having beneficial effects, and as being absent in women ([17]; [34], Chs. 6, 12). Many encourage women to experience their anger, rather than repress it, with the understanding that anger arises from injury, form a slight to their personhood, or that of someone they care about. If the anger is not expressed toward the cause of the injury, but is repressed and unrecognized, it takes other more destructive forms. One common form that repressed anger at injury takes in women is self-blame. Victims of rape and child sexual abuse frequently come to accept responsibility for their own victimization, rationalizing that such atrocities do not happen to the innocent, that they must have done something to attract or set off the abuser ([13], Chs. 7, 8, 10). Victims of marital rape and child incest abuse are often so dependent both emotionally and materially on their abusers that they fear the loss of love and support if they vent their anger by accusing the abuser. Even women victims of strangers frequently fear a lack of support from relatives, friends, and social agencies—a fear which is all too often realistic—and interpret this to mean that there is no basis for their anger; that it is appropriately aimed inward.

Anger aimed inward in the form of self-blame is terribly destructive, and often begins a process of loss of respect and concern for one's self as not worthy of care and protection. The fact that many victims of sexual abuse, especially young victims, are frequently revictimized later in life, is often explained through this learned failure to care for, and therefore to protect, themselves ([44], Ch. 11).

But all injuries to women are not sexual. Parents and teachers who steer top ranking girl students into nursing schools instead of medical schools, secretarial programs instead of academic tracks, companies who routinely pass over women for promotion, personnel directors who ask women applicants what form of contraception they use and do they plan to have children, all do women injury. The anger at this injury is often repressed because women know that such behavior is not intentionally vindictive, and is often well meant. But repression of such anger does not eliminate it.

All persons yearn for power, not necessarily power over others, but personal power—the power to choose and direct one's course, to make a difference, to achieve, to earn recognition. Many women in the traditional family have been denied freedom and opportunities to fulfill their yearning for power in legitimate ways. The role ascribed to them is supportive, with little room for independence. Denied legitimate methods of exercising personal power, some women, like some in other suppressed groups, choose illegitimate ways of exercising personal power, usually through manipulation of those to whom they are bonded in the family ([36], pp. 13–20). In the nineteenth and early twentieth century, middle and upper class women frequently used illness as a means of gaining attention and controlling other family members. The nagging wife, the controlling mother, are contemporary stereotypes not true of women as a whole, but nonetheless all too often real. They result at least in part from the restriction of women to a narrow role in which they are unable to recognize or satisfy their own ambitions.

Such responses of women to the restrictions of women's roles in the family are still present in our world, but as opportunities for some women open up we have become aware of another type of damage done to women by socialization for the patriarchal family, and that is fear of success ([14], pp. 238–241; [36], pp. 29–32, 119–122). Many women fear success in a variety of forms. Adult women sometimes fear job success out of concern that their husbands cannot accept wives who earn more or who have higher status positions; this fear may be well grounded, as such situations frequently figure in reasons given for divorce. Many young women deliberately fail to succeed both in school and in sports, especially when directly competing with men, for fear this will turn off boyfriends, or boys in general. Some women exhibit a more generalized fear of success as something not feminine, something they are unable to reconcile with themselves as women. Women seem to achieve best when they understand the endeavor in terms of developing or testing social skills. Women are least likely to achieve when success is achieved in direct competition; studies show that while competition raises achievement for boys, it decreases success for girls, even when the competitors are same sex ([31], pp. 247–254; [20]).

Women's repressed anger and the fear women carry of men take their toll on women's relations with men, even men they have no reason to fear, men who have not injured them. They create real tension in women who want to love and trust their husbands, but cannot entirely banish the whispered warnings of male violence and male failure to take women seriously which echo in women's heads every time their husband curses a reckless driver or complains about his secretary's incompetence.

All of this leads us to one of the greatest casualties of the patriarchal family structure: the marital relationship itself. There seems little doubt that the interpersonal intimacy which can characterize marriage is rendered infinitely less possible within the structure of patriarchal marriage. Both spouses suffer this lack of intimacy, though differently. Women seem to have greater resources for intimacy outside marriage than men, who are more dependent on wives for intimacy than wives are on them. But wives are much more likely to feel a conscious need for intimacy, and to mourn or resent low levels of intimacy in marriage. It is the power relation in patriarchal marriage which operates against intimacy. When one person has power over another—and the greater the power, the more profound the effect—trust becomes difficult. The powerless party is unlikely to fully trust the powerful party, and therefore avoids complete vulnerability. Who of us chooses to confess our fears and failures on the job to our boss? Co-workers are more likely confidants, and, especially for men, only when the co-workers are not in any way competitors. We are more likely to confide in fellow students than teachers, siblings than parents, unless the object of our confiding is to enlist the powerful one on our side against another. True marital intimacy requires trust so total that it allows us to abandon self-consciousness—to fail to consider how we appear to the other—and to merge with the other at some level. To merge with someone of superior power is dangerous, for we can disappear completely, be swallowed up by the other—which has been women's experience of the legal, political and economic consequence of marriage historically understood as "two in one flesh."

While the powerful person may have no fear of being controlled, punished, abandoned, swallowed or otherwise hurt, the role division in the traditional family leaves men also wary of marital intimacy. For the nature of power over others, which men are conditioned to see as central to masculinity, is that it is never vulnerable, never allows the lowering of the barrier of self-consciousness, lest power be lost. Fear of intimacy, especially with women, as an obstacle to identity, which may be left over from boys' early struggle for gender identity, may also contribute to men's resistance to marital intimacy, and to men's tendency to understand marital intimacy in terms of physical sharing in sex ([6], p. 364) rather than as an integration of physical with emotional intimacy.

Effects on Children

The area in which the traditional family's effects have received the least scrutiny is that of effects on children. The ideological right today bemoans the demise of the traditional patriarchal family; their argument that children are the foremost victims of its demise is widely accepted. Even liberals, who support the changes in women's role opposed by the right, often approach the issue of the family by asking how to compromise the legitimate aspirations of women with the real needs of children for the protective nurture of the traditional family. There is little systematic attempt to assess the positive and negative effects of the traditional family on children.

The most commonly posited benefit of the traditional family for children is the full time presence of mothers. In fact, this supposed benefit does not withstand much historical scrutiny, as it seems to suppose a modern, stable, two parent household with a full time female homemaker. For thousands of years women in the home worked—in the fields, in animal care, weaving, slaughtering, candle and soap making, not to mention cooking, washing and cleaning. Among the poor, married women were often employed outside the home as cooks, laundresses, in factories and mines, as seamstresses and maids, and in raising the children of the rich. It has probably been historically accurate to posit that contemporary working mothers with a 40 hour workweek spend more time interacting with their children than their ancestresses did.

We also need to look at the psychological research on the effect of female child care on young children referred to above, which leads girls and boys to different strategies for reaching gender identity—strategies which promote later deficiencies in intimacy and relationship for boys, and in individual identity for girls.

Liberal rights language is just beginning to be applied to children. It can be helpful to probe the rights of children, and the extent to which children's rights are recognized in the traditional patriarchal family. Children obviously have at least equal rights to material subsistence with adults. The role of fathers as breadwinners in the traditional family is assumed to supply the material needs of children. When fathers are adequately remunerated for work, children are usually benefitted.[6] However, the material dependence of children on fathers is often experienced by children—and often consciously presented by parents—as the basis of fathers' authority in the family, the reason that obedience is due to father: "So long as you live in my house, and I feed you, you do as I say." The dependence of the child on father's control of resources (or in female-headed households on mother's) conditions children to view reality as a realm where those with material resources call the shots. While this can stimulate in children a positive desire to aspire to economic self-sufficiency as an adult, it can also have very negative effects. It is a very real factor in children leaving home before they are prepared for independence, either as runaways or in order to marry too early. It can lead children to see the amassing of material resources as the means of being in total control of one's life (especially when fathers are not only powerful but non-expressive of feelings of failure, dependency, and anxiety), when in fact such freedom is impossible; all humans must learn to deal with dependency and the unavoidable arbitrariness of accidents, sickness, and death. This link between father's resources and father's authority can also lead children to desire control over others, to be as powerful as, or more powerful than, father. Worse, it can condition children to be deferential to those in later life who have more resources than they, as if those persons have a right to authority over them. Interestingly enough, the Judeo-Christian tradition has from its beginnings criticized attempts by the rich to use their wealth to manipulate and control the less fortunate, to deny them justice and rights, but has never recognized that the identification of the headship role with the breadwinner role of men predisposes children to resign themselves to the real power—if not the just right—of the rich to manipulate others less well endowed.

The emphasis on the obedience of children to parents, in the absence of any elaboration of the rights of children, fails to prepare children to recognize parental wrongdoing, whether towards them or others. Thus child victims of parental physical or sexual abuse, even when they consciously hate the abusive parent, frequently have no consciousness that the parental action is objectively wrong and could be condemned by, or much less stopped by, outside authorities. The difference in age and status between parents and children, not to mention the tremendous emotional and material dependence of children on parents, will always make it difficult for children to challenge parents' wrongdoing. But the model of the traditional family actually encourages the child to see the parent as the ultimate authority, incapable of wrongdoing. Even when children as adults could otherwise expect to be freed from obligations of parental obedience, the religious tradition has insisted that adult children honor and respect parents, without specifying any limits on that honor and respect (Ex. 20:12, 21:17; Mt. 19:18–19; Eph. 6:1–3). While it is one thing to demand that children provide material support for dependent elderly or disabled parents, unlimited honor and respect, as indicated in the Exodus condemnation of anyone who curses his parents, is quite another.

The terror and trauma of children trapped in physical, sexual or emotional abuse by parents cries to heaven, but because children have been silenced by our failure to instill in them a sense of their own right to freedom from abuse, only heaven hears their largely unspoken cries. We often read that many of these abused children grow up to be abusers, which is true. But we need to add to this picture the hundreds of thousands of child runaways whose chief reason for flight was abuse, and who all too often end up further exploited in our urban underworlds. We need to add to the picture the thousands of victims of parental incest who become self-destructive out of internalized anger and hatred, and commit suicide, or choose the slow death of drugs, alcohol, or the daily death of self-punishing sexual exploitation by others. We have a tendency to think that these cases, despite burgeoning statistics, are only exceptions to a general rule of parental nurture. But we have a great deal of psychoanalytic literature that describes other, more subtle but also disabling consequences on children of the power roles embedded in the traditional family.

Alice Miller, a German psychoanalyst, writes of her work with many "successful" persons whose parents have demanded and received the surrender of the child's self to meet the parents' needs. The loss of the self in such children cripples them emotionally:

> Children who fulfill their parents' conscious and unconscious wishes are "good," but if they ever refuse to do so, or express wishes of their own that go against those of their parents, they are called egoistic and inconsiderate. It usually does not occur to the parents that they might need and use the child to fulfill their own egoistic wishes. They often are convinced that they must teach their child how to behave because it is their duty to help them along the road to socialization. If a child brought up this way does not wish to lose his parents' love (and what child can risk that?) he must learn very early to share, to give, to make sacrifices and to be willing to "do without" and forego gratification—long before he is capable of true sharing or of the real willingness to "do without." Frequently such children use their own chil-

> dren, satisfying the needs of the suppressed child in themselves at the expense of their child, just as their parent did ([35], p. xii).

The very language we use to describe many of the reasons for having children are revealing, for they say little of respect for the dignity and identity of the child her/himself: to insure our immortality, to succeed more than I did; to be the ——— I never got to be; for company and security in my old age; to see myself in another person; to have someone who will love me; to have someone I can pour out my love on; to be a real woman (man). All of these reasons are based on the needs of the parent, and on using the child to fulfill one's need. The very description of women in the traditional family as necessarily mothers—and the long millennia that barren women have been despised or pitied—encourages women, in particular, to see children as fulfilling a basic need for women.

In many ways we do see children as property, a special kind of property which fulfills a variety of intimate needs for us. We give very little thought to the process by which children become adults (and later parents themselves), to how they are to move from being dependent objects to becoming subjects with free agency. Marriage counselors tell us that many of the most common marital problems stem from relationships between parent and child that remain unresolved ([15], Ch. 3). Most persons in our society marry long before having reached adulthood in terms of seeing themselves as peers of their parents. Most remain trapped by the emotional authority they were socialized to grant parents. One problem for marital intimacy resulting from this failure to throw off the emotional authority of parents takes the form of fearing to achieve greater emotional intimacy in one's marriage than one's parents achieved. The adult child has accepted the parents as the norm which cannot be surpassed; to attempt to do so is to be disloyal. Such disloyalty implies a recognition of parental failure at intimacy, not only within the parental marriage, but also a failure to satisfy the intimacy and affection needs of the child. Such recognition is often painful for the child, a festering sore that has often been long repressed. A failure on the part of the adult child to face parental failure in intimacy and one's own resentment toward the parent for such failure (and all parents sometimes fail their children) produces resistance to intimacy with one's spouse, often most obviously in the presence of one's parents.

Another obstacle to marital intimacy reported by marriage counselors stemming from the failure of adult children to understand themselves as peers, and not emotional dependents, of their parents, concerns identifying one's spouse with the parent of the same sex. We often marry seeking in a spouse the positive qualities we see in our opposite sex parent without the negative qualities we resent in that parent. Frequently, after marriage, we come to see in the spouse the negative qualities we most resent in the parent—whether or not the spouse really exhibits such qualities. When we have never resolved with the parent the resentments which linger from our childhood, when we have never recognized and forgiven the parent their failures with us, we often read into and resent in the spouse the qualities we resented and feared in the parent but could never openly face in the parent due to dependency and fear/reverence for parental authority. The wife who resented her father's consistent failure to listen to her, to take her seriously, may explode in anger at her husband's momentary preoccupation which causes him to miss some more or less inconsequential remark of hers, and may see a few such incidents over a period of years as evidence that he is just like her father: uncaring. The husband who resented his mother's attempts to control his every action and relationship through guilt and emotional manipulation may flare up at a wife who expresses a preference regarding some decision they face; he interprets her statement not as a preference, but as an attempt to control his decision, as his mother did.

In conclusion, the emphasis on children's obedience to parents in the Judeo-Christian tradition, and the underlying assumption that parents are natural protectors guided by the best interests of the child, have worked against any recognition of the rights of children. The absence of treatment of children's rights has failed to restrain parental abuse of children, helped prevent children from resisting parental abuse, and caused social blindness to the abuse of children. In addition, because within the tradition children are always children of their parents, subject to some degree of obedience, and never become peers, children are hindered in resolving the very real and powerful resentments against parents that they carry from childhood. These resentments are often pre-rational, deeply rooted angers (sometimes unreasonable) at the ways in which they were weaned, toilet trained, disciplined, and touched or not touched with affection, or even actually abused. Religious communities could be a source of real support for children in becoming adults if they encouraged children to see their parents as humans, not as god-like authorities, humans who are themselves wounded, who make mistakes and fail to love enough. For only if children can see their parents realistically, and forgive them their inadequacies, can they move on to the real issues of adulthood without projecting the problems of childhood on their adult relationships and situations. Such a resolution of our childhood resentments affects also our relationship with God, since the Judeo-Christian tradition presents God as parent. If we so often project our problems with our parents on our spouses, how easy it is to project these same problems onto our divine parent.

Conclusion

It is clear that the patriarchal understanding of the family within western religion is not merely an issue for theologians. Religion shapes both individuals and social relationships. Many different kinds of contemporary professionals—doctors, psychotherapists, social workers, and marriage counselors, among others—as well as a variety of non-religious institutions deal on an everyday basis with unhealthy effects of religious understandings of the family. Their concern is one source of support for the growing interest within many religious communities both in revamping the family in directions which would allow for healthier individuals and relationships among men, women and children, and in using social scientific criteria to give shape to these new directions.

The greatest obstacle to such revamping is ingrained reverence for religious tradition, which manifests itself in opposition to all changes in what is perceived as the revealed tradition. The best rebuttal to such opposition seems to be a demonstration of the internal contradictions within western religious traditions, in particular the existence within these traditions of potentially liberating perspectives which counter dominant practice regarding the family. Within Judaism, we can look to the nature of Yahweh as revealed both in divine intervention to liberate the suffering Hebrews enslaved in Egypt and in the law given to Moses, which took such pains to establish a strong community rooted in justice and concern for the weak. From this grounding, both Talmud and Mishnah elaborated further protections for women and children. In Christianity, Jesus's treatment of women, children, work, and power, together with the evidence of how the early church in Acts and the epistles implemented some of these teachings, form the basis for rethinking the family. This work has only barely begun.

Notes

1. See the speeches of twentieth century Roman Catholic popes, for example, [21], [22], [23]. In Protestantism, Martin Luther himself is often pointed to as the initiator of this romanticizing of the family ([29], pp. 89, 160–161, 191) though his appreciation of the joys of the family hearth and the conjugal bed are less fulsome than in the twentieth century popes, and seem a welcome relief from the often legalistic and ascetic treatment of family in the theology of his own day.

2. Mirra Komorovsky writes: "The need to maintain a 'manly' facade, the fear of acknowledging 'feminine' traits—all generate in the male a constant vigilance against the spontaneous expression of feelings. . . . Such guardedness adds stress to the ever-present external sources of tension" [28]. Jourard argues that being manly requires men to wear a kind of neuromuscular armor against expressiveness. He goes so far as to consider that the chronic stress thus generated is a possible factor in the relatively shorter lifespan of men as compared with women. But the deleterious effects of such self-control do not end with stress. A man who does not reveal himself to others is not likely to receive their confidences. It is precisely in the course of such interaction, however, that a person learns to recognize his own motivations, to label emotions, and to become sensitive to the inner world of his associates. Without an experience of psychological intimacy a person becomes deficient in self-awareness and empathy

[26], [3]. Still another recent writer ([11], p. 210) alleges that men are threatened by psychological probings of feelings. What passes for confidence in their relationships with women is nothing but their need for uncritical reassurance ([28], p. 158).

3. This range is based on two studies: ([25], p. 145) for the conservative figure of 20–30 percent, and ([44], p. 158) for the 48 percent, which is conservative in its own way: Russell's survey found that 82 percent of the victims of child incest were later victims of serious sexual assault as adults, whereas *only* 48 percent of those who had not been victims of child incest suffered serious sexual assault as adults. Thus the figure of 48 percent is not for the population as a whole, but for the population who were not victims of child incest. Figuring in the victims of child incest would raise the figure even higher.

4. As found, for example, in 1 Cor. 7:3–4: "The husband should give to his wife her conjugal rights, and likewise the wife to the husband. For the wife does not rule over her own body, but the husband; likewise the husband does not rule over his own body, but the wife."

5. This male medical establishment itself used Christianity in its bid to replace the midwives who preceded the male physicians: midwives were accused by the male physicians of pagan superstition because of their refusal to use the new mechanical forceps and their insistence on working with, and not against nature. As a result, thousands of midwives were burned at the stake as witches by the church [10]. The struggle over women's bodies continues [41].

6. For example, there is continuing emphasis through one hundred years of Catholic social teaching on the just wage as one sufficient for the support of the wage earner and his family in adequate comfort and security, without the necessity of his wife or children working ([29], p. 662; [26], pp. 626–629).

Bibliography

1. Andolsen, B.: 1985, "A Woman's Work Is Never Done," in B. Andolsen et al. (eds.), *Women's Consciousness, Women's Conscience: A Reader in Feminist Ethics,* Winston, Minneapolis, pp. 3–18.

2. Aries, E.: 1977, "Male-Female Interpersonal Styles in All Male, All Female, and Mixed Groups," in A. Sargent (ed.), *Beyond Sex Roles,* West, St. Paul, MN, pp. 292–299.

3. Balswick, J. O. and Peek, C. W.: 1971, "The Inexpressive Male: A Tragedy of American Society," *Family Co-ordinator* 20, 263–268.

4. Bird, P.: 1974 "Images of Women in the Old Testament," in R. Reuther (ed.), *Women and Sexism,* Simon and Schuster, New York, pp. 41–88.

5. Brown, J. C. and Bohn, C. R. (eds.): 1989, *Christianity, Patriarchy, and Abuse: A Feminist Critique,* Pilgrim, New York.

6. Bunker, B. B. and Seashore, E. W.: 1977, "Power, Collusion, Intimacy/Sexuality, Support: Breaking the Sex-Role Stereotypes in Social and Organizational Settings," in A. Sargent (ed.), *Beyond Sex Roles,* West, St. Paul, pp. 356–370.

7. Cantor, A.: 1976, "Jewish Women's Haggadah," in C. Christ and J. Plaskow (eds.), *Womanspirit Rising: A Feminist Reader in Religion,* Harper and Row, San Francisco, pp. 185–192.

8. Chodorow, N.: 1978, *The Reproduction of Mothering: Psychoanalysis and the Sociology of Gender,* University of California Press, Berkeley.

9. Clark, E. and Richardson, H. (eds.): 1977, *Women and Religion,* Harper and Row, San Francisco.

10. Ehrenreich, B. and English, D.: 1972, *Witches, Midwives, and Nurses,* Feminist Press, Old Westbury, CT.

11. Fasteau, M. F.: 1974, "Why Aren't We Talking?" in J. Pleck and J. Sawyer (eds.), *Men and Masculinity,* Prentice-Hall, Englewood Cliffs, NJ, pp. 19–21.

12. Fiorenza, E. S.: 1983, *In Memory of Her: A Feminist Theological Reconstruction of Christian Origins,* Crossroad, New York.

13. Fortune, M. M.: 1983, *Sexual Violence: The Unmentionable Sin,* Pilgrim, New York.

14. Frieze, I. et al.: 1974, "Achievement and Nonachievement in Women," in I. Frieze et al. (eds.), *Women and Sex Roles,* W. W. Norton, New York, pp. 234–254.

15. Gallagher, C. et al.: 1986, *Embodied in Love: Sacramental Spirituality and Sexual Intimacy,* Crossroad, New York.

16. Gordon, L.: 1977, *Woman's Body, Woman's Right: A Social History of Birth Control in America,* Penguin, New York.

17. Harrison, B. W.: 1985, "The Power of Anger in the Work of Love: Christian Ethics for Women and Other Strangers," in C. Robb (ed.), *Making the Connections: Essays in Feminist Social Ethics,* Beacon, Boston, pp. 3–21.

18. Hartman, H.: 1981, "The Family as the Locus of Gender, Class and Political Study: The Example of Housework," *Signs* 6, 366–394.

19. Hauptman, J.: 1974, "Images of Women in the Talmud," in R. Ruether (ed.), *Women and Sexism,* Simon and Schuster, New York, pp. 184–212.

20. Horner, M. S.: 1970, "Femininity and Successful Achievement: Basic Inconsistency," in J. M. Bardwick et al., *Feminine Personality and Conflict,* Brooks-Cole, Belmont, CA, pp. 40–74.

21. John XXIII: 1960, "Ci e gradito," *Osservatore Romano,* 8 December 60.

22. John Paul II: 1979, "All'indirizzo," *The Pope Speaks* 24, pp. 168–174.

23. John Paul II: 1979, "Chi troviamo," *The Pope Speaks* 24, pp. 165–167.

24. John Paul II: 1981, "Laborem exercens," *Acta Apostolicae Sedis* 73, pp. 577–647.

25. Johnson, A. G.: 1980, "On the Prevalence of Rape in the U.S.," *Signs* 6, 136–146.

26. Jourard, S. M.: 1971, *Self-Disclosure,* Wiley-Interscience, New York.

27. Keller, C.: 1986, *From a Broken Web: Separation, Sexism and Self,* Beacon, Boston.

28. Komorovsky, M.: 1976, *Dilemmas of Masculinity,* W.W. Norton, New York.

29. Leo XIII: 1891, "Rerum novarum," *Acta Sanctae Sedis* 23 [William Gibbon (ed. and transl.), *Seven Great Encyclicals,* Paulist, New York, pp. 1–30)].

30. Luther, M.: 1967, *Table Talk,* in T. S. Tappert (ed. and trans.), *Luther's Works,* Vol. 54, Fortress, Philadelphia.

31. Maccoby, E. and Jacklin, C.: 1974, *The Psychology of Sex Differences,* Stanford University Press, Berkeley.

32. Martin, D.: 1976, *Battered Wives,* Glide, San Francisco.

33. McLaughlin, E.C.: 1974, "Equality of Souls, Inequality of Sexes: Women in Medieval Theology," in R. Ruether (ed.), *Women and Sexism,* Simon and Schuster, New York, pp. 213–266.

34. Milhaven, J. G.: 1989, *Good Anger,* Sheed and Ward, Kansas City.

35. Miller, A.: 1981, *The Drama of the Gifted Child* [1979 *Das Drama des begabten Kindes*], Basic, New York.

36. Miller, J. B.: 1986, *Toward a New Psychology of Women,* 2nd ed., Beacon, Boston.

37. Minge-Klevana, W.: 1980, "Does Labor Time Decrease with

Industrialization? A Survey of Time Allocation Studies," *Current Anthropology* 21 (3), 279–298.

38. Plaskow, J.: 1976, "Bringing a Daughter into the Covenant," in C. Christ and J. Plaskow (eds.), *Womanspirit Rising: A Feminist Reader in Religion,* Harper and Row, San Francisco, pp. 179–184.

39. Pleck, J. H.: 1981, *The Myth of Masculinity,* MIT Press, Cambridge, MA.

40. Raines, J. C. and Day-Lower, D.: 1986, *Modern Work and Human Meaning,* Westminster, Philadelphia.

41. Rothman, B. K.: 1982, *In Labor: Women and Power in the Birthplace,* W. W. Norton, New York.

42. Russell, D.: 1983, *Rape in Marriage,* Macmillan, New York.

43. Russell, D.: 1984, *Sexual Exploitation: Child Sexual Abuse and Workplace Harassment,* Sage, Beverly Hills, CA.

44. Russell, D. E. H.: 1986, *The Secret Trauma,* Basic, New York.

45. Sales, E.: 1974, "Women's Adult Development," in I. Frieze et al. (eds.), *Women and Sex Roles,* W. W. Norton, New York, pp. 157–190.

46. Sennett, R. and Cobb, J.: 1972, *The Hidden Injuries of Class,* Vintage, New York.

47. Smith, R.: 1985, "Feminism and the Moral Subject," in B. Andolsen et al. (eds.), *Women's Consciousness, Women's Conscience: A Reader in Feminist Ethics,* Winston, Minneapolis, pp. 235–250.

48. Wertz, R. and Wertz, D.: 1979, *Lying-In: A History of Childbirth in America,* Schocken, New York.

13. Friendship as Inspiration: A Study in Theo-politics

Mary E. Hunt

This chapter first appeared in *Fierce Tenderness: A Feminist Theology of Friendship* in 1991.

> Still—in a way—nobody sees a flower—really—it is so small—we haven't time—and to see takes time, like to have a friend takes time.
>
> —*Georgia O'Keeffe*

Friendship Quilts

The theo-politics of friendship comes quite naturally in my neighborhood, just a block beyond the Washington, D.C., border. Washington, as Meg Greenfield wrote, is "the only place in the world where 'friend' is a bad word." She went on to say that here "friendship is thought of as something that can compromise you, make you less trustworthy, blind you to your larger institutional interests. And so finally it is seen as something that can ruin your otherwise promising career . . . sort of like being a kleptomaniac or a drunk."[1] This was especially true in the Reagan and Bush years when corruption among friends was the order of the day.

It might seem odd, then, that I would link theology and politics, much less friendship and politics, when I want to claim that friendship is a source of inspiration. But to do so I have chosen a lovely metaphor, the friendship quilt, that I hope will illustrate both the necessity and the content of such connections. The quilt provides an image for holding these together in a rich variety of ways.

Friendship quilts were a form of folk art that peaked in the

1840s–1850s.[2] They were a popular way to combine craft with sentiment, design with communication. Thousands of such quilts were made in New England. Many were given to pioneers as they headed west. Unlike common folk quilts that were used as covers, friendship quilts were often considered too precious to be used every day. So they were preserved in chests and on walls as decorations. This accounts for the number of them that are still in very good condition, preserving for us this imaginative and, I will argue, revelatory testimony to friendship. Typically a friendship quilt was made of pieces that were all of the same shape sewn together in a pattern. The most popular designs were the "Chimney Sweep" and "Album Patch." Some quilts were quite elaborate, others quite plain. They could have one maker or be the product of several women's work. What distinguished them was the fact that friends personalized them by signing their names, sometimes adding their address as well, thus immortalizing their friendships, especially when loved ones moved west.

Autograph books preceded friendship quilts as a way women recorded their affection for one another. Letters, of course, were popular, with the quilts sometimes functioning as a kind of address book, keeping friends in touch at a distance by having their data at hand. Information was put on the quilt—signature, date, place, and usually relationship to the person who was to own the quilt. Many times a message or a bit of advice, even a poem, was added. All was written in indelible ink or cross-stitched for longevity. Women were practical as well as artistic in these endeavors.

Friendship quilts were not simply given to women as wedding or going-away gifts, although that was a popular custom. They were exchanged by friends. Sometimes they were given by sisters to one another. They were passed down through the family as part of the inheritance because, like later family photo albums and now video tapes, they contained a record of women's lives that could not be duplicated.

Two curious features of friendship quilts make them an apt metaphor for the theo-politics of women's friendship. First, "with so many choices available for making friendship quilts, it is remarkable that the results were so similar. . . . It is true that, with time, certain standard patterns for the friendship quilt emerged."[3] Friendships themselves emerge from a variety of starting points, but the ones that endure and become prototypes for other such experiences share common characteristics such as generativity and an orientation toward community. Second, friendship quilts are among the only remaining evidence of the existence of some women. Before 1850 "only the names of 'heads of families' were listed on government census records. . . . A woman's name was listed on the census only if she herself were the head of the household, generally due to the death of her husband."[4] Women's lives were recorded in the family Bible and on the gravestone, but the former was often lost in successive generations, and natural forces like storms and erosion often did away with the latter. This is part of why women are invisible historically.

Incredibly, it was on friendship quilts that women wrote themselves into history. As Linda Otto Lipsett notes:

> It was not woman's desire, however, to be forgotten. And in one simple, unpretentious way, she created a medium that would outlive even many of her husband's houses, barns and fences: she signed her name in friendship onto cloth and, in her own way, cried out "Remember me."[5]

My observation is that it is not by coincidence that women wrote themselves into history. They were literally forced to buy their circumstances. Nor is it a coincidence that they used friendship quilts to do the job. These were concrete symbols of their most trustworthy relationships. They knew that the owners of such quilts would guard them carefully, look at them periodically to be reminded of their friends, and treasure them long after their friends had died. Even more than family, friends were enduring. The quilts, and the practice of making and preserving them, are a source of inspiration.

Theo-politics Explored

The friendship quilt stands as a metaphor for what women need in the theological world. Women have been systematically excluded from participating in theological reflection, kept from places where that reflection is chronicled and preserved as part of the legacy of a faith tradition. Women's experiences, hopes, and dreams, commitments, doubts, and religiously motivated work for justice have been absent, until very recently, from the theological mainstream. This has diminished men's work as well.

My choice of women's friendship as the experiential starting point for a study of feminist theology is linked to the friendship quilts. While each woman is unique, as was each quilt, there is enough overlap in women's experiences to see some similar patterns and to make some, albeit very limited, shared claims. Further, no one will preserve women's history and the integrity of women's experiences if women do not do it themselves. Women have to lift to public expression their own faith, name what is ultimately meaningful and valuable for us. The result, like a friendship quilt, is both useful and artistic. It will last as part of history. Otherwise, women's stamp on creation will be superficial at best. Women from many different racial and class backgrounds made quilts, a clue to preserve and display equally diverse theological claims.

Women do that best in community, or in groups of friends, what I call unlikely coalitions of justice-seeking friends. Like the women who made the friendships quilts, it is necessary to express, chronicle, save, and share information about women's lives and loves and to probe their meaning. This is what feminist theologizing does. Like stitching names on a patch for a quilt, different women's experiences are stitched into the fabric of theology through conscious and often costly efforts. For example, nineteenth-century women's theological writings are preserved now in the history of feminist theology only because later women befriended the materials. Through little help from the theological establishment, which to date still pays them scant attention, the work of earlier women is known. It is a legacy that has been preserved by women. Still I shudder to think how much has been lost, the tattered quilts of our collective history turned into dust rags. It cannot happen again.

Theo-politics signifies the fact that theology does not exist in a vacuum. It is part of a larger context, i.e., heterosexist patriarchy and much, much more. Similarly, theo-politics is not an objective science that stands on its own. It reflects some of the most deeply held values, including religious values, of a culture. The theo-political reason why women's friendships have not been taken seriously as data of revelation, as a source of inspiration, hinges on the word "power." This understanding of theo-politics comes from the liberation schools in the past twenty years. While African American, feminist, womanist, Latin American, Asian, and the other liberation theologies all have different characteristics based on their various starting points, they have in common the fact that they challenge the prevailing power dynamics in theology. They critique those as being imperialist and exclusive. They strive to replace existing power dynamics with a more participatory and egalitarian approach.

The theological establishment is still made up of those who hold sway in denominational seminaries and university-based theological schools. Affirmative action gains notwithstanding, they are still overwhelmingly white, male professors who believe that theology can only be done according to strict methodological rules that "happen" to correspond with theirs. While there is nothing inherently wrong with their approach as one among many ways of doing theology, the problem arises when it is seen as *the only* way. Openness to the liberation schools in the late 1970s and early 1980s is reported to be almost over. A rise in neoconservative theo-politics is making itself felt in many theological schools. Regrettably, future generations of students seem to be experiencing backlash, a return to the so-called classical, traditional, institutional approach to theology. Again, there is nothing inherently wrong with such theological projects, though I claim that they represent class, race, and gender agenda; they simply are not all there is. Challenges from liberationists have been opposed vigorously. In some cases the establishment has simply denied the validity of the work. In other cases teaching appointments, tenure, publication, or even critical discussion are denied to those who work out of a different framework. Deconstruction of the prevailing theological method has been the common project of liberationists, and to a certain extent, their success. I consider myself in this number as a feminist and hope that I am incorrect in my pessimistic view of contemporary theo-politics.[6]

Still there is a long way to go before the particular insights of the various liberation schools are incorporated by the other liberationists, much less by the mainstream. The trajectory is clear, that changing the persons who are part of the theologizing community will have an impact on the product. But much work remains if we are to claim interstructured approaches. For example, Hispanic women point out the need for culturally specific feminist analyses; likewise, liberation theologians in Latin America are learning to integrate feminist concerns.[7] While there is much to be done in this regard, I caution against losing the primary and common agenda, which is to challenge the hegemony of one particular style of theologizing. At base we are all engaged in shifting the power equation.

Theologizing, as understood by liberationists, is the organic and communal process of sharing insights, stories, and reflections on questions of ultimate meaning and value. The answers that a community gives to such questions are then evaluated in light of the tradition, weighed with respect to the culture in which they are set, and pondered in relation to the ineffable mystery we call the divine. Only then can tentative and always changeable, faithful, and serious answers be shared. Such a method has been disparaged as "untheological" so that certain value-laden presuppositions will always emerge as normative. The negative reaction of the theological establishment to most liberation theologies has been aimed at keeping certain kinds of people from engaging in this process. This highlights the political dimension of theology, the extent to which factors other than those that are seemingly logical and reasonable are at play. Masked as academic excellence or scholarly rigor, such efforts still have status-quo-preserving results.

Examples abound. In some theological schools Spanish is not considered a "theological language" even though major work is being done in Spanish (and Portuguese). This discourages students from doing dissertations on liberation theology, a subtle and effective way of keeping it from the mainstream. Another example is the firing of the respected feminist ethicist Elizabeth Bettenhausen from Boston University School of Theology for alleged "insufficient scholarship." While it is true that Elizabeth Bettenhausen has not published an opus in the form that the theological establishment recognizes as definitive, she is a highly regarded scholar who has contributed far more than some whose works gather dust. Her helpful work has given denominations, women's groups, her own students, and the theological world at large some important insights. Yet she is kept from the mainstream.[8]

Theo-politics is not the unique discovery of liberationists. It has been a well-known, if unnamed, phenomenon in the theological world for centuries. It has been at play when, for example, women's experiences were written out of history, when women were excluded from theological schools, and when ethical reflection did not include women's experiences as moral agents. Only when women and others who have been marginalized began to claim their rightful place in the center was theo-politics named as such.

Now that we all understand the rules of the game we can play fairly, although obviously race, class, and gender are automatically determinants of advantages and disadvantages. Claims made from the partial, limited, and contextual framework that surrounds the theological establishment will be evaluated as simply that. They are not to be discarded simply because of their privileged social location. But neither are they to be taken with any more seriousness because they are part of the establishment. This is what it means to shift the power dynamics. Accordingly, I name my starting point as feminist with the responsibility to define it and to limit my claims on the basis of its boundaries. I do so gladly, asking only that all theological exercises include the same step. Otherwise liberationists are even more disadvantaged if they limit claims while others continue with their blanket statements and their sense of entitlement.

Feminist Theology

Feminist theology in the United States takes many forms as women from various religious traditions, principally Jewish, Christian, Neo-Pagan, and Goddess, ask questions of ultimate meaning and value. Note that I am confining my sweep to the United States both because it is my context and because it is premature to evaluate feminist theology in a global sense. It is important to note, however, that feminist theology is far from a U.S. phenomenon. Excellent work is being done in Europe, especially in Holland and Germany, as well as by women in Latin America, Asia, and Africa.[9] I look forward to similar theological assessments that will reflect women's experiences of friendship in those contexts.

Few feminist theologians have taken friendship as a guiding category. Nevertheless, let me review a bit of the history of feminist theology, highlighting some of the immediately relevant sources for friendship, in order to locate my reflections in this theological tradition. Four distinct periods provide a useful outline: preparation, criticism, construction, backlash.

A period of *preparation* began in the late nineteenth century when Matilda Joslyn Gage wrote what many scholars consider to be the first scholarly work in contemporary feminist theology.[10] The work of Elizabeth Cady Stanton and her Revising Committee on *The Woman's Bible* proved that women were perfectly capable of exegetical work, albeit in their time without modern tools of biblical criticism.[11] Although neither of them made friendship a predominant theme, Stanton's celebrated friendship with Susan B. Anthony played a formative role in her own life and work. Stanton's collaborative work style, her belief in the power of women to make social change through the study of Scripture, and her faithful friendship with one of the leaders of the women's suffrage movement make her a convincing prototype of a woman-oriented scholar.

Stanton's regard for women was obvious: "If Miriam had helped to plan the journey to Canaan, it would no doubt have been accomplished in forty days instead of forty years."[12] And her sense that the Bible needed critical attention only becomes more urgent with time:

> Verily we need an expurgated edition of the Old Testaments before they are fit to be placed in the hands of our youth to be read in the public schools and in theological seminaries, especially if we wish to inspire our children with proper love and respect for the Mothers of the Race.[13]

The *critical* period, when all theological thinking had to be reconceived on the basis of feminist insights, began well into the twentieth century. Protestant women were ordained in many denominations, giving them a new form of religious leadership and of theological respectability. Catholic women, especially nuns, were busy founding schools and hospitals to carry out the social mandate of their faith even though they were not allowed into theological circles. Circuit riding preachers were spreading their news; some black women were founding their own pentecostal churches. It was not until the second wave of the women's movement was launched in the early 1960s and feminist claims were being heard in many professional arenas that critical feminist theology came forth.

The theological mainstream kept such "problems" at bay until 1960 when Valerie Saiving wrote the first article of what we now consider consciously feminist theology.[14] She lifted up the fact that women's and men's ways of being in the world are sufficiently different that human experience cannot be known on the basis of a male model. Since her writing, theology cannot be done as if male experience were normative. This foundational methodological insight changed the course of theology. While Valerie Saiving did not use varying experiences of friendship as a case study, she did contribute invaluable insights that can be applied to friendship. She stated her position clearly:

> It is my contention that there are significant differences between masculine and feminine experience, and that feminine experience reveals in a more emphatic fashion certain aspects of the human situation which are present but less obvious in the experience of men. Contemporary theological doctrines of love have, I believe, been constructed primarily upon the basis of masculine experience and thus view the human condition from the male standpoint. Consequently, these doctrines do not provide an adequate interpretation of the situation of women—nor, for that matter, of men, especially in view of certain fundamental changes now taking place in our own society.[15]

Contemporary feminist theology has so thoroughly incorporated Saiving's insight as to render it rather unremarkable today. My effort is to apply it to the particular experience of friendship since this is one of the areas around which fundamental gender-based conditioning is radically different. Thus the theological and ethical claims that arise from such friendships will also vary widely.

Mary Daly's work is probably the best known feminist theology. It is safe to say that she opened up the second period by the publication of *The Church and the Second Sex,* and later *Beyond God the Father,* the latter being the watershed volume in the field.[16] Mary Daly's impact was threefold. First, she gave women the experience that they could go beyond patriarchal religion and still survive. Religion is a voluntary activity, but for many the deeply ingrained teachings of a faith tradition produce a kind of spiritual paralysis when the foundation is shaken. Mary Daly cured all of that, or at least provided the strong medicine capable of effecting the cure, painful side effects notwithstanding.

Her courageous move to the boundary and beyond, while not followed by everyone, showed the way. She literally cleared the psychic space for others to move beyond the parameters of patriarchal religions. Having been freed in this way, women are quite ready to surrender other long-held patriarchal notions as well. In fact, it is easier to jettison old thinking on something concrete like friendship when the work has been done on something seemingly more foundational and more abstract like views of the divine. Mary Daly has given practice in living and thinking anew. Women can abandon old notions of friendship, leave aside degrading definitions, and thrive with confidence while creating a postpatriarchal world as friends. Women can theologize on women's own terms and need not worry about rejection from people and places that should be discounted. Most of all, women can shape and model new ethical awarenesses without fear. As religious agents women are responsible to act on what we know. That is Mary Daly's legacy.

Second, Mary Daly couched her vision in an exodus community with "Sisterhood as Cosmic Covenant."[17] Sisterhood is not an exact synonym for women's friendship, but it does describe a close theological antecedent to my concerns in this book. She went on to name Crones and Hags, later Websters and Women-Touching Women, always redefining the patriarchally tainted words to reflect their proper etymology and woman-friendly usage.[18] While her usages border on the neoromantic at times, her creativity and courage to name things in a new way is exemplary.

In calling for sisterhood, Daly was onto the fact that massive social and intellectual changes do not come quickly nor in private. They must be intuited, articulated, expressed and lived out in community. In fact, it is only in a communal setting that shared vocabulary starts to change, normative assumptions shift, and people begin to live differently. To do so alone is to run the real risk of being considered crazy. To do so in a community of sisters, or better, I would argue, in a community of friends, is to give and receive the necessary reinforcement to change habits and to sustain hope while others follow suit, albeit more slowly. I prefer "friends" to "sisters" because I want to underscore the voluntary nature of friendship, and because I want to distinguish it from any blood tie. However, given my conviction that family members can learn to be friends, there is reason to use the terms interchangeably. At least sisterhood is a close cousin, a name that many women use when talking about close friends: "We are as close as sisters." "She is just like a sister to me."

Some readers have trouble applying Daly's work to the practical order. But this, in my judgment, is a failure to incorporate her powerful model for change that includes, Be-Longing: The Lust for Happiness; Be-Friending: The Lust to Share Happiness; and Be-Witching: The Lust for Metamorphosis.[19] What Mary Daly means is that happiness shared by women friends is indeed transformative. It changes individuals and communities in ways hitherto unknown under patriarchy. Ironically, this concept of Mary Daly's is far more practical than people give her credit for, simply because they do not make the explicit connection between friendship and politics.

Mary Daly is eminently practical when she makes clear that not all women can be friends. Material constraints on time and energy as well as differences in personality limit the possibilities. More so, class, race, age, social location, and sexual preference play a large part. Still, the energy of women's friendship when we "be-friend" and are "be-friended" has been vastly underrated.

However, "the work of Be-Friending can be shared by all, and all can benefit from this Metamorphospheric activity."[20] She defines "Be-Friending" as "Weaving a context in which women can realize our Self-transforming, metapatterning in Being. Therefore it implies the creation of an atmosphere in which women are enabled to be friends."[21] While the language may strike some as cumbersome, the issues are clear. She avoids the greeting card approach to friendship by moving immediately to a global example. She focuses on the publication of Simone de Beauvoir's *The Second Sex* as an instance of women being Be-Friended. Writing is a generative activity, one of the hallmarks of friendship. The book provided women with a concrete referent to which to direct conversation, channel ideas and energy. Most of all, it was a touchstone by which to find other women who were thinking the same thoughts. Simply having read *The Second Sex* meant, in the early years after its publication, that the reader was thinking about previously unthinkable topics. Mary Daly allows that while Simone de Beauvoir was not personally involved with the thousands of women who read her book, "It can be said that she has been part of the movement of Be-Friending and that she has been a catalyst for the friendships of many women."[22] An author can hope for little more.

Third, Mary Daly developed a whole new context in which to set her vision of sisterhood. It is a world in which "Virgins" are "Marriage Resisters" and "Soothsayers" are "Courageous Truthsayers."[23] She has taken the next step with her vision and begun to gear up the powerful intellectual forces necessary to make it normative. She leaves herself open to the charges of neoromanticism or even elitism. Does a word really mean what I want it to? But her method is consistent and her contribution vital to living the new now. I suggest that any less favorable reading is finally anti–intellectual. She has proved prophetic once again. Without an entirely new context there is little point to theologizing about women's experience including friendship. It will only be lost or coopted in heterosexist patriarchy. If allowed at all, it will be taken as a grand and glorious exception, something for the literary set but not for all women. Mary Daly's change of context results, ironically, more forcefully than tinkering with taboos, in space for women on their own terms. Altering basic assumptions by redefining words turns out to be a more efficient way of making change than some have given her credit for. Regardless of whether one credits Mary Daly or not, it is amazing to see the ongoing power of her concepts.

The drawback, of course, is that one talks meaningfully only to the converted for a while until the rest catch up. But assuming that conversations are replicated at least among friends, there is good reason to hope that change can take place in this way. It is remarkable to hear people use phrases like "beyond God the father" or even "Crones and Hags" as if they had always been a part of polite conversation. This is Mary Daly's legacy, to give us whole new ways of thinking and being so that social change can happen. Without new words we would have no way to articulate new concepts. While I favor a more politically explicit agenda, I remain in her debt for the conceptual work that perhaps precedes, and surely at least goes along with, social change.

Changing the context must happen if friendship is to replace such a deeply rooted assumption as the marriage norm. Women need to give content courageously and without equivocation to the meaning of friendship. I like to think that I have been doing that since I told my mother about Susy, i.e., even children can do it if we listen to them. Being an astute scholar and an excellent pedagogue, Mary Daly knows just what she is doing. While I do not agree with her full philosophical program, I am persuaded that these three factors, inspiring women to imagine a way beyond patriarchy, providing a concrete conceptual alternative in "Sisterhood as Cosmic Covenant," and especially by redefining words, Mary Daly helped to set the stage for and provide an example of constructive feminist theological discourse on friendship.

The beginning of the *constructive* phase of feminist theology in the early 1980s did not signal the end of critical work. Far from it. But it did signal that new ideas and insights are flowering on their own terms, not simply in response to other work. Rosemary Radford Ruether and Elisabeth Schüssler Fiorenza are widely regarded as having made some of the most substantial constructive contributions. Even though they do not employ friendship as a guiding metaphor, I suspect that they might describe relationships with the divine, "Holy Wisdom" in Rosemary Ruether's formulation and "Sophia" in Elisabeth Schüssler Fiorenza's formulation, as friendly. Carter Heyward's work, mentioned earlier, is also part of this constructive moment. I suggest that exploring the desired relationship with the divine in each of these, we find a generative quality, as well as a concern for difference but not distinction, that is analogous to our best experiences of friendship.

The most explicit hints in constructive theological and ethical work on friendship are provided by Beverly Wildung Harrison in her insightful ethical writing.[24] It is not friendship as such that she lifts up, but a feminist Christian ethical framework in which we can view friendship on women's terms: "My basic thesis [is] that a Christian moral theology must be answerable to what women have learned by struggling to lay hold of the gift of life, to receive it, to live deeply into it, to pass it on. . . ."[25]

She goes on to affirm that

> we must learn what we are to know of love from immersion in the struggle for justice . . . [because] women have always been immersed in the struggle to create a flesh and blood community of love and justice and . . . we know much more of the radical work of love than does the dominant, otherworldly spirituality of Christiantiy.[26]

Beverly Harrison's insight into women's experiences of struggle for justice corresponds to my own claims about justice-seeking friends. She uncovers the "reified masculinist idolatry" of the Christian theological tradition that would downgrade mutuality for some mythic higher relationship with the divine.[27] A feminist vision, on the contrary, finds within human mutuality all of the richness that others ascribe to the divine. Beverly Harrison's is a tough but gentle love that issues in "a spirituality of sensuality."[28] This is a context in which women's friendships flourish.

Turning her ethical acumen to the connections between misogyny and homophobia, Beverly Harrison argues that to understand these one must "examine this problematic tendency of Christian theological tradition to neglect, ignore, or denigrate the body."[29] The identification of the body with lower things and the mind with higher things immediately sets up a dualistic framework in which sexual expression, even in marriage, is always of a lower order. For friends, especially friends of the same gender, to touch one another rather than to be together in a kind of disembodied, intellectual way, is simply unacceptable in this bifurcated worldview. The implications of Beverly Harrison's analysis, especially that patriarchal homophobia is "a pathological source of human sexual disorder," are helpful.[30] Given that homophobia is part of our social fabric, Harrison, coupling it with a patriarchal worldview, argues that we suffer from "learning security in intimate patterns of inequity."[31] Work to overcome such conditioning is difficult especially for women, but it can be done. Friendship is a relational mode in which security can be felt in intimate equality.

Such work, in my judgment, is best done by women in friendships with other women. Far from lacking the "otherness" that Freudians have foisted on us for too long, women loving women who are conscious of the dynamics of homophobic patriarchy have at least a chance to experience equality in relationship. Of course this has to be distinguished from any blurring of personal boundaries and identities that sometimes plagues woman. Lesbian women are said to have particular trouble keeping boundaries clear since sexual intimacy involves a certain melding. But to experience security in equality is a new and welcome experience for most women. Once having had it, we know the difference. Sometimes even without having it we long for it. One day men, too, may experience such equality on a routine basis. For now we are paving the way for what is not only "sensual pleasure, but sensual trust."[32]

Mary Daly hinted at this when she described the patriarchal reversal that happens when one is said to need a partner of the opposite sex in order to experience the fullness of "otherness." She pointed out that, ironically, women find more authentic "otherness" in other women. Our sameness as women provides a shared experience that allows the *particularity* of each one, the real "otherness" unmediated by patriarchal baggage, to emerge. How obvious yet how obscured this insight has been in patriarchal heterosexist society. Beverly Harrison's work is helpful for thinking about justice-seeking friendship. Friendship is one of the ways in which women "making the connections" are transforming an unjust world.[33] Harrison's wisdom on the issue begins the constructive work from well within the boundaries of the academic discipline of moral theology and from well beyond those boundaries in her own praxis.

In another style, Sallie McFague writes about friendship with special attention to friendship with the divine. Her work, however helpful, is disappointing in that she does not differentiate women's friendships in any way. She neglects to use many sources that express women's experiences of friendship. Instead she falls into the trap of establishment theology. She notes "Aristotle, Kant, Hegel, Bonhoeffer" among those who have written on the topic, and cites C. S. Lewis over and over without ever mentioning the reason why women's writings on friendship and women's friendships themselves have been passed over by Christian theologians.[34] At least she is dealing with friendship as a theological category, but much more needs to be said.

While each of the well-respected male scholars that Sallie McFague lists had something important to say about friendship, it is by no means clear that their insights were equally applicable to women's experiences. That is, after all, the achievement of feminist theology, to glean from women's as well as men's experiences and to let theology be shaped differently by each. Nor is it any longer academically respectable, i.e., after Valerie Saiving et al., to take male scholars' however brilliant insights at face value as if they were applicable to all humans. For example, the fact that C. S. Lewis could say that friendship is "the least *natural* of loves; the least instinctive, organic, biological, gregarious and necessary" is preposterous from a feminist perspective no matter how nuanced the statement may be.[35] Why even entertain it? This, coupled with his assumption that there is a wide gap between friends who are normally "side by side, absorbed in some common interest," and lovers who are normally "face to face, absorbed in each other" shows how far Professor McFague is from a feminist understanding of friends.[36] While this is ultimately an inadequate effort when evaluated from a feminist perspective, at least she lifts up friendship in relation to the divine, providing future scholars with a valuable stimulus.

A recent collection that is relevant to the constructive phase of feminist theology in this regard is *Embodied Love: Sensuality and Relationship as Feminist Values,* edited by Paula M. Cooey, Sharon A. Farmer, and Mary Ellen Ross.[37] The essays, though uneven, are stimulating. They come from a variety of perspectives and represent a wide spectrum of theological concerns. However, it is striking that little if any attention is paid to friendship as a constructive category in these essays. Many people's primary experience of embodied love, that is, the focal experience for many people of sensuality and relationship, is friendship. There is the real danger, even for feminists, of falling into abstraction when discussing difficult theoretical issues. Nonetheless, the volume provides a useful display of current debates between and among feminist theological constructionists. For example, Sheila Davaney raises an interesting question by asserting that Mary Daly, Rosemary Ruether, and Elisabeth Schüssler Fiorenza have more in common than they and others think they do. Differences notwithstanding, all three, Professor Davaney claims, assume a "correspondence between feminist visions and ontological reality and the at least implicitly made claim that feminist-conceived symbols refer to such a reality."[38] This type of debate is helpful in clarifying the theoretical frameworks in which future work will be set. But the volume leaves unanswered what models of relationality are emerging from feminist experience. I respectfully suggest that friendship is one model that the book leaves largely unexamined and therefore that the collection limps as a vehicle for really exploring the fullness of embodiment.

A few male ethicists are beginning to take up the issue of friendship during the constructive phase of feminist theology. James B. Nelson's work stands out. He has begun to incorporate feminist insights into his writing.[39] Focusing on men's lives, Nelson observes that men

> seem to handle our lives with an activity-achievement style, we handle others with a style of dominance and submission, and we handle our psyches with a style that

> prizes logical and cool level-headedness. None of these characteristics is particularly conducive to nurturing the capacities for intimacy and friendship.[40]

Nelson mentions that friendship is almost entirely absent from the contemporary theological scene. This is due primarily to the fact that "males have dominated the theological tradition, and men have had problems with friendship—particularly friendship with other men."[41] He wisely confines most of his work to men's relationships with each other. This is a prudent approach at a time when the catch-up work that men need can only be done by other men. Later on women and men can find common bonds. This method is eschewed by those who wish to keep everyone together even at the expense of the tough work that transitional separatism signals. White people had to learn this lesson during the civil rights struggles; North Americans are learning it now from Central and South Americans who need to name their own future. Professor Nelson is evidence of the fact that some men have heard most women's wishes in this regard.

James Nelson's major contribution to contemporary male views of friendship is his insistence on the extent to which deeply internalized homophobia prevents men from becoming friends. This is a common assumption in Men's Studies materials on friendship. But his treatment of it marks the first time that it has been brought into the Christian ethical mainstream. He asserts in his chapter on friendship with God that "to love God in the very midst of loving another human being is sheer gift—and revelation."[42] Although I recoil at the use of the word "gift" (it seems to be a favorite of those who refuse to grapple seriously with the seemingly inexplicable), I quite agree with him on revelation. Perhaps the fact that he does not spell out the implications of this statement accounts for why this book is classified under Psychology instead of Religion. Nonetheless, we concur that what has been obscured is only now coming into focus, that is, being revealed.

Some readers may wonder why I include James Nelson's work with constructive feminist theology. On the one hand, I include it parenthetically since it does not bear *directly* on women's friendship. It is not feminist theology per se. On the other hand, I include it without qualification or apology as a gesture of hope that such work, when taken in conjunction with volumes like this and others that feminist women and men are writing, will move us toward renewed female-male relationships. Meanwhile, I do my work confident that James Nelson is doing his, and that the synthesis is ahead of us. Read together, such work provides a sound basis for such a hope.

A new resource for feminist theological construction is the companion volume to *Womanspirit Rising,* the second collection of editors Judith Plaskow and Carol P. Christ, *Weaving the Visions.*[43] It is clear now that many perspectives inform feminist theology, that womanist theology is important on its own terms, and that "transforming the world" is the immodest but important goal of the entire enterprise. Of special relevance to ethical study are the essays in the section "Self in Relation" that echo many of the constructive themes contained in this work.[44]

The fourth phase of feminist theology is that which has developed in reaction to the constructive work, namely, *backlash.* As we enter the 1990s this can be found in some ultraconservative Christian women's groups that have co-opted women's issues. It is also found in antichoice efforts by Catholic bishops who claim to join women in an undifferentiated concern for fetal versus maternal lives. And it is most violent in right-wing diatribes against lesbian/gay people that are coming from conservative churches and political groups.

A more subtle and insidious form of backlash is found among backsliding liberals who are realizing that changes in the theological power equation have a greater impact on them than they had imagined. It is expressed when, for example, feminist theologians are compared, so that "softer" feminists are pitted against "harder" feminists. Competition for jobs, especially in church and seminary bureaucracies that are filling their small quotas, makes this polarizing obvious. Lesbian women are especially hard hit when set over against heterosexual women. Asian, African American, and Hispanic women, while seemingly on everyone's short list for jobs, continue to experience discrimination as they are played off against white feminists. Once hired, many of them report being so overwhelmed by work that they are too worn out to be creative, a subtle but sure way of limiting their contributions.

It is important to note that backlash does not signal the end of construction. To the contrary, it is usually a measure of the progress that has been made which some feel must be turned back. As such, backlash is a useful measure, perversely, a sign of progress made, but one that most of us would just as soon do without.

My feminist theological work on friendship, as history would have it, is set in the nexus of construction and backlash. I am indebted to the theologians whose work in the periods of preparation and criticism set the stage. I join the constructionists in a concerted effort to stem the tide of backlash. While we cannot ignore it, neither can we afford to let backlash dictate our constructive efforts.

It is not accidental that one of the first themes chosen by the Consultation on Lesbian Feminist Issues in Religion of the American Academy of Religion was friendship. It is a key to survival. The constructive work continues apace even in the face of serious and sustained backlash. It is not work for lesbian women only, but in fact for all who wish to bring to the light of theological day the data of women's experiences, the stuff of theological reflection.

Some Historical Examples of Women's Friendships

A complete history of women's friendship is beyond the scope of this book. In fact, Janice Raymond has laid out a genealogy of female friendships so thoroughly that it is more than enough to refer the reader to her work.[45] She focuses on the Beguines, Catholic nuns, and Chinese Marriage Resisters as three categories of women who put women first. Their friendships are a legacy for us. I admire this approach and I also agree with Janice Raymond on the importance of naming the friendships between famous women of our time such as "Helen Keller and Annie Sullivan, Margaret Mead and Ruth Benedict, and Eleanor Roosevelt and Lorena Hickok" so that we will have recognizable examples of what we are discussing.[46] Such role models are important for our own self-understanding. Homophobia and the trivializing of women are the only conceivable reasons not to make these friendships explicit.

I could add countless names of church women, many of whom would lose jobs and/or privilege if the full extent of their friendships were revealed. This threat is reason enough to bring a theological light to the subject. If the world would be shocked and punitive about the depth to which they love one another and the choices they make about the physical and emotional expression of that love, then we are missing more than I can ignore. The task of feminist theology is to prevent such a loss in future generations.

The powerful example of Ruth and Naomi, who promised each other that they would maintain their bonds even in the absence of financial security and social acceptance, graces the Hebrew Scriptures. In the text, especially Ruth 1:16–17, we find a clear expression of friendship between two women. I never cease to be amused when I hear this formula used for heterosexual wedding vows, providing the first pastoral clue that women's friendships are a good model for human relationships in general. It does not seem to follow that heterosexual marriages are a very good model for women's friendships. Some interpreters have tried mightily to play down the friendship factor in a stream of exegeses about the familial patterns that made such a promise so extraordinary. It was, they conclude, just a special kind of family bond. This leaves aside the detail that there was no blood relationship between them. Although kinship requirements gave their bond a dimension we do not experience today with in-laws, why not simply call their friendship by its name? That would elevate friendship over family, something that patriarchal societies fear.

In the New Testament another friendship constellation is sighted in the relationship between Mary and Elizabeth. Commentators have tried hard to describe them as cousins, missing the obvious friendly relationship that prevailed between these family members. Again the reader is puzzled as to why such an obvious link is passed over, until one admits that in a patriarchal context it is assumed that relations between women are mediated by a third party, usually if not always a man. Family meant male-centered, property-conscious family. Stressing that tie, at the expense of passing over the affective one, is considered routine exegesis. Paying attention to friendship reveals something more in the text and inspires something beyond it.

The more interesting cases, as Elisabeth Schüssler Fiorenza's innovative methodology would have it, involve the relationships between Mary and Martha, or the woman at the well and her friends, women whose lives and friends can only be reconstructed imaginatively.[47] I await more of this scholarly work in the belief that friendship is one of the most helpful exploratory and explanatory frameworks that will aid in reconstruction effort. Then we will have not only a fuller picture of our tradition, but one that reflects women on their own terms. Renita Weems in her biblical studies moves in this direction and provides useful questions for others to take it the next step.[48]

Monastic groups were a logical homosocial environment in which women's friendships could flourish. We are only now discovering the depth and expression of some of those friendships. As Janice Raymond noted, "the power of female friendship in convents derived from the fact that friendship is by nature a spiritual communion, but that women are not and never will be pure spirits. With nuns, as with all women, friendship is mediated through and only becomes Gyn/affection in the material world."[49] We lack a definitive study of the women's experience of the period, one that would match Adele M. Fiske's comprehensive treatment of male *Friends and Friendship in the Monastic Tradition*.[50] But we can and must imagine if our history is to be complete.

That study, while detailed and philosophically rigorous, is based on men's experience in previous centuries, e.g., Augustine, Boniface, Anselm, Bernard of Clairvaux, Aelred of Rievaulx. Professor Fiske's command of the original sources and her thoroughness in chronicling the period using friendship as a guiding metaphor make one wish that she had trained her sights on monastic women instead of or as well as men in monasteries. Still, I would be loathe simply to lift the insights from male experience and foist them onto medieval women, even nuns. The work remains to be done with a feminist hermeneutic of friendship as a guide.

While I agree with Augustine that "life without friends would be too hard to endure for a day," I am not sure that women were content with the spiritual kiss that Aelred thought included both friends and Christ. Dr. Fiske, writing prior to the "feministization" of theology, must be credited with a nascent feminist insight that friendship itself is a key category for interpreting human life, even if her work only told part of the story. Moreover, Adele Fiske was astute enough to limit her claims: "Each generation can understand fully only its own questions and answers."[51] This makes the fact that she did not turn her considerable research skills and insights to women's experience all the more regrettable as the dual data would have provided us with some rich material on the period as well as perhaps an early start on gender difference and the difference it makes. Of course it must be noted that part of the reason why scholars wrote as they did was because data simply were not available about women.

She concluded her study by positing that "the understanding of friendship is an index of the level of a civilization."[52] As women's experiences are taken seriously on women's own terms, the way of understanding women's friendships will indeed judge our society. Until now ignoring them seems to be a form of scorn.

Examples abound of women's friendship in the contemporary period. What is fascinating, however, is how details sometimes fade away. They are often erased, only to be restored in friendlier times. For example, the original name of the Sisters of Loretto was "The Little Society of the Friends of Mary under the Cross of Jesus."[53] The official title now is "Sisters of Loretto at the Foot of the Cross." As feminist consciousness grows, the group is returning to its roots that include this powerful relational component. Thinking about the original title, Marian McAvoy, former president of the group, wrote: "Perhaps because they were thinking of Mary as standing at the foot of the Cross, they knew that the need at such a time for Mary was for companions, friends."[54] She went on to encourage members to "grow in the ability to be friend—certainly friend to one another in community and to others whose welfare we seek in ministry; more than that, to try to relate to all so that no one is servant."[55] This is friendly advice that corresponds faithfully to the roots of the Loretto Community.

Realizing the importance of women's relationships with one another is crucial for the formation and development of any sort of community. Friendship takes the power away from an external authority and relies on committed bonds to prevail. Such a move to friendship bodes well for a canonically affiliated group that may eventually choose to sever ties with male authority and continue its woman-centered work in the world. Then women will finally be religious agents, able to name their own experiences, make decisions on the basis of them, and live accountably on the basis of these choices without male interference. Such agency is a rare but important goal that ought to be normative.

Another powerful example of women bonding is found among poor, *pobladora* women in Santiago, Chile. The Casa Sofía is a women's center that I visit regularly when I participate in "Women Crossing Worlds," a project of international sharing through WATER, the Women's Alliance for Theology, Ethics and Ritual. The project is our way of embodying the gospel imperative to go and make friends in all nations. And indeed it is because of our friends that we visit and share resources. Support groups flourish at the Casa. Women provide one another with literacy training, mental health care, and other practical assistance. The hidden yet most important aspect of that center is the bond women form in a society that would keep all of them powerless:

> Beyond a doubt, the overwhelming discovery in these groups is friendship. For many women, this fire comes alive for the first time in their lives, it then grows and expands and provides the strength to confront their often monumental difficulties. . . . The obstacles of repression, cynicism, and scoffing by those who would keep women at home or in church are at times overwhelming. . . . We no doubt need visionary, accompanying, passionate, stirring and remarkable friendship.[56]

To visit this center is to experience the warmth of women who know that their survival is contingent on their bonding. Theirs are not friendships of convenience but of necessity, born of the need to survive together against crushing odds. This insight into the need for friendship in order to survive inspires others of us to act accordingly. It parallels the early work of Charlotte Bunch, who insisted that necessity and not ideology grounds and sustains efforts at social change. While in no way denying the very real love these women feel for one another, it is made all the more powerful by the horrendous situation of political, economic, and social (especially macho) oppression in which they live.

Some might wonder why an overview of theological materials leaves out the contribution of male scholars in the history of women's friendship. The answer is simply that very few if any sources exist. In fact, the best bibliography I could unearth on the topic, which covered Western sources from Plato to Saint-Exupery, cited virtually nothing on women's friendships and few works by women.[57] This can only improve.

The same problem accrues when one tries to search, à la Sallie McFague, through the sources of male theology. While the insights are helpful in a general sense, the new material that will shape the tradition in innovative ways is what women's friendships reveal. Engaging male sources that do not take account of women's experiences seems to me to be counterproductive. It reinforces the false generic of human experience based on males, and it distracts from the task at hand, namely, focusing on women's lives. Those who would do so in the name of "the tradition" forget that the very tradition has been shaped without concern for women's well-being. While Martin Buber and others may have begun to move in the direction that feminist theology is now pursuing, they too lack specific attention to women. This does not mean that men's friendships or even female-male friendships are not important. It simply means that when scholars seek to discover what has yet to be considered it is women's friendships that appear. Women's friendships reveal something new and inspire something powerful.

Women's Friendship as Inspiration

Inspiration is a technical theological term that can also be used more informally. Women have traditionally shied away from such words due to something I label "theology anxiety." It is like "math anxiety," a peculiarly (though not exclusively) female problem, which has been outlined in feminist theory. Two strong parallels exist.

First, as with the teaching of mathematics, women were not given proper instruction in theology. At least with mathematics they could take the courses. The prohibitions were more subtle, such as the teacher calling on boys more than girls, or helping out the boys more than the girls with problems. In the theological world women were not admitted to many degree programs until quite recently. There are still theological faculties in this country, and many places around the world, where women are not permitted to study or to take advanced degrees in theology. Those are reserved for the clergy who are male. This lack of knowledge produces an understandable anxiety about the unknown. It results in control by those who can manipulate the jargon and concepts of the discipline to keep women as permanent outsiders. It will take several generations to overcome theology anxiety, but we are well on the way.

The second reason for theology anxiety, again like math anxiety, is that many women are not convinced that everything they have been taught is the way things *really* are. For example, in mathematics, many women are not convinced that two plus two must really equal four. Many intuit that numbers are "only" a linguistic and mathematical convention that has been used to make certain social interactions and scientific explanations easier. In this sense they are not ultimate but convenient. Many women do not impute unchangeable truth to numbers. Such women are not recalcitrant. They just refuse to give the discipline of mathematics too much power. With the odds stacked in favor of the discipline, this can cause anxiety even though it is a defensible position.

Likewise, many feminist theologians have gained deeper and deeper suspicions about the language and concepts that have been given in the name of a faith tradition. Women are now quite sure that God the Father, Jesus his only son (no daughters), and a male-dominated church are not adequate to pass on to children. Theology anxiety is correctly placed even though it creates serious problems for women who want to "make it" in a patriarchal church. Still it is well grounded in our exclusion and in our doubt. A healthy response to such anxiety is to theologize from women's own starting points. Of course no such work begins in a vacuum. Witness: the periods of preparation, criticism, and now construction/backlash. Women come to the notion of revelation with little of the usual baggage. So rather than enter into a technical comparison of various theories of revelation, most of which revolve around who decides what is revealed (and eventually who decides who decides, all of which is finally claimed to be revealed by someone to someone else, illustrating the *reductio ad absurdum* that has given theology a bad name), I prefer to begin with friendship, lifting up the dimensions of human experience that are made obvious and then note what it is that inspires imitation. This is a plausible way to develop a theory of how inspiration works, i.e., by observation rather than fiat. Of course more needs to be said, but this is a reasonable beginning approach, given the historical exclusion of women's experience from the data of revelation.

Several presuppositions come first. I begin with the assumption that revelation is ongoing or not at all. As a working definition I assume that revelation is that which continually reinforces, albeit always differently and usually to our great surprise, the fundamental goodness of creation and the simultaneous need for divine-human cooperation that keeps creation in process. Inspiration, far from being secrets blown into the minds of those who chronicle history, is simply the way in which generations glean insights from one another. I refer not to inspiration in the technical sense in which it is used for Scripture (though I think there are parallels here) but to the common passage of meaning and value through time.

Friendship, at least as women's friendships prove, reveals a good deal about ourselves, one another, the natural community in the world, and our relationship with the divine. It inspires those same dynamics in future generations. In each category we find, by way of women's experiences, something that we did not know before, something that women sense is connected to the fundamental way things are. This is why friendship can be said to function in a revelatory way, making obvious what has previously been obscured when women's friendships were not recognized or were consciously kept from view. This is how friendship inspires change.

Such language implies an ontological claim. Friendship is a real experience that cannot be negated. But it is at the same time a perspectival claim insofar as that which is revealed is contextualized in time and place. Still, certain claims must be made if women's experience is to move from the margin to the center. This move does not mean negating the claims made by those who already find the light of revelation shining on them, i.e., what comes from male experiences. Rather, it means extending and expanding the rays to encompass ever more diverse and even diffuse experiences. Put another way, it means looking at the heretofore dim as well as at the shining examples.

There is a deliberate move here away from what is revealed by the divine and passed on (i.e., inspired) to a more expansive, ultimately more trusting sense that much remains to be seen. Inspiration is what we can see without special apparatus if only we are encouraged to look. In this sense women's friendships can be said to inspire a good deal:

1. *Women's friendships reveal something about women themselves.* The most insidious problem created by the refusal to acknowledge women's friendships as existent, much less meaningful, is that without them women are kept from understanding themselves as loving human beings. If such love does not count, or if it must be seen as secondary, less important than the real thing that will come later if at all with a man, then women do not have a true picture of themselves.

Failure to acknowledge friendships with women as embodied love functions as one more barrier to women's self-love. Being prevented from loving those like ourselves casts into doubt the possibility of loving ourselves. In a patriarchal society this is quite convenient. But as women come into our own as moral agents we discover that such self-love, far from being solipsistic, is necessary for our healthy integration.

Likewise, because in friendships people express their worst capacities as well as their best, we all learn something about limitations. We see how capable we are of evil, of hurting and being hurt, of forgiving and being forgiven. Most of all we learn that without challenge and limits we will not necessarily do what is best for all involved. Friends are some insurance against our worst selves.

Friendship is an honest mirror, but it must be allowed to reflect or its power is lost. This may seem pedestrian, but it strikes at the heart of a patriarchal society's means of control, namely, alienation. Insofar as women need men in order to be a part of what is defined as the way things are, then it will be necessary to keep the lid on women's love for one another and for ourselves, indeed to keep the mirror hidden. Otherwise we risk massive social upheaval. Obviously I favor such upheaval. Women's friendships inspire it. But I acknowledge the deep dangers it portends for those who favor the status quo and whom the status quo favors.

When the mirror is used, friends find that they are part of the goodness of the created order. Not only are people empowered in the personal sense; there is no excuse for ignoring the brokenness of the human community. Accountability is increased since women are obliged to name clearly, unequivocally, and without fear even when it means exposing the limits of full humanity. Rather than romanticize women, we see how our authentic experiences, both positive and negative, serve to inspire future friends. Friendship implies a new way to think about our responsibility to participate in the divine-human matrix. Ours is not an outsized responsibility. It is a consequence of personal mortality. As Rosemary Ruether described this eschatology:

> We do not know what this means. It is beyond our power and our imagination. It is not then our direct responsibility. We can do nothing about the "immortal" dimension of our lives. It is not our calling to be concerned about the eternal meaning of our lives, and religion should not make this the focus of its message. Our responsibility is to use our temporal life span to create a just and good community for our generation and for our children. It is in the hands of Holy Wisdom to forge out of our finite struggle truth and being for everlasting life.[58]

Friendship is, finally, in the hands of Holy Wisdom, but we would be remiss if we did not name what we know and whom we love. That naming inspires new naming, beginning with ourselves.

2. *Women's friendships reveal something about one another.* We learn something about ourselves as loving and loveable persons through friendship, but we learn similar things about one another.

In friendship we are forced to confront the sometimes ugly reality of human perversity, the devastating fact that humans, including some of our friends, are capable of the most horrendous torture and deception. This is not a pretty picture, but it is part of the picture that cannot be negated lest inspiration be misconstrued as always positive.

Being with friends is the clearest way to understand embodiment. How else could we be except in the finitude of our physical selves? This is why touch and communication are so crucial. We say things without words to friends. Gestures, glances, silence, smiles take on shared meaning with intimates. Sexual relations are usually most satisfying when carried out between close friends. A meal, sports, prayer, work, theater are all heightened in the company of friends.

Anna Quindlen captures some of the spirit of this when she writes about conversation between women friends:

> Most of the time we talked and talked, not in a linear way, but as though we were digging for buried treasure. Why did you feel that way? And what did you say then? What are you going to do about that? How long did it go on? It was an extended version of the ladies' lunches in which we bring our psyches out from inside our purses, lay them on the table and fold them up again after coffee. . . . [59]

This is what it means to take embodiment seriously, to acknowledge that women's experiences are radically contingent but can be and ought to be shared. It does not make them better or worse than men's, simply different and worthy of attention. But it does signal why so-called "girl talk" is so much maligned in a patriarchal society.

The putdown of women's conversations is a defensive, trivializing reaction against what it is imagined women must be saying to one another. It is "efficient" to dismiss such conversation as something unimportant rather than acknowledge that different embodied experiences will inevitably result in lacunae in communication between women and men. Most men's notion of "girl-talk" is most women's idea of "buried treasure." So much for universal experiences! This underscores the need for women's friendships to be explored on their own terms if anything meaningful is to be said of friendship as a whole. Men too will learn the seemingly unlearnable about women only when women speak on their own terms.

3. *Women's friendships reveal something about the natural order.* We are taught to think of friends as people with whom we can relate. But I am increasingly struck by women's experiences of nature that reveal deep connections with the nonhuman realm that many people have written off as unimportant. While I admit certain biases in favor of human beings, I have long been persuaded that animals, plants, and other living things have much to teach us. I am of course wary of a romanticized view of nature that links women to it as if there were some inextricable relationship, once again repeating the "biology is destiny" mistake. Likewise I have my doubts about approaches to animal rights that privilege the needs of animals over the material needs of people who are poor. But somewhere there is a middle ground, one that women stand on to be able to hold together what many men see as competing claims.[60] I suggest that our experiences of balancing friendships, i.e., the woman who balances friendship requirements for herself and her fetus when making a decision about reproduction, give us practice in upholding the importance of the natural order alongside of the human order.

It is often said that "man's best friend is his dog," something all too believable given how many men treat some of their human friends. While I have rarely heard it said that women's best friends are their cats, it is interesting to imagine what it would mean. For example, May Sarton has written about "the fur person." I know many cat lovers who are as devastated by the loss of their pets as they are by the loss of a parent or a spouse. But the point is that friendships with animals, and a friendly posture toward the rest of the created order that women have long championed, reveal something about the oneness of the cosmos. The gradual blurring of lines between human and animal life means increasing friendliness to both.

Our nonhuman friends teach us the necessity of developing distinctions that are not categorical. These distinctions take account of the nuances of differences between and among us rather than, as patriarchy would have it, the hierarchical prioritizing of humans over animals as God is over humans. We are compelled by our friendship with animals to the kind of animal liberation activities that denounce medical and pharmaceutical experiments on defenseless animals, that urge eating lower on the food chain, and that seek to evaluate animals' rights to life and limb alongside of humans'. These are basically friendly postures that are transforming the way in which we live.

Likewise, ecology is the act of befriending the earth and its inhabitants, guaranteeing for future generations access to the natural world that we have enjoyed. In some parts of this country it is considered a fad that will fade; in some parts of the world it is seen as First World guilt for having caused environmental damage to begin with. In any case, ecology is a way of embodying the friendship that the earth deserves.

What is revealed in this expression of friendship is the essential harmony of the natural order. Periodic disturbances, like hurricanes, tornados, and the like are equally natural albeit unfriendly. Our interaction with the earth and its inhabitants, both human and nonhuman, is a part of this harmony. When the harmony is broken, as it so often is, we know the unfriendly results. But when things are in harmony, as in a walk through the woods with a beloved pet or when a summer storm has just passed, there are glimpses of this friendship we call ecology.

4. *Friendships reveal something about the divine.* Irrational reactions to inclusive language about God/ess are a clue to what is being revealed about our friendship with the divine. When She is our Mother instead of our Father, common assumptions about the nature, relationship, and function of the divine are called into question. When He is Father and never Mother we sense the imbalance. Feminist theologians have been quick to point out that the deity has no gender. Linguistic conventions for referring to "it" are simply that. But the violent reaction that accrues when religious language is changed, e.g., those who proclaim that the Bible is being castrated when the text is rendered in inclusive language, reveals that some deep chord has been struck. Friendship with the divine, whether he, she, or it, is inspired by human friendship, and

vice versa. This does not trivialize the divine nor elevate the human. It simply names friendship as the most adequate relational referent. As women begin to value friendships with women, the referent for divine-human friendship is given new content. It is, perhaps, too early to say how it is changing. But in a preliminary way it inspires new depths of friendship in both arenas.

This is more realistic than claiming that the divine is a many-breasted goddess whose goodness fairly oozes forth. Rather, as in all women's friendships, the potential for nurture and nastiness, comfort and challenge resides in all divine-human relationships. So, too, the divine friend surprises with Her revelations at times, inspiring humans to the same serendipity.

What then of inspiration? Women's friendships reveal something about ourselves, one another, the natural order and the divine that inspires anew. But what makes this inspiration and not simply some insight that could be disproved just as quickly? The simple answer is nothing, admitting that inspiration does not need to be something special that relies on belief or capitulation of will in order to be true. Rather, in the sense in which I am using the term, inspiration is obvious when it unveils some previously hidden data that will further humanize the world. That is what I claim women's friendships do.

These themes need to be probed as women's friendships are increasingly taken for granted. But the most telling characteristic, revealed simply in the act of taking women's friendships seriously, is justice. It is only *just* to lift up, name, and celebrate the bonds between and among women. It is only *just* to acknowledge love where it comes to rest. It is only *just* to recognize women's equality not only in the job market but among friends. It is only *just* to rectify the depravity and suffering that women experience at the hands of patriarchy. It is only *just* to acknowledge erotic love where it is. Justice, as I will stress later, is a hallmark of women's friendship. Glimpses of justice inspire action to assure more justice.

Notes

1. Meg Greenfield, "Friendship in Washington," *Washington Post,* July 20, 1983.

2. See Linda Otto Lipsett, *Remember Me: Women and Their Friendship Quilts* (San Francisco: Quilt Digest Press, 1985). This is a beautiful volume that details the history of friendship quilts and contains stunning pictures of these beautiful designs.

3. Ibid., 21.

4. Ibid., 28–29.

5. Ibid., 30.

6. See Mary E. Hunt, "Feminist Liberation Theology: The Development of Method in Construction" (Berkeley, Calif.: Graduate Theological Union, 1980), for a modest example of such deconstruction.

Elisabeth Schüssler Fiorenza's efforts to "decenter" biblical scholarship are an important part of this movement. See her brilliant essay "The Ethics of Biblical Interpretation: Decentering Biblical Scholarship," Society for Biblical Literature Presidential Address (December 5, 1987), *Harvard Divinity Bulletin,* Fall 1988, 6–9.

7. See Ada María Isasi-Díaz and Yolanda Tarango, *Hispanic Women: Prophetic Women in the Church* (San Francisco: Harper & Row, 1988).

Elsa Tamez's interviews with male theologians of liberation in *Against Machismo* (Oak Park, Ill.: Meyer-Stone Books, 1987) are fascinating accounts of their various ways of approaching the issues. It is clear from these interviews that there is plenty of work yet to be done if liberation is to be achieved.

Fortunately women in Latin America are developing their own liberation theology. Excellent examples include, *Apuntes y aportes de la mujer ecuménica,* edited by Alieda Verhoeven, Mendoza, Argentina: Acción Popular Ecumnénica Regional Cuyo, nos. 4, 5, 6 1987. Also *El rostro feminino de la teología,* Elsa Tamez et al. (San José, Costa Rica: Departamento Ecuménico de Investigaciones [DEI], 1986). These contain essays that were originally delivered as lectures for the Reunión Latinoamericana de Teología de la Liberación desde la Perspectiva de la Mujer, Buenos Aires, 1985. See Elsa Tamez, editor, *Through Her Eyes: Women's Theology from Latin America* (Maryknoll, N.Y.: Orbis Books, 1989).

8. See Marjorie Heins, *Cutting the Mustard: Affirmative Action and the Nature of Excellence* (Winchester, Mass.: Faber and Faber, 1987), for a full account of the firing of Nancy D. Richardson from Boston University

School of Theology. The case of Elizabeth Bettenhausen was set in the same web of conservative theo-politics and power wielding.

9. For example, *With Passion and Compassion,* edited by Virginia Fabella and Mercy Amba Oduyoye (Maryknoll, N.Y.: Orbis Books, 1988), provides a look at Asian, African, and Latin American women's theological writings.

European theologians like Marga Bührig, Catharina J. M. Halkes, Bärbel von Wartenberg-Potter are equally important. See Marga Bührig, *Die unsichtbare Frau und der Gott der Väter* (Stuttgart: Kreuz Verlag, 1987), and *Spät habe ich gelernit, gerne Frau zu sein* (Stuttgart: Kreuz Verlag, 1987). Among the many published works of Catharina J. M. Halkes see "Feministische theologie en bevrijding," in *Op zoek naar een West-europese bevrijdingstheologie.* Verslag knogresdag Kritische Gemeente Ijmond 1985, 6–18. See Bärbel von Wartenberg-Potter, *We Will Not Hang Our Harps on the Willows* (Bloomington, Ind.: Meyer-Stone Books, 1988).

10. Matilda Joslyn Gage, *Woman, Church and State,* copyright 1893, reprint edition (Watertown, Mass.: Persephone Press, 1980).

11. Elizabeth Cady Stanton and the Revising Committee, *The Woman's Bible* (New York: European Publishing Company, 1895; reprint, Seattle: Coalition Task Force on Women and Religion, 1974).

12. Ibid., 103.

13. Ibid., 184.

14. Valerie Saiving, "The Human Situation: A Feminine View," originally published in *The Journal of Religion,* April 1960; reprinted in *Womanspirit Rising,* edited by Carol P. Christ and Judith Plaskow (New York: Harper & Row, 1979), 25–43.

15. Saiving in *Womanspirit Rising,* 27.

16. Mary Daly, *The Church and the Second Sex* (Boston: Beacon Press, 1968), and *Beyond God the Father* (Boston: Beacon Press, 1973).

17. Mary Daly, *Beyond God the Father,* 115–78.

18. Mary Daly, *Gyn/Ecology: The Metaethics of Radical Feminism* (Boston: Beacon Press, 1978), and *Pure Lust: Elemental Feminist Philosophy* (Boston: Beacon Press, 1984).

19. Mary Daly, *Pure Lust,* especially chapters 10–12.

20. Ibid., 374.

21. Ibid.

22. Ibid.

23. Mary Daly, *Websters' First New Intergalactic Wickedary of the English Language* (Boston: Beacon Press, 1987), 176 and 163 respectively.

24. Beverly Wildung Harrison, "The Power of Anger in the Work of

Love: Christian Ethics for Women and Other Strangers," in *Making the Connections,* edited by Carol S. Robb (Boston: Beacon Press, 1985), 3–21.

25. Ibid., 8.

26. Ibid.

27. Ibid., 18.

28. Ibid., 8.

29. Beverly Wildung Harrison, "Misogyny and Homophobia," in *Making the Connections,* 135–51.

30. Ibid., 151.

31. Ibid.

32. This happy phrase originates with J. Giles Milhaven in his article "Sleeping Like Spoons," *Commonweal,* April 7, 1989, 207. Sensual trust is what friends embody; fierce tenderness is sensual trust.

33. See my essay "Friends in Deed," in *Sex and God,* edited by Linda Hurcombe (New York: Routledge and Kegan Paul Inc., 1987), 46–54.

34. Sallie McFague, *Models of God* (Philadelphia: Fortress Press, 1987).

35. Quoted in ibid., 159, from C. S. Lewis, *Four Loves* (New York: Harcourt, Brace and Co., 1960), 88.

36. Ibid., 91.

37. See *Embodied Love: Sensuality and Relationship as Feminist Values,* edited by Paula M. Cooey, Sharon A. Farmer, and Mary Ellen Ross (San Francisco: Harper & Row, 1987).

38. Sheila Davaney, "Problems with Feminist Theory: Historicity and the Search for Sure Foundations," in ibid., Paula Cooey et al., 79–95, especially 92.

39. James B. Nelson, *The Intimate Connection: Male Sexuality, Masculine Spirituality* (Philadelphia: Westminster Press, 1988). This work stands in sharp contrast with other contemporary male theological treatments such as Bob Mesle's "A Friend's Love: Why Process Theology Matters," *The Christian Century,* July 15–22, 1987, 622–25, where the focus is, typically, on the implications for theology rather than for human conduct. Such efforts, while useful insofar as they take friendship seriously as the most adequate and meaningful way of talking about the divine-human relationship, are finally inadequate and relatively meaningless because they are abstract and because they objectify the matter at hand.

40. James B. Nelson *The Intimate Connection: Male Sexuality, Masculine Spirituality,* 49.

41. Ibid., 48.

42. Ibid., 66.

43. Judith Plaskow and Carol P. Christ, *Weaving the Visions: Patterns in Feminist Spirituality* (New York: Harper & Row, 1989).

44. See ibid., part 3, "Self in Relation" 171–266.

45. See Janice Raymond, *A Passion for Friends: Toward a Philosophy of Female Affection* (Boston: Beacon Press, 1986).

46. Ibid., 4.

47. See Elisabeth Schüssler Fiorenza, *In Memory of Her* (New York: Crossroad, 1983), and *Bread Not Stone* (New York: Beacon Press, 1984), 15–22 and chapter 5.

48. See Renita Weems, *Just a Sister Away* (San Diego: Lura Media, 1988).

49. Raymond, *A Passion for Friends,* 114.

50. Adele M. Fiske, *Friends and Friendship in the Monastic Tradition,* a doctoral dissertation presented at Fordham University, later published, Cuernavaca, Mexico: Centrol Intercultural de Documentación, *CIDOC Cuaderno* no. 51, 1970. I am indebted to Virginia Anderson, M.D., for bring this remarkable source to my attention.

51. Ibid., Introduction, 15.

52. Ibid., chapter 20, 2.

53. See *I Am the Way,* the Constitution of the Sisters of Loretto, approved by the General Assembly, 1984, 2.

54. Marian McAvoy, S. L., "President's Report," July 1984, 29.

55. Ibid.

56. Carolyn Lehmann, "Where Wisdom and Friendship Dwell," Santiago, Chile: Casa Sofía, November 1986.

57. Bibliography for a seminar on friendship taught by Ralph B. Potter, Harvard Divinity School, Harvard University, 1980. This was considered by many scholars to be a definitive listing on a topic that is treated very lightly in the theological literature. Several of the items listed by women involve sociological or other related materials. Of the more relevant theological materials is the work of Anne Therese dem arguent de Coucelles, Marquise de Lambert (1647–1733), *The Works of the Marchioness de Lambert,* 2 vols. (London: W. Owen, 1769), "A Treatise on Friendship," vol. 1, 140–75.

58. Rosemary Radford Ruether, *Sexism and God-Talk,* 258.

59. Anna Quindlen, "Between Women, Talk is Digging for Buried Treasure," "Life in the 30's" series, *New York Times,* April 22, 1987.

60. The most comprehensive and convincing treatment of these issues is Carol J. Adams, *The Sexual Politics of Meat: A Feminist-Vegetarian Critical Theory* (New York: Continuum, 1989).

14. While Love Is Unfashionable: Ethical Implications of Black Spirituality and Sexuality

Toinette M. Eugene

This chapter first appeared in *Women's Consciousness/Women's Conscience* in 1985.

For you there shall be no longing, for you
shall be fulfillment to each other;
For you there shall be no harm, for you
shall be a shield for each other;
For you there shall be no falling, for you
shall be support to each other;
For you there shall be no sorrow, for you
shall be comfort to each other;
For you there shall be no loneliness, for you
shall be company to each other;
For you there shall be no discord, for you
shall be peace to each other;
And for you there shall be no searching,
for you shall be an end to each other.
—Kawaida Marriage Commitment

Introduction

Black spirituality and black sexuality, properly understood as aspects of the holistic life-style of Afro-American women and men, are a closer fit than hand and glove. Nonetheless, taken together these issues also represent two of the most serious ethical challenges that the contemporary black church must address.

While we may affirm the covenantal poetry above which is based on an African worldview and value system, we must also acknowledge another Afro-American reality which sorely lacks the spiritual and sexual fidelity expressed in the poem.

One of the most neglected ministries in the black church has been the holistic integration of sexuality and life. Although the black church has been one of the key supportive institutions for upbuilding family life and values,[1] the need to address issues and attitudes dealing with sexuality, with mutuality in male/female relationships, and with the more recent impact of black feminism has never been greater then today.

This essay investigates the relationships between black spirituality and sexuality in the quest for mutuality among black women and black men. I will examine these issues with particular reference to the unifying factor of black love. The focus is holistic, that is, it illuminates black spirituality and sexuality as they are experientially related. The assumptions of this approach are incarnational. Consequently, a theology of black male/female friendship which is mutual, community seeking, as well as other-directed, is a central, incarnational, and liberational premise for this work in an era in which any effort at committed love appears unfashionable.

Spirituality and Sexuality as Religious Aspects of the Contemporary Black Experience

We must acknowledge at the outset a widespread and well-known experience within the black community. Michelle Wallace, among others, agrees that experience of distrust has driven a wedge between black women and black men:

> For perhaps the last fifty years there has been a growing distrust, even hatred between black men and black women. It has been nursed along, not only by racism on the part of whites, but by an almost deliberate ignorance on the part of blacks about the sexual politics of their experience in this country.[2]

This basic distrust between black women and black men accounts for the inability of the black community to mobilize as it once could and did. The religious aspect of *black sexuality,* by which I mean the basic dimension of our self-understanding and way of being in the world as black male and female persons, has been distorted into a form of black sexism. Because of this basic distrust, the beauty of black sexuality, which also includes our sex-role understandings, our affectional orientations, physiological arousal and genital activity, and our capacity for sensuousness, has become debilitated. The power of black sexuality to contribute to our liberating mission to change our oppressive condition has been weakened. This basic distrust disables and distracts us as we strive to bring about the reign of God, which is a theological, as well as a political reality, for black women and black men.[3]

Theologian Jacquelyn Grant adds another significant aspect of the nexus between black spirituality and black sexuality: the effects of sexism on the kerygmatic and proclamatory mission of the black church. She insists:

> If the liberation of women is not proclaimed, the church's proclamation cannot be about divine liberation. If the church does not share in the liberation struggle of Black women, its liberation struggle is not authentic. If women are oppressed, the church cannot possibly be "a visible manifestation that the gospel is a reality"—for the gospel cannot be real in that context. One can see contradictions between the church's language or proclamation of liberation and its action by looking both at the status of Black women in the church as laity and Black women in the ordained ministry of the church.[4]

The holistic expression of black spirituality is a central part of what is at stake in liberating relationships between black women and men in the church and society.

Spirituality is no longer identified simply with asceticism, mysticism, the practice of virtue, and methods of prayer. Spirituality, i.e., the human capacity to be self-transcending, relational, and freely committed, encompasses all of life, including our human sexuality.

Specifically, Christian spirituality involves the actualization of this human transcendence through the experience of God, in Jesus the Christ, through the gift of the Spirit. Because God, Jesus, and the Spirit are experienced through body-community-history, a black Christian spirituality includes every dimension of black life. We must begin to re-employ the power of black spirituality as a personal and collective response of black women and black men to the gracious presence of the God who lives and loves within us, calling us to liberating relationships with one another and with all people on Earth.

Black Love as Foundational for the Expression of Black Spirituality and Sexuality

A black liberating love must serve as the linchpin to link black spirituality and sexuality. Black love is the agent of gospel liberation as well as the strongest asset of the black and believing community. Black love, expressed through the faithful witness of our spirituality and sexuality creates awareness of the living God who is in every place. Black love sustains our own ability to choose and to discern, and nurtures the sense of the bonding and *esprit d'corps* which allows black women and men to be distinctive in the style of our self-acceptance. Black love confirms and affirms our affection for God, self, and others, especially those who have also been oppressed.

Historically, black love enabled the incredibly crushed spirits of enslaved black women and men to look beyond their immediate, undeserved suffering to a God who would never forsake them in their hour of anguish and despair. Historically, it has been the religious aspect of black love which enabled black Christians to believe always in the worth of each human life: born and unborn; legitimate and "illegitimate"; single and several-times married; young and old; unemployed and inexperienced.

Any major misunderstandings or doubt about the ability of black love to link and liberate the power of spirituality and sexuality can be traced to the effects of our enslavement experiences. Historically, it was criminal for blacks to express extended love for one another or to establish lasting relationships of social interdependence and care. Blacks were wrenched from our African societies in which sexual behavior was orderly and under firm family and community controls. Under the system of slavery black people were bred like animals; white men were allowed to sexually coerce and abuse black women; black families were frequently broken up and legal marriage was often prohibited. Sexual instability was forced upon the Afro-American community.[5]

Racist myths and stereotypes perpetuated these distortions to this day, falsely detailing black hypersexual activity and an inability to maintain and nurture marital commitments. Racists also repeat ubiquitous rumors about violent relationships among black men and their women or wives. It is impossible for the many white Americans reared on this pathological mythology to think, speak, or write with historical accuracy or ethical understanding about the integrity of black love and relationships.

Despite these assaults, black love has continuously flowed between black people, almost like breath (the *nepesh,* the *ruah* or the *pneuma,* which scriptural studies tell us is like the breath of God), breathing life into dead or desperate situations. This death-defying capacity of black women and men to go on giving and receiving love has been incredibly preserved within a hostile and racist American environment. Such tenacious black love had its spiritual genesis in African soil where it developed unencumbered, at least in its beginnings, by the prejudices of American puritanical Christianity. We must hold on to this strong inheritance from our African past if there is to be any hope for nurturance, growth, and fruitfulness in black male/female relationships in our black church and society.

Racist assumptions and myths perpetuate the lie of a "black love deficiency." Black persons educated in the black religious experience have recognized that if black people today are to be liberated, we must continue to conceive of and model ourselves as a morally creative and spiritually generative race of women and men who choose to act out of our own positive *ethos.* We must continue to create and articulate our own positive expressions and standards of excellence rather than continue to be confined and defined by the negative images of a dominant social, sexual, cultural, and political system which does not value blackness as inherently good.

Black love ought always to serve as an essential normative and descriptive referent for the relationship found in black spirituality and sexuality. I arrive at this ethical "ought" or injunction for our future based on results which are verifiable in our brutal and painful past history as a people in this country. It may be historically demonstrated that in times past whenever black women and men consciously and consistently dared to express black love through an integration of their spirituality and sexuality, they became a source for liberating social transformation in both the black community and in the white world around them. The abolitionist and feminist Sojourner Truth, through her involvement in redressing the racist and sexist oppression of her times, is an excellent example of the way in which the integration of personal spirituality and sexuality may come to fruition in a prophetic paradigm for the sake of the reign of God. (I shall return to examine the religious experience of Sojourner Truth as a model for our theme.)

In the days gone by, black love expressed between black women and men was at worst illegal or at least highly unprofitable in every way for those trying to survive in impossible situations. Nonetheless deliberate choices were made by our foreparents which: 1) enabled Afro-American peoples to create and perform under great duress their own wedding rituals such as the slave marriage custom of "jumping the broomstick" or the practice of "marrying in blankets";[6] 2) promoted an internal sexual ethic in the slave communities which safeguarded marriages, secured the welfare of children and forbade indiscriminate or irresponsible sexual relations; 3) prompted hundreds of former slaves to search endlessly for a reunion with their spouses, children, and relatives after the Emancipation Proclamation of Lincoln.

These realities are foundational for an understanding that black love expresses a sacramental statement about the relationship of black spirituality to sexuality. Without a realistic assessment of the innumerable ways black women and men have endeavored to hold fast to each other, and to cherish one another, it is easy to generate theological premises and sociological strategies based on false foundations. For example, it is true that urban lifestyles and escalating unemployment have contributed greatly to the breakdown of many black marriages and families. However, it is equally critical to assert the historical fact that until the third decade of the twentieth century, the majority of black marriages and families were thriving and stable.[7]

This practical understanding of black integrity, fidelity, as well as familial stability, enables a clearer assessment of the pathologies of racism and sexism which affect black male/female relationships in church and society. Racism and sexism continue to hinder us from expressing the depths of black spirituality and sexuality as epitomized in black love.

Racism and Sexism as Critical Factors Affecting the Black Quest for Mutuality

Racism and sexism, operative in our midst, are the two primary negative factors which affect black male/female relationships. Any ethical reflection on the issue of sexism in relation to racism requires a coming to terms with the suffering and oppression which have marked past pathological relationships between black women and black men. Honest reflection on the issue of sexism in relation to racism may also highlight positive aspects of the challenge and conversion available to black and believing women and men who want to deal with their own spirituality and sexuality as a means of coming to terms with a new life in God.

Jacquelyn Grant explains the effects of sexual dualism on the self-image of black people. "Racism and sexism are interrelated," she says, "just as all forms of oppression are interrelated."[8] Racism and sexism have provided a theological problem within the Christian community composed of both black women and men who theoretically are *equally* concerned about the presence of freedom and justice for all. "Sexism, however, has a reality and significance of its own because it represents that peculiar form of oppression suffered by Black women at the hands of Black men. It is important to examine this reality of sexism as it operated in both the Black Community and the Black Church."[9]

A careful diagnosis of the sickness and the sin of sexism within the black church calls forth a challenge to ministers and laity alike. The failure of the black church and of black theology itself to proclaim explicitly the liberation of black women indicates, according to this assessment, that neither theology nor the church can claim to be agents of divine liberation or of the God whom the evangelist describes as the Author and Exemplar of black love. If black theology, like the black church, has no word for black women, then its conception of liberation is inauthentic and dysfunctional.

There are two basic forms which such sexism takes in black male/female relationships: sexist and spiritualistic splits or divisions within reality.

Sexist dualism refers to the systematic subordination of women in church and society, within interpersonal relationships between males and females, as well as within linguistic patterns and thought formulations by which women are dominated.[10] Hence the term "patriarchal dualism" may be also appropriate, or more simply, the contemporary designation of "sexism," may be used. *Spiritualistic dualism* has its roots in the body-spirit dichotomy abounding in white western philosophy and culture introduced at the beginning of the Christian era. Hence, the term "Hellenistic dualism" may also be appropriate. It must be noted in offering these descriptive distinctions about sexual and spiritual dualisms that African philosophy and culture was and still is significantly different from these white western conceptualizations.[11] It is this African worldview which has given rise to the holistic potentiality residing in authentic expressions of Afro-American spirituality and sexuality today.

Sexist dualism has pathologically scarred not only the white community from which it originated but has also had its negative effect within the black religious community.[12] Sexist dualism, which has been organized along racial lines, refers to "schizophrenic" male attitudes toward women in general who are imaged as either the virgin or the whore—the polemical Mary or Eve archetype represented by the female gender. The prevailing model of beauty in the white, male-dominated American society has been the "long-haired blond" with all that accompanies this mystique. Because of this worldview, black women have had an additional problem with this pseudo-ideal as they encounter black men who have appropriated this norm as their own.

Sexist as well as racist dualisms have elevated the image of the white woman in accordance with the requirements of a white worldview into becoming the respected symbol of femininity and purity, while the black woman must represent an animality which can be ruthlessly exploited for both sex and labor. Similarly the sexist dualism present within pseudo-biblical teaching argues that *woman* is responsible for the fall of "*man*kind," and is, consequently the source of sexual evil. This dualistic doctrine has had its doubly detrimental effect in the experience of many black women.[13]

The self-image and self-respect of many black women is dealt a double blow by both black religion and black society. Thus, black women are made to believe or at least accept on the surface that they are evil, ugly, insignificant, and the underlying source of trouble, especially when the sense of intimacy begins to break down in black love relationships.

This dualistic doctrine has nurtured a kind of compensatory black male chauvinism (as evidenced in typical black church patterns and black nationalism movements) in order to restore the "manliness" of the one who had traditionally been humiliated by being deprived (according to a white patriarchal model) of being the primary protector for his family. In such manner, sexist dualism has been a central limitation in the development of a black love which at its zenith is the most authentic expression we have of the unity of black spirituality and sexuality.

A disembodied spirituality has also been a central limitation in the development of black love. Spiritualistic dualism has been a central factor in persistent efforts to portray faithful black love as an unfashionable and hopelessly anachronistic way of establishing black liberation and black material success and achievement. Eldridge Cleaver obviously recognized the racism and sexism in this spiritualistic form of dualism. Cleaver readily identified bodily scapegoating as an aspect of the sickness within racist/sexist relationships: "Only when the white man comes to respect his own body, to accept it as part of himself will he be able to accept the black man's mind and treat him as something other than the living symbol of what he has rejected in himself."[14] Bodily scapegoating implies a discomfort with our own bodies which leads us to discredit any human body-person which differs too much in appearance and similarity from our own. This scapegoating is particularly evident in racist, white-black relationships. But it is equally obvious in the revealing and discrediting attitudes of some men, white and black, about the assumed menstrual "uncleanliness" of women, or the intrinsic "repulsiveness" of the pregnant female form.

Because blackness has long been understood as a symbol for filth as well as evil, a spiritualistic dualism prevalent in the worldview of many white persons has allowed them the racist option of projecting onto black persons any dirty or disgusting bodily feelings which they may harbor within themselves. Because of the fertility potential symbolized by the female menstrual and pregnancy cycles, a spiritualistic and sexist dualism has also been created and sustained by white and black males which has allowed them to act out their own latent anxieties and hostilities by sexually depreciating the value and worth of the black female person.

As long as we feel insecure as human beings about our bodies, we will very likely be anxious or hostile about other body-persons obviously racially or sexually different from our own embodied selves. Thus, the most dehumanizing spoken expressions of hostility or overt violence within racist and/or sexist experiences are often linked with depreciating the body or body functions of someone else. Worse yet, though, the greatest dehumanization or violence that actually can occur in racist and/or sexist situations happens when persons of the rejected racial- or gender-specific group begin to internalize the judgments made by others and become convinced of their own personal inferiority. Obviously, the most affected and thus dehumanized victims of this experience are black women.

Racism and sexism diminish the ability of black women and men to establish relationships of mutuality, integrity, and trust. Racism and sexism undermine the black communities in which we live, pray, and work out our salvation in the sight of God and one another. However, in coming to terms with racism and sexism as oppressions affecting us all, the black church does have access to the black community in ways that many other institutions do not. The black church has a greater potential to achieve both liberation and reconciliation by attending carefully to the relationships which have been weakened between black males and females.

Because the black church has access, and is often indeed the presiding and official agent in the process of sexual socialization, it has a potentially unlimited opportunity to restore the ancient covenant of Scripture and tradition which upholds the beauty of black love in its most profound meaning. Wherever black love is discouraged or disparaged as an unfashionable or unattainable expression between black women and black men, the black church has an unparalleled option to model these gospel values of love and unconditional acceptance. By offering from its storehouse an authentic understanding of black spirituality and sexuality, the black church becomes paradigmatic of the reign of God materializing and entering into our midst.

I have referred to spirituality as a commitment and life-style, as the growth and response of the human personality to the beauty and benevolence of a liberating God. For black Christians in particular, the praxis of spirituality is a conscious response to the call for discipleship by Jesus. It is intimately related to the moral and ethical conviction which moves us from the private, prayerful posture of bowed head and bent knee to the public, prophetic position of proclaiming before oppressor and oppressed alike: "Thus saith the Lord of Justice. . . ."

For black Christian women and men, the importance of the spiritual life cannot be overplayed. It is what unites those of African ancestry in the possession of a distinctive *ethos*. For black Christians, our African heritage allows us to comprehend spirituality as a *Lebenswelt*—as a life-experience—as well as a worldview. Our African heritage allows us to share in a collective mindset that recognizes yet does not rigidly separate the sacred from the secular, or insist on negative, polemic (i.e., Hellenistic) distinctions about the relative merits of the ideal and actual, the body and the spirit, or the profane and the pristine.[15]

Dualisms, sexist or spiritualistic, have no place within the seamless garment of authentic black religious experience. It is this integrative understanding implicit and inherent in the Afro-

American religious *Lebenswelt* that allows spirituality and sexuality to be considered together and as aspects of a holistic religious experience for black women and men in the church and society. Whatever one decides in the historical debate surrounding the actual degree of African retentions in the New World, it is certain that the black church in America has thrived on the dynamic qualities of an African spirituality. History has evidenced a faith affirmation among black religionists that indicates "both the individual and community have a continuous involvement with the spirit world in the practical affairs of daily life."[16]

A striking description of African Christian spirituality provides in summary format a black perspective:

> [African Christian] spirituality is a dynamic and outgoing concept. . . . There is nothing cerebral or esoteric about spirituality; it is the core of the Christian experience, the encounter with God in real life and action. Spirituality is the same thing as continuous or experiential prayer—prayer as a living communion with God who is experienced as being personally present in the relationships of humanity. It is the mode of living, the essential disposition of the believer, and it imparts a new dimension to the believer's life. In other words, it is not only a new way of looking at human life, but a new way of living it. It is unnecessary, perhaps, to draw any sharp dividing line between theology and spirituality. Theology should be spiritual theology . . . it should not be merely speculative, but should encourage active commitment.[17]

Because of this overarching emphasis in black spirituality on human persons, relationships, and values, the black church is in a prime position to invite and reestablish in creative ways a dialogue between black women and black men. Because the black church is seen to be the driving force of the movement toward the recovery of a meaningful value system for the black community, it has tremendous potential for fostering constructive, instructive, and reconciling discussion on issues of mutuality, sexuality and spirituality for black women and men. It is obvious that the foundational theory and the theology are all in place to accomplish this dialogue, yet the praxis is still limited or lacking if we are at all honest in our reflection upon our lived experience. The recovery of a meaningful value system enriching the relationships between black women and men still remains underdeveloped, or at best only moderately achieved.

The tendency to opt for a spirituality which is unrelated to our black bodily existence or the temptation to become too heavily fixated at the level of the physical, material, or genital expressions of black love keeps us off balance and unintegrated in religiously real ways. Thus, relationships between black women and men in the black church and community still struggle to reveal that *imago Dei* of which Scripture speaks:

> Then God said, "Let us make man in our image, after *our likeness*" . . . so God created . . . Male *and* female . . . (Gen 1:26f.)
>
> For as many of you as were baptised into Christ have put in Christ. There is neither slave nor free, there is neither male or female; for you are all one in Christ Jesus. (Gal 3:27f.)

It is impossible to adequately establish any Christian perspective on human sexuality without first returning to and affirming the value that God has forever made human flesh and "body-persons" the privileged place of the divine encounter with us. Perhaps, as we are able to deepen our understanding of black spirituality as an embodied, incarnational, holistic and earthy reality and gift given to us by the God who became enfleshed to dwell with us as a "body-person," we may become better at the praxis which this implies.

If God has so trusted and honored the human body by taking on a human form and accepting human sexuality as a way of entering into relationship with all humanity, how much more must we strive to imitate the model of spirituality and sexuality offered to us by the Word-Made-Flesh. God freely chose to become a body-person as we are. I am persuaded to think that many of us are simply too afraid to take ourselves that seriously and act "freely mature with the fullness of Christ himself" (Eph 4:13).

In the process of exploring theologically how this ontological blackness points to the *imago Dei* in black humanity we are immediately referred back to the context of the feminist challenge. To theologically explore ontological blackness requires us to engage in open and nondefensive dialogue with others about creative use of sexually inclusive *language* for God as well as sexually inclusive *images* which serve to symbolize God. Although we may take great pride and satisfaction in the language and image of the phrase "God is Black," there is still a black feminist question which is appropriately raised for our consideration: "Have we simply shifted from imaging and thinking of God in white male terminology into conceiving and speaking of God as a black male figure?"

James Evans offers a straightforward reply to this concern in his article on "Black Theology and Black Feminism."

> If blackness is an ontological symbol [pointing out the *imago Dei* in humanity] then it means more than physical blackness and also more than maleness. . . . Blackness must mean the racism and liberation from it experienced by black men. It must also mean the racism/sexism and the liberation from them experienced by black women. If blackness as an ontological symbol refers to authentic humanity, then it cannot become simply a "living testament" to failure in white male/female relationships, but must point to new relationships.[18]

This consideration of new relationships between black women and black men and with a God whom we choose to image as black and as androgynous within our contemplation and conversation necessarily urges us onward in the ethical task of reintegrating and restoring the fullness of meaning to black spirituality and sexuality. The search for ways of expressing and experiencing an inclusive vision of God calls us to the task of offering and receiving black love which joins and sustains our spiritual and sexual lives in appropriate ways.

Through a deepening trust and mutuality in our relationships with God, self, and others, the expressions of black love which may seem so unfashionable or unsophisticated to the world may serve to bond black women and men even more closely together in our worst periods of trial and tribulations as well as in our best moments of joy and achievement.

Feminism and Friendship as Embodied Examples of Black Love

There are hopeful signs on the horizon pointing to an increasing sense of mutuality and deepening of understanding in black male/female relationships. Black women who are feminists do want to deepen their exchange of experiences with black men, and to make plans together for a future full of hope. As Jeanne Noble puts it: "Black women want to be involved. . . . Black women want to be partners, allies, sisters [with black men]! Before there is partnering and sharing with someone, however, there is the becoming of oneself. And the search and discovery of authentic selfhood on the part of black women has begun."[19] Black feminism as a concept is *not* meant to describe militant, manhating females who are strict separatists without sensitivity for anyone but themselves—a sort of chauvinism in reverse. Black feminism is defined as a self-acceptance, satisfaction, and security of black women within themselves. Similarly, in the case of black men who understand themselves as feminists, black feminism for them is an attitude of acceptance of black women as peers—an attitude which is verifiable in their behavior and efforts on behalf of and in solidarity with black women. Black feminism proceeds from the understanding, acceptance, and affirmation of black women as equal and mutual in relation to black men, to an increasing openness of mind and heart to be in solidarity with and in self-sacrificing compassion and action for others who have also been oppressed or marginal in society. This solidarity includes being in communion and consultation with all Third World peoples, and implies dialogue and discussion with white women's liberation actions as well as with gay liberation movements in this country.

As black men and women come to understand and to express this kind of black feminist perspective in relation to one another and for the sake of bringing about the reign of God in our world, this kind of black love is not always going to be fashionable or acceptable to everyone. However, by accepting the divine demand to struggle against both sexism and racism, black feminists (both men and women) can experience and express a black love that is both redemptive and refreshing. There are those who have been there in the struggle before us and can show us the way. A renowned example of black Christian feminism, and a model of the quest for mutuality between black women and men and all oppressed others, was the emancipated slave and celebrated mystic, Sojourner Truth.

Born into slavery in upstate New York at the end of the eighteenth century, Isabelle Bomefree received a call to begin a new life in 1843. At the age of forty-six she took a new name that summed up her vocation and conviction to be a Sojourner or pilgrim of the Truth. She suddenly felt called to leave her employment in New York City and set out to do God's work in the world. For the next forty years she moved about the country lecturing, singing, and helping the cause of abolition of slavery. After the Civil War she worked tirelessly and selflessly for the betterment of the lot of freed slaves as well as for all women's rights. She knew well that black love expressed in black spirituality and sexuality was not always welcomed warmly as a means of liberation or reconciliation in the places where she was called to minister. As a black Christian feminist on a quest for mutuality among all peoples, she offers an embodied example for our consideration.

A tall, forceful woman with a booming voice, we are told she spoke plainly about prayer to God. In the autobiographical account of her life, which she dictated since she was unable to write, she recounted in *The Narrative of Sojourner Truth* this religious experience that she had when she was still a slave:

> . . . (Sojourner) told Mrs. Van Wagener that her old Master Dumont would come that day, and that she should go home with him on his return . . .
>
> . . . before night, Mr. Dumont made his appearance. She informed him of her intention to accompany him home.

> He answered with a smile, "I shall not take you back again; you ran away from me." Thinking his manner contradicted his words, she did not feel repulsed, but made herself and child ready . . . [to] go with him. . . .
>
> . . . But ere she reached the vehicle, she says that God revealed himself to her, with all the suddenness of a flash of lightning, showing her "in the twinkling of an eye, that he was *all over*"—that he pervaded the universe—"and that there was no place God was not." She became instantly conscious of her great sin of forgetting her Almighty Friend and "ever present help in time of trouble."
>
> . . . She plainly saw that there was no place, not even in hell where he was not; and where could she flee? Another such "a look" as she expressed it, and she felt that she must be extinguished forever, even as one, with the breath of his mouth "blows out a lamp," so that no spark remains.
>
> . . . When at last the second look came not, and her attention was once more called to outward things, she observed that her master had left, and exclaiming aloud, "Oh God, I did not know you were so big," [she] walked into the house.[20]

The rest of Sojourner's life was a long conversation with her "Almighty Friend," God. All who met her would always be struck by the calm self-possession of this stately black woman. The most characteristic aspect of her spirituality was the vivid sense of God's presence everywhere (a distinctively African worldview), and her simple manner of praying everywhere.

Sojourner's suffering was as direct a result of her blackness as it was a result of her ministry, and it was a significant element in her spiritual development. And, "because of this humility," according to Heb 5:7–8, "this prayer was heard." Daughter though she was, she learned obedience in the school of suffering, and once transformed, she became a model of liberation and of the quest for mutuality for us and for the encouragement of all who will learn from her example.

Through her intimate relationship with God, Sojourner Truth offers us a model for a theology of friendship which may serve to further our understanding of the quest for mutuality between black women and men as well as with all other persons. Sojourner Truth understood and related to God consistently and continuously as her dear and "Almighty Friend." The narrative of her life declares that, "she talked to God as familiarly as if he had been a creature like herself; and a thousand times more so, than if she had been in the presence of some earthly potentate."[21]

Relationships which are mutual, community-seeking, and other-directed are critical in the encouragement of any lasting commitments between black women and men. They are also critical for the development of friendships or intimacy between couples or groups who wish to embody the meaning of what has been defined as black love. It is these characteristics of mutuality, communality, and disinterestedness (in the best sense of its meaning as an unbiased personal interest or advantage in a relationship) that have the most potential to transform our culture and to create the preconditions necessary for the reign of God to take root and to grow in our midst.

Such a theology of friendship seems much more adequate than just a theology of sexuality standing alone, or just a simple rendition of spirituality offered for application in our times. A theology of friendship is more adequate and appropriate for us because it acknowledges that it is not sexuality or spirituality *per se,* but friendship which determines what the quality of a relational life can be with God and others.

When we can accept and relate to God as our "Almighty Friend," we are no longer left only with the limiting notions of God available to a patriarchal system—i.e., Father, Lord, and King. Nor are we stuck with the alternate prevailing terms of Mother Hen, or the recently reclaimed feminine Holy Spirit or Holy Wisdom which are often rolled out to balance the gender images of God. With Sojourner Truth as a witness we may discover the androgynous, unfettered notion of God as Friend—a notion which can serve to strengthen and encourage the quality of all of our intimate and personal relationships as well as our broader social connectedness.

Some characteristics which may prove useful for understanding God as Friend are mutuality, the urge toward community, and disinterestedness. Mutuality has been suggested by theologians and others who are concerned with how God is affected by humankind and *vice versa*. One feminist theologian describes it in this way:

> Mutuality is that quality of the otherness of God which is really God's oneness with us. To characterize otherness as mutuality is to say that God can only be understood in human terms, but that very understanding is affected by our belief in God. In short, mutuality means that our relationship with God is freely chosen on both sides (unlike family or government images like Father and Lord in which the relationships are not necessarily intentional and gratuitous).[22]

A related characteristic of mature friendships, i.e., a sense of and need for communality, is an essential quality of the Christian and triune God. The idea of the reign of God, the gathering of all that is into a harmonious community, is another way of describing the God-human cooperation which results in salvation and liberation. Jesus is the Force in Christianity, the Friend whose relationship with us is manifested in our being part of the Christian community of God. Our membership is authenticated, as it was in Sojourner Truth's case, by the works of love and justice which we embrace. This is not the pietistic, "What a friend I have in Jesus." Rather, it is the lived experience we have of a historical group of friends. Jesus' friendships with his immediate community of women and men disciples are a model for our contemporary Christian life. This is the community which derives its identity from the laying down of life for friends. We can conclude that the missionary vocation which springs forth from Christianity is in fact a call and an invitation for black women and men in particular to go forth in ministry and mutuality together to make friends with all people all over the world.

The sexist and spiritualistic dualisms previously discussed

would have us believe that "the world, the flesh, and the devil" are a collective evil which militates against our enjoyment of any meaningful relationships. However, when we begin to recognize and respect one another as embodied persons with a body-soul unity, and when we begin to see the world not as some grimy abstraction but as the clean and earthly clay from which we were created, then a final characteristic of a theology of friendship can come into play. Other-centeredness, disinterestedness, or a willingness and desire to place others ahead of our own personal ambition, is the quality of relationality which is essential to making the love expressed between black women and men a reflection of God's love for us and others. In this world when a philosophy of "make way for me first" is so prevalent, other-directedness as an aspect of the theology of friendship can help us to see how the world is really oriented not just for our individual pleasure but for our collective future. The pleasure of a few cannot be allowed to determine the future of everyone, or it will soon become no future for anyone. While self-centeredness and narcissism remain the fashionable norm regulating the self and larger society (including our governmental policies and positions on nuclear disarmament, and over-involvement in Third World nations' political liberation decisions), we must work at expressing a currently unfashionable praxis of black love.

While love is unfashionable
let us live
unfashionably.
Seeing the world
a complex ball
in small hands;
love our blackest garment.
Let us be poor
in all but truth, and courage
handed down
by the old
Spirits.
Let us be intimate with
ancestral ghosts

and music
of the undead.
While love is dangerous
let us walk bareheaded
beside the Great River.
Let us gather blossoms
under fire.[23]

Notes

1. For an excellent theological treatment of the unique relationship between the two institutions of the black family and the black church, see J. Deotis Roberts, *Roots of a Black Future: Family and Church* (Philadelphia: Westminster Press, 1980). See also Andrew Billingsley, *Black Families in White America* (Englewood Cliffs, NJ: Prentice-Hall, 1968) and Herbert G. Gutman, *The Black Family in Slavery and Freedom, 1750–1925* (New York: Pantheon, 1976) for extensive documentary examinations of this issue.

2. Michelle Wallace, *Black Macho and the Myth of Superwoman* (New York: Dial Press, 1979), 13.

3. See J. Deotis Roberts, *A Black Political Theology* (Philadelphia: Westminster Press, 1974), for further explanation of the reign of God as both a theological and political reality.

4. Jacquelyn Grant, "Black Theology and the Black Woman," in *Black Theology: A Documentary History, 1966–1979,* ed. Gayraud Wilmore and James Cone (Maryknoll: Orbis, 1979), 423.

5. See Wade Nobles' "African-American Family Life," in *Black Families,* ed. Harriet Pipes McAdoo (Beverly Hills, CA: Sage Publications, 1981), 77–86.

6. See Gutman's *The Black Family in Slavery and Freedom, 1750–1925,* 273–84 for fuller discussion of black slave marriage rituals. "Jumping the broomstick" served as the most common practice to transfer a "free" slave union into a legitimate and respected slave marriage. "Marrying in blankets" referred to the ritual by which a slave woman brought her blanket or bedroll to place beside that of her intended husband to signify their intent to share life and love together as a committed couple. In a

note Gutman records that this simply symbolic action so disturbed Yankee missionaries that they even imposed "severe strictures" on South Carolina slaves "marrying in blankets."

7. See Herbert G. Gutman as cited in Edward P. Wimberly, *Pastoral Counseling and Spiritual Values: A Black Point of View* (Nashville: Abingdon, 1982), 62.

8. Grant, "Black Theology and the Black Woman," 422.

9. Grant, "Black Theology and the Black Woman," 422.

10. James B. Nelson has made extensive use of the concepts of "sexist and spiritualistic dualism" in *Embodiment: An Approach to Sexuality and Christian Theology* (New York: Pilgrim Press, 1976). See especially Chapter Three. I have attempted to turn his categories into explicit reflection on black sexual experience.

11. See John Mbiti, *The Prayers of African Religion* (New York: Orbis, 1975) and *Concepts of God in Africa* (London: SPCK, 1970) for further connections made on the nexus between black spirituality and an integral worldview.

12. See Rosemary Radford Ruether, *New Women, New Earth: Sexist Ideologies and Human Liberation* (New York: Seabury, 1975), Chapter Five.

13. Grant, "Black Theology and the Black Woman," 422.

14. Eldridge Cleaver, as quoted by Robert Bellah in *The Broken Covenant: American Civil Religion in Time of Trial* (New York: Seabury, 1975), 105.

15. See John Mbiti, *African Religion and Philosophy* (Garden City, NY: Anchor Press, 1969), for additional emphasis on the integration of African life-styles and value systems: epistemology and axiology.

16. Gayraud S. Wilmore, *Black Religion and Black Racialism* (Garden City, NY: Anchor Press, 1973), 197.

17. Aylward Shorter, ed., *African Christian Spirituality* (Maryknoll: Orbis, 1978), 47.

18. James H. Evans, Jr., "Black Theology and Black Feminism," *The Journal of Religious Thought* 38 (Spring–Summer, 1982), 52.

19. Jeanne Noble, *Beautiful Are the Souls of My Black Sisters* (New York: Prentice-Hall, 1978), 343.

20. Sojourner Truth, as quoted by Olive Gilbert in *The Narrative of Sojourner Truth* (Chicago: Johnson Publishing Company, 1970), 46–48.

21. Gilbert, *The Narrative of Sojourner Truth,* 43. *The Narrative* also relates Sojourner's affection for her friend Jesus in detail, pp. 48–52, 119–22, and elsewhere.

22. Mary E. Hunt, ". . . A Feminist Theology of Friendship," in *A*

Challenge to Love, ed. Robert Nugent (New York: Crossroads, 1983), 153.

23. Alice Walker, "While Love Is Unfashionable," in *Revolutionary Petunias and Other Poems* (New York: Harcourt, Brace, Jovanovich, 1972), 68. In an interview the author indicates that this poem was written during the period of her marriage to a white man and while they lived in a southern state with laws against miscegenation. I have used the same poem to encapsulate the difficulties and devotion entailed in the love expressed by black women and men for each other. Although the applications of the poem may differ, the larger context in which Walker explains her black feminist freedom to love in her own fashion and with whom she chooses does not appear to be violated.

Part Four

BIOETHICS

15. Elements of a Feminist Approach to Bioethics

Barbara Hilkert Andolsen

This chapter first appeared in *Religious Methods and Resources in Bioethics* in 1994.

> . . . when thousands of American women are dying from diseases we *can* treat, when thousands more succumb to diseases that more research might prevent, and when thousands of babies are born with unnecessary handicaps because their mothers' medical care was inadequate, then something is deeply wrong.
>
> *Leonard Abramson, President of U.S. Healthcare ([1], p. A17)*

The health and well-being of women are in needless jeopardy in the United States. Unnecessary risks to health are not shared equally by men, at least not by the more privileged men. Nor are unnecessary risks shared equally by all women. Feminist ethicists articulate an approach to bioethics in the midst of this social reality.

One distinctive aspect of feminist ethics is the insistence of its proponents that gender is an important category to consider in both descriptive and prescriptive moments in ethics. Gender is a term that draws attention to the culturally constructed meanings of masculinity and femininity, which are social elaborations upon human biological sexual differentiation. Paying close heed to gender reveals that socially structured sex roles are important for understanding most social practices and issues, including ethical issues.

Damaging inequalities in the treatment of women are too often ignored or even accepted as morally legitimate, in part, because many ethicists apply "sex-blind" moral norms to cases relevant to women without due consideration of women's social circumstances. Such "universal" moral arguments ignore the social context, particularly the pervasiveness of gender hierarchies in which men are dominant. For example, too many ethicists disregard the possible disparate and detrimental effects of justice understood as formal equality, if the subjects of nominally "equal" treatment are facing unequal material and social circumstances. The most helpful work in feminist ethics frames particular biomedical ethical issues against a social and historical background in which unequal gender relationships are carefully delineated.

In this essay I will show the importance of attention to gender in the description of bioethical problems. I will emphasize the need to be alert to the interstructuring of gender, race, and class. I will propose a cautious appreciation of the strengths of a mode of ethical reasoning consistent with a moral attitude of "care." I will explore some connections between feminist ethical methodology and feminist assumptions about moral agency. Finally, I will seek to make new connections between ethics and elements of feminist theology.

Gender Analysis and Social Description

Feminist ethicists, particularly those in the field of theology, insist that all ethical analysis has an important social dimension. Attention to the social structural position of women is an essential requirement for an adequate description of almost any bioethical problem. There is a growing recognition among feminists that any adequate feminist social analysis must be complex—sensitive to the multiple social locations of women in a multitiered structure of gender hierarchy.

An important, and too often unexamined, aspect of the doing of ethics is how we recognize an issue as an ethical issue and how we select certain ethical issues as worthy of more careful examination. A key element in a feminist ethical method is that ethical questions be viewed, at least initially, from the vantage point of women. (I say initially, because feminists are ultimately concerned about the well-being of all persons, including men, and about the good of the entire natural world.) When feminists view medical ethical questions from the standpoint of women's well-being, new gender-related questions are brought into high relief.

For example, one piece of the social analysis essential for a feminist bioethics is an examination of how the social power to define health and disease is distributed between the sexes. Today predominantly *male* medical experts still exert power over women's bodies by defining certain physiological states experienced exclusively by women as diseases or potential medical crises that should be controlled by [male] medical management. Thus, physicians become the relevant authorities who define the appropriate responses to female bodily experiences such as childbirth or menopause. Doctors are still predominantly male, and women, more often than men, are patients in need of medical care. There is a danger that women will become passive "patients" who give unilateral power over their bodies to medical experts. The social roles of doctor and patient and active man and passive or receptive woman can reinforce each other in a fashion that increases women's dependency on doctors and makes it more difficult for women to exercise an appropriate degree of autonomy in medical matters.

Hormone replacement therapy is an example of morally ambiguous, technological control exercised by predominantly male medical experts over women's bodily states. In the past half century, doctors, particularly endocrinologists, have redefined menopause as a hormone deficiency disease or as an "endocrinopathy" ([41], pp. 2–3). They then recommend wide scale treatment of older women with synthetic estrogen (and sometimes progestin) to reverse this so-called deficiency. In my opinion, there is a legitimate place for hormone replacement therapy for some, perhaps many, older female patients. Hormone replacement therapy for menopausal women suffering from severe "hot flashes" or vaginal atrophy can improve the quality of life for these women. Long term treatment may lessen a woman's risk of osteoporosis, stroke, or coronary heart disease.

A recent epidemiological study suggests that treatment with unopposed estrogen may significantly lower an older woman's risk of death from heart disease, which is the leading cause of death in older women [40]. However, other alternatives such as regular, vigorous exercise and good nutrition also have positive effects in lowering the incidence of osteoporosis and heart disease.

The decision to place a woman on a regimen involving prolonged hormone replacement therapy is a weighty one. Hormone replacement therapy has potentially serious negative side effects. These include nausea, mastalgia, increased risk of surgery for gynecological problems, gallstones, thromboembolisms, hypertension, cardiovascular disease, breast cancer, and endometrial cancer ([41], p. 4). The risk of cancer may be lessened by prescribing progestin in combination with estrogen, but progestin may significantly lessen the positive impact of synthetic estrogen in preventing heart disease.

The autonomy of women may be subtly undermined when a normal female biological change is defined as pathological. If postmenopausal women suffer from a deficiency disease, then medical treatment to mitigate the effects of that *disease* seems clearly to be medically and morally good. The decision process subtly privileges doctors as medical experts who diagnose and treat pathologies. I will return to the question of female autonomy and hormone replacement therapy later in this essay.

Women may be harmed if normal female physiological functions are viewed as pathologies which ought to be controlled by medical management. Women are also harmed, because they lack the power to assign a *needed* medical label to certain other threats to their physical well-being. Such a power to name disease is necessary to mobilize health care resources in response to these threats to women's health. For example, the power to define disease is a particularly urgent issue for women who are infected by the human immunodeficiency virus (HIV). Many HIV-infected women first present themselves to a physician with gynecological problems, such as vaginal infections or pelvic inflammatory disease. Yet, until 1993, no gynecological indicators were a part of the official United States definition for AIDS set by the Federal Centers for Disease Control.[1]

For HIV-positive women, there were serious personal implications if they did not fit the official medical definition for an AIDS patient. Without an accurate diagnosis, some seriously ill poor women found it hard to qualify for social welfare benefits, such as

Supplemental Security Income (SSI) payments, i.e., social security funds for the disabled.[2] Poor women terminally ill with AIDS too often spent the last months of their lives in an exhausting and debilitating round of visits to Social Security offices, welfare agencies, and legal services offices ([16], p. A19). The harm done to women by medical and social policies that marginalized them was even worse in this instance, because "women on average die of AIDS in half the time of men with the disease" ([16], p. A19). And "African American women [with AIDS] in 1988 died at nine times the rate of European American women" ([4], p. 24). Some women with AIDS died before they could get the social welfare benefits to which they were entitled. The majority of the women who were thus harmed were African-American and Latina women.

Fortunately, the Social Security Administration has begun to take increased note of AIDS related pathologies in women. And, after a Congressional probe, the CDC did agree to provide an expanded official definition for AIDS. A key aspect of the revised definition is an additional standard for severe compromise of the immune system. (This measure is a CD4+ T-lymphocyte count of less than 200 per microliter.) This aspect of the definition is potentially equally applicable to women and men, heterosexual or gay. The fundamental reason that CDC provides a standardized definition of AIDS is for epidemiological purposes. A definition of AIDS that stresses a gender neutral, immunosuppression standard provides a sufficient measure of gender equality for purposes of tracking the epidemiological scope of this public health crisis.

Still, it is important that both the public and health care practitioners be well educated about special medical problems experienced by HIV-infected *women*. The CDC recognized this concern when it also added invasive cancer of the cervix to the list of diseases that are used by the agency as an indicator of full-blown AIDS. However, invasive cervical cancer is only one of the gynecological disorders to which HIV-infected women are unusually susceptible. Therefore, one remaining, crucial issue is provision of health education that facilitates early diagnosis and treatment of HIV infection in women.

Another important issue is women's ability to direct a reasonable share of available medical research resources to their health care priorities. The National Institutes of Health reported that in 1987 NIH spent only 13.5 percent of its budget on women's health research. Much of the rest of NIH's resources went to fund research into diseases that afflict both women and men. But many of these studies that would appear to benefit both women and men are not always equally beneficial to women. This is because major studies of diseases (also) prevalent in women have often been performed on an exclusively male population. As a result it is often not clear whether important biomedical findings apply to female patients.

For example, a well-known study found that consumption of a single aspirin per day was helpful in the prevention of coronary heart disease. Although heart disease is a major killer of older women, there were no women included in the study. Researchers drew their experimental subject population from a group of older physicians. At the time the study was done, there were not enough female physicians over 50 to create an adequate statistical sample, so women were simply not studied. Therefore, this study does not establish whether the consumption of a prophylactic aspirin a day is beneficial to women at risk of heart disease[3] ([30], pp. 1601–02).

It is also difficult to get adequate research funds to study medical issues that affect primarily women. For three years in a row (1988–90), the National Cancer Institute refused to fund a major prospective study of the effect of fat in the diet on the development of breast cancers. NCI rejected the study again in 1990 because an advisory committee doubted that "women, especially low-income women, could be counted on to stick to a prescribed diet, and . . . [to] reliably remember and accurately report what they ate" ([38], p. 25). Feminist health care activists questioned whether there would have been a similar level of distrust of the ability of male subjects to comply with an experimental protocol. The advisory board also expressed concern about the recruitment of minority women and poor women for the study. The board insisted that the study should have a broad based subject population, so that the results would be applicable to women from diverse groups. The criteria of race- and class-inclusiveness in relevant subject populations is morally laudatory. Still, it is morally ironic that NCI denied funding for a study of great importance to women because of concern about inclusiveness, when NCI rarely turns down male-oriented projects on such grounds ([38], p. 25).

When treatments are developed that could protect women's health, those treatments are not always used appropriately in women's health care. There may be a morally offensive sexual bias in the way in which physicians respond to women's medical complaints. One study on bypass surgery for women suffering from coronary heart disease revealed that many women were not referred to surgeons until their cardiovascular disease was more severe. More male cardiac patients were sent to heart surgeons after exercise treadmill tests indicated heart problems. Patients referred after such tests had better outcomes after surgery ([20], p. 564).

Women, who were less likely to be referred for the exercise stress test, were more often seen as candidates for bypass surgery after a serious heart problem unmistakably manifested itself. More women died after bypass surgery, because more women were in poorer medical condition when the surgery was performed. However, this situation is complex, because women, for physiological reasons, tend to develop serious heart disease later in life than do men. Therefore, female candidates for bypass surgery are older, as well as sicker, and age is also a risk factor that leads to poorer outcomes for women. Still, in the words of the chief investigator on this study: "For women's symptoms to be acted on, they have to be significantly sicker. They have to prove there is something going on" ([21], p. A15). It is an injustice to take women's health complaints less seriously than similar complaints voiced by men.

Looking carefully at women's health care issues means that a feminist ethical method will involve an honest appreciation of complexity and ambiguity. Even these brief descriptions of hormone replacement therapy and bypass surgery show that women's health care issues can be complicated. In the face of so much injustice suffered by women in society generally and in the health care system in particular, it is tempting to write a description of hormone replacement therapy as patriarchal contempt for and control of aging women's bodies. Or to describe poorer survival rates after bypass surgery as the result of sexual discrimination that leads to inferior health care treatment for women. There is more than enough sexism in the history of women's medical "care" to justify such skepticism. But there are other factors which must be considered, too.

There are important physiological differences between women and men and differential medical treatment of women may be based on real, medically relevant bodily differences. Moreover, individual medical practitioners and their women patients are making treatment decisions under circumstances of imperfect knowledge. Some cardiologists do not send female patients for exercise stress tests, because they say that test results are more difficult to interpret for female heart patients. There has never been a randomized, controlled clinical trial that could definitively answer questions about hormone replacement therapy's risks and benefits. A feminist bioethical method must be sensitive to complexity and ambiguity in the formulation of ethical questions.

Nevertheless, attention to gender is a mandatory requirement for an adequate description of the vast majority of bioethical questions. We should examine how the social power to define disease is distributed and who reaps the benefits or bears the burdens created by socially constructed definitions of disease. We also should examine the gender patterns in the distribution of social resources for research leading to the prevention and cure of disease. Finally, we must examine whether women receive medical treatment of similar quality to that afforded to men when women suffer from similar diseases. In addition, an adequate feminist social analysis will be attentive to morally significant differences among women.

Gender, Race, and Class

One important contribution of feminist religious ethics is careful attention to the interstructuring of social oppression in the definition of moral problems. While all women share certain vulnerabilities as women, the social circumstances of women differ. Race, class, sexual orientation, and handicapping conditions, among other considerations, make the life experiences of various women different in important ways. Feminist ethicists, particularly those who are theological ethicists, give careful attention to the ways in which these factors, in interaction, affect the life chances of various women. This means that in seeking to describe any bioethical issue, feminist ethicists should pay attention to factors such as race and class.

For example, one cherished principle in contemporary bioethics is the principle of respect for patient autonomy. I will have more to say about an adequate concept of autonomy later. However, respect for patient autonomy certainly includes informing a patient about the range of treatments available for a given medical condition and enlisting the patient's participation in selecting an acceptable course of treatment. Yet the process of arriving at informed consent is not the same for all women. Social class is a key variable in determining the range of autonomy permitted to a patient.

Sue Fisher, a sociologist, observed the decision making process in the treatment of precancerous lesions of the cervix. She noted now such decisions were made in two different locations in the same medical center. One was a clinic staffed mainly by residents; the other was a service where attending physicians saw private patients. She found that hysterectomies were more often persuasively recommended as the initial treatment of choice for poor women who used the clinic. In contrast, doctors recommended less invasive surgical biopsies with careful monitoring for middle-class women. Two groups of physicians treated women patients with similar medical conditions differently, in part because the residents who treated poor, minority women needed training material upon which to practice their surgical technique. The residents in the clinic also viewed low-income, minority women as less able to comply with the long-term medical monitoring program required along with the less extensive surgery ([10], pp. 42–58).

Race, ethnicity, and social class are also important factors influencing access to good quality health care and, therefore, factors influencing health outcomes for specific groups of women. One good example is the early detection of breast cancer and, therefore, survival rates after a diagnosis of breast cancer. A recent study of the public hospitals in New York City found that poor women, who were disproportionately African-American and Latina, were less likely to be scheduled for routine mammograms.[4] Lack of aggressive screening programs for poor, minority women was one factor in their higher mortality rates. Poor women were diagnosed with breast cancer at a much later stage in the disease process and, therefore, their five-year survival rate was much worse than that of women from more affluent neighborhoods. Nationally, the five-year survival rate for breast cancer patients whose cancer is detected early is 90 percent.[5] At Harlem hospital, where late detection is the norm, the survival rate was 22 percent ([29], pp. 1, 4). Lack of access to convenient and affordable breast cancer screening programs for poor women might be a factor partially explaining why "black women's five-year survival rate [in breast cancer cases] is 13 per cent lower than than [sic] for white women" ([38], p. 24).

It is crucial to examine the intersection of gender and class in a feminist approach to bioethical issues, because seemingly beneficial public health care policies may have disparate effects on women from different classes. For example, starting in 1991, laboratories that process pap smears were required by Federal law to comply with stricter standards for clinical supervision of the technicians who examine pap smears. In view of "the already chronic shortage of specialists who administer the pap smear tests," knowledgeable commentators predicted that hospitals will be forced into "a bidding war" to recruit and retain key laboratory personnel in order to comply with tougher federal standards ([2], p. 1A). That, in turn, would raise the cost for performing the pap smear test. When similar legislation was passed in New York State, the laboratory charge for a routine pap smear went from $10 to $30 ([2], p. 5A). Dr. Marshall Austin, a South Carolina cytopathologist, predicted that even fewer poor women will be able to afford regular cervical cancer screening. He commented, "Low income women, if they have to choose between buying a bag of groceries and having a pap smear, they'll buy the bag of groceries" ([2], p. 5A). Thus, this Federal policy may increase the accuracy of pap smear results available to more affluent women at a trivial cost increase for those women, while it decreases poorer women's access to this critical screening test.

Any comprehensive social analysis intended to illuminate bioethical issues germane to women should include an examination of the interstructuring of gender, race, and class. Other factors such as age, sexual orientation or handicapping condition also may be important. A feminist ethic rooted in the experience of diverse women calls for a challenging, even daunting, multi-faceted social analysis.

An Ethic of Care

A feminist perspective also invites us to reexamine women's experiences to discover the strengths that diverse women might bring to the process of making biomedical ethical decisions. A segment of the feminist community highly values research that shows that many women have a distinctive style of moral analysis and decision making. Following the ground-breaking study by Carol Gilligan, *In a Different Voice,* some ethicists describe women as focusing on optimizing the value of care for persons within relationships. By contrast, they hold that men have a propensity to stress an abstract procedural method for deciding between conflicting and sometimes mutually exclusive rights.

Unfortunately, from my perspective, Gilligan and some of those who have expanded upon her work call this abstract masculine style of moral reasoning an ethic of "justice." Gilligan, who is a psychologist interested in moral development, has adopted a severely constrained philosophical notion of justice as one aspect of her care/justice dichotomy. For Gilligan, justice is that virtue that permits the moral agent to make a fair and impartial adjudication of conflicting moral claims. I contend that another style of reasoning about justice questions, one more adequate for feminist ethical work, is possible. I will say more about a feminist mode of justice-reasoning below. Nevertheless, despite my serious disagreement with Gilligan's use of the word "justice," I will follow her usage in this section of the essay.

In the Gilligan-inspired discussion about care, justice-reasoning is described as the insight available to an impartial observer who assesses the moral weight of conflicting claims. The justice approach involves a careful balancing of the moral scales. The impartial observer adjudicates moral claims through an appeal to the primacy of certain moral principles in a carefully justified hierarchy of moral principles. The justice style of reasoning demands detachment and a high level of abstraction.

Justice-reasoning is a freeze frame approach to the moral process. It usually stops the action at key moments of decision. The emphasis in this mode of rationality is upon reaching a definitive conclusion about the right or good thing to do. The stress is upon *the decision* as the culmination of a reasoning procedure. Iris Murdoch has an apt description of the moral agent who uses this abstract reasoning style. Murdoch declares that the moral self, "thin as a needle, appears in the quick flash of the choosing will" ([25], p. 53).

I maintain that this abstract mode of reasoning is associated with race, class and gender privilege. Moral detachment is a luxury more accessible to the powerful and affluent. It is easier to assume this transcendent perspective when everyday, mundane experiences do not impinge in painful or threatening ways on abstract consciousness. Privileged persons (often men) frequently rely on a wide range of caring labor provided by less privileged persons (often women) who do the hands-on labor necessary to sustain the bodily existence and comfort of the more privileged. In such a circumstance of freedom from bodily labor, privileged persons can more readily claim for themselves the right and duty to achieve an Olympian, disembodied, impartial vantage point on abstract questions of rights and justice.

Care-Reasoning

An ethic of care calls our attention to a different style of moral reasoning. In the moment(s) of caring, the one-caring is especially attentive to the reality of the one-cared-for. The one-caring pays very close attention to the particular circumstances in which the one-cared-for finds herself or himself. As educator D. Kay Johnston remarks: "This [caring] is not done intuitively; rather, it is done by attending to all the variables in a particular situation. This logic does not systematically discard variables, but integrates as many variables as possible" ([18], p. 67).

The one-caring values disciplined thought, not in its own right, but as a skill that can and should be used in the service of the one-cared-for. The one-caring does engage in careful analysis and thoughtful deliberation. She analyzes the other's needs, critically examines alternative means to meet those needs, selects the "best" course of action, and monitors its impact upon the one-cared-for. All of those reasoning processes must be *firmly connected to the concrete reality of the one needing care.*

Care-reasoning seeks to determine the best response to the perceived needs of real people, not the most valid claim among a heterogenous set of abstractly defined rights. The aim of care-reasoning is not to identify and privilege abstract moral principles appropriate to resolving a given set of "problems" or "issues," but to understand the multiple moral demands within a specific, richly textured situation. The one-caring strives to increase options to benefit others, not to solve a problem within the preordained terms set by traditional philosophic definitions of moral principles.

Relationships are central in care-reasoning. In some of the literature of care, dyadic language predominates. The central, moral relation is between the one-caring and the one-cared for. This is particularly true of philosopher Nel Noddings's *Caring: A Feminine Approach to Ethics and Moral Education* [27]. But this dyadic language may be unnecessarily confining and misleading. Care oriented reasoning can and should pay close attention to the needs of multiple others. The one-caring attempts to draw everyone affected by a decision into a circle of care. With care-reasoning, the emphasis is on relationships and maintaining the most positive conjunctions possible in a matrix of relationships. For example, in biomedical ethics, a care mode of reasoning allows us to consider the needs of family or other loved ones of the patient in a more straightforward manner than some examples of so-called justice-reasoning permit.

Attorney Susan Wolf provides a good example of the differing implications of these two styles of moral reasoning in a commentary on the Nancy Cruzan case. Wolf is reacting to the justice-reasoning employed by the Missouri Supreme Court and later upheld by the United States Supreme Court. The judges impartially applied the principle of respect for autonomy of the competent patient. In this case, a central moral question became: Had Nancy Cruzan (who was then in a persistent vegetative state)—while a competent, autonomous individual—expressed a clear and convincing wish not to receive artificial nutrition and hydration should she ever subsequently be in a persistent vegetative condition?[6] If so, the courts asserted her autonomy should be respected, and her wishes should govern treatment. If Cruzan, *as an independent decision maker,* had not asserted a clear and convincing wish to forego treatment under such circumstances, then the state of Missouri's interest in preserving life could be granted a higher priority and the State could (and did initially) require that treatment continue.

Wolf adopts a care perspective, when she analyzes the Cruzan case. She insists that the courts should recognize that we are not radically isolated, autonomous moral agents. Rather, many of us have loving relationships in which we trust family members and other loved ones to make appropriate decisions for us based on their enduring attitude of care toward us. Wolf finds the decision of the Missouri Supreme court morally deficient, in part, because "the court enforces a regime of isolation. . . . Nancy . . . is cut off from those who love her and whom she loved" ([42], p. 40).

Wolf operates from a perspective in which human relationality is a basic assumption. As Noddings puts it: "relation will be taken as ontologically basic and the caring relation as ethically basic" ([27], p.3). From such a perspective, it appears to Wolf that the Court made a poor decision because it ignored relationality. In the eyes of the Court, "it is irrelevant that her family knows her best, nurtured the very person whose preferences the court takes as unknowable. It does not matter that they love her most" ([42], p. 40). From a caring perspective, however, it matters profoundly that they love her most.

According to Wolf, we are most likely to reveal our value orientation toward medical intervention to those closest to us—our family and friends. Moreover, our values are shaped relationally, and a loving family of origin has an important influence on the values we espouse. The Cruzan family nurtured Nancy's values and continued a dialogue with her about those values. Therefore, the Cruzan family is particularly well situated to speak on behalf of Nancy when she can no longer speak for herself. When the

Cruzans' "intimate knowledge" of Nancy is coupled with their "special solicitude" for her, the Cruzan family establishes a powerful claim to make decisions about Nancy's medical treatment ([42], p. 40). An ethic of care, with its attention to relationality, makes it easier to perceive and value the Cruzan family's claim to decide what is best for Nancy and for those who love her.

Some Caveats about "Care"

Human caring is a precious value. It is attractive to reexamine the ethics of the health *care* system reasserting the importance of moral care. It rings true in the experience of many women that caring is a precious ethical contribution often rendered by women, but little recognized or rewarded. Yet the ethic of care needs to be examined critically and advocated cautiously.

Among my concerns is a fear that treatments of caring reasoning which focus on female care givers suggest (often unintentionally) that caring is an innate female character trait. Seeing care as uniquely feminine may create an impression that caring is *univocally* manifest by all women under all social and historical circumstances. On the contrary, the process of caring is different for women (and men) who find themselves in differing social situations.

Gender, class, race, and sexual orientation are among the important variables that can influence for whom and in what way we care. For example, sociologist Karen Sacks, who studied relationships in a Southern hospital, found that African-American ward secretaries felt a special obligation to care for African-American patients who would not otherwise receive an adequate level of medical attention. Intraracial bonding in a situation of institutional racism became the motivating force for particular expressions of care. In one dramatic episode, an African-American female patient's condition suddenly deteriorated during the night shift. The African-American ward secretary and the African-American LPNs tried without success to get the white RNs to call a code. The nurses refused, contending that the patient's condition was not that serious. Finally, the LPNs rolled the cardiopulmonary resuscitation cart to the patient's room, and one of the LPNs summoned the doctors herself. When the doctors arrived, the patient was dead ([36], pp. 181–82). In this incident, racial alliances and racial tensions affected the ability of various members of the health care team to respond to an African-American female patient as "one-cared-for."

More attention also needs to be given to the *costs of caring* under conditions of scarce resources, including the scarce resources of time and human energy. Even Noddings, who presents an idealized phenomenology of care in which the care giver is engrossed in the needs and desires of the one-cared-for, recognizes that care giving can take an inordinately heavy toll on the care giver. According to Noddings, the care giver is then in danger of being caught up in his/her own "cares and burdens" ([27], p. 18). The care giver can even be so worn down by the demands of care giving that he or she is then in need of care.

When considering medical ethics, it is important to do a social analysis of who bears the burdens of care in situations of illness, disability or dying. For example, elderly patients who are unable to do self-care tasks are now often discharged from hospitals earlier in their "recovery" period. Indeed, new Medicare reimbursement policies put pressure on hospitals to discharge more elderly patients in unstable conditions, thereby thrusting greater burdens onto predominantly female care givers—usually wives and daughters. The burden of caring for the frail elderly is shifted from government provided health care services to predominantly female relatives. Too frequently the physical and emotional costs borne by these female care givers are unjustly high. "There is often an unspoken assumption that female caregivers will manage without support until their emotional exhaustion or stress-produced physical illness creates a crisis in caregiving, to which the community will finally make a crisis response" ([7], p. 13). Women are asked to assume a disproportionate share of the burdens of caring for the frail elderly in this society. Such injustices may go unchallenged unless we situate an ethic of care within a broader framework of a commitment to gender justice.[7]

There is another moral irony associated with caring that must be pointed out. Some women—generally more economically privileged women—exploit the caring skills of other less well-to-do women, often women of color. Economically privileged white women find needed relief from the arduous bodily tasks of caring for ill or disabled dependents by hiring, at very low wages, the services of home health aides or nursing home attendants. These lower-level health care workers are working-class women, often women of color. Thus, when examining how burdens of caring are allocated, feminist ethicists should ask hard questions about the behavior of economically, ethnically, and/or racially privileged women. *Intragender* justice should be an important moral standard in any feminist bioethics.

A superficial use of an ethic of care may also obscure the institutional character of many biomedical decisions. Who among the persons involved with a patient is obligated to "care for" the patient? Ought we to assume that the family is always in an emotionally supportive relationship with a patient and is focused on the patient's greatest good? (Certainly health care personnel, who see many dysfunctional families, should not sentimentalize family caring.) When difficult moral choices have to be faced, who has access to the wealth of detail necessary for a care-reasoning approach? A larger role for the care-reasoning perspective in biomedical decision-making would probably require a team approach by the medical care providers. Nurses and social workers would no doubt have an important role to play *in a collaborative process of discerning a caring response* to a particular patient. Sometimes licensed practical nurses or housekeeping or clerical staff members might be the ones who have an essential insight about how best to "care" for the patient.[8]

Another crucial question in an ethic of care is for whom are we obliged to care? Since each of us is a social being embedded in complex, interdependent, social structures, the limits of our responsibility to care are not readily apparent. Yet, since "caring" is such an attentive, holistic response, it is clearly not possible for a single moral agent to care for everyone with whom his life is somehow intertwined. How impersonal or indirect does a social relationship have to become before it is inappropriate, or even hypocritical, to speak of "caring?"

By way of example, let us return to the issue of women with AIDS. The largest number of women infected by the human immunodeficiency virus live in sub-Saharan Africa ([5], pp. 222–23). These women often have only the most minimal health care resources available to them. One international health care expert declares: "Indeed, the cost of a single HIV antibody test (roughly $1 to $4) approaches the annual per capita health expenditure for many African countries" ([6], p. 121). Many African women have no access to the pharmacological treatments being used in Europe and the United States to prolong the lives of people with AIDS. Even routine preventive measures, such as screening of the blood available for transfusion, are economically far more difficult in the developing nations. Persons with AIDS in developing nations compete with many other persons with other serious illnesses for access to severely constrained health care resources.

In what ways, if any, is it legitimate to speak of people from the United States as caring for African women who are HIV-positive? When we ask about the limits of care, it becomes clear that an ethic of care does not provide a comprehensive ethical stance adequate to address all biomedical ethical concerns. Stanley Hauerwas reminds us of an important strength of the ethic of [liberal] justice. "Such theories are not meant to tell us how to be good in relation to some ideal, but rather to insure that *what we owe to others as strangers, not as friends or sharers in a tradition,* is nonarbitrary" ([15], p. 17, emphasis added). Perhaps we need to supplement an ethic of care with an ethic of impartial justice that clarifies our moral responsibilities to distant strangers to whom we are bound by complex political and economic, but not affective, ties.

It is important to note that the two styles of reasoning—a care approach and a justice approach—are not mutually exclusive. The same person can learn both styles of reasoning and apply both modes in a search for the right, good, or fitting action in a morally complex situation. A study by Johnston, for example, showed that adolescent subjects of both sexes were familiar with both types of reasoning and could use both styles of reasoning if prompted to do so. Johnston found that ". . . the girls as a group choose both orientations more frequently than the boys who tend as a group to use the rights [justice] orientation more exclusively. In other words, boys use the moral orientation of care much less often than girls use the moral orientation of justice" ([18], p. 60–61). It is encouraging that people can use both approaches, because it suggests that more flexible and creative moral responses to perplexing moral questions are possible.

Still, it is disturbing that the young men in this study were less likely to make use spontaneously of the style more culturally connected with women's experience.[9] Despite their ability to think in a care oriented way when questioned specifically, male adolescents were less likely to use the care-reasoning mode without prompting. Perhaps adolescent males are particularly concerned about seeming unmasculine if they volunteer a care approach to moral questions. Another disquieting possibility is that these young men underrate care-reasoning precisely because it is a style culturally associated with women. If care-reasoning is actually devalued as a lesser form of thought characteristic of (inferior) women, then men (and some women) will be denied an enriched moral understanding.

Care, Liberal Justice, and Gender Justice

As I have indicated above, Gilligan and her followers attach a specific meaning to "justice" as it contrasts with "care." The concept of justice in the "ethic of care" literature is a seriously constrained moral ideal. It is highly influenced by the model of moral decision making promoted by certain proponents of philosophic liberalism. The emphasis is upon formal, procedural justice. Deliberations about procedural justice require a particular type of abstract reasoning. This view of justice is rooted in a particular view of the autonomous moral agent about which I will say more below. Liberalism celebrates a form of moral reason that achieves impartial fairness by transcending all particular interests, loyalties, and relationships.

As I have indicated above, so-called justice-reasoning involves establishment of an a priori hierarchy of moral values. The agent homes in on the key principles or values in question, setting those principles or values in sharp relief. Facing a sharply delineated conflict of values, the moral agent determines what decision is consistent with the higher value in a preexisting hierarchy of values. The most skillful moral agent is able to engage in clear, abstract reasoning about a theoretical scale of values and to persuade others of the soundness of his or her reasoning.

By contrast, the method employed by many feminists, not just those emphasizing care, involves a more concrete and complex style of moral reasoning. Most feminist ethicists are more attentive to the particularities and ambiguities of moral questions. Feminist thought often is more aware of moral complexity, in part, because it presupposes relationality. The needs, concerns, views, and actions of multiple others involved in a moral predicament are all potentially germane to feminist ethical decision making.

Among certain theological feminist ethicists, the concern for relationality opens out into an explicit awareness of economic, social and cultural influences on moral questions. These social ethical feminists give careful consideration to the richness of social historical experience. They examine in some detail the cultural and historical patterns that have created particular configurations of bioethical moral questions today. They give careful attention to variations related to factors such as gender, race, class or sexual orientation. Most feminist ethicists do not strive to remain high above everyday experience in order to get a detached, schematic perspective on moral issues and moral values. Rather, many feminists try to dive deep into women's multifaceted experiences, in order to grapple with moral values as relational possibilities in the everyday world.

Thus the notion of (liberal) justice-reasoning is very different from the ideal of gender justice to which some feminists appeal. Feminist ethicists acknowledge frankly their particular loyalties to women and their specific commitments to the well-being of women. Such feminist thinkers contend that special attention to women is necessary because women are at special risk of being treated unfairly. A key background assumption here is the presumption that social institutions have been and continue to be riddled with sexism. The gender justice method is explicitly partisan on behalf of oppressed women. It is important to note, however, that not all women suffer identical forms of oppression.

Thus some feminist thinkers are beginning to reconceptualize justice as rooted in relationality, not detachment. Gender justice is not what we envision after we have transcended all our particular loyalties and our actual relationships. Instead, gender justice is a standard for right relationships among human beings which is articulated in a social world in which women are subject to multiple forms of injustice. Gender justice is a standard that we create, modify, and sustain in the midst of our concrete struggles to transform all oppressive gender relationships and hierarchies.

Gender justice, as I am using the phrase, is a substantive as well as a procedural moral concept. This is in contrast to certain liberal conceptions of justice as procedural justice only. According to certain philosophers, such as Robert Nozick, justice is achieved by scrupulously following certain procedural rules for fair treatment among human beings [28]. If just procedures are followed, any outcome is unquestionably just. Vast inequalities in the distribution of social power and material resources are just, as long as ethically proper procedures led to that distribution.

I am unwilling to make any such sharp separation between a gender justice oriented mode of analysis and the substantive outcomes that result from a gender justice approach. I cannot specify criteria for substantive gender justice judgments in detail here. However, I do contend that gender justice requires substantively that all women receive a share of social power adequate to pursue their genuine interests and the common good. Gender justice demands that women receive, at least, a decent minimum of the (material) goods and services necessary to pursue their individual and collective aims. Therefore, gender justice requires that women participate equally with men in the definition of disease and health, and that they receive a more equitable share of social resources devoted to health care.

Justice can be a much richer concept than an exclusively procedural fairness—fairness defined by some impartial, ideal observer. Feminists ought not concede that justice is and can only be what some dominant, male voices have thus far declared it to be. Feminist theorists need to move beyond contrasting "care" with a particular, stereotypical, liberal, philosophic notion of justice. Feminist ethicists need to envision a new relationship between "care" and justice understood as a value which encompasses gender justice.

Autonomy, Embodiment, and Relationality

There are close and important links between one's ethical method and one's presuppositions concerning moral agency. Central to a feminist bioethics is a positive view of the moral agency of women. Yet contemporary feminists are working within a cultural context in which women's ability to be autonomous in the classic liberal sense—to be rational, objective, independent decision makers—has been denied and continues to be questioned.[10] As feminist theory has developed, many feminists have responded to the denigration of women's capacity for moral autonomy by questioning the intellectual adequacy of the dominant, modern model of the autonomous self. Thus, many feminist scholars are prominent among the critics of the Enlightenment model of the solitary individual who is the sole master of his ethical destiny. The notion of a transcendent, self-sufficient moral agent is, of course, closely connected to the impartial observer who employs what Gilligan has called justice-reasoning.

As pictured throughout the modern era, the radically autonomous or self-governing moral agent controls and ultimately transcends his body, its desires, and its emotions. His personal relationships and his memberships in specific groups or communities is morally irrelevant. As political scientist Rosalind Petchesky notes, " 'the [liberal] individual' [is] conceived as isolated, atomized, exclusive in *his* possessions, disconnected from larger social fabrics" ([31], p. 665, emphasis in original).

Many feminists reject these liberal presuppositions about the moral agent. They are seeking new understandings of women (and men) as embodied moral subjects who exercise autonomy as a moral power in relationships. Most feminist thinkers insist that human beings are not first and foremost solitary intellects moving into voluntary relationships on (at least implicitly negotiated) terms that are reciprocally fair. Rather human beings often find themselves involved in bodily relationships that they did not choose, but upon whose nurture they are dependent in important ways. Our history of bodily relationships makes us who we are and enables (or obstructs) our entrance into future relationships. These future relationships include both those we choose and those in which we become enmeshed without our choosing them. Moral agents are not isolated, but interdependent, and much of that interdependence is rooted in *our bodily needs* for help, support, and love from one another.

Embodiment

Related to feminist critiques of the disembodied, isolated, rational moral agent is a feminist concern for the female self as a body subject. This is a complex issue for feminist ethicists. Too many great figures in Western ethics have identified woman with mute bodily experience, juxtaposed to man's (disembodied) rationality. This male emphasis on the essential bodily nature of women has been harmful to women. Women have been considered by some men to be too carnal and too easily swayed by emotion to be morally trustworthy decision makers. The charge that women are too emotional is closely related to the accusation that they are too bodily. For strong emotions are experienced by embodied subjects as vivid, tangible changes in body states. Philosopher Elizabeth Spelman notes the irony that, in medical relationships, as in many other relationships, women continue to be identified particularly with the body. Simultaneously, women are denied effective control over their female bodies. ". . . [T]hough defined as body, she [woman] is estranged from it because what happens to it is in the hands—literally—of the [male] doctor" ([39], p. 225).

Feminist scholars are trying to find new, positive ways to discuss women's moral experiences as bodily experiences. Every relationship we have, including every moral relationship, is known in and through our bodies. Philosopher Mary Rawlinson reminds us "embodiment . . . is the inscription or presence of the subject in the world. All other inscriptions or traces of the subject in the world are generated by hand or voice" ([33], p. 158). Perhaps there are a few other bodily ways of making our consciousness known in the world, such as an eloquent look in the eye, but every way of making ourselves and our desires known is through the body. In addition, it is through our bodies that we acquire knowledge about concrete situations that call forth our moral responses. Our relationships with other persons and with the natural world are all experienced in and through the body. It is always as body selves that we participate in a process of communication that results in shared moral decision making and the unfolding of communal moral relationships. Thus embodiment and relationality are inextricably interlinked.

I suggest that feminist ethicists need to construct additional rich, experientially based descriptions of key episodes in the lives of women as embodied moral subjects. The menopausal woman, for example, is an embodied subject experiencing her bodily nature in a new and different way. Menopause is not just a biological process that takes place within a woman's body. During menopause, a woman comes to a new understanding of who she is as an embodied subject, and she tries to integrate changing bodily possibilities into a new sense of herself and her life project. Menopause presents an opportunity to achieve a new consciousness as a body subject.

I have not discovered any discussions of medical interventions related to menopause written from the philosophical perspective of the menopausal or post-menopausal woman as an embodied moral subject. Yet menopause is a time of important transition for embodied female subjects. If is a time of physical change and loss, but also of potentially positive transition for women.

For any particular woman, menopause brings about specific changes that mark a milestone in her aging process. An adequate description of the menopausal embodied subject would have to include a carefully considered social, cultural, and historical component. For example, physical aging is more difficult in a culture, such as the contemporary United States, that highly values youth, especially in women. Race, class and sexual orientation are all factors in how a woman experiences her aging body and how it is perceived by others in society.

The realization that women are identified with their bodies, but deprived of the power to control those same bodies, might illuminate some moral dangers associated with hormone replacement therapy in a sexist culture. From the perspective of some physicians, all women who survive into menopause are defective bodies afflicted with endocrinopathy. But a stance that objectifies women as defective bodies can subtly, or not so subtly, undermine respect for the autonomy of postmenopausal women.

A feminist approach to bioethics which sought to articulate the experience of menopausal women as embodied subjects would give us an important new angle for an ethical assessment of hormone replacement therapy. Providing a richly textured account of female moral subjectivity would tend to focus attention sharply on the menopausal woman as the one who should make an informed decision about whether to use synthetic hormones. It would also help us understand that the morally relevant decision is one based not only on statistics concerning relative risk from heart disease and cancer, but also a decision legitimately influenced by the meaning of breast cancer and heart disease in a particular woman's embodied consciousness.

Relationality

Human beings are relational beings and any adequate notion of human "autonomy" must take account of human relationality. When feminists are attracted to the concept of autonomy, it is rarely the absolute power of the isolated, disembodied, individual will that they crave. For many feminist thinkers, "freedom . . . is not total autonomy but differentiated relationality. Never mere liberty from relational entanglement, freedom enables the development of authentic human centeredness and mutual relations. . . ."[11] ([41], p. 86). Autonomy, then, is not some moral power that guarantees that one can assert one's independent will, but *an embodied power in relationship* that allows one to get one's own body-based needs, desires, emotions, perceptions, and values taken seriously. Autonomy is the power to act as an embodied subject *among other embodied subjects* in the unfolding of a particular history of moral relationships.

One nascent feminist theory of autonomy recognizes that all moral decisions are made by persons who are embedded in particular webs of relationships. A moral method that stresses abstract reasoning as a means to transcend the compromising aspects of relationality is ultimately misguided, for there is no way for relational human beings to escape their relationality. Therefore, some feminists focus on engendering morally positive relationships. They especially value relationships that generate and sustain the female self's ability to function as a moral subject. Autonomy has to do with the ways in which persons share control and power within relationships. Noddings points out that genuine caring requires respect for the freedom of the other who is one-cared-for. The one-cared-for is encountered "as subject—not as an object to be manipulated nor as a data source" ([27], p. 72).

Moral autonomy then is not an isolated faculty inherent in rational individuals. Moral autonomy is the power within specific socio-historical relationships to formulate and to pursue particular moral aims. As the work of ethicist Ruth Smith makes clear, socio-historical conditions are crucial in the formation of the "autonomous" self. Smith reminds us that "we are not social in general but in specific historical ways, ways which make our rationality and our moral freedom not a priori givens but problems to be struggled with within the social structure of relations . . ." ([37], p. 248).

Within societies that promote masculine superiority, the struggle to be taken seriously as moral agents is a particularly arduous one for women. For example, a recent study of judicial decisions in a set of similar medical ethical cases shows that female autonomy continues to be less respected and protected by the United States' legal system than male autonomy. The study involved decisions to terminate treatment being rendered to patients most of whom had previously been competent, but who were currently incapable of expressing their wishes concerning further treatment. There was less judicial respect for a person's expression of values consistent with a wish to forego aggressive treatment, when the subject was a woman. Men's prior statements concerning personal values were more likely to be upheld, because these male declarations were more likely to be judged thoughtful and convincing. Women's expressions of personal values were more likely to be questioned as incoherent or irrational and to be overridden. Judges seemed to stereotype women as less rational, and therefore, less capable of expressing a clear, considered judgment before a protracted period of incompetence. The researchers concluded: "women are disadvantaged in having their moral agency taken less seriously than that of men when a controversial medical decision is evaluated by a court" ([24], p. 92).

In a society still deeply scarred by sexism, it is more difficult for women to articulate their wishes about what happens to their bodies and their lives. It is also more difficult for women to get those wishes taken seriously. Gaining respect for oneself as an "autonomous" moral agent is even more arduous for some women than for others. It is frequently more difficult for poor women—who may not have had the opportunity to develop verbal skills impressive to highly educated doctors—to get taken seriously as autonomous subjects. For example, as noted above, doctors allow stereotypes about poor, minority women to skew their presentation of treatment options once precancerous cervical lesions are detected. A poor woman is more likely to be encouraged to choose a hysterectomy, rather than less extensive surgery, because doctors do not trust a poor, minority woman to comply with a long-term monitoring plan. A poor, minority woman is often presented with an unnecessarily constrained set of choices. Her autonomy is inhibited, and she must make extra efforts to assert her legitimate prerogatives as a moral subject.

Under social conditions that include a pervasive distrust of women's capacity to make well-considered moral judgments, it has been crucial for feminist ethicists to defend fiercely women's capacity to make sound moral determinations about their actions and lives. Yet, as feminist theorist Elizabeth Fox-Genovese recognizes, when women demand their power of self-determination in a social situation still tainted by assumptions of female inferiority, "the reappropriation of self can be reappropriation not just for the individual but for the community itself" ([11], p. 233). For female patients and health care workers to demand respect for their capacity for moral agency is also to demand a shift in the distribution of decision-making power in health care relationships, including institutional relationships.

The category of autonomy remains an attractive one for me, as a feminist ethicist, in so far as it can be reconceptualized to support women's moral power *in relationship*. What I want to stress is the importance of every female patient's having the opportunity to speak with moral authority when negotiating with health care providers. Feminist presuppositions about relational moral agency and a feminist commitment to a reasoning process sensitive to particularity and complexity entail shared medical decision making in which women have strong and respected moral voices. Respect for women as embodied subjects requires a medical decision making process in which women have extensive social power to participate fully in decisions about how they will be treated.

Theology/Spirituality

A difficult question in feminist theological ethics is how to make connections between our moral vision and shared theological symbols and stories. Multifaceted feminist examinations of religion and spirituality are underway. Jewish feminists are striving to uncover or to create stories, images, rituals, and theological constructs that are consistent with "the liberation of all women and all people" and "the creation of a society that no longer construes difference in terms of superiority and subordination" ([32], p. xv). Other feminists seek to connect spiritual insight with moral integrity through the thought and practice of Goddess religions, including WICCA. Still other female ethicists are exploring the theological resources in their own African-American, Hispanic, or Asian-Pacific traditions.[12] In this essay, I will concentrate primarily on Euro-American Christianity, because it is the particular religious tradition within which I struggle with the problem of integrating feminist moral apprehensions with a theological horizon of meaning.

The problems involved in creating an adequate Christian feminist theological ethic are daunting. Describing fully any proposal for such an ethic would go far beyond the limits of this essay. However, since this is a volume on the methodological contributions of *theological* ethics to bioethics, let me indicate some challenges confronting the Christian feminist ethicists and some of the alternative responses that are being probed by them. In this section I will focus on feminist theological insights that have important implications for ethics. While these theological assertions have implications for a wide range of ethical questions, I have selected them with an eye toward their significance for a feminist *bioethics*.

As theologian Cornell West reminds us, "belief in God itself is not to be understood in a noncontextual manner. It is understood in relation to a particular context, to specific circumstances" ([17], p. 204). Thus, speaking in the midst of a protracted feminist struggle, I must begin by clearly acknowledging that the Christian religion has been a key tool for legitimating patriarchy and domination in western civilization. Once this is faced squarely, we must then explore Christianity's capacity to purge itself of patriarchy and domination in order to become consistent with a moral vision for the full human dignity of all women (and men). As theologian Rita Brock says: "The feminist vision of healing, wholeness, and spirituality must save Christianity from its patriarchy—if Christian theology is to remain true to its claims that all human begins are created in the divine image, that divine power is love in its fullness, and that the community of divine power is one of justice and peace" ([3], p. 50).

Christian feminist theologians face the confounding task of "reappropriation of a difficult past in the interest of constructing an acceptable future" ([11], p. 231). One response by contemporary feminist theologians has been to reexamine Christian history to discover ways in which Christian women, empowered by their contact with a Divine Presence, have acted so as to manifest their dignity as ones beloved by God/dess.[13] Some feminist biblical scholars, for example, are reconstructing our view of Jesus and the community of disciples (including a significant contingent of women) who gathered around him. These feminists seek to present a plausible case for an interpretation of the earliest Christian community as a discipleship of equals. This paradigm of the Jesus community as an egalitarian community becomes one inspiration for contemporary efforts to achieve gender justice.

As biblical scholar Elisabeth Schüssler Fiorenza explains this project: "The vision and praxis of our foresisters who heard the call to coequal discipleship and who acted in the power of the Spirit must be allowed to become a transformative power that can open up a feminist future for women [and men] in biblical religion" ([9], p. 343). Schüssler Fiorenza presents the earliest Christian communities as prototypes for communities in which women and men enact in their daily relationships the belief that they are radically equal before God. Such a feminist hermeneutic provides a critical evaluation of biblical history that uses as its central criterion coherence with the struggle for justice and wholeness for all, especially women ([8], pp. 8–15).

Some feminist exegetes emphasize *the active role of women* in the Jesus community and *Jesus's openness to women's needs and their initiatives.* Such a reading of Scripture allows us to see courageous assertiveness as a female virtue and equal regard for women as a male virtue. For example, a feminist reading of the healing of the woman with the chronic hemorrhage ([26], Mark 5:24–35) could have interesting resonances with a feminist approach to bioethics. Feminist hermeneutics make it possible for me, as an ethicist, to find in this story a message that affirms a woman's taking the initiative to regain bodily wholeness. The story also connects female health and wholeness with a human drive toward right relationship. Additionally, it shows that right relationship is often achieved with some difficulty.

In this biblical story, the woman has been suffering from a bloody discharge for twelve years. She has sought medical treatment from many medical practitioners, but the only results are a worsening of her condition and impoverishment because of medical costs. The woman with the hemorrhage suffers, not just because of her physiological condition, but also because of the cultural meaning of her physical illness. Her discharge renders her perpetually unclean (taboo). She is continuously unfit for participation in the religious life of her community. Moreover, she is a source of pollution for anyone else who touches her—any physical contact with her renders the other ritually unclean as well. Her taboo status deepens the audacity of her action, as she surreptitiously reaches out to touch the cloak of Jesus, whom she recognizes as a vehicle for healing power.

Brock's telling of this story emphasizes the initiative taken by the ill woman. "The woman is, nonetheless, determined to be whole. She is able to acknowledge, from the depths of herself, her heart, her desperate need to be healed, to be restored to right relationships." Having faith that she will be healed by the power manifest in Jesus, "she summons the courage to violate a patriarchal social taboo. Though an unclean woman, she touches Jesus in public." Brock observes: "In the touching, she is, literally, saved, not just cured in a medical sense, but saved. Her courage in violating a taboo has made her whole" ([3], p. 84).

Feminist biblical scholarship emphasizes the empowering quality of Jesus's relationships with women. In his encounter with the hemorrhaging woman, Jesus is initially perplexed by the awareness that "healing power . . . [has] gone out from him" ([26], Mark 5:30). Jesus asks who has touched him. When the woman, fearful but still courageous, comes forth to tell of her new wholeness, Jesus ratifies her action. He shows no sign of repugnance in the face of her socially stigmatizing illness. Rather he confirms that her faith has saved her, ratifies the healing her faith-inspired audacity has wrought, and offers her peace. Scripture scholar Vernon Robbins comments: "In other words, as the positive qualities of Jesus unfold, so the positive qualities of the woman unfold" ([34], p. 510).

In this story, healing takes place in a mutually empowering relationship between Jesus and the woman. Biblical commentator William Lane recognizes in the account of the healing ". . . a mutual event in which the personal relationship between Jesus and the woman released power" ([22], p. 193). A fresh reading of this story draws attention to its positive presentation of a woman's initiative for health and wholeness. In its own way, it is a tale of autonomy in relationship. The woman is personally empowered to become whole through her actions in relationship with Jesus and with God. Jesus's perplexity and the woman's courage, despite her real fearfulness, show that right relationship is not easily achieved and requires a commitment to struggle to maintain and deepen relationship.

A feminist reading of this biblical tale thus points toward a major theme in the work of Christian feminist theologians.[14] Many feminist theologians are developing a "metaphysic of connectedness" that serves as "both revelatory paradigm and moral imperative" ([13], p. 7). Connectedness is good and we have a moral obligation to preserve and extend connection. God/dess is known as both the web of life *and* the power in relationship displayed by communities struggling for justice and wholeness. The stress on relationality emerging in such feminist theological reflections is consistent with the insistence on the importance of relationality in the ethic of care and with a reconceptualized notion of autonomy as power in relation.

Many contemporary feminist theologians—both Euro-American Christians and those from other traditions—share an intimation of the Divine as the Web of Life. God/dess encompasses the entire matrix of creation. Human beings are but one element in a cosmic pattern in which all beings share in the power of the sacred. God/dess is the power of relationship that flows throughout that web of life. God/dess is known when we feel our deep connectedness to the earth and the cosmos. Our own wholeness and healthfulness are dependent upon actions consistent with a respect for the integrity of the cosmos.

Through participation in right relationships and genuine communities—no matter how fleetingly these goods are experienced in a sinful world—many feminists recognize God/dess as the power that creates and sustains right human relationships. Thus, some feminist theologians recognize and celebrate Divine Presence revealed in community. A holy people dedicated to work for social justice is a pivotal reality in the work of many feminist theologians.[15] Thus, for example, in Brock's work, relationship and community are "the whole-making, healing center" of reality ([3], p. 52). God/dess is the ground that undergirds the moral strength of courageous women (and men). The God/dess enables human beings to display a tenacity that "will not abandon the total web of our connections in spite of failures of our energy and the recurrent disintegrations of community" ([19], p. 224). God/dess is the ultimate source of our hope and our fortitude in the struggle for justice, peace, wholeness and holiness.

The theological affirmation of God/dess as the power of relation is interwoven with a particular ethic of responsibility. The central moral response to God/dess as Power in Relation is behavior that forges and sustains right relationships. Acts by the God/dess on behalf of preservation, liberation, and wholeness for humanity and the cosmos take place significantly—although, not exclusively—through human actions. This feminist vision is a spirituality that involves *reciprocal* divine-human agency and responsibility. We are co-creators with God/dess of human and cosmic well-being, wholeness, and holiness. In the words of Mary Grey, "seeking to co-create in forming more just patterns of relating, new forms of mutuality, is both actively making God incarnate, and becoming not *passive* but *receptive* to the ways in which God is already active as energizing presence" ([13], p. 14, emphasis in original).

Therefore, efforts to open the biological and medical sciences more fully to women, so that women have a greater capacity to name their physiological ills and to define their health are examples of making right relationships and thereby co-creating human wholeness and flourishing. An important theological question for believers who are health care practitioners is how groups of health care workers might be understood as jointly acting so as to make God/dess present in the world. The medical community, if it is to be a community of equals in right relationship to one another, would have to manifest greater respect for the contributions made by all members of the health care team, including those—frequently minority women—in the jobs which currently carry lower pay and lower prestige.[16]

Finally, I will examine another methodological question in theology that has ethical implications. What language and metaphors may Christian ethicists and theologians responsibly select to describe our relationship with divine being? In a culture still characterized by gender hierarchies, the language that theological ethicists choose to use for the deity has important implications for an ethic of gender justice. Heavy or exclusive reliance on familiar masculine terms such as Father, Lord, or God is inconsistent with an ethic that stresses gender equality.

There are two available alternatives. An ethicist can select gender neutral language such as Creator, Redeemer, Lover, or Friend. However, I suggest that ethicists should sometimes select female language and imagery for the Divine. I concur with Plaskow that "only deliberately disruptive—that is, female—metaphors can break the imaginative hold of male metaphors that have been used for millennia" ([32], p. 160). It is the disjunction and uneasiness that accompany use of explicitly female pronouns, words, and metaphors for Ultimate Power that reveal our deeply internalized assumptions about intrinsically superior male authority and power. To call the Ultimate Power in the universe "She," "Mother," or "Goddess" is congruent with an ethic that values autonomy as power in right relationship for women. Female metaphors and language for the divine are one element in a cultural transformation that allows women and men to rely on women's ability to exercise power beneficially. Thus, it is an ethically significant act when women and men choose to call upon the name of Goddess.

An example of reframed theological imagery for the divine occurs in the work of theologian Sallie McFague. McFague has explored alternate images of the divine suitable for a time of nuclear threat and ecological crisis. All her work has promising implications for feminist theological ethics. I will concentrate here on her vision of God as a Mother who has a fierce, passionate commitment to the survival and fulfillment of all humanity (and the cosmos itself). Therefore, McFague asserts, "the mother-God as creator is necessarily judge, at the very basic level of condemning as the primary (though not the only) sin the inequitable distribution of basic necessities for the continuation of life in its many forms" ([23], pp. 113–14).

Considering the prior discussion of the ethic of care and its relationship to justice, McFague's decision to focus on justice as an ethical attribute of God our Mother is very interesting. McFague highlights the Mother's just love that serves as a model for the fair distribution of life-sustaining goods to all creatures ([23], p. 106). In McFague's paradigm of God as mother-judge, the fundamental human evil is a selfish disregard for the continued existence and well-being of the Mother's other creatures. Sin is a deliberate rupture of delicate, life-sustaining webs of relationship. The central human virtue is a "bedrock justice: the establishment of the conditions of a just order in which the necessities of existence are shared" ([23], p. 117). Humanity should join with God our Mother in fostering life through promoting justice. Somewhat paradoxically, given our earlier juxtaposition of justice and care, McFague tells us that God our Mother calls us "to bring about justice through care" for human beings and for the rest of creation ([23], p. 119). I would add that She also calls us to foster care by promoting structures of justice that enable us to provide reliable, continuing succor to one another. In addition, the Mother-Judge requires that the burdens of care be distributed equitably to women and men.

On one level there is a continuity for Christian bioethics in the preceding theological assertions about God our Mother. It is a standard Christian claim that God is a Creator-Parent who wills life and fulfillment for all God's children. Generations of prophetic Christians have denounced social systems in which essential goods are denied to the least of God's children. Yet that God who is Creator-Parent is usually—and very importantly—God our Father. In a reciprocal process, male metaphors for God both reflect and reinforce the patterns of gender hierarchy found in male dominant societies. The heavy predominance of masculine imagery for "God" (in itself a masculine term) is a subtle and powerful means of legitimation of male authority throughout the culture—including throughout the medical system. It is no accident that in a male dominated health care system, doctors, who are more often men, are tempted "to play God."

Repeated use of the metaphor God our Mother would have important implications for our fundamental orientation in bioethics. Still, this image has ethically significant limitations as well. If we use singular terms such as the Goddess or Mother to name Ultimate Power, we may replace an oppressive singular male image with an oppressive singular female image. In a racist society, She is likely to be imaged as the Great White Goddess, if we do not explicitly reject any notion that She is white. A sole white Goddess will not bring wholeness and right relationship to anyone, least of all white people, in a racist society.

Moreover, Mother is a stereotypically feminine term. It comes complete with a dangerous amount of cultural baggage. Some women who have chosen not to be mothers or who have infertility problems might find exclusive reliance on God our Mother demeaning to them as non-mothers. God our Mother could easily become a sickeningly sentimental image associated with undemanding, all-accepting maternal love. McFague's association of Mother and Judge is important precisely because it undercuts such sentimentality. God/dess as Mother will not, by itself, be a sufficient new vision of the Divine. Having acknowledged some limitations of this image, I still assert that God/dess wills that all Her daughters (and sons) have effective access to the health care necessary to protect and sustain life. By implication a theological ethic rooted in worship of "God as Mother" would result in a prophetic denunciation of the current United States' health care system that allows thousands of women and their children to die of diseases that we could prevent or treat. (It also allows thousands of men, especially poor men and men of color, to die unnecessarily.) Appeals to God our Mother might seem deliberately clumsy in a society conditioned to use male imagery. It would create a theological rupture in which we might be sensitized to the injustices of a medical system still plagued by gender inequalities—a medical system in which privileged men, usually white, heterosexual men get the benefit of more research and better treatment. Evoking God our Mother would be consonant with moves to empower women as patients and as health care practitioners.

Conclusion

The disorienting image of our co-responsibility with God our Mother for the well-being of all persons can provide a fresh vantage point from which to consider biomedical ethical questions. In a society still shaped by gender hierarchies in which males are dominant, ethicists should stress a compensatory gender justice. Every health care issue should be analyzed in terms of its impact on women. There is often a gender justice dimension to questions about what gets defined as a disease or medical crisis, how research funds are allocated, and which treatment modalities are offered to which patients. An adequate feminist social analysis includes attention to the concrete social locations of various women. Race, class, sexual orientation, and handicapping conditions must receive careful attention.

A feminist perspective encourages us to examine the distinctive moral strengths that diverse women offer to enliven our understanding of the moral life. We should have a cautious appreciation of the "ethic of care" style of moral reasoning that seems more readily adopted by women (at least under present social, historical conditions). The ethic of care approach assumes human relationality and attempts to maximize harmony among the needs of specific persons as ones-cared-for. We need to be more attentive to the particular ways care is manifest in specific social, historical circumstances—for example, the ways in which care is provided, or neglected, for African-American patients in an institutionally racist context. We also need to see that the burdens of the moral imperative to care are fairly distributed among the members of society. Unfortunately, advocates of the ethic of care contrast care with an unduly constrained notion of justice. Feminists need to understand justice in a less abstract, more relational, more substantive fashion.

Central to a feminist bioethics is a fresh appreciation of the moral dignity of women as embodied, relational moral subjects. Autonomy has a different meaning for such a subject. Autonomy is that shared power in relationships that allows one to get one's own body-based needs, desires, emotions, perceptions, and values taken seriously. Autonomy is a power to act as a moral subject among other moral subjects. Women's efforts to reappropriate their moral power in relationships implies a fundamental shift in the ways in which women are treated throughout the health care system, both as patients and as health care workers.

The problem of the integration of moral insights into a theological horizon of meaning remains one of the most challenging questions facing feminists who do theological ethics. This essay explores some emerging fresh directions. Feminist biblical interpretations of passages such as the healing of the woman with the chronic hemorrhage reveal the power of women's faith-inspired, courageous initiatives for their well-being and wholeness. Healing power is experienced in a mutual relationship among the woman, Jesus, and God/dess, but that right relationship is only achieved through moral struggle.

A "metaphysic of connectedness" is increasingly central to feminist theology and ethics. God/dess is the Web of Energy that enlivens the cosmos and the Power of Relation known in and through communities struggling for justice and wholeness. As Beverly Harrison tells us: "a feminist moral theology envisages a society, a world, a cosmos, [in which] . . . there are 'no excluded ones' " ([14], p. 20). This metaphysics of connectedness serves as a basis for a moral imperative to act to preserve the integrity of the cosmic web of life and to effect right relationships.

In a society still characterized by gender hierarchies in which males are dominant, the words and metaphors we use to name Ultimate Reality are morally significant choices. Exploration of language such as God our Mother can provide a fresh angle of vision on our moral responsibility to join with the Mother in doing what fosters life and fulfillment for all Her creatures. Since we are all created in Her image, women as well as men can be trusted to exercise "autonomy" properly understood as moral power in relationships to pursue projects that sustain and deepen life and relationality. Feminist theological bioethics challenges us to analyze all biomedical issues against the horizon of a belief in the God/dess who will tolerate no excluded ones.

Notes

1. This is the case, in part, because of the historical accident that, in the United States, AIDS was first recognized in a male population. Obviously, the first male victims did not display disorders of the female reproductive tract. However, even though a large number of female persons with AIDS have been identified, medical authorities were slow to begin changing the definition to reflect female experience.

2. This problem exists partially because the welfare bureaucracy adopted for purposes of determining eligibility for benefits a definition of AIDS that had been created for epidemiological purposes.

3. A recent study of the benefits of low doses of aspirin for preventing heart disease in women seems to indicate that aspirin consumption is also beneficial for women. However, the scientific design of this study on nurses was less rigorous than the study on men discussed above.

4. Another indication, to me, of the importance of just distribution of the social power to direct social resources to the solution of health care problems is the fact that this report was issued under the leadership of a female Comptroller, Elizabeth Holtzman. When women have greater social and political power, their health care needs get more careful attention.

5. Some scientists and women's health care activists question whether early detection of breast cancer is as critical to good outcomes as prevailing wisdom suggests. See [37], p. 23.

6. Rendering the Cruzan case more complex, some persons contended that it is impossible to give informed consent to forego treatment under certain hypothetical future conditions. This argument holds that we cannot really know what we would want under conditions that we have not actually experienced. Yet, holding that hypothetical "informed" consent is a contradiction in terms creates a justice-reasoning "Catch 22" for patients in a persistent vegetative state (PVS). You cannot make a valid informed choice to forego treatment now in the event that you are reduced to a persistent vegetative state in the future, because you do not actually know—in an experiential way—what it is to be a PVS "patient." If later you do become a PVS "patient," you are then unable by virtue of your neurological condition to request withdrawal of treatment. So there is literally no time when an autonomous moral agent can refuse medical treatment, if he/she should become a PVS "patient."

7. By gender justice, I mean a procedural and substantive conception of justice that is consistent with a recognition of the fundamental equal dignity of women and men. I will say more about gender justice in the next section of this essay.

8. By care in this sentence, I do not mean exclusively medical treatment. Rather I mean a holistic care that encompasses signs of respect for the one-cared-for and means of humane comfort.

9. I presented a version of this work at a faculty colloquium. One female faculty member urged me not to describe the ethic of care as a feminine approach, because she feared that anything feminine would be denigrated as less valuable and would therefore be avoided by men.

10. Men from socially subordinated ethnic or racial groups are often stereotyped in ways that undermine their perceived capacity for moral autonomy, too. Such men are caricatured as stupid, emotional, and carnal—the antithesis of the autonomous [privileged male] self.

11. Harrison was describing process thought in the section of her work from which this quote is taken. However, the quote is also descriptive of a concern for autonomy and relationality as corollary concepts which is congenial with emerging feminist theories of autonomy.

12. Some of these women would term their work womanist; others might choose other identifiers.

13. I use the term God/dess to denote the Ultimate Power in the Universe, a Power which is neither male nor female, but in which both women and men have their being.

14. This is an important theme for some Jewish theologians and for theorists in the women's spirituality movement as well.

15. Communal holiness is not present exclusively in groups that explicitly name themselves as religious communities.

16. In the future, pay and working conditions consistent with right relationship would also have to be provided for such workers.

Bibliography

1. Abramson, L.: 1990, "Uncaring Women's Health Care," *New York Times* (May 14), A17.

2. Anon.: 1990, "New Pap Smear Rules to Hike Cost of Tests," *The News* (Greenville, SC) (December 29), 1A, 5A.

3. Brock, R. N.: 1991, *Journeys by Heart: a Christology of Erotic Power,* Crossroad Press, New York.

4. Byron, P.: 1991, "Women and AIDS: The U.S. Scandal," *Ms.* 1 (Jan/Feb), 24–29.

5. Chin, J.: 1990, "Current and Future Dimensions of the HIV/AIDS Pandemic in Women and Children," *Lancet* 336 (July 28), 221–24.

6. Christakis, N.: 1989, "Responding to a Pandemic: International Interests in AIDS Control," *Daedalus* 118 (Spring), 113–34.

7. Faulkner, A. O. and Micchelli, M.: 1988, "The Aging, the Aged, and the Very Old: Women the Policy Makers Forgot," *Women and Health* 14 (3/4), 5–19.

8. Fiorenza, E. S.: 1984, *Bread Not Stone: The Challenge of Feminist Biblical Interpretation,* Beacon Press, Boston, MA.

9. Fiorenza, E. S.: 1984, *In Memory of Her: A Feminist Theological Reconstruction of Christian Origins,* Crossroad Press, New York.

10. Fisher, S.: 1986, *In The Patient's Best Interest: Women and the Politics of Medical Decisions,* Rutgers University Press, New Brunswick, NJ.

11. Fox-Genovese, E.: 1991, *Feminism without Illusions: A Critique of Individualism,* University of North Carolina Press, Chapel Hill.

12. Goldman, L. and Tosteson, A.: 1991: "Uncertainty About Postmenopausal Estrogen: Time for Action, Not Debate" [editorial], *New England Journal of Medicine* 325 (September 12), 800–802.

13. Grey, M.: 1991, "Claiming Power-in-Relation: Exploring the

Ethics of Connection," *Journal of Feminist Studies in Religion* 7 (Spring), 7–18.

14. Harrison, B.: 1983, *Our Right to Choose: Toward a New Ethic of Abortion,* Beacon Press, Boston, MA.

15. Hauerwas, S.: 1977, "From System to Story: An Alternative Pattern for Rationality in Ethics," *Truthfulness and Tragedy: Further Investigations in Christian Ethics,* University of Notre Dame Press, Notre Dame, IN, pp. 15–39.

16. Hilts, P.: 1991, "AIDS Definition Excludes Women, Congress is Told," *New York Times* (June 7), A19.

17. hooks, b.: 1990, "Black Women and Men: Partnership in the 1990s—a Dialogue between bell hooks and Cornel West," in *Yearning: Race, Gender and Cultural Politics,* South End Press, Boston, MA, pp. 203–214.

18. Johnston, D. K.: 1988, "Adolescents' Solutions to Dilemmas in Fables: Two Moral Orientations—Two Problem Solving Strategies," in C. Gilligan et al. (eds.), *Mapping the Moral Domain: A Contribution of Women's Thinking to Psychological Theory and Education,* Center for the Study of Gender, Education and Human Development, Cambridge, MA, pp. 49–71.

19. Keller, C.: 1986, *From a Broken Web: Separation, Sexism, and Self,* Beacon Press, Boston, MA.

20. Khan, S. S. et al.: 1990, "Increased Mortality of Women in Coronary Artery Bypass Surgery: Evidence for Referral Bias," *Annals of Internal Medicine* 112 (April 15), 561–67.

21. Kolata, G.: 1990, "Study Finds Bias in Way Women Are Evaluated for Heart Bypasses," *New York Times* (April 15), A15.

22. Lane, W.: 1974, *The Gospel According to Mark,* William B. Eerdmans Publishing Company, Grand Rapids, MI.

23. McFague, S.: 1987, *Models of God: Theology for an Ecological, Nuclear Age,* Fortress Press, Philadelphia, PA.

24. Miles, S. and August, A.: 1990, "Courts, Gender, and "the Right to Die'," *Law, Medicine, and Health Care* 18 (Spring–Summer), 85–95.

25. Murdoch, I.: 1970, *The Sovereignty of Good,* Routledge and Kegan Paul, Boston, MA.

26. *New American Bible:* 1971, Thomas Nelson, Publishers, Nashville, TN.

27. Noddings, N.: 1984, *Caring: A Feminine Approach to Ethics and Moral Education,* University of California Press, Berkeley, CA.

28. Nozick, R.: 1974, *Anarchy, State and Utopia,* Basic Books, New York.

29. Office of the Comptroller (New York City), Office of Policy Management: 1990, *Poverty and Breast Cancer in New York City,* October.

30. Palca, J.: 1990, "Women Left Out at NIH," *Science* 248 (29 June), 1601–02.

31. Petchesky, R.: 1980, "Reproductive Freedom: Beyond "A Woman's Right to Choose'," *Signs* 5 (Summer), 661–85.

32. Plaskow, J.: 1990, *Standing Again at Sinai: Judaism from a Feminist Perspective,* Harper and Row, San Francisco.

33. Rawlinson, M.: 1982, "Psychiatric Discourse and the Feminine Voice," *Journal of Medicine and Philosophy* 7 (May), 153–77.

34. Robbins, V.: 1987, "The Woman Who Touched Jesus's Garment: Socio-Rhetorical Analysis of the Synoptic Accounts," *New Testament Studies* 33, 502–15.

35. Ruddick, S.: 1989, *Maternal Thinking: Toward a Politics of Peace,* Ballantine Books, New York.

36. Sacks, K. B.: 1984, "Computers, Ward Secretaries, and a Walkout in a Southern Hospital," in K. B. Sacks and D. Remy (eds.), *My Troubles Are Going to Have Trouble with Me,* Rutgers University Press, New Brunswick, NJ, pp. 173–190.

37. Smith, R.: 1985, "Feminism and the Moral Subject," in B. Andolsen, C. Gudorf and M. Pellauer (eds.), *Women's Consciousness, Women's Conscience: A Reader in Feminist Ethics,* Harper and Row, San Francisco, CA, pp. 235–50.

38. Solomon, A.: 1991, "The Politics of Breast Cancer," *Village Voice* (May 14), 22–27.

39. Spelman, E.: 1982, "Book Reviews," *Journal of Medicine and Philosophy* 7 (May), 217–227.

40. Stampfer, M. et al.: 1991, "Postmenopausal Estrogen Therapy and Cardiovascular Disease," *New England Journal of Medicine* 325 (September 12), 756–62.

41. Utian, W.: 1990, "The Menopause in Perspective: From Potions to Patches," *Annals of the New York Academy of Sciences* 592 (June 13), 1–7.

42. Wolf, S.: 1990, "Nancy Beth Cruzan: In No Voice At All," *Hastings Center Report* 20 (January/February), 38–41.

16. The Argument for Unlimited Procreative Liberty: A Feminist Critique

Maura A. Ryan

This chapter first appeared in *Hastings Center Report* in 1990.

As growing numbers of infertile heterosexual and gay and lesbian couples, along with single individuals, seek to parent through techniques that facilitate conception or permit the use of a genetic and/or gestational donor, and the boundaries of the "scientifically possible" enlarge, we are confronted with a host of increasingly urgent questions. Can the components of parenting—genetic, gestational, and social—be separated at will without harm to the participants? Do new forms of non-coital and donor-assisted reproduction threaten the foundations of the family, and hence, social existence as we know it? Are there "natural" limits to human intervention in the procreative process? Ought artificial reproduction be permitted to become a commercial venture? Does the right to engage in coital reproduction, protected for married couples under the U.S. Constitution, extend into a right to engage in noncoital reproduction; if so, for whom, and under what circumstances?

Questions of liberty and individual rights are emotionally charged ones in American public discourse. Moreover, family autonomy has long been held as a value worthy of such firm protection in our courts and legislatures that policies of minimal interference by the state into domestic life have been maintained even where it has meant a certain institutional blindness to the reality of spousal and child abuse. This context explains why the question of procreative liberty is important in current public policy debates surrounding the "new reproduction." Decisions with respect to the limits that may be placed on efforts to procreate, on which parties may be permitted to seek technological assistance in procreation, on the amount of public protection or funding to be extended, and on the conditions under which funding or protection might be warranted turn, many legal scholars believe, on the question of whether we have a right to procreate. Some maintain that the Constitution provides for virtually unlimited right of access to reproductive means.

The freedom to decide whether one will bear and nurture children, and under what circumstances, has been a central issue in the women's liberation movement. As persons whose self-identity and social role have been defined historically in relation to their procreative capacities, women have a great deal at stake in questions of reproductive freedom. Early feminists expended significant energy to secure the right to use contraceptive measures and to seek legal abortion, as well as to gain recognition of their rights as consumers of gynecological and obstetrical care. To say that feminism has promoted procreative liberty for women is not, however, to say that contemporary feminists have welcomed recent developments in reproductive technology without reservation.[1] Nor is it to say, despite the central importance given to the protection of women's autonomy in reproductive decisions, that feminists in general would treat procreative liberty as an unrestricted value. Rather, a feminist perspective includes commitments to human relationality as well as autonomy, and attention to the social context of personal choices. Thus questions of individual freedom, even in matters of reproduction, must be raised in conjunction with other equally compelling considerations about what is needed for human flourishing and what is required for a just society.

I want to highlight these themes by attending to the arguments for an unlimited right to procreate raised most cogently by John Robertson.[2] This position, based primarily on the importance of procreation for individuals, contains several elements that are troubling from a feminist perspective. My concern will not be with matters of constitutional law, but instead with the underlying model of procreative liberty, and its consequences for our understanding of reproduction and our attitudes toward human persons in general and children in particular.

The Case for Full Procreative Liberty

Robertson's argument for the protection of a right to reproduce noncoitally or collaboratively (that is, with the participation of a gamete donor or gestator who is not one's spouse) is based on a historical protection of intramarital reproductive rights and the societal interest in safeguarding family autonomy. Since courts have recognized persons' rights to reproduce coitally, and not to reproduce coitally, their right to pursue those ends by noncoital means, if necessary, must also be protected. As a consequence of the natural lottery, infertility ought not prevent some from pursuing what has been recognized as of value to all.

Because childbearing and rearing have been viewed as experiences of great significance to persons, constitutive of individual identity and notions of a meaningful life, the courts have tended to take a position of noninterference in procreative decisions, particularly where married couples were involved. However, while an individual's right *not* to conceive, gestate, and rear has been explicitly protected in cases like *Griswold v. Connecticut* and *Roe v. Wade,* as has the right of parents to rear according to their own beliefs in cases like *Wisconsin v. Yoder,* the right *to* procreate has been addressed only implicitly. Robertson argues that one could and should infer from the right of couples to avoid procreation a correlative right to procreate, and from the unregulated freedom of married couples to add to their families coitally a freedom to do so noncoitally. No clear distinction should be allowed to stand, when procreative means exist, between fertile and infertile couples:

> The reason and values that support a right to reproduce coitally apply equally to noncoital activities involving external conception and collaborators. While the case is strongest for a couple's right to noncoital and external conception a strong argument for their right to enlist the aid of gamete and womb donors can also be made.[3]

Since reproductive rights are derived from the central importance of reproduction in an individual's life and are limited only by a capacity to participate meaningfully and an ability to accept or transfer rearing responsibilities, all those persons meeting this minimum criteria, whether married or not, ought to be free to pursue it.

Having argued that procreative autonomy is finally rooted in "the notion that individuals have a right to choose and live out the kind of life that they find meaningful and fulfilling," Robertson will allow for the use of technology for any reason that would realize the couple's "reproductive goals":

> The right of married persons to use noncoital and collaborative means of conception to overcome infertility must extend to any purpose, including selecting the gender or genetic characteristics of the child or transferring the burden of gestation to another.[4]

Because procreative interests are for some persons dependent on the offspring's having certain gender or genetic characteristics, procreative liberty includes, according to Robertson, the freedom to manipulate egg, sperm, or embryo to achieve the desired offspring, and the freedom to stop implantation or abort a fetus with undesirable characteristics. A couple is not free to alter genetic material in a way that would cause serious harm to the offspring (that is, harm so great as to make life not worth living), but they may do whatever else will facilitate the development of an offspring possessing those characteristics and traits that make having a child meaningful for them.[5] Claims of harm made in the name of society (threats to the ideal of the family, etc.) are not compelling enough in his view to override individual rights.

Many people have taken issue with this position on the grounds that a right to assistance in reproduction simply does not follow from the right not to be compelled to bear a child.[6] It is one thing to say that no one ought to be made to reproduce, or no one ought to be prevented from reproducing by decree; it is quite another to say that society ought to provide whatever is necessary for reproduction to occur.[7]

While sharing these reservations, I wish to raise a different set of objections: The view of offspring presupposed in such a position is unacceptable from a feminist perspective; further, treating the act of reproducing in such a way has serious implications for efforts to bring about a society free of oppression. My concerns lie chiefly in three areas: the tendency in this position to treat children as property; the use of "rights" language and a contract model to define the family; and an imbalance of concern for reproductive ends versus reproductive means.

Attitudes toward Children

The success of Robertson's argument depends upon accepting the view that persons can be the object of another's right. Since he is not arguing for the protection of the right to engage in procreative activities, but the freedom to "acquire that sort of child that would make one willing to bring a child into the world in the first place,"[8] he is asserting the right to acquire a human being (and one with particular characteristics). Nor is Robertson referring simply to the right of persons to share in the experience of child nurture (since ability to adopt would satisfy that), but to have a genetically related child. As a feminist, I would agree that persons ought to be protected in their right to determine when and in what manner they will reproduce, and that they should be free to shape familial life in a way meaningful for them. But such a right should not be understood as unlimited, as extending as far as the acquisition of a concrete human being. Every exercise of freedom has a history and a context; our liberty is thus conditioned both by our potential for causing harm to others and by our responsibility for the quality of our common lives. A view of unlimited procreative liberty does not give sufficient attention to the ways in which not only individual offspring could be harmed, but the human community. Nor does it take seriously enough the possibilities for conflicts between claims.

First, such a position fails to respect offspring as autonomous beings, as ends in themselves. While a child's special dependency requires a condition of compromised autonomy vis-à-vis his or her caretakers, still that child comes into this world as a human person with the potential for self-determination. Although we might grant that the experience of reproduction appropriately fulfills needs and desires for the adults involved, advocating a model where children are brought into this world *chiefly* for that purpose gives too much weight to parental desires and too little to the protection of the offspring's essential autonomy. I am not saying that the desire to reproduce must be altruistic to be morally acceptable, nor that the experience of reproduction ought to be, or even could be, free of parental hopes and expectations for that offspring. My challenge is to a framework wherein the basis for unlimited procreative liberty is an individual desire for a particular type of child, a desire that is seldom weighed appropriately against the reality of the child-to-be as a potential autonomous human being. At what point does a being, who has been conceived, gestated, and born according to someone's specifications, become herself or himself? And if a child comes into the world primarily to fulfill parental need, are there limits to what a parent may do to ensure that the child will continue to meet the specified expectations?

With others, I share the fear that this understanding of procreative liberty incorporates a notion of children as products, on the assumption that individuals have a right to a particular kind of child and ought to be free, insofar as it is possible without causing grave physical harm, to manipulate the reproductive process so as to acquire the desired offspring. Currently, collaborative reproduction is a lengthy, arduous, and quite costly experience. How might parents look upon offspring when they enter the process with the belief that a certain kind of child is *owed* to them, and after they have paid a high price for that child? Certainly well-meaning people can bring children into the world through artificial reproduction and value them highly because of what they have gone through to have them. But this view of reproduction carries nonetheless the sense of "ordering" or "purchasing" children in accordance with specific parental desires, which in the end objectively devalues the child.

Not unlike, and just as dangerous as the thinking that makes women the property of their husbands, is the underlying view that children are not first and principally autonomous persons who also function as members of families and societies but rather the proper object of a parental right. We place our children at serious risk when we fail to see them first as existing for their own sakes and when we allow ourselves to think of them as malleable goods.

There are, in addition, serious problems in accepting as the standard for deciding how technology will be used to intervene in the reproductive process the adult initiator's definition of "procreative excellence." Since we are talking about a potentially autonomous human being, questions about the manipulation of genetic features, etc., ought to be asked first from the point of view of the offspring's best interests, not the prospective parent's desires. The decision then would be whether a certain genetic characteristic ought to be altered to facilitate that child's flourishing rather than whether a feature ought to be manipulated to make that offspring more acceptable to the parent.

A position of unlimited procreative liberty rooted in individual desire risks harming as well the quality of our lives together in community. Since reproduction in this view is tied so closely to one's private conception of a meaningful life, we are never talking about offspring per se, but a very specific type of offspring—a child with those genetic and gender characteristics that allow it to be incorporated into and contribute to the initiator's overall life project.

In a world where mixed-race and handicapped children are not now being adopted because they are "undesirable" we need to ask who determines, and should be permitted to so determine, what human characteristics are "desirable." My claim is not that parents are wrong to want a healthy, and genetically similar, child nor that persons may not have any good grounds for intervening in a pregnancy, for example one in which it is obvious that given certain characteristics the child will place great burdens on the parent or the family. My criticism is directed at an implied yardstick of acceptability, and the determination of reproductive standards based on personal whim. Such a model stands at odds with a feminist vision of community where all are welcome and persons are challenged to deal creatively with differences.

In addition, we need to weigh the consequences of using a model of reproductive desirability which includes choices about the preferred sex of one's offspring, for efforts to promote equality between persons in society. This is not to suggest that such a practice, if widespread, would result in more boys being chosen than girls. We have no way to know that nor reason necessarily to assume it. What is dangerous, in light of the reality of sexism in our society, is the perpetuation of the belief that an offspring's gender should be a determinative factor in her or his value to parents, or to anyone else. The primary question is whether the project to provide the subjectively desirable child is where social energies and resources in reproductive medicine ought to be directed.

The underlying ideal of perfection shaping this perspective and the belief that all so-called imperfection, even in so complex a process as reproduction, can or should be eliminated, needs thus to be questioned seriously. Reproduction and nurture are processes that are never totally within our control, no matter how sophisticated our technology. The formation of a child's character and personality, the development of his or her talents, have to do with a great deal more (such as education, historical events, significant role models) than genetic blueprint. A genetically normal, or "genetically perfect" offspring in this model can for a variety of reasons turn out to be the sort of person his or her parents would not have objectively speaking "been willing to bring into the world." Thus the claim that a parental right to a satisfying reproductive experience justifies the manipulation of genetic material is flawed, for the sort of guarantee sought cannot be provided by control of conception.

The attempt to exert this level of control over the creation of offspring is not only an illusory project but a mistaken one. I do not want to advocate a total passivity toward nature or to suggest that the use of technology in altering the conditions of conception and gestation is always inappropriate. But the feminist value of cooperation with and humility toward nature suggests a middle road between technical domination of the natural reproductive process and passivity. This middle road entails, at least, some attention to the essential elements of particular personhood, and thus a weighing of which features of our offspring we ought to attempt to determine in advance and which we should accept as characteristics of that unique being.

It is not only the sense of "reproducing for excellence" that is troubling about the case for unlimited procreative liberty but the presupposition that since children are property, all relationships between offspring and interested adults can be wholly a matter of contract. This way of thinking about the family is in some ways reflective of an old and familiar pattern, one about which feminists ought to be very cautious.

The Contractual Model of Family

Robertson admits that when we begin to have multiple participants in reproduction "it becomes unclear which participants hold parental rights and duties and will function socially and psychologically as members of the child's family."[9] Such confusion can be alleviated, however, by a presumption that the contract between the parties will determine obligations and entitlements toward the child, rather than the commonly held definitions of paternity and maternity. Whether collaborative arrangements can or will result in family disruption and identity confusion for the offspring or in productive and satisfying "alternative" family experiences will depend in part on the clarity and quality of these contracts. Experience with donor sperm, Robertson argues, suggests that the contract between parties will play the decisive role in determining rearing rights and duties to the offspring. Generally speaking, the presumption of rightful parentage ought to go to the initiating couple according to the agreements made prior to conception.

If these practices become institutionalized, there is no doubt that well-constructed contracts will be enormously helpful for clarifying parental rights and duties and that all the parties, including potential offspring, would benefit from legal protection. There are serious problems, however, with accepting a simple contract solution to the confusion of collaborative reproduction; it is both inadequate and perpetuates an ideologically dangerous model of the family. For example, claiming that the pre-conception contract can be sufficiently clear as to determine parental relationships in advance denies the complexity of reproduction as an affective and social experience as well as a biological one. Accounts of surrogate mothering, for example, suggest it can be quite difficult to decide the shape of one's reproductive role beforehand when we are engaged in a project about which we can come to have very deep feelings. In addition, the nature of what reproductive initiators are contracting about is qualitatively different than the object of ordinary contracts. We do not have at this time, and may never have, a good way to determine the value of specific reproductive contributions or to weigh conflicts between contributors (for example, what is the market value of gestation versus gamete donation?). At the very least, to use sperm donation as a paradigm for workable contracts reflects inattention to the vast differences, emotional as well as physical, in the nature of various collaborative roles. Moreover, it masks inequalities between parties with respect to risk and benefit. A contract that may well be sufficient to determine rearing duties and rights with respect to a sperm donor may not address at all the complex physical and affective situation of the surrogate mother.

Our understanding of the experience can perhaps be reinterpreted as Robertson suggests, so that what comes to count as reproduction is the donation of genetic material for one person, or the experience of gestation for another. Yet while there are very good reasons for preserving the freedom of individuals to choose their level of participation in procreation, to say that the meaning of reproduction can be reduced to one of these partial roles is to perpetuate an impoverished notion of what it means to be a parent. Assigning various rights and obligations to abstract roles may facilitate the execution of collaborative contracts, but risks treating the various components of reproduction as though they fit into neat compartments, and as though the conception-gestation-rearing relationship is entirely negotiable. Feminists do not want to affirm a view of reproduction that makes the moral connections between conception, gestation, and rearing such that conception generates an absolute duty to rear; at the same time, however, concerns for embodiment and thus for reproduction as a whole process mitigate against treating parental obligations and entitlements in isolation from the experiences of conception, pregnancy, and birth.

There is, of course, a kind of tacit agreement, at least in our society, involved in every gestation and birth with respect to the resultant offspring's nurture (and in a sense, also with respect to parental entitlements). Whatever model has been used thus far to understand the relationship, however, has not taken the form of an entirely free contract. Prior to the development of technology, we identified the mother as the woman giving birth to the child and the father as the man whose sperm initially fertilized the egg—those persons with biological and experiential connection, rather than those who have contracted for parental rights and duties. Even when we describe situations where another individual has taken over rearing responsibilities for a child not his or her issue, we continue to refer to that person as an "adoptive" or "foster" parent. We do this not to say anything about the quality of rearing, but to preserve a truer sense of identity and biological continuity for the child, acknowledging that no matter what function the rearing adult serves, he or she cannot ever become the child's father or mother in the traditional sense. I do not want to hold that there could be no legitimate reasons for separating genetic, gestational, and rearing components of reproduction, or that persons who conceive a child will always be the best rearers of that child and that they must therefore be the rearers in all cases. Experience shows that children can be raised well in situations other than the traditional biologically related family. However, the genetic-gestation-rearing connection in procreation ought not be disregarded a priori in the way suggested by the contract model, both for the sake of protecting the offspring's sense of identity as a value and for preserving an awareness of the importance of the task involved when human life is being created.

While "rights" and "entitlements" in childbearing do have much to do with an agreement to accept responsibility, the biological parent-child relationship is still deeply significant, particularly if we are speaking of the intimate mother-child bond in a normal gestation experience. It may be acceptable to say that a woman who has conceived, carried, and birthed a child may legitimately choose to transfer rearing obligations to another, but it does not seem correct to say then that this experience of procreation places *no* claim on her as a mother unless she chooses to assume one under the terms of a contract, or that her claim to this child is identical to the claims of all other contracting parties prior to the contract. Both the experience of having conceived and carried a child and the implicit agreement to nurture grounds parental entitlements; these two dimensions must be seen as elements of the same experience even where a decision is made to separate them. Given the significant burdens and challenges of childbearing and the length of time the commitment ordinarily encompasses, this interconnection is important to protect when possible. Implicit in my critique is the great irony of collaborative reproduction: it is precisely the value of this biological connection, which must be open for renunciation on the part of the donor or gestator, that drives the search for new methods and justifies the infertile party's right to assistance.

The Involuntary Nature of Kinship

The authority of the collaborative contract, coupled with a property view of children, generates a troubling picture of the parent-child bond. One of the false notions perpetuated in such a model of parental entitlement is that we are free to choose all obligations, and able to formulate all the conditions of our lives to meet our expectations. While most contracts and commitments are based on things such as shared purpose, equal benefit, common attraction, etc., and are entered into and terminated voluntarily, until recently, the agreement to conceive, gestate, and rear a child has been of a different nature. While in the best of circumstances we make a choice to parent, and a series of choices about how children will be raised and the shape our family life will take, a great deal of the experience of reproduction is not in our control. The common expression "This child has a face only a mother could love" speaks, of course, to the fact that a parent's bond to her child transcends all cultural standards of beauty, etc., but also alludes to a deeply entrenched understanding of the "givenness" and duration of parental responsibilities. These have included acceptance of a relatively unknown outcome, of inequalities in benefits and burdens, and also of a certain irrevocability. "A face only a mother could love" says something as well about acceptance and fidelity to children, even to those whose looks or gender or genetic characteristics are not what the parent would have desired or what meets society's standards. We have accepted the fact that, unlike a product in the market, children cannot be returned or exchanged if found to be other than what was expected.

The commitment a parent undertakes is not dependent on

that child's behavior or the return of like affection or the fulfillment of expectations in life, although those factors can certainly influence a parent's subjective experience and may at times modify obligations. A child does not enter into a committed relationship with his or her parents in the same way that a parent, by virtue of the decision to bear offspring, does with the child; still, there is some measure of givenness in the child-parent relationship as well. We are free throughout life to choose friends, a mate, employers, etc. but not our family of origin. One of the things that family life can teach us is that we are born into some obligations, and some are born to us, and life includes the acceptance of those kinds of indissoluble and predefined obligations as well as the ones we freely incur. The involuntary quality of kinship can also teach us how to accept others as intimately connected to us, even when they fail to live up to our standards or when they do not possess the physical or personal qualities most attractive to us. To image reproduction as primarily a contractual process, where all the elements are open for negotiation, threatens to lose sight of this sense of transcendent commitment.

From the perspective of feminist ethics, the contractual view of procreative liberty assumes and perpetuates a traditional patriarchal model of the family (centered around rights and ownership), a model that has proven oppressive and sometimes dangerous for persons, especially women. A contract approach is initially attractive as it appears to bring about greater flexibility in the definition of family and the protection of procreative liberty (among the values feminists want to promote). But when persons are treated primarily as the object of another's right, and significant relationships are defined wholly according to legal arrangements rather than the experiences of nurture, the symbolic framework is that of the patriarchal family. Janet Farrell Smith has argued that this property model of parenting, having at its center a notion of rights, is inherently gender-biased and is protective of dangerous authority patterns. It is problematic in her view both because its structure of relationship is "male" in form and because males have traditionally been the exclusive holders of familial rights.[10]

What makes such a model destructively gender-biased, according to Smith, is its rootedness in an extractive view of power rather than a developmental one and its relation to the authority patterns of the traditional patriarchal family. The major elements of such a property model of human relations,

> namely ownership and proprietary control, have had more to do with fathering than with mothering. The realities of motherhood, on the other hand, have had more to do with care, nurturance and day-to-day responsibility. These represent a very different set of moral and political ideals.[11]

The concepts of right and entitlement used in the contractual model correspond to the values preserved in traditional notions of patriarchal fathering (control and ownership) rather than to those of care and responsibility associated with mothering. While many feminists would not want to posit "distinctively female" values or ideals, most would reject familiar structures that treat persons as property and would call instead for a style of parenting that is respectful of a child's autonomy and encourages individual flourishing. They would, as well, reject models of the family that attach authority to rigidly defined roles in favor of models based on equality between partners and cooperation in the performance of family tasks.

As Smith argues, promoting a property (or "rights-centered") model, whether through vigorous protection of familial autonomy or by the rhetoric of "right to procreate" can only reinforce an ideal of the family that not only does not encourage more respectful and cooperative parenting styles but may further facilitate the abuse of parental power. In the context of Robertson's argument, familial autonomy means a protection of parental control as rightful parent (owner) over minor children (a control that in the past has extended to wives). But this sort of familial autonomy underlying arguments for clarity of contract serves largely to protect proprietary interests rather than to facilitate intimacy or the development of creative, more humane forms of parenting for women and men.[12] Since the problem is not only that males have been the exclusive holders of rights to property (including their wives and children) but that this way of imaging the family denies the reality of women and children as fully human, it may not be enough simply for feminists to argue for equality between women and men in the holding of these rights. Rather, the very language of rights, implying as it does some exclusive access to property, must be seen as inappropriate when describing the structure of the family.

Reproductive Ends and Means

One of the weaknesses of the argument for unlimited procreative liberty is a tendency to split ends from means, to overemphasize goals while giving little moral consideration to the methods employed to achieve them or to the price paid. Robertson's concern to promote the procreative initiator's interests is not adequately balanced, for example, by a concern for the persons who will participate as the means to the stated reproductive goals. Except where he discusses contract stipulations (requirements for informed consent, freedom from coercion, screening procedures, etc.). Robertson does not speak of donors and gestators as though they really have interests to be weighed; he argues, in fact, that unless grave harm is being done, their interests cannot override individual procreative liberty. As we saw earlier, the offspring as a particular child is treated not as an end in himself or herself, but as the means to a goal (a fulfilling parenting experience). The question of how such treatment may affect that child's quality of life, sense of identity, or development is hardly raised.

The problem is not that the holding of a reproductive end is wrong in itself, but that it may be mistaken to assume that an end-state can be clearly demarcated from the processes that lead up to it.[13] The primary assumption that reproduction is highly valued by individuals and therefore that freedom of access should be promoted treats reproductive freedom for the most part as a value that could be pursued in isolation of other claims (except the minimal obligation not to do grave harm to an offspring). Feminists reject such thinking as inadequately attentive to the reality of events as processes and to the fact that the means we use to bring about any end are part of the total reality of the event in question. Thus it is not enough to assert that providing genetically related children to infertile individuals is a good to be promoted; questions must be raised about the nature of the arrangement by which that might occur, the impact of that project on the individuals involved and on the larger human community, and the claims other goods are simultaneously exerting.

It is wrong to suppose that an individual procreative right can be posited and its unlimited exercise upheld without careful consideration of the moral nature of the means necessary to attain its end. Interest in a genetically related child cannot be seen as an independent end, the value of which automatically discounts concerns for the present and future state of the offspring, for the physical and emotional safety of the collaborators, or for the place of the experience of reproduction in our collective value system. In addition, the particular techniques used in collaborative reproduction need separate evaluation. We might accept the use of artificial insemination by a donor, for example, on particular grounds (as that the risks to donor are small and the benefit great), but have serious reservations about the practice of surrogacy. An adequate argument for procreative liberty as a good would have to include a fair description of the necessary means since they cannot be separated from the end-state.

Because reproduction has a social dimension, and reproductive practices have profound real and symbolic impacts on the community, the promotion of individual procreative liberty can never be an abstract end. The value of collaborative reproduction for individuals needs to be weighed against the costs these practices may exact, not only in the lives of those individuals directly involved, but also with respect to the promotion of full human community. An assessment of procreative liberty that takes seriously the contextual nature of our choices asks, in addition to whether the "new reproduction" is good for individuals, how it relates to social concerns (to efforts to secure an adequate standard of living for all persons, to progress in the quality of class, gender, and race relations, etc.).

A commitment to the creation of a just society requires that an individual desire for a genetically related child cannot be held up as an end commanding significant public resources and energy if as a "good" it encourages the exploitation of vulnerable persons or fosters negative attitudes toward persons or groups of persons. At a minimum, questions need to be raised about the influence of institutionalizing these practices on our views toward women: will opportunities to serve as egg donors or gestators facilitate progress toward equality with men for women, or does this type of service further identify women in an oppressive way with their reproductive capabilities? If individuals have a right to a genetically related child, do others have an obligation to donate genetic material, and how will the extent of the obligation be determined? What are the potential consequences of medicalizing reproduction in terms of women's right to control over their own bodies? And who will the women be who serve as donors?—will the poor, who have always been exploited by the rich, be used to perform even this form of domestic service?

To take account of the context in which individual procreative liberty is pursued, we also need to weigh the expense and energy channelled in the direction of these reproductive services against the realities of poverty and overpopulation. We need to ask whether we should support the right of individuals to go to any length to acquire the type of child they want when there are so many children already living who are not being taken care of. And, recognizing that collaborative reproduction ordinarily has as its object a white child, we need as well to examine the kind of racial attitudes being perpetuated. We cannot treat the pursuit of a genetically related child, or the protection of individual procreative liberty, as though they are abstract goods that are never in conflict with other relevant goods, nor can we consider procreative liberty from the point of view of its end alone. Given the nature of the procreative task, *how* we reproduce is as significant as *whether* we do.

Promoting Full Humanity

The promotion of women's right to self-determination, especially in matters of reproduction, has indeed been a critical item on the feminist political agenda. But for most feminists, protection of individual autonomy is never treated as the single value to be considered in the analysis of a situation. A commitment to viewing persons as embodied and relational, as well as autonomous, mitigates against an abstract notion of freedom that does not take seriously enough the way in which personal choices alter the shape of the world in which they occur. Questions of personal liberty, including how far our right to procreate extends, can only properly be asked from the point of view of our reality as relational beings whose power for reproduction is a capacity with profound personal and social implications. It is never even theoretically unlimited.

The objectification of children, impoverishment of meaning in the experience of reproduction, damage to notions of kinship, the perpetuation of degrading views of women—all these concerns may be deemed "symbolic harms" that are not compelling enough to override personal liberty. But attention to women's experience has taught feminists that there are no "merely symbolic" harms; we interpret and shape experience through our symbols and therefore how we think about persons, events, and biological processes has a great deal to do with how we behave toward them. We need, then, to pay careful attention to what is being said of personhood, of parent-child relationships, of reproductive capacities, and so on in arguments for unlimited procreative liberty. If we hope to use reproductive technology in a way that promotes the full humanity of all persons, in a manner that is truly creative rather then destructive, then we must be attentive to the potential for harm on all levels. We have an ever-expanding power to reshape the experience of reproduction; whether we will prove in the future to have done so in the service of human life or not will have more than a little to do with how we came to think about it and what we allowed to be of value today.

Acknowledgments

The author would like to thank Professors Margaret Farley and Richard L. Fern for helpful comments on earlier drafts.

Notes

1. While a few feminists have heralded developments in technology as the ground of possibility for women's true liberation, most have remained more cautious, foreseeing potential for further oppression as clearly as hope of equality. See Shulamith Firestone, *The Dialectic of Sex: The Case for Feminist Revolution* (New York: Bantam Books, 1971), 238; Christine Overall, *Ethics and Human Reproduction: A Feminist Analysis* (Boston: Allen and Unwin, 1987).

2. John Robertson, "Procreative Liberty and the Control of Conception, Pregnancy and Childbirth," *Virginia Law Review* 69 (April 1983), 405–462; "Embryos, Families and Procreative Liberty: The Legal Structures of the New Reproduction," *Southern California Law Review* 59 (1986), 942–1041.

3. Robertson, "Embryos, Families, and Procreative Liberty," 961.

4. Robertson, "Procreative Liberty," 450.

5. Robertson, "Procreative Liberty," 432.

6. See Overall, *Ethics and Human Reproduction,* chapter 8; also Richard L. Fern, "The Fundamental Right to Marry and Raise a Family," unpublished manuscript (1987).

7. The parallel would be marriage, that is, there is a recognized right to noninterference in the decision to marry but no obligation on society's part to provide a mate. See William J. Daniel, "Sexual Ethics in Relation to IVF and ET: The Fitting Use of Human Reproductive Power," in *Test-Tube Babies,* William Walters and Peter Singer, eds. (Melbourne: Oxford University Press, 1982), 73.

8. Robertson, "Procreative Liberty," 430.

9. Robertson, "Procreative Liberty," 424.

10. Janet Farrell Smith, "Parenting and Property," in *Mothering: Essays in Feminist Theory,* Joyce Treblicott, ed. (Totowa, NJ: Rowman and Allanheld, 1983), 199–210.

11. Smith, "Parenting," 208.

12. Smith, "Parenting," 206.

13. For a discussion of a feminist critique of dualistic means-ends reasoning, see Jean Grimshaw, *Philosophy and Feminist Thinking* (Minneapolis: University of Minnesota Press, 1986), 187–226.

17. Whose Bodies? Which Selves? Appeals to Embodiment in Assessments of Reproductive Technology

Paul Lauritzen

This chapter first appeared in *Embodiment, Morality, and Medicine* in 1995.

> Now men are far beyond the stage at which they expressed their envy of women's procreative power through couvade, transvestism, subincision. They are beyond merely giving spiritual birth in their baptismal-font wombs, beyond giving physical birth with their electronic fetal monitors, their forceps, their knives.
>
> *Now they have laboratories ([3], p. 314).*

This passage from Gena Corea's book *The Mother Machine* typifies the reaction of one important strand of feminist thought to the new technologies of reproduction and birth. It is fairly representative, for example, or the grave suspicion with which feminists associated with FINRRAGE (Feminists International Network of Resistance to Reproductive and Genetic Engineering) have greeted such possibilities as *in vitro* fertilization, embryo flushing and transfer, and gene therapy. According to this general line of thinking, the new reproductive technologies should be resisted because they concentrate power in the hands of a predominantly male and patriarchal medical establishment by disembodying procreation. By separating procreation from women's bodies, reproductive technology simultaneously reduces women to bodies, or body parts, and strips women of one traditional source of power, namely, the power to procreate. Hence Corea's warning. Previously men were denied direct control over the process of procreation; they might give birth symbolically or intervene medically in this process, but these were only simulacra of control. The existence of *in vitro* fertilization, however, and the distinct possibility of *in vitro* gestation turn resemblance into reality. Laboratory conception and gestation are a threat to women.

At the same time that FINRRAGE has mobilized to resist the new reproductive technologies, opposition has come from other quarters as well. The most substantial opposition has come from groups at the opposite end of the political spectrum, most notably the Roman Catholic Church. For example, the Catholic Church has also condemned *in vitro* fertilization, embryo flushing and transfer, and genetic engineering. Indeed, the Vatican has rejected virtually every application of the new reproductive technology (NRT), and, like FINRRAGE, the Vatican is worried about disembodiment. Thus, in the Vatican *Instruction* [2] on reproductive technology, we hear an echo of Corea's concern. We must take seriously the embodied nature of our existence, and failure to do so results in the reduction of a person to a product. So, for example, we find the Vatican insisting that "an intervention on the human body affects not only the tissues, the organs and their functions but also the person himself on different levels" ([2], p. 8).

This apparent convergence of two such different traditions of thought is interesting in itself. It is doubly so when, as in this volume, attention is focused on "how the realities of embodiment influence moral relationships in practical health care settings." Despite very serious differences between these traditions of thought—even on issues of embodiment—they agree in their rejection of reproductive technology, and they do so for reasons connected to worries about treating procreation as an out-of-the-body laboratory production. So examining how appeals to embodiment function in feminist and Vatican critiques of reproductive technology promises to be quite useful to the overall project of this volume. Moreover, if we attend to the similarities and differences between feminist appeals to embodiment and those of the Catholic Church, we may come to appreciate how the meaning of embodiment may vary from context to context. We may see, for example, how a religious appeal to embodiment in the Christian tradition takes quite a different form from an appeal to embodiment rooted in feminist thought, even if there are also substantial similarities between the two appeals.[1]

Feminist Opposition to Reproductive Technology

We can begin, then, with feminist opposition to reproductive technology. That one significant strand of feminist resistance is fueled by concerns about embodiment is clear. Yet, how precisely does the appeal to embodiment function in this particular feminist critique of reproductive technology? To answer that question, we can return to Gena Corea's work. According to Corea, reproductive technology is best understood in terms of two analogies that have implications for how we think about women's bodies and thus for how we think about, and treat, women. On the one hand, techniques for assisting human reproduction bear a striking resemblance to techniques used to facilitate reproduction in livestock. On the other hand, the commercial transactions frequently associated with reproductive technology bear a striking resemblance to those associated with sexual prostitution. Let us consider each of these analogies in turn.

Corea makes the comparison between reproductive technology in humans and scientific breeding of animals repeatedly and forcefully in her writings (see [3], [4], and [5]). Consider, she says, the techniques commonly used for breeding animals. Artificial insemination, superovulation, estrus synchronization, ova recovery, embryo evaluation, embryo transfer, and caesarean section are all available to animal breeders, just as they are to physicians of reproductive medicine [4]. Indeed, many applications of this technology used in infertility clinics have been adapted from their original use in the livestock breeding industry. This, says Corea, should give us pause because women have frequently been symbolically associated with animals in western thought, as "parts of nature to be controlled and subjugated" ([3], p. 313).

The point of the comparison between reproductive medicine and animal breeding is to invite an inspection of the attitudes that stand behind the practice of animal breeding. Once we see the attitudes driving animal reproduction, we may come to ask whether similar attitudes do not also drive reproductive medicine. And, as Corea shows, there is no mistaking the attitudes of animal breeders.

> When reproductive engineers manipulate the bodies of female animals today, they are clear, blunt and unapologetic about why they are doing it. They want to turn the females into machines for producing "superior" animals or into incubators for the embryos of more "valuable" females. They want, as one entrepreneur told me, to "manufacture embryos at a reduced cost." They aim to create beef cows yielding "quality carcasses of high cutability," and dairy cows producing more milk on the same amount of feed ([3], p. 312).

Or as a manager for Wall's Meat Company put it, this time in relation to the production of pork, "[t]he breeding sow should be thought of, and treated as, a valuable piece of machinery whose function is to pump out baby pigs like a sausage machine" ([4], p. 41).

Corea's point is clear: When the bodies of animals are treated in this fashion, when the animal is essentially reduced to its reproductive parts, the animal ceases to have any individuality or spiritual worth ([4], p. 39). The upshot of reproductive technology is thus that the animal is reduced to a reproductive commodity and nothing more. The worry is that we may come to think of women and their bodies in precisely the same terms.

This worry informs Corea's second analogy as well. If comparing reproductive medicine to livestock production is meant to highlight the possibility that employing reproductive technology may lead us to think about women's bodies as commodities, comparing reproductive medicine to prostitution is meant to highlight the fact that our society already conceptualizes women's bodies in market terms. Drawing on Andrea Dworkin's work, Corea shows that the reduction of women to commodities has already taken place. As Corea notes, our society already markets parts of women's bodies. Pornography is a thriving industry and sexual prostitution is widely perceived to be harmless and is thus tolerated as largely benign.

But if women can sell vagina, rectum, and mouth, Corea asks, why not wombs, embryos, or eggs? Given how women are conceptualized in our society, the answer, of course, is that there is no reason to object to the marketing of women as reproductive commodities, and indeed, Corea says, that is precisely what we see with the development of a commercial surrogate mother industry and egg "donor" programs.

In fact, says Corea, we do not need to attend merely to the obvious comparison case, namely, surrogate motherhood. Talk to women who have been through *in vitro* fertilization programs. Quoting from an Australian study of women who had been treated in IVF programs, Corea draws attention to the dehumanizing aspects of the treatment.

> It [the IVF treatment] is embarrassing. You leave your pride on the hospital door when you walk in and pick it up when you leave. You feel like a piece of meat in a meat-works. But if you want a baby badly enough you'll do it ([5], p. 86).

Corea notes, for example, that many women report undergoing a process of emotional distancing during IVF. They attempt to separate mind from body and in fact come to feel disconnected from their bodies in ways that interfere with bodily love making with their partners. Here, Corea says, the comparison to prostitution is direct and disturbing.

> What kind of spiritual damage does it do to women when they emotionally separate their minds and bodies? . . . We have heard some prostitutes say that during intercourse with strangers who have rented the use of their bodies, they too separate their minds from their bodies as a means of self protection. We have heard some people with multiple personalities say that during extreme sexual abuse and torture in childhood, they split off into separate personalities in order to make what was happening to them endurable. In order to survive.
>
> What does it do to women in IVF "treatment" pro-

> grams when, to varying extents, they separate their minds and bodies in order to make all the poking and prodding and embarrassments endurable? ([5], p. 86)

Corea is not the only feminist asking such questions, nor is she the only one to focus on the importance of embodiment to assessments of reproductive technology. Barbara Katz Rothman, for example, has made essentially the same point in her book, *Recreating Motherhood* [11].[2] In a chapter on the ways in which technological ideology shape how we think about ourselves, Rothman summarizes one important line of resistance to technological thinking in terms that are strikingly similar to those set out above. "It is an objection," Rothman says "to the notion of the world as a machine, the body as a machine, everything subject to hierarchical control, the world, ourselves, our bodies and our souls, ourselves and our children, divided, systematized, reduced" ([11], p. 54). Rothman's earlier work also focused on the effects of technology on conceptions of selfhood. In *The Tentative Pregnancy* [12], for example, she documents the effects of technologies of prenatal diagnosis on the experience of pregnancy, demonstrating that the existence of amniocentesis generates the same sort of emotional distancing, the same sort of splitting of the self, as Corea documents in regard to *in vitro* fertilization.

In fact, a careful reading of feminist responses to the technologies of reproductive medicine shows this to be a pervasive theme: reproductive technology encourages women to separate their selves from their bodies, and the resulting fragmentation leaves women vulnerable. Women become vulnerable because, with fragmentation, comes a willingness to treat women's bodies as biological machines that can be manipulated and controlled. Reproductive technology thus alienates women from their bodies and thereby strips them of an important source of personal fulfillment and power. As Margaret Farley puts it, "For many feminists the sundering of the power and process of reproduction from the bodies of women constitutes a loss of major proportions. Hence, the notion of moving the whole process to the laboratory (using not only *in vitro* fertilization but artificial placentas *et al.*) is not one that receives much enthusiasm" ([7], p. 301).

Catholic Opposition to Reproductive Technology

If we turn now to the Vatican's response to reproductive technology, we see that the Catholic Church is also concerned about issues of embodiment. Consider, for example, the *Instruction* on reproductive technology issued by the Congregation for the Doctrine of the Faith in 1987, in which the position of the Church is set out at length. For our purposes, the introduction and the first two sections of this document are of particular interest, because the introduction sets out the basic moral considerations that are then applied in sections one and two to arrive at particular conclusions about reproductive technology. A careful reading of these three sections reveals that Vatican opposition to reproductive technology is supported by two lines of argument, both of which are rooted in concerns about embodiment. The first line of argument is set out in the introduction in terms of what the Vatican describes as "a proper idea of the nature of the human person in his bodily dimension" ([2], p. 8). The Congregation asks: What moral criteria must be used to assess reproductive technology? The first answer it gives is that any adequate criteria must recognize the bodily and spiritual unity of the person. In the Vatican's view, a person is a "unified totality," and thus it is wrong to treat a person in a way that reduces that person either to mere body or mere spirit. It is particularly important to keep this principle in mind, the Vatican says, when addressing ethical issues in medicine because there is a tendency in medicine to treat the body as "a mere complex of tissues, organs, and functions." Indeed, this is one of the central difficulties with reproductive medicine: it approaches human reproduction as if it were nothing more than the union of bodily parts, namely, of gametes. So one of the most serious problems with reproductive technology, the Vatican concludes, is precisely that it fails to treat the person as a unified whole. Instead, it treats the body in just the way the Vatican says it must not be treated, as a mere complex of tissues and organs. In other words, this technology treats our bodies functionally, the consequence of which is that persons get objectified and treated merely as means to an end. When this happens, technology is not simply assisting, but dominating the process of reproduction.

The second line of argument used to oppose interventions in the reproductive process is less obviously rooted in a concern about embodiment, but, once again, a careful reading of the text highlights the relevance of considerations of embodiment. This second line of reasoning is related to what the Vatican calls "the special nature of the transmission of human life in marriage." In the Vatican's view, since human procreation is the fruit of a "personal and conscious act," it is irreconcilably different from the transmission of life in other animals. It is intentional and purposive and therefore governed by laws. What laws? Laws, says the Vatican, given by God and "inscribed in the very being of man and woman."

As the language here suggests, the appeal is to a natural law conception of human nature, according to which we must understand the telos of human sexual life, marriage, and the family in order to discern the range of acceptable reproductive interventions. Moreover, the appeal is to a particular understanding of this telos, one in which intercourse, love, procreation, marriage, and the family belong together. In the Vatican's view, procreation is properly undertaken in the context of a loving monogamous marriage through an act of sexual intercourse. Here, then, is a second standard by which to assess interventions in the reproductive process. Any type of assisted reproduction that conforms to the procreative norm just articulated, i.e., any procreative attempt that includes sexual intercourse between partners in a loving monogamous marriage, helps facilitate the natural process of procreation and is therefore acceptable. Any intervention that fails to conform to the norm is a departure from the natural law with respect to human sexuality and is therefore morally problematic.

Two points are worth noting at this juncture. First, in rejecting reproductive technology as a violation of natural law, the Vatican is invoking the "inseparability thesis," set out in *Humanae Vitae,* and which supports Catholic opposition to contraception. Just as the Catholic Church condemns contraception because it separates what is never permitted to be separated by allowing for sex without procreation, so it condemns reproductive technology because it provides for the possibility of procreation without sex. This is important to note because many critics of the inseparability thesis have argued that, by insisting that each and every act of sexual intercourse must be open to procreation, the Vatican itself accepts a sort of "physicalist" understanding of sexuality that is incompatible with the holistic picture of the person as a "unified totality" of body and spirit that grounds the first line of argument against reproductive technology discussed above.

This observation suggests a second one. To say that reproductive technology separates procreation from sex is not equivalent to saying that reproductive technology disembodies procreation. So opposition to reproductive technology is not just opposition to those techniques, like IVF, that actually disembody conception, but opposition to how the body is used and viewed by reproductive technology generally. To be sure, the Vatican objection is not merely reducible to the consequentialist concern that all forms of reproductive technology move us toward the objectionable endpoint of extracorporeal gestation. Nevertheless, whether emphasis is placed upon the bodily and spiritual unity of a person, or upon the importance of keeping sex and procreation together, the Vatican is concerned that reproductive technology leads us to treat our bodies merely as a source of gametes, and that so treating our bodies is the first step to disembodying procreation altogether. We already have extracorporeal conception; can extracorporeal gestation be far behind? Ultimately, then, one important source of Vatican resistance to reproductive technology is that it encourages the disembodiment of procreation.

At this point it is worth noting that Vatican opposition to reproductive technology appears strikingly similar to feminist opposition to this technology, and that both groups couch their opposition in terms of the unfortunate consequences of disembodying procreation. Indeed the language of complaint is almost identical. Technological intervention in the process of procreation reduces reproduction to a production process in which humans are themselves reduced to products. Given the similarity of complaint, may we conclude that Vatican appeals to embodiment are essentially identical to feminist appeals to embodiment?

Janice Raymond [10] has argued that the answer to this question should be an emphatic and unequivocal "no!" The similarities, she says, are apparent only. In fact, according to Raymond, feminists should resist this equation, not only because it will be used by their opponents to discredit them as latter day Luddites, but because it is offensive to women. Linking fetalists—the term she uses for conservative religious opponents of reproductive technology—and feminists, she writes, "is an insult of the first order to women. It's tantamount to saying that behind every female idea or movement is male impetus, that women cannot stand on our own and create a woman-defined opposition to the NRTs for autonomous feminist reasons . . ." ([10], p. 60). "Feminists and fetalists," she says flatly, "are not aligned in any way" ([10], p. 65).

Raymond's total rejection of the similarities between Vatican opposition and feminist opposition is too extreme, but her argument is instructive nonetheless, for it demonstrates how an appeal to embodiment is inextricably tied to the context in which it is made. We therefore do well to take up her argument in some detail.

Raymond begins by noting that there are essentially two groups that have mounted substantial opposition to reproductive technology, feminists and the Roman Catholic Church, and that supporters of reproductive technology have an interest in trying to link feminist opposition to Catholic opposition as a way of discrediting both. Not only will advocates of reproductive technology adopt this "politics of guilt by association," but some conservative religious groups may attempt "to co-opt feminist language, ethics, and politics for their own cause" ([10], p. 60). So there may be a variety of reasons why individuals or groups might seek to conflate feminist opposition and Catholic opposition. Nevertheless, there are philosophical and political differences that make these traditions irreconcilable.

Raymond acknowledges that both the Catholic Church and feminists appeal to the language of embodiment in their critique of reproductive technology, but she says they "are talking about different bodies." ([10], p. 61) Feminists locate their appeal to embodiment within a context of opposition to violence against women. "Feminists," Raymond writes:

> are concerned about the ways in which the NRTs destroy a women's bodily integrity and the totality of her personal

> and political existence. Many feminists criticize the way in which the "technodocs" sever the biological processes of pregnancy and reproduction from the female body while at the same time making ever more invasive incursions into the female body for eggs, for implantation, for embryo transfers, and the like. Through such incursions, women can only come to be distanced from their autonomous bodily processes. And the net result of this is that women's bodies are perceived by themselves and others as a reproductive resource, as a field to be seeded, ploughed and ultimately harvested for the fruit of the womb. The feminist value of "embodiment" translates to bodily integrity and the control of one's body ([10], pp. 61–62).

By contrast, Raymond argues, Catholic opposition to disembodiment is located within a context of opposition to violence against fetuses. Consequently, in the Vatican *Instruction,* a document that, as we saw, appeals repeatedly to the language of embodiment, an entire section is devoted to a discussion of the effects on women. "Nowhere," writes Raymond about the Vatican *Instruction*,

> is there one mention of the "disrespect" that is accorded to the woman's "human life" by these technologies. One might expect that a document whose title purports to talk about the "origin" of human life might at least mention women. But the so-called "dignity of procreation" is applied in a general sense to the dignity of the human person and certainly not specifically to the dignity and integrity of the woman's body. . . . Nowhere is there any recognition that the body of the woman becomes an instrument in the technological procreative process and that this constitutes an assault against the dignity of women and a form of violence against women. The abstract inviolability of fetal life reigns supreme; the real and present violability of a woman's life, on which the new reproductive technologies depend for their very existence, is once more invisible ([10], pp. 63–64).

Moreover, Raymond argues, even when the Vatican is not focused exclusively on the bodies of fetuses, even when women's bodies come into view, the consequences of reproductive technology on women's bodies are seen against the backdrop of concern about sexuality, parenthood, or marriage, and not against a backdrop of concern about the bodily integrity of women, nor of concern that women have control of their bodies. So whereas feminist appeals to embodiment are rooted in a commitment to subverting "the entire fabric of sexual subordination and the ways in which that subordination has insured for men both sexual and reproductive access to women," Vatican appeals to embodiment are rooted in a pro-natalist world view that embraces compulsory motherhood for women and thus subsumes ". . . the autonomy and independence of the woman to the 'interests' of the family . . ." ([10], p. 62).

Given the striking similarities that we noted above between feminist opposition to reproductive technology and Vatican opposition, is Raymond right? The answer is that Raymond is both partly right and partly wrong. Although Raymond is right to point out the very real differences between some of the feminist objections and some raised by the Catholic Church, she is wrong to dismiss as quickly as she does the mutual concern about disembodiment. To be sure, there are good reasons for feminists to be skeptical about Catholic opposition to reproductive technology. As we saw, the rather glaring omission of any explicit discussion of how reproductive technology affects women is one. Nevertheless, a healthy skepticism here does not justify Raymond's hasty dismissal of Vatican concerns about disembodiment.

For example, Raymond claims that while the Vatican uses the language of embodiment in criticizing reproductive technology, it is only concerned about women's body derivatively. That is, the Catholic Church is only concerned about women's bodies to the extent that these bodies serve the reproductive interest of men or are necessary to safeguarding the bodies of fetuses. She says, "for feminists, women are our bodies," and the unstated implication is that for the Catholic Church this is not true. If we look closely at the Vatican *Instruction,* however, we see nearly identical language, language that, I believe, is meant to express the same worry. Quoting Pope John Paul II, the Congregation for the Doctrine of the Faith endorses a claim that might well be summarized as, "touch the body, touch the person." "Each human person," we read, "in his absolutely unique singularity, is constituted not only by his spirit, but by his body as well. Thus, in the body and through the body, one touches the person himself in his concrete reality" ([2], p. 8). "Touch the body, touch the person" might well be substituted without loss of meaning for "women are our bodies."

Yet if this comparison highlights the fact that Raymond states her case too strongly by claiming that the Vatican and feminists are not aligned in any way, it also reveals the truth of her observation that the context of appeals to embodiment is all important. Feminists apply the insight behind the aphorism "women are our bodies" from a context in which there is an explicit and unequivocal commitment to women's bodily integrity and to securing personal and political liberty for women. So feminists move directly from a concern about the disembodiment of procreation that appears to come with reproductive technology to an explicit discussion of how this technology affects women's bodies and thus women's hope for freedom and equality.

By contrast, the Catholic Church appeals to embodiment from within a context in which there has not traditionally been a significant commitment to women's equality. The upshot is that when the Vatican talks about embodiment, it is not typically speaking about women's bodies. So although "touch the person, touch the body" in fact articulates the same view of the human person as "women are our bodies," the former aphorism refers primarily to male bodies. Thus, when the Vatican turns to apply this insight in an assessment of reproductive technology, we should not be altogether surprised—though we may still be outraged—by the fact that it takes up the effects this technology has on the bodies of fetuses, but says nothing about its impact on the bodies of women.

Indeed, Raymond's emphatic repudiation of Vatican appeals to embodiment forces us to confront the fact that the Church's discussion of the effects of disembodiment takes place against the backdrop, not merely of an undistinguished record of commitment to the rights of women, but against a significant legacy of denigration of the body, women, and sexuality. Margaret Farley, for example, has pointed out that any appeal to embodiment within the Christian tradition must come to grips with the fact that the Christian tradition has frequently embraced a dualism that pits spirit against body, man against woman, reason against emotion, a dualism that has served to oppress women. "Body/spirit," Farley writes,

> is in many ways the basic dualism with which historical religious have struggled since late antiquity. Women, as we have already noted, have been associated with body, men with mind. Women's physiology has been interpreted as "closer to nature" than men's in that many areas and functions of a woman's body seem to serve the human species as much or more than they serve the individual woman. Women's bodies, in this interpretation, are subject to a kind of fate—more so than men's. Women are immersed in "matter," in an inertness which has not its own agency. This is manifest not only in the determined rhythms of their bodily functions, but in a tendency to act from emotion rather than from reason, and in women's "natural" work which is the caring for the bodies of children and men" ([7], p. 291).

Has the Church come to grips with this legacy in its appeal to embodiment in the *Instruction* on Reproductive Technology? Raymond has shown decisively that the answer to this question is "no." The lesson to be drawn here is that the Church's own best insights have been undermined by a continuing legacy of sexism and dualistic thinking. If the Vatican was not in fact blinkered by the regrettable bifurcation of reality that runs deep in the tradition, if instead the Vatican took seriously an incarnational theology that, in Carolyn Walker Bynum's words, treats the "body as locus, not merely of pleasure but of personhood itself," ([1], p. 19) then the Vatican appeal to embodiment in the *Instruction* on Reproductive Technology would in fact commit it to attend seriously to women's bodily autonomy and to the threat posed to women's bodies by reproductive technology. It is regrettable that the *Instruction* does not do justice to the Church's own vision of the human person as "a unified totality" of body and spirit, but we should not dismiss the vision itself as sexist or misogynist for that reason.

If Raymond's juxtaposition of feminist criticism with Vatican criticism of reproductive technology helps us to see that any appeal to embodiment must be taken in context, and, if attending to the context of Vatican appeals to embodiment helps us to discern the shortcomings of Catholic opposition to reproductive technology, it is worth asking whether this juxtaposition does not also highlight the shortcomings of some feminist appeals to embodiment. I want in closing to suggest that it does and, indeed, to show how the *Vatican Instruction* might offer an important corrective to one strand of the feminist critique precisely at the point where the context of feminist appeals to embodiment undermines feminist insights.

To see once again that the comparison of feminist and Catholic opposition to reproductive technology is instructive, we may return to the analogy Gena Corea draws between sexual prostitution and the commodification of reproduction. We saw above that this comparison is made to highlight the dangers of an activity that appears to commodify women's bodies in a cultural context where women's bodies are already for sale in the marketplace. To explain the full force of this analogy, however, we must ask why sexual prostitution is morally problematic.[3] If feminism is committed to the bodily autonomy of women, why should women not be able to sell their bodies if they so choose? This is a difficult question for feminism, and it is instructive to see how one strand of feminist thought has answered this question. One answer to the question has essentially been to suggest that prostitution is so degrading and so dehumanizing, that no woman would choose to be a prostitute unless she were coerced.

It is this line of reasoning, for example, that Catharine MacKinnon has in mind when she writes that the fact that ". . . prostitution and modeling are structurally women's best economic options should give pause to those who would consider women's presence there a true act of free choice" ([9], p. 180). As MacKinnon points out, in other contexts, we readily acknowledge that people do degrading work for lack of better economic options, and we neither deny that the work is degrading nor deceive ourselves by thinking that the work is freely chosen. Indeed, even where a woman "chooses" prostitution in a context where she is not doing so, say, to feed herself or her children, we have good reason to suspect that other forms of coercion are at work. Perhaps self-esteem has been so undermined by a society that systematically devalues women that there is not a sufficient sense of self worth to recognize the degradation of prostitution.

Thus, whether we are talking about economic coercion or other, perhaps less obvious forms of coercion, the important point is that this approach to prostitution challenges the presumption that prostitution is freely chosen. What MacKinnon says of pornography could also be said of prostitution. "I will leave you wondering . . . ," MacKinnon writes, "why it is that when a woman spreads her legs for a camera, she is assumed to be exercising free will" ([9], p. 180). Why is it, critics of prostitution might ask, that when a woman sells her body for money, she is assumed to be exercising free will? To reverse the presumption here is to take the view that sexual prostitution in itself could not possibly fulfill any legitimate interest for a person of self-respect. Hence, if a women is selling her body, there is reason to suspect coercion.

I have argued elsewhere that this is in fact a powerful argument and that the critique of "liberal" conceptions of autonomy implicit in it is also significant (see [8]). For our purposes, it is important to see how the logic of this argument must be extended to reproductive technology if the comparison of assisted reproduction to sexual prostitution is to carry any weight. Take, for example, the argument that IVF turns a woman into a sort of reproductive prostitute. Part of the force of this argument comes from the suggestion that women are coerced into IVF, just as they are coerced into becoming prostitutes. Yet, if we consider the claim that to offer IVF to a childless woman is coercive, we discover that for this claim to be plausible we require a conviction comparable to the belief that eliminating prostitution could not conflict with any legitimate interest a women of self-respect might have.

In one sense, of course, this is not true even of prostitution. If a woman sells her body in order to feed herself or her children, she is obviously pursuing a legitimate interest. Nevertheless, the point opponents of prostitution and of reproductive technology wish to make is that there is nothing in the activity of selling one's body or in the procedures of assisted reproduction that is itself rewarding for women, and, consequently, if women choose either activity, the only explanation is that they have been coerced. The problem with pressing this line of argument, however, is that there is a more direct connection between assisted reproduction and the good of bearing and begetting a child than between prostitution and the good of feeding children. The upshot is that opponents of reproductive technology can only utilize this analogy with prostitution effectively, if they are simultaneously prepared to reject or devalue the importance of begetting and bearing children.

Unfortunately, when we examine the work of some who have opposed IVF on the grounds that it may be coercive, we see precisely this sort of skepticism about the value of children. For example, in an article entitled "'Women Want It': *In-Vitro* Fertilization and Women's Motivations for Participation," Christine Crowe argues that women participate in IVF programs largely because they accept the dominant ideology of motherhood in Western culture, an ideology that includes the belief that biological motherhood is valuable. "IVF," Crowe writes, "relies upon women to perceive motherhood as desirable" ([6], pp. 547–48). Or consider Robyn Rowland's explanation of the pressures facing infertile women. Under the heading "pro-natalism and the experience of infertility," Rowland writes:

> To understand the impact of infertility, we need to understand that we live within a society which says that it is good to have children. That is, one which has pronatalist values. . . . The exclamations of wonder whenever we see something young, vulnerable, and cuddly such as a kitten are also reinforcing the desire for children ([13], p. 85).

Rowland is certainly correct that childless women face enormous pressure in Western societies, but does recognizing this fact, and the coercion that may come with it, also require rejecting any affirmation of children, as this passage appears to suggest?

Here we see how the context of feminist appeals to embodiment may also subvert the full significance of embodiment. To appeal to embodiment from within a context that emphasizes the way in which pregnancy, childbirth, and the care of children have been oppressive to women, poses the danger of neglecting the value of the decidedly embodied experience of pregnancy and the embodied goodness of children.

This is not to say that all, or even most, feminists who have opposed reproductive technology out of concerns over embodiment devalue children. Nor do I wish to deny that pregnancy is sometimes oppressive for women and perceived by women as such. Nor would I deny that having and rearing children can be unfulfilling or even disastrously burdensome. Still, those feminists who have categorically discounted the value to women of pregnancy and parenthood have not taken embodiment seriously enough. Given a preoccupation with combatting an ideology that sacralizes pregnancy and motherhood, it is easy to conflate the socially sanctioned belief that having children is desirable (and pregnancy uniquely fulfilling) with the very different proposition that women cannot be fulfilled unless they have children. Thus, in their eagerness to reject the latter claim, some feminists have been blinded to the fact that women may legitimately value carrying and caring for children. To celebrate is not to sacralize, and any view that fully embraced the importance of embodiment, could not but celebrate the experiences of bearing and rearing children.

In the final analysis, careful attention to Vatican and to feminist appeals to embodiment reveals striking differences that in turn highlight the shortcomings of both Vatican and some feminist opposition to reproductive technology. At the same time, however, we can see striking similarities. Both traditions of thought draw our attention to the potential dangers of disembodying procreation, and in doing so, both traditions properly highlight the importance of attention to issues of embodiment when reflecting morally on medicine. It is perhaps ironic, therefore, that, in assessing reproductive technology in light of the embodied character of human life, critics in both traditions go so wrong. For, surely, no adequate account of embodiment and reproductive technology would conclude that this technology always or necessarily violates the embodied quality of human procreation. On the contrary, for many infertile individuals, reproductive technology mediates embodiment, not the reverse (see [7]). That both Catholic opposition and some feminist opposition to reproductive technology appear blind to this fact demonstrates how important the context of appeals to embodiment can be.

Notes

1. For a fuller discussion of feminist and Catholic opposition to reproductive technology, see [8]. See also [14], [15].

2. It is important to note, however, that Rothman does not reach the same conclusions about reproductive technology as Corea, even though she shares Corea's worries about disembodiment.

3. In fact, I cannot hope to unpack this analogy fully here. To do so would require a complete analysis of the relationship between a prostitute and client, and an examination of that relationship compared to the relationship among infertile individuals, physicians, and gamete donors. I will focus only on the comparison between an infertile woman and a prostitute.

Bibliography

1. Bynum, C. W.: 1991, *Fragmentation and Redemption,* Zone Books, New York.

2. Congregation for the Doctrine of Faith: 1987, *Instruction on Respect for Human Life in Its Origin and on the Dignity of Procreation,* Unites States Catholic Conference, Washington.

3. Corea, G.: 1985, *The Mother Machine,* Harper & Row, New York.

4. Corea, G.: 1987, "The Reproductive Brothel," in G. Corea *et al.* (eds.), *Man-Made Women,* Indiana University Press, Bloomington, pp. 38–51.

5. Corea, G.: 1988, "What the King Can Not See," in E. H. Baruch, A. F. D'Adamo, Jr. and J. Seager (eds.), *Embryos, Ethics, and Women's Rights,* Harrington Park Press, New York, pp. 77–93.

6. Crowe, C.: 1985, "Women Want It: *In Vitro* Fertilization and

Women's Motivations for Participation," *Women's Studies International Forum* 8(6), 547–52.

7. Farley, M.: 1985, "Feminist Theology and Bioethics," in B. H. Andolson, C. E. Gudorf and M. D. Pellauer (eds.), *Women's Consciousness, Women's Conscience,* Harper and Row, San Francisco, pp. 285–305.

8. Lauritzen, P.: 1993, *Pursuing Parenthood,* Indiana University Press, Bloomington.

9. MacKinnon, C.: 1987, *Feminism Unmodified,* Harvard University Press, Cambridge.

10. Raymond, J.: 1987, "Fetalists and Feminists: They Are Not the Same," in P. Spallone and D. L. Steinberg (eds.), *Made to Order,* Pergamon, Oxford, pp. 58–66.

11. Rothman, B. K.: 1989, *Recreating Motherhood,* W. W. Norton, New York.

12. Rothman, B. K.: 1985, *The Tentative Pregnancy,* Viking Press, New York.

13. Rowland, R.: 1987, "Women as Living Laboratories: The New Reproductive Technologies," in J. Figuerra-McDonough and R. C. Sarri (eds.), *The Trapped Woman,* Sage, Newbury Park, pp. 81–111.

14. Ryan, M.: 1993, "Justice and Artificial Reproduction: A Catholic Feminist Analysis," Ph.D. dissertation, Yale University, New Haven, CT.

15. Ryan, M.: 1990, "The Argument for Unlimited Procreative Liberty: A Feminist Critique," *Hastings Center Report* 20(4), 6–12.

18. Abortion and the Sexual Agenda: A Case for Prolife Feminism

Sidney Callahan

This chapter first appeared in *Commonweal* in 1986.

The abortion debate continues. In the latest and perhaps most crucial development, prolife feminists are contesting prochoice feminist claims that abortion rights are prerequisites for women's full development and social equality. The outcome of this debate may be decisive for the culture as a whole. Prolife feminists, like myself, argue on good feminist principles that women can never achieve the fulfillment of feminist goals in a society permissive toward abortion.

These new arguments over abortion take place within liberal political circles. This round of intense intra-feminist conflict has spiraled beyond earlier right-versus-left abortion debates, which focused of "tragic choices," medical judgments, and legal compromises. Feminist theorists of the prochoice position now put forth the demand for unrestricted abortion rights as a *moral imperative* and insist upon women's right to complete reproductive freedom. They morally justify the present situation and current abortion practices. Thus it is all the more important that prolife feminists articulate their different feminist perspective.

These opposing arguments can best be seen when presented in turn. Perhaps the most highly developed feminist arguments for the morality and legality of abortion can be found in Beverly Wildung Harrison's *Our Right to Choose* (Beacon Press, 1983) and Rosalind Pollack Petchesky's *Abortion and Woman's Choice* (Longman, 1984). Obviously it is difficult to do justice to these complex arguments, which draw on diverse strands of philosophy and social theory and are often interwoven in prochoice feminists' own version of a "seamless garment." Yet the fundamental feminist case for the morality of abortion, encompassing the views of Harrison and Petchesky, can be analyzed in terms of four central moral claims: (1) the moral right to control one's own body; (2) the moral necessity of autonomy and choice in personal responsibility; (3) the moral claim for the contingent value of fetal life; (4) the moral right of women to true social equality.

1. The moral right to control one's own body. Prochoice feminism argues that a woman choosing an abortion is exercising a basic right of bodily integrity granted in our common law tradition. If she does not choose to be physically involved in the demands of a pregnancy and birth, she should not be compelled to be so against her will. Just because it is *her* body which is involved, a woman should have the right to terminate any pregnancy, which at this point in medical history is tantamount to terminating fetal life. No one can be forced to donate an organ or submit to other invasive physical procedures for however good a cause. Thus no woman should be subjected to "compulsory pregnancy." And it should be noted that in pregnancy much more than a passive biological process is at stake.

From one perspective, the fetus is, as Petchesky says, a "biological parasite" taking resources from the woman's body. During pregnancy, a woman's whole life and energies will be actively involved in the nine-month process. Gestation and childbirth involve physical and psychological risks. After childbirth a woman will either be a mother who must undertake a twenty-year responsibility for child rearing, or face giving up her child for adoption or institutionalization. Since hers is the body, hers the risk, hers the burden, it is only just that she alone should be free to decide on pregnancy or abortion.

This moral claim to abortion, according to the prochoice feminists, is especially valid in an individualistic society in which women cannot count on medical care or social support in pregnancy, childbirth, or child rearing. A moral abortion decision is never made in a social vacuum, but in the real life society which exists here and now.

2. The moral necessity of autonomy and choice in personal responsibility. Beyond the claim for individual *bodily* integrity, the prochoice feminists claim that to be a full adult *morally,* a woman must be able to make responsible life commitments. To plan, choose, and exercise personal responsibility, one must have control of reproduction. A woman must be able to make yes-or-no decisions about a specific pregnancy, according to her present situation, resources, prior commitments, and life plan. Only with such reproductive freedom can a woman have the moral autonomy necessary to make mature commitments, in the area of family, work, or education.

Contraception provides a measure of personal control, but contraceptive failure or other chance events can too easily result in involuntary pregnancy. Only free access to abortion can provide the necessary guarantee. The chance biological process of an involuntary pregnancy should not be allowed to override all the other personal commitments and responsibilities a woman has: to others, to family, to work, to education, to her future development, health, or well-being. Without reproductive freedom, women's personal moral agency and human consciousness are subjected to biology and chance.

3. The moral claim for the contingent value of fetal life. Prochoice feminist exponents like Harrison and Petchesky claim that the value of fetal life is contingent upon the woman's free consent and subjective acceptance. The fetus must be invested with maternal valuing in order to become human. This process of "humanization" through personal consciousness and "sociality" can only be bestowed by the woman in whose body and psychosocial system a new life must mature. The meaning and value of fetal life are constructed by the woman; without this personal conferral there only exists a biological, physiological process. Thus fetal interests or fetal rights can never outweigh the woman's prior interest and rights. If a woman does not consent to invest her pregnancy with meaning or value, then the merely biological process can be freely terminated. Prior to her own free choice and conscious investment, a woman cannot be described as a "mother" nor can a "child" be said to exist.

Moreover, in cases of voluntary pregnancy, a woman can withdraw consent if fetal genetic defects or some other problem emerges at any time before birth. Late abortion should thus be granted without legal restrictions. Even the minimal qualifications and limitations on women embedded in *Roe v. Wade* are unacceptable—repressive remnants of patriarchal unwillingness to give power to women.

4. The moral right of women to full social equality. Women have a moral right to full social equality. They should not be restricted or subordinated because of their sex. But this morally required equality cannot be realized without abortion's certain control of reproduction. Female social equality depends upon being able to compete and participate as freely as males can in the structures of educational and economic life. If a woman cannot control when and how she will be pregnant or rear children, she is at a distinct disadvantage, especially in our male-dominated world.

Psychological equality and well-being is also at stake. Women must enjoy the basic right of a person to the free exercise of heterosexual intercourse and full sexual expression, separated from procreation. No less than males, women should be able to be sexually active without the constantly inhibiting fear of pregnancy. Abortion is necessary for women's sexual fulfillment and the growth of uninhibited feminine self-confidence and ownership of their sexual powers.

But true sexual and reproductive freedom means freedom to procreate as well as to inhibit fertility. Prochoice feminists are also worried that women's freedom to reproduce will be curtailed through the abuse of sterilization and needless hysterectomies. Besides the punitive tendencies of a male-dominated health-care system, especially in response to repeated abortions or welfare pregnancies, there are other economic and social pressures inhibiting reproduction. Genuine reproductive freedom implies that day care, medical care, and financial support would be provided mothers, while fathers would take their full share in the burdens and delights of raising children.

Many prochoice feminists identify feminist ideals with communitarian, ecologically sensitive approaches to reshaping society. Following theorists like Sara Ruddick and Carol Gilligan, they link abortion rights with the growth of "maternal thinking" in our heretofore patriarchal society. Maternal thinking is loosely defined as a responsible commitment to the loving nurture of specific human beings as they actually exist in socially embedded interpersonal contexts. It is a moral perspective very different from the abstract, competitive, isolated, and principled rigidity so characteristic of patriarchy.

How does a prolife feminist respond to these arguments? Prolife feminists grant the good intentions of their prochoice counterparts but protest that the prochoice position is flawed, morally inadequate, and inconsistent with feminism's basic demands for justice. Prolife feminists champion a more encompassing moral ideal. They recognize the claims of fetal life and offer a different perspective on what is good for women. The feminist vision is expanded and refocused.

1. From the moral right to control one's own body to a more inclusive ideal of justice. The moral right to control one's own body does apply to cases of organ transplants, mastectomies, contraception, and sterilization; but it is not a conceptualization adequate for abortion. The abortion dilemma is caused by the fact that 266 days following a conception in one body, another body will emerge. One's own body no longer exists as a single unit but is engendering another organism's life. This dynamic passage from conception to birth is genetically ordered and universally found in the human species. Pregnancy is not like the growth of cancer or infestation by a biological parasite; it is the way every human being enters the world. Strained philosophical analogies fail to apply: having a baby is not like rescuing a drowning person, being hooked up to a famous violinist's artificial life-support system, donating organs for transplant—or anything else.

As embryology and fetology advance, it becomes clear that human development is a continuum. Just as astronomers are studying the first three minutes in the genesis of the universe, so the first moments, days, and weeks at the beginning of human life are the subject of increasing scientific attention. While neonatology pushes the definition of viability ever earlier, ultrasound and fetology expand the concept of the patient *in utero*. Within such a continuous growth process, it is hard to defend logically any demarcation point after conception as the point at which an immature form of human life is so different from the day before or the day after, that it can be morally or legally discounted as a nonperson. Even the moment of birth can hardly differentiate a nine-month fetus from a newborn. It is not surprising that those who countenance late abortions are logically led to endorse selective infanticide.

The same legal tradition which in our society guarantees the right to control one's own body firmly recognizes the wrongfulness of harming other bodies, however immature, dependent, different looking, or powerless. The handicapped, the retarded, and newborns are legally protected from deliberate harm. Prolife feminists reject the suppositions that would except the unborn from this protection.

After all, debates similar to those about the fetus were once conducted about feminine personhood. Just as women, or blacks, were considered too different, too underdeveloped, too "biological," to have souls or to possess legal rights, so the fetus is now seen as "merely" biological life, subsidiary to a person. A woman was once viewed as incorporated into the "one flesh" of her husband's person; she too was a form of bodily property. In all patriarchal unjust systems, lesser orders of human life are granted rights only when wanted, chosen, or invested with value by the powerful.

Fortunately, in the course of civilization there has been a gradual realization that justice demands the powerless and dependent be protected against the uses of power wielded unilaterally. No human can be treated as a means to an end without consent. The fetus is an immature, dependent form of human life which only needs time and protection to develop. Surely, immaturity and dependence are not crimes.

In an effort to think about the essential requirements of a just society, philosophers like John Rawls recommend imagining yourself in an "original position," in which your position in the society to be created is hidden by a "veil of ignorance." You will have to weigh the possibility that any inequalities inherent in that society's practices may rebound upon you in the worst, as well as in the best, conceivable way. This thought experiment helps ensure justice for all.

Beverly Harrison argues that in such an envisioning of society everyone would institute abortion rights in order to guarantee that if one turned out to be a woman one would have reproductive freedom. But surely in the original position and behind the "veil of ignorance," you would have to contemplate the possibility of being the particular fetus to be aborted. Since everyone has passed through the fetal stage of development, it is false to refuse to imagine oneself in this state when thinking about a potential world in which justice would govern. Would it be just that an embryonic life—in half the cases, of course, a female life—be sacrificed to the right of a woman's control over her own body? A woman may be pregnant without consent and experience a great many penalties, but a fetus killed without consent pays the ultimate penalty.

It does not matter (*The Silent Scream* notwithstanding) whether the fetus being killed is fully conscious or feels pain. We do not sanction killing the innocent if it can be done painlessly or without the victim's awareness. Consciousness becomes important to the abortion debate because it is used as a criterion for the "personhood" so often seen as the prerequisite for legal protection. Yet certain philosophers set the standard of personhood so high that half the human race could not meet the criteria during most of their waking hours (let alone their sleeping ones). Sentience, self-consciousness, rational decision-making, social participation? Surely no infant, or child under two, could qualify. Either our idea of person must be expanded or another criterion, such as human life itself, be employed to protect the weak in a just society. Prolife feminists who defend the fetus empathetically identify with an immature state of growth passed through by themselves, their children, and everyone now alive.

It also seems a travesty of just procedures that a pregnant woman now, in effect, acts a sole judge of her own case, under the most stressful conditions. Yes, one can acknowledge that the pregnant woman will be subject to the potential burdens arising from a pregnancy, but it has never been thought right to have an interested party, especially the more powerful party, decide his or her own case when there may be a conflict of interest. If one considers the matter as a case of a powerful versus a powerless, silenced claimant, the prochoice feminist argument can rightly be inverted:

since hers is the body, hers the risk, and hers the greater burden, then how in fairness can a woman be the sole judge of the fetal right to life?

Human ambivalence, a bias toward self-interest, and emotional stress have always been recognized as endangering judgment. Freud declared that love and hate are so entwined that if instant thoughts could kill, we would all be dead in the bosom of our families. In the case of a woman's involuntary pregnancy, a complex, long-term solution requiring effort and energy has to compete with the immediate solution offered by a morning's visit to an abortion clinic. On the simple, perceptual plane, with imagination and thinking curtailed, the speed, ease, and privacy of abortion, combined with the small size of the embryo, tend to make early abortions seem less morally serious—even though speed, size, technical ease, and the private nature of an act have no moral standing.

As the most recent immigrants from nonpersonhood, feminists have traditionally fought for justice for themselves and the world. Women rally to feminism as a new and better way to live. Rejecting male aggression and destruction, feminists seek alternative, peaceful, ecologically sensitive means to resolve conflicts while respecting human potentiality. It is a chilling inconsistency to see prochoice feminists demanding continued access to assembly-line, technological methods of fetal killing—the vacuum aspirator, prostaglandins, and dilation and evacuation. It is a betrayal of feminism, which has built the struggle for justice on the bedrock of women's empathy. After all, "maternal thinking" receives its name from a mother's unconditional acceptance and nurture of dependent, immature life. It is difficult to develop concern for women, children, the poor and the dispossessed—and to care about peace—and at the same time ignore fetal life.

2. From the necessity of autonomy and choice in personal responsibility to an expanded sense of responsibility. A distorted idea of morality overemphasizes individual autonomy and active choice. Morality has often been viewed too exclusively as a matter of human agency and decisive action. In moral behavior persons must explicitly choose and aggressively exert their wills to intervene in the natural and social environments. The human will dominates the body, overcomes the given, breaks out of the material limits of nature. Thus if one does not choose to be pregnant or cannot rear a child, who must be given up for adoption, then better to abort the pregnancy. Willing, planning, choosing one's moral commitments through the contracting of one's individual resources becomes the premier model of moral responsibility.

But morality also consists of the good and worthy acceptance of the unexpected events that life presents. Responsiveness and response-ability to things unchosen are also instances of the highest human moral capacity. Morality is not confined to contracted agreements of isolated individuals. Yes, one is obligated by explicit contracts freely initiated, but human beings are also obligated by implicit compacts and involuntary relationships in which persons simply find themselves. To be embedded in a family, a neighborhood, a social system, brings moral obligations which were never entered into with informed consent.

Parent-child relationships are one instance of implicit moral obligations arising by virtue of our being part of the interdependent human community. A woman, involuntarily pregnant, has a moral obligation to the now-existing dependent fetus whether she explicitly consented to its existence or not. No prolife feminist would dispute the forceful observations of prochoice feminists about the extreme difficulties that bearing an unwanted child in our society can entail. But the stronger force of the fetal claim presses a woman to accept these burdens; the fetus possesses rights arising from its extreme need and the interdependency and unity of humankind. The woman's moral obligation arises both from her status as a human being embedded in the interdependent human community and her unique lifegiving female reproductive power. To follow the prochoice feminist ideology of insistent individualistic autonomy and control is to betray a fundamental basis of the moral life.

3. From the moral claim of the contingent value of fetal life to the moral claim for the intrinsic value of human life. The feminist prochoice position which claims that the value of the fetus is contingent upon the pregnant woman's bestowal—or willed, conscious "construction"—of humanhood is seriously flawed. The inadequacies of this position flow from the erroneous premises (1) that human value and rights can be granted by individual will; (2) that the individual woman's consciousness can exist and operate in an *a priori* isolated fashion; and (3) that "mere" biological, genetic human life has little meaning. Prolife feminism takes a very different stance toward life and nature.

Human life from the beginning to the end of development *has* intrinsic value, which does not depend on meeting the selective criteria or tests set up by powerful others. A fundamental humanist assumption is at stake here. Either we are going to value embodied human life and humanity as a good thing, or take some variant of the nihilist position that assumes human life is just one more random occurrence in the universe such that each instance of human life must explicitly be justified to prove itself worthy to continue. When faced with a new life, or an involuntary pregnancy, there is a world of difference in whether one first asks, "Why continue?" or "Why not?" Where is the burden of proof going to rest? The concept of "compulsory pregnancy" is as distorted as labeling life "compulsory aging."

In a sound moral tradition, human rights arise from human needs, and it is the very nature of a right, or valid claim upon another, that it cannot be denied, conditionally delayed, or rescinded by more powerful others at their behest. It seems fallacious to hold that in the case of the fetus it is the pregnant woman alone who gives or removes its right to life and human status solely through her subjective conscious investment or "humanization." Surely no pregnant woman (or any other individual member of the species) has created her own human nature by an individually willed act of consciousness, nor for that matter been able to guarantee her own human rights. An individual woman and the unique individual embryonic life within her can only exist because of their participation in the genetic inheritance of the human species as a whole. Biological life should never be discounted. Membership in the species, or collective human family, is the basis for human solidarity, equality, and natural human rights.

4. The moral right of women to full social equality from a prolife feminist perspective. Prolife feminists and prochoice feminists are totally agreed on the moral right of women to the full social equality so far denied them. The disagreement between them concerns the definition of the desired goal and the best means to get there. Permissive abortion laws do not bring women reproductive freedom, social equality, sexual fulfillment, or full personal development.

Pragmatic failures of a prochoice feminist position combined with a lack of moral vision are, in fact, causing disaffection among young women. Middle-aged prochoice feminists blamed the "big chill" on the general conservative backlash. But they should look rather to their own elitist acceptance of male models of sex and to the sad picture they present of women's lives. Pitting women against their own offspring is not only morally offensive, it is psychologically and politically destructive. Women will never climb to equality and social empowerment over mounds of dead fetuses, numbering now in the millions. As long as most women choose to bear children, they stand to gain from the same constellation of attitudes and institutions that will also protect the fetus in the woman's womb—and they stand to lose from the cultural assumptions that support permissive abortion. Despite temporary conflicts of interest, feminine and fetal liberation are ultimately one and the same cause.

Women's rights and liberation are pragmatically linked to fetal rights because to obtain true equality, women need (1) more social support and changes in the structure of society, and (2) increased self-confidence, self-expectations, and self-esteem. Society in general, and men in particular, have to provide women more support in rearing the next generation, or our devastating feminization of poverty will continue. But if a woman claims the right to decide by herself whether the fetus becomes a child or not, what does this do to paternal and communal responsibility? Why should men share responsibility for child support or child rearing if they cannot share in what is asserted to be the woman's sole decision? Furthermore, if explicit intentions and consciously accepted contracts are necessary for moral obligations, why should men be held responsible for what *they* do not voluntarily choose to happen? By prochoice reasoning, a man who does not want to have a child, or whose contraceptive fails, can be exempted from the responsibilities of fatherhood and child support. Traditionally, many men have been laggards in assuming parental responsibility and support for their children; ironically, ready abortion, often advocated as a response to male dereliction, legitimizes male irresponsibility and paves the way for even more male detachment and lack of commitment.

For that matter, why should the state provide a system of day care or child support, or require workplaces to accommodate women's maternity and the needs of child rearing? Permissive abortion, granted in the name of women's privacy and reproductive freedom, ratifies the view that pregnancies and children are a woman's private individual responsibility. More and more frequently, we hear some version of this old rationalization: if she refuses to get rid of it, it's her problem. A child becomes a product of the individual woman's freely chosen investment, a form of private property resulting from her own cost-benefit calculation. The larger community is relieved of moral responsibility.

With legal abortion freely available, a clear cultural message is given: conception and pregnancy are no longer serious moral matters. With abortion as an acceptable alternative, contraception is not as responsibly used; women take risks, often at the urging of male sexual partners. Repeat abortions increase, with all their psychological and medical repercussions. With more abortion there is more abortion. Behavior shapes thought as well as the other way round. One tends to justify morally what one has done; what becomes commonplace and institutionalized seems harmless. Habituation is a powerful psychological force. Psychologically it is also true that whatever is avoided becomes more threatening; in phobias it is the retreat from anxiety-producing events which reinforces future avoidance. Women begin to see themselves as too weak to cope with involuntary pregnancies. Finally, through the potency of social pressure and the force of inertia, it becomes more and more difficult, in fact almost unthinkable, *not* to use abortion to solve problem pregnancies. Abortion becomes no longer a choice but a "necessity."

But "necessity," beyond the organic failure and death of the body, is a dynamic social construction open to interpretation. The thrust of present feminist prochoice arguments can only increase the justifiable indications for "necessary" abortion; every unwanted fetal handicap becomes more and more unacceptable. Repeatedly assured that in the name of reproductive freedom, women have a right to specify which pregnancies and which children they will accept, women justify sex selection, and abort unwanted females. Female infanticide, after all, is probably as old a custom as the human species possesses. Indeed, all kinds of selection of the fit and the favored for the good of the family and the tribe have always existed. Selective extinction is no new program.

There are far better goals for feminists to pursue. Prolife feminists seek to expand and deepen the more communitarian, maternal elements of feminism—and move society from its male-dominated course. First and foremost, women have to insist upon a different, woman-centered approach to sex and reproduction. While Margaret Mead stressed the "womb envy" of males in other societies, it has been more or less repressed in our own. In our male-dominated world, what men don't do, doesn't count. Pregnancy, childbirth, and nursing have been characterized as passive, debilitating, animallike. The disease model of pregnancy and birth has been entrenched. This female disease or impairment, with its attendant "female troubles," naturally handicaps women in the "real" world of hunting, war, and the corporate fast track. Many prochoice feminists, deliberately childless, adopt the male perspective when they cite the "basic injustice that women have to bear the babies," instead of seeing the injustice in the fact that men cannot. Women's biologically unique capacity and privilege has been denied, despised, and suppressed under male domination; unfortunately, many women have fallen for the phallic fallacy.

Childbirth often appears in prochoice literature as a painful, traumatic, life-threatening experience. Yet giving birth is accurately seen as an arduous but normal exercise of life-giving power, a violent and ecstatic peak experience, which men can never know. Ironically, some prochoice men and women think and talk of pregnancy and childbirth with the same repugnance that ancient ascetics displayed toward orgasms and sexual intercourse. The similarity may not be accidental. The obstetrician Niles Newton, herself a mother, has written of the extended threefold sexuality of women, who can experience orgasm, birth, and nursing as passionate pleasure-giving experiences. All of these are involuntary processes of the female body. Only orgasm, which males share, has been glorified as an involuntary function that is nature's great gift; the involuntary feminine processes of childbirth and nursing have been seen as bondage to biology.

Fully accepting our bodies as ourselves, what should women want? I think women will only flourish when there is a feminization of sexuality, very different from the current cultural trend toward masculinizing female sexuality. Women can never have the self-confidence and self-esteem they need to achieve feminist goals in society until a more holistic, feminine model of sexuality becomes the dominant cultural ethos. To say this affirms the view that men and women differ in the domain of sexual functioning, although they are more alike than different in other personality characteristics and competencies. For those of us committed to achieving sexual equality in the culture, it may be hard to accept the fact that sexual differences make it imperative to talk of distinct male and female models of sexuality. But if one wants to change sexual roles, one has to recognize preexisting conditions. A great deal of evidence is accumulating which points to biological pressures for different male and female sexual functioning.

Males always and everywhere have been more physically aggressive and more likely to fuse sexuality with aggression and dominance. Females may be more variable in their sexuality, but since Masters and Johnson, we know that women have a greater capacity than men for repeated orgasm and a more tenuous path to arousal and orgasmic release. Most obviously, women also have a far greater sociobiological investment in the act of human reproduction. On the whole, women as compared to men possess a sexuality which is more complex, more intense, more extended in time, involving higher investment, risks, and psychosocial involvement.

Considering the differences in sexual functioning, it is not surprising that men and women in the same culture have often constructed different sexual ideals. In Western culture, since the nineteenth century at least, most women have espoused a version of sexual functioning in which sex acts are embedded within deep emotional bonds and secure long-term commitments. Within these committed "pair bonds" males assume parental obligations. In the idealized Victorian version of the Christian sexual ethic, culturally endorsed and maintained by women, the double standard was not countenanced. Men and women did not need to marry to be whole persons, but if they did engage in sexual functioning, they were to be equally chaste, faithful, responsible, loving, and parentally concerned. Many of the most influential women in the nineteenth-century women's movement preached and lived this sexual ethic, often by the side of exemplary feminist men. While the ideal has never been universally obtained, a culturally dominant demand for monogamy, self-control, and emotionally bonded and committed sex works well for women in every stage of their sexual life cycles. When love, chastity, fidelity, and commitment for better or worse are the ascendant cultural prerequisites for sexual functioning, young girls and women expect protection from rape and seduction, adult women justifiably demand male support in child rearing, and older women are more protected from abandonment as their biological attractions wane.

Of course, these feminine sexual ideals always coexisted in competition with another view. A more male-oriented model of erotic or amative sexuality endorses sexual permissiveness without long-term commitment or reproductive focus. Erotic sexuality emphasizes pleasure, play, passion, individual self-expression, and romantic games of courtship and conquest. It is assumed that a variety of partners and sexual experiences are necessary to stimulate romantic passion. This erotic model of the sexual life has often worked satisfactorily for men, both heterosexual and gay, and for certain cultural elites. But for the average woman, it is quite destructive. Women can only play the erotic game successfully when, like the "*Cosmopolitan* woman," they are young, physically attractive, economically powerful, and fulfilled enough in a career to be willing to sacrifice family life. Abortion is also required. As our society increasingly endorses this male-oriented, permissive view of sexuality, it is all too ready to give women abortion on demand. Abortion helps a woman's body be more like a man's. It has been observed that *Roe v. Wade* removed the last defense women possessed against male sexual demands.

Unfortunately, the modern feminist movement made a mistaken move at a critical juncture. Rightly rebelling against patriarchy, unequal education, restricted work opportunities, and women's downtrodden political status, feminists also rejected the nineteenth-century feminine sexual ethic. Amative, erotic, permissive sexuality (along with abortion rights) became symbolically identified with other struggles for social equality in education, work, and politics. This feminist mistake also turned off many potential recruits among women who could not deny the positive dimensions of their own traditional feminine roles, nor their allegiance to the older feminine sexual ethic of love and fidelity.

An ironic situation then arose in which many prochoice feminists preach their own double standard. In the world of work and career, women are urged to grow up, to display mature self-discipline and self-control; they are told to persevere in long-term commitments, to cope with unexpected obstacles by learning to tough out the inevitable sufferings and setbacks entailed in life and work. But this mature ethic of commitment and self-discipline, recommended as the only way to progress in the world of work and personal achievement, is discounted in the domain of sexuality.

In prochoice feminism, a permissive, erotic view of sexuality is assumed to be the only option. Sexual intercourse with a variety of partners is seen as "inevitable" from a young age and as a positive growth experience to be managed by access to contraception and abortion. Unfortunately, the pervasive cultural conviction that adolescents, or their elders, cannot exercise sexual self-control undermines the responsible use of contraception. When a pregnancy occurs, the first abortion is viewed in some prochoice circles as a *rite de passage.* Responsibly choosing an abortion supposedly ensures that a young woman will take charge of her own life, make her own decisions, and carefully practice contraception. But the social dynamics of a permissive, erotic model of sexuality, coupled with permissive laws, work toward repeat abortions. Instead of being empowered by their abortion choices, young women having abortions are confronting the debilitating reality of *not* bringing a baby into the world; *not* being able to count on a committed male partner; *not* accounting oneself strong enough, or the master of enough resources, to avoid killing the fetus. Young women are hardly going to develop the self-esteem, self-discipline, and self-confidence necessary to confront a male-dominated society through abortion.

The male-oriented sexual orientation has been harmful to women and children. It has helped bring us epidemics of venereal disease, infertility, pornography, sexual abuse, adolescent pregnancy, divorce, displaced older women, and abortion. Will these signals of something amiss stimulate prochoice feminists to rethink what kind of sex ideal really serves women's best interests? While the erotic model cannot encompass commitment, the committed model can—happily—encompass and encourage romance, passion, and playfulness. In fact, within the security of long-term commitments, women may be more likely to experience sexual pleasure and fulfillment.

The prolife feminist position is not a return to the old feminine mystique. That espousal of "the eternal feminine" erred by viewing sexuality as so sacred that it cannot be humanly shaped at all. Women's *whole* nature was supposed to be opposite to man's, necessitating complementary and radically different social roles. Followed to its logical conclusion, such a view presumes that reproductive and sexual experience is necessary for human fulfillment. But as the early feminists insisted, no woman has to marry or engage in sexual intercourse to be fulfilled, nor does a woman have to give birth and raise children to be complete, nor must she stay home and function as an earth mother. But female sexuality does need to be deeply respected as a unique potential and trust. Since most contraceptives and sterilization procedures really do involve only the woman's body rather than destroying new life, they can be an acceptable and responsible moral option.

With sterilization available to accelerate the inevitable natural ending of fertility and childbearing, a woman confronts only a limited number of years in which she exercises her reproductive trust and may have to respond to an unplanned pregnancy. Responsible use of contraception can lower the probabilities even more. Yet abortion is not decreasing. The reason is the current permissive attitude embodied in the law, not the "hard cases" which constitute 3 percent of today's abortions. Since attitudes, the law, and behavior interact, prolife feminists conclude that unless there is an enforced limitation of abortion, which currently confirms the sexual and social status quo, alternatives will never be developed. For women to get what they need in order to combine childbearing, education, and careers, society has to recognize that female bodies come with wombs. Women and their reproductive power, and the children women have, must be supported in new ways. Another and different round of feminist consciousness raising is needed in which all of women's potential is accorded respect. This time, instead of humbly buying entrée by conforming to male lifestyles, women will demand that society accommodate itself to them.

New feminist efforts to rethink the meaning of sexuality, femininity, and reproduction are all the more vital as new techniques for artificial reproduction, surrogate motherhood, and the like present a whole new set of dilemmas. In the long run, the very long run, the abortion debate may be merely the opening round in a series of far-reaching struggles over the role of human sexuality and the ethics of reproduction. Significant changes in the culture, both positive and negative in outcome, may begin as local storms of controversy. We may be at one of those vaguely realized thresholds when we had best come to full attention. What kind of people are we going to be? Prolife feminists pursue a vision for their sisters, daughters, and granddaughters. Will their great-granddaughters be grateful?

19. Abortion and Organ Donation: Christian Reflections on Bodily Life Support

Patricia Beattie Jung

This chapter first appeared in *Abortion and Catholicism: The American Debate* in 1988.

In this essay I intend to explore two interrelated topics: first, I will delimit the responsibility to give bodily life support; second, I will analyze Christian justifications for both the giving and refusing of bodily life support. Both of these topics have been neglected in much of the literature dealing with bodily life support. Many, including most recently the Iowa State Supreme Court, have asserted that such a gift cannot be legally required and therefore its giving ought not be coerced.[1] But few have defended that assertion, beyond claiming as the courts have that compulsory bodily life support would violate an individual's right to privacy. However, one may ask: why is this particular invasion of privacy intolerable, whereas others are legally sanctioned, if not enjoined?[2]

In her book *Abortion and the Roman Catholic Church,* Susan T. Nicholson argues that the teachings of the Roman Catholic Church on bodily life support are inconsistent. Abortion following rape is forbidden, while the responsibility to offer other forms of bodily life support, she thinks, is quite limited. She quotes Gerald F. Kelly in this regard: "One must help a needy neighbor only when it can be done *without proportionate inconvenience* and with a reasonable assurance of success" (1951:553–54) (emphasis hers). Obviously, Nicholson believes that the rape victim has no special parental responsibilities toward the fetus, and is only a neighbor to it. She concludes, with only passing attention to what she calls the "special nature of bodily life support," that the Roman Catholic proscription of abortion following rape is wrong.

There are a number of difficulties with her argument. First, it is not at all clear that rape victims have no parental responsibilities (this is discussed in more detail in note 7). However, the charge of inconsistency still stands of course because the Roman Catholic Church (and common law) has never demanded of parents that they offer other forms of bodily life support to their children except under the circumstances detailed by Kelly. The law has never mandated organ donation by parents to children even when Kelly's conditions are fulfilled.

Second, it is not clear that Kelly's statement of the principle of beneficence is all that limited. It is not evident that in all *imaginable* cases of problem pregnancies the "inconvenience" of the pregnancy would be out of proportion with the good that could predictably ensue from a decision to sustain the life support. Indeed, one could imagine a utopian situation of optimal medical, financial, and emotional support where it would be clearly disproportional to abort on the basis of a cost-benefit analysis. Beverly Wildung Harrison, in her book *Our Right to Choose,* recognizes this as a logical (though not at present a historical) possibility.

> In such a utopian world, where women's lives were really valued (a world, let us insist, quite unlike the one we know!), it probably would be possible to adhere to an ethic which affirmed that abortions should be resorted to only *in extremis,* to save a mother's life. (1983:18).

The same argument could be developed in regard to other forms of bodily life support, including bone marrow and organ donations, etc. In this essay, however I will argue that bodily life support cannot be morally required of persons. It is my contention that no person can demand access to another person's body—to their blood, for example—and that abortion, along with other refusals to give bodily life support, ought not be forbidden.

Second, let us assume for the sake of argument that traditional Roman Catholic teachings as epitomized in Kelly's maxim are indeed quite limited and hence contradict the Roman Catholic prohibition of abortion following rape. Why conclude that the injunction against abortion should be dropped? Indeed, perhaps the moral error in the tradition lies on the other side of the polarity, in its minimalism. Why not argue that persons are absolutely required to give assistance to others, including all forms of bodily life support? Nicholson did not demonstrate, but instead merely asserted, that the gift ethos which currently informs transplantations is ethically fitting or appropriate. I intend to *demonstrate* that there are good reasons for interpreting *both* organ donation and childbearing as gift relations.

In this essay, I will articulate some of the reasons why a Christian ought to initiate and/or sustain the giving of bodily life support; I will also examine the feminist suspicion of the gift ethos. While the giving of bodily life support has traditionally been exhorted and almost always respected and admired, its intelligibility and meaningfulness for Christian feminists is problematic. In light of their deconstruction of traditional rationales for such sacrificial giving, I will describe in the final section of this essay what the gift of bodily life support and its refusal might mean. This will be discussed in terms of both childbearing and organ donation.

Reframing the Activity: A Defense of the Analogy

First, it is necessary to define bodily life support. By this term, I mean to designate any form of assistance that entails an invasion of the giver's body to sustain another's life. This activity arises with particular frequency in two biomedical contexts: obstetrics and transplantation. Indeed, it is my contention that childbearing and various kinds of live organ donation are morally analogous activities.[3]

Donations from living persons, whether of (1) a renewable part of the body, such as skin, blood, and bone marrow, (2) a paired organ, such as an eye or a kidney, or (3) (for the sake of argument) unpaired vital organs, such as the heart or liver, are forms of bodily life support. Similarly, pregnancy is a form of bodily life support. An optimal pregnancy involves the massive (though temporary) physical modification and the minor (permanent) bodily transformation of the mother—all for the sake of and in support of fetal life. At worst it may involve mutilation (caesarean section or hysterectomy) done solely for the benefit of the fetus, though at present such procedures frequently benefit both mother and child. Pregnancy, like organ donation, is a form of bodily life support that can gravely threaten the life of the donor.

When women's experience of pregnancy is taken seriously, the invasive element in the experience is quite prominent in the reframing of the activity. In an essay aptly entitled "The Moral Implications of Regarding Women as People: New Perspectives on Pregnancy and Personhood," Caroline Whitbeck makes the following claim:

> Possession and inspiration provide the closest analogy to the ultimately unique experience of pregnancy. The difference in the experience of a wanted pregnancy and that of an unwanted pregnancy is as different as the two experiences of inspiration and possession. (Perhaps all or most experiences of inspiration have some element of possession in them and vice versa, and similarly with wanted and unwanted pregnancies.) (1983:264)

One obvious strength of my proposed analogy is that it takes seriously not only women's life-supporting role *in* pregnancy, but also their experience *of* it.

Analogies in moral argument are usually not proposed without a purpose. My intent in highlighting the similarities between these various activities is to allow the moral tradition behind organ donation to inform the arguments about abortion, and *vice versa*. The ethos that pervades the medical literature dealing with organ and tissue transplants is that of gift giving.[4] Indeed the gift metaphor so pervades the discussion of informed consent in such matters that motives of duty or guilt are judged suspect because, it is argued, they reflect the donor's misunderstanding of the discretionary nature of the act or a less than voluntary "consent" to it. The ethos that pervades the medical and traditional Christian literature dealing with abortion is that of the duty of nonmaleficence, and the legitimate violations thereof.

By drawing an analogy between these forms of bodily life support,[5] I hope to increase our understanding of both the limits of and the reasons for the responsibility one person may have to give bodily life support to another. If a moral analogy between childbearing and organ donation can be established, then perhaps it will yield clues as to why abortion ought not be prohibited. Perhaps it will also yield clues as to why the giving of bodily life support through either organ donation or childbearing ought to be encouraged. It should, in addition, be noted that the analogy will enable this argument to be developed in a context free of sexist biases. As a feminist, I believe it is altogether appropriate to apply a "hermeneutics of suspicion" to the moral tradition surrounding the current abortion debate. Upon comparison, it is hard to miss the disparity between what "conservatives" have demanded of women who are pregnant and what those same persons view as obligatory in regards to other forms of bodily life support, which not incidentally can be offered by men.[6]

It is also the case that most moral analogies are not self-evident. Given the controversial implications of this analogy, a defense of it is clearly in order. One may object to the claim that these activities are morally analogous on at least the following five grounds. With the exceptions of the second and final objections, each criticism of the proposed analogy can be interpreted as an argument for the claim that there is a *stricter* responsibility to bear children than to donate organs, and that while the former is a duty, the latter is supererogatory.

1. First, it can be argued that it is not possible to compare organ donation with pregnancy because by definition pregnancy entails *special* (parental) obligations not necessarily entailed in organ transplants. The analogy (so the objection goes) obscures a distinctive feature of pregnancy that is morally significant, if not decisive, insofar as this *special* obligation creates a *stricter* obligation to sustain a pregnancy than to donate organs. One could argue, as Nicholson has, that since a rape victim does not participate voluntarily in the sexual act that produces fetal life, she has no *parental* obligation to the fetus, and therefore "the moral problem of abortion following rape" ought to be "conceptualized as that of

the bodily life support *one human being owes another*" (1978:80) (emphasis mine). This rebuttal, however, does not withstand careful scrutiny.[7]

In cases of transplants or pregnancy, contractual responsibilities can come into play and donors may have various degrees of parental and other special obligations. The point is, however, that critics of this analogy assume that parental duties require one to give bodily life support. Yet, what strikes them as obvious in regard to pregnancy and motherhood is somehow obscured when they consider what ought to be required of histocompatible donor fathers (and mothers). Consistency requires that childbearing and paternal (parental) organ donation *both* be viewed as either obligatory or discretionary.

2. It may also be objected that fetal life is not morally convertible with other forms of human life.[8] This is indeed a hotly debated equation. However, it is not my intention to defend this key assumption, but to adopt it for the sake of the argument that follows. Therefore, this essay is addressed to three different audiences: (1) those who hold this assumption about fetal life to be true; (2) those who wish to examine this issue exclusively as it relates to organ donations (and hence will ignore portions of this argument); and (3) those who wish to explore the moral ramifications of this reconceptualization of pregnancy, even though they don't hold this presumption about fetal life. I hope to make it evident that, while the status of fetal life is clearly an important question, it is not *the* decisive issue in the abortion debate, even from within the most conservative framework. Much can be gained by exploring other frequently overlooked issues which profoundly affect bodily life support.

3. A third objection to this analogy can be made on the basis of the so-called passive-active distinction. In the case of transplants, bodily life support involves the question of our responsibility to *give* and our right to *withhold* support. However, in the case of pregnancy, bodily life support is a "given" (except perhaps in cases involving surrogate motherhood or the use of the "morning after" pill) and the central issue is the question of the *withdrawal* of bodily life support. Refusal in the former case is a passive instance of "allowing to die," whereas in the latter it is an active instance of

"killing." Within the framework of this objection, the duty not to kill is viewed as stricter than the responsibility to save and so the responsibility to continue pregnancy is stricter than the responsibility to supply organs.

In responding to this objection, I must begin by explaining that throughout this essay I will assume that abortion implies primarily the severing of the host or donative relation. It does not necessarily imply either the death or killing of the fetus.[9] It is of course true that at present the withdrawal of maternal support early (before the twenty-week mark) in the gestation process invariably results in fetal death. It is also true that some abortion techniques (the D & C/aspiration and the saline-injection methods, for example) kill the fetus. Thus, as it is commonly practiced, abortion also implies killing the fetus, though sometimes "only" allowing it to die.

Proponents of this objection recognize that not all imaginable instances of "allowing to die" are justifiable. Likewise, they recognize that not all imaginable instances of "killing" are unjustifiable. They claim, however, that, all other morally relevant factors being equal, one must have more reason to kill than to decline to save primarily because, it is argued, such a practice would erode the trust essential to the health-care partnership. (Interestingly, in other contexts of death and dying, the duty not to withhold life support is generally viewed as stricter than the obligation not to withdraw life support because of the time required for diagnostic and prognostic judgments). At any rate, the validity of this premise is the topic of much debate among many ethicists both within and without the biomedical context. Once again for the sake of argument, let us take up the most conservative perspective and assume that this premise is true. What would its implications be for the topics under consideration?

It would follow that allowing a person to die, say, of renal failure by refusing to donate a kidney takes less justification than killing the potential recipient, all other morally relevant factors being equal. Similarly, it would follow that abortion techniques which merely terminate the host relation, even though they might invariably result in fetal death, would be preferable to those methods that entail the killing of the fetus, all other morally relevant factors being equal. On the basis of these implications proponents of this objection conclude that since abortion frequently implies killing the fetus, it requires more justification than the refusal to donate organs. Indeed, they frequently jump to the further conclusion that pregnancy can therefore be required, but organ donation is discretionary.

My response is twofold. First, as I understand current abortion practices, the methods employed to terminate pregnancy vary because as a matter of fact all other morally relevant factors are not equal—specifically, the techniques which best ensure maternal well-being can vary considerably at different stages in the gestation process. Second, it does not necessarily follow that pregnancy can be mandated. It may simply be the case that organ donation is more discretionary than childbearing.

4. Fourth, this analogy may be objected to on the grounds that the physical relationship of pregnancy is natural and normal, whereas the nurturance and dependency associated with organ donation is pathological or biologically nonnormative. Both are instances of "giving life," which is good. However, Lisa Sowle Cahill suggests that, "all other things being equal," pregnancy constitutes an *intrinsic* good to be preserved, whereas the donative relation is to be avoided when possible. Childbearing is a premoral good toward which human communities are naturally inclined. Thus she concludes a more serious or weightier set of reasons is necessary "to justify the destruction of such a 'positive' relation of dependency (physical or otherwise)" than of an intrinsically "negative" one (1981:14).

This is a formidable objection to the proposed analogy, particularly since Cahill is careful not to interpret this argument as supportive of an absolute prescription for procreation. Indeed, she suggests that contemporary moral theology is right in its efforts to avoid the dangers of physicalism. However, totally ignoring the moral significance of corporeality is equally problematic for her. Hence, the analogy I propose obscures according to Cahill the nonpathological character of the bodily life support constitutive of pregnancy.

It is certainly true that the gestation process is normal, in that the fetal need for dependency is neither caused by a disease nor does it originate from some sort of trauma.[10] Furthermore, one would be foolish to argue with Cahill when she suggests that the donative relationship, unlike pregnancy, ought to be avoided when possible through the prevention and/or curing of various diseases and injuries. Indeed I will even grant that pregnancy constitutes an *intrinsic* good to be preserved. Consequently, because there is *some* kind of responsibility to maintain all intrinsically good states of affairs, there is *some* kind of responsibility to continue pregnancy in every case and this is not true in regard to organ donation.

However, Cahill jumps from these premises to the conclusion that childbearing (unlike organ donation) is a *prima facie* duty or obligation mandated by the natural requirements of justice. I reject her conclusion for the following two reasons. First, neither childbearing (unlike child rearing) nor organ donation are responsibilities which can be equitably distributed among all members of the human community. Second, they are both *bodily* forms of life support. Therefore they are highly discretionary gifts, and ought to be encouraged but not required.

In summary, Cahill's argument reveals a significant point of disanalogy. However, this difference is only relevant to an evaluation of these activities insofar as they ought to be enjoined. One cannot conclude, as does Cahill, that this difference renders one activity (pregnancy) obligatory, while the other is merely supererogatory. The reframing I propose reveals that *neither* form of bodily life support can be legitimately required.

5. Finally, some feminists might object to the proposed analogy on the grounds that childbearing (unlike organ donation) is an activity that only women can do. Furthermore, they argue, it is a responsibility shouldered at present in a world which is largely hostile to both women and children. Thus, they argue, the responsibility to donate organs is stricter than that which can be ascribed to childbearing, all other factors being equal.

Clearly, because of its requirements for histocompatibility, the responsibility for most types of organ donation cannot be equally allocated. Nevertheless, this natural lottery is not influenced by gender factors, which are of particular significance given the reality of most women's lives within patriarchy. Here again we are confronted with a formidable objection. This is clearly a morally significant point of disanalogy. However, I believe it is relevant only to a comparison of pregnancy and organ donation as acts of supererogation. Because both forms of life support are (1) bodily and (2) incapable of equal allocation, *neither* can be viewed as a duty or obligation. It is this insight which I believe the proposed analogy makes clear, and which I will defend at length later in this essay.

In summary, despite notable differences these activities—organ donation and pregnancy—are morally analogous in significant ways. I intend to argue that the moral traditions behind these instances of bodily life support will fruitfully illumine one another. Indeed it is my contention that this mutual reframing of the activities will yield insights crucial to the development of cogent arguments regarding both the grounds for and the limits of our responsibilities to give bodily life support. Before proceeding to these tasks, it is necessary to clarify what it means to say an activity ought to be done if it is not thereby morally required.

Reframing the Notion of Ought

In his pamphlet *Supererogation: An Analysis and a Bibliography,* Willard Schumaker suggests that there is more to morality than what is minimally required of us.

> Supererogation is possible because while we always have a right to our fair share of benefits and can always rightly be forced to accept our fair share of burdens, it is sometimes morally preferable for us to take less than our fair share of the benefits of our common life or to voluntarily accept more than our fair share of burdens; and whenever we do so for altruistic reasons, we are acting supererogatorily. (1977:33)

For example, simply because it is morally permissible in some situations not to forgive does not mean that one ought not forgive or that such praiseworthy forgiveness is of only marginal significance to moral life.

As Schumaker points out, Kant is correct in his claim that if persons were just, then there would be no dire need for charity. However, it is equally true and significant that as a matter of fact persons are not always just (1977:42). Indeed, Kant's program, even when interpreted as entailing a form of moral community, establishes only those principles and rules necessary for a barely human social existence. There is no need, I would argue, for either philosophical or theological ethicists to restrict themselves to such a truncated conception of their reflective tasks. There is a need, even if not a Hobbesian one, to establish the necessary conditions of morality. It is an appropriate and important task. However, the content of the moral life is not exhausted by such work.

Since it is my aim in this essay to explore some of the reasons why Christians ought and ought not to offer the gift of bodily life support, I must sketch something of the framework through which I interpret and evaluate this activity. Thus, this essay will be explicitly both theological and political. It will criticize a modern liberal theory of community in light of an explicitly Christian vision.[11] In summary, there are at least two broad levels of responsibility. First, there are those "oughts" which are requisite for a barely human social existence. These minimal obligations are duties, the fulfillment of which is appropriately required by all moral communities. Second, these are those "oughts" which stem from other visions of communal life which exceed or go beyond that of a barely human existence. The "oughts" are best thought of as self-imposed—and in that sense, discretionary—responsibilities which stem from an agent's commitment to a particular vision of life. They are imposed by the self's desire to be in its fullness a certain kind of person and to create a certain kind of community.

It is my intention in this essay to examine the limits of and grounds for the responsibility to give bodily life support. In the next section of this essay, I will analyze what it is about this kind of *gift*—this gift of one's *bodily* self, as distinguished from a gift of one's property—that makes it a choice to be encouraged and commended but not required by either church discipline or civil law. In the final part of the essay, I will explore why, in light of the Christian vision of life, a believer "ought" or "ought not" to give bodily life support.

Bodily Life Support Should Not Be Required by Canon or Civil Law

All human beings have an obligation or duty to give some minimal degree of assistance to others in life-threatening situations. Conversely, by virtue of a person's humanity, he or she may lay claim to or have a moral right to minimal assistance from others in perpetuating his or her own life. This thesis is put forward in order to distinguish my position from others. It is at least intelligible (though I believe erroneous) to delimit the responsibility to give bodily life support by attempting to demonstrate that there is no general positive duty to give assistance to others and hence no specific duty to offer bodily life support.[12] I intend to clarify the "special nature" of bodily life support by explaining its immunity from what I regard as the legitimate general requirements of both social justice and beneficence.

Minimal Assistance Ought To Be Required by Law

The obligation to assist others has roots in both justice and beneficence. The obligation to give assistance to another can be derived from two very different conceptions of justice. On the other hand, it can spring from a reciprocal theory of justice. Minimal assistance is required because all persons have received and continued to expect to receive such "mutual aid" from others. On the other hand, it can be argued that there are certain primary goods—like self-preservation, health maintenance, and procreation—toward which human communities are naturally inclined, and therefore justice requires *prima facie* that all persons pursue these communal goods.

Each theory, albeit a very different manner, helps illumine the moral intuition that a starving "thief" can have a right to or can legitimately claim the "stolen" bread. To the degree that an agent is responsible for his or her neighbor's "need"—that is, has profited in some fashion from the exploitation which produced and sustains it—to that same degree, he or she is required by justice to go beyond this minimal level of assistance. In some cases then, the starving "thief" may be said to have a right to this "donor's" bread.

However, no single donor can be justly required to carry a genuinely communal burden. It is not always the case that *this* starving thief has a right to *this* donor's bread. For these reasons the tradition has rooted the general obligation to give assistance in beneficence as well as justice. Charity is possible for three reasons: (1) not all persons carry their fair share of social burdens; (2) some communal responsibilities cannot be fairly distributed, but rather fall by virtue of the natural and/or historical lottery on the shoulders of single individuals or institutions; (3) persons can voluntarily give up their fair share of social benefits.

What has all this to do with bodily life support, specifically with childbearing and organ donation? First, it establishes that non-bodily life support can be required by the demands of justice of both individuals and communities. However, it also establishes that such life support can sometimes be at least in part a matter of charity. Why? Because for a variety of reasons, single individuals are asked to shoulder a burden, the responsibility for which is not theirs alone. It is important to understand that *both* organ donation and childbearing are always in part (if not largely) acts of charity.

This has been clearly recognized in regard to organ donation and is expressed well in the gift ethos which illumines that activity. Even though in theory the responsibility for some types of organ donation (for example, blood) could be fairly distributed, in fact many people cannot (say, for health reasons) or do not carry their fair share of this communal burden. Thus most blood donors give more than might be theoretically required of them by justice. Indeed many give who will never use their fair share of the communal blood supply. The beneficent character of organ donation is vividly dramatized when the requirements for histocompatibility become more complex, as in bone-marrow transplants. In such a case a donor is asked to carry alone a burden for which their responsibility (as that, say, of a distant cousin) may be minuscule.

Likewise, childbearing is always in part (if not largely) an act of charity. This however has not been widely understood nor is it reflected in the traditional ethos surrounding abortion. The life support of children is a *joint* parental responsibility as well as a communal one. Yet during the gestation period this burden cannot be equitably distributed even in theory. Mothers alone carry children to term. The fact that *every* pregnant woman carries far more than her fair share of this responsibility is simply and vividly dramatized when pregnancy results from rape or the failure of contraceptive measures, and when it threatens the mother's life or is accompanied by total paternal or social abandonment.

However, simply because both organ donation and childbearing are acts (at least in part) of charity does not automatically mean they ought not be required. Because justice cannot always enjoin this "donor" to give his or her loaf of bread to the starving "thief" does not mean that such a gift is purely discretionary. As David Little points out in "Moral Discretion and the Universalizability Thesis," beneficence can give rise to obligations. The robust passerby can be blamed if he or she fails to save the drowning child by rolling him or her out of the puddle. The donor can be blamed for failing to feed the starving thief, even if the thief has no right to this donor's bread. Thus I must show what is it about the gift of a womb or other bodily organ that makes it discretionary? Why should *bodily* life support not be required?

Bodily Life Support Is a Gift

In struggling to identify the logic of beneficent acts, Little identifies some of the criteria for determining the extent to which assistance is discretionary. In my opinion one factor influencing the determination of the discretionary quality of a beneficent act is the extent to which the "gift" in question is truly a gift. Some gifts are more genuinely gifts than others. Compare a gift of money to the gift of a friendship. The latter is more truly a gift, and thus more discretionary (other relevant factors being equal), because friendship belongs more to and is more expressive of the giver than is money.

The giving of bread to the starving thief is only minimally discretionary because the bread belongs to the donor only in a minimal way. Even if one assumes on a penultimate level, as did Thomas Aquinas, that the notion of private property best serves communal needs and responsibilities vis-à-vis the goods of the earth, it does not follow that one can ultimately possess or own wealth or property. One is finally only a steward over such goods. The saving of the drowning child is more discretionary than the giving of the bread because an agent's actions, labor, skills, etc., belong more to him or her—are more personal—than property. Hence, they are more of a gift. (In the *particular* case cited by Little, the rescue is still required because the costs and risks of the saving activity are so minimal. Even though the "gift" is more purely a gift, its giving remains obligatory.)

What is the extent of the discretionary nature of bodily life support? Can it ever be said that a needy "thief" has a right to this "donor's" blood, bone marrow, or womb? What kind of gift is this? Is the giving of such assistance through organ donation or pregnancy ever obligatory? If persons have a general obligation to assist others based on the demands of both justice and beneficence, may this not include bodily forms of life support? If not, why not? Persons do not have a duty to give bodily life support to others. Nobody, simply as a human being in need, has a claim to the use of another's body. Charles Fried, in his discussion of "bodily integrity" as a negative right in his book *Right and Wrong,* offers a fruitful explanation of the "special nature" of bodily life support. While he admits that agents have a general obligation to assist minimally persons in urgent need, this moral requirement does not include bodily life support. So, for example, blood donations are in his judgment purely "discretionary" options. This is so because when the demands of justice or beneficence conflict with those of autonomy, the latter generally take precedence over the former. (There are, of course, exceptions for Fried. Some demands of justice—for example, the duty to contribute a fair share—override some conceivable preferences.) However, bodily integrity for Fried is essential to "the sense of possession of oneself" and hence an agent cannot use another person's body against his or her will without violating the more primary obligation to respect that person as a person (1978:154).

This is quite correct. In accord with James M. Gustafson, I would argue that "man's 'sovereignty over himself', to use Kierkegaard's phrase, is fundamental to any serious moral view of life" (1968:112). Bodily integrity is viewed descriptively as a foundation of agency or condition necessary for human action. In Alan Donagan's *The Theory of Morality* (1979), such a condition becomes the basis for a normative judgment. In order for a person to act morally, his or her bodily integrity must be respected by others. (Indeed, we do not hold persons accountable for choices made under undue duress or coercion.) Therefore the agent must respect these same features of agency in others.[13]

But why draw the line at *bodily* life support? Why not view an agent's body regardless of gender as one of life's goods (like food, property, etc.) which can like other objects be possessed, exchanged, confiscated, and/or rightly claimed by another? Why is bodily integrity a condition necessary for agency? Bodily life support cannot be required precisely because the human body is not like the other goods of creation which an agent can objectify without distortion. The body is not like other possessions. One does not have a body—one is embodied.

Granted, there are many lived experiences of the body which tempt persons to objectify the body, and stoically to treat it like a stranger. For example, agents are often affectively besieged by their physical needs and must occasionally fight them off, as if they were foreign invaders. Or again, several medical techniques have at their foundation an analogy between the body and a machine in need of upkeep or repair. According to Paul Ricoeur, "here lies the temptation of naturalism, the invitation to deprive the experience of the body of its personal traits and to treat it as any other object" (1966:87).

If so much our experience of the body tempts us to treat it like an object, then why not accept the invitation? Why view such an invitation as treasonous? Primarily it is because such objectifications break down, according to Ricoeur. Upon close inspection they do not fit our *personal* experience of the body, *le corp propre.* "I do not know need from the outside, as a natural event, but from within as a lived need. . . ." (1966:87). In *Freedom and Nature,* Ricoeur adopts Gabriel Marcel's basic intuition about the ultimate unity of the subject and object. This is for Ricoeur the real meaning and mystery of incarnation. This primordial link, "this inherence of a personal body in the Cognito" (1966:88), is most evident when the experience of embodiment is analyzed on the *prereflective* level. In his philosophy of the will, Ricoeur uses the phenomenological method to unravel Marcel's enigmatic insight and to elaborate systematically the meaning of incarnate agency. In his analysis this elusive unifying link between consciousness and body which is incarnation is disclosed to be "already functioning" prior to reflection at the core of the decision-making process.

For example, Ricoeur analyzes muscular effort, a typical experience of the body as object. By attending to the prereflective level of this experience, he is able to demonstrate that the body can be experienced not only as recalcitrantly alien but also, and primarily, as an available servant to the will. The prereflective experience of bodily docility is difficult to capture because it shrinks away from attention. However, as Ricoeur notes, "only willing which is already effectively deployed can encounter limitations. External resistance presupposes the docility of the body" (1966:310).

Persons do not have a right to or a claim upon parts or the use of another's body because living bodies are primordially personal. All objectifications of the body are abstractions from this lived unity. Therefore, while the needy "thief" may have a just right to another's property or wealth, such claims may not be extended to another's body without direct violation of the obligation to respect persons as persons. While beneficence may impose upon all agents a requirement to give certain kinds of "gifts"—gifts which are only marginally gifts—it can never require of agents so pure and personal a gift as the gift of one's body. This is a claim for the most part accepted but inconsistently applied by traditional bioethicists.

For example, in their now famous debates about experiments on children, *both* Paul Ramsey and Richard A. McCormick (albeit to a lesser extent) recognize the moral significance of this axiom. For Ramsey, it grounds his absolute prohibition of any nontherapeutic experiments on children. For McCormick, it grounds his prohibition of any nontherapeutic experiments on children which (1) are more than minimally invasive, or (2) carry any significant risk. Even for McCormick, *only* routine weighings and blood workups can be tolerated. Both men (although again to varying degrees) recognize the moral significance of bodily integrity when analyzing the ethics of organ donation. However, neither Ramsey nor McCormick (like many moral theologians) recognize as significant the claim to bodily integrity made by women in regard to their reproductive capacity in general, and both tend to deny its significance in the abortion debate.

In a recent essay entitled "Abortion and the Sexual Agenda: A Case for Pro-Life Feminism," Sidney Callahan reinforces this position. Therein she notes that no one ought to "be forced to donate an organ or submit to other invasive physical procedures for however good a cause" (1986a:232). But this right to bodily integrity does not apply to childbearing, according to Callahan, because when pregnant "one's own body no longer exists as a single unit but is engendering another organism's life" (1986a:234). I would concur with Callahan when she claims that a woman's right to control her own body does apply to self-regarding choices about mastectomies, contraception, and sterilization, and I have taken as axiomatic her premise that the fetus is not like a cancerous tumor or subhuman parasite. Further, I agree that childbearing is clearly an other-regarding activity and that this other can be intelligibly regarded as a person, whose very life is dependent upon maternal bodily support. Yet isn't such also the nature of organ donation: that is, isn't the "good cause" the preservation of another person's life? It strikes me as blatantly inconsistent to grant potential donors the right to refuse to participate in transplant procedures, yet view childbearing as required.

The analogy I have proposed illumines the fact that a woman denied access to either birth control or abortion is forced into childbearing—a highly invasive experience with significant risks—against her will. Ramsey, McCormick, and Callahan would never tolerate such abuse of either children or reluctant organ donors.[14] Were they consistent, they would not be able to tolerate this abuse of pregnant women. As it stands, they contribute to and endorse that long tradition which regards women's bodies as objects to be controlled by others, if not by their fathers or husbands, then by the state.

Like McCormick, I believe agents ought to give minimal bodily assistance even to strangers. Indeed, in the concluding portion of this essay I will outline some of the distinctively Christian reasons for such gift giving. However, McCormick errs when he argues this can be *required* of agents by the demands of justice. He moves in this direction in order to emphasize (in contrast to Ramsey and others) the essentially communal nature of justice. Corporate obligations are constitutive of the moral life. He is correct when he argues that persons are not properly construed as autonomous, if that translates into an atomistic form of individualism. It is counterintuitive to deny that there are certain communal goods—including health maintenance and disease control—toward which human communities are inclined and that agents are required to pursue these goals.

While I am most sympathetic with McCormick's emphasis on the communal character of persons and with his wariness of the current surge of liberal interest in "autonomy," I believe he is mistaken in his attempt to link the responsibility to give *bodily* life support with the requirements of justice. The communal character of human agency can be accurately portrayed only when it is recognized that persons are not parts of but rather "wholes within a whole" (Ramsey, 1970).

One final comment about bodily integrity seems in order. Many prolifers, especially Roman Catholic, view antiabortion legislation as analogous to antislavery and feminist "equal rights" legislation. From within this perspective the antiabortionist, abolitionist, and feminist are all viewed as seeking legal recognition of and protection for groups whose full humanity has not been generally respected. Sidney Callahan, in a joint interview with her husband on their book *Abortion: Understanding Differences,* represents this perspective well.

> Just as women and blacks were considered too different, too undeveloped, too biological to have souls or rights as persons, so the fetus is now seen as mere biological life. (1986b:4)

Women who "want" abortions are viewed, like slaveowners and slave dealers, as coerced into forfeiting their "rights" by prolife legislation.

But are these really analogous types of legislation? The alleged conflict of rights in the national debate over slavery appears in retrospect to be obviously bogus, once slaves are recognized as persons and not merely property. At most, there was conflict between human rights and individual (as well as regional) financial interests. However, as my argument displays, even when fetuses are recognized as persons, an authentic conflict of rights can remain. The right jeopardized by antiabortion legislation is not the right to dispose of fetal "property" as one sees fit, but rather the right to have control over one's own body. This basic right to bodily integrity can and sometimes does stand in direct conflict with the other's basic right to life.[15]

None of the ethicists who, like McCormick, would argue that some measure of bodily life support via participation in routine studies can be required of persons contend *on the grounds of justice* that organ transplants can be required or that abortion following rape can be prohibited. This would demand that a single individual carry an unjust share of the social burden. While the rape victim as a member of society shares partial responsibility for this fetal life (in addition to her portion of parental responsibility), it is blatantly unfair to ask her to carry the full burden of life support. I would only reiterate here that this is true (though to a lesser degree) of *every* pregnant woman.

In summary, one may wish to argue that beneficence may legitimately require of all persons the giving of certain kinds of "gifts"—particularly of objectifiable possessions. Nevertheless, the more personal the gift, the more "gifty" and discretionary it becomes. I can think of no more personal and intimate type of gift than the gift of one's bodily self—whether given sexually, in pregnancy, through various forms of organ donation, or as sacrificed for another. The more a gift belongs to, indeed *is,* another, the more truly it is a gift. In his discussion of *Sacraments as God's Self-Giving,* James F. White meditates at length on the nature of gift giving:

> When we give a gift we do not ordinarily say, "This is my body," or "This is me," but this is what we mean. And the receiver understands the gift this way, and not merely as an anonymous object. (1983:20)

One can only give in the purest sense of gift giving what one is. Thus, communal responsibility ought not be conceptualized in such a way as to distort the bodily integrity of persons. Likewise, it should not place unfair burdens on individuals. Furthermore, not even minor forms of bodily life support which theoretically could be fairly distributed (like blood donations) can be required of persons because of the special nature of embodiment.[16]

The ethos of gift giving that currently pervades the practice of organ transplantation is the only ethos appropriate to the "special nature" of *all* forms of bodily life support. This ethos should be extended to our moral understanding of both pregnancy and abortion. Health-care professionals (and, I would add, moral theologians) are appropriately described by Fox and Swazey (1978) as "keepers of the gates," that is, as agents who facilitate gift giving and who guard against the theft or confiscation of what by its very nature can only be freely given. In her discussion of the wider moral framework of abortion, Beverly Wildung Harrison in *Our Right to Choose* makes the following assertion.

> We need also to acknowledge the bodily integrity of any moral agent as a foundational condition of human well-being and dignity. Freedom from bodily invasion . . . is no minor or marginal issue morally; rather, it is central to our conception of the dignity of the person (1985:196).

My purpose in this section has been to explain and justify this axiom. The conclusion that neither pregnancy nor organ donation should be mandatory does not imply that all or even most refusals to offer bodily life support (through organ donations or childbearing) can be morally justified. Bodily integrity is a necessary but not self-evidently sufficient condition of morality.

Bodily Life Support: A Christian Feminist Assessment of Its Meanings

The overarching purpose of this section of my essay is to assess the gift ethos in light of the feminist suspicion of any moral framework that might call for the self-sacrifice of women. Though I have explained why I believe bodily life support should not be mandated for any person, I have yet to examine what it might mean for a Christian to give or refuse to give such gifts either through organ donation or childbearing.[17] Clearly *ought* in this instance does not mean *required*. Furthermore, as the proposed analogy reveals, the decision to bear a child, like that to donate organs, is a complex decision through which the gift giver attempts to serve and balance a number of competing values.

Though they may be obvious, a brief rehearsal of some of these competing responsibilities is in order insofar as it will establish the context for my analysis of self-sacrifice and its refusal. Let us begin by listing some of the factors that might enter into a decision for or against donating an organ. The donor's general physical and emotional health and life-situation, the value of and likely impact of donation upon his or her life-plan (including present as well as future career considerations and family and social-life ramifications), the extent to which the community (family, church, and townspeople) will support (both financially and emotionally) the donor and his or her dependents, the value of the recipient's life as well as the recipient's best interests (which are not in all cases *obviously* served by extending that person's life), and any special responsibilities of a contractual origin that the donor may have to either the recipient or others—*all* of these factors are normally considered relevant to a decision regarding organ donation.[18] Obviously, there is considerable room for conflict among these goods and it is not always possible to balance them. In some circumstances they may be mutually exclusive; that is, sometimes morally legitimate concerns must be sacrificed for the sake of other concerns.

Decisions regarding childbearing are analogous. *All* of the factors identified above are likewise morally relevant to a woman's decision to abort or bear a child. In her essay "A Family Perspective on Abortion," Theodora Ooms notes that when one listens carefully to women who speak about their childbearing and abortion decisions, the language of "care, responsibilities and relationships" is emphasized (1986:98). Abortion is never a "simple" choice based on a single factor, such as the value of fetal life or maternal health. Pregnancies become problematic when no way of balancing the various responsibilities outlined above can be found.

Whether terminated *or not,* these pregnancies never have morally "happy" endings. At best in such tragic circumstances, one aims to follow the least-evil course of action. As Whitbeck demonstrates women do not ever "want" abortions. Medea is a false image of women; it is the product of misogyny. Those who take women's experience seriously could never describe an abortion, whether spontaneous or induced, as "a matter of little consequence." Further, women ought not be deceived about or veiled from the developmental reality of aborted fetal lives. Paternalism, however beneficent in origin, robs women of the opportunity to face their situation and their decision truthfully, with integrity, courage, and self-respect. Within this wider understanding of the problem, let us first unravel and then critically assess the traditional claim that Christians ought to give bodily life support, even when this entails self-sacrifice.

From the Kantian "moral point of view," others are properly perceived as strangers and decisions about bodily life support are "purely personal" and "private." In contrast, within the Christian story a (nonpatriarchal) family model is the lens through which persons are perceived as morally linked to one another by obligations of mutual respect, service, and support. These are not merely "special relations" constituted by optional social contracts. These rights and obligations in regard to one another are not related merely to the performance or failure to perform certain acts. They are not subject only to voluntary control. They are also "thrust on" agents who find themselves "stuck with" needy others.

According to Hauerwas, life is out of human control, and this is not problematic for him. Nor does it trouble him that these relations may bring neither happiness nor self-fulfillment on a penultimate level to agents. That is not what the moral life is chiefly all about, given this vision. The moral life is more contingent than social-contract theorists would have us believe.

> It is the Christian belief, nurtured by the command of Jesus, that we must learn to love one another, that we become more nearly what we were meant to be through the recognition and love of those we did not "choose" to love. (1981:227)

Therefore, simply because there is no voluntary or contractual relation to the needy recipient does not mean there is no responsibility to offer bodily life support. (This does not, however, mean one cannot distinguish between varying degrees of responsibility inherent in varying forms of relationships.)

Persons find themselves linked—by virtue of blood or tissue type, or by virtue of their sexual or social nature—to other persons in need of bodily life support. These needy others are experienced as unalterable "givens" in an agent's life. Their burdensome and difficult presence is experienced as totally beyond voluntary control. It is not now, even if it might be in the future, humanly possible to reverse in all cases the process of renal failure or prevent in all cases the rape-induced or otherwise unwelcome conception (unless it is verified that this is in fact what the "morning after" pill does). These are part of the radically involuntary necessities which ground and limit human freedom. Though such givens are unalterable they need not crush human freedom because, like other brute facts of life, they are not only unalterable but also received. Agents have a choice about how they are going to respond to such burdens and difficulties. This choice informs and is informed by the dispositional stance the agent has assumed in relation to the finitude and frailty of human existence in general.

Such a faith stance is not mere intellectual assent to dogmas, but entails a commitment to see and relate to "reality" through a certain lens or canonical set of presumptions. We can only know what it means to give bodily life support to those whose need crashes into our lives within the context of a particular faith framework. For example, one can interpret and evaluate the decision of a rape victim to bear the fetus to term only in light of a particular vision of reality.

Traditional Christian Faith Presumptions

As Hauerwas notes, "the Christian respect for life is first of all a statement, not about life, but about God" (1981:226). Indeed, in the first instance it is a statement about God's ultimate sovereignty over all of life. A voluntarist commitment to or love of the potential recipient is not the necessary moral precondition for the giving of bodily life support. On the contrary, such bearing of the other is the condition for the understanding of what love is in a world where God, not humankind, is in ultimate control.

Before God humans stand in radical poverty, their life and value hang, as it were, by a providential thread. From this perspective, human existence and worth come as a gift from God. Apart from this presumption of nakedness, any human activity—including the giving of bodily life support—will become a form of idolatrous self-aggrandizement. Thus, for the Christian to offer bodily life support is to convict oneself to a life of radical poverty in a world where God is sovereign.

Implicit in such an adoption of the other is a latent valuation. It is a sign of the ultimate trustworthiness of life. It is also a symbol of hope, for the world provides little objective evidence that such confidence is justified. Presuming that life is a gracious gift from God does not entail being deceived about the frailty and faultedness of human existence. Like the presumption of a person's innocence, this belief is indefeasible. While it readily admits the existence of counterexamples (like guilty persons), they do not undermine the presumption itself. It is for Christians a faith claim made from under the shadow of the Cross. For example, it is not to assert that objectively renal failure or fetal deformations are gracious gifts. Rather it is to assert that the lives of those who suffer from such evils, despite their costly and burdensome features, remain gracious gifts. It is to consent to one's own frail and faulted life as gracious gift. It is not to seek or to yield passively to suffering, but rather to adopt it when unavoidable.

The Moral Implications of the Traditional View

Furthermore, the faithful agent is one whose particular responses to others and whose life as a whole is characterized by these presumptions. The Christian not only comes to perceive life as gracious gift but becomes a gift giver, extending favors and mercy to others. To see faithfully one's life as graced is, in a word, to live graciously. In *Sharing Possessions,* Luke T. Johnson concluded that "the mandate of faith in God is clear: we must, in some fashion, share that which has been given to us by God as a gift" (1981:108). To grasp, hoard, or hold on to the world's goods, including ourselves, is not a proper thanksgiving. As Johnson notes in his exegesis of Sirach, "it is not enough to keep from oppression and injustice; covenant with God demands that we deliver the oppressed" (1981:99). Or again, as Hauerwas points out, to believe in the parenthood of God is to learn to see others, including strangers and even enemies, as siblings. "We must be a people who stand ready to receive and care for any child, not just as if it were one of our own but because, in fact, each is one of ours" (1981:229).[19]

Thus, sharing the gift of life seems to be a consequence of accepting the cosmology of Christian faith. Monika K. Hellwig writes of this dominical calling.

> In a wide sense we are all called to be parents to one another, to bestow on others the life and blessing with which we have been blessed, that is, to bless others with the substance of our own lives. (1976:44)

This leads to at least one other kind of reason Christians may offer for such self-giving. This latter reason focuses not so much on what Christians are called to do, but rather on who they are called to be.

Christians are called to be images of God in the world. The paradigmatic example of such an image is the kenotic Christ (Phil. 2:5–8), whose outpouring is celebrated in the Eucharist. For Christians the death of Jesus is *not* adequately portrayed as the surrogate sacrifice of the perfect scapegoat, the merits from which they passively profit. Instead the death of Jesus is seen as foundational to a covenant community in which Christians are active participants. That is why the central action of the Eucharist is not the passive, individual reception or eating of food, but the communal sharing of it, according to Hellwig. Christians are to be living incarnate signs to the world of that divine self-giving. This explains why the primitive church told the tale of her early martyrs in eucharistic terms. Those early Christians who witnessed the sacrifice of the martyrs were clearly conscious of the prototypical character of their gift. From this point of view, it seems very fitting that organ donation be described in eucharistic language—that is, as the shedding of blood and the breaking of the body given as testimony to one's experience of God.[20]

Traditionally, the church has recognized at least one woman's pregnancy as having this same prototypical character. In their perception of and devotion to Mary, the Mother of God, Christians have borne witness to certain beliefs about the purpose of human existence. In his book *The Life of the World,* the Russian Orthodox theologian Alexander Schmemann discerns in the celebration of the *Theotokos* the exclamation that "from all eternity all creation was meant and created to be the temple of the Holy Spirit, the *humanity* of God" (1963:61). In her very bearing of the Christ, Mary imaged God's self-gift. Her traditional status as the paradigmatic disciple of Christ is rooted in her willingness to give of her own flesh so that the world might see the face of God.

In her reflections on the meaning of the eucharistic claim that one person can be the bread of another, Hellwig writes:

> Literally and physically this is always true of the mother of the unborn or unweaned child, and it is not accidental that the Bible uses the image of mother to describe God's nurturing. . . . Nor is it accidental or unduly fanciful that mystics have spoken of Jesus and his relationship to the Church in terms of motherhood. (1976:27)

My purpose here has been threefold. First, I wished to give some indication of how central self-giving, indeed sacrifice, is to Christian faith and to the sacramental expressions which constitute the church. Second, I sought to highlight the explicit connection that has been made in the tradition between childbearing and God's own self-giving. Far from being owed anyone or a right, childbearing is most appropriately viewed as a gracious gift, not unlike God's own gratuitous Presence. Third, I have suggested that organ donation can be rendered intelligible and meaningful within this same vision of life.

Feminist Reformations of the Tradition

At this point it is important to delineate and respond to the feminist critique of this view of the Christian faith experience. It might be outlined as follows. People, women especially, need to take charge of and responsibility for their lives. They need "to own," not relinquish, control over their lives. Second, for many people, women especially, sin is experienced primarily as self-negation or neglect, not as hubris or self-aggrandizement. The call to gracious living appears at best to romanticize servitude and at worst to sacralize victimization. Feminists have documented the sadomasochistic expressions such theology has given rise to in the church's history.

They have further documented that in fact Christianity has operated with a double standard: women are called to self-renunciation and submission, whereas men are empowered and given leadership positions. Harrison is well worth quoting at length on this point.

> The morally normative, *sacrificial* behavior expected from women in relation to childbearing and childrearing never applies to the public actions of men. Men's lives are to be governed by strict conformity to "duty" construed narrowly as observing established conventional behavior. Women, by contrast, are expected to achieve a "supererogatory" morality. Although women have moral obligations in relation to procreation, this sort of theology double-binds us. We are admonished to be obedient and passive but simultaneously are told that we were born to be more responsible than men for nurturing human well-being and embodying an ethic of sacrifice. We live in a world where many, perhaps most, of the voluntary sacrifices on behalf of human well-being *are* made by women, but the assumption of a special obligation to self-giving or sacrifice by virtue of being born female, replete with procreative power, is male-generated ideology. (1985:62)

In light of such discrepancies as these, it strikes me as wise to be suspicious of attempts to sanctify the "crucifixion" of women facing burdensome and unwanted pregnancies. It is equally appropriate to be wary of arguments that might force "martyrdom" on potential organ donors.

Clearly feminists are correct in asserting that God is neither a divine child abuser nor a sadist. God's self-giving in the Incarnation led to the slaughter of Calvary not by divine design but by reason of sin, as expressed in *both* the Promethean drive for power *and* self-negation, with its corresponding abrogation of personal and social responsibility. However, Christian feminists would be wise to be suspicious of other additional cultural assumptions produced by patriarchy—including the prevailing desire to avoid suffering at all costs. It is appropriate to be wary of all that results, to use Dorothee Soelle's term, in the "narcotizing of life." It is the experience of pain, she argues in *The Strength of the Weak,* that enables us to empathize on a personal level and eventually connect on a political level with others. Sidney Callahan speaks to this point directly when she notes that "the fetus is to a woman as a woman has so often been to the dominant male—in a position of weakness and vulnerability" (1986b:4).

In my own attempt to weave together these feminist and traditional Christian insights, I have reached the following tentative conclusions. First, it is important to distinguish servitude from servanthood. Though suffering accompanies both, servitude is an involuntary oppression that objectifies, subordinates, and violates persons, whereas servanthood is a voluntary vocation that seeks to break the cycle of powerlessness, domination, and violence in which we are all trapped.[21] Though within both frameworks a service may be offered unilaterally, within a system of servitude this is normative. In contrast, mutuality and solidarity characterize servanthood. The difference is *not* found in the distinction between a sadistic master (servitude) and a masochist slave (servanthood), as some would argue. On the contrary, servanthood, as I define it, breaks altogether with the master/slave paradigm, by seeking to empower and liberate all. Power in this new context stems not from dominion over and isolation from others, but is rather a strength rooted in connection and solidarity with others, *especially* the weak.

Second, the willingness to carry an unwanted child to term can be meaningfully understood as a sign of solidarity with the weak among us. And, correspondingly, a decision to abort in this context can be seen as an analgesic choice, a headlong flight from suffering. Communities that offer no web of support for persons facing such choices, who do not recognize as heroic the choice so to serve, must be held responsible for their systemic support of slavery. To offer those who suffer only opiates is in the long run to support oppression.

Many on both sides of the abortion debate continue to romanticize pregnancy and motherhood. This romantic myth blinds many to the real problems and devastating conflicts pregnant women frequently face. It blinds others to the work, delayed gratification, suffering, and sacrifice constitutive of even planned ordinary pregnancies. Romanticism about motherhood reflects a failure of persons on both sides of the abortion debate to take the experience of women seriously.

Third, the refusal to carry a burdensome child to term can be meaningfully understood as an important symbol of self-affirmation for some women. By this I do not mean raw egoism or selfishness (though such remains a possibility). Instead I refer to that measure of self-love and self-respect which is not only the prerequisite for and enabler of other-love but also its fitting correlate. Correspondingly, a decision to continue a pregnancy could be interpreted as a blind slavery to a life the responsibility for which one has forfeited. Communities, ecclesial or civil, which seek to mandate childbearing only reinforce the powerlessness and violation many women have systematically experienced within those same communities.

In making this assertion I wish to distinguish my own position regarding suffering and self-sacrifice from that expressed by Lisa Sowle Cahill. In her essay "Abortion, Autonomy, and Community," she argues that feminists who affirm the moral maturity and adulthood of women must encourage them to "recognize that some human situations have unavoidably tragic elements and that to be human is to bear these burdens" (1986:271–72). While I concur with Cahill's rejection of the avoidance of the tragic via both romanticism and masochism, I wish to assert that elements of what is authentically human can be expressed *both* in the decision to abort and in the decision to bear the burdensome child. Self-love and other-love are both normatively human forms of love. What makes the choice tragic is precisely the fact that neither available option can express human love in its fullness.

Such a "double reading" of the choices women make about childbearing offers small comfort to those who sought in this part of my essay a "solution" to the abortion problem. It does however clarify for Christian feminists what it might mean to make such choices in a world that is truly an original blessing, however marred by original sin.

Finally, somewhat parallel judgments can be reached in regard to the practice of organ donation. As first noted by Parsons, Fox, and Lidz (1972), Christianity can frame the giving of bodily life support in such a way as to make it both intelligible and commendable. Through the donation of various types of organs, persons may enflesh certain truths about the purpose and character of all creation. Thus, the inability on the part of some (for example, Fellner and Schwartz, 1971) to understand or encourage live donation between unrelated persons may reflect not limits intrinsic to bodily life support, but rather the convictions constitutive of the modern liberal vision of life. In the future as the risks of graft-versus-host disease are minimized, unrelated live donations, at least of bone marrow, will become increasingly significant from a medical standpoint. It would seem to be a tragic form of myopia if the medical community continues to judge unrelated live donations as inappropriate, if not automatically suspect.[22] Unrelated live donation is not only intelligible but may be a sacramental act for some.

Clearly, however, health-care professionals need to remain wary of those "volunteers" manifesting masochistic tendencies. As "keepers of the gate" they ought to be especially cautious of compensation structures that might ensnare those who are economically oppressed into a personally treasonous forfeiture—into the objectification and sale of their body. This is already a reality at many inner-city blood banks. The power of biomedical commerce to erode the gift ethos which surrounds most other forms of organ donation should not be underestimated.

Notes

1. In this case William Head, a leukemia victim, wished to participate in an experimental procedure involving bone-marrow transplants from a nonrelated donor. Because computer records indicated that Mrs. X might be a possible matching donor for Mr. Head, she was invited to participate in the research program. She refused, indicating she was unwilling to be a donor "unless it was for a relative." After being informed of her decision, Mr. Head sought a court order which would compel the researchers to reinvite Mrs. X, informing her that a specific patient might be helped by her donation. For more information about this case and Judge J. McCormick's 1983 ruling, see *Cases in Bioethics,* ed. Carol Levine and Robert M. Veatch (1984:83–85). For additional legal precedents against compulsory organ donation, see *McFall v. Shrimp,* No. 78–17711 In Equity (C.P. Allegheny County, Penn., July 26, 1978).

2. Here I have in mind such things as requests for information regarding one's sexual partners for the sake of either encouraging paternal economic support for an unwed mother and child, or containing the spread of venereal disease. Or, perhaps more relevant, if the police have reason to suspect that someone's life is in danger, they may invade one's home without a search warrant or the owner's permission.

3. This analogy has its deepest roots in the fictional case created by Judith Jarvis Thompson in her article "A Defense of Abortion," *Philosophy and Public Affairs* 1 (1971) 47–66. It is further developed by Susan S. Mattingly in her essay "Viewing Abortion from the Perspective of Transplantation: The Ethics of the Gift of Life," *Soundings* 67, no. 4 (1984) 399–410.

4. This literature would include such books as: Ray Yorke Calne, M.D., *A Gift of Life* (New York: Basic Books, 1970); Renee C. Fox and Judith P. Swazey, *The Courage to Fail* (Chicago: University of Chicago Press, 1974); J. Hamburger and J. Crosnier, "Moral and Ethical Problems in Transplantation," in *Human Transplantation,* ed. Felix T. Rapaport and Jean Dausset (New York: Grune and Stratton, 1968); Roberta G. Simmons et al., *Gift of Life* (New York: John Wiley, 1977); and such essays as: W. J. Curran, "A Problem in Consent: Kidney Transplantation in Mi-

nors," *New York University Law Review* 34 (1959) 891 ff.; J. Dukeminier, Jr., and D. Sanders, "Organ Transplantation: A Proposal for Routine Salvaging of Cadaver Organs," *New England Journal of Medicine* 279 (1968) 413–19; A. M. Sadler, Jr., and B. L. Sadler, "A Community of Givers, Not Takers," *Hastings Center Report* 14, no. 5 (1984) 6–9; and William F. May, "Religious Justifications for Donating Body Parts," *Hastings Center Report* 15, no. 1 (1985) 38–42.

5. It is mistaken to think of metaphorical comparisons as establishing a substitutionary relationship between the terms. Rather the analogical wager sets up an interaction (not interchange) between the terms, the fruit of which is new insight into that which is compared. Though the argument that constitutes the body of this essay is not developed analogically (in the substitutionary sense rejected above), it does rest upon the insights yielded by such a reframing of the activities. In his book *Women and Equality: Changing Patterns in American Culture* (New York: Oxford University Press, 1977), William H. Chafe argues that the popular analogy between women and blacks has permitted us new understandings of "social control." At this level of generalization it is very useful. It is less (or altogether not) useful, Chafe argues, in exhibiting the material conditions which accompany either sexual or racial oppression. The analogy developed in my essay will permit us new understanding of the reasons for and limits of the obligation to give bodily life support. For a more detailed discussion of the nature and role of metaphorical thinking, see the now classic essay by Max Black entitled "Metaphor" (1954–1955).

6. This same "hermeneutics of suspicion" should be applied to the growing consideration of prophylactic (for the fetus) cesarean section at term. For more detailed information about the current shape of this discussion, read the brief note submitted by George B. Feldman and Jennie A. Freiman on that topic to the *New England Journal of Medicine* (May 9, 1985: 1264–67). Consider as well the growing discussion among both jurists and biomedical ethicists about forcing pregnant women to undergo fetal therapies. See the essay by H. Tristram Engelhardt, Jr., "Current Controversies in Obstetrics: Wrongful Life and Forced Fetal Surgical Procedures," *American Journal of Obstetrics and Gynecology* 151 (Feb. 1, 1985) 313–18.

7. In this essay the question of whether voluntary participation in sexual acts *alone*—or more pointedly, with the failure of contraceptive measures—establishes a parental relation cannot be addressed in detail. However, I wish to suggest that even if contractual considerations have a legitimate role to play in the determination of the extent of special parental obligations, they do not settle the matter. Family obligations are at

least in part noncontractual in origin. Clearly a rape victim does not have as much of a *parental* obligation to her child as one who "planned" her pregnancy; nevertheless, she still has some parental obligation.

Children do not choose their parents; persons do not volunteer to be part of a family. Instead we find ourselves inescapably and inextricably "stuck with" our family and obligated to them, whether or not these parents, siblings, or children benefit us. My point is that contract theory alone cannot explain the moral significance of a person's willingness to have and care for children, particularly those who are unexpected, burdensome, or otherwise unwelcome, since these children highlight the nonvoluntary, uncontrollable, and risky nature of even "planned" parenthood.

It is simply erroneous to assume, in Lisa Sowle Cahill's words, that "only freedom creates moral obligation" (1981:15). In contrast to this liberal fallacy, Cahill accurately suggests that persons are social not only by contract but also by nature. Agents are naturally interdependent and bound by the obligations of this interdependence. Thus pregnancy and gestation can be viewed as primordial and prototypical examples of this natural social interdependence.

8. Even though this essay is deeply indebted to the work of Thompson (referred to in note 3), I agree with Whitbeck when she argues that it is almost absurd to envision the fetus as a dependent "adult-stranger." Such an analogy is visualized in photographic and cinemagraphic essays when fetuses as mini-astronauts floating about in "inner" space connected by an umbilical life line to their "mothership." Some weaknesses in this analogy are obvious: fetuses are neither adult nor strangers; mothers are not objectifiable things like spaceships. A strength of the analogy is equally obvious: the fetus is usually dependent upon the mother for survival, though some in the third trimester may be viable.

According to Whitbeck, "a claim more worthy of examination is the claim that human fetuses are relevantly like newborn human beings" (1985:254). Some strengths of this analogy are obvious: fetuses are immature and blood relations; mothers are persons, not objects controlled by others; like neonates, fetuses have voracious appetites and place nearly constant, at times quite taxing, demands on their caretakers. Furthermore, like newborns, fetuses are speechless: they cannot articulate their needs or defend themselves. They are extremely vulnerable: this is a form of dependence quite unlike that of the astronaut. A weakness of this analogy is also obvious: though both the newborn and the fetus are dependent, the neonate's survival is not tied exclusively to the care of one particular individual.

Though neither analogy is perfect, the second one is more illuminative and less problematic. Yet, it has not informed *much* of the abortion debate. Why? Women's experience has been excluded from the pool of wisdom upon which our collective moral imagination feeds. Astronauts are apparently more familiar to those who have controlled the terms of the abortion debate than neonates.

9. Beyond the twenty-week mark, the fetal survival rate can increase if the abortion is done by hysterotomy (a technique resembling a C-section) or by the injection of prostaglandins (which simulate a normal delivery). When combined with the increased availability of neonatal intensive care nurseries, these factors generate two new moral questions. First, how should postabortion neonates be treated? Second, given a reasonable chance of fetal viability, should certain methods of abortion be legally mandated?

In his commentary on a 1976 California bill which attempted to establish guidelines on this matter, Leroy Walters reached the following conclusions. (1) All newborns should be treated equally. As "wards of the state," postabortion neonates should be given neither compensatory nor punitive treatment. (2) Women should not be required to assume higher risks for the sake of a viable fetus, "just as the law should not require parents to rescue their children from burning buildings." If, however, among abortion methods there emerges an alternative which lowers the risks for both the pregnant woman and fetus, then the state can (and I would add ought to) mandate the safer method, for the right not to offer bodily life support (to terminate pregnancy) is not identical with the right to fetal death (Levine and Veatch, eds., 1984:5–6). Furthermore, from within its perspective a woman's right to terminate pregnancy is not identical with the right to fetal experimentation. No one has ever argued that a histocompatible parent's refusal to donate a kidney to a child suffering from renal failure can be interpreted as proxy consent to nontherapeutic research on the "dying" recipient. The case, should there be one, for experimenting on abortuses rests elsewhere.

10. In one sense pregnancy may be said to result from trauma, as in the case of rape, or from a psychological disease such as immaturity among the retarded. Notice, however, that in both instances it is the "donor" who is either traumatized or diseased. The (fetal) "recipient's" dependency remains nonpathological in origin.

11. This critique will be developed along the lines proposed by Stanley Hauerwas in his work, *A Community of Character* (1981). There he seeks to develop an ethical theory of the classical type which can account for the moral life's dependence upon a certain vision of community. Therein he engages in a polemic against modern political liberalism. As

Ronald Dworkin indicated in his essay "Why Liberals Should Believe in Equality," liberalism is not a single political theory. "There are, in fact, two basic forms of liberalism and the distinction between them is of great importance" (1983:32). While both versions seek to encourage equality and legal neutrality vis-à-vis self-regarding and/or supererogatory actions, these conclusions are based on quite distinct rationales. In one form of liberalism, equality is the fundamental value and the concern for public neutrality is a derivative injunction served only to the extent made necessary by the prior commitment to egalitarianism. In the other form of liberalism, neutrality is the decisive value. It is this latter form of liberalism that Hauerwas attacks, citing as defects its basis in moral skepticism and its essentially negative political vision. Its emphasis upon individual freedom and its discrediting of dependence on and ties to others are viewed as symptomatic of this ethos for the uncommitted.

12. Within the Anglo-Saxon legal tradition, strangers have no duties to aid or rescue one another. Indeed, when it reviewed the old common-law crime of "misprision of a felony," the U.S. Supreme Court of 1822 ruled that strangers were not required even to report crimes to legitimate authorities. Lest this portion of my argument be misinterpreted, I believe a sound moral case can be made against this aspect of our legal heritage and that we ought to be expected in some minimal way to be our "sibling's keeper." Thus, I would argue that both moral and legal pressure should be brought to bear on those who can assist victims of crime, such as the witnesses of Kitty Genovese's murder in New York and the spectators of the gang rape of the woman in Big Dan's Bar in New Bedford, Massachusetts.

13. This essay diverges from the theory of Donagan in that it seeks to do more than delineate what must be protected by articulating a vision of what must be encouraged. In this sense, it has a much less restricted notion of what is properly construed as moral argument.

14. Ramsey, it should be noted, even argues against the "routine salvaging of cadaver organs" on the grounds that "a society will be a better human community in which giving and receiving is the rule, not taking for the sake of good to come." This is so even when the good at stake is life itself. "The moral sequels that might flow from education and action in line with the proposed Gift Acts may be of far more importance than prolonging lives routinely." Even corpses ought not to become involuntary "donors" (1970:210). The communal revulsion to the unauthorized harvesting of cadaver pituitary glands for humanitarian purposes in the mid-1960s was a contributing factor to the development of the Uniform Anatomical Gift Act of 1968. Prochoice groups express an analogous kind of shock in response to forced pregnancy.

15. In his essay "Abortion: A Changing Morality and Policy?" McCormick articulates a theoretical framework which seems compatible with the position I am developing, yet he fails to delineate its implications explicitly.

> For an act . . . to be the lesser evil (all things considered), there must be at stake human life or its moral equivalent, a good or value comparable to life itself. This is not what the traditional formulations say, but it is where the corpus of teachings on life taking leads. (1979:39)

For example, human freedom as expressed in political sovereignty has long been accepted as such a value within the just-war tradition. I have been arguing in regard to abortion and organ donation that human freedom expressed in bodily integrity is also such a value.

16. There is a counterexample to this argument which must be considered. Bodily life support has traditionally been *required* of soldiers during war. Further, one might imagine compulsory pregnancy and/or mandatory organ donation reasonable should the survival of the nation and/or species ever come to depend upon it. In addition, though we have awarded decorations of honor, such as the Purple Heart, to those honorably wounded in action against the enemy, strictly speaking we have not interpreted such sacrifices as above and beyond the call of civic duty. Only when a soldier takes up more than his (or her) fair share of the risk would we judge the sacrifice to be supererogatory and confer a meritorious award (such as the Bronze Star). Although there is considerable debate about the extent of one's civic responsibilities in peacetime, there is a wide consensus that military (or alternative, though still potentially life-threatening) service can legitimately be mandated during a national emergency. This practice would appear at first glance to undermine my claim that bodily life support ought not be required. However, I reject that conclusion for three interrelated reasons.

First, though this has varied throughout the history of the draft, many kinds of deferments and exemptions have been granted. Though not necessarily all legitimate, the factors considered relevant have been gender-, age-, health-, education-, career-, fortune- (a la the lottery), religious-, moral-, and family- (especially dependent) related. Therefore, society has clearly recognized the illegitimacy of making such a requirement exceptionless.

Second, while the rationale for each classification varies, several of the deferments are rooted at least in part in the conviction that this potential conscript would be asked to shoulder more than this fair share of the burden. Only if the situation worsens or as a last resort would it be appropriate to draft him, if ever.

While some are comfortable with compulsory military *service* during peacetime, most would argue that hazardous duty should remain voluntary. Bodily life support is a sacrifice that can be mandated only in a national emergency. Thus it would seem that the military "counter-example" under consideration is in fact an exception which proves the rule. As a society we have not required bodily life support for the sake of single individuals but instead mandate such sacrifice only *in extremis*.

17. My attention to the distinctively Christian rationales behind the gift ethos should not be interpreted as a claim that *only* Christians can intelligibly engage in bodily life support. There are lots of non-Christian frameworks which can render gift giving meaningful.

18. This is clearly not meant to be a comprehensive list. It is, however, a representative sample of the variety of factors relevant to such decision making.

19. Dorothee Soelle in her book *The Strength of the Weak* (1984) tells a Jewish story that makes a similar point. "An old rabbi once asked his students how one could recognize the time when night ends and day begins. 'Is it when, from a great distance, you can tell a dog from a sheep?' one student asked. 'No,' said the rabbi. 'Is it when, from a great distance, you can tell a date palm from a fig tree?' another student asked. 'No,' said the rabbi. 'Then when is it?' the students asked. 'It is when you look into the face of any human creature and see your brother or your sister there. Until then, night is still with us.' "

20. It is important to note there that such language and images are not unique to Christianity. In her recently published diaries, Etty Hillesum, a Dutch woman murdered at Auschwitz, wrote of her efforts to comfort and aid fellow Jews as follows: "I have broken my body like bread and shared it out. . . ." The unleavened bread of Passover was always understood to be not only a sign of freedom but the bread of affliction as well. See *An Interrupted Life: The Diaries of Etty Hillesum, 1941–1943,* trans. Arno Pomerans (New York: Pantheon Books, 1985), p. 195. It might also be noted that William F. May in the essay on cadaver donation cited above speaks of organ donation as a "fitting and direct sign" of the Christian's eucharistic participation (1985:42).

21. At first glance, my emphasis on the voluntary character of servanthood may appear to contradict my earlier rejection of liberalism. By voluntary I am referring not only to those burdens that may accompany

contractual agreements but also to those unexpected burdens the bearing of which we may choose either to refuse or consent to.

22. At some medical schools, renal specialists automatically view unrelated donors as "crazy" and declare them to be "obviously" incompetent.

References

Black, Max
1954–1955 "Metaphor." *Proceedings of the Aristotelian Society* 55:273–94.

Cahill, Lisa Sowle
1981 "Abortion and Argument by Analogy." Paper presented at the annual meeting of the American Academy of Religion, San Francisco.
1984 "Abortion, Autonomy, and Community," In *Abortion: Understanding Differences,* edited by Sidney and Daniel Callahan. New York: Plenum Press. Pp. 261–76.

Callahan, Sidney
1986a "Abortion and the Sexual Agenda: A Case for Pro-Life Feminism." *Commonweal* 113, no. 8 (April 25) 232–38. Reprinted in this volume, pp. 422–39.
1986b "Abortion: Understanding Our Differences," with Daniel Callahan. *Update* 2, no. 2 (March) 3–6.

Dworkin, Ronald
1983 "Why Liberals Should Believe in Equality." *New York Review of Books* 30 (Feb. 3) 32–34.

Fellner, Carl H.
1971 "Altruism in Disrepute: Medical versus Public Attitudes toward the Living Organ Donor." *New England Journal of Medicine* 284 (March 18) 582–85.

Fried, Charles
1978 *Right and Wrong*. Cambridge: Harvard University Press.

Gudorf, Christine E.
1984–1985 "To Make a Seamless Garment, Use a Single Piece of Cloth." *Cross Currents* 34, no. 4 (Winter) 473–90.

Gustafson, James M.
1968 *Christ and the Moral Life.* New York: Harper and Row.

Harrison, Beverly Wildung
1981 *Our Right to Choose: Toward a New Ethic of Abortion.* Boston: Beacon Press.

Hauerwas, Stanley
1981 *A Community of Character.* Notre Dame, Ind.: University of Notre Dame Press.

Hellwig, Monika K.
1976 *The Eucharist and the Hunger of the World.* New York: Paulist Press.

Johnson, Luke T.
1981 *Sharing Possessions.* Philadelphia: Fortress Press.

Kelly, Gerald F.
1951 "Notes: The Duty to Preserve Life." *Theological Studies* 12 (Dec.) 550–56.

Levine, Carol, and Robert M. Veatch, editors
1984 *Cases in Bioethics.* Hastings-on-Hudson, N.Y.: The Hastings Center.

Little, David
"Moral Discretion and the Universalizability Thesis." Unpublished essay.

McCormick, Richard A.
1979 "Abortion: A Changing Morality and Policy?" *Hospital Progress,* Feb., 36–44.

Nicholson, Susan T.
1978 *Abortion and the Roman Catholic Church.* Knoxville: Studies in Religious Ethics.

Ooms, Theodora
1984 "A Family Perspective on Abortion." In *Abortion: Understanding Differences,* edited by Sidney and Daniel Callahan. New York: Plenum Press. Pp. 81–108.

Parsons, Talcott, Renee C. Fox, and Victor M. Lidz
1972 "The Gift of Life and Its Reciprocation." *Social Research* 39 (Autumn) 367–415.

Ramsey, Paul
1970 *The Patient as Person.* New Haven: Yale University Press.

Ricoeur, Paul
1966 *Freedom and Nature.* Evanston: Northwestern University Press.

Schumaker, Willard
1977 *Supererogation: An Analysis and a Bibliography.* Edmonton, Alberta: St. Stephen's College.

Soelle, Dorothee
1984 *The Strength of the Weak.* Philadelphia: Westminster Press.

Whitbeck, Caroline
1983 "The Moral Implications of Regarding Women as People: New Perspectives on Pregnancy and Parenthood." In *Abortion and the Status of the Fetus,* edited by William B. Bondeson et al. Dordrecht, Holland: D. Reidel. Pp. 247–72.

White, James F.
1983 *Sacraments as God's Self-Giving.* Nashville: Abingdon Press.

Part Five

SOCIAL ETHICS

20. Toward Renewing "The Life and Culture of Fallen Man": *Gaudium et Spes* as Catalyst for Catholic Feminist Theology[1]

Anne E. Patrick

This chapter first appeared in *Questions of Special Urgency: The Church in the Modern World Two Decades After Vatican II* in 1986.

In discussing "The Proper Development of Culture," *Gaudium et Spes* (hereafter cited as *GS*) ranges widely over theological, ethical, and educational matters pertaining to "the cultivation of the goods and values of nature" (no. 53). The tone of this section of the conciliar document is largely positive, conveying an openness to new possibilities and a hope that proper development of culture will lead to "a world that is more human" (no. 57). Twenty years later, the church continues to grapple with the items this text identified as sufficiently novel to warrant our times being called "a new age of human history" (no. 54), items which include cultural and religious pluralism, new developments in the physical and human sciences and in technology, and increasing aspirations toward autonomy and responsibility on the part of women and men across the globe. But when one surveys the section, "The Proper Development of Culture," in light of the entire document of *GS,* and in light of subsequent developments in the church, there is a change in the scene since 1965 that stands out for its significance and impact, a change which seems not to have been anticipated by the document and yet is arguably, at least in part, a result of *GS*. This development is the enhanced sense of full personhood and moral and social responsibility now articulated by

Catholic women, a number of whom are solidly established as professional theologians.

How did it happen that women, once presumed to be silent and acquiescent, docile and supportive of male ecclesiastical authority, came to take positions in opposition to "official" Catholic teachings on questions ranging from God-language and women's ordination to conception control, homosexuality, and even abortion?[2] An extraordinary development has taken place in Roman Catholicism since the appearance of *GS,* and this chapter indicates the connection I see between the words of this document and the emerging feminist critique of the tradition by Catholics who regard themselves as loyal members of the church. It is my impression that the rhetoric of *GS* struck forcefully on a female population that was ripe for implementing its ideas and carrying them beyond anything anticipated by the Fathers of the Council.[3] My claim here is that the limited vision of social justice articulated by this document paved the way for a more adequate Christian feminist vision of justice among Catholics who might otherwise have felt it necessary to choose between either a traditionally Catholic or a secular feminist philosophy of life and view of justice. What made the difference was the opening of theological education and research to women, which lessened the insularity of male theologians and at the same time gave women the tools to argue our case for justice in the forum that was responsible for legitimating our subordination.

Gaudium et Spes: Product of Androcentric Culture

There is no reason to suppose that the Council Fathers ever anticipated the sort of contributions Rosemary Radford Ruether, Elisabeth Schüssler Fiorenza, or Margaret A. Farley would make to Catholic theology. It is true that no. 55 recognizes that in general women as well as men are eager to mold the culture of the societies to which they belong:

> In each nation and social group there is a growing number of men and women [*virorum ac mulierum*] who are con-

> scious that they themselves are the craftsmen [*culturae artifices*] and molders of their community's culture. All over the world the sense of autonomy and responsibility increases with effects of the greatest importance for the spiritual and moral maturity of mankind. This will become clearer to us if we place before our eyes the unification of the world and the duty imposed on us to build up a better world in truth and justice.

However, the egalitarian reference to women and men together here is highly unusual; although *GS* does employ *mulier* alone in various contexts, it generally avoids *vir,* using instead forms of the ambiguous term *homo,* which are nearly always rendered in the generic masculine ("man" or "men") in English.[4] Thus women are not specified in the crucial paragraph that voices the hope that "more of the laity [*plures laici*] will receive adequate theological formation and that some among them will dedicate themselves professionally to these studies and contribute to their advancement," in which the Fathers also declare that "Those involved in theological studies in seminaries and universities should be eager to cooperate with men [*hominibus*] versed in other fields of learning by pooling their resources and their points of view" (no. 62). There is every likelihood that readers of this paragraph would infer a presumption on the part of its authors that intellectual circles were overwhelmingly, if not exclusively, male. For this they could hardly be blamed, given that women were excluded from the early sessions of Vatican II and were admitted only as silent observers during the final two sessions. Indeed, as Albertus Magnus McGrath recalls in her study *Women and the Church,* the noted British economist Barbara Ward was not allowed to address the Council Fathers, her paper instead being delivered at the third session by a man.[5]

During the Council there were, of course, a number of significant statements made concerning justice for women, and Archbishop Paul Hallinan of Atlanta filed a proposal during the final session that women be encouraged to become "teachers and consultants" in theology.[6] But although Hallinan's proposal was widely noted by the press, it never reached the assembly floor, and the text of *GS* does not specifically promote the involvement of women in theology.

Thus, although the document does represent some progress on the question of justice for women, its tone and contents (especially when rendered in English) betray a decidedly androcentric bias, indeed a blindness to the sexism in its understanding of human rights and dignity. Nonetheless, the language of the document at least leaves open the possibility that women might interpret in their favor statements the text left ambiguous, for there are no passages specifically ruling out the participation of women in theology. Furthermore, by affirming intellectual freedom in theology, the highly significant final sentence of the section on culture states a principle that contributed both to male support of women's involvement in the discipline and also to the development of feminist positions by both male and female theologians:

> But for the proper exercise of this role [of theologian], the faithful, both clerical and lay [*sive clericis sive laicis*], should be accorded a lawful freedom of inquiry, of thought, and of expression, tempered by humility and courage in whatever branch of study they have specialized (no. 62).

Later in this essay, I probe in some detail the document's limitations where justice for women is concerned, but what needs to be stressed first are two factors that offset these limitations and enabled *GS* to be the ground-breaking document it was. These are essentially theological affirmations, which permeate the document and which make it possible for Catholics who read it to carry its spirit beyond the literal sense of the text.

Key Theological Affirmations

In the first place, it is impossible to exaggerate the import of the document's stress on the essential equality of all persons (*homines*) and of its recognition that ". . . forms of social or cultural discrimination in basic personal rights on the grounds of sex . . . must be curbed and eradicated as incompatible with God's design" (no. 29). Here the Fathers incorporate into their own text a critical principle that continues to be seized upon by their readers as a basis for carrying the spirit of *GS* beyond the implementation envisioned by most of its episcopal authors.

In the second place, along with this important affirmation that God intends a society in which the essential equality of woman is recognized, the Fathers also affirm a more dynamic, historically conscious understanding of God's will for humanity than had previously held sway in post-Reformation Catholicism, with all that this implies in terms of openness to the genuinely *new.* The tone of confidence with which this document speaks of the abiding presence of God's Spirit in history, with the accompanying recognition that even ideals may develop and improve, had the potential to counter a spirituality that feared to transgress static divine orders. Indeed, in contrast to this negative spirituality, *GS* invited believers to look beyond the forms that symbolized past understandings of God's will and concentrate instead on the essential divine values of truth, justice, and love that pulse at the heart of the tradition. Early in *GS,* the words of section no. 11 establish a new sort of piety, one far different from the passive, defensive piety associated with the period following the "modernist crisis," which had sought to protect itself from worldly influences, retreating to the safety of prescribed and seemingly immutable patterns of Christian life:

> The people of God believes that it is led by the Spirit of the Lord who fills the whole world. Moved by that faith it tries to discern in the events, the needs, and the longings which it shares with other men of our time, what may be genuine signs of the presence or of the purpose of God. For faith throws a new light on all things and makes known the full ideals which God has set for man, thus guiding the mind toward solutions that are fully human.

These two theological affirmations—that God wills for society to reflect the essential equality of the sexes and that history is the locus of the activity of God's Spirit—gave expression to a perspective that was already experienced, if not articulated, by many Catholics, especially women and men in societies where God's liberating intent with respect to women had already been felt in "secular" feminist movements for women's educational and political rights. For these women and men, to read *GS* (especially no. 29) was to discover a powerful rebuttal to the old arguments against women's advancement in society. It was to hear at last a belated disavowal on the part of the international hierarchy of such prejudiced episcopal interventions against social equality as Cardinal Gibbons' 1911 words against women's suffrage in the United States: "When a woman enters the political arena, she goes outside the sphere for which she was intended. She gains nothing by that journey. On the other hand, she loses the exclusiveness, respect and dignity to which she is entitled in her home."[7]

Women and Theology

But beyond this, to read *GS* was to be invited to make connections that even its authors had not made, to move by a logic implicit in the text from affirmation of women's rights in society to affirmation of women's rights in the church, beginning with the right to theological education and to participation in the advancement of theology itself. In the two brief but eventful decades since this document appeared, a profound change in the theological scene has occurred, a change that can be summed up by saying that the nouns "woman" and "theologian" are no longer mutually exclusive terms. This fact that women are now teaching and writing theology as professionals in the Catholic church testifies to tremendous efforts on the part of justice-minded women and men. Risk, sacrifice, suffering, and unflagging labor have been required for women to earn the necessary academic credentials, enter the theological forum, and begin to influence the discussion. These accomplishments, which I briefly review, represent a creative application of the injunctions of *GS* no. 62 to extend participation in theology beyond the ranks of the clergy and to promote "lawful freedom of inquiry, of thought, and of expression" among theologians.

In 1985, when women can study theology in virtually all the

American doctoral programs open to men, it is easy to forget what things were like a generation ago. But relatively equal access to theological education is a very new item indeed for women. All the female members of the Catholic Theological Society of America (CTSA) whose doctorates in theology date from the 1950s are graduates of a single far-sighted program at Saint Mary's College, Notre Dame. These women earned Ph.D.s rather than the traditional canonical degree for Catholic theologians, the S.T.D., and at least one American Catholic woman in the 1950s wanted that traditional ecclesiastical degree enough to go abroad in pursuit of it. Mary Daly recalls her experience in the autobiographical preface to the 1975 edition of *The Church and the Second Sex:*

> There was no place in the United States where a female was allowed to study for the "highest degree" in this field, the "canonical" Doctorate in Sacred Theology. Since I would settle for nothing less than the "highest degrees," I applied to study in Fribourg, where the theological faculty was state-controlled and therefore could not legally exclude women. . . . [M]y classmates were nearly all priests and male seminarians . . . in the crowded classrooms there frequently were empty places on each side of me. . . .[8]

Another American woman also earned an S.T.D. abroad in the 1960s, namely, Sister Agnes Cunningham, S.S.C.M., who in 1968 completed a dissertation for the theology faculty at Lyons entitled "Toward a Theology of Christian Humanism."[9] Daly, a laywoman, had supported herself in Switzerland by teaching philosophy to American students who were in Fribourg for "junior year abroad" programs. Cunningham's education had been financed by an anonymous lay benefactor who had approached her religious superiors with the idea of backing the preparation of a sister theologian as an experiment. Daly's financial struggle was certainly the more typical experience for women, both religious and lay, who have earned doctoral degrees in Europe, Canada, and the United States in subsequent years.

It is also noteworthy that when women were first admitted to doctoral studies in theology at The Catholic University of America, they were confined to the Ph.D program and were not eligible for the S.T.D., an inequity that was repaired by the early 1970s. Meanwhile, Ph.D. programs had become available to women at Marquette, Boston College, and a number of other Catholic universities by the late 1960s. By this time also a handful of Catholic women had entered doctoral programs in some of the traditionally Protestant schools, including Chicago, Yale, and Union/Columbia, among others. Rosemary Radford Ruether, the most influential Catholic woman theologian today, earned her Ph.D. from Claremont in 1965. In large part this development was an outgrowth of the new ecumenical movement launched by Vatican II, and in many cases it was the result of foresight on the part of leaders of women's religious communities, as well as of initiative on the part of the individual women who undertook to study theology in an ecumenical context. For these women to finance their educations and succeed in situations where most of the students and all the faculty were male was a major accomplishment, whether they studied in Catholic universities or in other institutions of higher learning; the fact that the situation is better for women studying theology today is due in great measure to their pioneering efforts.

Once the degrees were earned, women who wanted to contribute as theologians had to find employment and make their way into the professional organizations. There are now 349 women (approximately 25% of whom are Catholic) listed at doctoral or professional levels in the most recent directory published by the Women's Caucus of the American Academy of Religion.[10] In 1980, this figure stood at 168. Not all these women are employed, but many have found good positions and have contributed to the profession through various publications and through involvement in the College Theology Society, the American Academy of Religion, the CTSA, and in professional groups specializing in such areas as biblical studies, church history, liturgy, and Christian ethics. Jill Raitt, a Catholic theologian who earned the Ph.D. from The University of Chicago in 1970, served as president of the American Academy of Religion during 1981. Anne E. Carr, a 1971 University of Chicago graduate, was the first woman tenured in that university's Divinity School. Monika Hellwig, who obtained the Ph.D. from The Catholic University of America in 1968, became the first woman to receive the John Courtney Murray Award for Distinguished Achievement in Theology in June, 1984. Mary Collins, a 1967 Ph.D. graduate from The Catholic University of America, began her term as the first woman president of the North American Academy of Liturgy in January, 1985.

Women's progress in the CTSA has been relatively rapid, given its unpromising beginnings. In *The Church and the Second Sex,* Mary Daly describes in the third person her own disillusioning experience of nineteen years ago:

> In 1966 an American woman who holds a doctorate in theology traveled to Providence, Rhode Island, to attend the annual meeting of the Catholic Theological Society of America, of which she is a member. . . . When she attempted to enter the ballroom of the hotel in which the meeting was being held in order to attend a buffet for members of the society, she was prevented from doing so by one of the officers, a priest. When she insisted upon her right to enter, the priest threatened to call the police. She replied that in this case it would unfortunately be necessary for her to call the newspapers. After a long and humiliating scene, she was finally permitted to enter. This was the debut of the female sex in the Catholic Theological Society of America.[11]

Surely this experience contributed to Daly's decision, formalized by the early 1970s, to leave the Catholic church and proclaim herself a post-Christian feminist. Some justice-minded men of the CTSA, however, were resolved to open things up, for by 1969 Agnes Cunningham had been elected to the board of directors of the society, and one or two women have served on the board every year since 1975. Cunningham, in fact, progressed during the 1970s through the offices of secretary, vice-president, and finally president of the society, giving the first presidential address by a woman in 1978. Monika Hellwig, elected vice-president in 1984, will become the second female president of the CTSA in June, 1986. About 10% of those attending the meeting where Hellwig was elected were female, and admissions statistics show an increasing percentage of women entering the society. In 1983, for example, more than one-third of the 45 new members accepted were female.

There is no question that the rapid entry of women into the profession has influenced the discussion, for the topics being treated by theologians generally reflect in some measure the agenda that many women have carried into the theological forum. A notable instance is the justice issue of sacramental sex discrimination, often termed the women's ordination issue. The gathering of 1200 women in Detroit at the first Woman's Ordination Conference in 1975 was enormously significant, for it was the first time a sizable number of theologically trained female scholars and ministers convened to do theological reflection on the status of women in the Roman Catholic church. Speakers for that occasion included Rosemary Radford Ruether, Margaret A. Farley, Anne E. Carr, and Elisabeth Schüssler Fiorenza, as well as Richard McBrien, Carroll Stuhlmueller, and George Tavard. It is likely that the caliber of the theological papers given at the meeting had something to do with the Vatican's 1977 reiteration of the traditional position against women's ordination.[12] It is also significant that American Catholic theologians responded to the Vatican declaration by publishing a closely reasoned analysis and refutation of its arguments against ordaining women. Forty-four women and men contributed to this project, which was edited by Leonard Swidler and Arlene Swidler and published as *Women Priests: A Catholic Commentary on the Vatican Declaration.*[13] The work bears testimony to the fact that matters were far from settled by the Sacred Congregation for the Doctrine of the Faith, and that American theologians had taken to heart the words of *GS* no. 62 acknowledging that the "proper exercise" of their role requires "a lawful freedom of inquiry, of thought, and of expression, tempered by humility and courage in whatever branch of study they have specialized."

The influence of women's agenda on the theological discussion is also apparent in the fact that the CTSA commissioned a study of women in church and society, published in 1978, as well as in the fact that many male and female scholars now take care to avoid sexist language in their ordinary discourse and in their references to Divine Reality as well. Other examples of the influence of women's concerns on theology abound. Special issues of journals such as *Liturgy, Theological Studies,* and *New Catholic World* have been devoted to these matters. Raymond E. Brown's Hoover Lecture of January, 1975, advertised as an address on New Testament studies and ministry, surprised its ecumenical audience by its content: a discussion of the question of women's ordination.[14] Bernard Cooke's article on "Non-Patriarchical Salvation," which appeared in the tenth anniversary issue of *Horizons* in 1983,[15] and Daniel Maguire's 1982 presidential address to The Society of Christian Ethics, entitled "The Feminization of God and Ethics,"[16] also reflect the influence of feminist theology, as does the fact that when the moral theology seminar of the CTSA took stock of matters it needed to concern itself with during the 1980s, the first item on an agenda proposed by Richard A. McCormick in 1982 was "Feminism in the Church."[17]

It should be clear from the above that the labors of women have had considerable impact on contemporary theological discussion. It should also be apparent that the trend is for this influence to increase, judging from such items as the recent establishment of the Women's Theological Center in Boston, the opening in 1984 of an M.A. program in Feminist Spirituality at Immaculate Heart College in Los Angeles, and the inauguration in 1985 of the *Journal of Feminist Religious Studies.*

Anne E. Carr observes in a 1983 article that the emergence of organized feminist groups of ministers and scholars within the Protestant and Catholic churches over the last two decades has led to a distinctive form of the "theology of liberation":

> Like its Black and Latin American counterparts, feminist theology begins with the concrete experience of women (consciousness-raising), understands itself as a collective struggle for justice (sisterhood), and aims toward a transformation of Church and societal structures consistent with the practical implications of the Gospel.[18]

The literature of Christian feminism, she adds, involves three tasks: critiquing the past, recovering "the lost history of women" in the tradition, and "revisioning Christian categories in ways which take seriously the equality and the experience of women."[19] Carr observes further that the Christian feminist movement is decidedly ecumenical, with Protestant and Catholic theologians alike involved in various aspects of a common project:

> They use the central and liberating Gospel message of equality, mutuality, and service *and* their own experience to criticize those elements in the tradition which capitulate to take-for-granted patriarchal norms. And they use the central biblical tradition of justice and equality to criticize sexist patterns and practices in culture and society.[20]

Another Catholic feminist, Janet Kalven of the Grail movement, describes the project in even more basic terms. What religious feminists are about, according to Kalven, is "simply drawing out the implications of affirming that women are full human beings made in the image of God."[21]

A Feminist Reading of *Gaudium et Spes*

To illustrate what feminist theology can involve, I conclude this chapter with a feminist analysis of *GS,* concentrating on Part One and on the chapter from Part Two dealing with "Culture." As I have indicated, there is no question that this document conveyed Good News to the faithful, and particularly to women. Its insistence on the full humanity of woman—fully equal to man and created with him in the divine image—represents a decisive break with a long tradition of misogynist Christian anthropology, which had taught that woman is ontologically inferior to man and less reflective of the divine image. The import of this new understanding of woman's full humanity cannot be overstated, and its articulation by Vatican II in 1965 is to be celebrated.

Nevertheless, the context in which this new teaching is affirmed—the document *GS* and other conciliar and postconciliar documents—makes clear that the *implications* of this new affirmation of woman's full humanity have yet to be recognized and carried out to their logical conclusions in the church. This was not, of course, a task for Vatican II; rather it is an ongoing charge for the faithful who have benefited from the legacy of *GS, Lumen Gentium, Dignitatis Humanae,* and other momentous conciliar documents. To critique *GS* in light of its crucial insight of woman's full humanity, then, is to affirm as well its other central theological insight, namely, its recognition that it is God's Spirit who moves in the historical quest for fuller solutions to the mystery of ideal human existence on earth (no. 11). In what follows here, then, I draw out some implications of the document's affirmation of woman's equality by describing five limitations of *GS* that a feminist perspective judges in need of rectifying. These concern the areas of language, nature and culture, social analysis, ethical norms, and theological affirmations.

Language. The first thing that strikes a feminist reader of the English translations of *GS* is their use of "generic" masculine nouns in countless instances where a more felicitous rendering of the Latin would have allowed the language of the document to affirm woman's full humanity by including her unambiguously in the *words* about humanity. In view of the fact that as early as 1974 the *Journal of Ecumenical Studies* adopted an editorial policy proscribing the generic use of "man," it can only be regretted that there is not yet available an English translation of *GS* that employs "men and women" or "persons" in contexts where the Latin uses plural forms of *homo.*

To be sure, not everyone recognizes the moral seriousness of the feminist complaint about language. It requires a good deal of empathy and no small amount of moral imagination to appreciate the harm that is done so subtly to the psyches of males and females alike when the very structures of speech imply that one form of human being sufficiently encompasses all that is essential to humanity, that it can stand *in place of* the other form, apparently without significant remainder. Without getting into the question of whether in fact forms of *homo* functioned as generic masculine forms in Latin culture, one can recognize that today nothing would be lost and much would be gained had the opening line of *GS* been translated so as to make it unambiguously evident that the Fathers cared about "The joy and hope, the grief and anguish" of the women as well as the "men of our time."

The issue of language in this document is not merely a matter of translation, however, for the Latin text itself is replete with usages that have the effect of rendering females invisible. Of particular significance is the frequent use of forms of *frater* and *filius* in contexts where the full inclusion of women in the Christian community would require *soror* and *filia* as well. Again, the point is not trivial, though it is not yet universally acknowledged. In a culture where the superiority of males has been assumed, it is taken for granted that "brotherhood" encompasses an ideal for human community and that "God's sons" is an adequate way of speaking of God's children. However, from the perspective of those who appreciate the power that language has over thought and who recognize the injustice perpetuated by sexist language, the words employed in *GS* no. 55 to express the Fathers' interpretation of the duty "to build up a better world in truth and justice" can only be understood as ironic: "We are witnessing, then, the birth of a new humanism, where man [*homo*] is defined before all else by his responsibility to his brothers [*fratres*] and at the court of history."

These words are ironic, albeit unintentionally so, because until people recognize that *the ideal of "brotherhood"*—which excludes half of the world's population from consideration—*is part of the problem of global injustice,* there can only be very limited progress toward the better world for which the authors of *GS* hoped. The wisdom of certain strains of popular Catholicism, which finds it proper to specify both sexes in such classic texts as the Easter hymn *O filii et filiae* and the Litany of the Saints, has something to teach official Catholicism in this regard.

Nature and culture. A second problematic area concerns the views on nature and culture that undergird *GS*. Here the difficulty is perhaps best described as one involving a "root metaphor" that governs the conciliar understanding of these realities. The metaphor derives from Genesis 1:28 ("And God blessed them, and God said to them, 'Be fruitful and multiply, and fill the earth and subdue it; and have dominion over the fish of the sea and over the birds of the air and over every living thing that moves upon the earth' ") and is essentially a metaphor of domination of nature. Section no. 9 speaks approvingly of "a growing conviction of mankind's ability and duty to strengthen its mastery over nature," and no. 57 refers to a divine design whereby "mankind's" task is "to subdue the earth and perfect the work of creation." The metaphor implies that humanity is superior to "nature" and is divinely authorized to be violent in its regard. What such a concept of culture as "mastery over nature" fails to provide is the sense of humanity's *continuity* with the rest of nature and, indeed, of our interdependence with the earth and the rest of the physical universe. There is an unresolved tension in the document between its several approving references to "conquering," "subduing," and "mastery" in relation to earth and nature (all implying a degree of violence)—see nos. 9, 34, 38, 53, 57, and 63—and the ideal it proclaims at the close of no. 92: ". . . we ought to work together without violence and without deceit to build up the world in a spirit of genuine peace."[22]

Not unrelated to this is the tendency of the document to regard woman's "nature" rather differently from the way it treats the "nature" of "man."[23] When the document speaks of human nature in general, it stresses the element of mystery, the sense that God alone can supply the full answer to the question which each person is to oneself. When *GS* speaks of woman's nature, however, it conveys a sense of fixity that contrasts with an earlier reference to a "dynamic and more evolutionary concept of nature" in general (no. 5). Thus one reads in the chapter on culture (no. 60):

> At present women are involved in nearly all spheres of life: they ought to be permitted to play their part fully according to their own particular nature. It is up to everyone to see to it that woman's specific and necessary participation in cultural life be acknowledged and fostered.

The passage is ambiguous, for were a truly evolutionary view of woman's "nature" intended, it could indeed be a summons to women's liberation. But the term "specific" with respect to woman's participation in cultural life suggests that this is not the case, and subsequent church documents have made it clear that official Catholicism has not applied teachings about the dynamic and mysterious quality of "human nature" so fully to female forms of that nature as to male. Indeed, this became apparent the day following the promulgation of *GS,* when the Fathers of the Council addressed several closing letters to various constituencies. Their message to women indicates that past attitudes were still very much in the ascendency. Even the existence of this message itself is telling, since there is no document addressed simply "to men," although there are messages addressed to "rulers," "men of thought and science," "artists," and "workers." This very arrangement of categories carries the implication that women are thought of primarily in terms of sexual roles, while men are regarded in terms of diversified vocational contributions. Indeed, this is made clear in the opening sentence of the message to women: "And now it is to you that we address ourselves, women of all states—girls, wives, mothers, and widows, to you also, consecrated virgins and women living alone—you constitute half of the immense human family."[24] The message goes on to mention that "the vocation of woman" is in the present era "being achieved in its fulness," a statement whose tone of assurance that the church already knows what this vocation is stands in marked contrast to what is said in the message to workers ("very loved sons"): "The Church is ever seeking to understand you better."[25]

Social analysis. A third area of concern regarding *GS* involves the social analysis it provides, which for all its acuity in so many respects is regrettably limited on two points of importance, especially to women. In the first place, there is a sense in which women are only partly visible to this analysis. While it is good that women's progress toward our rights is generally affirmed by the document, it is cause for regret that the limited nature of this progress, especially in the developed countries, is not acknowledged. Blindness to the real situation of women is particularly evident in the line from no. 9, ". . . women claim parity with men in fact as well as of rights, where they have not already obtained it." Leaving aside for the moment the question of whether "parity," with its weaker connotation of "equivalence" rather than "equality," is an adequate norm for progress toward justice, what amazes a feminist reader of this sentence is the implicit claim that women have achieved a fair situation in some parts of the world. The claim in not documented, and indeed it would be impossible to defend, given the actual status of women worldwide. As the sociologist Constantina Safilios-Rothschild observed *ten years after* the promulgation of *GS:*

> . . . despite some progress in some areas, the status of women is still quite low. . . . If we accept that a society is modern when it "is successful in removing social and structural constraints and in establishing appropriate compensatory mechanisms so that all individuals, regardless of their categorical membership such as age, sex, race, religion, ethnic origin, or social class, can have equal access to a wide range of options in all life sectors," no society can claim to have achieved modernity. . . . [Even in Western, developed] societies . . . sex discrimination has not been eliminated and probably it has not even decreased. It has only changed form: from open, direct discrimination to subtle, sophisticated sex discrimination, which tends to be more effective and difficult to fight.
>
> The status of the majority of women who live in the Third World is still low and ongoing social changes either do not affect their status or tend to even further deprive them of options and opportunities.[26]

The factors examined by Safilios-Rothschild in the cross-cultural study that resulted in the conclusion quoted above were educational and vocational training, employment and other economic roles, marriage and the family, power and political participation, and health and nutrition. Today most analysts of women's status worldwide would support her conclusion that it generally remains lower than man's status.[27]

Given that the text of *GS* was approved with such a notable misconception about women's actual status left to stand in no. 9, it is not surprising that other suggestions of the "invisibility" of women occasionally appear, such as the failure of the document to mention rape or domestic violence, both of which are suffered frequently by women worldwide, in its list of crimes against life and human integrity and dignity (no. 27).

A second problematic aspect of the social analysis in the document is its tendency to press the valid distinction between the church and the rest of society so far that the religious institution escapes the criticism that is leveled against the broader society.[28] Whereas no. 26 affirms in general that "the social order requires constant improvement," the more specific sociological reference to the church in no. 44 is considerably weaker:

> The Church has a visible social structure, which is a sign of its unity in Christ: as such it can be enriched, and it is being enriched, by the evolution of social life—not as if something were missing in the constitution which Christ gave the Church, but in order to understand this constitution more deeply, express it better, and adapt it more successfully to our times.

A feminist social analysis, of course, would claim that the church order ought to be a *model* of justice and equality for society in general, rather than simply a gradually enhanced reflection of "the evolution of social life," and would provide detailed practical suggestions toward achieving this goal.

Ethical norms. Paragraph no. 26 also articulates a social ideal that includes ethical norms—particularly justice and love—which are solidly endorsed by feminists. The key passage reads:

> The social order requires constant improvement: it must be founded in truth, built on justice, and enlivened by love: it should grow in freedom towards a more humane equilibrium.

What *GS* fails to acknowledge, however, is the way in which norms of justice and love can themselves paradoxically function to legitimate oppression if they are not subject to criticism from a perspective that appreciates the full humanity of women. In an article supplying just such a critique, Margaret A. Farley demonstrates the need for theology to draw out the implications of the change from

". . . past assumptions regarding fundamentally hierarchical patterns for relationship between men and women and today's growing acceptance of egalitarian patterns of relationship." She points out that "the 'old order' was clearly one in which women were considered inferior to men and in which women's roles were subordinate, carefully circumscribed, and supplementary." And this "old order" resulted in *theories of justice* that "systematically excluded the possibility of criticizing sexism." By contrast, the "new order," which Farley and other feminists applaud, "is based upon a view of women as autonomous human persons, as claimants of the rights which belong to all persons, as capable of filling roles of leadership in both the public and private spheres, as called to equality and full mutuality in relation to both men and women."[29]

What Farley then suggests is that theological ethics needs to develop new interpretations of the traditional principles of love and justice, interpretations that will give impetus to rather than impede progress toward a society that recognizes women as full persons. Whereas *GS* evinces no sense that Christian ideals of love and justice have been in any way problematic for women, Farley's feminist perspective allows her both to critique inadequacies in traditional understandings of these ideals and to offer constructive alternatives in their stead. Thus, with respect to "Christian love" she proposes that its component of "equal regard" is empty if it does not include real equality of opportunity, that its dimension of "self-sacrifice" is false if tied in with misconceptions about female "passivity," and that its aspect of "mutuality" is inadequate if based on analogues found " . . . in the mutuality of relationships between parent and child, ruler and subject, master and servant" rather than on a full recognition of the equality of women and men."[30] With respect to justice she argues that adequate understandings of both individual and common good require a shift from strict hierarchical models of social organization to more egalitarian ones, noting that ". . . in fact the good of the family, church, etc. is better served by a model of leadership which includes collaboration between [male and female] equals" than one which places a single male leader at the head of the community.[31] In the end, new understandings of justice and love are found to be mutually reinforcing norms for this Christian feminist ethic:

> That is to say, interpersonal communion characterized by equality, mutuality, and reciprocity may serve not only as a norm against which every pattern of relationship may be measured but as a goal to which every pattern of relationship is ordered. Minimal justice, then, may have equality as its norm and full mutuality as its goal. Justice will be maximal as it approaches the ultimate goal of communion of each person with all persons and with God.[32]

Such a perspective would find the ideal of parity expressed in *GS* no. 9 inadequate insofar as this concept, usually associated with agricultural economics, implies that less-than-equal shares are just ones. "Parity" is not analyzed in the document, but it is the sort of norm which, when applied to human society, tends to accept unequal distribution of literacy, income, and food on grounds that needs for schooling, remuneration, and nourishment differ according to gender roles, men and boys "naturally" requiring more of all because of their actual or prospective positions of dominance.

A feminist perspective also finds inadequate the ideal of "brotherhood," which is articulated so often in *GS,* precisely because the word reinforces patterns of vision that select out the sisters from our midst (who, across the globe, are less educated, poorer, and hungrier than their brothers in every major society) and thus undermines the very laudable traditional norm articulated in no. 27, the injunction to look upon the neighbor "as another self." So long as one does not *see* the *specifics* of female neighbors, that long will one's neighbor-love remain inadequate in their regard.

Theological affirmations. Finally, a feminist analysis of *GS* must attend to what is said, and perhaps more important, what is implied about Divine Reality in this text. Here again, the problem can best be approached by the avenue of metaphor. It is an accepted theological principle that all language about God involves analogy, which means that no human expressions about Divine Reality are ever adequate to the Mystery to which they refer. In the Western religious traditions the metaphor of human fatherhood, which carries, unfortunately, the weight of longstanding patriarchal associations, has traditionally been emphasized in descriptions of Divine Reality and in the language of worship. Many scholars have pointed out, however, that even ancient biblical texts do not limit their language about God to male images such as father, warrior, and lord (although indeed these predominate), but also employ on occasion female metaphors to describe divine qualities and activities.[33] What is problematic about the language used in *GS* to refer to God is that it relies so heavily on male imagery that it risks reinforcing a naive but widespread tendency to take the metaphor of God as "father" too literally, with the resultant reinforcement of the patriarchal values such language has long legitimated. There are resources within the tradition for countering this tendency, but the Council Fathers, like most Christians two decades ago, were evidently unaware of the connections between societal injustice toward various oppressed groups and patriarchal religious language. Their treatment of atheism can hardly be faulted for not recognizing what was only beginning to be apparent in Western culture, namely, that patriarchal God-language is one of the ways in which "believers" can be said, in the words of *GS* no. 19, "to conceal rather than to reveal the true nature of God." Twenty years later, however, it has become clear that the rejection of Christianity lamented by the Council Fathers is sometimes due to the idolatrous use of religious language that continues to support the "father-rule" so many associate with values and behavior they see as harmful to humanity and threatening to the rest of creation as well.[34]

Thus, were a Council to address the issue of alienation from Christianity today, it would be essential to build on the insights of feminist theologians such as Rosemary Radford Ruether, Elisabeth Schüssler Fiorenza, and Bernard Cooke, who claim that the tradition was originally distinguished by a nonpatriarchal understanding of Divine Reality, which can be expressed in terms of the "Abba" experience of Jesus[35] as well as in terms of the "Sophia-God" experience of Jesus. As Fiorenza concludes from her study of early Christian sources:

> To sum up, the Palestinian Jesus movement understands the ministry and mission of Jesus as that of the prophet and child of Sophia sent to announce that God is the God

> of the poor and heavy laden, of the outcasts and those who suffer injustice. As child of Sophia he stands in a long line and succession of prophets sent to gather the children of Israel to their gracious Sophia-God. Jesus' execution, like John's, results from his mission and commitment as prophet and emissary of the Sophia-God who holds open a future for the poor and outcast and offers God's gracious goodness to *all* children of Israel without exception. The Sophia-God of Jesus does not need atonement or sacrifices. Jesus' death is not willed by God but is the result of his all-inclusive praxis as Sophia's prophet. This understanding of the suffering and execution of Jesus in terms of prophetic sophialogy is expressed in the difficult saying which integrates the wisdom and *basileia* traditions of the Jesus movement: "The *basileia* of God suffers violence from the days of John the Baptist until now and is hindered by men of violence" (Matt 11:12). The suffering and death of Jesus, like that of John and other prophets sent to Israel before him, are not required in order to atone for the sins of the people in the face of an absolute God, but are the results of violence against the envoys of Sophia who proclaim God's unlimited goodness and the equality and election of *all* her children in Israel.[36]

It is indeed good that Vatican Council II, particularly in *GS,* began a process of restoring to a central place in Catholic piety an appreciation of God's power and presence that stresses the metaphor of the gentle, inviting, and guiding Spirit, who affirms creation and inspires and sustains human hope and community (nos. 11, 93). Surely the fruits of Catholic feminist theology, which the episcopal authors did not anticipate from their work, bear witness today to the truth of the affirmation from Ephesians 3:20–21 with which they conclude the document *GS* (no. 93). In sisterly solidarity with these brothers, then, I also conclude: To this Sophia-God, who by the "power at work within us is able to do far more abundantly than all we ask or think . . . be glory in the Church and in Christ Jesus, to all generations, for ever and ever. Amen."

Notes

1. My title cites the *Pastoral Constitution on the Church in the Modern World* (*GS*), no. 58. This and subsequent citations of the English translation of this text are from Austin Flannery, O.P., ed., *Vatican Council II: The Conciliar and Post Conciliar Documents* (Northport, N.Y.: Costello Publishing Co., 1975). Citations of the Latin text are from *Sacrosanctum Oecumenicum Concilium Vaticanum II: Constitutiones Decreta Declarationes,* vol. 1 (Vaticanum Typographium, 1967). As to the meaning of "feminist," I employ the term here in a broad sense to indicate a position that involves (a) a solid conviction of the equality of women and men, and (b) a commitment to reform society, including religious society, so that the full equality of women is respected, which requires also reforming the thought systems that legitimate the present unjust social order. Both women and men can thus be "feminist," and within this broad category there is enormous variety in levels of commitment, degrees of explicitness of commitment, and, of course, in opinions regarding specific problems and their solutions. Feminism is a concept that is best understood in dialectical relationship to the concept of sexism. For an insightful analysis of these concepts, see Patricia Beattie Jung, "Give Her Justice," *America* 150 (April 14, 1984): 276–78. In focusing on the Catholic feminist theology that has developed in part as the result of *GS,* I am conscious of the limits of my work. Clearly, many other dimensions of what the document said about "culture" could have been discussed, and clearly, my own perspective is limited by my status as an educated white woman from the United States. There remains a great need for the voices of women of color and of women from less privileged backgrounds to be heard in the theological forum. As long as the voices of nonwhite experience are out of the mainstream of theological inquiry, so long will this discipline risk being skewed and out of line with life. It simply will not do if the justice won by women in theology is shared only by white women from the upper and middle classes of Western society.

2. For examples of positions recently articulated by women that challenge certain Catholic teachings while remaining solidly grounded in the Catholic tradition, see Rosemary Radford Ruether, *Sexism and God-Talk: Toward a Feminist Theology* (Boston: Beacon, 1983); Joan Timmerman, *The Mardi Gras Syndrome: Rethinking Christian Sexuality* (New York: Crossroad, 1984); as well as essays by women contributors to Robert Nugent, ed., *A Challenge to Love: Gay and Lesbian Catholics in the Church* (New York: Crossroad, 1984); Leonard Swidler and Arlene Swidler, eds., *Women Priests: A Catholic Commentary on the Vatican*

Declaration (New York: Paulist, 1977); and the periodical *Conscience.* Catholic women writers, not all of whom are theologians, are by no means unanimous in their analyses, programs, and degrees of dissent from official teachings. In this, of course, they resemble male writers on religious subjects. The above examples are but a sampling from a vast and growing body of feminist literature bearing on Catholic life and thought. I have treated these developments at some length in two articles, from which I occasionally borrow in the present essay, with the permission of Paulist Press. These are: "Women and Religion: A Survey of Significant Literature, 1965–1974," in Walter Burghardt, ed., *Woman: New Dimensions* (New York: Paulist, 1977), 161–89, and "Coming of Age: Women's Contribution to Contemporary Theology," *New Catholic World* 228 (March-April 1985): 61–69. I also want to acknowledge here the assistance given me by two feminist thinkers, Anne E. Carr and Janet Walton, who read an earlier version of this chapter and made valuable suggestions for revisions.

3. Perhaps my own case will help to illustrate the phenomenon of the extraordinary existential impact of *GS* upon some women. I first read the document in the edition edited by Walter M. Abbott, S.J. (New York: America Press, 1966) during a thirty-day Ignatian retreat in the summer of 1967. Schooled in a strict interpretation of the vow of poverty, I had not since 1958 possessed a book like this that spoke so directly to my life and aspirations, and for some reason I felt entitled to take the then remarkable step of underlining and marking this ninety-five-cent paperback so that I could easily find key passages again. Passages that struck home particularly were those dealing with the rights of all, including women, to educational and cultural development. In 1967, I had been teaching high school students for seven years, but despite assiduous application to college extension courses during summers and weekends, I was far from completing my B.A. degree. The words of the document gave expression to my own basic sense of the wrongness of this situation, which I realized even then was tied in with the status of women religious in the church, and they offered a spirituality to counter the prevalent one that legitimated injustice and waste of talents. These words inspired me to take initiatives I would not not have considered earlier. I arranged with my religious superiors to be released from classroom duties for three months during the 1968–69 school year, and that spring I completed my B.A. at age twenty-eight, two years earlier than I would otherwise have done and eleven years after I had entered church service. That summer of 1969, I began to study German, the first step in a long program of further study that would finally allow me to become active in the Catholic Theological Society of America in 1978. By 1972, I was heavily involved in organizing Catholic women

religious and beginning to publish my developing feminist views. As I reflect on these developments, I feel that had the breakthroughs of *Pacem in Terris* and *GS* not taken place, it is quite likely that my talents and energy would long since have left the world of institutional Catholicism and been invested instead in "secular" pursuits, a course taken by countless women ahead of me. For another account of the impact of Vatican II and *GS,* see Mary Daly, *The Church and the Second Sex,* both the original and the revised "feminist post-Christian" editions (New York: Harper and Row, 1968 and 1975).

4. Indeed, the term *vir* is not indexed in the Vatican edition of the conciliar documents, although the parallel term *mulier* is included in the index. It is also interesting to note certain other distinctions the index draws or fails to draw: *Fraternitas, Fratres et Sorores Religiosae,* and *Fratres separati* are all listed. The last of these terms, heard often at the Council, inspired Gertrud Heinzelmann to entitle her collection of interventions regarding women made during Vatican II *Die getrennten Schwestern: Frauen nach dem Konzil* (Zurich, 1967).

5. Garden City, N.Y.: Image Books, 1976, 8. This volume appeared earlier under the title *What a Modern Catholic Believes about Women* (Chicago: Thomas More Press, 1972), where the incident is described on p. 5. Mary Daly discusses the place women and women's concerns were given at Vatican II in *The Church and the Second Sex* (1975), 118–31.

6. Daly, *The Church and the Second Sex* (1975), 131. Hallinan's statement appears in George Tavard's *Woman in Christian Tradition* (Notre Dame, Ind.: University of Notre Dame Press, 1973), 127–28.

7. Quoted by Rosemary Radford Ruether in "Home and Work: Women's Roles and the Transformations of Values," in Walter Burghardt, ed., *Woman: New Dimensions* (New York: Paulist Press, 1977), 77.

8. Daly, *The Church and the Second Sex* (1975), 8. As Daly indicates in this post-Christian feminist introduction to her earlier work, she completed doctorates in both philosophy and theology at Fribourg. Had Vatican Council II not taken place, she declares in the same introduction, she might never have written *The Church and the Second Sex.*

9. Mary I. Buckley, now of St. John's University (N.Y.), earned the Th.D. in 1969 from the University of Münster, as did Elisabeth Schüssler Fiorenza in 1970.

10. See Lorine M. Getz and Marjorie L. Roberson, compilers, *A Registry of Women in Religious Studies* (New York: The Edwin Mellen Press, 1984). This directory is available for $10 from Women's Caucus: Religious Studies, c/o Boston Theological Institute, 210 Herrick Road, Newton Centre, MA 02159.

11. Daly, *The Church and the Second Sex* (1975), 141–42.

12. For the proceedings of the Detroit Conference, see Anne Marie Gardiner, ed., *Women and Catholic Priesthood* (New York: Paulist, 1976).

13. New York: Paulist, 1977.

14. This lecture was later published under the title, "The Meaning of Modern New Testament Studies for the Possibility of Ordaining Women to the Priesthood," in Raymond E. Brown, *Biblical Reflections on Crises Facing the Church* (New York: Paulist, 1975), 45–62.

15. *Horizons* 10/1 (Spring 1983): 22–31. This journal is published by the College Theology Society, an organization that developed to meet the needs of growing numbers of Catholic theologians, many of them laypersons, who were not teaching in seminaries. Its membership is not limited to Catholics, and the organization continues to focus on the concerns of those teaching in colleges and universities.

16. This address is published in the 1982 edition of *The Annual of the Society of Christian Ethics*.

17. "Moral Theological Agenda: An Overview," *New Catholic World* 226 (January-February 1983): 4–7.

18. "Coming of Age in Christianity: Women and the Churches," *The Furrow* 34 (June 1983): 347.

19. Ibid., 348.

20. Ibid., 351.

21. Janet Kalven, "Women's Voices Began to Challenge after Negative Vatican Council Events," *National Catholic Reporter* (April 13, 1984): 20.

22. I suggest that the biblical metaphor should be recognized as suffering from the limitations of the patriarchal culture from which it emerged and the text should be reinterpreted so as to emphasize a different metaphor, one of caring or stewardship. The import of biblical attitudes toward the earth and nature has been amply discussed by Christian theologians since the appearance of Lynn White's famous article, "The Historical Roots of Our Ecologic Crisis," in *Science* 155 (1967): 1203–7. See, for example, Ian G. Barbour, *Technology, Environment, and Human Values* (New York: Praeger, 1980) and Roger Lincoln Shinn, *Forced Options: Social Decisions for the 21st Century* (New York: Harper and Row, 1982), and various works by Ruether.

23. The theme of "nature" is an important and much debated one in feminist writing. For theological contributions to this discussion, see Valerie Saiving's essay of 1960, "The Human Situation: A Feminine View," reprinted in Carol P. Christ and Judith Plaskow, eds., *Womanspirit Rising* (New York: Harper and Row, 1979), 25–42; and Ruether's *Sexism and*

God-Talk, especially 72–92. For instances of the secular feminist discussion, see Sherry B. Ortner, "Is Female to Male as Nature Is to Culture?" in M. Z. Zimbalist and L. Lamphere, eds., *Woman, Culture and Society* (Stanford: Stanford University Press, 1974), 67–87; and Penelope Brown and L. J. Jordanova, "Oppressive Dichotomies: The Nature/Culture Debate" in The Cambridge Women's Studies Group, *Women in Society: Interdisciplinary Essays* (London: Virago Press, 1981), 224–41.

24. Walter M. Abbott, S.J., ed., *The Documents of Vatican II* (New York: America Press, 1966), 732–33.

25. Ibid., 735–36.

26. "The Current Status of Women Cross-Culturally: Changes and Persisting Barriers," an article first published in *Theological Studies* 36 (December 1975) and reprinted in Burghardt, *Woman: New Dimensions,* 27. Safilios-Rothschild is quoting her own earlier research in the above passage.

27. For example, Lucille Mathurin-Mair, a Jamaican who is Secretary General of the World Conference of the UN Decade for Women, has recently observed that today, "Women stand in the wings, as political expediency gives lowest priority to those social and economic sectors which serve society's vulnerable groups, of whom Third World women and their families constitute the most numerous and the most vulnerable. Not surprisingly, the current United Nations review of the Decade [1975–85] concludes that '. . . the condition of the majority of women in the developing world has changed, at most, marginally . . .' " See her article, "The Quest for Solidarity," in *New World Outlook* (January 1985): 56. This entire issue of the magazine, a monthly published by the General Board of Global Ministries of the United Methodist church, is devoted to the theme of "Women Challenging the World."

28. The implications of this tendency are evident in such observations as the following passage from the 1977 Vatican Declaration, reaffirming a traditional position against women's ordination: "Thus one must note the extent to which the Church is a society different from other societies, original in her nature and in her structures." Here the distinction between the church and other societies is used to counter arguments that modern social developments indicate the need to alter a longstanding tradition. See "Declaration on the Admission of Women to the Ministerial Priesthood," in Austin Flannery, ed., *Vatican Council II: More Postconciliar Documents* (Grand Rapids, Mich.: Wm. B. Eerdmans, 1982), 342. The tendency also accounts for the discrepancy sometimes noted between official church concern for violations of human rights in various extra-ecclesial political entities and unconcern for violations of human rights within the institutional

church. For a recent discussion of this problem, see Leonardo Boff, *Church: Charism and Power* (New York: Crossroad, 1985), 32–46.

29. "New Patterns of Relationship: Beginnings of a Moral Revolution," in Burghardt, *Woman: New Dimensions,* 53–54.

30. Ibid., 56–57.

31. Ibid., 69.

32. Ibid., 69–70.

33. For a rich discussion of this dimension of the Old Testament, see Phyllis Trible, *God and the Rhetoric of Sexuality* (Philadelphia: Fortress, 1978).

34. In *Sexism and God-Talk,* Ruether describes an understanding of patriarchy widely shared by other religious feminists: "By patriarchy we mean not only the subordination of females to males, but the whole structure of Father-ruled society: aristocracy over serfs, masters over slaves, king over subjects, racial overlords over colonized people" (p. 61). Thus, the patriarchal system is understood most fundamentally to be a system in which some dominate others, and besides being associated with sexism, it is also linked with racism, classism, militarism, violence, and ecological irresponsibility.

35. The significance of the NT references to *Abba* and *Pāter* remains at issue among scholars. Besides the above-cited works of Cooke and Ruether, see Robert Hamerton-Kelly, *God the Father* (Philadelphia: Fortress, 1979), and Phyllis Trible's critical review of this book in *Theology Today* 37 (1980): 116–19. More recently, Madeleine I. Boucher has provided detailed exegetical evidence to counter the positions of Joachim Jeremias and Hamerton-Kelly regarding the alleged "centrality" of the "father symbol" for God in the religious understanding of Jesus. In a paper presented to the Catholic Biblical Association of America meeting in New Orleans August 12, 1984, "The Image of God as Father in the Gospels: Toward a Reassessment," Boucher suggests that "the increasing frequency of the father image for God (much more common in Matthew and John than in earlier materials) may have been not so much a theological as a christological development. It is the understanding of Jesus as 'the Son' that leads to language about God as 'the Father' (typescript, 19). Boucher is currently preparing a book-length study of the use of *Abba* and *Pāter* in the NT.

36. Elisabeth Schüssler Fiorenza, *In Memory of Her: A Feminist Theological Reconstruction of Christian Origins* (New York: Crossroad, 1983), 135.

21. Bridge Discourse on Wage Justice: Roman Catholic and Feminist Perspectives on the Family Living Wage

Christine Firer Hinze

This chapter first appeared in *The Annual: Society of Christian Ethics* in 1991.

Justice for working people has been a persistent concern in modern Christian social ethics. A hallmark of the modern Roman Catholic approach to economic justice has been its advocacy of the worker's right to a family living wage. In the United States, the Catholic case for a living wage was impressively articulated and advanced by ethicist and reformer Monsignor John A. Ryan (1869–1945). Ryan's classic Catholic defense of a family living wage was inevitably shaped by the ideological and practical features of the work-home relation that formed the historical context for its development. Since Ryan's time, however, significant cultural and economic shifts affecting workers and families have occurred. In particular, changes pertaining to the roles and rights of women call into question the case for a family living wage as it has been structured in the century of Catholic social thought since *Rerum Novarum*. Social theorists and contemporary cultural critics—chiefly feminists—who have analyzed the "family wage system" set these changes and these questions in high relief.

The questions raised cut to the quick of the Catholic conception of the good society. To address them, Catholic ethicists must reconsider assumptions about gender, power, and social flourishing that have decisively influenced traditional thinking about wage justice. Such critical examination can, I believe, open the way for retrieving the normative concept of a family living wage as part of a vital, radically transformative approach to worker justice. If the norm is to be revitalized, distortions that have bedeviled past thinking about "family," about "making a living," and about "work" and the "wage" due it, must be identified and exorcised. Intertwined in all these are apprehensions about women and their activity. Unravelling this knot of issues will require an ideological turn, coupled with the awareness that ideology critique carries its own occupational hazards.

This consideration of the family living wage draws upon two distinctive moral traditions: progressive strands of modern Catholic social thought and socially transformative strands of radical feminist theory.[1] Catholics and feminists often find themselves in intense and even fundamental dispute. Yet they share an ardent commitment to individual and social well-being and to the pursuit of economic justice. Both communities have given careful and extensive attention to matters of wage justice. Engaging these two literatures will, I hope, not only shed light on the issue at hand, but contribute to the forgoing of what philosopher Nancy Fraser calls "bridge discourse." Bridge discourse can enhance analytic lucidity and transformative power by amalgamating disparate and sometimes isolated conversations and agendas into "hybrid publics."[2] Such forays, as Fraser observes, are risky; one takes the chance of offending everyone. Yet, given the pluralistic context in which Christian ethicists seek to comprehend and pursue social justice today, building bridges and cultivating hybrids seem timely, indeed indispensable, tasks.

Roman Catholic Advocacy of a Family Living Wage

From Leo XIII's 1891 encyclical *Rerum Novarum* forward, papal teaching on modern industrial society has made the just treatment of wage workers a central moral concern.[3] In line with the natural law approach favored by Catholic moralists—and in contrast to influential individualist and collectivist alternatives—work is interpreted through an anthropology that posits the dignity of each person, realized within three primary social relationships deemed natural to humans: the political, the economic, and the familial.

The political realm contributes to the common good by coordinating and protecting through law the well-being of groups and individuals. The economic sphere serves human flourishing by providing fair access to the goods of creation intended for all. In modern industrialized economies, the majority of persons are dependent for such access on wages attained through their labor. Human dignity is upheld in this setting only if workers are assured that, through honest labor, they can obtain the material conditions necessary for survival and a reasonable degree of security and material well-being. For Leo XIII and his successors, this translates into the worker's right to a "living wage." Important as the political and economic dimensions of social life are, this modern natural law tradition particularly cherishes the family, "the first, essential cell of human society."[4]

The family, as an intimate "community of love," "school for a deeper humanity," "nurse and mother" of a wholistic attitude toward the nature and dignity of persons in society, and "school of work," is regarded as the primary milieu for personal, interpersonal, and intergenerational growth and sustenance. As a "domestic church," family is an essential locus for spiritual education and formation. Family contributes to the common good by nurturing the bonds and values necessary if civic and economic life is to subsist and prosper, yet in a real sense the civic and the economic spheres are there *for the sake of* the family. Family, for instance, functions as a warrant for private ownership in the papal writings.[5] In *Gaudium et spes,* marriage and family are described as the foundation of political life, and the well-being of political society is presented as intimately linked to the well-being of the community founded by marriage. Family needs and is obligated to the polis, yet retains an integrity and freedom within its sphere that ought not be violated by state or economic interference. A priority of family over economy is asserted analogous to the priority of individual over state and labor over capital. Economic justice is therefore understood as necessarily including measures that promote and protect family life. A right to a *family* living wage—that is, a wage sufficient to assure a basic level of material security for both the adult household head, normally male, and his dependents, normally, wife and children—is implied in Leo XIII's *Rerum Novarum* and is explicitly articulated in Pius XI's *Quadragesimo Anno*.

The consistent concern in this literature with labor and with workers' rights reflects a traditional emphasis in Christian social thought upon the moral priority of the basic needs of those who are economically vulnerable, over against the protection of the superfluities of the economically advantaged. Set as it has been within a normative vision of society as a harmonious, hierarchically interdependent organism, the conflictual, even radical implications of this basis have frequently been muted. Yet official Catholic support for union organizing and for strikes, and for state planning to ensure a decent livelihood for all, has been augmented over the years by a heightened recognition of the need to combat underlying institutional imbalances of power. Though the overarching goal of a peaceful and harmoniously ordered community endures, Catholic sensitivity to the dynamics of power, the reality of sinful systems and structures, and the necessity of struggle for social justice has increased over the past century, becoming especially evident in the social encyclicals of the present pope and the later writings of his predecessor, Paul VI. Seen in light of these developing sensibilities, the living wage is a means of *empowering* the poor to fulfill their material needs, to cultivate their abilities and aspirations, and to participate in just, enlivening social relationships.

In developing his argument for a family living wage, John A. Ryan was self-consciously faithful to the Catholic natural law tradition and the papal social teachings of his day. Simultaneously, he employed an inductive analysis and evaluation of the specifics of the U.S. economy to fashion a moral and practical argument that was distinctly American. As ethicist and social reformer, Ryan contended with both the theoretical and practical aspects of the issue of economic justice, and as a sophisticated and influential American Catholic case for wage justice, his work remains unsurpassed.[6] Not surprisingly, his work displays the tension, characteristic of the tradition, between a theological affirmation of equal rights and dignity for all and a hierarchical, organic picture of social relations that legitimates differential access to institutional power, burdens, and benefits according to one's function in the social organism. The tension is most obvious in treatments of gender roles, but it also affects other areas, such as models of social transformation and of class relations. We shall see in Ryan's writings the difficulties that this uneasy marriage of egalitarian and hierarchical models wrought.

John A. Ryan's Case for a Family Living Wage

Ryan's 1906 treatise *A Living Wage* contends that "the workingman's right to a decent livelihood is, in the present economic and political organization of society, the right to a Living Wage."[7] Ryan defines "workingman" as "the adult male of average physical ability who is exclusively dependent upon the remuneration that he is paid in return for his labor." An individual living wage denotes remuneration sufficient to provide the laborer with a decent livelihood (81–82). What is meant by a decent livelihood? This is, Ryan explains, "that amount of the necessities and comforts of life that is in keeping with the dignity of a human being . . . that minimum of conditions which the average person of a given age or sex must enjoy in order to live as a human being should live" (72–73).

Here is a first noteworthy feature of Ryan's understanding of a living wage. On the one side, a *living* wage supersedes the bare minimum needed to stave off hunger, disease, or exposure to the elements. The laborer who responsibly conforms with "nature's universal law of work" is entitled to at least the minimum of the material conditions of "reasonable" living. "This implies the power to exercise one's primary faculties, supply one's essential needs, and develop one's personality" (117). On the other side, the living wage, while more ample than bare subsistence, reflects Ryan's support for the right to acquire moderate but not unlimited material security. To champion a living wage was by no means to underwrite an unbridled quest for acquisition or upward mobility for laborers any more than for capitalists.[8]

A *living* wage, then, refers to an ample minimum, limited by norms prohibiting greed and obliging consideration of the grave needs of others. A living *wage* signifies the whole return due the laborer for his hire: "Food, clothing, shelter, insurance, and mental and spiritual culture—all in a reasonable degree—are, therefore, the essential conditions of a decent livelihood. *Remuneration inadequate to secure all of these things to the laborer and his family falls below the level of a Living Wage*" (136, emphasis added). Ideally, the worker should be paid a money wage that would enable him or her to provide for all these needs directly, rather than through benefits such as social insurance.[9] But regardless of the mode of delivery, the test of a living wage, and of economic justice, is whether the worker and his family gain access to all of the benefits mentioned.

Ryan's references to "the worker and his family" direct us to a second pivotal feature of his moral argument: he presents a case not simply for a personal, but a *family* living wage. Several elements stand out in Ryan's defense of every adult male worker's right to a wage sufficient to support not only himself, but also (potentially or actually) his wife and children. First, Ryan argues not on the basis of the rights of the family or any of its members, but rather on the basis of the dignity and rights of the individual man. He claims that remuneration for work is a right derived from the worker's own essential and intrinsic worth, whose primary end is his own welfare. Ryan, consistently, now contends that the primary end of the right to a family living wage is also the welfare of the male worker. "The right to the means of maintaining a family . . . is not finally derived from the *duty* of maintaining it—from the needs of the family—but from the laborer's *dignity,* from *his* own essential needs" (119, emphasis original).

Further, in founding the right to a family living wage in the dignity of the male worker, who is presumed to be the conduit through whom the material needs of wife and children are met, Ryan relies on a strictly defined sex-role script drawn from both his contemporary cultural context and from traditional theological and natural law sources favoring a hierarchical/organic picture of society.[10] The basic lineaments of the male role as household head are dictated by unchanging nature, and ultimately, God (118). The subject of the right to a family wage is the adult male, and he is subject to this right by virtue of his patriarchal destiny in the social and familial order. Ryan admits that "if the support of wife and children did not in the normal order of things fall upon the husband and father, he would not have a right to the additional remuneration required for this purpose." But the right of a male worker to the conditions of being the head of a family seems to Ryan to be obvious; and this right implies the right to a family living wage "because nature and reason have decreed that the family should be supported by its head" (119).

Nature and reason have also decreed a role for women, and it is not in the public workplace. Ryan's comments betray an image of woman as ordained for the domestic, non-wage-earning realm. Ryan supports an individual living wage for the growing numbers of women in the work force in his own day, and he seems to favor some form of family allowances to assist women who become the sole economic support of their children due to widowhood, desertion, or other calamities. Nonetheless, he consistently depicts the "normal" flourishing of women—and the flourishing of family and society—in terms of the confinement of wives and mothers to domestic duties in the home. Normally, a single working woman has the right to remuneration sufficient to support herself individually, but not to a family living wage. The single working male retains the right to a family living wage for savings against the day when he will exercise his male family rights.[11]

Ryan's enduring concern with a living wage for working persons is in line with the moral priority the Christian moral tradition has accorded the less advantaged in the economic realm. As a right due every full-time adult worker, the living wage is deemed not a matter of charity to the poor but of justice. Ryan also expressly identifies the living wage as an effective instrument in a scheme of distributive justice that would widely disperse moderate economic power and security. As a distributive strategy, it reflects the canons Ryan elaborates in *Distributive Justice,* where he gives the canon of human needs a central role.[12]

Ryan's defense of the family living wage was a focal point in his agenda for social reform guided by legislation. This plan does not reject American capitalism in favor of a socialistic alternative, but rather opts for "the existing system, greatly, even radically amended."[13] Ryan is usually categorized as a progressive rather than a radical, a practical reformer rather than a revolutionary. Yet elements of his position entail changes more thoroughgoing than the term *practical reform* conveys. Advocating what John Coleman calls "a widespread people's capitalism embracing industrial democracy and consumer and productive cooperatives," Ryan's vision of change went further than that of many of his progressive and even his socialist counterparts.[14]

Ryan models a strategy in U.S. Catholic social thought that is of potential significance to others who seek deeply-reaching economic and social transformation, yet who, like Ryan, must judge when ameliorating reform is a useful or necessary step on the long road to more radical change. We can detect in Ryan's work hints of an approach that harbors a long-range vision of profound social transformation and begins to enact it by selecting short-range, reformist strategies. I call this a "radical transformationist" stance.

Allegiance to larger normative goals in this kind of approach requires two things, both found in Ryan's writings. First, particular reformist moves must be seen not as ends but as beginnings and must be assessed in light of their success in advancing a larger vision of social renovation. Second, a radical transformationist approach recognizes that steps toward social and economic reconstruction remain superficial and short-lived unless accompanied and energized by intellectual and moral conversion: education of mind and change of heart on the part of large numbers of persons. One aspect of that conversion, mentioned but not developed by Ryan, involves embracing a simpler, less acquisitive lifestyle and rejecting what later popes would call consumerism and materialism. He writes, "For the adoption and pursuit of these ideals the most necessary requisite is a revival of genuine religion."[15] Nevertheless, he clearly does not believe the problem of injustice will be rectified by personal conversion and individual conviction; conversion must lead people to organize together, for only combined power will effect larger social change:

> It is true that the efficiency of social effort is limited by the character of the individuals through whom the effort is made. . . . But it is also true that organized effort will add very materially to the results that can be accomplished through moral suasion addressed to individuals. This very obvious truth is superlatively true in our time,

> when man's social relations have become so numerous and so complex. Both methods are necessary. There must be an appeal to the minds and hearts of individuals, and the fullest utilization of the latent power of organization and social institutions [330–31]

The Feminist Challenge to Family Wage Ideology and Practice

At the time of Ryan's death in 1945, cultural mores concerning family and work, legislative trends in the wake of the New Deal, and a thriving post-war economy provided a congenial environment for the family wage norm. A broad middle-class consensus linked maturity and happiness to the roles of father-husband-wage-earner for men and wife-mother-homemaker for women. The expectation that the male breadwinner ought to earn a family wage and that he would use it to support his spouse and children, was essential to this mindset. In the 1960s, however, this "family wage system" began a period of decline. Chief among the undermining forces were changing work and familial patterns, and challenges to the system's supporting ideology. Some of the most trenchant and damaging critiques of the family wage arrangement, though by no means the only ones, have come from feminists.[16]

Feminists' indifference to or attacks upon the family living wage as the centerpiece of a program for securing wage justice must be understood against the background of their own perspective on economic injustice. Feminists have been concerned with (1) establishing the *economic* value of work performed in the home and, at the same time, (2) dismantling the system of practices built on the belief that work traditionally done in the home is uniquely women's calling and women's glory. While Catholic teaching has traditionally stressed the value of the activities of women in child-bearing, child-rearing, and maintaining kinship relationships, Catholic thought has characteristically presented the domestic sphere as an alternative to economic life rather than as any kind of expression of it. Even more seriously, the traditional theoretical underpinning of the Catholic arguments in support of a family living wage advances with remarkable explicitness precisely the system of beliefs that these feminists condemn. Clare Fischer, for instance, identifies a complicitous alliance between the modern family wage system and the denial of socio-economic value to traditional "women's work." This deeply rooted cultural denial has made the practice of under-remunerating those who perform domestic labor seem legitimate, even natural. Fischer identifies three ideological structures that support the mistreatment of women and domestic work endemic to the family wage system: the division of labor according to gender, the division of labor according to location, and the assumption that these divisions reflect some important intrinsic (natural) difference between women and men.[17]

The *sexual division of labor* separates body and mind according to gender and then perceives them as reconciled in the distinctive efforts of the two sexes. Associating the public world of men with "mind" reinforces the asymmetric value and power relations between the public sphere and the more "bodily" sphere of women. The *division of work according to location or space* "assumes the symbolic and real division and unification of the sexes by way of the woman as wife/mother in the home, and man as breadwinner in the marketplace." Late nineteenth-century developments in industry and middle-class values helped shape a split between work and hearth that idealized both the domestic realm and woman as wife and mother. The home, with woman at the heart, came to be seen as a blessed retreat for children and men from the polluting effects of the city. Woman's role as guardian of domesticity and morals made it unthinkable that she should abandon home for wage work. Women who sought paid employment were perceived as "either unfortunate or perverse." The gendered distinction of spheres was widely embraced as a virtuous arrangement that gave every family member a special destiny in the building of a strong nation.[18]

Unfortunately, be relegating the meaning of "work" to paid labor performed outside the home (as in the question asked of married women, "do you work?"), this division denies public acknowledgment and economic value to the wealth of socially contributive work performed in and around domestic space. The "home-work" thus belittled encompasses a rich constellation of tasks involved in homemaking and housekeeping. It also includes volunteer work, involuntary unpaid work in consumer-related activities, and the reproductive work of assuring social and economic continuity through the raising of children.[19]

The first two ideological patterns feed into the third, involving *the assumption of distinctive personalities according to gender, and segregation of occupational aspirations and opportunities accordingly.* The combination of these three ideological structures, charges Fischer, has nourished a gender-based occupational hierarchy that under-values, under-privileges, under-rewards, and disempowers women, both inside and outside the home.[20]

As I noted, Ryan and the Catholic social tradition are vulnerable to this feminist criticism. Popes and moral theologians have relied on authorities who assume that male-female biological differences form a natural basis for asymmetries in capacity, characteristics, and social roles.[21] Such assumptions detract from the force of claims about the value of domestic work also found in modern Catholic teaching. For example, Pope John Paul II's 1981 encyclical on human work, *Laborem Exercens,* reiterates Catholic support for a family living wage; it also offers a broad definition of work that underscores the right to remuneration attaching to *both* "economic" labor and the "social" labor associated with family life. The test of a just system is whether work, thus construed, receives a just wage, explicitly described as a family wage.

> Just remuneration for the work of an adult who is responsible for a family means remuneration which will suffice for establishing and properly maintaining a family and for providing security for its future. Such remuneration can be given either through what is called a family wage—that is, a single salary given to the head of the family for his work, sufficient for the needs of the family without the spouse having to take up gainful employment outside the home—or through other social measures such as family allowances or grants to mothers devoting themselves exclusively to their families [19].

These words avoid an exclusively masculine reading of the bread-winner role, yet the traditional view of the mother as primary guardian of children and the home remains. The pope continues:

> It will redound to the credit of society to make it possible for a mother . . . to devote herself to taking care of her children and educating them in accordance with their needs. . . . Having to abandon these tasks in order to take up paid work outside the home is wrong from the point of view of the good of society and of the family when it contradicts or hinders these primary goals of the mission of a mother [19].

The pope's strong appeals for equal treatment of women and for work arrangements that support parental responsibilities are likewise hobbled by a perduring understanding of woman as mother, and mother as primary parent. "The true advancement of women requires that labor should be structured in such a way that women do not have to pay for their advancement by abandoning what is specific to them and at the expense of the family, in which women as mothers have an irreplaceable role" (19).[22]

Is it disingenuous to anticipate the emergence of "bridge discourse" and "hybrid publics" in the context of such a seemingly intractable disagreement? There are promising signs. Within the Catholic community, some scholars and religious leaders are re-examining traditional Catholic interpretations of sex difference and gender roles. A spectrum of Catholic moral thinkers continues to affirm that "the implications of sexual differentiation extend beyond the minimum requirements of species propagation," and warns against a dualist denial of any relation between sexual and human identity.[23] Yet these thinkers vigorously reject the thesis that biology dictates rigid distinctions in personality, social roles, or power. On the feminist side, even feminists who denounce the record of patriarchy in Roman Catholicism might find a point of agreement with Catholic writers who reject schemes that would simply "treat women like men" in an effort to achieve economic justice. Over the last decade, feminists have been reconsidering the implications of gender differences for their political and economic agendas. Debate has centered on the questions of how to admit and respect differences—between or among men and women—while preventing unjustly differential access to resources, opportunities, and power.[24] This knotty issue is directly relevant to the project of conceiving a new, feminist-informed family living wage argument.

There are, then, tentative indications that the construction of bridges may already be underway. To this we might add that whatever their ideological differences, these representatives of Roman Catholic and feminist social thought share three important convictions: (1) The problem of wage justice represents a moral challenge and a public policy issue of commanding importance because the wage structure that currently characterizes the United States economy is manifestly unjust. (2) Wage justice cannot be achieved in a policy context that attends only to the situation of individual workers; family life and relations of support and dependency must be taken into account. (3) Labor within the confines of the household contributes in a major way to the common good and should be recognized and rewarded in conformity with its real value.

Renovating the Family Living Wage for the 1990s

Critique of family wage ideology would doubtless have had little impact had it not been accompanied by dramatic changes over the last three decades in the practices and compositions of workplace and family. The trends are well known: the dramatic rise in participation of women, especially married women, in the paid work force; the continuing gap in pay between men and women, with women making on the average less than seventy cents to each dollar earned by men; the doubling of female-headed households over the last two decades; the persistently higher under- and unemployment rates for minority women; and the continuing clustering of the female labor force (80 percent) in low-paying occupational categories (clerical, sales, service, factory).[25] Ironically, as the numbers of women in the paid labor market swell, women as a group are getting poorer—the "feminization of poverty" noted by sociologist Diana Pearce. Barbara Ehrenreich points out that the fastest growing segment of America's female poor are single mothers. She quotes the findings of Caroline Bird who asserts that in the 1970s, the number of "ill-paid, dead-end 'women's jobs' increased so much faster than better paid 'men's work' that by 1976 only 40 percent of the jobs in this country paid enough to support a family." Ehrenreich comments that in the economy of the 1980s the only way most households have been able to make a family wage is by adding up the wages of all individual family members.[26]

Both as ideal and as reality, the family-wage norm has waned. Is it a norm with retrieving? I am convinced it is. The great numbers of households in which adults are unable to support their families with the wages they are able to attain for their work is just as morally intolerable today as it was in Ryan's time. Such families, so many of them headed by women, testify to the continued relevance of framing wage questions in terms of basic human rights and social morality. The injustice these families suffer is still usefully expressed as the denial of sufficient remuneration to ensure a decent livelihood for self and family—that is, as the denial of a family living wage.

If the family living wage is to recapture public attention as a compelling agenda, however, both is rationale and its description require revision. It plainly will not do to frame the moral agenda for a family living wage *in the form or with the justification* familiar to Ryan and much modern Catholic social teaching. That form and justification were bound to patriarchal presuppositions that have bred an overly individualistic construal of men's public economic rights, while socially and economically devaluing women and children, homemaking and parenting. Economic justice today will require a new, more equitable, marriage of home and workplace. A revitalized case for the family living wage must incorporate and advance three major changes in the context for its discussion: (1) work connected with home and family, and any work performed by women, must now be valued and remunerated in ways comparable to the valuing and remuneration of the economic contributions of men; (2) responsibility for the rearing of children is being socially reshaped and this transitional period demands creative policy initiatives; and (3) the global dimensions of the U.S. economy must be taken into account. Let me consider these each in turn.

The Catholic tradition's appreciation for the value and importance of homemaking and parenting can be fused with a feminist affirmation of the rights and dignity of women to produce an adequate valuation of women's traditional contribution without circumscribing opportunities for women in the workplace and professions. John Paul II states, "Experience confirms that there must be a social re-evaluation of the mother's role, of the toil connected with it and of the need that children have for care, love and affection. . . ."[27] The pope mistakenly attributes domestic activity solely to mothers; yet he is right that home-work and parenting-work demand social re-evaluation. An honest assessment of the effort and time required for reasonable degrees of housekeeping, homemaking, and child care brings to light a fact obvious to practitioners: homemaking and parenting constitute, in themselves, *at least* the equivalent of one full-time occupation. If both partners are employed full time outside the home, the question is only whether the work relating home and children will be performed by those partners as full-time "second shift" (with duties either shared between partners or resting, as most studies show, primarily on the working mother/wife), be turned over to paid or unpaid others, or not get done at all.[28]

Declaring homemaking and parenting bona fide, socially enriching, and publicly indispensable occupations whose responsibilities devolve in some way on every adult householder, seems innocuous enough. That impression is deceiving. To think of domestic work in this way cuts directly across privatized and interest-maximizing cultural images of work and family. To accept home-work as real work is to acknowledge that the wage-worker, householder, or parent is reducible neither to an isolated individual nor to a social role, but is a person enmeshed in a complicated network of relations and obligations. To admit that familial relations and home-work at times can and should take precedence over conventionally wage-rewarded economic activities, not just for women but for all workers, also flies in the face of common perceptions of careers as linear paths to be plied with undistracted and single-minded concentration. A social and economic system that began to treat domestic work, and public occupations that carry out traditional domestic functions, as equitably-valued, remunerable vocations, would surely augur the demise of the current gender-based occupational hierarchy. To call home-work real work, in short, is to foment radical change.

Secondly, we must think in fresh ways about the responsibilities of child-rearing in our socially altered world. I have already discussed the pervasive ways in which the unsustainable but still widely prevalent assumption that only women can and should parent has contributed to economic injustice. Changes in the public valuation of children will also be required. The flood of women into the workplace has forced some improvising on privatized parenting and child care, but the deficient response of United States social policy to the so-called child-care crisis (and the persistent framing of this crisis as a women's issue) attests to an alarming lack of common accountability for children. Provision for the care and nurturing of the rising generation is a public as well as a familial responsibility.[29]

The third point, supported in both Catholic and feminist literatures, is that wage-worker justice in one country can no longer be pursued in isolation from the global dimensions of the economy.[30] The trend toward moving domestic manufacturing jobs into countries that offer higher profits and a "cheaper, more docile" labor force is well known. Many of these situations replicate to a shocking degree the abuses of nineteenth-century laissez-faire industrial capitalism in the North Atlantic, especially the exploitation of the labor of poor women. The fact that 85 percent of assembly line workers in developing countries are women, preferred precisely because of their economic vulnerability, underscores on the international scene what is true domestically: because women are disproportionately affected by wage injustice, they must take center stage in schemes for change.[31] These facts also highlight the need to set programs for worker justice within an inclusive, complex construal of the common good.

This is, then, a decisive moment, demanding creative, concrete response. The work of John Ryan provides strategic guidance in the politics of implementation as well as in the development of moral theory. One lesson bequeathed by Ryan is that ethicists can serve social transformation by helping convince relevant publics that the morally required course can also meet reasonable tests of practicality and expediency. Some regard Ryan's "principle of expediency"—that good ethics can also be good economics—as his most innovative contribution to U.S. Catholic economic ethics. Ryan recognized that expediency would never do as an overarching principle for Christian economic ethics. Yet as Charles Curran points out, to argue that the moral course and the economically expedient course may at least intersect squares with the Catholic natural law view that the goal of moral activity is genuine flourishing, in the context of a common good whose material conditions economic activity provides.

Ryan addressed the objection that requiring all employers to pay a family living wage would result in capital losses, inefficiency, bankruptcies, job flight, and general economic harm. His rebuttal attempts to give due weight to the legitimate concerns of business and industry, the social obligations attaching to property and capital, and the natural right of workers to a decent livelihood. In a similarly nuanced response, contemporary advocates of the family living wage will explicitly attend to the ramifications and responsibilities of what Pope John Paul II calls the "indirect employer": those influences, persons, conditions, and institutions (chief among these the state) that affect the direct employer's ability or willingness to justly remunerate employees.[32] Feminist analysis brings to light the extent to which the society as bearer of ideology must be considered as a dimension of the indirect employer.

Ryan also teaches us how important it is to cherish and preserve an animating concern for assuring dignified access to basic levels of material well-being to those who currently lack them. Over the past three decades, critics have sounded the death knell for the traditional theory and practice of a family living wage. Simultaneously the ranks of working or underemployed poor have swelled with people, largely women, who are losing ground or are unable even to make the amount sufficient to be called minimally just under Ryan's definition. In the face of these realities, top priority must continue to be given to the struggle for *minimal* wage justice that preoccupied ethicists like Ryan.

Rethinking the Terms: "Family," "Living," "Wage"

The pro-family wage turf of the 1970s and 1980s was dominated by the forces of religious and social traditionalism. In the 1990s, support for a family living wage flowing from the hybrid public joined by radical transformationist feminism and progressive social Catholicism could fuel a different and more powerful movement for change than that so far accomplished by conservatives.[33] The family living wage agenda this unlikely partnership might beget would be animated by a fresh understanding of each of its central terms.

Family and the roles of its members in relation to home and work would be newly considered from a non-sexist perspective. One feature of this vantagepoint would be its appreciation for the heterogeneity of forms family is actually taking today. The Catholic tradition holds out lifelong, monogamous, heterosexual marriage as the normative context for children and family. The encounter with feminist and pluralist values, and the experience of the persistence of variety, argue for elasticizing, without abandoning, the traditional Catholic norm.[34] Varied expressions of family would be not merely tolerated but actively supported. This is an admittedly difficult feat—to continue to affirm a norm without excoriating, marginalizing, or demeaning those who by necessity or according to their best judgments take a different path. Steps toward this goal are taken when Catholics respectfully attend not only to contemporary variations on the "traditional" family, but also to the heterogeneity of familial forms and styles that have historically existed outside the narrow confines of the dominant race, class, and culture.

In building its normative picture of family, a Catholic and feminist hybrid public could jointly affirm the dignity and worth of the intimate circle of family life in its various forms and stages; the need to realize in any family form a genuine and equal partnership of men and women; the constitutive value that meaningful work holds for the flourishing of each family member and of the family unit itself; and the fact that labor must be set within a broader picture of family life that makes provision for, as Ryan would put it, the reasonable bodily, intellectual, moral, spiritual, and cultural development of all members. This means time and space for rest and celebration, for civic participation, for work for justice, for religion. Feminists and popes can both call the family "a school for deeper humanity," and both have a high stake in preserving this privileged locale for the care and nurture of persons.

This vision of family leads directly to new thinking about what the word *living* in "a living wage" entails. In a major poll conducted in 1989 by the *New York Times,* over 80 percent of working men and women with small children stated that they felt unable to devote proper time and energy to their children.[35] Making a living must surely imply having the sustenance, time, and energy to live with and in one's family; all this is included in the meaning that "a decent livelihood" held for John Ryan. By this yardstick, however, a great many jobs today, including some of the most cash-productive, fall far short. Workers today continue to deserve, and too many do not attain, access to these aspects of decent living. Redirecting policies and resources in order to assure those minimums will be aided by appeals to the moral limits on acquisition and ownership that the Catholic moral tradition has stressed.

The word *wage* in "family living wage" will also have a different meaning in the 1990s. Progressive Catholics and radical feminists can agree that work has moral significance. This moral regard, bestowed equally upon work located in the home and outside the home, can ground claims about the right to a just return for one's domestic as well as one's non-domestic labor. Ryan implicitly admitted the right of the full-time homemaker to a living wage, but assumed that this right was normally honored by channeling wages through the male household head. Feminists debate whether work in the home should be subject to money payment, but, like mainstream writers, have developed no consensus as to whether homework fits properly under the category of waged labor. The ideological and practical questions involved are many and are badly in need of critical scrutiny.

I support explicitly extending *wage* to mean the whole remuneration given the worker. Benefits, insurance, opportunities for time off, and other forms of payment, such as family allowances, may augment or substitute for cash wages to form a sum total that may be deemed a living wage. Again, Ryan's formulation can guide: the total remuneration must provide the minimum material conditions for a decent livelihood, empowerment for a reasonable degree of flourishing. While it will be difficult to specify this in dollar amounts for 1990s families, quibbling over how to precisely define "just level of remuneration" will not excuse policymakers from recognizing and counteracting grossly unacceptable levels and conditions where they currently exist.

Reformist Proposals; Transformative Prospects

If we can agree that childrearing and home-work should be regarded a full-time occupation, *for which just remuneration in some form is due,* we then face difficult policy questions: how much remuneration? delivered in what form? from whom? under what system of accountability? Given that change starts from where we presently stand, what is the most promising path toward realizing the family living wage agenda sketched here? Let me propose for debate a two-staged approach.

A first step, one that may already be gaining some implied consent in contemporary U.S. practice, is to press for full employment and for a "family living wage" (an amount sufficient to reasonably support self, spouse, and children) for every adult wage worker, male or female, regardless of marital or family status. This goal has the advantage of being simple and clear, and it avoids applying different wage scales to people in different life situations—an option that was rejected by Ryan for prudential reasons (though he accepted wage differentials for single women and single men). Today the female employee is at least as likely as her male counterpart to be head or sole breadwinner of her household. Since at present, white women employed full time make, on the average, only two-thirds the salary of white men—black and Hispanic women only about one half of white male salaries—the struggle to achieve comparable worth for female-concentrated occupations is of critical importance.[36] Such an approach can draw on many of the arguments advanced by Ryan, extending the designation of individual familial rights and duties to adult women as well as men. Choice and monetary freedom would be maximized for individual adults in this "liberal" expansion of Ryan's proposal.

If this level of remuneration were accorded all adult workers, dual-earner households could in theory afford for either worker to forego earnings during periods of high familial intensity, or to pay a fair rate to competent assistance in upholding domestic duties while both parents work outside the home. Single household heads could afford full-time domestic and child care help[37] and could, at least theoretically, choose to work part time at different points in the family and child-rearing cycle. Lacking some family allowance system, single parents would not, however, have the option of caring for their own home and children full time. Nor, given present workplace practices, could dual-earner families expect to periodically switch to part-time status without paying penalities in salary scales, advancement, and job security.

These limitations return us to a central point. Short of qualitatively upgrading the social and economic value placed on the domestic activities of citizens, and adjusting the mutual expectations of employers and employees accordingly, simply upping or equalizing wage scales will not change much. To truly accomplish the sense of "family living wage" introduced here, "living wage" must come increasingly to mean not just cash amounts, but hours and conditions of work, career tracks, benefits and leave policies, pension and insurance plans that conduce to the fulfillment of one's domestic, along with one's public vocation.[38]

To be complete, this program for worker and family economic justice will have to address two critically important sets of issues that I can only mention here. First, a thicket of specific economic and political questions concerning policy goals, strategies, and means of compliance and enforcement, surround my reformist proposal that a family living wage be extended to all full-time workers. As Ryan saw, no appeal for social change, regardless of its moral validity, can gain a hearing unless it evidences sufficient attention to these often detailed and technical questions. A persuasive brief for extending a family wage must also analyze the relationship between higher wages and unemployment, and must consider how a wage system that honors domestic rights will refract in reforms of the public welfare system.[39]

Behind these specific questions about reform are more foundational questions that also demand attention. The institutions and ideology of the capitalist, free-market economy that have underpinned the notion of a family living wage must be subjected to more thorough critique and reconsideration. If the logic of capitalism is to commodify work and reduce its value to the wage it commands, how can remunerating people for home-work avoid corrupting this sphere of human practice? Would extending a family wage to each individual adult decrease the incentive to marry, undermining traditional marriage as a social institution? Might this renovated approach call, finally, for reweaving the economic and cultural fabric out of which the family living wage was originally cut?

As strategic and foundational concerns of this sort are encountered, the initial, seemingly straightforward plan may begin to give way to pressure for more radical changes in the family-work relation. We may find ourselves called, at this second stage, to "utopian envisagement" of what ought to be and "anticipatory action" to bring the present order into better conformity with the normative vision.[40] A more deeply transformative goal can be advanced: a concrete historical ideal of a social order that balances and coordinates economic and domestic participation, in the context of a pluralistic common good. Of course, for the vast majority of workers today, even in elite professional settings, such an order is at best a dimly perceived hope. Yet such an orienting ideal is, I believe, entailed both in a Catholic vision of a family living wage liberated from oppressive distortions and in descriptions of the sought-for society proffered by feminists.[41] Such images are not in themselves policy answers. Yet they can serve as lodestars to those engaged in the tedious and messy labor of articulating middle axioms and executing courses of action that might move the present closer to God's future.

The feminist spirit we have tapped here presses toward radical change. But, in the spirit of Ryan—who also harbored some radical predilections—the work of transformation can begin, I think, with building consensus on particular reforms that ensure the minimum to those who lack it, simultaneously moving toward an enriched public understanding of what is minimally due. So refashioned, the family living wage can be a compelling norm that attracts the support of hybrid publics.

In the present domestic and international circumstances, pursuing such a full-fledged economic and social goal may seem quixotic. Yet a glance at the milieu of social and economic crisis in which Ryan developed his ethics, and at the great disparity that then existed between the norms he articulated and the actual situations of workers, reminds us that neither assurance of success nor certain economic prospects fed Ryan's dedication to the task. What impelled him forward was the need to alleviate the suffering of the economically vulnerable—and honor their God-given dignity and rights.

The difficulty of specifying a contemporary program for wage justice and the daunting problems facing its implementation should neither paralyze ethical analysis nor dissuade us from testing every promising means of instantiating in policy the norms we analyze in theory. Here again Ryan, theorist and reformer, remains a model. Ryan knew that every concrete initiative laid him open to being called either dogmatic or oversimplistic. Yet, he insisted,

> neither honesty nor expediency is furthered by an attitude of intellectual helplessness, academic hyper-modesty, or practical agnosticism. If there exist moral rules and rational principles applicable to the problem of wage justice, it is our duty to state and apply them as fully as we can. Obviously we shall make mistakes in the process, but until the attempt is made, and a certain (and very large) number of mistakes are made, there will be no progress. We have no right to expect that ready-made applications of the principles will drop from Heaven.[42]

Probing, articulating, and negotiating steps toward flourishing in that space between heaven and the ground we presently occupy—these are perduring tasks of a Christian ethic of wage justice.

Notes

1. "Radical transformationist feminist" denotes a variegated group of writers who judge existing social structures to be radically diseased by

patriarchy, yet who are committed to transformative struggle with and within those existing structures. Among Christian feminists, radical transformationists, who often align themselves with liberation theology, include Rosemary Radford Ruether, Beverly Wildung Harrison, and Dorothee Sölle.

2. Nancy Fraser, *Unruly Practices: Power, Discourse, and Gender in Contemporary Social Theory* (Minneapolis: University of Minnesota Press, 1989), 11–13, 174.

3. For a comprehensive study, see Donal Dorr, *Option for the Poor: A Hundred Years of Vatican Social Teaching* (Maryknoll, N.Y.: Orbis, 1983). On the question of the coherence of modern papal social teaching, see Michael Schuck, *That They Be One: The Social Teaching of the Papal Encyclicals* (Washington, D.C.: Georgetown University Press, 1991).

4. *Gaudium et spes,* in *Vatican Council II: The Conciliar and Post Conciliar Documents,* ed. Austin Flannery, O.P. (Northport N.Y.: Costello Publishing Co., 1977), 52.

5. *Rerum Novarum,* 9; *Quadragesimo Anno,* 45; *Mater et Magistra,* 45, 112; *Pacem in Terris,* 21—in *Seven Great Encyclicals* (Paramus, N.J.: Paulist Press, 1963).

6. For a balanced appreciation and critique of Ryan, see Charles E. Curran, *American Catholic Social Ethics* (Notre Dame, Ind.: University of Notre Dame Press, 1982), 84–91.

7. John A. Ryan, *A Living Wage: Its Ethical and Economic Aspects* (London: Macmillan & Co., 1906), 81.

8. Ryan distinguishes three separate levels of wealth: (1) wealth sufficient to provide the necessities of life; (2) wealth sufficient to provide the conventional necessities and comforts of one's own social plan or station in life; and (3) wealth that is superfluous to maintaining the standards of decent livelihood or one's station in life. Everyone has a natural right to the first level, which determines the basic living wage. Ryan attempts to enumerate the specifics included in this frugal, yet more-than-basic, level of material comfort and security (and to estimate the dollar amounts needed to acquire them at various times and in various geographical regions). He includes a moderate amount for amusement and recreation, clothing that will allow one dignity in the society of one's peers (for example, one good set of dress clothing and several changes of underclothes), organizational memberships, some periodical and other literature, and money for charity and religion. In addition to *Living Wage,* 117, see John A. Ryan, *Distributive Justice: The Right and Wrong of Our Present Distribution of Wealth,* new revised edition (New York: Macmillan

Co., 1927), chap. 21, esp. 273. John Coleman observes that Ryan seemed to regard upper-middle-class wealth (or the lower reaches of it) as the utmost moral limit to material possessions—this would refer to the second level. Anyone attaining wealth at the third level would morally have it entirely subject to the call of grave necessity. John A. Coleman, *An American Strategic Theology* (New York: Paulist Press, 1982), 94–95.

9. Ryan recognizes that in the American legislative and business milieu, some of this remuneration takes the form of benefits such as social insurance. He places the main responsibility for social insurance on the business sector. The principle of subsidiarity and the rightful autonomy of the worker and family dictate that state-legislated insurance be avoided when possible; if deemed necessary, such public insurance plans should be supported by a levy on business. Ryan, *Distributive Justice,* 380–81. For a different contemporaneous view, see Barbara Nachtrieb Armstrong, *Insuring the Minimum: Minimum Wage Plus Social Insurance Equals a Living Wage Program* (New York: Macmillan, 1932).

10. Hierarchical and organic images of society have a long lineage in western Christian thought. The importance of social hierarchy in the thought of Thomas Aquinas, for instance, is treated in Katherine Archibald, "The Concept of Social Hierarchy in the Writings of St. Thomas Aquinas," *The Historian* 12 (1949–50): 28–54; reprinted in *St. Thomas Aquinas on Politics and Ethics,* ed. and trans. Paul E. Sigmund (New York: W. W. Norton, 1988), 136–41.

11. For Ryan's argument that unmarried working women ought to be paid a *personal* living wage equivalent to that paid unmarried men doing the same job, see *Living Wage,* 107–9; and *Distributive Justice,* 333–35. For his argument that, nonetheless, even single adult male workers have a right to the higher, *family* living wage, see *Distributive Justice,* 395; *Living Wage,* 109 n. 1. For his belief that women should not, except in cases of calamity, work outside the home, see *Living Wage,* 133. For his discussion of what is due in the "abnormal" situation of a single female household head who is a wage earner, see *Distributive Justice,* chap. 16. For Ryan's brief discussion of family allowances, see *Distributive Justice,* 335. Note that for Catholic natural law theory, the "normal" serves as a powerful moral guide both in judging men's and women's nature and roles, and in determining the substantive meaning of the standard of a decent livelihood. A similiar appeal to "normal standards" occurs when Ryan specifies a minimum living wage as one which renders access to "that quantity of goods and opportunities which fair-minded men would regard as indispensable to humane, efficient, and reasonable life" (*Distributive Justice,* 321). Such appeals reflect confidence that close observation of

human nature and experience can yield trustworthy moral insight. Yet when uncritically employed this method can assume and reinforce existing power relations and their ideological supports, as when Ryan writes, "The welfare of the whole family, and that of society likewise, renders it imperative that the wife and mother should not engage in any labor except that of the household. When she works for hire she can neither care properly for her own health, rear her children aright, nor make her home what it should be for her husband, her children, and herself. . . . The wife become a wage worker is no longer a wife" (*Living Wage,* 133). Definitions of what is normatively normal may unwittingly be controlled by the class, gender, and ethnic biases of their formulators. Even feminist sensitivities do not guarantee escape from the blinding power of the "normal"; the tendency of U.S. social reformers to judge what is normal and beneficial for poor women from the vantagepoint of their own middle-class mores and assumptions is documented in Shelia Rothman, *Woman's Proper Place: A History of Changing Ideals and Practices, 1870 to the Present* (New York: Basic Books, 1978).

12. Ryan, *Distributive Justice,* chap. 16. The prominence of the criterion of actual human need is also illustrated when Ryan discusses what is due in the "abnormal" situation of the single female household head who is a wage earner. "In view of the large number of women wage earners who have to support dependents, they ought to be included in any family allowance system. The objections drawn from the integrity of the family, the normal place of the mother, and the responsibility of the father, seem insufficient to outweigh the actual human needs of so many thousands of working women and their children" (*Distributive Justice,* 335).

13. Morris Hillquit and John A. Ryan, *Socialism: Promise or Menace?* (New York: Macmillan, 1914), 13.

14. Coleman, *American Strategic Theology,* 88. See also Curran's helpful discussion of Ryan's program for social transformation in *American Catholic Social Ethics,* 51–58. In pressing the radical import of Ryan's long-range vision I differ with commentators, among them Curran, who stress Ryan the progressive reformer and who judge that Ryan's realism and practicality limited him to ameliorative programs. Ryan's advocacy of economic democracy suggests something more. Ryan's vision of industrial democracy was a radical proposal, more so than perhaps Ryan at the time perceived. The tumult caused by the use of the term *economic democracy* in early drafts of the recent U.S. bishops pastoral letter on the economy (*Economic Justice for All* [Washington, D.C.: National Conference of Catholic Bishops, 1986]) supports this claim.

15. Ryan, *Distributive Justice,* 397. Though Ryan employs the phrase

"revival of genuine religion" with some regularity, he neither makes clear what such a revival would entail nor elaborates religion's specific place in his moral vision which relies heavily on natural law philosophy.

16. For works that trace the development of the assumption of the worker's right to a family living wage from the late nineteenth through the middle twentieth centuries under the aegis of the "family wage system," see e.g., Barbara Ehrenreich, *The Hearts of Men: American Dreams and the Flight from Commitment* (Garden City: N.Y.: Anchor Books, 1983), esp. chap. 1; Mark Kline Taylor, *Remembering Esperanza: A Cultural-Political Theology for North American Praxis* (New York: Maryknoll, 1990), 87–97; Arthur Brittan, *Masculinity and Power* (Oxford: Basil Blackwell, 1989), 113–18. For a discussion of "the aberrant 1950s" as a period of unprecedented and atypical cultivation of the family wage system and the gender prescriptions attached to it, see Sylvia Ann Hewlett, *A Lesser Life: The Myth of Women's Liberation in America* (New York: William Morrow & Co., 1986), chaps. 10, 11. For feminist criticism of the family wage system Eleanor Rathbone, *The Disinherited Family: A Plea for the Endowment of the Family* (London: Edward Arnold & Co., 1924), esp. chaps. 2–4; Jean Bethke Elshtain, "The Family Crisis, The Family Wage, and Feminism," in Jean Bethke Elshtain, *Power Trips and Other Journeys: Essays in Feminism as Civic Discourse* (Madison, Wis.: University of Wisconsin Press, 1990), 61–72. Ehrenreich, and others also document revolts by some men against the theory and practice of male-as-breadwinner. See *Hearts of Men* chaps. 4–8; Hewlett, *A Lesser Life,* chap. 13.

17. Clare B. Fischer, "Liberating Work," in *Christian Feminism: Visions of a New Humanity,* ed. Judith L. Weidman (San Francisco: Harper & Row, 1984), 123–24. "Each of these represents an ideological structure that generates and sustains difference and hierarchy in the work world [and home]. Each possesses a nuanced value-orientation that promotes and legitimates the devaluation of and discrimination against women in their daily activity of earning a wage, [and] of securing an adequate environment for the family. All three structures are intertwined in the fundamental assumption about the *naturalness* of differentiated labor [and remuneration] according to gender."

18. Ibid., 133–36. An insightful analysis of the cult of motherhood is found in Sara Ruddick, "Maternal Thinking," in *Rethinking the Family: Some Feminist Questions,* ed. Barrie Thorne with Marilyn Yalom (New York & London: Longman, 1982), 76–94.

19. Fischer cites Nona Y. Glazer, *The Invisible Intersection: Involuntary Unpaid Labor outside the Household and Women Workers* (Berkeley,

Calif.: The Center for the Study, Education, and Advancement of Women, University of California, 1982). See also Elshtain, *Power Trips,* and Arlie Hothschild with Anne Machung, *The Second Shift: Working Parents and the Revolution at Home* (New York: Viking, 1989).

20. Fischer, "Liberating Work," in *Christian Feminism,* ed. Weidman, 135–39.

21. One might begin with Thomas Aquinas, *Summa Theologicae* I-I, Q. 92, but a *locus classicus* is Pope Pius XI's critique of female emancipation in the 1930 encyclical *Casti connubii:* "this false liberty and unnatural equality with the husband is to the detriment of the woman herself, for if the woman descends from her truly regal throne to which she has been raised within the walls of the home by means of the Gospel, she will soon be reduced to the old state of slavery (if not in appearance, certainly in reality) and become as amongst the pagans the mere instrument of man" (in *Seven Great Encyclicals,* 75).

22. The pope does not envision a similarly irreplaceable domestic and parental role for the father. The implication remains: the male is indispensable in the breadwinner role and is allowed and appreciated in—*but not fundamentally meant for*—the domestic role. For the female, the reverse is assumed. John Paul II's stance on the equality and public role of women is far more positive than that of some of his predecessors, and more is said about the role of the father in other documents. See, e.g., John Paul II, *Familiaris consortio: Apostolic Exhortation on the Family* (Washington, D.C.: U.S.C.C., 1982), 22–25. Yet the problems noted here are never fully overcome.

23. Lisa Sowle Cahill, *Between the Sexes* (Philadelphia: Fortress Press, 1985), 96, 98. See also, U.S. Catholic Bishops, "One in Christ Jesus, A Pastoral Response to the Concerns of Women for Church and Society," *Origins* 19/44 (April 5, 1990): paras. 23–26.

24. For a theologically-informed treatment of the implications of difference for feminists, see Susan Brooks Thistlethwaite, *Sex, Race, and God: Christian Feminism in Black and White* (New York: Crossroad, 1989). For the vigorous debate over heterogeneity among feminist philosophers and social theorists, see the thematic issue "Reason, Rationality, and Gender" (ed. Nancy Tuana) of *Newsletter on Feminism and Philosophy* [*of the American Philosophical Association*] 88 (June 1989). One crucial practical arena for this debate is the current struggle over "comparable worth." The comparable worth principle, which has gained legislative and judicial acceptance in a number of states, beginning in Minnesota in 1984, holds that "jobs dissimilar in nature can be compared in terms of knowledge, skill, effort, responsibility, and working conditions, and that jobs equiva-

lent in value in these terms should be paid equally." Sara M. Evans and Barbara J. Nelson, *Wage Justice: Comparable Worth and the Paradox of Technocratic Reform* (Chicago: University of Chicago Press, 1989), 11.

25. These trends are documented in Fischer, "Liberating Work," in *Christian Feminism,* ed. Weidman, 122, and are also discussed in Evans and Nelson, *Wage Justice,* chaps. 2, 3; and Hewlett, *A Lesser Life,* esp. chaps. 4, 15.

26. Ehrenreich, *Hearts of Men,* 172–73. For the quotation of Caroline Bird, see p. 173; exactly seven decades before the period studied by Bird, John A. Ryan decried as morally unconscionable the fact that only about 40 percent of American workers were paid a decent living wage. Ryan, *Living Wage,* chap. 8.

27. John Paul II, *Laborem Exercens,* 19.

28. Hochschild, *Second Shift,* 2–4, inter alia.

29. Studies of family policies in various countries highlight the atypically individualistic and privatized approach toward the care of children taken in the United States. These findings are summarized in Hewlett, *A Lesser Life,* 127–28.

30. Pope John Paul II underscores this point in his most recent social encyclical, declaring that in third world contexts, the objective of a decent family living wage is still a far distant goal. *Centesimus Annus,* in *Origins* 21/1 (May 16, 1991): 34.

31. For revealing studies of the situation of women in global industry, see Rachel Grossman, "Women's Place in the Integrated Circuit," *Radical America* 14/2 (January/February 1980): 29–49; and Naomi Katz and D. S. Kemnitzer, "Fast Forward: The Internationalization of Silicon Valley," in *Women, Men, and the International Division of Labor,* ed. J. Nash and P. Fernandez (New York: SUNY Press, 1983).

32. John Paul II, *Laborem Exercens,* 17. See also Gregory Baum, *The Priority of Labor* (New York: Paulist Press 1982), 53–54.

33. Some conservative pro-family organizations favor a family wage system that would support an at-home wife and be increased according to the number of children involved. Like Connaught Marshner, chair of the Pro-Family Coalition interviewed by Ehrenreich, these "New Right" leaders do not seem to recognize that implementing such a plan might involve a massive, even revolutionary downward redistribution of wealth. Ehrenreich, *Hearts of Men,* 174–75.

34. See Lisa Cahill's similar suggestion in *Between the Sexes,* chap. 8.

35. *New York Times,* August 21, 1989, 1.

36. U.S. Bureau of the Census, 1986 figures quoted in Evans and Nelson, *Wage Justice,* 43.

37. This would be practically true only if the amount of money paid the household head actually included the wherewithal for a just wage for domestic work.

38. See Barbara Hilkert Andolsen, "A Woman's Work Is Never Done," in *Women's Consciousness, Women's Conscience,* ed. Barbara Andolsen, Christine Gudorf, and Mary Pellauer (Minneapolis: Winston, 1985), 15–16. "Enormous changes will be required in order to integrate family and work in a structure humane to all parties." Such seemingly disparate issues as land-use patterns that segregate businesses from residential housing; inflexible hours of work or mandatory overtime for service and factory workers; and career tracks for many professional careers which demand work hours that preclude domestic participation during the very years when parenting and household responsibilities are greatest, all need to be challenged in the quest for a more genuinely equitable relation between home and work.

39. Ryan questioned the assumption that higher wages, widely distributed, would be detrimental to employment rates. See "Higher Wages and Unemployment" (1931) in John A. Ryan, *Seven Troubled Years: 1930–1936* (Ann Arbor, Mich.: Edwards Brothers, Inc., 1937), 19–22. For a judicious treatment of the welfare issue that also contends that a family living wage should be attainable by one full-time adult worker per family, see David Ellwood, *Poor Support: Poverty in the American Family* (New York: Basic Books, 1988).

40. I am borrowing the language used by Letty M. Russell in *Household of Freedom: Authority in Feminist Theology* (Philadelphia: Westminster Press, 1987), chap. 1. Russell and others propose that eschatology, with its envisagement of God's intended future, be adopted as a starting point for feminist and liberationist ethics. The difficulties involved in applying the vocabulary of eschatology to public policy issues have yet to be addressed.

41. See Rosemary Radford Ruether, "Spirit and Matter, Public and Private: The Challenge of Feminism to Traditional Dualisms," in *Embodied Love: Sensuality and Relationship as Feminist Values,* ed. Paula M. Cooey, Sharon A. Farmer, & Mary Ellen Ross (San Francisco: Harper & Row, 1987), 75. Describing a Christian feminist vision of society, Reuther writes, "we seek a society built on organic community, where the processes of child raising, of education, of work, of culture have been integrated in such a way as to allow both men and women to share child nurturing and homemaking, on the one hand, and creative activity and decision making in the larger society, on the other hand."

42. Ryan, *Distributive Justice,* 355–56.

22. Women's Ways of Working

Carol Coston

This chapter first appeared in *One Hundred Years of Catholic Social Thought: Celebration and Challenge* in 1991.

What would happen if Maria Montessori and Virginia Woolf were to meet Leo XIII and Pius XI and dialogue with them about work? Could a feminist educator and writer find any common ground with Catholic social thought?

Who are these women and what do they have to say about the meaning of work? About women as workers? About values in the workplace?

What does the church's social tradition say in response? Are there convergence points? If there are areas of agreement between Catholic social thought and feminism, how have contemporary Catholic women tried to integrate both perspectives into their worklives? And finally, what guidance can this give to Catholic social thought in the future?

Defining Work Through Women's Experience

In the United States bishops' pastoral *Economic Justice for All,* work has a threefold significance for people: 1) a way to meet their material needs, 2) a way to exercise self-expression and self-realization, 3) a way to contribute to the well-being of the larger community (no. 97).[1]

In my experience of women's organizations, this definition is consistent with "women's ways of working." Women particularly contribute to the well-being of the community in that the majority of teachers, social-service workers, health-care providers and volunteers in non-profit organizations are women. "Well-being of the community" is another way to express a key element in Catholic social tradition—the common good. Some goals of the common good, as articulated in *Mater et Magistra* and applicable to this essay, are "to make accessible the goods and services for a better life to as many persons as possible . . . to provide employment for as many workers as possible . . . that harmony in economic affairs and a friendly and beneficial cooperation be fostered" (nos. 79–80).

Women have traditionally been the volunteer or underpaid backbone of innumerable organizations dedicated to the common good and through this have often exercised creative self-expression. Some women are able to do this and also meet their material needs, but millions more must work in mind-numbing and back-breaking jobs which are not forms of creative self-expression.

This chapter focuses on ways in which four women-led organizations—two from the early 1900s, two from the 1970s—reflect the common good in their purpose or mission and incorporate other principles and values contained in Catholic social thought within their internal processes. The Montessori "Children's Houses" and Rachel's Women's Center provide direct services in ways which help participants empower themselves to grow and change. The Women's Cooperative Guild and NETWORK work for systemic change within the social-justice tradition. Each of these four models of women's organizations will be expanded upon.

Maria Montessori Meets Leo XIII

Pope Leo XIII and Maria Montessori were both in Rome in 1891. I do not know if they ever met personally, but if they did they may have discussed women's proper role in the workplace. While Leo was preparing for *Rerum Novarum,* Maria was struggling to enter the University of Rome Medical School.

The medical school refused her first application, and her father was unalterably opposed to Maria's chosen career. Maria, however, was determined not to accept a woman's traditional role and was finally admitted in 1892.

In 1896, after earning scholarships each year and making extra money through private tutoring, Maria, rising above individual and institutional sexism, became the first woman to graduate from a medical school in Italy.

Curiously, although Leo's most specific reference to women (which, incidentally, appeared in the "Child Labor" section of *Rerum Novarum*) would indicate a definite bias toward keeping women in the home, there is some evidence that, in response to Montessori's admittance to the medical college, he later opined that medicine was an acceptable profession for a woman.[2]

A few months after graduating, at age 26, Dr. Montessori represented Italy at an international women's congress in Berlin and gave a speech on the conditions of working women in Italy. Excerpts from Dr. Montessori's speech and Pope Leo's encyclical—where he consistently referred to "man's labor" and "workmen"—give us a hint of what their conversation about the role of women in the workplace might have been like.

LEO: Women, again, are not suited to certain trades; for woman is by nature fitted for home-work, and it is that which is best adapted at once to preserve her modesty, and to promote the good bringing up of children and the well-being of the family (no. 33).

MARIA: I speak for the six million Italian women who work in factories and on farms as long as eighteen hours a day for pay that is often half of what men earn for the same work and sometimes even less.

Afterward, she asked the delegates to approve a proposal for equal pay for equal work by women, beginning with those working in state-owned factories. They did so unanimously.[3]

Following a stint working with children in Rome's insane asylums, Dr. Montessori directed a day-care center in a slum area housing project. Through her work with these sixty 3- to 7-year-old children (whose parents were illiterate), she began to develop a unique approach to education which culminated in the world-renowned Montessori Method. It is beyond the scope of this essay to describe her organizational model in detail, but many of her insights on children at work and the values learned are relevant to this discussion on women's ways of working and will be referred to later.

Virginia Woolf Meets Pius XI

In 1931, when Pius XI wrote *Quadragesimo Anno,* he referred almost entirely to "workingmen," only briefly expressing concern about the "virtue of girls and women" in modern factories. Although the pope does suggest (in the section on "Support of the Workingman and His Family") that it is acceptable for women, as part of the family, to contribute to "common maintenance" in a rural home or that of artisans or small shopkeepers, he clearly does not approve of women working elsewhere.

Ironically, that same year Virginia Woolf published *Life as We Have Known It,* a book by members of the Women's Cooperative Guild in England, in which they describe their jobs, families, and political awakening. Woolf admires and supports these working women who had no choice about whether or not to be wage-earners. In her "Introductory Letter" to the book, Woolf recalls her impressions of them at one of their Cooperative Congresses as "humorous and vigorous and thoroughly independent." She was impressed with the dignity and determination with which each of the "delegates" represented the concerns of her particular constituency.[4]

Excerpts from Pope Pius XI's encyclical *Quadragesimo Anno* and Virginia Woolf's "Introductory Letter" give us a hint of what a conversation between them about the role of women in the workplace might have been like.

PIUS: Mothers will above all devote their work to the home and the things connected with it; intolerable, and to be opposed with all Our strength, is the abuse whereby mothers of families, are forced to engage in gainful occupations outside the domestic wall to the neglect of their own proper cares and duties (no. 71).

VIRGINIA: Most of the women had started work at seven or eight, earning a penny on Saturday for washing a doorstep. . . . They had gone into factories when they were fourteen. They had worked from seven in the morning till eight or nine at night and had made thirteen or fifteen shillings a week. . . . They had seen half-starved women standing in rows to be paid for their match-boxes while they snuffed the roast meat of their employer's dinner cooking within.[5]

Pius XI apparently saw no good coming from women working outside the home, nor did he refer to them in sections on "Workingmen's Unions." On the other hand, Woolf praised the Women's Cooperative Guild for providing these working-class women with multiple opportunities to improve their educational, job training, social and organizational skills.

Model #1: "Children's Houses"

In 1907 Dr. Montessori officially opened the first Children's House in a slum area housing project. A group of wealthy bankers invited her to direct a day nursery for the tenants of their newly renovated buildings. These builders wanted to protect their investment from the fifty children of poor working parents who "ran wild throughout the building, defacing the newly whitewashed walls and . . . other petty acts of vandalism."[6]

For her part, Dr. Montessori saw this as an opportunity to test some of her educational ideas on normal children. The child care was free to those working parents who agreed to send the children there on time, "clean in body and clothing, and provided with a suitable apron." She also invited the mothers to be actively involved in this education process: "Once a week, at least, the mothers may talk with the Directress, giving her information concerning the home life of the child, and receiving helpful advice from her."[7]

Dr. Montessori stressed the importance of freedom for students and of providing them choices for "auto-education" activities. Further, she felt that no child could be free unless he or she were independent. Discipline was developed through opportunities for constructive work. Work became its own reward and artificially induced competitions or rewards and punishments were banned.

Both community life and personal initiative were developed because the children felt a sense of ownership and responsibility for the classroom. They maintained daily order by returning materials to shelves, polishing the tables, and caring for the animals and plants. The children also felt and demonstrated responsibility for each other. For example, they took turns distributing the noon meal, which they ate in common.

Montessori and Leo XIII's Approach to Women Workers

In his encyclical Pope Leo did not discuss what happened to children when women had to become wage-earners. Montessori, however, assumed that poor women had to work outside the home. So she focused her energies on setting up Children's Houses to provide for the education, health, moral and physical development of their children. These became the forerunners of today's head start and full-service child-care centers.

Model #2: Women's Cooperative Guild

The Women's Cooperative Guild was established in 1883 as a way for women in local Cooperative Societies to become a more powerful force in the Cooperative Movement, to share in its administration and to strengthen its impact on public policy. By 1930 the Guild had sixty-seven thousand members and nearly fourteen hundred branches.

The experience of being part of the Guild encouraged the women to identify social problems—long hours, little pay, and a lack of running water and electricity—and provided forums to develop strategies for change. The Guild Annual Meeting also helped stretch the women's concerns to broader public policy issues. Woolf noted that the delegates expressed positions on the taxation of land values, reform of the divorce laws, the minimum wage, care of maternity, education of children over 14 years of age, and adult suffrage. The women learned "to speak out, boldly and authoritatively, about every question of civic life . . . [including] peace and disarmament and the spread of Cooperative principles . . . among the nations of the world."[8]

The Guild experience also helped women workers. Virginia Woolf, as a writer and publisher, must have been pleased to publish the seventeen "Extracts from Letters Written in 1927" in which the women describe the influence of their Guild experience on their reading. One woman wrote: "I have, of course, to keep well abreast of current topics and for that I have to read the daily papers or such parts as may be of value. . . . But I must admit that everything I can get hold of relating to International matters have a keen interest for me." Another wrote: "My reading, of course, is done in time stolen from my sleeping hours, and, I am bound to confess, any meal times when alone or with my little son, who also reads."[9]

Popes Leo XIII and Pius XI shared with the Guild a definition of work as a way to meet material needs and each actively supported the value of just wages for the worker. However, the encyclicals focused almost exclusively on the male worker and his needs, while Montessori, Woolf, and the Guild recognized and supported women wage-earners.

These two popes did not refer specifically to work as creative self-expression or self-realization. This, however, was an important second definition of work for Montessori and members of the Guild. Montessori set up her Children's Houses to facilitate this value. The Guild women held that their organizational work was creative, educational, and empowering.

A third definition of work, as contributing to the well-being of the larger community, was affirmed by the popes as well as the

Guild, Montessori, and Woolf through their support for workers associations.

The popes encouraged associations that directed "the activities of the group to the common good," although the references were generally to men's associations. Using a more inclusive approach, Montessori viewed the associations formed around the Children's Houses as ways not only to care for the children and provide services for working women, but also to serve as models for other tenement-clubs, which could provide alternatives to gambling-houses and saloons.

The Women's Cooperative Guild, which was founded in 1883 and thus preceded both encyclicals, worked for the common good by voicing the neglected needs of married working women. "They supported vigorously the establishment of School Clinics. They brought forward a National Scheme for the care of Maternity . . . for the inclusion of Maternity Benefit in the Insurance Act."[10]

Whereas Pius XI worried about women's virtue in the workplace, the Guild offered protections and support systems. It not only provided work opportunities for women, but through its nearly fourteen hundred branches the Guild offered safe spaces for women to meet, a workshop wherein they "could remodel their lives, could beat out this reform or that."

The Guild also took the concern for the common good in the workplace beyond national boundaries through its International Cooperative Women's Guild. For example, in 1930, at its Congress in Vienna, 250 delegates from twenty countries discussed "whether the economic position of women should be best solved by State family allowances or factory work." In addition, the International Guild "has steadfastly stood for Peace, and has laid before the League of Nations the strong demand of its members for Disarmament."[11]

Model #3: Rachel's Women's Center

Rachel's, begun in 1979, provides direct services to homeless women as a contribution to the common good—a service in the church's charity tradition of responding directly to the needs of the poor. Rachel's current director, Mary Ann Luby, is a Catholic sister and the bulk of financial, board, and staff support comes through the efforts of Catholic women.

Mary Ann Luby's basic approach is to value the women's human dignity and to offer them all the opportunity "to get their lives together." Mary Ann believes that every human has the potential for change and that change largely occurs through human relationships.

As a day shelter for homeless women in the District of Columbia, the Center tries to implement these values by offering a broad range of services which provides a holistic and integrated approach similar in concept to that designed by Maria Montessori for poor women and children in Italy.

These services address physical needs through food programs, drug and alcohol addiction sessions, and health assessments; spiritual needs through bible studies and structured discussions on women's issues; social needs through cultural workshops, outings, and knitting classes; emotional needs through assertion training, general problem solving, and support groups sessions; and educational needs through job-training skills.

Mary Ann believes in addressing more than just the primary human needs. Her philosophy in operating the Center goes beyond providing food and shelter to include a belief in the importance of helping the women build self-esteem. Without self-esteem it is almost impossible to get out of the shelter system and into independent living.

Participation is another important value at Rachel's and the high degree of participation by its occupants makes it unique among local shelters. Through weekly house meetings, the women are consulted on almost all program development. Mary Ann believes that the women know better than anybody else what they need, so she spends a lot of time listening to them. Several of the women who were drug addicts, for example, came to ask for a weekly drug and alcoholics anonymous meeting. Together they wrote a grant proposal and a set of goals and have continued to meet ever since.

The women also participate in planning celebrations such as holidays and birthday parties. Because the women are involved in the initial planning, they feel more ownership of and responsibility for the events. Mary Ann acknowledges that these events are "more profound when the women have done them."

Similarly, the women participate in the cleaning of Rachel's by signing up for a chore each morning when they come in. Thus they become active participants in shaping their environment and develop a sense of responsibility for "their space," just as the Italian students did in the Children's Houses.

A final example of their active participation is the women's involvement in advocacy on issues that affect the homeless. Rachel's women are encouraged to attend congressional and local hearings, give testimony, and lobby on their own behalf—rather than always having others speak for them.[12]

Model #4: NETWORK, A Catholic Social-Justice Lobby

NETWORK, begun in 1971, works for the common good by seeking systemic change through the legislative and political process. This advocacy is in the justice tradition of Catholic social thought, particularly emphasized since Vatican Council II. NETWORK was started by forty-seven Catholic sisters and from its inception has been women-led.

What Rachel's and NETWORK have in common is that they try to integrate their vision of the common good into the organization's mission, in the goods or services it produces, and into their internal processes. They particularly try to integrate the values of participation, empowerment, and cooperation. In doing this they follow in the footsteps of Montessori, the feminist educator, and the Guild—a feminist organization.

Just as Rachel's somewhat echoes a Montessori organization, so too does NETWORK echo the Women's Cooperative Guild; both were started by women, kept women in leadership positions, and organized themselves to influence public policy. Both groups developed ways for poor women at a local level to articulate their needs to policy makers at a national level.

NETWORK has a Washington office, which does research and lobbying on national legislation. Information and action suggestions are then sent to the thousands of members, who are organized by congressional districts.

NETWORK is rooted in Catholic social justice teachings and, as such, perceives its mission as seeking the common good in public policy, especially for the economically poor. This is done through supporting legislation which provides: 1) just access to economic resources, 2) fairness in national funding, and 3) justice in global relationships.

Just as the Guild convened regular forums for its members to provide mutual support and to give direction to its advocacy work, so too does NETWORK. The membership is consulted regularly through the publication, in phone conversations with state coordinators and congressional district contacts, in regional workshops, and national legislative seminars.

Through its "Bridge Building Project," NETWORK attempts to insure that its advocacy positions are rooted in the experience of those who suffer most from unjust policies. This year NETWORK convened two groups of women to assist in shaping its policy positions. The first were Catholic sisters in direct ministry with the economically poor, along with women who themselves suffer from poverty; the second were housing advocates, including women who were formerly homeless. This second group drafted a position paper on housing, which NETWORK distributed to all members of Congress. NETWORK also organized a major lobbying campaign around the statement involving its local membership and the media.

In addition to its legislative goals, NETWORK is committed to creating an alternative organizational model from a feminist perspective. A goal of the NETWORK staff and board is that the organization mirrors internally the same principles and values it advocates in national legislation. Thus, *how* things are done is as important as *what* is done.

Some elements of this alternative model are the following:

1. Co-responsibility for the goals of the organization
2. Participatory decision-making
3. Equality of persons
4. Commitment to reflection on shared values
5. Emphasis on cooperation rather than competition

6. Integration of professional activities with spiritual, personal, and communal life.

Because of space limitations, only a few of the operational ramifications of these elements are highlighted.

Participatory Decision-Making and Equality of Persons

NETWORK functions with a participatory management style at both the staff and board level. The guiding assumption is that people should be involved in all major decisions that affect their individual work lives and the health and direction of the organization. All staff participate in key decisions such as budget setting, salary scale, large capital expenditures, new programs or staff positions, and public policy positions. All staff attend and participate in board meetings and committees.

In deliberating on the salary issues, NETWORK agreed with the definition of work as a means for workers to meet their material needs; but it also had to operate under the financial constraints facing most non-profit advocacy groups. In addition, the NETWORK women realized how undervalued women's work had been traditionally, especially "support staff" positions such as secretarial work. Thus, the decision to have everyone on the staff receive the same salary was based on the underlying belief that all persons are inherently equal, though differently gifted, and of different experience and competencies. It is the fundamentally equal dignity of the person as worker that gives each person and her role in the organization equal value.

The actual salary level assumes a modest standard of living and a high commitment to NETWORK's mission. It reflects Pius XI's definition of a just wage as "sufficient to meet adequately ordinary domestic needs" (no. 71).

But NETWORK would probably find Virginia Woolf's definition of poverty more appropriate to its salary decision: "By poverty is meant enough money to live upon. That is, you must earn enough to be independent of any other human being and to buy that modicum of health, leisure, knowledge and so on that is needed for the full development of body and mind. But no more."[13]

NETWORK Strives for Integration in the Workplace

The women at NETWORK recognize that a healthy approach to political ministry is to integrate their professional activities with their spiritual, personal, and communal lives. To help achieve this, NETWORK sets aside several days each year for a reflection process on political ministry. These days help the women discover the relationship between faith values and work on legislative issues. The reflection culminates with symbol, ritual, and prayer, which help express a deepening commitment to their ministry for justice.

NETWORK staff members also take time to create and celebrate rituals that develop the organization's communal life. The staff year begins with a commitment ritual around contract signing and, at an Epiphany ritual, each staff member is affirmed for her participation contributions to NETWORK. Rituals are an important part of the NETWORK-directed seminars and workshops. These activities recall the ritualized procedures of the Guild's Annual Congress, the birthday celebrations at Rachel's, and the many seasonal rituals within the Catholic tradition.[14]

Can Feminism in the Workplace Guide Catholic Social Thought?

These four women-led organizations have lived out a definition of work as self-expression, a means of meeting material needs, and a way to contribute to the common good. Each group and its leadership has also sought consistency between its outward mission and its internal processes. I believe the ways in which they have done this can be useful to the institutional church in any future articulation of Catholic social thought.

What might these women emphasize if consulted? Or as Virginia Woolf asked in *The Three Guineas:* What are the lessons "educated men" can learn from "daughters of uneducated women"?

Montessori Would Speak Up for Women Wage-earners

Maria Montessori and the working women benefiting from the Children's Houses would ask the popes and their advisors to accept the fact that millions of women have no choice: they *must* work for wages outside the home. Therefore, lecturing them about their "proper role" in the home is not helpful; they know full well their maternal responsibilities and carry them through the days—some, literally, on their backs—or in their anxious hearts.

A majority of the women in the world work more hours daily than men and in most cases carry a double load. For example, women do agricultural, domestic, or professional work for ten or more hours daily, and then add several hours more for their own household work, while the men relax under the trees, in the pubs, or in front of television sets.

Maria Montessori would suggest that the encyclicals focus more on articulating what support systems and wages are needed by working women and whose responsibility it is to provide them.

The Women's Guild Would Urge Participation

The Women's Cooperative Guild would probably emphasize women's representation and broad participation in the workplace. They recognized how an organization is strengthened when each member feels she has a *real role* in shaping its direction and setting its financial and programmatic priorities. The Guild women empowered themselves through participation in local, national, and international gatherings, through self-education programs and through political advocacy.

The institutional church, by contrast, does not yet really seek women's broad participation or welcome their active involvement in decision-making. As a result, women are walking away in droves and finding their personal sense of religious commitment more fulfilled in other institutions, such as the Guild. For example, a 70-year-old Guild member, writing in 1920, describes her retirement setting "along a ditch":

> There is a railway bank at the end of the path covered with grass and beautiful dandelions. I can sit outside the little shed and see the church tower of old Hampstead Church and think of all the good work that has been done in the Guild Office. I go there all day on a Sunday, and am sure there is as much spiritual feeling going along a ditch as there is in hearing a sermon . . . thank God that I became a Guild member for more reasons than I can explain.[15]

The Guild might also suggest that the popes could use some women writers such as Virginia Woolf. Woolf's spirited descriptions of the "humorous and vigorous and thoroughly independent" Guild women and her keen observations of Guild meetings make for livelier reading than the ponderous prose of *Quadragesimo Anno* on the "uplifting of the proletariat."

Rachel's Women's Center Would Recommend Listening to Women

Both the staff and the women served at Rachel's would recommend: "Listen to the women." Just as homeless women were best able to advise on their particular needs and to help set appropriate policies and procedures for running their Center, so too should the teaching church listen to women from many countries, lifestyles, and educational backgrounds. It is fairly clear that Leo XIII and Pius XI listened primarily, if not entirely, to men in drafting these first encyclicals. As a result, women and their needs as wage-earners were not taken seriously, nor was attention given to their child-care concerns.

Similarly, in contemporary Catholic social teachings, women's ongoing childcare needs are not given enough serious and thoughtful attention, nor are women's concerns and dilemmas around child-bearing. The predominant focus in church statements on public policy and in allocation of church resources continues to be on the abortion issue. So once again, in an area they know the most about, women are made passive recipients of church policies and magisterial pronouncements, rather than active participants in shaping them.

NETWORK Would Counsel Consistency between Theory and Practice

As a political lobby group founded in the early 1970s, NETWORK studied and supported John XXIII's encyclicals, the Vatican II documents, Paul VI's *Call to Action,* and the Synod statement on *Justice in the World.* The group was influenced by the teachings' emphases on participation, cooperation, need to move to political action, justice as a constitutive element of preaching the gospel, listening to the experiences of the poor, just wages and the common good described in broad terms as in *Mater et Magistra*—"the sum total of those conditions of social living."

NETWORK staff saw the power of challenging others, religious and lay, to become involved in political ministry, to integrate their faith commitment with their public lives as citizens. But the staff also knew that the values they advocated in public had to be reflected in their internal structure as well. Nancy Sylvester, I.H.M., NETWORK's National Coordinator, explains:

> It is one thing to testify and lobby on minimum wage or urge that local people should be involved in decisions that affect their lives, but if you don't also advocate for this in your own organization, the public soon sees the inconsistency and you lose credibility.

To the extent that the official church carries social-justice values forward in political actions, public statements, and use of church resources, the teachings can be motivational and directional. However, when church workers and the public at large observe huge disparities between theory and practice, the teachings lose their moral force.

Personal Reflection on Past and Future Social Justice Teachings

For twenty-five years my work has been in the social-justice arena: first in educating against racism and the Vietnam War, then as a political lobbyist and activist with NETWORK, and now in the area of alternative investments. I view this work as a ministry for the common good, and in the 1960s and 1970s I felt supported by the theory and practice of Catholic social teachings, which I read and studied. I was proud of what Catholicism stood for, especially when it advocated for the needs of the world's poorest, encouraged broad-based participation in both politics and the church, and spoke out fearlessly for all human rights. However, since then I have been keenly disappointed and disillusioned by inconsistencies between theory and practice. I often find it difficult to believe that the institutional church takes its own teachings seriously. The following examples illustrate this.

Inconsistent Messages Regarding Political Activity

Paul VI's encyclical *Call to Action,* which described politics as a way to live out the Christian commitment, inspired many women religious to take up political ministry. Several even felt called to public office—both elected and appointed. These women worked directly with the poor and offered constituents a fresh perspective on the role of public servants. Yet John Paul II forced several United States religious to choose between their political ministry and their congregations because he declared it was unacceptable for religious to hold political office.[16] This directive against political activity seems to run counter to his own well-publicized meetings with politicians and heads of state and his statements during public appearances—all highly political acts.

Common Good More Than Abortion

John XXIII taught in *Mater et Magistra* that the common good includes all the conditions of social living and urged national governments to create employment, care for the less privileged, and provide for the future. In *Pacem in Terris* he outlined a whole series of rights and duties within a well-ordered society; yet, many in the United States hierarchy continue to use the abortion issue as the single litmus test for political candidates.

Moreover, in 1984, when twenty-four United States women religious, prompted by an over-all concern for the common good, joined others in publicly asking for a dialogue on the issue of abortion in an ad in the *New York Times,* these women and their communities bore the brunt of an authoritarian and disproportionate reaction from the Vatican.

Women's Ways of Working and the Future of Catholic Social Thought

Women's organizations, such as the four described in this essay, can offer future church documents rich experiences in creating alternative workplaces. Their voices need to be heard during the formulation of church teaching, not after the fact. Women need to participate fully in evaluating the effect of past teachings and suggesting future changes.

If not, Catholic social teaching and the world will be the poorer for it. And women's productivity, creativity, spirituality, and thought will find other outlets that give meaning and expression to their lives and values.

If the churches then become more empty on Sunday, look for the women gathered "along a ditch" by a dandelion-covered railway bank. They'll be there finding that "spiritual feeling" and giving thanks for women's ways of working.

Notes

1. Since the encyclicals are easily available in many editions, I will simply reference in parentheses the number of the section quoted.

2. Rita Kramer, *Maria Montessori* (New York: G. P. Putnam, 1976), p. 35.

3. Ibid., p. 55.

4. Virginia Woolf, "Introductory Letter," *Life as We Have Known, It,* ed. Margaret Llewelyn Davies (New York: W. W. Norton Company, 1975), p. xxvii.

5. Ibid., p. xxxi.

6. Kramer, p. 110.

7. Maria Montessori, *The Montessori Method* (New York: Schocken Books, 1964), pp. 70–71.

8. Woolf, pp. xvii–xxxvi.

9. Ibid., pp. 116–20.

10. Margaret Llewelyn Davies, "Notes on the Women's Co-operative Guild," in Woolf, p. xii.

11. Ibid., p. xiii.

12. The information and quotations regarding Rachel's Women's Center are taken from an interview by Nancy Chupp with Mary Ann Luby on May 14, 1990.

13. Virginia Woolf, *The Three Guineas* (New York: Harcourt Brace and Company, 1938), p. 122.

14. Information on NETWORK is taken from materials and oral interviews provided by Nancy Sylvester, current national coordinator of NETWORK, and from my own experience as NETWORK's director for eleven years.

15. Woolf, *Life as We Have Known It,* p. 55.

16. The women religious were Sisters of Mercy Agnes Mary Mansour, Elizabeth Morancy, and Arlene Violet. Each made the painful choice to withdraw from formal membership in the congregation in order to pursue her personal sense of ministry in public office. Jesuit priest Robert Drinan was also forced to choose between remaining in the United States Congress or in the Jesuits. He chose to remain a Jesuit.

23. Healing the World: The Sacramental Tradition

Rosemary Radford Ruether

This chapter first appeared in *Gaia and God: An Ecofeminist Theology of Earth Healing* in 1992.

In this chapter I trace a line of Christian tradition that regards Christ as the cosmic manifestation of God, appearing both as the immanent divine source and ground of creation and its ultimate redemptive healing. Although this cosmological understanding of Christ as both creator and redeemer of the cosmos, and not just of human beings separated from the cosmos, is central to much of New Testament thought, Western Christianity since the late medieval and Reformation periods has ignored this holistic vision. Thus modern searchers for a cosmological spirituality have assumed that this is lacking in Christianity and can only be found in non-Christian perspectives, such as pagan "nature religions" or Asian religions.

Although the cosmological tradition in Christianity needs reinterpretation to be adequate for ecological spirituality, nevertheless it has been absent. Its possibilities and limits will be discussed in this chapter. I will then explore what it would mean to restore for today the cosmological center of theology and spirituality. Once the cosmos becomes the mediating context of all theological definition and spiritual experience, how does this change our understanding of both "God" and "humans"?

Hellenistic Roots of Cosmological Christology

New Testament and early cosmological Christology built on theologies of cosmogenesis in Oriental Hellenism, particularly as these had already been assimilated into Hellenistic Judaism. The mediation of these ideas through Judaism allowed Christians to assimilate ideas of Hellenistic philosophy, while denying their "pagan" origins. Christian theology took over the Hellenistic Jewish apologetic myth that Plato had learned his philosophy from Moses. Thus the similarity of Christian theology to contemporary Platonic thought could be explained away by making Platonism derivative of biblical revelation.[1]

Christianity also took over from Judaism an ideology of religious "purism," over against paganism as "false religion." This dualism still shapes Christian self-understanding, causing it to obscure and deny its actual syncretistic reality. Today this role of Christianity as synthesizer of major Hebraic, Oriental, and Greco-Roman thought should be recognized as a strength, rather than a "secret" to be denied. Certainly Christianity's success as the "winning" religion of late antiquity can hardly be explained apart from this synthesizing process. Today's eco-spiritual crisis demands a synthesizing creativity of even greater expansiveness.

What is called here Oriental Hellenism encompasses both schools of Greek philosophy that had synthesized the Platonic, Stoic, and Peripatetic cosmologies,[2] and also movements that restated this mystical philosophy as "Oriental wisdom," for example, the *Chaldean Oracles* and the Hermetic literature.[3] Out of this speculative milieu there also emerged the Gnostic literature. But the writings I trace here rejected Gnostic anti-cosmic dualism. Instead they affirmed the cosmos as the expression of immanent divinity, within which humans stood as microcosm to macrocosm.

In Middle Platonism the Platonic concept of the transcendent world of Ideas and the Aristotelian concept of the Divine Mind were combined. Also combined were Plato's concept of the World Soul and the Stoic concept of the Logos, which Stoics saw as the immanent life-power of all beings. There thus developed a cosmogonic story with either a two-part or a three-part sequence. Neoplatonism in Plotinus fully develops the three-part sequence.[4]

The cosmos is seen as originating in a transcendent divine being, who is the source of all things. This divine being brings forth from "himself" a perfect "image" and self-expression, in which the intellectual essences of all things are contained. This second God is then also identified with the Demiurgos, who shapes the cosmos from the intellectual "blueprint" contained in "his" own mind. The world soul, in turn, expresses this divine Logos in immanent form as the sustaining power of the cosmos. Human souls are seen as partaking in the substance of this world soul or immanent Logos of the cosmos.[5]

This cosmogonic picture was used in Jewish Wisdom literature to describe divine Wisdom as a secondary manifestation of the Creator God who is God's agent in creating the universe, and is also the immanent power that sustains the universe. Wisdom is understood also as the presence of God speaking in revelation. Through Wisdom human souls come to know God and grow into virtuous "sons" of God.[6]

Philo, the major philosopher of Hellenistic Judaism, developed a more elaborate philosophical theology. He saw God bringing forth a secondary expression, the divine Logos, who is the manifestation of the divine mind. From this Logos radiate the "Dynameis" or energies of God that create the world. The cosmos is sustained by the power of this immanent Logos. Each human soul, in turn, reflects the divine logos. Humans and cosmos thus are seen as "brothers" and parallel "sons of God."[7]

The Christian Synthesis: Cosmic Christology

The term *Christ* originally referred to the Messiah, a figure in Jewish apocalyptic thought that was seen as appearing at the end of world history to destroy the forces of evil and renovate the universe, installing the saints of God there in a blessed existence. In Jewish apocalyptic thought, there had been no identification of this figure of the Messiah with cosmogenesis, even though he was sometimes seen as "preexistent."[8] The Christianity reflected in the synoptic Gospels also lacks this identification of Christ with the cosmogonic Logos. However, when we turn to the more speculative Christian thought found in Paul, the Gospel of John, and the book of Hebrews, this identification of Christ as redeemer with the cosmogonic Logos has been put together into a unified vision of the beginning and the end of "all things." One of the fullest expressions of this cosmological Christology is found in Colossians 1:15–20:

> He is the image of the invisible God, the firstborn of all creation; for in him all things in heaven and on earth were created, things visible and invisible, whether thrones or dominions or rulers or powers—all things have been created through him and for him. He himself is before all things, and in him all things hold together. He is the head of the body, the church; he is the beginning, the firstborn from the dead, so that he might come to have first place in everything. For in him all the fullness of God was pleased to dwell and through him God was pleased to reconcile to himself all things, whether on earth or in heaven, by making peace through the blood of his cross.

It is likely that the original form of this hymn stressed primarily the cosmological logos. It has been edited to add the Christological references to "the church," "the firstborn from the dead," and "the blood of the cross."[9] The resulting synthesis brings together the two dramas of creation and redemption in the figure of the Logos-Christ. This one divine being is seen as (1) the manifestation of God, (2) the immanent presence of God that creates and sustains the cosmos, and (3) the divine power remanifest at the end of time, healing the enmity that has divided the cosmos and reconciling the cosmos to God.

The divine person encountered in Jesus is thereby identified with this Logos-Christ. His redemptive act "through the blood of the cross" is seen as the paradigmatic manifestation of one and the same divine being of the beginning and the end of "all things." As firstborn from the dead and head of the body, the Church, Christ is seen as the power of the new creation, not severed from the cosmos created in the beginning, but the principle through which this cosmos was originally created and now is renewed and reconciled with God. The Church itself is seen cosmologically. It is not simply a group of human believers in this figure, but is the paradigmatic community of the whole renovated cosmos.

The references to "thrones," "dominions," "rulers," and

"powers" reflects a Judaeo-Persian apocalyptic cosmology, in which God is seen as ruling the cosmos through angelic agents. The regions of earth, both the primary elements and the nations, and the planetary spheres, were understood as ruled by angelic governors. These angelic spirits were believed to have revolted against God, creating an alienated universe in which evil triumphs over good.[10]

The manifestation of the cosmogonic Logos in the end time thus can be understood as a reincursion of God's primal creative power, subjugating these dissident angelic powers and thereby bringing about a reunified cosmos, reconciled to God, and filled with God's plenary goodness. The culmination of this process of subjugation of the unruly cosmic powers, and the reconciliation of the cosmos with God, is, as Paul puts it in 1 Corinthians 15:25, "So that God may be all in all."

This bold effort to unify cosmogony and eschatology in early Christianity, however, was jeopardized by the conflicting strands of Hebrew and Greek thought that they sought to synthesize. The Hebrew concept of "creation" demanded a cleavage between the being of God and that of created beings, including humans. Jewish thought originally saw humans as essentially mortal. Redemption was a fulfilled, blessed existence on earth within mortal limits, that is, one hundred years.[11]

Greek thought, by contrast, saw the relation of God and cosmos as emanational. There is ontological continuity between God, the Logos of God, and the cosmos. Each of these realities expresses being on different levels of existence. Thus the world soul and the human soul partake in the being of the divine Logos, which manifests the ultimate source of being. But Greek thought also sees the cosmos as split between a higher planetary realm of immortal being and a sublunar world of mortal being. The soul belongs to the higher realm and has been cast down "unnaturally" into a body. Its task is to escape from the body through turning the mind "upward" and so return at death to disincarnate, immortal blessedness in the stars.

Classical Christianity presented several efforts to unify these disparate worldviews. With the Hebrew view, Christianity insisted that humans were a psychophysical union. The body was essential for wholeness of existence, and the resurrection of the body was intrinsic to salvation. Christ must have a real body, not merely an "appearance" of body. Both of these ideas were to cause great difficulty to those imbued with Platonic thought. Patristic Christianity fended off various efforts to deny a bodily incarnation to Christ and the bodily resurrection of both Christ and humanity.[12]

At the same time, Christianity accepted the Platonic prejudice against "becoming." The transience and mortality of material existence was evil. The solution, found already in Paul, is the strange concept of the "spiritual body," a created vehicle of the soul, but stripped of its mortality. This concept of the transfigured body in redeemed life was applied, not only to humans, but to the whole cosmos. Christians shared with Hellenism the view that the whole cosmos was alive, pervaded by dynamic energy that Christianity identified with the immanent Logos of God. Evan animals and plants had soul, and the human soul shared with them the animal and vegetative soul.[13] Human psychophysical existence was inseparable from this cosmic whole, within which humans stood as microcosm.

One ambitious effort to create a theology in which creation, incarnation, and consummation are unified in one cosmic whole is found in the second-century anti-Gnostic churchman, Irenaeus. For Irenaeus, creation is itself an incarnation of the Word and Spirit of God, as the ontological ground of bodily existence. The incarnation of the historical Christ is the renewal of this divine power underlying creation. In the incarnation divine power permeates bodily nature in a yet deeper way, so that the bodily becomes the sacramental bearer of the divine, and the divine deifies the bodily.

The Christian sacraments are paradigmatic of this deeper mingling of body and spirit, renewing the life power of creation. As Irenaeus puts it in his refutation of gnostic negation of the body:

> But indeed vain are they who despise the entire dispensation of God and disallow the salvation of the flesh, and treat with contempt its regeneration, maintaining that it is not capable of incorruption. But if this indeed does not attain salvation, then neither did the Lord redeem us with

> his blood, nor is the cup of the Eucharist the communion of His blood, nor is the bread which we break the communion of His body. For the blood can only come up from the veins and the flesh, and whatsoever else makes up the substance of man, such as the Word of God was actually made. . . . And as we are his members, we are also nourished by means of the creation. . . . He has acknowledged the cup, which is part of creation, as His own blood, and the bread, which is also part of creation, he has established as His own body, from which he gives increase to our body.[14]

But since for Irenaeus (as for Paul and for all subsequent Christianity) salvation has to do with transcending mortality, the only way he can finally think about redemption—not just of the human being, but of the cosmos as a whole—is by assuming that, through being infused by the immortal life of the divine, it will overcome its mortality. This redemption of creation, following the biblical apocalyptic tradition, takes place in two stages. First, there is the millennial blessedness of earthly life. Irenaeus describes the millennium in images drawn from Hebrew prophecy:

> Then the whole creation shall, according to God's will, obtain a vast increase, that it might bring forth and sustain fruits, such as Isaiah declares. . . . And they shall come and rejoice in Mount Zion, and shall come come to what is good, and into a land of wheat and wine and fruits, of animals and of sheep; that their soul shall be as a tree bearing fruit, and they shall hunger no more.[15]

Then the whole cosmos will be transformed into a "new heaven and earth," immortalized, and fully united with the divine life of God. This final union with the Being of God fulfills the promise of the original creation:

> And in all these things and by them, the same God the Father is manifested, who fashioned man and gave the promise of the inheritance of the earth to the fathers,

> who brought forth the creature from bondage at the resurrection of the just and fulfills the promises for the Kingdom of his Son. . . . For there is one Son, who accomplished his Father's will, and one human race also in which the mysteries of God are wrought . . . the wisdom of God, by means of which his handiwork, confirmed and incorporated with his Son, is brought to perfection; that is His offspring, the First-begotten Word, should descend to the creature . . . and that it should be contained in Him, and, on the other hand, the creature should contain the Word, and ascend to Him, passing beyond the angels, and be made after the image and likeness of God.[16]

This effort to incorporate the lush Hebraic view of earthly blessedness into eternal salvation was dropped by mainline Christianity after the third century. Christ is seen as establishing his millennial reign through the political power of the church and Christian rulers, but this has no effect on renewal of nature, nor does it bring forth a new era of justice between humans.[17] Millennial visions continue in Christianity, but as the preserve of heretical, counterestablishment groups. Dominant Christianity sees the earth as going downhill toward destruction. Although the cosmos too will participate in the resurrected, immortal "new heaven and earth," the focus is on humans and on planetary spheres, not on other forms of earthly life.[18]

Disintegration and Renewal of Cosmological Theology

Although a millennial vision of redeemed earth was discarded by dominant Christianity, the cosmogonic Logos, as the principle of creation, continued in medieval Christianity, both Eastern and Western, as the basis of a view of nature as an ontological "ladder" of ascent to God. This view of nature was transmitted to Western Christianity particularly by the writings of Dionysius the Areopagite.[19]

This understanding of nature as emanational stages of descent (the levels of being from God to angelic hierarchies to humans to animals and plants, rocks, mountains, and rivers) is continuous. The "way down" from God to the humblest creature is also the "way up." Hence, as we have seen in Bonaventure's *The Mind's Road to God,* the contemplative ascent to God begins with the contemplation of visible things, and moves upward to contemplative union with the being of God.

This worldview began to disintegrate in the late Middle Ages. Nominalism rejected the Platonic ontological epistemology, which saw in every plant, animal, or other being a disclosure of an eternal essence in the Mind of God. "Ideas" became mere "names" for collections of individuals. For nominalism, also, the universe no longer disclosed the divine essence, but merely the "ordained will" of God. God was no longer the top of a continuous ontic and epistemological hierarchy, disclosed in visible things. Rather, God dwelt in a transcendent otherness radically inaccessible to the human mind and spirit.[20]

Thus one could no longer begin with the perception of visible things and move upward through the mind's categories to union with the mind and being of God. The ladder of ascent had been broken, both ontologically and epistemologically. The distance between God and humans could only be bridged by divine revelation, not by any "natural" speculative or mystical capacities of humans. Nominalism reinforced the renewed Augustinianism of the Reformation in its emphasis on the unbridgeable gap between "fallen nature" and God, making it hostile to mysticism and to sacramental views of nature.

However, the Renaissance period also saw a great revival of cosmological mysticism, reinforced by new access to its ancient Hellenistic sources. Byzantine scholars, fleeing from the Turkish conquest of Constantinople, would bring to Italy the corpus of Hermetic literature and the *Chaldean Oracles,* as well as Platonic and Neoplatonic works previously unknown in the West. Italian scholars, like Ficino (1433–99), working under the patronage of Cosimo De Medici, translated these works, initiating a renewed Neoplatonic cosmic mysticism, often only lightly disguised as Christianity.[21]

Renaissance scholars were misled by the belief that the Hermetic literature represented an ancient Egyptian wisdom contemporaneous with Moses. They believed it to be a pristine wisdom parallel with the oldest roots of the Bible. Revelation in Christ renewed and fulfilled this ancient wisdom. Thus the Renaissance reduplicated the ancient chronological error that justified the fusion of biblical and Neoplatonic thought.[22]

In the early sixteenth century, Copernicus would challenge the ancient geocentric cosmology, making the earth as one planet among others circling the sun. But, for Renaissance Neoplatonists, this removed the distance from earth to the planetary spheres. The permeation of the whole universe by the animating world soul, consubstantial with the human soul, allowed Renaissance magicians, such as Paracelsus (1493–1541) and Giordano Bruno (1548–1600), to see themselves as empowered to roam freely throughout the cosmos, communing with the nearest plants and rocks and the farthest planets through the faculties of the soul that had affinities with these earthly and celestial elements.[23]

But Bruno was burned to death in 1600 as a heretic. In the seventeenth century, both orthodox theology and orthodox science would distance themselves from Neoplatonic magic. Yet Neoplatonism, in more chastened form, did not die out, but would be continued among the Anglican school of Cambridge Platonists, such as Ralph Cudworth (1617–88) and Henry More (1614–87). These thinkers sought to bridge the sharp dualism of revelation and reason by reestablishing the ontological relation between the divine mind and the human mind. For More, God also indwells in the universe as Spirit of Nature or World Soul.[24] Renewed by grace, the human spirit could once again ascend from outer to inner things and attain to contemplative experience of the divine through Nature.

The eighteenth and nineteenth centuries saw a continual stream of philosophical idealism, which sought to bridge the division of mind and matter with some concept of the divine as the unifying source of both thought and physical things. For the heterodox Jewish philosopher Spinoza (1632–77), God was *natura naturans,* the underlying substance from which arose the physical world and the human mind (*natura naturata*), as mutual reflections of each other.[25]

German idealists Johann Gottlieb Fichte (1762–1814) and Friedrich Wilhelm Schelling (1775–1854) would also expound philosophies of Nature that saw God as the unitary Being underlying both thought and physical things. G. W. F. Hegel (1770–1831) sought to bridge spirit and matter through a dialectical process of thesis (spirit), antithesis (material expression), and synthesis (matter-spirit union), which in turn became the new thesis.

This European quest for a philosophy of nature that united matter and spirit continued to be haunted by the unresolved syncreticism in Christianity of Greek and Hebrew thought. Those who moved toward a more pantheistic communion with deity immanent in nature, such as the English poets Coleridge and Wordsworth, would toy with modes of thought more "pagan" than Christian.[26] In reaction to these trends, Christian theology would seek to establish its "purely biblical" roots by rejecting any presence of God in nature. Yet other Christians would seek to mediate between this opposition, restating forms of cosmological Christology.[27]

Types of Contemporary Ecological Theology

Although the ecological crisis interjects a new urgency into this quest for a theology of nature, in many ways the tensions between Christian and anti-Christian proposals represent a restatement of this classic tension between Greek and Hebrew thought. For neo-pagan thealogians such as Carol Christ, the pagan gods and particularly the goddesses are being reborn to save us from antinatural Christianity. For Christian ecological thinkers, however, the biblical God and Gaia are not at odds; rightly understood, they are on terms of amity, if not commingling.

Three somewhat different versions of Christian cosmological theology circulate in the contemporary quest for ecological spirituality. One of these is Creation-centered spirituality, represented particularly by Matthew Fox. Another has been developed by followers of the French paleontologist-philosopher Pierre Teilhard de Chardin (1881–1955), and a third is based on the process theology of Alfred North Whitehead (1861–1947). I will characterize each of these briefly, and then discuss the key elements in them for an ecofeminist theology of nature.

For Fox, original blessing is the intrinsic nature of things. True Christian spirituality remains rooted in this vivid sense of original goodness. Evil is present in history, but as distortion and alienation from original blessing, not as primary reality. Evil can be evaluated as evil only in its negation of primary goodness, which remains our true "nature." Goodness is fundamentally relational. It is the life-giving and celebratory interconnection of all things. Evil is the denial of that interconnection.[28]

In his *The Coming of the Cosmic Christ,* Fox reclaims the classical cosmological Christology we have discussed in this chapter. Christ is not simply confined to the historical Jesus, nor only related to human souls. Christ is the immanent Wisdom of God present in the whole cosmos as its principle of interconnected and abundant life. The cosmic Christ is not only the foundational basis of original blessing in creation, but is its *telos* or direction of fulfillment. Creation moves toward increasing fulfillment of this abundance of life. The cosmic Christ is thus another name for original and final blessing. It is both immanent divinity present in all things in their interconnection, and the fulfilled being of the cosmos, which it seeks to realize.[29]

For Christians, Jesus is the paradigmatic manifestation of cosmic wisdom and goodness. But he is only one such manifestation. The same wisdom and goodness underlies all other religious quests and has been manifest in many other symbolic expressions, such as the Tao, the Buddha, the Great Spirit, and the Goddess. Thus the truth manifest in Jesus is in no way exclusive, but links Christians in "deep ecumenism" with all other religions, not just the "Great Religions," but also native religions that have been despised as "paganism."[30]

Fox also calls for dialogue with secular wisdom cultures, such as psychotherapy, whose antireligious views have often been based on critique of the distortions of religion. The recovery of an ecological spirituality also means that we have to redevelop the "right brain" or intuitive part of our experience and culture atrophied by masculine dominance. This means attention to the arts and liturgy, dance and bodywork, to reawaken our deadened capacities for holistic experience.

I think that Fox is basically on target in these affirmations and values. His chief defect is a certain superficiality. He has, as it were, mapped the territory that needs exploring, but others have to follow up in greater depth.[31] Particularly problematic is his tendency to distort the Christian past by dividing it into two traditions, creation-based and fall/redemption. Although there is some element of truth in this distinction, he appropriates it in too simplistic a manner, exaggerating the similarities to his own views among medieval mystics, such as Meister Eckhardt or Hildegard of Bingen, with whom he identifies himself.[32]

In Fox's account the ambiguities of all these Christian thinkers, and the elements of social hierarchy and spirit-matter dualism in them, are erased. Fox tends to brush off the significant differences between these expressions of past Christian tradition and his view of creation spirituality, rather than grappling with the meaning of these differences. The deep questions of sin and death, which were central to Christian theology, need new answers for today, and not simply a denial that these are real questions.

The second and third types of ecological theology to be summarized here represent important efforts to incorporate new scientific understanding, the new earth story of evolution and the new subatomic physics or quantum mechanics. Teilhard de Chardin, whose writings only became available in the late 1950s due to church censorship, used the new insights from evolution to restate the sweeping cosmic vision of salvation history found 1,700 years earlier in Irenaeus. Not just humans, but all of nature is part of this salvation drama.

For Teilhard, the universe is a total system that ascends in successive systems of organization, from the atomic to the planetary level. This ascent to increasing organizational complexity is also a moral and spiritual ascent, moving toward the unification of consciousness in what Teilhard calls "the Omega Point." The different stages of the evolution of matter, from atomic energy to molecular organization to cellular life to plants and animals and finally humans, are not merely changes of quantitative complexity, but are qualitative leaps to new levels of existence.[33]

The universe evolves along the axis of the complexification of matter. Increasingly complex organization of matter increases the internal "radial energy." It is this interior aspect of the complexification of matter that Teilhard sees as responsible for "boiling points" that bring breakthroughs to new levels of existence. There arises from molecular organization the living cell, then increasingly complex organic beings that become more and more aware, and then human self-consciousness. Everything that appears in the process of cosmogenesis is latent from its beginning, but this does not change the reality of its historical birth, which can appear only when a critical level of evolution is reached.

Teilhard's thought would mesh well with the Gaia hypothesis, for he sees the planet earth as a living organism.[34] Earth is one living organism, not only spatially, but across time. The planet earth grows through stages of development that are not repeatable, any more than the stages of organic growth from fetus to adult are repeatable. Like an organism, it will also eventually die.

The link between geosphere and biosphere is the organic cell, the highest unit of the molecular structure and the simplest unit in the organic structure. The breakthrough to life expresses a new level of centerness and unification, in which the whole structure becomes an organism participating in a common center and a common life. Unlike nonorganic structures that can be split up and each part survive, when the vital center of an organism is cut, the whole structure disintegrates.

Once organic life appears, its profusion ramifies into ordered types. The phyla become self-perpetuating along the lines laid out by specific types, and they cease to be able to cross-fertilize each other. There is a pattern of experimentation in evolution. First there appears the rudimentary type, then a series of modifications and experimentations with that type, until the most efficient form of that species is reached and its reproduction is stabilized around that form. Less successful experiments die out, and evolutionary changes within that species cease. The suppression of penults gives the impression of greater differences between phyla than originally existed when evolution of that group of related species was in progress.

For Teilhard, the evolutionary tree has a privileged axis or *telos*. This *telos* is toward increasing interiorization and centricity, increasing coordination around the directing center of the organism. With vertebrates we arrive at an animal, not held together by an external shell, but from within by a central nervous system. From vertebrates to reptiles to mammals, the nervous system develops a unifying center in the brain. The increasing size and convolutions of the brain correspond to increasingly intelligent species of mammals, until we arrive at *Homo sapiens,* in which conscious thought appears.

For the last 100,000 years, humans have been the privileged axis of evolution, while the animal and plant kingdoms, from which humans arose, diminish. Now the age of animals is over, and the earth is more and more a human earth. Once the level of thought is reached, evolution takes place socially rather than organically. Humans are more adaptable than animals because they add new evolutionary developments, not as adaptations of their bodies, but as culture and technology. Human evolution through culture and technology is through the complementarity of increasing individuality and increasing collectivity.

Teilhard unabashedly sees Christian Western history as the privileged axis of cultural evolution. From the Neolithic revolution, there arose a limited number of classical civilizations, of which the Greco-Roman world was one. From the Renaissance to the twentieth century, a new stage of modernity began, which is now reaching around the globe, transforming all surviving Neolithic and classical cultures. Teilhard sees this new global stage of consciousness and technology as making possible a "noosphere" or world mind that is increasingly unified and centralized. Human minds together increasingly become one unitary Mind.

Teihard sees this evolution toward unitary Mind as, in some sense, the evolution of immanent deity or the cosmic Christ. As increasingly collective consciousness develops, finally the organic substratum of the planet will die away, and Unitary Mind will be born from the finite earth into eternal life. The universe will fall away and die after having given birth to God, the ultimate communal consciousness, in which all that has gone before is gathered up and made immortal.[35]

This world picture contains some disturbing elements that need to be rejected. One is the way in which traditional hierarchical order has been "laid on its side," in an evolutionary concept of "progress," together with the confident faith in Western civilization and modernity as the privileged axis of this progress. The anticolonial movements and the ecological crisis have put this confidence in Eurocentric progress in grave question. Second, there is the sanguine acceptance of extinction of species as the acceptable price of progress. Does this not imply an acceptance of ethnocidal destruction of other peoples and cultures as also to be tossed aside by the triumphal march of Eurocentric progress?

Finally we must question the vision of the material underpinnings of consciousness as being tossed aside in the eschatological, culminating stage of evolution, a conclusion that contradicts the foundational insight of life and consciousness as the interiority of complexified matter. Surely this means that mind and body, the inside and the outside, cannot finally be separated. What is compelling about Teilhard's thought for today is precisely this insight that mind is the interiority of matter, and it is continuous from the simplest molecule to the most complex organism.

Process theology, as developed by Christian theologians such as John Cobb and Marjorie Suchocki,[36] from A. N. Whitehead's work,[37] has many affinities with the thought of Teilhard de Chardin. Like Teilhard, process theology sees an element of "mentality" present even in the random movements of subatomic particles. "Mentality" is a capacity for interaction, which becomes increasingly self-determining and conscious as matter organizes itself at successive layers of organizational complexity.

Process theology postulates, as underlying this process, a dipolar God. The Primordial Nature of God contains the whole of potentiality of all existing entities at every moment of actualization. This Primordial Nature of God provides the "initial aim" or best potential option for each entity at each occasion of existence. This "initial aim" relates to the total context of the past of that entity at that moment, and thus is interrelated with all that has been, ultimately, in the whole universe.

Each entity has, however, its own subjectivity. It adapts or actualizes this aim of God through actualizing one possibility that can only partially fulfill that aim, and can even thwart that aim in negative choices that are destructive. Thus the God of Process theology "lures," but does not coerce. It offers continual new possibilities, but the choice belongs to existent entities that can negate their own best options. There is freedom and risk in divine creativity, and with this risk, the possibility of evil. This possibility of evil increases as consciousness and power increase on the part of existent entities.

As entities opt for particular choices, these actualizations are taken into the being of God as God's Consequent Nature. The reality of God is thus shaped through interrelation with self-actualizing entities. God not only lures and offers new life, but also suffers, experiencing the pain of destructive choices as well as the pleasure of good choices.

Process theologians also postulate that this Consequent Nature of God, reflecting the memory of all that has been, is taken up in some way into the Primordial Nature of God, not only preserving immortally all that has been, but also incorporating it into the total vision of what could and should have been, to reconcile the evils and missed opportunities of history. In this way all that has been is not only remembered in the eternal being of God, but is redeemed as well.[38]

Toward an Ecofeminist Theocosmology

Ecofeminist theology and spirituality has tended to assume that the "Goddess" we need for ecological well-being is the reverse of the God we have had in the Semitic monotheistic traditions; immanent rather than transcendent, female rather than male identified, relational and interactive rather than dominanting, pluriform and multicentered rather than uniform and monocentered. But perhaps we need a more imaginative solution to these traditional oppositions than simply their reversal, something more like Nicholas of Cusa's paradoxical "coincidence of opposites," in which the "absolute maximum" and the "absolute minimum" are the same.[39]

Something like this coincidence of opposites has appeared, surprisingly, in subatomic physics. Newtonian physics had seen reality as composed of indestructible atoms, like hard billiard balls, moved by external force in a fixed space. God was seen as constructing this world from outside it, like a clock-maker, and setting it to run by its own internal mechanism, but in no way participating in it as an immanent life-force. Eventually this external God was banished altogether as an unnecessary hypothesis. The universe came to be seen as a mechanistic system arising from random accidents.

But, as physicists continued to probe matter, seeking its ultimate "building blocks" or smallest "simple units," out of which everything else was composed by mechanistic combinations, they discovered smaller and smaller units. The atom was made up of vast space in which tiny particles or electrons moved around an extremely concentrated core or nucleus that contained most of the mass of the atom. The relation of the two can be envisioned if we imagine blowing up an atom to the size of the dome of St. Peter's Basilica in Rome. The nucleus would then be the size of a grain of salt.[40]

The nucleus itself was recognized to be held together by a distinct energy, nuclear energy, the same energy that fires the sun, but found rarely in earth in "loose" form. As the physicists penetrated the nucleus, they discovered that this too was composed of various particles, protons and neutrons. As techniques for detection of yet smaller particles increased, more and more particles were counted, until finally it became apparent that the whole concept of "particles," or elementary "building blocks" of matter, needed to be abandoned. What the physicists were discovering were energy fields in which energy "events" appeared and disappeared. Particles appeared out of energy and dissolved back into energy.

At the subatomic level, the classical distinction between matter and energy disappears. Matter is energy moving in defined patterns of relationality. At the level of the "absolute minimum," the appearance of physical "stuff" disappears into a voidlike web of relationships, relationships in which the whole universe is finally interconnected and in which the observer also stands as part of the process. We cannot observe anything "objectively," for the very act of observation affects what we observe.

As we move below the "absolute minimum" of the tiniest particles into the dancing void of energy patterns that build up the "appearance" of solid objects on the macroscopic level, we also recognize that this is also the "absolute maximum," the matrix of all interconnections of the whole universe. This matrix of dancing energy operates with a "rationality," predictable patterns that result in a fixed number of possibilities. Thus what we have traditionally called "God," the "mind," or rational pattern holding all things together, and what we have called "matter," the "ground" of physical objects, come together. The disintegration of the many into infinitely small "bits," and the One, or unifying whole that connects all things together, coincide.

How do we connect ourselves and the meaning of our lives to these worlds of the very small and the very big, standing in between the dancing void of energy that underlies the atomic structure of our bodies and the universe, whose galaxies, stretching over vast space and time, dwarf our histories? Even our bodies, despite the appearance of continuity over time, are continually dying and being reborn in every second. Over a period of seven years, every molecule of our body has been replaced.

In this universe of the very small and the very big, can the human only appear lost, crying out with Pascal, "The eternal silence of those infinite spaces terrifies me!"[41] Or is it a universe in which it makes sense to speak of values, of life and death, good and evil, as meaningful distinctions within which we can hope for a "better world"? Is it a universe with which we can commune, as heart to heart, thought to thought, as I and Thou?

As humans stand peering down through their instruments into the subatomic realm and outward into the galaxies, it cannot but be evident that, for us, the human remains the "mean" or mediator between the worlds. This is so because what we perceive can only be known and evaluated from the context of our own standpoints. But also because we are faced with the recognition that humans alone, amid all the earth creatures and on all the planets of these vast galaxies, are capable of reflective consciousness. We are, in that sense, the "mind" of the universe, the place where the universe becomes conscious of itself.

Reflective consciousness is both our privilege and our danger. At least for the last several thousand years of cultural history, male ruling-class humans have used this privilege of mind to set themselves apart from nature and over dominated women and men. Thereby they denied the web of relationships that bind us all together, and within which these males themselves are an utterly dependent part. The urgent task of ecological culture is to convert human consciousness to the earth, so that we can use our minds to understand the web of life and to live in that web of life as sustainers, rather than destroyers, of it.

But also, as Teilhardian and Process thought have argued, reflective consciousness, while it distinguishes the human from animals, plants, cellular bacteria and nonbiotic aggregates of molecules, it does so only relatively, not absolutely. The capacity to be conscious is itself the experience of the interiority of our organism, made possible by the highly organized living cells of our brains and nervous systems that constitute the material "base" of our experience of awareness.

Consciousness is one type of highly intense experience of life, but there are other forms present in other species, sometimes with capacities that humans lack, as in fish that can hear ranges of sound or animals that can see ranges of light not possible to our ears and eyes. Nor can we simply draw a line between us, together with large-brained mammals, and other beings, as a distinction of "living persons" and "dead bodies." For plants too are living organic beings that respond to heat, light, water, and sound as organisms, and even chemical aggregates are dancing centers of energy.

Human consciousness, then, should not be what utterly separates us from the rest of "nature." Rather, consciousness is where this dance of energy organizes itself in increasingly unified ways, until it reflects back on itself in self-awareness. Consciousness is and must be where we recognize our kinship with all other beings. The dancing void from which the tiniest energy events of atomic structures flicker in and out of existence and self-aware thought are kin along a continuum of organized life-energy.

Our capacity for consciousness, which allows us to roam through space and time, remembering past ages, exploring the inner workings of all other existing beings on earth or on distant planets, also makes us aware of the ephemeral nature of our "self." Our capacity for consciousness is sustained by a complex but fragile organism. Cut that organism at its vital centers, in the brain or in the heart, and the light of consciousness goes out, and with it our "self."

It is this juxtaposition of the capacity of consciousness to roam through space and time, and its utter transience in its dependence on our mortal organisms, that has generated much of the energy of what has been called "religion" in the past. Much of this religious quest has sought to resolve this contradiction by denying it, imagining that consciousness was not really dependent on the mortal organism. The mental self could survive, and even be "purified" and strengthened, by the demise of the body. This concept of the "immortal self," survivable apart from our particular transient organism, must be recognized, not only as untenable, but as the source of much destructive behavior toward the earth and other humans.

An ecological spirituality needs to be built on three premises: the transience of selves, the living interdependency of all things, and the value of the personal in communion. Many spiritual traditions have emphasized the need to "let go of the ego," but in ways that diminished the value of the person, undercutting particularly those, like women, who scarcely have been allowed individuated personhood at all. We need to "let go of the ego" in a different sense. We are called to affirm the integrity of our personal center of being, in mutuality with the personal centers of all other beings across species and, at the same time, accept the transience of these personal selves.

As we accept both the value and the transience of the self, we can also be awakened to a new sense of kinship with all other organisms. Like humans, the animals and the plants are living centers of organic life who exist for a season. Then each of our roots shrivels, the organic structures that sustain our life fail, and we die. The cutting of the life center also means that our bodies disintegrate into organic matter, to enter the cycle of decomposition and recomposition as other entities.

The material substances of our bodies live on in plants and animals, just as our own bodies are composed from minute to minute of substances that once were parts of other animals and plants, stretching back through time to prehistoric ferns and reptiles, to ancient biota that floated in the primal seas of earth. Our kinship with all earth creatures is global, linking us to the whole living Gaia today. It also spans the ages, linking our material substance with all the beings that have gone before us on earth and even to the dust of exploding stars. We need new psalms and meditations to make this kinship vivid in our communal and personal devotions.

But, even as we take into our spirituality and ethical practice the transience of selves, relinquishing the illusion of permanence, and accepting the dissolution of our physical substance into primal energy, to become matter for new organisms, we also come to value again the personal center of each being. My eye catches the eye of a bird as it turns its head toward me on the side of the tree, and then continues its tasks. Brendan spies me coming up the path, and with flashing red fur is at the door, leaping in circles with unfeigned delight. My body, stretching in the sun, notices a tiny flower pushing up through the soil to greet the same sun. And we know our kinship as I and Thou, saluting one another as fellow persons.

Compassion for all living things fills our spirits, breaking down the illusion of otherness. At this moment we can encounter the matrix of energy of the universe that sustains the dissolution and recomposition of matter as also a heart that knows us even as we are known. Is there also a consciousness that remembers and envisions and reconciles all things, as the Process theologians believe? Surely, if we are kin to all things and offspring of the universe, then what has flowered in us as consciousness must also be reflected in that universe as well, in the ongoing creative Matrix of the whole.

As we gaze into the void of our future extinguished self and dissolving substance, we encounter there the wellspring of life and creativity from which all things have sprung and into which they return, only to well up again in new forms. But we also know this as the great Thou, the personal center of the universal process, with which all the small centers of personal being dialogue in the conversation that continually creates and recreates the world. The small selves and the Great Self are finally one, for as She bodies forth in us, all the beings respond in the bodying forth of their diverse creative work that makes the world.

The dialogue can become truncated. We can seek to grasp our ego centers of being in negation of others, proliferating our existence by diminishing that of others, and finally poisoning the wellspring of the life process itself. Or we can dance gracefully with our fellow beings, spinning out our creative work in such a way as to affirm theirs and they ours as well.

Then, like bread tossed on the water, we can be confident that our creative work will be nourishing to the community of life, even as we relinquish our small self back into the great Self. Our final gesture, as we surrender ourself into the Matrix of life, then can become a prayer of ultimate trust: "Mother, into your hands I commend my spirit. Use me as you will in your infinite creativity."

Notes

1. The idea that Plato was indebted to Moses is a commonplace in Hellenistic Jewish thinkers, such as Philo: Richard Baer, *Philo's Use of the Categories of Male and Female* (Leiden: Brill, 1970), 6. It also is taken for granted in Patristic writings; see Justin Martyr, *1st Apology,* 59, and *Hortatory Address to the Greeks,* 25–26, 31.

2. See Philip Merlan, *From Platonism to Neoplatonism,* 3d ed. (The Hague: Martinus Nijhoff, 1975).

3. *The Chaldean Oracles,* edited by Sapere Aude (London: Theosophical Publishing Society, 1895); also Hans Lewy, *Chaldean Oracles and Theurgy: Mysticism, Magic and Platonism in the Later Roman Empire* (Paris: Etudes Augustinienne, 1978) and Garth Fowden, *The Egyptian Hermes: A Historical Approach to the Late Pagan Mind* (Cambridge: Cambridge University Press, 1986).

4. R. E. de Witt, *Albinus and the History of Middle Platonism* (Cambridge: Cambridge University Press, 1937); also Plotinus, *Enneads,* translated by Stephen MacKenna (London: Faber, 1969).

5. *Corpus Hermeticus,* text and French translation by A. D. Nock and A.-J. Festugiere (Paris: Société d'édition "Les Belles Lettres," 1960), 2 vols.

6. Proverbs 8; and Wisdom of Solomon 6–8.

7. See E. R. Goodenough, *By Light, Light: The Mystic Gospel of Hellenistic Judaism* (New Haven: Yale University Press, 1935).

8. See Sigmund Mowinckel, *He That Cometh: The Messiah Concept in the Old Testament and Later Judaism* (New York: Abingdon Press, 1955), 324–25.

9. Patrick Rogers, *Colossians* (Wilmington: Michael Glazier, 1980), 13–17.

10. For an analysis of the terms in the New Testament and their pre-Christian roots, see Walter Wink, *Naming the Powers: The Language of Power in the New Testament* (Philadelphia: Fortress Press, 1984).

11. One hundred years was seen as the fullness of human life: see Isaiah 65:20.

12. The heresy of docetism haunted the struggle in the first five centuries of Christianity to define the "two natures" in Christ. The view that Jesus only appeared to take on a body, but did not have a real material body, was most explicitly stated in Gnostic Christianity, such as Valentinianism. In the fourth century, the Neoplatonic philosopher turned Christian bishop, Synesius of Cyrene, openly declared his inability to believe in the bodily resurrection: see Jay Bregman, *Synesius of Cyrene: Philosopher-Bishop* (Berkeley: University of California Press, 1982), 120.

13. See D. S. Wallace-Hadrill, *The Greek Patristic View of Nature* (New York: Barnes and Noble, 1968), 66.

14. *Ad Haer.* V.2.2.

15. *Ad Haer.* V.34.2, 3.

16. *Ad Haer.* V.36.3.

17. This is Augustine's view, passed on as the dominant view for the Latin medieval church: *City of God* 20.7.

18. For example, Chrysostom, *Commentary on Romans,* 14: see Wallace-Hadrill, *The Greek Patristic View of Nature,* 115–20.

19. C. E. Rolt, *Dionysius the Aeropagite on the Divine Names and the Mystical Theology* (London: SPCK, 1940).

20. See particularly Heiko Oberman, *The Harvest of Medieval Theology: Gabriel Biel and Late Medieval Nominalism* (Cambridge: Harvard University Press, 1963), 30–46.

21. Frances A. Yates, *Giordano Bruno and the Hermetic Tradition* (New York: Random House, 1969), 12–13.

22. The antiquity of Hermes Trismegistus is attested to in the church fathers, and thus the Renaissance thinkers believed they had it on the best authority: for example, Augustine, *City of God* 18:29.

23. See particularly William Huffman, *Robert Fludd and the End of the Renaissance* (London: Routledge, 1988).

24. Henry More, *Manual of Metaphysics* (1671); see C. A. Patrides, ed., *The Cambridge Platonists* (Cambridge, MA: Harvard University Press, 1970).

25. See excerpts from Spinoza's *Ethics* in *The Age of Reason: Seven-*

teenth Century Philosophers, edited by Stuart Hampshire (New York: New American Library, 1956), 99–141. Also R. G. Collingwood, *The Idea of Nature* (New York: Oxford University Press, 1970), 103–12.

26. Wordsworth returned to more orthodox Christianity in his later years, becoming an admirer of the Oxford movement, while Coleridge came to be seen as a founder of the "Broad Church Movement": Basil Willey, *Nineteenth Century Studies: Coleridge to Matthew Arnold* (New York: Harper & Row, 1949), 1–50.

27. For Hegel's view and the transition to the modern view of nature, see Collingwood, *The Idea of Nature,* 121–32.

28. See Matthew Fox, *Original Blessing* (Santa Fe, NM: Bear and Co., 1983), 117, 157, 229.

29. Matthew Fox, *The Coming of the Cosmic Christ* (San Francisco: Harper & Row, 1988), 129–55.

30. Fox, *The Coming of the Cosmic Christ,* 235–39.

31. See Rosemary Ruether, "Matthew Fox and Creation Spirituality," in *The Catholic World* (July/August, 1990): 168–72.

32. Barbara Newman, author of *Sister of Wisdom: St. Hildegard's Theology of the Feminine* (Berkeley: University of California Press, 1987), has conveyed to me her critique of Fox's mistranslations and misinterpretations of the writings of Hildegard of Bingen. See her review in *Mystics Quarterly* XV.4 (December 1989): 190–94.

33. Pierre Teilhard de Chardin, *The Phenomenon of Man* (New York: Harper and Brothers, 1959).

34. See James Lovelock, *Gaia: A New Look at Life on Earth* (New York: Oxford University Press, 1979); also *The Ages of Gaia: Biography of our Living Earth* (New York: Norton, 1988).

35. See Teilhard de Chardin, *Phenomenon of Man,* 285–90; also his *The Divine Milieu* (New York: Harper & Row, 1960), 133–39.

36. See John Cobb and David Ray Griffin, *Process Theology: An Introductory Exposition* (Philadelphia: Westminster Press, 1976); also Marjorie Suchocki, *God-Christ-Church: A Practical Guide To Process Theology* (New York: Crossroad, 1989).

37. Alfred North Whitehead, *Process and Reality: An Essay in Cosmology* (New York: Macmillan, 1929), 519–33.

38. See particularly Marjorie Suchocki, *The End of Evil: Process Eschatology in Historical Context* (Albany: State University of New York Press, 1988), 97–114; also her *God-Christ-Church,* 183–216.

39. See Jasper Hopkins, *A Concise Introduction to the Philosophy of Nicholas of Cusa* (Minneapolis: University of Minnesota Press, 1978), 7–

43; also Pauline M. Watts, *Nicolaus Cusanus: A Fifteenth-Century Vision of Man* (Leiden: Brill, 1982), 33–74.

40. The analogy comes from Fritjof Capra, *The Tao of Physics* (New York: Bantam Books, 1976), 54.

41. Blaise Pascal, *The Pensées,* edited by J. M. Cohen (Baltimore: Penguin Books, 1961), 57.

24. Feminism, Liberalism, and Catholicism

Mary C. Segers

This chapter first appeared in *Catholicism and Liberalism: Contributions to American Public Philosophy* in 1994.

The global women's movement and the varieties of feminist theory informing this movement require imaginative thinking about how issues of gender justice and equality affect attempts to address tensions between liberalism and Catholicism in the American milieu. This essay will consider liberal and Catholic traditions from a feminist perspective and argue that feminist theory presents an alternative vision of social justice which criticizes yet incorporates elements from liberalism. It also maintains that while Catholic thought and practice have not adequately addressed the challenge of contemporary feminism, Catholic tradition is rich in resources which feminists can use to press the case for theoretical and practical change in church and society.

There are three reasons for such a study. The first is apologetic (in the sense of an apologia or defense). Many deficiencies of contemporary liberal capitalist society—abstract individualism, subjective and relativist conceptions of the good, the cultural excesses of an untrammeled exercise of individual choice, the decline of the family, and a decrease of volunteerism in community life—are attributed at least in part to the contemporary feminist movement. Some worry that as women become more concerned with asserting their worth as individuals, they will lose what Carol Gilligan has identified as a special moral emphasis on care and responsibility for others and, as a result, society will be diminished. I think this characterization of the effects of the women's movement is inaccurate and seek to defend feminism against such criticisms.

Second, liberal feminism, that strand of feminist theory upon which I focus here[1] derives from the liberal tradition historically and builds upon its central notions of human dignity and individual rights. Yet liberal feminism is critical of liberal social thought and has moved beyond it in important respects. Not coincidentally, feminism generally—even liberal feminism—provides a critical perspective on American liberalism that should be of interest to Catholics and others with communitarian concerns.

A third factor is the use in Catholic circles of a distinction between "Christian feminism" and "radical feminism."[2] The latter phrase is a catch-all term for all varieties of feminist theory outside "true Christian feminism." Since most secular and religious feminists regard Catholic tradition as deeply patriarchal, they view the church hierarchy's attempts to define "true Christian feminism" with irony and skepticism. Nevertheless, the church's efforts to respond to the challenges of the women's movement by coopting the feminist label indicates the need to discuss the relation between Catholicism and feminism. It is necessary to review some major feminist criticisms of Catholic thought as well as positive elements in the Catholic tradition that might promote justice for women in modern society.

The discussion has four parts. The first briefly defines feminism and the varieties of feminist theory. The second examines what feminism has appropriated from liberal theory as well as ways feminism has criticized and progressed beyond liberalism. The third analyzes Catholic conceptions of womanhood articulated in recent papal teaching and summarizes the major feminist criticisms of Catholic Christianity. It also indicates positive elements in Catholic tradition and practice that some women have appropriated in their quest for social justice. The final section summarizes points of contact between liberal feminism and Catholicism that offer alternatives to the dominant cultural ethos of American liberalism.

The Feminist Challenge

Feminism can be defined in terms of what feminists oppose as well as what they support. Thus Nancy Holmstrom defines a feminist as "anyone, male or female, who opposes the exploitation and oppression of women," while Gloria Steinem states that "Feminism is the belief that women are full human beings. It is simple justice."[3] Nevertheless, despite its many varieties, feminism insists that women be taken seriously as moral agents. An instrumentalist conception of women is rejected by all feminists, no matter what their ideology. As Dame Rebecca West wrote in 1913, "I myself have never been able to find out precisely what feminism is: I simply know that people call me a feminist whenever I express sentiments that differentiate me from a doormat or a prostitute."[4]

Feminist theory is a more systematic articulation of feminist goals and commitments. Feminist thought is astonishingly diverse; it is not one but many theories or perspectives. The varieties include liberal, Marxist, radical, socialist, psychoanalytical, existentialist, and post-modern feminism as well as eco-feminism, pro-life feminism, and libertarian feminism.[5] In general, each feminist theory attempts to describe women's oppression, to explain its causes and consequences, and to prescribe strategies for women's liberation. Many different theoretical currents flow into feminist thought; the "women question" has been around for at least two centuries and socialist, liberal, and Marxist theoreticians have felt compelled to address it. There is much disagreement about the causes and nature of the oppression of women, and the remedies for it. Nevertheless, diverse feminist theories do not so much compete with as complement one another. Each feminist theoretical perspective is a partial, provisional answer to "the woman question."[6] The different varieties of feminist thought overlap and enrich one another. One of these varieties is liberal feminism.

Liberalism and Liberal Feminism

The relation of feminism to liberalism is complex. Feminism has emerged from liberalism, yet clearly transcends it. As Susan Okin notes, "Though by no means all contemporary feminists are liberals, virtually all acknowledge the vast debts of feminism to liberalism. They know that without the liberal tradition, feminism would have had a much more difficult time emerging."[7]

Historically, the development of liberal feminism from liberalism is evident in the work of such feminists as Mary Wollstonecraft and John Stuart Mill. In *Feminism, Marriage, and the Law in Victorian England,* Mary Lyndon Shanley describes how traditional liberal concepts of individual rights, natural freedom, and consent or contract were powerful tools in the hands of feminist reformers in the nineteenth and early twentieth centuries.

> Individualistic and contractual ideas, particularly the notion that consent is at the root of all human obligations, were crucial to early divorce law reform. Ideas about contract were also at the heart of the battle against the common law doctrine of coverture, which took away a woman's independent legal status when she married. . . . The argument made by opponents of women's suffrage that women were adequately represented by their fathers, husbands, or brothers (who voted, in effect, for the "household") was for a while successful, but was ultimately doomed in a polity based on the notion that government was created by the free consent of individuals endowed with "inalienable rights."[8]

In the 1960s and 1970s, feminists used similar liberal principles to secure legislative statutes and court decisions undermining the sexual division of labor and enabling more women to participate in the public world of marketplace and politics. Indeed, it is liberal feminism that has been most influential in American society, providing the justification for many of the political, legal, and social reforms of the 1970s and 1980s.[9]

Liberal feminists maintain that women's subordination "is rooted in a set of legal and customary constraints that block women's entrance or success in public life. Because society has the false belief that women are, by nature, less intellectually and physically capable than men, it excludes women from the academy, the forum, and the marketplace."[10] As a result of such exclusionary policies, the true potential of many women goes unfulfilled and society is deprived of the contributions they could make. As remedies, liberal feminists appropriate from the parent tradition principles of individual rights, equality of opportunity, natural freedom, consent or contract, an emphasis on education as a means of social reform, and a focus on law as a key to political and social change. They place special emphasis upon women's dignity and individual rights.[11] Moreover, liberal feminists are usually committed to major economic reorganization and considerable redistribution of wealth, since one of the political goals most closely associated with liberal feminism is genuine equality of opportunity in education and employment.

While feminists utilize major elements of the liberal tradition, they also strongly criticize important aspects of it. According to these critics, liberalism is flawed by a false gender neutrality, a failure to recognize that the liberal state historically has not been and is not now neutral in its politics toward women, children and families. It is faulted for its failure to recognize that the family, a basic unit of private life, is very much a political institution to which principles of justice should apply. Liberalism's formalistic ethic of rights is said to deny difference by bringing all separate individuals under a common measure of rights, an impartial standard of equal treatment which in reality is partial—i.e., is derived from men's experiences of the world of work and public life.[12] Finally, a major difference between liberalism and contemporary feminist thought centers on the public-private dichotomy. Feminists contend that liberal polities have been slow to extend to women crucial political and legal rights largely because of traditional distinctions between public and domestic realms. Traditionally, this public-private dichotomy has assumed that men inhabit both realms, easily moving from one to the other, while women inhabit only the realm of family life, where they are properly subordinate to their husbands. The "autonomous individuals" dear to most classical liberal thinkers were traditionally male heads of households.[13]

Indeed, liberal feminism has outgrown its parent tradition in significant respects. Feminist theorists have criticized the abstract individualism associated with the liberal view of the self, liberalism's conception of social relations as largely contractual or voluntary, and the liberal view of political community. Sometimes liberal feminists sound like communitarians in their critique of some fundamental premises underlying liberal thought; however, as we shall see, there are major reasons why feminists find communitarian perspectives inadequate as an alternative to liberalism.

Let us first consider the abstract individualism associated with the liberal view of the self. According to this atomistic individualism, society is composed of individual human beings who are unsituated, unencumbered, and unrelated. This "disregards the role of social relationships and human community in constituting the very identity and nature of individual human beings."[14] Thus it is an essentially false depiction of human beings because it ignores factors of interdependence including, among other things, the fact that men's autonomy rests on women's subordination. As Susan Okin states, "Claims that the subjects of classical liberal theory are autonomous, basically equal, unattached rational individuals rest on the often unstated assumption of women's unpaid reproductive and domestic work, their dependence and subordination within the family, and their exclusion from most spheres of life."[15] Or, in Naomi Schmeman's words, "Men have been free to imagine themselves as self-defining only because women have held the intimate social world together, in part by seeing ourselves as inseparable from it."[16]

From a feminist perspective, therefore, a major task for women is to extricate themselves from webs of social interdependence. Men may need to sensitize themselves to the social construction of their identities, but women need to do exactly the opposite—to realize some degree of autonomy and assert some independence from social definition. Seyla Benhabib and Drucilla Cornell express this idea eloquently:

> The vision of the atomic, "unencumbered self," criticized by communitarians, is a male one, since the degree of separateness and independence it postulates among individuals has never been the case for women. . . . Precisely because to be a biological female has always been interpreted in gendered terms as dictating a certain psychosexual and cultural identity, the individual woman has always been "situated" in a world of roles, expectations and social fantasies. Indeed, her individuality has

> been sacrificed to the "constitutive definitions" of her identity as a member of a family, as someone's daughter, someone's wife and someone's mother. . . . If unencumbered males have difficulties in recognizing those social relations constitutive of their ego identity, situated females often find it impossible to recognize their true selves amidst the constitutive roles that attach to their persons.[17]

Like communitarians, feminists reject liberalism's vision of atomistic individualism because it draws a picture of the self that is incomplete and because it encourages people to think of themselves first, fostering egoism and rewarding selfishness. Unlike communitarians, however, feminists see validity in liberal notions of individuality and individual rights, especially for women. Feminists "begin with the situated self but view the renegotiation of our psychosexual identities, and their autonomous reconstitution by individuals as essential to women's and human liberation."[18]

In addition, some feminists have argued that justifications for liberal principles of political equality and individual liberty need not logically imply a commitment to abstract individualism.[19] Alternative justifications—advanced historically, for example, by liberals such as John Stuart Mill—employ arguments based on utility, the protection of people's interests, and representative government. Susan Wendell contends that one might maintain that political equality is "the best system for helping people to protect their own interests . . . [and] that it has proven dangerous to the interests, happiness or self-development of human beings to allow others to make major decisions affecting their lives without their representation or consent. . . . [Moreover] while human beings are often bad at ensuring our own wellbeing or development, history seems to indicate that we are even worse at ensuring other people's wellbeing, and therefore the best arrangement is individual liberty and political equality."[20] These practical considerations yield arguments supporting liberal principles without assuming a state-of-nature condition of free unsituated individuals. Thus liberal feminism need not imply a commitment to abstract individualism. Indeed, as indicated above, there are good reasons why liberal feminists do not assume such a view.

A second liberal feminist critique of the parent liberal tradition concerns its conception of social relations as largely contractual or voluntary. "The boundaries of human relations are drawn by the nature of the self, understood in liberalism as competitive, privatistic, isolated, and self-interested."[21] These assumptions limit the potential bonds that can be created between people to ones that are instrumental and self-imposed. The individual is not seen as related to other individuals in intrinsic ways.

Again, the feminist critique on this point stresses how partial, limited, and therefore inaccurate the liberal account of human relations is. Feminists argue that the liberal analysis not only leaves out a broad range of human experience, but that it systematically ignores the experiences of women and children. As Virginia Held writes, "If the epitome of what it is to be human is thought to be a disposition to be a rational contractor, human persons creating other human persons through the processes of human mothering are overlooked."[22] Elizabeth Wolgast adds that "Atomism cannot . . . represent non-peer relationships like those of parent and child, teacher and student, or any where one person takes care of the interest of another."[23]

The model of interpersonal relations preferred by liberal feminists to that of traditional liberalism is one that allows for organic connections among people, relations of dependency and interdependency of many kinds. A model such as this captures the diversity of human relationships and does not ignore women and children. Liberal feminism therefore resists the tendency to "contractualize" relationships and opts for something difficult. In Held's words:

> Instead of importing into the household principles derived from the marketplace, perhaps we should export to the wider society the relations suitable for mothering persons and children . . . relations . . . characterized by more care and concern and openness and trust and human feeling than are the contractual bargains that have

developed so far in political and economic life, or even that are aspired to in contractarian prescriptions.[24]

Finally, the liberal feminist critique of traditional liberal theory is directed at its view of political community. While liberalism claims to provide a neutral state which protects the rights of individuals to pursue their private interests and goods as they define them, a feminist critique of liberal politics challenges this pretense to gender neutrality. The standard view is that by its non-intervention, the state maintains its neutrality concerning what goes on within the private sphere. However, gender scholars point out that the liberal state has regulated and controlled the family in innumerable ways that have tended to reinforce patriarchy. In nineteenth-century England, the common law doctrine of coverture deprived women of legal personhood upon marriage, including rights to own property, to veto a husband's decisions, to sue for separation or divorce, or to retain custody of one's children. By exempting the family from principles of justice applicable to the public sphere, nineteenth-century liberal thought, supposedly neutral, rationalized and justified women's domestic and political subjection.

Similarly, twentieth-century feminists question the neutrality of a state that has condoned sex discrimination in employment, continues in public policy to privilege the nuclear family over all other familial arrangements, and refuses to intervene in cases of domestic violence on "privacy" grounds. They also worry that extending formal rights to individuals may not amount to much if people do not have the financial resources necessary to exercise those rights. In a formal sense the state may be a neutral arbiter between competing interests, but in reality the state simply recognizes and legitimates an existing balance of forces, a balance in which one of the strongest forces is that of male dominance. Perhaps this is why Catherine MacKinnon argues that "liberal neutrality" in fact amounts to "substantive misogyny." In the context of sexual inequality, a government which refuses to take sides in the name of "neutrality" is in reality taking sides with the more powerful, men, allowing them to maintain their dominance through a state policy of non-interference.[25]

To summarize, liberal feminism is not classical liberalism. Historically, it has emerged from the liberal tradition and it is indebted to liberal theory for fundamental concepts of liberty, individual dignity and equality of opportunity. But it distances itself from other, more negative aspects of liberalism: abstract individualism, a contractarian view of social relations, and the concept of the neutral state. Moreover, liberal feminists reject an understanding of equal rights and equal opportunity that assumes that what is most worth having and doing is what men think worth having and doing. The equal opportunity doctrine does not necessarily commit liberal feminists to either a meritocratic model of society or a competitive form of individualism. In fact, equal opportunity turns out to be a surprisingly radical political goal for liberal feminists because it means, for example, educating men and women equally, and ending the "double work-day" for women by requiring men to share parenting and homemaking. Liberal feminists do not promote self-fulfillment to the exclusion of concern for others nor are they committed to the denigration of women's traditional role as homemaker. The equal opportunity formula does not propose that women should become just like men; rather it suggests a fluidity of social roles for women and men according to individual ability and aspiration.

Finally, while liberal feminism has outgrown traditional liberalism, it has not embraced, in uncritical fashion, communitarianism. Feminists and communitarians both find fault with liberalism, but they do not agree on remedies for the deficiencies of liberal capitalist society. While communitarians are concerned with the loss of "traditional boundaries," feminists are concerned with the costs of those boundaries, especially for women. Communitarians tend to gloss over or ignore the oppression of women in traditional communities; this is especially true of the family. Whereas feminists are wary of an ahistorical idealization of the traditional family, communitarians tend to speak uncritically of "the family" as a universal and undifferentiated unit. Furthermore, communitarian thinkers have generally had little commitment, and sometimes great hostility, to gender equality. In fact, as Penny Weiss notes, some feminists wonder why there is so much interest in community among feminists, and so little interest in feminism among communitarians.[26]

Catholicism and Feminism

Liberal feminists and traditional liberals may have their differences, but they are united in criticizing the views of the institutional Catholic church on women's role in church and society. Indeed, in analyzing the interaction of liberalism and Catholicism in American public life, feminists will invariably find much to applaud in liberalism and much to criticize in Catholic conceptions of womanhood. While secular feminists are likely to dismiss Catholic Christianity as hopelessly patriarchal and anti-feminist, religious feminists struggle valiantly within the church to increase awareness of sexism and to prod the church into action on issues of gender justice. Their trenchant critique of Catholic views on women is especially noteworthy precisely because they do not dismiss Catholic tradition as irremediably flawed, but try instead to salvage positive elements from Catholic social teaching which feminists can use to promote gender justice.

Feminists and scholars in women's studies in religion have criticized Catholic Christianity for its traditional conception of women as primarily wives and mothers, for the denial of voice to women in church life, for its long history of fear and distrust of women.[27] As a cultural force in Western history, the church has, for the most part, either excluded women from education or selectively educated them primarily for social rules in domestic life. Institutionally, the Catholic church in the United States actively opposed women's suffrage and has been slow to support women's greater political participation. Most gender scholars are not surprised by the church's failure to champion women's rights in the public (political) sphere. To them, this failure of the institutional church is merely the public reflection of an exclusion of women from priestly ordination and a refusal to include women in high administrative posts within the official church. There seems to be a parallelism between public and private, between the treatment of women in church polity and in the liberal state.

The issues raised by Catholic feminists—new ecclesiological models, questions of authority, revisionist understandings of "women's place"—have challenged the papal, curial, and episcopal authorities and created tensions within the church in the United

States. These tensions have carried over to the church's external relations with the larger society and government. Traditional views on women's role as wife-and-mother are reflected, for example, in the primacy accorded by the church to the abortion issue in American politics. Indeed, because of their heightened concern with abortion, the American bishops have been single-issue-oriented in their approach to issues of women's rights and public participation. Compared with the bishops' extensive pro-life lobbying, the record of the American church on other questions of women's rights has been modest indeed. On issues such as equal credit opportunity, comparable worth, equal educational opportunity, childcare, child support, and social security for spouses, the bishops' support has been lukewarm and qualified. Moreover, the American hierarchy has used the abortion issue to justify its refusal to support other public policy initiatives—the Equal Rights Amendment, the Pregnancy Discrimination Act of 1978, and the Civil Rights Restoration Act of 1988—designed to end discrimination against women and improve the quality of their lives.[28]

Judging by the record, then, the Catholic hierarchy does not really support women's full participation in the public life of the church or the public sphere of civil society. Moreover, it is difficult to think this is unrelated to the traditional conception of women in official church teaching. As Mary Jo Weaver notes, "Official Catholic teaching about women is a religious form of sex-role stereotyping which Catholic feminists oppose."[29]

A useful way both to analyze Catholic conceptions of womanhood and to delineate feminist criticisms is to examine Pope John Paul II's 1988 apostolic letter *Mulieris Dignitatem.* This letter was written in response to a request by the 1987 World Synod of Bishops on the Laity for a deeper consideration of church teaching on women. *Mulieris Dignitatem* includes the pope's reflections on several topics: Catholic conceptions of womanhood; papal reflections on marriage; the defense of Catholic traditional teaching against feminist criticism; papal Mariology; the policy implications of the pontiff's traditional view of women's special role as mothers; and his emphasis upon nurturing and caring as special feminine qualities.

The pope's apostolic letter is important, first, because of the influential role of papal statements in Catholic teaching. Such statements generally set the tone for subsequent pronouncements of episcopal conferences, individual bishops, clerical preachers and diocesan educators at lower levels of the church hierarchy. Concretely, this means that if the American bishops decide to issue a pastoral letter on women's concerns, as they did in 1988, they will make sure their pastoral letter reflects the views stated in the pope's apostolic letter. Second, the pope's letter is significant because it is a strikingly clear and complete expression of the ideology or worldview which feminists strongly challenge. Since it is a contemporary statement of authoritative church teaching on the status of women, it will shape official discussion topics for years to come. After examining the pope's letter, I shall recount briefly the views of several Catholic feminists in evaluating the pope's conception of the role of women. Finally, I shall suggest some positive elements in Catholic tradition which would enable the church to better affirm and support women.

Mulieris Dignitatem (On the Dignity and Vocation of Women) is written in the form of a philosophical reflection on the theology of women; it is also the first pontifical statement which attempts to answer feminist objections to the use of exclusive language in liturgy and worship and feminist claims to priestly ordination.[30] The letter begins with an extended meditation on biblical texts from Genesis (1:27–28; 2:18–25) and Ephesians (5:25–32) as establishing the equality of the sexes before God and the sanctity of marriage. Human beings are made in the image and likeness of God, and as free, rational creatures they are to imitate the loving communion of a Trinitarian Creator. However, men and women are created to complement one another. "Whatever violates the complementarity of women and men, whatever impedes the true communion of persons according to the complementarity of the sexes offends the dignity of both women and men."[31]

John Paul II emphasizes the significance of marriage in Genesis and the Christ-Bridegroom/Church-Bride analogy in Ephesians as definitive of the dignity and vocation of women. Woman is to be open to love in order to love in return. She is equal with man, but has "feminine" qualities—not defined by the pope—which specially qualify her to care for human persons in family and society. This theological construction of Genesis and Ephesians explains why marriage and family are important, as central religious symbols, for the church. A whole ecclesiology is made to turn on the nuptial analogy in Ephesians. Women as loving wives and mothers are to image the church as the loving, faithful Bride of Christ, the Bridegroom. In this interpretation, as women go, so goes the church; that is, if the conduct of women is disorderly, then church order and the social order are threatened.

Women, then, are seen primarily in relation to marriage and family. The pope refers to "the naturally spousal predisposition of the feminine personality" (*MD* 20). The role of women is to witness prophetically to the order of love. They do this through motherhood and virginity; these are "two particular dimensions of the fulfillment of the female personality" (*MD* 17). Mary, mother of Jesus, is the model for women since she was both virgin and mother.

A good part of the pope's exhortation is given over to defending Christian tradition against some aspects of the feminist critique while accommodating other parts of the feminist challenge. For example, the pope minimizes the role of Eve in the story of the Fall and original sin, so as to counter the identification of women with sinfulness. He reinterprets the celebrated passages in Ephesians 5:25–32 to imply mutuality and an egalitarian relationship between marriage partners rather than relations of subjection and authority (*MD* 24).[32] With respect to language and terms such as "the fatherhood of God," he contends that anthropomorphism is characteristic of biblical language, that maternal imagery was sometimes used to depict God, and that, in any case, God as pure spirit is beyond the language of gender (*MD* 8).

The pope seeks to counter arguments for the admission of women to the ordained priesthood. He maintains that the Jesus of the Gospels was a promoter of woman's true dignity, whose words and works always expressed the respect and honor due to women. The pontiff therefore insists that Christ's calling only men as his apostles was an intentional and deliberate action, not an unthinking acquiescence in the prevalent customs of his age and culture.

Mulieris Dignitatem is also informed by the strong Mariology characteristic of John Paul II. The pope offers Mary as "a model of discipleship and a sign of hope to all, and at the same time as a special symbol and model for women" (*MD* 24). Christ reveals to us how men should live while Mary is the model for women of true dignity and feminine humanity. The pope focuses especially on the Annunication and Mary's willing consent to be united with God as the mother of his son. John Paul II suggests that Mary's fiat is the exemplary attitudes for women; he repeatedly emphasizes the analogy between Mary's gracious acceptance of motherhood and that of ordinary women (*MD* 19).

The conclusion seems inescapable that women find their dignity and vocation primarily through marriage and motherhood and that women should, like Mary, be good mothers thereby cooperating in God's salvific plan.[33] The pope's language suggests a mystification of motherhood and an exaggerated expectation of maternal sensitivity. In his words, a pregnant woman's

> unique contact with the new human being developing within her gives rise to an attitude toward human beings—not only toward her own child, but every human being—which profoundly marks the woman's personality. It is commonly thought that women are more capable than men of paying attention to another person and that motherhood develops this predisposition even more. (*MD* 18)

According to the pope, both parents should share in child-rearing, but "the mother's contribution is decisive in laying the foundation for a new human personality" (*MD* 18). Thus complementarity for this pope means that, though men and women are essentially equal (both are created in God's image), women bear primary responsibility for parenting and for the welfare of the family.

The pope is willing to draw out the policy implications of this traditional view of women's special role as mother. Since parenthood "is realized much more fully in the woman, especially in the prenatal period," he contends that "No program of 'equal rights' between women and men is valid unless it takes this fact fully into account" (*MD* 18). In *Laborem Exercens,* John Paul II's 1981 encyclical On Human Work, he urged that since motherhood and care of children and family are primary tasks of women, a "family wage" is mandatory in a well-ordered society. That is, wages must be sufficient to enable women to stay at home caring for their children. He also called for the restructuring of the labor process so that working women might carry out their primary maternal responsibilities while being gainfully employed (note that the pope said little about changing society to enable fathers to combine career and fatherhood).

Mulieris Dignitatem concludes by emphasizing caring love as the fundamental special calling of women universally. Not only must women care for children and family; they must exemplify love and caring for all human beings. In the post-modern age, they must take care of the marginalized persons left behind by advancing science and technology; they must clean up after men, so to speak (*MD* 30). The pope indicates no awareness that women themselves might be in science and technology, but instead continues and reinforces age-old sex-stereotyping of human abilities and predispositions.

To summarize: the church's response to the feminist challenge—at the level of the papacy—has been, first, to reassert the traditional view of woman as wife and mother with some modification to accommodate changing social conditions. It is clear that women are to be at the service of the family in the papal worldview. John Paul II continues the emphasis in Catholic social thought upon the importance of the family as the basic unit of society (*MD* 31). The pope generally ignores the responsibilities of fathers and sees care of the family as especially entrusted to women. Thus while women should have access to public life, the private role of wife and mother is primary. There is little awareness of diversity of family types in different societies and little recognition of the feminist insistence upon equitable division of labor within families.

Second, the papal response to the feminist critique is characterized by considerable ambiguity. In his writings, John Paul II indicates an awareness of women's oppression and condemns the objectification and exploitation of women.[34] He holds the church up as a defender of woman's dignity, yet reaffirms the ban on women's ordination. He does not seem to recognize that unequal treatment of women and men within the church might be related to discrimination against women in society.

Third, the pope reiterates the traditional view that while men and women are equal before God, women are not identical with men but have complementary qualities which fit them to be companions and helpmates. In this typically functionalist, biologically deterministic approach, being determines function, and the physiological and psychological differences between the sexes indicate a divine intention about their respective roles. However, it is difficult to know exactly what to make of sex differences. As one Catholic feminist has remarked, it is uncertain whether there is a measurable connection between sex and gender differences and the conclusions we should draw about them in our public life.

> If men and women are different, does that mean only men should be priests—or only women? Or does it mean that priests should come in equal proportions of both sexes? If women are likely to have tender hearts, as one curial official recently warned, does that mean they should not serve on marriage tribunals, or does it mean that no marriage tribunal should be without them? If men are less likely to have tender hearts, should that restrict them to football fields and basketball courts while women deal with questions like third-world debt?[35]

Proponents of complementarity are usually quick to assert that differences do not mean diminishment, that although women are different, they are not inferior. But Mary Jo Weaver insists that "We must ask what inferiority means in the church. How would it be demonstrated? Is the usual complementary choice for Catholic women—motherhood or a convent—a way to keep women in powerless positions? And is powerlessness linked with inferiority?"[36] Other feminists note that in the traditional Catholic view, women serve as complements to men, but are not complementary companions and helpmates to women. They criticize the language of complementarity as designed "not to name a relevant reality but to evade real equality in the church." Margaret Steinfels contends that if advocates of complementarity are to be taken seriously, then let them install women in positions of power within the institutional church, so that the link between difference and inferiority-powerlessness can be broken. Arguing that the ban on ordination does not mean a ban on women in organizational leadership, she advocates that women be appointed to positions as chancellors, heads of tribunals, heads of curial congregations, members of the college of cardinals, and Vatican diplomats. Such appointments would signify a commitment to genuine equality within the church.

Fourth, *Mulieris Dignitatem* contains considerable ambiguity about feminine symbolization in Christian theology. For example, men and women are both called to consecrated virginity as well as to marriage and parenthood; yet virgin and mother (parent) symbols are feminine, and the pope wishes to draw special implications from these symbols as to how women should behave (he speaks of "feminine" characteristics and conduct). On ordination, only men can be priests (imaging the person of Christ, the Bridegroom), although the church as Christ's bride includes all Christian women and men. The pope is ambiguous on such symbolization, using it in two ways. But this is precisely where the feminist theological critique is relevant. It insists that contemporary theologians and churchmen (churchwoman also) cannot discount the gendered character of many Christian symbols. Anne Carr puts it this way:

> Jesus was a male; the dominant biblical images of God are male. And inherently male symbols are no help to alienated women *because* they have functioned so effectively in history to legitimate the subordination of women. This point may not be trivialized. Feminist reflection on the doctrines of God and of Christ, that shows that God is not male and that Jesus' maleness is a purely contingent fact, must further attend to the effective history of these doctrines, their practical and political uses. Only if the effects of these symbols and doctrines are transformed now and in the future can it be claimed that the symbols and doctrines are not intrinsically patriarchal, that they can be made available to women. A pragmatic criterion of the future emerges that holds that the truth of theological formulation lies in its effects. Given the effects of the past, any adequate contemporary formulation of the doctrine of God or of Christology must unmask past ideological uses

> of the symbols and attend to their transformative, ethical, and futural [sic] horizons of interpretation.[37]

What resources in the Catholic tradition would enable it to better acknowledge, recognize, affirm and support women? Obviously, the contemporary church's human rights tradition and its concern for social justice is a starting place. Another resource is the work of feminist theologians and ethicists which has, for the most part, been underutilized by the church hierarchy. It might help if church authorities tried to discern the complexity of contemporary feminist thought, instead of speaking only of "Christian feminism" and dismissing all the other varieties of feminist thought as "radical feminism." Still another positive step is exemplified by Archbishop Rembert Weakland of Milwaukee's "listening sessions" in which he set about trying to hear women speaking frankly on the basis of their own experiences. Finally, admitting women to positions of high church authority would certainly give some credibility to papal and episcopal claims that the church really supports equality of the sexes.

Conclusion

Just as liberalism challenged the Catholic worldview in the nineteenth and early twentieth centuries, feminism is surely a major challenge to Catholic Christianity in the last quarter of the twentieth century. However, as I have indicated, feminism also criticizes and qualifies liberalism to a significant extent. Indeed, because of the pervasive, deep, and lasting effects of patriarchy, feminists apply a healthy skepticism to *all* claims made by established authorities, institutions, and traditions. Adopting a critical, feminist perspective means standing on the margins of society and asking *who* defined the reigning conventions and practices, and *who* benefits primarily from these existing social arrangements? Neither Catholicism nor liberalism can withstand scrutiny from a feminist perspective; both must adapt to meet this new challenge which, when all is said and done, concerns the well-being of half of humanity.

Nevertheless, if the criterion of this scrutiny is the degree to which an institutional tradition opposes the oppression of women and works diligently to promote equity and equality, then liberalism looks somewhat better than Catholicism in terms of ideology and practice. Liberals at least recognize the problem of sex-stereotyping and sex-based discrimination, and they espouse principles of equality of opportunity, human dignity, and individual rights which naturally can contribute to the struggle for gender justice.

Catholicism also emphasizes human dignity and global human rights, but the church seems light years behind liberalism and liberal feminism in efforts to support the advancement of women. Limitations on the church's ability actively to support the women's movement include the following. First, its official teaching endorses a biological determinism or anatomy-is-destiny approach that conceives women's natural, primary role to be that of wife and mother. Acceptance of this traditional way of conceptualizing women's role in society seems to render many churchmen insensitive to the realities of injustice against women in private and public life. Second, a narrow, rigid teaching on sexuality, evident in the prohibition of artificial contraception as a means of limiting the size of the family is far from persuasive to many Catholics and many feminists. Third, the refusal to ordain women or to give them high administrative positions within the church undermines church support for the advancement of women in secular society. In addition, feminist theologians and Scripture scholars have shown how the church is also limited by linguistic sexism in liturgy, spirituality, and in theological conceptions of God. And they have emphasized the fact that much Catholic moral theology on the position of women in society was written by men, from the perspective of men. This continues in efforts by contemporary American churchmen to write pastoral statements defining women's role in church and society. Needless to say, such a practice is contrary to the thrust of the feminist movement which stresses decision-making and role definition by women themselves.

Cumulatively, these limitations of the institutional church amount to a refusal to accord women full status within the ecclesia of Catholic Christianity, and an attempt to circumscribe women's moral decision-making. Compared to this legacy, the liberal tradition is obviously more progressive and seems, to women at least, to offer more hope and greater relevance. If there is a spectrum or scale of progress towards women's empowerment, Catholicism would have to be seen as lagging behind liberalism because it has not yet granted women the signs and symbols of basic respect, individual dignity, and equal opportunity necessary to the full inclusion of women in social life. Liberal feminism by contrast would occupy a point on the scale in advance of liberalism; that is, liberal feminism has improved upon liberalism by rejecting some negative aspects of the liberal tradition while reaffirming greater individualism, freedom, and equality for women.

The liberal tradition is of course very complex. It should be emphasized that liberal feminists are more committed to political liberalism with its emphasis on individual rights and equal opportunity while they are distinctly less comfortable with laissez-faire economic liberalism and with cultural liberalism (defined as a kind of libertarianism in matters of culture, morals and style). In distancing itself from the parent tradition, liberal feminism has been more influenced by the critique of liberalism made by radical feminists and socialist feminists rather than the critique emanating from communitarians or Catholic cultural conservatives.

How can Catholic tradition affirm and support women? What is or could be a Catholic contribution to the feminist project? Catholicism is a rich heritage which contains many resources of potential use to the feminist cause. Through the centuries, Catholic tradition and practice has furnished us with many examples of heroic, pioneering women who made significant contributions to the public good: Joan of Arc, Teresa of Avila, Elizabeth Seton, Katharine Drexel, Dorothy Day. In the United States, religious sisterhoods nursed wounded soldiers during the Civil War, built and operated schools, hospitals, colleges, and social service agencies, and worked in other ways to build a decent, humane society. There must be some powerful, attractive sources of commitment within Catholic tradition to have inspired these kinds of activities.

In liturgy and spirituality, Catholic tradition also contains sources of nurturance and sustenance for religious feminists. In contrast to a first generation of feminist theologians whose pioneering work was critical of the tradition, a second generation has emerged whose work is more synthetic. Sandra Schneiders, Anne Carr, and Elizabeth Johnson belong to this second generation of feminist theologians whose work joins the insights of feminist theory with the riches of Catholic thought.[38] The Scripture scholar Schneiders, for example, wonders why among the hundreds of images of God in the Bible—God as mother, father, friend, sower, baker, lamb, gate, water, wind, fire, light—Christians have chosen the image of Christ the king as their predominant image. She maintains that the overwhelming message in Scripture is that humans cannot define God: "God is beyond anything we can box into one image or category." She argues that Catholics, particularly Catholic women, have been offered a very limited and sometimes unhealthy spirituality, and insists that "We need some theological therapy of the religious imagination." To do this Catholics should avoid all sexist language and come to understand that just as men in Scripture "are role models for all Christians, so too are the women in Scripture role models for all Christians, male and female."[39] It is this kind of deconstruction and reconstruction of the tradition which religious feminists propose.

Finally, Catholic social thought is potentially an important resource for feminists in the struggle for gender justice. Catholic social teaching tries to chart a middle way between the negative aspects of capitalism and the liabilities of socialism. Its concepts of human dignity, rights correlative with duties, the common good, subsidiarity, and participation in economic life comprise a rich tradition which could be tapped. Without revision, however, there is some question as to how much assistance this tradition could provide. Catholic social teaching itself badly needs a solid infusion of feminist theory in order to offset its general neglect of "the woman question."

Thus while liberal feminism has outgrown liberalism, Catholic thought has yet to appropriate fully those positive elements of the liberal tradition that would help to promote women's greater recognition and self-value as individuals. This means that there is some distance—some would say a great divide—between Catholic tradition and liberal feminism. But there is also some room for dialogue between these traditions. On three issues—pornography, contract pregnancy, and abortion—there are some surprising and interesting common themes which liberal feminists and Catholics can explore.

Radical feminists such as Catharine MacKinnon and Andrea Dworkin have characterized pornography as debasing and exploitative of women, and have sought civil statutes to protect women's rights. The Catholic church has also opposed pornography—though for different reasons. What is surprising is that liberal feminists, who might be expected to defend First Amendment rights of individuals to determine what they see and read, have agreed with their radical feminist sisters in questioning whether pornographers should be allowed to sell their wares. I think especially here of two liberal feminists, Susan Wendell and Elizabeth Wolgast, who have argued against pornography in ways that suggest some commonalities with Catholic thought. Both authors argue that a good case can be made, on the basis of Mill's principle of liberty alone, for restricting pornography that portrays violence and coercion of women and children. Mill's principle, they contend, permits interference with expression when it causes serious harm to others, provided that the harm cannot be prevented by acceptable means other than restricting the expression. Insofar as pornography is exploitative of women and children or is felt by women to be demeaning and insulting, its protection by the government under the First Amendment cannot be easily argued in a society committed to equal respect for individual persons.[40]

Catholic moral teaching condemns pornography as corrupting of people's minds and imaginations and as depicting sexuality in a manner that is debasing and demeaning as well as exploitative of women and children. It would appear that Catholic sexual ethics and liberal feminist views agree at least in their opposition to violent pornography.

A second point of contact between Catholic perspectives and those of some liberal feminists concerns contract pregnancy (also known as surrogacy or surrogate motherhood). The Catholic church officially opposes contract pregnancy on grounds that it interrupts the essential, necessary relationship between human sexuality, marriage, and parenthood. The church maintains that surrogacy violates human dignity because it exploits women and treats children as commodities. The church also views surrogacy as a threat to the integrity of the family and an attack on the institution of marriage that will weaken further its place and role in society. Finally, the hierarchy recognizes that the practice of surrogacy may put pressure on poor women to participate in such arrangements to help support themselves and their families.[41]

Again, among feminists surrogate motherhood is controversial. The feminist debate on surrogacy pits supporters of contract pregnancy as a legitimate expression of women's autonomy against critics who deplore surrogacy as destructive of families and who worry that poverty will force women to resort to contract pregnancies for income. Under such circumstances, it makes little sense to these feminists to speak of women's "freedom" to bear children for others in return for payment. Indeed, some liberal feminists criticize surrogacy as the quintessential expression of contractarian liberalism with all its shortcomings. Contractarian liberal arguments for enforcing pregnancy contracts are said to conflate contract and freedom, and to present contract as the paradigmatic bond linking people to one another in human society. As Mary Lyndon Shanley argues, "The model upon which contract pregnancy rests—of the self-possessing individual linked to others only by contractual agreements—fails to do justice to the complex interdependencies involved in human procreative activity, family relations, and human social life in general."[42] This criticism sounds markedly similar to the official church criticism stated above.

Of course, a critical difference between feminist opposition to surrogacy and the Catholic hierarchy's opposition is the church's insistence upon the absolute inseparability of the unitive and procreative dimensions of sexual intercourse. This position leads the church to reject all forms of artificial conception (just as it rejects all forms of artificial contraception). However, feminists approach reproductive technologies with more flexibility and evaluate them with respect to their safety and efficacy in terms of the goal of childbearing, not the physical integrity of a single act of intercourse. Feminists also give much greater emphasis to a class and gender analysis of artificial reproduction. Nevertheless, despite their differences, a curious but complementary blending of concerns and principles links Catholics and feminists on the matter of contract pregnancy. As Shannon notes, "The methodology of the bishops and feminists is not similar. Yet each group, beginning from different starting points, identifies similar concerns and comes to similar conclusions."[43] Perhaps there is room here for dialogue—to develop further the shared critique of atomistic individualism and contractarian liberalism which underlies arguments for the enforcement of pregnancy contracts.

A third point of contract between Catholic perspectives and those of liberal feminists concerns public policy on abortion. Liberal jurisprudence resists coercive laws restricting abortion as a violation of women's autonomy and as poor public policy. While liberal feminists support the legality of abortion, many have moral reservations about the high incidence of abortion in the United States. Nevertheless, for these feminists, the way to reduce the incidence of abortion is not to burden or coerce involuntarily pregnant women but to press for reform policies to create alternatives for such women. This sounds remarkably similar to what some Catholic pro-lifers are currently doing regarding abortion policy in the United States—educating public opinion and sponsoring programs which offer alternatives to abortion for involuntarily pregnant women. This is not to minimize basic differences between Catholics and feminists concerning the moral status of fetal life and the primacy of women's autonomy. Rather, it is simply to point out possible areas of agreement and cooperation between these two groups at least with respect to public policies to assist women.

It would be naive to suggest that these points of contact are anything more than openings for dialogue. One must be realistic about the grounds for rapprochement between feminism and Catholicism. Nevertheless, it would seem that these two traditions have nothing to lose by exploring their common critique of classical contractarian liberalism.

In this essay, I have tried to show that liberal feminism is not "ultraliberalism," and that liberal feminists have thoughtfully appropriated positive elements from the liberal tradition while distancing themselves from excessively individualistic strains of contractarian thought. Feminism offers a conception of the person as a social self, whose identity is shaped from the start by social interdependence. Catholic social thought also emphasizes the social situatedness of the person. But before Catholics and feminists can find common ground, the church must make a major effort to address the feminist critique. One possibility is a feminist project of recovery of the riches of the Catholic tradition—done within the church by religious feminists. In such a project, Catholics have much to learn from the nuanced views of liberal feminists.

Notes

1. The fact that I discuss liberal feminism does not mean that I am a liberal feminist or that I prefer this variety of feminism to other feminist perspectives. I focus on liberal feminism because of the issues studied in this volume, the relation between liberalism, Catholicism, and American public philosophy. I myself think that liberal feminism is properly balanced and enriched by other feminist theories, e.g., socialist feminism and radical feminism.

2. This distinction was made during a March 1989 meeting in Rome between American archbishops and the heads of Vatican curial congregations to discuss the state of the American Catholic church; see *Origins,* February 23, March 23, and March 30, 1989; also *The New York Times,* March 12, 1989; *National Catholic Reporter,* March 10, 1989; and *Origins* 18 (September 22, 1988): 242.

3. Gloria Steinem, "Reflections," in Lynn Gilbert and Gaylen Moore, eds., *Particular Passions* (New York: Clarkson Potter, 1981), 167. The source for Nancy Holmstrom's definition was her lecture at the Newark campus of Rutgers University in March, 1986.

4. Dame Rebecca West, quoted in *The New York Times Book Review* by John Leonard, May 28, 1982, 25. I acknowledge that this quotation from West is troubling. I do not subscribe to the elitism implicit in this statement which ignores the fact that prostitution is often undertaken as an alternative to poverty. However, while the reasons for engaging in prostitution may be mitigating circumstances, they do not diminish or alter the instrumental use of women which underlies prostitution.

5. See, for example, Rosemarie Tong, *Feminist Thought* (Boulder, CO: Westview Press, 1989); Alison Jaggar, *Feminist Politics and Human Nature* (Totowa, NJ: Rowman & Allanheld, 1983); Zillah Eisenstein, *The Radical Future of Liberal Feminism* (New York: Longman, 1981); and Jean Bethke Elshtain, *Public Man, Private Woman: Women in Social and*

Political Thought (Princeton University Press, 1981) for more on types of feminist theory.

6. Tong, *Feminist Thought,* 1.

7. Susan Moller Okin, *Justice, Gender, and the Family* (New York: Basic Books, 1989), 61.

8. Mary Lyndon Shanley, "Afterword: Feminism and Families in a Liberal Polity," in Irene Diamond, ed., *Families, Politics, and Public Policy* (New York: Longman, 1983), 357–358. See also Shanley, *Feminism, Marriage, and Law in Victorian England: 1850–1895* (Princeton University Press, 1989).

9. Prominent liberal feminists include Pat Schroeder, Eleanor Smeal, Elizabeth Holtzman, Bella Abzug, and Geraldine Ferraro, as well as leaders and members of the National Organization for Women. Liberal feminists (loosely defined) include philosophers and political theorists such as Susan Okin, Elizabeth Wolgast, and Mary Lyndon Shanley.

10. Tong, *Feminist Thought,* 2.

11. Susan Wendell, "A (Qualified) Defense of Liberal Feminism," *Hypatia: A Journal of Feminist Philosophy* 2/2 (Summer 1987): 66.

12. See Zillah Eisenstein, *The Female Body and the Law* (Berkeley: University of California Press, 1988) for analysis of the problem of equal treatment in liberal theory; see also Iris Marion Young, *Justice and the Politics of Difference* (Princeton University Press, 1990), chap. 8.

13. Susan Moller Okin, "Humanist Liberalism," in Nancy L. Rosenblum, ed., *Liberalism and the Moral Life* (Cambridge, MA: Harvard University Press, 1989), 39–40.

14. Marilyn Friedman, "Feminism and Modern Friendship: Dislocating the Community," in Cass R. Sunstein, ed., *Feminism and Political Theory* (University of Chicago Press, 1990). 143.

15. Okin, "Humanist Liberalism," 41.

16. Naomi Schmeman, "Individualism and the Objects of Psychology," in Sandra Harding and Merrill B. Hintikka, eds., *Discovering Reality* (Boston: D. Reidel, 1983), 240.

17. Seyla Benhabib and Drucilla Cornell, eds., *Feminism as Critique* (Minneapolis: University of Minnesota Press, 1987), 12.

18. Ibid., 12–13.

19. Michael Walzer also contends that "Contemporary liberals are not committed to a presocial self, but only to a self capable of reflecting critically on the values that have governed its socialization." See his "The Communitarian Critique of Liberalism," *Political Theory 18/1* (February 1990): 21.

20. Benhabib and Cornell, *Feminism as Critique,* 70–71.

21. Penny A. Weiss, "Feminism and Communitarianism: Exploring the Relationship" (unpublished paper presented at the 1990 Annual Meeting of the American Political Science Association, San Francisco, August 31, 1990), 14.

22. Virginia Held, "Non-Contractual Society: A Feminist View," in Marsha Hanen and Kai Nielson, eds., *Science, Morality and Feminist Theory* (University of Calgary Press, 1987), 120.

23. Elizabeth H. Wolgast, *Equality and the Rights of Women* (Ithaca, NY: Cornell University Press, 1980), 154.

24. Held, "Non-Contractual Society," 122.

25. Catherine MacKinnon, *Feminism Unmodified: Discourses on Life and Law* (Cambridge, MA: Harvard University Press, 1987), 15. See also Weiss, "Feminism and Communitarianism," 24.

26. Weiss, "Feminism and Communitarianism," 1.

27. For a sampling of feminist theology and scholarship in women's studies in religion, see the writings of Elisabeth Schüssler Fiorenza, Rosemary Radford Ruether, Mary Daly, Anne Carr, Margaret Farley, Mary Hunt, and Bernadette Brooten. See also the following volumes in the Harvard Women's Studies in Religion Series: C. W. Atkinson, C. H. Buchanan, and M. R. Miles, *Immaculate and Powerful: The Female in Sacred Image and Social Reality* (Boston: Beacon Press, 1985); and C. W. Atkinson, C. H. Buchanan, and M. R. Miles, *Shaping New Vision: Gender and Values in American Culture* (Ann Arbor: UMI Research Press, 1987).

28. The bishops' opposition to the ERA developed initially in the mid 1970s because the Equal Rights Amendment appeared to be a blank check for possibly radical social change which the bishops feared. Later in the decade and in the early 1980s, the possible linkage of abortion rights with the ERA deterred the NCCB from supporting the ERA. For the story of the failure of the US Catholic Church to support the 1920s ERA, see Antoinette Iadarola, "The American Catholic Bishops and Woman: From the Nineteenth Amendment to the ERA," in Yvonne Y. Haddad and Ellison Banks Findly, eds., *Women, Religion, and Social Change* (Albany: State University of New York Press, 1985), 457–476.

29. Mary Jo Weaver, *New Catholic Women: A Contemporary Challenge to Traditional Religious Authority* (San Francisco: Harper & Row, 1985), xiv.

30. In 1976, the Vatican Doctrinal Congregation issued, with the permission of Pope Paul VI, its "Declaration on the Admission of Women to the Ministerial Priesthood" (*Inter Insigniores*), reiterating the church's ban on female priests. This Declaration is contained in Leonard Swidler

and Arlene Swidler, eds., *Women Priests: A Catholic Commentary on the Vatican Declaration* (New York: Paulist Press, 1977), 37–52.

31. "Human Rights and the Rights of Women," an *ad limina* address by Pope John Paul II to American bishops from the western United States, September 2, 1988, in *Origins* 18/15 (September 22, 1988): 243. See also *Mulieris Dignitatem,* no. 6.

32. The Pope reinterprets the celebrated passages in Paul's Letter to the Ephesians—"Wives, be subject to your husbands, as to the Lord. For the husband is the head of the wife. . . . Husbands, love your wives, as Christ loved the church and gave himself up for her"—to imply mutuality and an egalitarian relationship between married partners: "Whereas in the relationship between Christ and the church the subjection is only on the part of the church, in the relationship between husband and wife the 'subjection' is not one-sided but mutual" (*MD* 24).

33. An earlier pope was more straightforward and explicit about the Christian duty of women as mothers. Leo XIII wrote that the purpose of marriage was not only the propagation of the human race but "the bringing forth of children for the church, 'fellow citizens with the saints, and the domestics of God.' " Pope Leo XIII, *Arcanum* (*On Christian Marriage*), no. 10, in Claudia Carlen, ed., *The Papal Encyclicals: 1878–1903* (Raleigh, NC: McGrath, 1981), 31.

34. *Familiaris Consortio* (*The Role of the Christian Family in the Modern World*) (Boston: St. Paul Editions, 1981), 41–42.

35. Margaret O'Brien Steinfels, "The Church and Its Public Life," *America* (June 10, 1989): 554. This was the 1989 John Courtney Murray Forum Lecture delivered at Fordham University on May 18, 1989. The reference to women and tender hearts is to a remark made by Cardinal Edouard Gagnon, former President of the Pontifical Council for the Family, at the March 1989 meeting between American archbishops and the Pope and curial officials in Rome. Referring to the presence on diocesan marriage tribunals of women trained in canon law, Cardinal Gagnon stated: "Women religious can be very helpful in dealing with marriage cases, but we have to be careful that their tender hearts do not play tricks on them." *The New York Times,* March 12, 1989; also *The Washington Post,* March 10, 11, and 12, 1989; also "Catholics for a Free Choice," *Conscience* 10/2 (March-April 1989): 7–8.

36. Weaver, *New Catholic Women,* 52.

37. Anne E. Carr, *Transforming Grace: Christian Tradition and Women's Experience* (San Francisco: Harper & Row, 1988), 109.

38. Among the first generation of religious feminists drawn from the Catholic community, one might include Mary Daly, Rosemary Ruether,

and Elisabeth Schüssler Fiorenza. Admittedly, the work of some feminist theologians and ethicists is both critical and synthetic: I am thinking especially of Schüssler Fiorenza, Bernadette Brooten, Margaret Farley, Mary Hunt, and Rosemary Ruether.

39. "God Is More than Two Men and a Bird," Editors' Interview with Sandra M. Schneiders, *U.S. Catholic* (May 1990): 20–27.

40. See Elizabeth H. Wolgast, *The Grammar of Justice* (Ithaca, NY: Cornell University Press, 1987), 112–120.

41. Thomas A. Shannon, "Bishops, Feminists, and Surrogate Motherhood," in Mary Segers, ed., *Church Polity and American Politics: Issues in Contemporary American Catholicism* (New York: Garland Publishing, 1990), 251–271.

42. See Mary Lyndon Shanley, "A Critique of Contractarianism in Feminist Theory: 'Surrogate Mothering' and Women's Freedom" (unpublished paper presented at the 1990 Annual Meeting of the American Political Science Association, San Francisco, California, August 31, 1990).

43. Shannon, "The Bishops, Feminists, and Surrogate Motherhood," 251.

25. Liberating Compassion: Spirituality for a New Millennium

Francine Cardman

This chapter first appeared in *The Way* in 1992.

A young Korean woman stood before the crowd, barefoot and clad in the simple white clothing of a peasant. She called upon the tortured spirits of the ancestors and of the planet, the victims of human greed, hatred and religious intolerance, invoking their presence and voice. For only when we hear their cries and see the signs of their liberation, she claimed, "are we able to recognize the Holy Spirit's activity in the midst of suffering creation."

The keynote address of Dr. Chung Hyun Kyung to the Seventh Assembly of the World Council of Churches meeting in Canberra, Australia, in February 1991 unleashed what the press quickly labelled a "firestorm" of criticism, a reaction that has followed her home to Seoul.[1] She was charged with syncretism, labelled unorthodox, taken to task for not being sufficiently Christian or Trinitarian in her theology of the Spirit. Yet many people, especially those from the so-called "third world" and especially women, found the reality of their lives validated in Dr. Chung's moving presentation. In the commotion following her speech, a woman remarked to her that she really ought to be in the women's room at that moment rather than on the assembly floor. When she asked why, she was told that she should see how many women were there crying—in gratitude, relief and joy.[2]

Why were the women weeping? Why were others, men and women, raging? What does the Holy Spirit have to do with the spirits of history's martyred and victimized? What do Seoul and Canberra, the *minjung* of Korea and the aboriginal peoples of

Australia have to do with Jerusalem? Is there a Christian spirituality wide enough to encompass all these realities? Is the spirit of compassion deep enough and strong enough to carry us not only into a new country but also into a new age for all earth's creatures?

Chung Hyun Kyung's address and the reactions to it are a dramatic enactment of the crucial questions facing Christian spirituality in the last years of the second millennium of the time we have so characteristically claimed as *Anno Domini.* Issues of inculturation, empowerment, liberation, solidarity and western decentering are signs of profound changes already under way in the Church. In their most fundamental form, these questions challenge Christian faith and life to a radical reorientation to the world. The change in perspective and proportion that is called for is akin to the visual reorientation worked by maps of the world drawn on the Peters projection. In these maps, geographical landmass rather than cultural weight determines the scale of the continents.[3] Similarly, Christianity looks different when it is accurately contextualized. Globally, Christianity is a minority religion; its center of gravity is rapidly shifting from the "first world" to the "third world"; its voices are increasingly multilingual and pluralistic.

The tears and joy, anger and fears at Canberra were, at least in part, a response to the reality of reorientation taking place in the midst of the assembly. Change of this sort is not only political or cultural in its implications, though it is that. It is also profoundly spiritual, reaching to the roots of the hope and meaning we have for ourselves and for our world. To understand why this process of change is the matter of spirituality, I want to look first at the root meaning of spirituality and then consider some basic issues in that light.

Spirit and Spirituality

The most basic meaning of "spirit" is breath or life force, the body's animating principle. It is intrinsic to body and world, not separate from them; it moves in and through history, not outside it. When informed by consciousness, this spirit moves with direction and intent toward what it seeks to know and love. In human beings, this conscious, willing, moving spirit might best be known as *heart;* as embodied *eros,* as the place and means of connected knowing that leads to action, to loving and doing. Thus spirituality is about the ways in which this spirit relates to body, world and history.[4] It is the attentiveness which persons give to the reality of self, others, the natural world and whatever we name as holy, as source, depth and mystery (some would say, as the divine) in our lives. Spirituality is the direction, meaning and value we give to the totality of experiences.[5]

There are, then, many spiritualities, many ways of being human in the world. They are embodied in particular forms, shaped by particular cultural matrices and religious traditions. Within a tradition such as Christianity, there are distinctive spiritualities, ways of being Christian, each with its characteristic expressions and emphases, but all relating in some fashion to the God who is made known through Jesus Christ and the Holy Spirit. I would like to argue that, at its heart, this encounter of God and humankind is the revelation of love and freedom in history. Whatever form Christian spirituality takes, it seeks to embody and empower that loving and freeing action and carry it forward in the world.

One way of envisioning the revelatory activity of Christian spirituality and its relationship to the world is in terms articulated by Paul in his Letter to the Romans. In chapter 8, Paul describes what it means to live by the Spirit:

> For all who are led by the Spirit of God are children of God. For you did not receive a spirit of slavery to fall back into fear, but you have received a spirit of adoption. When we cry, "Abba! Father!" it is that very Spirit bearing witness with our spirit that we are children of God. . . . (14–16)

We still live in a time of suffering, yet we anticipate a glory about to be revealed. All creation suffers and waits with us, longing for the freedom that will be the revelation of the children of God.

> We know that the whole creation has been groaning in labour pains until now; and not only the creation, but we ourselves, who have the first fruits of the Spirit, groan

> inwardly while we wait for adoption, the redemption of our bodies. (22–23)[6]

We are heirs, yet we wait for adoption; we are no longer slaves yet we wait for freedom. Creation itself remains captive to futility in the space between "already" and "not yet." But as the call and response of spirit and Spirit grows stronger and more mutual, captivity is undone and freedom is made known now.

Seen in the light of the late twentieth century, this ancient text is startlingly relevant. It touches the deep feelings raised by the debate at Canberra and reaches beneath them to the fundamental human and religious questions: what is it that we hope for? why is it so long coming? how do we live so as to redeem the time? Whatever his sources of insight, Paul knew something that we have mostly forgotten: that the fate of the earth and the fate of humankind are intricately related. The making known (revealing, *apokalypsin*) of the children of God is the means by which creation itself shall be set free from the bondage of decay. The adoption that we wait for is the redemption of our bodies; not only our individual body, but the body politic and the world body. Another way to put this is to say that the redemption that we hope for is personal, political and global in its dimensions. That hope is anticipatory in a double sense; even as we long for its fulfilment, we act to make it present in history.

A spirituality that embodies such hope must encompass the realities of change and struggle at this time in the world's life. Most especially, it must take account of the major reorientation that is occurring as the result of the intersection of feminist, liberationist and ecological movements. Each of these perspectives is personal, political and global in its outlook. Together they constitute a new way of being in the world that I (with many others) would argue is crucial for our well-being and even survival as we approach the next millennium.

Decentering

Inherent in the feminist, liberationist and ecological movements is a strong critique of domination in all its forms—cultural, religious and ideological, as well as political. From their distinct but related vantage points, each of these movements rejects the notion that difference must be equated with otherness and otherness embodied in varying degrees of powerlessness. Rather, difference and particularity are understood as essential elements of reality and the basis of any authentic, i.e., non-dominating, relationship. Real difference and real connection demand a multiplicity of viewpoints, of subjects, of experiences. In a pluralistic world, there is no clear demarcation between center and periphery, but rather a shifting constellation of relationships that informs knowledge and action. Reorienting oneself to pluralism is a spiritual as well as an epistemological and practical process. It requires a radical decentering on the part of the privileged whose reality has occupied the center, whatever its defining terms (e.g., economic, geopolitical, sexual, even christological). At the same time, it moves the dispossessed to claim a center of subjectivity for themselves. In the process, the world is reconfigured.

The gradual decline of white, western, male hegemony in world politics and some areas of culture is only the most obvious instance of this ongoing reorientation. Another is the growing sense among very different peoples of humankind's relative place among the "earthcreatures," as an interdependent part of the biosphere, not its master.[7] Increasingly there is the recognition that human deadliness to nature is in direct proportion to our alienation from it. The emergence of creation spirituality is one needed corrective to the domination of nature. As long as it remains grounded in the concrete realities of historical struggle and human suffering, creation spirituality offers hope for integral liberation—the end of a politics of domination and the healing of the nature/culture split so characteristic of western history.[8]

The beginnings of other, equally significant shifts in perspective can be observed in contemporary Christian theology and spirituality as well. Feminist challenges to androcentric theology demand a rethinking of the attribution of maleness and its cultural characteristics (domination chief among them) to divinity, whether to God as Father or Jesus Christ as his only Son. For many, the exclusivity of Christian claims about Jesus Christ is deeply problematic, given the importance feminism attaches to particularity, difference and pluralism. Ecumenical and interreligious dialogues are making similar demands, particularly in respect to the uniqueness and finality of Christology.[9] A reorientation of Christian claims about Jesus, locating them in the context of a more expansive understanding of God's revelation in the world through the work of the Spirit, would be an important first step toward meeting these challenges. Christocentric liberation praxis need not be undercut by this shift; at the same time, solidarity with other liberation struggles is strengthened by it. If there is to be a future to this planet, it is imperative that the quest for Christian unity be part of a larger quest for human community and for a way to live in harmony with the rest of creation.

Attending to the web of relationship that is continuously being woven from the multiplicity of human experience leads to new understandings of power and its exercise.

Empowering

Implicit in the critique of domination and the practice of decentering is a revisioning of the nature and use of power. Feminist, liberation and ecological views commonly put this in terms of the distinction between "power over" and "power from within" (or, "power with"). Power does not exist absolutely, but is created in and for relationship. Exercised in mutuality, power is not diminished but enhanced; it increases rather than overwhelms freedom. Nurtured and used with care, it is a renewable human as well as natural resource, not a zero-sum commodity.

Understanding power in this way leads to a new sensitivity to the kinds of degrees of violence endemic to much of contemporary society. Advertising and entertainment media that objectify and commodify women's bodies; national security states worldwide; destruction of the rainforest and the ozone layer; battering and child abuse; the alienating and invasive medical technology that postpones death in stunningly life- and body-denying ways: these are only a few of the forms of everyday, institutionalized violence in our world. They all derive from the dominating exercise of power. Coming to know the violence around us compels us to attend to the realities of power and powerlessness in our own hearts.

Countering violence and creating new ways of exercising power from within, both personally and societally, is a challenge for the powerless as well as for the powerful. For the dominant, giving up exclusive and oppressive forms of power is experienced as a loss; at the same time, the mutuality engendered by the shared creation of power offers new possibilities for meaningful relationship and growth of self. For the dominated, too, change means a kind of loss as well as gain: claiming self and agency, remembering resistance, and honouring victims while also letting go of victimization and the defences of powerlessness. For both groups, establishing a new relationship to power involves spiritual and political transformation.

One area in which the reassessment of power is already having significant ramifications for Christian spirituality and theology is the feminist critique of sexual and domestic violence.[10] The revelation of violence at the heart of family life and heterosexual relationships is a searing indictment of patriarchal privilege in marriage and of punitive child-rearing practices that have long found legitimation in the theology and life of Christian Churches. Survivors of many kinds of family violence are finding the power within their individual and collective voices and using the authority of their experience to challenge theology and spirituality that perpetuate such abuse. Rejection of values that have been taken as fundamental to Christian spirituality—such as self-sacrifice, obedience, submission, and suffering—and the dismantling or displacement of theological constructs that support them—such as the predominant understandings of sin and redemption, atonement and Jesus's relation to the Father—are a call for a thorough-going transformation of Christian expression. Violent and disempowering models of God and humanity need to be replaced by images and experiences of mutuality that empower persons to live in ways that promote freedom and love, wholeness and connection.[11]

Both decentering and empowering are spiritual practices that have the potential of reorienting humankind to the world, to each other, and to whatever we regard as holy in the concrete circumstances of our lives. They do this by opening us to compassion.

Compassion

The ability to embrace otherness while honouring difference is the beginning of compassion. Acceptance of the reality and the otherness of our own pain allows us to be touched by the pain of others. Compassion does not confuse the reality of the other with our own, or seek to overcome the pain of separation by the imposition of sameness. It acknowledges distance and limitation, yet reaches beyond them in love.

Wherever love reaches out to suffering, there spirit is at work in history for the redemption of our bodies. Because love is made-known in acts of justice, healing and liberation are integrally connected. Compassionate love moves us to action, impelling us to struggle against suffering and injustice. There are times, though, when the causes of suffering are so impenetrable that love can only stand and suffer with the other. Yet in refusing to allow evil to break the bonds of relationship, a spirituality of compassion extends the possibilities of life for all of us. Opening our hearts to the anguish of the world gives rise not to resignation, but to solidarity and resistance.[12] Compassion is both the mother and the daughter of hope.

Compassion engenders hope by reminding us that victims do not have to stand alone. To stand together in suffering is already to resist. To make even this small act of resistance is to assert that suffering is not the last word, that victimization can be transformed into agency and power. In its turn, such hope generates the energy that allows us to extend the reach of our compassion.

By invoking the names of victims and martyrs at the Canberra assembly, Chung Hyun Kyung reached back compassionately into history to extend the hope of freedom to the present and future. When she had finished reading from the scroll that bore the names, she set it aflame and held it aloft. Rising like incense, like prayer, the smoke from the scroll touched the hidden places of the heart, loosening the bonds of suffering, freeing memory and desire, passion and action, marking a way toward the next millennium.

In like fashion, the cries of the spirit throughout the world continue to call us to love and freedom.

Notes

1. A slightly abridged version of her address and a variety of reactions to it can be found in *Christianity and Crisis* vol. 51, nos. 10–11 (July 15, 1991), pp. 220–232. See also *The Ecumenical Review,* vol. 43, no. 2 (1991). For further development of some of the themes presented in her address, see Chung Hyung Kyung, *Struggle To Be the Sun Again: Introducing Asian Women's Theology* (Maryknoll, NY, 1990).

2. She reported this to me in conversation in July 1991.

3. The English version of this map is published by Oxford Cartographers Ltd, Oxford, UK, and available through Friendship Press, New York. For a helpful introduction to the map and its significance, see *A New View of the World: A Handbook to the World Map: Peters Projection,* by Ward L. Kaiser (New York, 1987).

4. I am quite persuaded by Jon Sobrino's insistence that spirituality demands "(1) honesty about the real, (2) fidelity to the real, and (3) a certain 'correspondence' by which we permit ourselves to be carried along by the 'more' of the real," *Spirituality of Liberation: Toward Political Holiness* (Maryknoll, NY, 1988), p. 14.

5. There is considerable discussion among contemporary writers about the meaning of "spirituality," with a growing consensus about its relationship to this world and the body as well as to some element of transcendence. Sandra Schneiders surveys aspects of the current discussion in "Spirituality in the Academy," *Theological Studies* vol. 50, no. 4 (1989), pp. 676–697.

6. Quoted from the New Revised Standard Version (Oxford, 1989).

7. "Earthcreatures" is Carter Heyward's phrase, in *Touching Our Strength: The Erotic as Power and the Love of God* (San Francisco, 1989).

8. Matthew Fox is probably the leading proponent of creation spirituality, popularized in his many books. For a recent presentation, see his *Creation Spirituality: Liberating Gifts for the Peoples of the Earth* (San Francisco, 1991). The Spring 1989 issue of *Listening* (vol. 24, no. 2) was devoted to an evaluation of Fox's work; Roberto S. Goizueta is particularly critical of what he sees as a recent tendency of Fox to absorb the political in the mystical, history in cosmology, "Liberating Creation Spirituality," *ibid.,* pp. 85–115.

9. For concise statements of the questions with somewhat different conclusions, see Paul Knitter, "Key Questions for a Theology of Religions," *Horizons* vol. 17, no. 1 (1990), pp. 92–102 and Roger Haight, S.J., "Towards an Understanding of Christ in the Context of Other World Religions," *East Asian Pastoral Review* vol. 26, no. 4 (1989), pp. 248–265. For

a more extended discussion, see Knitter, *No Other Name?* (Maryknoll, NY, 1985).

10. Groundbreaking pastoral and theological work in this area was done by Marie M. Fortune, *Sexual Violence: The Unmentionable Sin* (New York, 1983). See also the essays in *Christianity, Patriarchy, and Abuse: A Feminist Critique,* ed. Joanne Carlson Brown and Carole R. Bohn (New York, 1989) and Mary Potter Engel, "Evil, Sin, and Violation of the Vulnerable," in *Lift Every Voice: Constructing Christian Theologies from the Underside,* ed. Susan Brooks Thistlethwaite and Mary Potter Engel (San Francisco, 1990), pp. 152–164.

11. Sallie McFague explores the need for new images and proposes the models of God as mother, lover and friend in *Models of God: Theology for an Ecological Nuclear Age* (Philadelphia, 1987).

12. See Joanna Macy, "The theoretical foundations of despair and empowerment work," in *A New Creation: America's Contemporary Spiritual Voices,* ed. Roger Gottlieb (New York, 1990), pp. 335–353, for a clear statement of how the experience of pain and despair empowers change and connection.

List of Contributors

Barbara Hilkert Andolsen is Helen Bennett McMurray Professor of Social Ethics, Monmouth University, West Long Beach, New Jersey.

Maria Pilar Aquino is Associate Professor of Theological and Religious Studies, University of San Diego, San Diego, California.

Lisa Sowle Cahill is Professor of Christian Ethics, Boston College, Chestnut Hill, Massachusetts.

Sidney Callahan is Professor of Psychology, Mercy College, Dobbs Ferry, New York.

Francine Cardman is Associate Professor of Historical Theology, Weston Jesuit School of Theology, Cambridge, Massachusetts.

M. Shawn Copeland is Associate Professor of Theology, Marquette University, Milwaukee, Wisconsin.

Carol Coston is Director, Partners for the Common Good 2000, Welfare, Texas.

Toinette Eugene is Associate Professor of Christian Social Ethics, Garrett-Evangelical Theological Seminary, and member of the Doctoral Faculty, Northwestern University, Evanston, Illinois.

Margaret A. Farley is Gilbert L. Stark Professor of Christian Ethics, Yale University Divinity School, New Haven, Connecticut.

Christine E. Gudorf is Professor of Religious Studies, Florida International University, Miami, Florida.

Christine Firer Hinze is Assistant Professor of Theological Ethics, Marquette University, Milwaukee, Wisconsin.

Mary E. Hunt is Co-Director of WATER (Women's Alliance for Theology, Ethics, and Ritual), Silver Spring, Maryland.

Ada María Isasi-Díaz is Associate Professor of Ethics and Theology, The Theological School, Drew University, Madison, New Jersey.

Patricia Beattie Jung is Associate Professor of Theology, Loyola University of Chicago, Chicago, Illinois.

Paul Lauritzen is Associate Professor of Ethics, John Carroll University, University Heights, Ohio.

Marie Augusta Neal is Professor Emerita of Sociology, Emmanual College, Boston, Massachusetts.

Anne E. Patrick is Professor of Religion, Carleton College, Northfield, Minnesota.

Susan A. Ross is Associate Professor of Theology and Director of the Women's Studies Program, Loyola University of Chicago, Chicago, Illinois.

Rosemary Radford Ruether is Professor of Theology, Garrett-Evangelical School of Theology, Evanston, Illinois.

Maura A. Ryan is Assistant Professor of Christian Ethics, University of Notre Dame, Notre Dame, Indiana.

Elisabeth Schüssler Fiorenza is Krister Stendahl Professor of Divinity, Harvard Divinity School, Cambridge, Massachusetts.

Mary C. Segers is Professor of Political Science, Rutgers University, Newark, New Jersey.